# TORAT YEHOSHUA
## ACCORDING TO THE ORIGINAL
## HEBREW BOOK OF MATTHEW

## BRUNO SUMMA
### 2019

Torat Yehoshua
According to the Hebrew Book of Matthew

For permissions: brunosumma@yahoo.dk


Other books from the same author:

The Torah to the Galatians
B. Summa 2018

The Knowledge of Good and Evil
B. Summa 2018

First publish 05/18/2019

# CONTENTS

TORAT YEHOSHUA     1

INTRODUCTION     5

PART I     19

PART II     67

PART III     419

PART IV     480

PART V     555

PART VI     641

# INTRODUCTION

# INTRODUCTION

The time has arrived! An awakening, as never seen before, all over the world has been taking place. An awakening by many people in a search for true knowledge about the Torah, the People of Israel and the real biblical origins, specially concerning the new testament and its roots. When we look at the whole church's history, and I even dare say, mankind's history, there has never been such a ceaseless "thirst" for the God of Israel, as I have seen these past few years.

Throughout the Western world, the eyes of many who follow Christianity have been opened and, for unexplainable reasons, they are seeing that the truth is not quite what they have learned from religions, the true is not actually in what the church has been teaching for the past almost two thousand years.

I have been witnessing this since the year of 2012, when many Christians began to talk to me and to question me about the Torah and its relationship with Yeshua. I was struck by the inner desire that each of them had. The feeling that was passed on to me was of a certain "despair" about an understanding concerning the One God and a "need" of freedom from the doctrines that have held them as hostages throughout their lives. Another thing I have realized is how some people, who often do not even know what the Torah is about, or have never cared about the existence of a God, are touched when they listen to something, even a simple matter, about His Word. It has happened to me a few times, in daily conversations, with no intentions at all, I end up saying something about the Torah and it goes deep inside their heart, in a way that amazes me. The life´s transformation that follows up next, is even more tremendous.

This is not something that comes from man, but rather from God, the Creator. When a person is a chosen one, there is no way out. Even though one never had heard about

God and His Word, just by hearing little things from the Torah, it instantly changes that person's ways. This has become a commonplace now a days. The search, the longing, and the thirst for the Creator's truth became a regular matter and not something punctual. In my view, it is fantastic, because it shows the closeness that we are of the coming of Mashiach.

God created for Himself a People, the People of Israel, and not a religion. Christianity, Judaism, and all others are nothing more than human creations that often enslave rather free. What God seeks is a people and not a cluster of people within a temple following human rules. Thais is why the Torah is vital, for it is not a religion, it is a way of life. It is through it that the individual is defined as People of God or as rest of the nations.

## TORAT YEHOSHUA

"Torat Yehoshua" means the Torah of Yeshua, or the Torah according to the understanding and teachings of Yeshua. This is not a book for the traditional Christian, nor for people who are strongly attached to religions, such as Judaism or any Christian strand. If one believes the truth is found in those religions, then it is good for him to remain in them. The purpose of this book is to bring a new understanding to those who search answers that go beyond religions, theologies, dogmas and human theories.

If the reader searches for answers that will challenge his faith and an understanding that frees him from human dogmas, then this book may help him. I do not intend to convince anyone of anything through it. It was conceived through what Adonai allowed me to understand, and it represents nothing more than a sharing of that understanding. I have no intentions of proving anyone wrong. The intention is to be a tool that might help those who seek something more from the Creator.

I have always been reluctant to write books about

Yeshua, since the New Testament has never been the main focus of my studies. The materials I place in this book have been acquired at different moments during my lifetime and it all have been kept hidden since 2012, as well as the original gospel of Matthew, as set forth at the end of this book.

All the studies in this book will focus on a Jewish/rabbinic understanding of Yeshua's teachings, so they will be presented in a completely different and opposite way from what is commonly taught by Christian churches and theologies. All that is exposed, will be proved by ancient teachings from the sages of Israel.

By reading the book of Matthew, in its original hebrew version, Yeshua clearly showed me the basis of his faith. Unlike of what many think and teach, that jesus rebelled against his own faith and thus founded a new belief, the true Yeshua proclaimed Judaism and always preached both Torah and the Old Testament, through a rabbinic vision, by using the Oral Torah as examples.

Without the Oral Torah, I am certain that it is impossible to understand who he was and what he was talking about, for he was addressing a Jewish audience, he was an expert in the Torah and had a life according to the Oral Torah, therefore, teachings in these conformities make total coherence. Interpretations of his words without this basic knowledge, lead to serious and deep errors that are difficult to be corrected later on.

Everything that will be presented in these studies will be based on the Written Torah and on the Oral Torah. Alongside, I will also bring up the commentaries from the sages and rabbis, with some explanations and observations that I have made myself. For this reason, understanding these studies can be somewhat difficult for those who are not accustomed to such way of thinking, teaching and ideology.

## THE BOOK OF MATTHEW IN HEBREW

Unlike what the church teaches, the book of Matthew,

the book of John, the book of Luke, and the book of Mark, were NOT written in the Greek language, but rather in the Hebrew language. Throughout the book of Matthew it is possible to confirm this, because of the numerous word puns that its author makes, word puns that are only possible in Hebrew writings.

The version of the book of Matthew that I present in this book, was a hand copy made by a Jewish physician named Shem-Tov Ben-Isaac Ben-Shaprut. Shem-Tov was born in a town called Tudela, in the kingdom of Castile in Spain, during the fourteenth century. Due to the strong Spanish inquisition that was decimating thousands of Jews, Shem-Tov was obliged, as well as his entire community, to study the new testament. This was due to the fact on how the inquisition proceeded. Christians had the custom to take the Jews to public squares, and under threat of death, they were obliged to answer some questions that where placed before them by the Inquisitiors. The Inquisitors, as they knew that no Jew knew nothing about the New Testament, they used to ask questions that would normally address the life of jesus.

The Jews of his community, in order to prepare themselves for such events, began to study the writings of the Gospels. One of his colleagues, while on a trip to the Middle East, was able to find a copy of a book called Matthew and through it, everyone else in this community began to manually make a copy. The copy I have is just that of Shem-Tov, which was made around the year 1380 CE and because it was a hand copy, something that demanded too much, there are some minimal errors of writing throughout the manuscript.

This manuscript, which is now hidden in the British Library, was disappeared for 507 years, until a scholar named George Howard from the University of Georgia, found it and published it in 1987. This is not the only manuscript of the book of Matthew in Hebrew, there is a copy of another author in Moscow and a third in Florence, Italy.

However, instead of using the George Howard's English translation, I decided to retranslate it, so I could be able to address some of its teachings in a different way. The translation, alongside its Hebrew version, are found at the end of this book.

## ORIGINALITY

To read the book of Matthew in its original language and to compare it with translations made from the Greek language reveals many things. Many of the differences found are striking and enlightening. However, most of the differences found in this book may not change much concerning one's understanding if one does not understand first-century Jewish culture and how orthodox rabbinical Judaism works. Therefore, I will try to bring to light, with the help of God, some "weirdness" that are found in this manuscript, and then compare them with the western language translation. By doing so, we will be able to see that there are more than a simple difference of words and terms, but a difference of message and context.

The book of Matthew, after the years I have spent studying it, is definitely and irrevocably a book written in Hebrew. The ancient Hebrew, known as *Yvrit Tanakhi*, follows a system of poetic writing. In old Hebrew, it is normal a repetition of terms, as well as the habit of using words that have the same root, giving an unique sonority to the text when read. Another custom of this ancient Hebrew, also very common in the Old Testament, is a narrative made in the passive form. This idea sounds very strange in the Western languages, but it is common in the biblical Hebrew.

Such customs of writing are known as Hebraism, and the book of Matthew is full of them. These are things that, as they are difficult to translate into other languages, it is also impossible to formulate these hebraisms through a translation from a foreigner language into Hebrew.

Here are a few examples of these typical hebraisms

that appear throughout the book of Matthew and are commonplace in the Old Testament:

*And she shall give birth to a son and will call him **YESHUA**, for he **YOSHIA** my people from their iniquities.*

Matthew 1:21

Naming people using "verbs" in order to show their life goal is something unique to the Hebrew language. It does not only happened with Yeshua, but practically with all the great men of the bible. This thing is completely lost in the Greek version.

*At that time Yeshua said to his talmidim: the Kingdom of Heaven is like a king who sat to make a reckoning with his servants and ministers. And when they begin to make the reckon, comes one that owes ten pieces of gold. And he has nothing to give and his lord commands him to be sold along with his children and with all that he owns **to pay (LESHALEM)** that value. And the servant falls before his master and asks him to be merciful on him and give him time, for **he will pay (ISHALEM)** all the debts. And then his master took pity on him and forgave him all the debt. And the servant went out, and found another that owed him a hundred pieces of silver, and grasped him, and attacked him, and said, Trust me and be patient with me, **I will pay (ASHALEM)** everything. And he was not willing to listen to him, so he took him to jail until everything was **paid (SHALAM)**. And the servants of the king saw what was done, and were very angry, and went and told their master. Then the lord called him and said to him: cursed servant, did not I forgive you of all the debt that you had with me?*

*So why did you not forgive the servant when*
*he pleaded you, as I forgave you?*
*And his master was angry with him and commanded to*
*afflict him until all his debts were **paid (ISHALEM)**.*
*So will you do my Father in heaven if you do not forgive*
*each man his brother with a **complete (SHALAM)** heart.*

Matthew 18:23-35

Throughout the same parable, words from the same root appear six times, such a feat, besides being very common in Hebrew, is practically impossible to achieve through a translation from other languages into Hebrew.

*And I tell you that you are **rock (EVEN)** and **I will build***
*(**EV'NAH**) on you my BEIT TEFILAH. And the gates*
*of the Gehinam shall not prevail before you.*

Matthew 16:18

We also have Hebraism in Matthew 16:18, by which many justify the Greek originality of the text. It turned out to be only a coincidence at the time of the translation into the Greek language, for hebraism is also there. One more linguistic example:

*And he **saw (vayir'u)** the multitude and **feared** (**vayir'u**) much ...*
Matthew 9:8a

In the above verse, we have another hebraism that is lost with translation, although "saw" and "feared" have nothing to do with each other, in Hebrew, the words are similar. This method would not be possible if the Hebrew book would come from a translation. Other than these examples above, there are thousands more throughout the book of Matthew.

It makes no sense, a Jew, of Hebrew origin, in the territory of Israel, speaking of things about Israel, teaching the people of Israel, to write in Greek. It makes no sense, for reasons more than obvious, there should be no doubt about the originality of its language.

There are some quotations made by the early church fathers concerning the book of Matthew:

*Matthew ... ... a gospels about christ, first published in Judea in HEBREW ... In Hebrew it has been preserved up to this day in the library in Caesarea ... I also had the opportunity to have a copy made for me by the Nazarenes of Beroea ... ... who use it.*
Jerome, 392

*They have worked hard, by the best of their ability, in order to do translate it from Hebrew.*
Clement of Rome, concerning the Gospels, 118CE

The formatting of the book of Matthew does not follow the Western versions formats. Its separation is not in chapters and verses, but rather the book is divided into 114 parts, which were set up to differentiate the themes that the author approached, something very common in Hebrew. I will leave both separations, both original and western, for an ease of understanding.

## GEMATRIA

Gematria is a numerological system by which the Hebrew letters has a correspondence to certain numerical values. This system is part of the Kabbalah and is a very powerful tool for interpreting biblical texts.

Each letter of the Hebrew alphabet is represented by a number. One can then calculate the numerical value of the Hebrew words of the Bible for a more mystical understanding and a do hidden exegesis of what the Word of God is teaching. In the world of biblical exegesis, many commentators and sages of the Torah base their arguments on the numerical equivalence of words. When a word has a numerical value equal to that of another word, there is a mystical connection between the two words. This shows that both words can be used in both contexts, that is, one can take the place of the other and vice versa, revealing a unique understanding of biblical passages.

Many sages believe that Adonai created the universe through the letters of the Hebrew alphabet and therefore, there is a hidden power behind each one of them. The numbers that each represents, serves to hide the secrets of the Creator from the sight of the common man.

On the other hand, we must be very careful with the Gematria, because it is a tool for exclusively Biblical use. To make use of it in a secular way as means of divination or prediction of the future is something vehemently forbidden by the Torah and by God several times. This method has so much power that many pseudo-cabalists now a day, offer this teaching to lay people for secular use. Many occult sects also know this tool and use it to strengthen their spells and witchcraft. Therefore, I emphasize, Gematria should not be used outside a biblical context and should not be learned by secular ways, such as books of unknown authors and people without direct connection with the divine Torah, it can only be taught and learned by rabbis who use it as a tool for biblical interpretation.

Gematria is a tool that I use a lot throughout this book. There are many ways of using it, but I will use the two most simple forms: the absolute value, which is the sum of the numbers attached in each letter from certain words or the reduced value, which is the sum of the numbers of the absolute value, reaching a number between 1 and 9.

For this, I will use two table charts for calculation, one that includes the SOFIT letters and another one, that does not include a special value for the SOFIT letters:

| | | |
|---|---|---|
| א 1 | ט 9 | פ 80 |
| ב 2 | י 10 | צ 90 |
| ג 3 | כ 20 | ק 100 |
| ד 4 | ל 30 | ר 200 |
| ה 5 | מ 40 | ש 300 |
| ו 6 | נ 50 | ת 400 |
| ז 7 | ס 60 | |
| ח 8 | ע 70 | |

GEMATRIA WITH NO SOFIT

| | | |
|---|---|---|
| א 1 | י 10 | ק 100 |
| ב 2 | כ 20 | ר 200 |
| ג 3 | ל 30 | ש 300 |
| ד 4 | מ 40 | ת 400 |
| ה 5 | נ 50 | ך 500 |
| ו 6 | ס 60 | ם 600 |
| ז 7 | ע 70 | ן 700 |
| ח 8 | פ 80 | ף 800 |
| ט 9 | צ 90 | ץ 900 |

GEMATRIA WITH SOFIT

## OMITTED VERSES

The following verses are not found in the book of Matthew in Hebrew. They may be later additions of the church, such as the already confessed added verse 19 from chapter 28. Or additions made by the people who translated it from Hebrew into Greek, with the intention of explaining something that would aid in translation, or perhaps they are found in other manuscripts.

5: 6 - 5: 7 - 5:47 - 10:33 (first part) - 10:38 - 14:34 - 16: 6 - 16: 7 - 18: 4 - 23:21 - 26:19 - 27: 36 - 27:61 - 28:19

## INTENTIONS OF THE BOOK

This manuscript, after being discovered, remained without being studied for many years. My intention is to explain it, for the first time, for everyone who has an interest in a more precise understanding of the origin of the new testament.

Another point is to show Yehoshua Ben Yosef, a Jew,

15

Israeli, Rabbi, Pharisee, Orthodox, follower of the Torah, master in the Oral Torah and in the Midrash, who declared himself Maschiach Ben Yosef and came behind the lost sheep of the House of Israel.

The Yeshua dealt within this book, according to the original book of Matthew, is not the Christian jesus, it is not the jesus of Rome, it is not the jesus that the Western world knows. This book is about a real person, not a myth.

## TERMINOLOGY

For those who do not know the Hebrew language or are not accustomed to rabbinical terminology, it is vitally important that the following terms be studied and understood before reading this book, because they are terms used a lot by the Book of Matthew and I so also use them in my studies, because it is a terminology that loses its essence when translated:

**Written Torah** - The first five books of the Bible - Genesis, Exodus, Leviticus, Numbers, Deuteronomy - also known as the Law of Moses. The Torah is the holiest of all books, for it is the only one that reveals the true "self" of the Creator of all things.

**Oral Torah** - According to the sages, the Oral Torah was the explanation of the written Torah that God gave to Moses while he was on Mount Sinai, which was passed down orally for generations. It deals with details of the commandments from the Written Torah that are not so "clear".

**Mishnah** - It is another for the Oral Torah, it addresses all the commandments from the Torah.

**Gemarah** - These are rabbinical commentaries on the Mishnah. It is also known as the Talmud, and it has numerous laws created by the sages and imposed upon the Jewish people over the years.

**Midrash** - Sages' commentaries on the biblical passages, the Midrashim were composed in Aramaic and possess an unique wisdom.

**Talmud** - Mishnah + Gemarah + some external teachings.

**Tzadik** - This is a vital term for understanding the words of Yeshua. A TZADIK is a person who observes and obeys the Laws of the Torah. This term was translated as "righteous" and thereby lost all its essence. Being a Tzadik, is the life's goal of any Jew who loves God.

**Kasher** - Although this term is associated with nourishment, the word kasher is an adjective given to anything that is in conformity with the Torah. A person who follows the Laws of God faithfully is a kasher person.

**Kashrut** - Biblical dietary laws according to Leviticus 11.

**Talmid (Talmidim, plural)** - "Student" in Hebrew.

**Mamon** - Although many claim this is the name of a demon, mamon is only a common word in Aramaic, it means "money".

**Gehinam** - Known as hell, for some it is only a temporary purgatory.

**Tshuvah** - Another very important term vastly used in the New Testament. Tshuvah in a direct translation means "answer", but it is a rabbinic term to refer to repentance. Unlike Christian repentance that is nothing but something inner oneself, Tshuvah is more like an action, whoever does Tshuvah is the person who decides to adopt a lifestyle according to the Torah.

**Olam Hazeh** - Earthly world, the life we live in the flesh.

**Olam Habah** – World to come or era of Mashiach. Synonym for eternal life.

**Mitzvah (Mitzvot, plural)** - Torah's Commandment.

**Chupah** - Hut where weddings are made.

**Mashiach** - Messiah, the anointed one.

**Bessorah** - Good News or Gospel.

**Tanakh** – Torah + Prophets + Writing = The Hebrew bible or old testament.

**EVERY PASSAGE FROM THE TANAKH, FROM THE MIDRASHIM, FROM THE TALMUD AND FROM THE RABBINICAL COMMENTARIES USED IN THIS BOOK, HAVE BEEN TRANSLATED FROM ITS ORIGINAL LANGUAGE (HEBREW OR ARAMAIC) BY THE AUTHOR HIMSELF, LEST IT IS MENTIONED WHERE THE TRANSLATIONS IS FROM. FOR THIS REASON, THOSE PASSAGES MIGHT PRESENT SOME DIFFERENCES WHEN COMPARED TO THE MOST USUAL WESTERN LANGUAGE'S TRANSLATIONS.**

**THIS BOOK MAY BE OFFENSIVE TO SOME PEOPLE DUE TO THEIR CREED AND FAITH. IF THE READER DEEPLY BELIEVES IN THE CHURCH, IN THEIR DOGMAS, THEOLOGIES AND TEACHINGS, AND SEE THEM AS AN ABSOLUTE AND IRREVOLVABLE TRUTH. PELASE DO NOT READ THIS BOOK.**

# PART I

# HISTORICAL

# SECTION I
## YEHOSHUA'S BACKGROUND

In order for a true understanding concerning the person that Yehoshua was, something that goes beyond his teachings and works, we need to seek information about what has not been reported in the books of the New Testament, such as his childhood and education. Although Yehoshua had an elevated existence, he was also a human being, he was a child, a teenager, a young adult and a full adult, and all these phases formed his characteristics as an individual. My intention here is not to discover the personal characteristics of Yehoshua, but rather to present from where the influences that gave the tone of his teachings throughout the New Testament, came from. Since we have no Biblical or Talmudic accounts of his life before the beginning of his ministry, we must look at how was the standard education practiced in the first-century's land of Israel.

First of all, it is necessary to remove from one's mind many concepts created by the ancient church. We have in popular belief, a Yehoshua who was a simple person with no basic education and a country boy. But with a careful reading of his teachings, it is clear that Yehoshua had an amazing education, being an expert in the Torah, the Tanakh, the Oral Torah, the customs, and all the rabbinical teachings of his day. If we had to bring an image of Yehoshua to our days, he would certainly be like an orthodox Jew, dressed in black and white, with the *Tzitzit* tied around him, a long beard and a handsome hat.

We cannot look at Yehoshua and see the jesus created by the church, a poor, uneducated and unprepared person. We should look at Yehoshua according to the person he really was, a Jew, a Pharisee, a Rabbi, an expert on the Torahs, from a wealthy family and with a very strong and unique teaching personality.

I believe that this image of an uneducated Yehoshua comes from a misunderstanding about the inhabitants of ancient Galilee. For to the Jews from big cities, such as Jerusalem, the Galileans were seen as countrymen, peasants and without intellectual ability as a cosmopolitan person had. But Galilee, for being close to border regions, had greater contact with diverse cultures, which enriched it culturally in a different way from what used to happen with the big cities in the interior of Yehudah, and such influence created a mentality in Galilee that was different from the rest of Israel.

If we look at the level of knowledge that the Galileans possessed, we will see that it far outweighs the people from big cosmopolitan centers. Galilee was the cradle of many of the greatest rabbis in the history of Judaism and their teachings are stil practiced and lived up to this day in many synagogues and communities. Among them we have Yohanan Ben Zakkai, Hanina Ben Dosa, Abba Yose Holikrofi, Zadok and Yehoshua Ben Yosef. Many important things also happened in this region, such as the birth of a movement known as "the Zealots" and it was at this place that the rebellion against the Roman empire began, causing the destruction of the Temple.

For a sage of the first century, there would be no better place to study the Torah and the scriptures than the region of Galilee, for it was in this region that the wisest and most lenient rabbis of history was formed.

## EDUCATION

Although the new testament does not tell anything about Yehoshua's childhood and education, it was certainly no different than the other Galileans. Both the education and the life stages of a typical first-century Jew is described by the Talmud, in the Pikei Avot:

*Yehudah Ben Teima said: at five years of age is the age for*

*the study of the scriptures, at ten years of age for the study*
*of the Mishnah, at thirteen years of age for the beginning of*
*observance of the Mitzvot, at fifteen years of age for the study of*
*the Talmud and at thirty years of age is the age of total strength.*
Pikei Avot 5:21

Every children from Galilee followed this form of education, the schools of that time were not only devoted to teaching math and history, but they were primarily focused on the scriptures and everything that was connected to them.

First-century synagogues had an annex called *Beit Sefer* (school), where the children used to go to receive all the education necessary for a secular life as well as a religious life. Many of the students used to leave school at the age of thirteen, because they needed to start working, but others, at fifteen, used to leave school to go under the tutelage of a rabbinical school to become Torah scholars and rabbis. From the high knowledge of the scriptures that Yehoshua possessed, I believe he continued his studies and affiliated himself with Beit Hillel, for both Hillel and Yehoshua possessed a strong similarity in their teachings, for countless times, Yehoshua makes an approach in his teachings in the same way Rabbi Hillel used to.

Every student who continued his study of Torah, was considered the true worshiper. According to the Jewish mentality, worship is not only about chanting songs and praises, but about a true dedication for the study of the Word of God, this is what defines the true worshiper:

*A person must practice mitzvot in life, for after he dies he*
*will be free from the observance of the Torah and can no*
*longer be a worshiper of the Holy One, Blessed Be He.*
Talmud of Babylon, Tractate Shabbat 30a

This shows that the most sacred place was precisely the *Beit Sefer*, as well as being under the tutelage of a rabbi, for it was precisely in these places where the greatest act of worship was practiced, the study of the Torah.

## UPBRINGING

Although there were scrolls and a well developed method of writing and reading, all written material at that time was extremely expensive, so the vast majority of the people of Israel did not have the Torah and no form of scriptural writing at home. Only the richest had some scrolls with some verses from the Tanakh. Because of this, learning the Written Torah and the Oral Torah required a great deal of memorization. Up to this day, where we have easy access to the scriptures, many rabbinic schools still use the process of repetition and memorization.

Yehoshua, like all the Pharisees around him, had the Torah, the Tanakh, the traditions and the Oral Torah fully memorized, as something that ran inside his veins, something very rare to find in other religions, for this demands years and years of study. In order to become a renowned rabbi, a secular life must be left behind.

*Hillel said, "He who repeats a hundred times is not comparable to who repeats a hundred and one times."*
Talmud of Babylon, Tractate Chagigah 9b

*He who does not return to the study of the Torah several times is like a man who plants and does not reap.*
Talmud of Babylon, Tractate Sanhedrin 99a

Many methods of memorization were developed by the sages and were taught in schools throughout Israel. Students studied the Torah six days a week and in the seventh no new subjects were given, they used that day to recite what they learned during the week to memorize them. Nowadays, in the more orthodox districts of Israel, it is common to see people walking around talking alone, in fact, they are reciting the Torah and the Talmud for total memorization.

The memorization and learning of the two Torahs in Israel have always been the most important parts of the Jewish faith, this is how they kept the Oral Toral alive for many centuries without ever having been written. A Catholic priest, around the year 400 CE, went to Israel to learn the Hebrew language and in one of his reports, he states that he did not see a child who did not know the bible from Adam until Zeruvbabbel.

Yehoshua, as a good Jew, went through all of this, his teachings show that he possessed an unparalleled knowledge of the Written Torah and the Oral Torah, the way he uses both, shows that the sacred texts were part of his essence. Therefore, it becomes impossible to understand him, if one do not have the same theological structure and the same way of thinking he had. The difference from Yehoshua's education, in comparison to Western Christian education, led the world to a very poor, and sometimes erroneous, interpretation of all that he taught.

The breaking of paradigms is necessary for any study concerning the Word of God, especially for a mind indoctrinated according to Christian theology, which was originated, in its essence, by the fathers of the church, who were nothing more than pagans seeking a God that they knew very little about. Unfortunately, the influence of their teachings and thoughts has entered in the church in a way that, today it affects all Christians, for they believe more in theology than in the bible itself. If one is not willing to look at the scriptures without pre-established concepts, the truth will never be revealed to him.

# SECTION II
## THE PHARISEES

The Hebrew word for Pharisee is *p'rushim*, which means "separatists". This title was given them because of their dissociation with the common people of Israel and specially, with the Sadducees. The Pharisees saw the ordinary citizens as impure people, who had little knowledge of the Scriptures and did not care about the law of the Oral Torah. They sought to distinguish themselves from what they might have called "commons". Other sources point out that the reason for this title was precisely due to the difference they had from a group a little older than them, the Sadducees.

### The Sadducees

All we know today about the Sadducees comes from outside sources, since they were not accustomed to record their history. The Sadducees were a type of caste within Judaism that began to form around the year 150 BCE. They are directly connected with the influence that the Maccabbeus gained within Israel through their victories over the Macedonian army.

It is believed that the Sadducees movement was founded by a person named Tsadok and they became a class of aristocrats who dominated the entire political and priestly areas of Israel. They had control over the *Sanhedrin* and had full power over the appointment of priests; though some of the priests were not part of the Sadducees, the vast majority was.

The Sadducees were the upper class from the time of Yehoshua, they were powerful, influential and wealthy people, they worked hard to please Rome, thus maintaining peace all over Yehudah. It was a class totally linked to politics, to finance, and had nothing to do with religion. Both

Yehoshua and Paul make strong criticisms about them, for they often put in the priestly office people who were not part of the tribe of Levi, they placed the secular gains above the commandments of God, and they made the people of Israel more and more slaved to the Romans, since this was extremely profitable for them.

Beside of all the political filth and maneuverings within the Temple, it was they who possessed authority over the Written Torah, for they controlled the *Sanhedrin*. The Sadducees possessed a doctrine that contradicted in some vital points the doctrine of the Pharisees, these are the four main points:

1- They denied that God was involved in the daily life of men;
2. They denied the resurrection of the dead;
3- They denied the afterlife, they believed the soul disappears after death;
4 -They did not believe in a spiritual structure, denying angels and demons.

Because they did not care about religion, they have never cared for Yeshohua until he arrived at the Temple and caused a confusion by turning over the tables of the vendors. The trade in the Temple was something created and encouraged by the Sadducees, especially in times of the feasts, such as Passover for example, when it was necessary for each man to bring an offering to be burned to God. This idea came from the need of many people, who used to live far from Jerusalem and had to make long journeys to the Temple, bringing along their offerings, which were often animals. The idea was to sell these animals on their land and come to Jerusalem with the money in their pocket, in order to buy another animal at the entrance of the Temple, so it could be offered.

Of course, if we look closely, we have the feeling that it would be an excellent idea that would help a lot of people, but the fact is that every commercial transaction under the Roman empire generated taxes, both by the sale of the animal and also by the purchase of another one, thus becoming something very interesting for both Rome and the Sadducees, who also profited somehow from these transactions.

When Yehoshua directly attacked the affairs of the Sadducees and begins to point out the political and priestly maneuvers they made, they began to pay more attention to him and the unfolding of his death began at that very moment.

For all this reason, a group was born, with a very strong popular appeal, that disagreed with the Sadducee's religious and political ideas, this group began to be called separatists, or in this case "the Pharisees". The Sadducees ceased to exist in the year 70 CE after the destruction of the Temple by the Romans, the Pharisees still exist up to this day, known as the Orthodox Jews.

## The Pharisees and the Oral Torah

It is not known for certain when the Pharisaic movement began, but many scholars believe that it was in parallel to the Sadducees, for many were against the control and manipulation they began to do with things that concerned God, for they mixed Hellenistic ideas with holy things. This struggle originated the commoner Pharisees and the aristocrats Sadducean. Around the year 130 BCE the quarrel between the two groups was so strong that all the Pharisees detached themselves from the *Sanhedrin* and from any activity which was established by its members.

The Pharisees differed from other groups by their rigid observance of the Oral Torah and distinct interpretation of the *Mishnah*. They taught that the Oral Torah explains in detail some points that are succinct in the Written Torah and therefore, it was of paramount importance because it made the commandments of God more accessible to everyone's understanding.

According to the Pharisees and the Orthodox Jews, the Oral Torah was delivered to Moses at the same time he received the Written Torah on Mount Sinai and that was the way Moses orally taught the Torah to the people. The Oral Torah, also known as the Talmud, is of vital importance, for even though the teaching of Yehoshua was based on the Tanakh, the tool he used to explain it, always been the Oral Torah and it was for this reason, he had a lot of impasses with the teachings of some Pharisees.

Yehoshua had a very clear understanding of the Oral Torah, much larger than any Christian or Jew can imagine. His relationship with the Talmud was one of love and hate, often reaffirming what is written in it, but sometimes, going totally against it, as we will see many times in this book. Although many believe that the Torah is what defines the orthodox Judaism, just as it was with Pharisaism, what actually defines them is precisely the Oral Torah, every rule of conduct, clothing, eating, behavior, observance, prayer, fasting, and many other things go far beyond what is described by the Torah, those are rules and customs created by the ancients and eternalized in the Talmud, and it is precisely these laws and customs that characterize a Jew and not the Torah itself.

### The Fence Around the Torah

*Anyone who transgresses the words of the sages shall receive a death sentence, as it is written, "Whosoever breaks the fence shall be bitten by a snake".*
Talmud of Babylon, Tractate Eruvim 21b

The Pharisees counted 613 commandments contained in the Torah, among them, 248 are positives, which one must do and 365 are negatives, which one should not do. This group, like the modern Orthodox Judaism, has an extreme fear of breaking any of these commandments and therefore, they have created what they call "fence around the Torah", which is nothing more than the creation of laws around these commandments, in order to keep the person as far as possible from breaking any Law contained in the Torah. Such "fences" are called "traditions" by the New Testament.

Clear examples of these traditions are the innumerable rules concerning the observance of Shabbat, the vast majority of which are non-biblical, the rules of a true kosher meal, the garments we see today, the way prayer and Torah studies are conducted and various other rules that literally cover all the life of a Jew.

The real problems began to appear when, the Pharisees themselves, began to define that the religiosity and devotion to God of a person is defined by his observance of their laws, laws that were created by the rabbis and not only by the observance of the Torah's Laws. Such customs did not generate great discord among the people, but it was one of Yehoshua's greatest objections, the other one was their hypocrisy when they fulfilled some Law from the Written Torah. Unfortunately, because the church has little knowledge about these customs and teachings, they do not understand where his teachings came from and believe that he has established a new law that has replaced the Torah.

We can use as an example the Pharisees' habit of fasting, it was a customary by the sages to teach that God commanded his people to fast twice a week, every Monday and Thursday, and for the fasting to be valid, according to their tradition, one should make himself sad, as proof of humility before the Creator, and also to feel the pain of a sacrifice on his own skin. Yehoshua makes a very brief comment on this rabbinic custom:

*Again he said to them, when you fast do not be as the hypocrites who make themselves to appear sad and who*

*change their faces to show their fasting before men, amen*
*(truly) I say to you, they have received their reward already.*
*But when you fast, wash your heads*
*That you might not appear to men to be fasting,*
*but to your father who is in secret, and your*
*father who is in secret will complete will.*

Matthew 6:16-18

Yehoshua was by no means contrary to the Pharisee's custom of fasting, perhaps if some one wanted to fast every day, Yehoshua would certainly support him, but the point he debated is precisely the "commandment" regarding the need to feel some kind of sadness at the moment of fasting. The interesting thing is that the feeling of sadness is not something controlled by the human being, nobody is sad when one wants to, it is something that simply happens, so the only way to appear sad is showing it by one's face.

Another example we can use of how Yehoshua used to criticize some of the less known Jewish customs is found in chapter 11:

*And when Yohanan came, he did not eat nor drink,*
*they said of him: he is possessed by demons.*
*And the men will eat and drink and say that he is a*
*glutton, drunkard and friend of violent and sinful*
*men. Fools judging the wise.*

Matthew 11:18-19

In this passage, Yeshoshua criticizes some people who spoke ill of Yohanan, the immerser. Who, because of not eating and drinking, was possessed by demons, while these same people were gluttonous and drunkards. Yehoshua, in this part, refers to a document dating to the first century, which states that all Pharisees, who truly served God, deserved a rich feast of food and drink every hour of the day and should love to feast, eat and drink from the moment they wake up until bedtime. Yehoshua made a clear criticism, which seems to me to possess a certain ironic tone, to that convenient tradition stipulated by some rabbi.

The Pharisees possessed great authority and influence over the masses, due to their dedication to the study of the Written Torah and the Oral Torah. All synagogue, prayer, celebration of the feasts and teachings of the Scriptures were performed by them. Just as in the present day, the great majority of synagogues, teachings, rituals of conversion and interpretation of the Torah are in the hands of the orthodox rabbis.

On the other hand, we should note that Pharisaic theology is almost perfectly aligned with the new testament's teachings. Many believe that Yehoshua was an Essene, it is true that the customs of this group closely resemble what Yehoshua taught, but this was due to the fact that these teachings also resembled the Pharisaic mentality. There are two very important points that we should take into consideration when we think that Yehoshua was Essene, the first is that this group did not believe in the resurrection of the dead, which right away goes against one of the most important deeds of Yehoshua, the second is, they were against any kind of public ministry and Yehoshua clearly had one. Only these two points are good enough to overturn any hypothesis that he was part of that society.

### The Nine Types of Pharisees
To go deeper about the hypocrites and those whom Yehoshua criticized so much, we should look at nine common types of Pharisees, as described by the Jewish Encyclopedia:

**1- Shechem Pharisee** – The one who likes to show his observance, so everyone might see it;
**2- Slow Pharisee** – The one who is always delaying others when he wanted to perform some mitzvah, so that all would

end up seeing it;

**3- Blind Pharisee** – The one who is always bumping the walls because he has to close his eyes, so he would not to look at women;

**4- Manipulator Pharisee** – The one who uses the laws to take advantage on others;

**5- Proud Pharisee** – The one who is always telling others about his good deeds, but he walks in hypocrisy;

**6- Wry Pharisee** – The one who erroneously teaches the Torah;

**7 - Innocent Pharisee** – The one who does not know what he does;

**8- Fearful Pharisee** – The one who was a true Tzaddik, just as Job was;

**9- God Lover Pharisee** - like Abraham, The one who has a very strong affection for God.

The sages in the Talmud, Tractate Sotah 22b, claim that if it were for the first seven types of Pharisees on this list, God would destroy the world, because of the enormous hypocrisy they possessed. However, because of the last two kinds, he decided to keep His creation. As we can read at Chapter 23 of the book of Matthew, Yehoshua casts "the seven woes upon the Pharisees", and they fit perfectly with the first seven types in this list:

**Shechem Pharisee** - Woe on you hypocrites, Pharisees and sages, who build up the tombs of the prophets and honor the monuments of the sages. (see 29);

**Slow Pharisee** – Woe on you sages and Pharisees, hypocrites, who look like graves, beautiful and white on the outside, but inside you are full of dead bones and filthy. (see 27);

**Blind Pharisee** - Woe on you, blind in the chair, who say that he who swears by the Temple is not bound (to fulfill), but he who swears by whatever is consecrated to the Temple is bound to pay. (see 16);

**Manipulator Pharisee** - Woe on you, Pharisees and sages, hypocrites, devour and divide the widow's assets through DERESH ARUKH, so you will suffer great punishment. (see 14);

**Pride Pharisee** - Woe on you, sages and Pharisees, who decimated mint, dill and pomegranate. But commit robberies. It is better to honor the Torah sentences, which are: Chesed, truth and faith. The Torah is worth of following, never forget that. (see 23);

**Wry Pharisee** – Woe on you Pharisees and sages, hypocrites, who close the doors to the Kingdom of Heaven to men and those who want to enter you do not let them enter. (see 13);

**Innocent Pharisee** - Shame on you, Pharisees and sages, who submerge the cups and the dishes on the outside and inside is full of evil and impurities. (see 25).

Yehoshua does not criticize the Pharisees in general, nor even Pharisaism, but rather some types of behavior that were very common within this group. Such behaviors are very common within any religion, we can still see them today within Judaism in all its spheres and also within the church, all of them.

The new Testament also talks about these last two groups of Pharisees, such as Nicodemus, Joseph of Arimathea and Rabbi Gamliel, as well as many others who followed Yehoshua. Flavius Josefvs wrote about the Pharisees: "*The Pharisees are recognized for their impressive ability to interpret the word of God*" and that is why this is the only group that still exists today, known as Rabbinic or Orthodox Judaism.

### The Pharisaic Mercy

Compared to the other two groups, the Sadducees and the Essenes, the Pharisees were those who had greater compassion for their neighbors, taught the scriptures out of love and were truly God-fearing. They practiced a great leniency when it came to the application of punishments concerning the breaking of the Laws of God and always sought divine justice in everything they did.

> *A Sanhedrin that carries out a death penalty*
> *every seven years is a murderous court.*
> Mishnah Makkot 1:10

They did what they could to avoid any kind of punishment that would cost someone's life and they developed various laws and customs to avoid that. An interesting case was a custom they had, if there was a death sentence, to alleviate the suffering of the condemned, the Talmud teaches about some mixtures that could be made and given to the condemned one, so the pain suffered would be easier on him and the punishment less suffered, such attitude appears in a not very clear way in the book of Matthew:

> *And they gave him wine mixed with MARAH (Extract*
> *from an extremely bitter plant). But when he began*
> *to drink, he noticed it and did not drink.*
> Matthew 27:34

One of these formulas is precisely the mixture of wine with *marah* and it was used as an anesthetic for pain and for sure, the person who tried to give this to Yehoshua, was a Pharisee, for thus was determined by the Oral Torah.

### The Rabbinical Authority

One of the fundamental principles of pharisaic/rabbinic faith is the absolute authority of the rabbis to interpret the Scriptures, whatever they say and decide, in religious terms, even when they are wrong, it becomes law. When a rabbi says that the sky is no longer blue, instead it is red, it becomes law and truth within the community in which he is a part of.

A story told in the Talmud of Babylon, makes this concept very clear:

> One day Rabbi Eliezer was engaged in a debate about
> a particular type of oven that could not be used, for
> it would not remove impurities from food. But all
> the other rabbis there claimed the opposite.
> Because Rabbi Eliezer was unable to convince the other rabbis,
> Rabbi Eliezer was very frustrated and to solve such a situation,
> he resolved to invoke a miracle, so Rabbi Eliezer shouts: "If I am
> right, let the trees confirm." Then a loud noise was heard from
> outside and when the rabbis went to look at what was happening
> through the window, all the trees in the garden were prostrate.
> Everyone in the room was impressed and turned to Rabbi Eliezer
> and said, "We do not listen to mere trees." Then Rabbi Eliezer
> tried again and shouted, "If I am right, may the river confirm."
> Everyone in the room ran outside and saw that the river that
> passed through the city, began to flow in the opposite direction.
> At that moment all the rabbis were extremely impressed and
> said, "We do not listen to waters." Rabbi Eliezer, deeply irritated,
> shouted again, "If I am right, may the Heavens confirm".
> Then they all heard a voice from heaven, saying, "Why do you
> disagree with Rabbi Eliezer, since he is correct?" And the rabbis
> said, "We do not listen to the heavens, since the Torah is not
> there, it is here under our care". Then God smiled and said, "My
> children have overcome me, my children have overcome me."
> Talmud of Babylon, Tractate Bava Metzia 59b

The passage of the Torah they use to corroborate this idea is found in Deuteronomy 30:12, but they use only the beginning of this verse, "*it is not in the heavens*" and in a totally out of context way, they use it to affirm that, as the Torah is not in heavens, rather in earth, in the hands of men, it is up to them to decide how to interpret it. This idea may be a bit strange, for example, since we live on this earth and not in the heavens, does it mean that our lives are not in the hands of the Creator? I find that a bit disturbing.

On the other hand, the rabbis also teach *"Everything is in the hands of heavens, except the fear of heavens"*. If we put both concepts side by side, we will have a huge contradiction, because on the one hand they affirm that as the Torah is on earth, being subject to the decisions of man, our lives lived on earth, in contrast, are in the hands of heavens . A huge inconsistency.

Apart from hypocrisy, this is the kind of contradiction of rabbinical teachings that Yehoshua repudiated. He refuted the rabbinic traditions and interpretations that contradicted the God-given Torah. Such thing, we will see throughout the entire book of Matthew.

### Yehoshua, the Pharisee

Yehoshua was a typical Pharisee, his teachings proved this clearly, but he had differing opinions about some rabbinical rules that went against or replaced some of the Written Torah, which for him, was above all else.

The greatest clashes that Yehoshua had and which gave the impression that he attacked Pharisaism itself were, in fact, only harsh criticisms against hypocrisy, and this all were done in order to defend the Pharisaic movement itself and the Torah. The way he did this was by teaching that serving God could not be by an external attitudes *per se*, but rather obeying God should be as result of faith and love that one possesses for Him. Also, no man made rule could ever overcome what is written in the Law of Moses. Unfortunately, the new Testament treats the Pharisee as a homogeneous group and contrary to the new religion of christ, but in fact, these clashes were only with some small groups of Pharisees, who came from different schools. The great mass of this group clearly agreed with Yeshohua, and this we can see in many others Pharisaic teachings.

*The heavens know everything, and the great court of the*

*heavens will bring the exact punishment to those who wear*
*the mantle of tzadikim, but in fact, are unworthy inside.*
Talmud of Babylon, Tractate Sotah 22b

*Do not fear the Pharisees or the Sadducees, but in*
*fact fear the hypocrites who resemble the Pharisees,*
*who have acts similar to the wicked Zimri.*
Talmud of Babylon, Tractate Sotah 22b

This shows that within the Pharisaic movement existed the problem of hypocrisy, as in all modern and ancient religions. The greatest sages were against this kind of attitude. Therefore, the criticisms that Yehoshua used to make cannot be seen as a criticism of a group, or of this movement, but of some individuals who were part of this group. Besides all the criticisms he made, he ended up aligning himself with the Pharisaic movement and mentality, making him even more a truly Pharisee.

**Pharisees, enemies of christ**

The term *Pharisee* became synonymous with "hypocrisy" and "killer of christ" from the earliest days of Christian theology. It was precisely this group that inspired some church fathers to compose extremely anti-Semitic works, as in the case of John Chrysostom and Martin Luther:

*The synagogue of the Jews is a worse place than a brothel or a bar:*
*a refuge for robbers, a cave of wild beasts, a temple of demons,*
*a den of thieves and perverts, a house of devils, a congregation*
*of christ-slayers. They are all worthy of being slaughtered.*
John Chrysostom, Adversus Judeos, vol.68

*Jews are little demons destined to hell. Burn their synagogues,*
*force them to work and treat them severely. They are useless, we*
*should treat them like mad dogs, lest we be partners in their blas-*
*phemies and vices, so we don't receive the wrath of God upon us.*
Martin Luther, father of Protestant and Evangelical
churches

Just as the Pharisees were the "bad guys" of the New Testament, they were also the good guys. I believe that before the church judges the Pharisees, it should look at history itself, not just the Catholic history, but all Christians strands histories, for the cradle is the same for them all. We see many strands where women are forbidden to wear makeup, earrings, only wear skirts, men cannot wear shorts, and even in extremist cases, some denominations claim that a woman who chews chewing gum is a sinner. Such attitudes and doctrines differ in nothing from what was practiced and taught by the Pharisaism of the time of Yehoshua. We must understand certain things about Pharisaism, for they were the first to develop places of worship (synagogues), they were those who began the "evangelism" by sending missionaries all over the places, they came up with the idea that each human being has the ability to have an intimate relationship with the Creator, it was they who developed the spiritual structure of angels, demons and, above all, it was they who educated Yehoshua.

Both Christianity and Judaism owe much to this group and to the sages that came out of there.

### The Pharisaic Worship to God

Due to the Babylonian exile, it became necessary for the people of Israel to develop other forms of how to worship God and, according to the Pharisees, one of the most important of them, is the study of the Torah. It was because of the lack of knowledge of the word of God that the people failed, a failure that caused the disobedience by which God allowed the destruction of the Temple. Every synagogue of the first century, as well as today, is basically divided into two parts, the *Beit Tefilah* (house of prayer) and *Beit Midrash* (house of study). Both houses are within the same *Beit Knesset* (synagogue) and have distinct functions.

The *Beit Tefilah* is where the scrolls of the Torah are

found and is the place where people gather for the reading of it on the night of Shabbat and for all kinds of prayer and worship. The *Beit Midrash* is where the Scriptures are studied, both the Written Torah and the Oral Torah, according to the understanding of the orthodox group that maintains that synagogue.

The interesting thing is that Yehoshua mentions this structure in a conversation with Peter, as reported in the book of Matthew:

*And I tell you that you are the stone and I build on you my BEIT TEFILAH. And the gates of Gehinam will not prevail before you.*
Matthew 16:18

Due to the innumerable modifications of the new Testament made by the church, we have lost the essence of what Yeshoshua was doing and this led many to believe that he was founding a new religion. What Yehoshua was setting, in that conversation with Peter, was just a *Beit Tefilah*, a house of prayer. What strikes me at most is that, he does not say a *Beit Knesset* or even a *Beit Midrash*, he only mentions the place where the Torah is read and the prayers are held, this shows that the structure of the *Beit Midrash* should be maintained. In simpler terms, Yehoshua brought a new interpretation of the Torah, which allowed a more intimate contact with the Creator and this generated a new way of praying, of approaching God, far beyond the customs of his time, but the studies, the form of teaching, what should be learned, should be maintained, i.e. the Pharisaic method of teaching. The teaching of the Written Torah and things from the Oral Torah, that do not oppose to the Written Torah, should be taught and practiced, and it is at this point that many don't get it. This is just one of the reasons that caused the church to be so far from the true People of Israel.

### Pharisaic Reaction to Miracles
According to Jewish literature, Yehoshua was not the

only one who performed miracles. Rabbis like Onias and Hanina Ben Dosa are remembered for the numerous healing miracles they have performed, from healing a simple deaf to healing people with more serious illnesses. Miracles and casting out demons were not uncommon in first-century Judaism, and Yehoshua even makes a critical comment about miracles that were made by some Pharisees:

> And if I cast out demons for Baal Zevuv, then why your sons do not expel them? They will be your judges.
> Matthew 12:27

However, there was a miracle that no one had ever done, the healing of a leprous man, and such a phenomenon is vastly mentioned in the New Testament as proof of Yehoshua's Messianism, since only Mashiach would perform acts that no man could perform. When Yohanan, the immerser, orders his talmidim to ask Yehoshua if he really was Mashiach, among many deeds, Yehoshua mentions that the lepers were pure, showing a feat not common throughout Jewish history of performed miracles.

According to the Torah, every leprosy heal should be reported to a priest, who should declare that the person has become ritually pure or not. At that moment, an offer must be given in the Temple to confirm the healing before God:

> On the eighth day he shall bring two lambs without blemish, one of them in its first year of life without defect, three tenths of a measure of chosen flour mixed with oil for the food offering, and one log of oil.
> This must be presented before Adonai by the man to be cleansed at the entrance of the tabernacle of the congregation by the priest who shall make the cleanse.
> Leviticus 14:10-11

Although many people believe that Yehoshua abolished the Torah, in fact, he encouraged and required its practice. In one of the cases that he heals a leprous man, he commands this person to introduce himself to the priest and to make an offering, as determined by the Law:

> *Yeshua stretched out his hand, touching him, and*
> *said: I desire that you be purified and at that time*
> *the leper was cleansed of his leprosy.*
> *And Yeshua said to him, Be careful when you*
> *tell this to the men, go to the priest and offer an*
> *offering as ordered by the Torah of Moses.*
>
> Matthew 8:3-4

This fact is of the utmost importance, for in addition to showing that he performed miracles beyond those performed by the Pharisees, he taught the importance of observing the Torah in its smallest details.

Yehoshua was a great Pharisee, connoisseur of the Written Torah and the Oral Torah, it was very clear in his teachings that no commandment should be added to those already given by God. Those who help others to follow the commandments of God, will be well accepted by Him. However, what Yehoshua was really against to, is when one adds something in the Law of God and teaches it as if it were God Himself who determined it. Those were the reasons that caused the biggest clashes between him and some Pharisees.

# SECTION III
## THE TORAH'S

The People of Israel were born from a promise made by God to Abraham, at a time in history where few people served the True God. The merit Abraham had before God, by renouncing the idolatry of his time and of his home, made him worthy to be the first patriarch of a people formed and chosen by God. This promise was fulfilled in its full form at the Mount Sinai, at the moment when Moses goes to its top and receives the Torah from the very hands of God.

The Jewish mysticism tells us that the Torah was created by God in its entirety before the creation of the world, just as an engineer draws a plan before beginning his work, God created the Torah, as His plant, to create all the things described by the book of Genesis, for God used it to put order in the world He had just created. The moment it is delivered on Mount Sinai, is the moment of its materialization and revelation of who the true Creator God is, and how He should be followed and loved.

The word Torah means "target", for it is the target that all who follow God must hit. Although strongly associated with Judaism, because it is the cervical spine of the Jewish people's faith, in fact, it was handed over to a people, not to a religious sect, it was delivered as a guide of life for those who want to follow the One True God. It is vitally important that all can unravel the Torah from the Jewish religion, so they may understand that it serves to gather those who fear God under His wings.

Within modern Judaism, as it was in the first century, there are two Torahs, the *Torah she-bichtav* and the *Torah she-b'al'pei*, which are the Written Torah and the Oral Torah. This second is what really defines the religiosity and the religious rituals of the Jewish religion. Understanding both is of utmost importance to anyone who wants to understand the

New Testament, for it is composed of books written by Jews and for Jews. Jews who were strongly connoisseurs and influenced by both Torahs, including Yehoshua.

## THE WRITTEN TORAH

The Written Torah is the real holy book, it is the only part of the bible that was not inspired by God, but revealed by God, which gives a much greater weight to its importance. The word Torah refers to the first five books of the Bible - Bereshis (Genesis), Shmot (Exodus), Vayikra (Leviticus), Bamidbar (Numbers) and Devarim (Deuteronomy) - but the term Torah has a meaning that goes beyond a name of a collection of ancient books, this term covers foundations, laws, concepts, revelation and all about who truly is the One God.

The weight of the written Torah is indescribable, Yehoshua, the apostles, Paul, and all who appear in the New Testament lived, preached, taught, and propagated the Torah, both among the Gentiles and among the Jews. It was the basis of all the teaching of Yehoshua and he has always put it above any other man made teaching. His life has been devoted to this book and he has brought a proper interpretation of it and that is what best defines his ministry in life.

Many people, especially Christians, believe that the Torah has been abolished by Yehoshua, if that were the case, Yehoshua would be a heretic, blasphemous and far from having the authority to declare himself to be son of God, for he would be putting an end to the greater work of the One who he called the Father. Who really abolished the Torah were the fathers of the church, Catholicism, Protestantism, the evangelical church and all other denominations that were born from the church of Rome, without exception, all Christian branches are and always will be connected to the paganism of the Catholic Church, even if some do not believe in its saints, idols and doctrine.

The restoration that will come before the age of Mashiach is precisely the return of the understanding of the importance of the Torah throughout the world, and those who accept its yoke will be the lost sheep of the house of Israel, both Jews and Gentiles.

## THE ORAL TORAH

The sages say that when Moses was on Mount Sinai, all that God gave to Moses to write was spoken by the mouth of God Himself, and this was the form Moses orally taught the Written Torah to the people. All that is passed verbally, even more at a time when writing was made in scrolls, is much clearer and more detailed, so the sages say, that the Oral Torah has all the details omitted in the Written Torah.

*Those are the laws, rules and TOROT (plural of Torah)*
*that Adonai established, through Moses on Mount*
*Sinai, between Him and the People of Israel.*
Leviticus 26:46

*The plural is used because there are two Torah's, one*
*written and the other by the words of the mouth.*
Rashi, Leviticus 26:46

In this passage from the book of Leviticus, in its original language, the word Torah actually appears in the plural, alluding thus to the two Torahs which were delivered by God on Mount Sinai. It is quite possible that God revealed many things to Moses that went beyond what was written, as we see in the following passage:

*I speak to him mouth to mouth, clearly and not by enigmas*
Numbers 12:8

Most of the *mitzvot* (commandments) of the Written Torah are not explained, the observance of the Shabbat is one of them because it has no specific instruction other than the prohibition of labor. All the explanations of how all the 613 Laws found in the Written Torah are to be observed, are found in the Oral Torah.

According to Rabbi Aryeh Kaplan, the Oral Torah, for many years, has only been passed on orally, because it should had to be something passed from master to disciple, thus making it not possible to be learned by anyone alone, which prevents various ambiguities. Another point that the sages teach about the importance of the Oral Torah is that God already knew that the holy book would fall into the hands of the Gentiles and so, it would be victim of poor and erroneous interpretations, so the Oral Torah was an exclusivity for the Jewish people; so this people would not cease to be unique and singular. The Oral Torah does not only explain the Written Torah, but it is this Torah that defines the Jewish people and sets it apart from all other religions in the world.

### The Mishnah

Moses, during his lifetime, taught the Oral Torah, mainly to his disciple Yehoshua Ben Nun, who in turn, passed it on to the elders of Israel, who taught the prophets and judges of the Sanhedrin. The Sanhedrin was the supreme court of Israel where the judges, who judged the cases according to the Torah were. During the period of the second Temple, these judges began codifying the teachings of the Oral Torah, which is now called the Mishnah.

In the year 188 CE, a rabbi named Yehuda Ha-Nasi gathered all the *Mishnot*, the Torah's commentaries, the explanations and the jewish traditions and brought them together in a single book, that became the Talmud as we know today. This was due to the fear he had for a second diaspora of the Jewish people and such traditions could be forgotten.

### The Talmud

Just as there are two Torahs, there are also two Talmuds, the Talmud of Jerusalem and the most important, Talmud of Babylon.
Whenever the sages studied the Torah and the *Mishnah*, they used to give their opinions about it, they used to analyze it,

and thus engaging in discussions with other rabbis to clarify what was written in the Written Torah, or in the *Mishnah*, and such deeds became known as *Gemarah*, which is nothing more than the rabbinical commentaries on the Mishnah, which is, the Oral Torah.

In the year 505 CE the *Mishnah* was compiled, alongside with its commentaries, known as *Gemarah*, the *baraita* that are external works to *Mishnah* and the *halachah* that is the Jewish law itself, and then the Talmud was born. Because it was written in the Babylon region, the name adopted was the "Talmud of Babylon". A compilation of books that have 517 chapters and 63 tractates, which is the main rulebook within the Jewish religion, stronger than its brother, the Talmud of Jerusalem. Although they were only written after the time of Yehoshua, such concepts, laws, rules and teachings, were already widely taught and lived in his time. Every first-century Jew was educated according to the teachings we find today in the Talmud, as well as Yehoshua certainly was.

According to the sages, the Talmud must be accepted by all the Jewish people as being the true source of Torah laws and therefore, it should not be revoked by any authority and it is precisely at this point that the whole problem, that Yehoshua had, begins.

Without a shadow of a doubt, Yehoshua was educated according to the Talmud, as we read his teachings in the book of Matthew, this is more than proven. Yehoshua was never against the existence of the Oral Torah, the *Mishnah*, the *Gemarah*, or any of the Jewish traditions, for on several occasions, his teachings followed what was taught there by the manner determined there. But he had a very clear thing in his head and that's what he spent his life teaching about, no law, no rule and no commandment, that come from a man, CANNOT, in no way, go against any commandment of the Written Torah, and, above all, no commandment pertaining to the Talmud should be taught as something that

"God has commanded".

Apart from the hypocrisy, which is something natural of the human being, the biggest clashes that Yehoshua had, dealt exclusively with the Oral Torah and how it transformed the behavior of the people before God.

## THE ETERNITY OF THE TORAH

The Torah is an everlasting book, even if the heavens and the earth pass away, the Torah will continue to exist. No sage, prophet, rabbi, apostle and not even Mashiach can annul or abolish the Torah. Anyone who comes in the name of Adonai, even if he performs miracles and healings, if he changes or denies a single comma from the Torah, he is a false prophet, a false sage, or a false Mashiach. Anyone who believes in a Mashiach who has abolished the most sacred book of all, believes in a mythical being created by pagan minds with doubtful intentions. In the age of Mashiach, the truth will be revealed and the world will recognize the Torah as the true and only divine command for mankind.

# SECTION IV
## SHAMMAI AND HILLEL

I can assert with conviction that it is impossible to understand the person who Yehoshua was, as well as his teachings, if we do not have at least a good knowledge about the faith he professed and about the historical and social context in which he was inserted in. The Judaism of his day, as well as today, is strongly influenced by the Oral Torah, also known as the Talmud, which encompasses all rabbinical debates about the interpretations of the laws from the Torah.

First-century Judaism already had the Oral Torah well-defined, which stipulated and regulated the lives of all Jews, the schools of that time heavily focused on the teachings of the *Mishnah* and *Gemarah*, which deals with the debates and applications of rabbinic laws.

Two of the greatest Talmud's rabbis are contemporaries of Yehoshua, Rabbi Hillel and Rabbi Shammai, both of whom have more than three hundred debates and discussions throughout the Talmud, making them the two greatest lawmakers in the rabbinical world. Understanding the lives of these two rabbis is of the utmost importance in order to understand Yehoshua, for he was likely a member of the school of Hillel, which had a strong influence in the Galilean region, for this reason, Yehoshua was greatly influenced by his vision and talmudic teachings. In the other side, Shammai's school was very strong in the Jerusalem area and its students had many discussions with the students from Hillel's school.

Yehoshua's teachings were based on the Torah and on the Tanakh, but the tool he used was the Talmud, both in a positive or in a critical way, many of the clashes he had with other Pharisees were precisely clashes that already existed between these two schools, which shows us that the Pharisees who confronted him, in fact, were most likely students from Shammai's school, for some of the disagreements Yehoshua had with some Pharisees were things that the two rabbis already disagreed.

## RABBI HILLEL

Hillel was born in Babylon and was brought to Yehudah at the age of fourteen, he was descended from David's lineage by his mother's side and was appointed by the sages of his time as a *Nasi* (leader of the Sanhedrin). Hillel was known as someone who preserved love, humanism, human rights, kindness, compassion and had an unbreakable patience.

Hillel was one of the first formulators of the *halachot* (Jewish laws) and how a Jew should observe the Torah correctly. He was also known to have made a great spiritual revolution within Judaism, for he was one of the first to speak of a mystical connection between God and man, how God could speak and communicate with each individual in a clear and direct way. Despite those ideas were criticized at his time, today is very well absorbed by Judaism, as it was by Yehoshua and Christian faith.

Hillel was a man of peace, he always answered all the questions that were asked to him, he had a great appreciation for all human beings, so strong that his school was the only one that accepted non-Jews, thus teaching the Torah to all the nations.

Hillel was indeed a revolutionary in his time and we can see much of his way of thinking in the teachings of Yehoshua, for they resemble much what was taught by this rabbi. He is the author of the famous phrase: *"Do not do to others what you do not want to be done for you"*.

He also had a strong political influence, as he developed several laws that helped keep the Jewish economy alive in his day.

*And whatever you want men to do to you, do to
them, that's all the Torah and the prophets.*
Matthew 7:12

*A non-Jew came to Hillel and Hillel converted him and said,
"What you do not want for yourself, do not do to your neighbor,
that is the whole Torah, the rest is commentaries, go and study".*
Talmud of Babylon, Tractated Shabbat 31a

## RABBI SHAMMAI

Shammai was known for being an extremely righteous man and correct in his ways, but with very little patience. He had a very firm stance towards the foreign oppression under which Yehudah was, and for this reason, he became the *Nasi* after Hillel's death.

Shammai always took the observance of the Laws of God in a very hard and radical way, he accepted no concessions and no excuses when it comes to obedience to the Creator. His students were easily recognized, for it was possible to see in them the radical and exalted ways of Shammai.

Despite Shammai's radicalism, he was a man who had extreme love for the Torah and his people.

*The sages taught in a baraita: One should always be
patient as Hillel and never impatient as Shammai.*
Talmud of Babylon, Tractated Shabbat 30b

## BEIT HILLEL AND BEIT SHAMMAI

Hillel and Shammai came from the same school, both were disciples of Rav. Shemaya and Rav. Avtalyon and so, at first, they had few points of discord, being only three. But due to the social problems of the time, they ended up dividing themselves in two different schools, Beit Hillel and Beit Shammai and from there, they ended up in disputes in more than three hundred cases.

In most of these quarrels, Beit Shammai was much more restricted concerning the interpretations of laws, while Beit Hillel had a more lenient approach, the Talmud ended up being supportive of Beit Hillel in a number of cases although Beit Shammai's school was far more numerous than Beit Hillel.

The dispute was so big between the two schools that there are records of Hillel's students threatening the lives of Shammai's students, which eventually formed two distinct communities within the Jewish people of the first century, both in terms of studies, interpretations, schools, way of life, synagogues and even women, because it was created a prohibition of marriage between people from the other school.

*The Gemarah suggests: Come and listen, even if Beit Shammai and Beit Hillel disagree in a number of cases, they should not prevent anyone from marrying women from the other community.*

Talmud of Babylon, Tractate Yevamot 14b

Yehoshua, because of the region where he was raised, and as seen in his teachings, was clearly a Pharisee from Beit Hillel, all the compassion, kindness, spirituality and the way he used to get into conflict, show the way of thinking that we see in the writings of Hillel. In order to understand what Yehoshua taught, it is important to understand the Torah according to the mentality taught by Beit Hillel, since many of the things Yehoshua taught may not be fully clear without understanding the way of thinking of this rabbi.

On the other hand, it is vital to understand Beit Shammai's line of thought, for many of the Pharisees who came to provoke Yehoshua were from the Shammai's school and they used their teacher's teachings to create debates, just as happens in the Talmud. The Pharisees that provoked Yehoshua were doing something very common between the two schools and between many rabbis in the Talmud. Most of debates took place because Yehoshua used his own interpretation of the Torah, which was more related to the Written Laws than to the laws of men, and that was the real difference in comparison to the Shammai's mentality.

Many of this book's studies, concerning Yehoshua's teachings, will be based on the interpretations of Hillel and Shammai, so that through the teachings of these two rabbis, we can understand the true message.

> *Rabbi Abba said that Shmuel said: "For three years*
> *Beit Shammai and Beit Hillel disagreed".*
> Talmud of Babylon, Tractated Eruvim 13b

# SECTION V
## MASHIACH

Many people who follow jesus consider him the messiah and know that, in order to be the messiah, bringing forth salvation to mankind is a must. However, that does not exactly define what Mashiach is. As many know, the Hebrew word Mashiach means "anointed", for he was chosen and anointed by God to lead His people. The word "Mashiach" appears 39 times throughout the Tanakh and the belief in his coming is part of the 13 foundations of the Jewish faith, as described by Maimonides.

Mashiach will have a God-given authority to rule over all the nations of the world, to impose God's Laws, to teach the true will of the Creator, to end iniquity, and to bring the true meaning of man's creation. Therefore, a faith in a messiah who abolished the Torah is like to believe in a mythical being created by human minds, which is no different from the paganism of ancient times.

### TWO MASHIACHIM

Our sages teach that there will be two *Mashiachim*, one named Mashiach Ben Yosef and the second Mashiach Ben David. In fact, Ben Yosef and Ben David do not represent two people, but two distinct missions that will be performed by Mashiach.

The Oral Torah has several Tractates that deal with this belief, let's look at a few:

*Rabbi Ben Dosa says: the earth will lament over the*
*Mashiach that will be murdered ... ... This explains that*
*the reason is the murder of Mashiach Ben Yosef.*
Talmud of Babylon, Tractate Sukkah 52a

*The beginning of the war of Gog and Magog will begin*
*with the coming of Mashiach Ben David.*

Kol HaTor 1:14

Mashiach Ben Yosef will be the first representation of Mashiach, as reported by the sages, he will be murdered by men. According to an archaeological finding, called "*stone manuscript of the dead sea*", dated about 110 years before Yehoshua's birth, this Mashiach Ben Yosef, after his death, would resuscitate.

Mashiach Ben David, will have the mission to rule over the entire world, to defeat his enemies, to restore the Temple and he will establish a thousand year reign. Throughout this book, I will deal with both representations of Mashiach, however, I will approach more the Ben Yosef version, for it is this one whom Yehoshua claims to be, the Mashiach Ben Yosef.

## Authority of Mashiach

*The Scepter shall not depart from Yehudah, nor
the lawgiver from between his feet; until Siloh
come, and the people shall assemble.*

Genesis 49:10

The Hebrew word SILOH (שילה), according to the *Midrashic* interpretation, is the same as (לו שי) - *tribute to him* - as we can find in the book of Psalms:

*Make vows and pay to Adonai your God; everyone around
you shall bring tributes (שי) to the fearsome.*

Psalms 76:12

Yaakov, in some mysterious way, already knew about Mashiach, as we see in the passage where he blesses his son Yehudah. Somehow, he speaks of the coming of a certain *Siloh* and to him will assemble the people, then in the book of Psalms, we have the same term referring to someone to whom everyone must bring tributes and that someone is fearsome. This shows us the authority that Mashiach will have, he will be King over all peoples, who will render him tributes and he will be feared by all.

## Mission of Mashiach

For an understanding of Mashiach, knowing his mission is essential.

*The earthly mission of Mashiach Ben Yosef has three fronts: revelation of the mysteries of the Torah, returning the exiles and removing the unclean spirit from the earth.*

Kol HaTor 1:11

### 1- REMOVAL OF THE SPIRIT OF IMPURITY

*I will see him, but not now; I will contemplate him, but not now. A star shall come from Yaakov, and a scepter shall ascend out of Israel, which shall smite the Moabites, and shall destroy all the sons of Seth.*

Numbers 24:17

In this passage we have words uttered by the prophet Bil'am, a prophet who came to prophesy against the People of Israel while they were in the desert, the words that came out from the mouth of this man are extremely mystical and full of hidden messages.

Mentioning again Yaakov, it is prophesied that a star will come from him, the name of Yaakov was changed to Israel, then this "star" will come from Israel, which represents Mashiach.

The second thing concerns his origin, for the term *"shall smite the Moabites"*, is the same term that appears in II Samuel 8:2, when it is reported that King David *"smote the Moabites"*, using exactly the same Hebrew terms. Now we can have a connection of this star, that come from Israel, with the house of David.

Lastly, it will be his final mission to destroy Seth's sons. Seth, as son of Adam, begat all nations, so the term *"sons of Seth"* refers to the nations that do not recognize and do not follow the God of Israel. Mashiach will have no mercy upon them, he will not come to preach to such people, he will not come to teach them to repent, but he will come to destroy all the nations which are God's enemies. And that is the meaning of *"to remove the unclean spirit from the earth"*.

## 2- TO TEACH TORAH

As the definition about the deeds of Mashiach is strongly approached by the Oral Torah, it is for it that we should look at in order to understand many things:

*(Gen 41:45) "He who explains what is hidden" - This was said about Yosef, and is one of the missions of Mashiach Ben Yosef, for he will reveal the hidden Torah for all generations.*
Kol HaTor 2:122

One of the main missions of Mashiach is to teach the Torah and this is of the utmost importance. The sages say that all the other books of the Scriptures will become just historical books, for the only one that will remain valid as a "bible" is the Torah itself, this because of Mashiach's explanation as to how it should be lived, leaving aside the need for prophets and sages.

Yehoshua, to be seen as Mashiach, in addition to never being able to abolish the Torah, he must concentrate 100% of his teachings on the Torah and how it is to be observed and lived, this is one of the main functions of Mashiach.

## 3- TO RETURN THE EXILED

This is a well known prophecy, repeated in many parts throughout the Tanakh, the return of the Jewish people to the land of Israel today is a reality after nearly two thousand years.

*Then Adonai, your God will restore your fortunes and take you back in love. He will gather you again from all the nations where Adonai your God will spread you.*
Deuteronomy 30:3

The sages say that the first verses of Deuteronomy 30 refers precisely to Mashiach and his deeds. Verse 3 deals exactly with this, the great work of God to bring His people back to the land of Israel.

Yehoshua, as a great connoisseur of rabbinical teachings, knew all of this three thing very well, and thus made three comments about it:

1) SPIRIT OF IMPURITY

*At that time Yeshua said to his talmidim, do not think that I came to put in the nations (peace), but rather desolation.*
Matthew 10:34

Actually, only the concept "jesus" by itself, already brought much war and death between nations and peoples. But the term "desolation" that he uses, which was erroneously translated as "sword", refers to the term *HaShkutz Shomem*, which appears in the book of Daniel and can be translated as "Abomination of Desolation". Such a term is used to refer to idolatry and pagan nations. Idolatry is the lowest level of impurity and the most hated thing by God.

What Yehoshua is saying is that he will cause the Abomination of Desolation, but as it is expressed in Hebrew, it gives the understanding that he will impose himself against the nations that practice idolatry, thus removing all the impurities by destroying them.

2) TORAH

*Take my yoke as your yoke and learn from my Torah, for I am humble, I am good and pure in heart and you will find rest in your souls.*
Matthew 11:29

Self-explanatory passage, Yehoshua is very clear in saying "my Torah", that is, "*my interpretation of Torah, the way I understand it, how I teach it, and how I reveal it to the world*".

I would like to make a brief analysis of the term

"yoke", because it gives the impression of something negative. In rabbinic language, when a student comes under the supervision of a rabbi, this student is said to have taken the "yoke" of that teacher. The yoke is nothing more than a piece made of wood and placed on the neck of two oxen to unite them and to make them to walk in compass, side by side. The term "yoke" was not used as a burden on the shoulders, but as something that makes two people walk in the same compass, just as it is the intention of the student who walks side by side with his master.

Yehoshua, by using such a term, summons people to walk side by side with him according to his interpretation of Torah, that is, according to his *halachah* (Jewish laws - halachah means "walk" in a direct translation).

3) EXILED

*And Yeshua said to them, I was not sent except*
*to the lost sheep of the house of Israel.*

Matthew 15:24

Many Christian preaches teach that Yehoshua referred to the sinners of Israel, that he came to forgive them and to teach them. However, the term Beit Israel (House of Israel) is used by *Gemarah* to refer to the northern kingdom, known as the Kingdom of Israel, which was invaded by the Assyrians and its people dispersed and assimilated by the world, up to this day, it is not known where they were taken to and neither who are their descendants.

Mashiach will also rescue these people and reunite them again with the rest of the people of Israel. Some sages say that the non-Jew who accepts the yoke of the Torah is somehow a descended from those people, who have been scattered throughout the world. (this will be approached again later on in this book).

### Salvation of Mashiach
We cannot speak of Mashiach without bringing up

"salvation". Even though for many Jews, Yehoshua is not Mashiach, his messianism cannot be denied by the Gentiles, for it was through his life, ministry, and death that many received knowledge about the true God and His word. It is undeniable that, if they depended on the Jews people, especially the Orthodox Jews, Gentiles would have no knowledge about the Living God at all, for in all my life, I have not seen one single Jew taking the word of God to the nations.

Christianity may have several faults, but it was the tool that God used to become known to the entire Western world, and this was done through the figure of Yehoshua Ben Yosef. Unfortunately, the concept of salvation that was grafted by the church in the mind of the Christian people, is not quite the one we have in the bible, especially in the New Testament.

According to many Christian lines of thought, when a person accepts jesus and gets baptized, he guarantees salvation, of course there will be rules to be observed, such as maintaining a puritan life according to the rules created by the church and a constant presence in the temple where the service takes place. Salvation has become a commercial item with a very high financial return for those who preach it, for such a concept can generate a certain fear within the individual through malicious preaching, which ends up bringing him into the bosom of the Christian faith for fear of eternal damnation. Salvation cannot be the motive of a life before the Creator, but the consequence of that life. If one cares about what God determines, salvation is automatically guaranteed.

However, many people confuse salvation with eternal life, but they are not the same things, eternal life is a self-explanatory term, but salvation is a state that must be acquired and then maintained, by simply accepting jesus and being baptize does not mean a free ticket to eternal life, however, a lifestyle does.

According to Paul of Tarsus, salvation is when the person is within the People of Israel as writen in Romans 11. To be part of this "olive tree" and to remain in it, is precisely what we can call "salvation". Becoming part of this people does not mean becoming a Jew, it means serving the God of Israel and keeping His ordinances faithfully, for it is those commandments that distinguish His people from the other nations of the world.

To put it more briefly, Yehoshua's death did not guarantee salvation *per se* to anyone, but his death assured the Gentile the access to the word of God, which, if followed, will lead the Gentile to salvation and automatically to eternal life, this is true biblical salvation.

An interesting example is hitler, a self declared Christian, who at some point in his life was baptized and accepted jesus as savior, on the other side we have more than six million cruelly murdered Jews, who did not accept jesus nor even got baptized. Were those six million in hell and hitler in heaven?

# SECTION VI
## YEHOSHUA IN THE TALMUD

All of the greatest sages in the Jewish history, both positively and negatively, are mentioned by the Talmud. This happens due to their teachings, examples of how life should be lived or even advices about marriage and parenthood. But the truth is, every Torah's scholar, who has caused some kind of repercussion in his days, ends up appearing in one of the Tractates.

With Yehoshua it was no different. There are some mentions about him in the Talmud, three of them by the name "Jesus, the Nazarene", others with a nickname, so he is not easily discovered. Such quotations are rarely brought up or debated, for they do not quite well fit with what Christianity believes and professes. The story at first, may be a bit shocking, but with a little further analysis, it is possible to see to a flaw about Yehoshua in those tales from the Talmud.

### Yehoshua Ben Perahya

*When they returned to Eretz Israel, Rabbi Yehoshua Ben Perahya entered a certain inn. The owner was standing before him and feeling honored by his presence. Rabbi Yehoshua Ben Perahya then sat down and was praising the owners saying, "How beautiful is this place". Jesus, the Nazarene, one of his pupils, said to him, "My master, the wife of the innkeeper is cockeyed". Rabbi Yehoshua Ben Perahya said to him: "how rude, is that what you're looking at?" Then he excommunicated Jesus. Every day Jesus came before him, but the Rabbi would not accept his return. One day Rabbi Yehoshua Ben Perahya was reciting the Shma when Jesus appeared. At this occasion, the Rabbi decided to accept him back, then signaled for him to wait, but Jesus thought he was being rejected by him again. So he went out and raised a stone and worshiped it as an idol. Rabbi Yeshoshua Ben Perahya said to him: "Come back from your*

*sins." Jesus said to him, "This is the tradition I have received*
*from you, anyone who sins and makes the masses sin, will*
*not have opportunity for forgiveness". The Gemarah explains*
*how he made the masses sin: For the teacher said, "Jesus,*
*the Nazarene did witchcraft and incited the masses, and*
*subverted the masses, and caused the Jewish people to sin.*
Talmud of Babylon, Tractate Sotah 47a

This passage from the Talmud tells a story about a very revolted student of a famous rabbi. The interesting thing is, despite a seemingly offensive story about this Jesus, the true criticism and teaching that the Talmud wants to pass on, concerns the attitudes of Rabbi Yehoshua, for he was very harsh on the student, thus generating a revolt inside of him.

This account is in Aramaic and has been very little commentated or discussed for many years, because, if such a story falls on the hands of the church, a lot of rabbis would end up having to give explanations in order to not lose their heads.

Yehoshua Ben Perahya was a great sage, for a period time, he was the leader of the *Sanhedrin* and had several students and followers, his line of thought was dominant in his time throughout the territory of Israel. From his school came prominent rabbis, such as Rabbi Shimon Ben Shatah, who was master of other famous rabbis, such as Rabbi Avtalyon and Rabbi Shemaya, who in their turn were master of Rabbi Hillel, and it is at this point that we see that this story has something odd, since the connection of Beit Hillel and Yehoshua is very clear.

Certainly, this "jesus, the nazarene" from the Talmudic story above, a student of Yehoshua Ben Perahya, existed. What this student, named Jesus, the Nazarene, has done or not done, it doesn't matter, the fact is that he is not the same Yehoshua reported by the book of Matthew, for Yehoshua Ben Perahya lived about 200 years before the birth of Yehoshua, if it were a five years error, or ten, or maybe twenty, we might have some doubt, but two hundred years is a very discrepant mistake and for sure, they are not the same.

Certainly, this story from the Talmud, which many ex-Christians who become pseudo-Jews, use to justify that jesus was a sinner, is flawed. I am not saying that this story is not real, but it is not about the same person.

## Stoning

The name "Jesus, the Nazarene" is mentioned again in another Tractate, as one who practiced witchcraft, idolatry, and made the people sin. Interestingly, this Jesus from this second Tractate matches exactly on what was reported in the Tractate mentioned above, so I believe, the Talmud continues the story of that same jesus, rabbi Yehoshua's student. I repeat, it is not the same one as reported by Matthew.

*On the night of Passover they hung the body of Jesus*
*the Nazarene after they had killed him by stoning,*
*for he practiced witchcraft, incited the masses to*
*idolatry, and led the Jewish people astray.*
Talmud of Babylon, Tractate Sanhedrin 43a

According to the Talmud, this Jesus, Rabbi Yehoshua's student, was stoned and then had his body hanged, because of the sins already mentioned. Of course, by the context similarities that both passages have, the jesus to which both of them refer, is the same one. This individual, who was suffocated by the religious rules and absurdities of the Jews, revolted, became embroiled in witchcraft, idolatry, and had many followers, for he certainly did wonders. So he was arrested, judged and condemned to death by stoning.

In the time of Yehoshua, under the Roman sovereign, Rome did not allow death penalties imposed by non-roman courts, for this reason that Yehoshua had to be taken before

Poncivs Pilatvs, in order to obtain a roman endorsement to kill him. However, death by stoning is not a method used by the Roman courts, so if this Jesus was stoned, it was before the dominion of the Roman empire over Israel and that began only in 63 BCE, thus confirming a date long before the birth of Yehoshua, the one who is reported in the book of Matthew.

## Onkelos

Due to the revolt that began in the year 66 CE, The Roman emperor Vespasian sends to Israel an enormous force of Roman soldiers led by a general named Titvs. For a little more than three years, Jewish militia fought the Romans on several fronts throughout the land of Israel, culminating in the total destruction of Jerusalem, the Temple and the expulsion of the Jews from all the territory of Yehudah, this is a diaspora that endures up to this day.

Titvs had a nephew named Onkelos Bar Kelonimos, a nobleman and a Roman scholar. One day he decided to go after something that was good for his soul and ended up finding Judaism.

*Onkelos went on and raised Titvs from his grave through necromancy and asked him: who are the most important people in the world where you are? Titvs told him: the Jews. Onkelos asked him: Should I join them? Titvs said to him: "Their commandments are too many, and you will not be up to the task, you'd better stand up against them and you'll be famous."*

*Then Onkelos went on and lifted Bil'am (Balaam) from his tomb through necromancy and asked him: who are the most important people in the world where you are? Bil'am said to him: the Jewish people. Onkelos asked him: Should I join them? Bil'am said to him: You should neither go after their peace nor their war, forget about them.*

*Onkelos then prayed to the God of the Jews and Yeshua*

*appeared before him. Onkelos asked him: who are the most*
*important people in the world you are? Yeshua said to*
*him: the Jewish people. Onkelos asked him: Should I join*
*them? Yeshua said to him: seek their welfare and not their*
*destruction, go, be a good Jew and study the Torah, for*
*they are the "apple" of God's eyes (Zechariah 2:12).*
Talmud of Babylon, Tractate Gittin 57a

Onkelos hears the advice of Yeshua and becomes a Jew. He then decides to translate the Torah from Hebrew into Aramaic and makes a true revolution within the Jewish faith. The translation he made, is a word by word translation and for this reason, was able to maintain the originality of the text, however, by doing so, he was able to do away with some ambiguities, becoming a widely used reference translation when there are doubts in the original.

In any Torah's scroll, in any *Sefer Torah* purchased in any country in the world, any original text of the Torah found written, the only name that ALWAYS appears along those texts, is precisely the Onkelos's name, for his translation always comes along with the original version. Today, his name is an inseparable part of the Torah, a person of weight within the Judaism, and it all began with a counsel from Yehoshua.

**Yeshua and the Disciples**
*Regarding the judgment of Yeshua, the Gemarah quotes*
*another Baraita, where the sages teach: Yeshu had five*
*disciples, Mattai, Nakai, Netzer, Buni and Toda.*
Talmud of Babylon, Tractate Sanhedrin 43a

This quotation from the Talmud has already caused much controversy, for among the five disciples mentioned, only Mattai (probably Matthew) is easily identifiable. There are scientific theses, debates between historians and scholars, but none of them with any concrete conclusions as to who these people were.

Joseph Klausner, in his book *Jesus of Nazareth*, claims that this text was a fabrication during the Amoraic period, by the time that the Talmud was already completed, and it was placed there to cause confusion within the church.

# PART II
# TEACHINGS

# SECTION I
## BERESHIS

*In the beginning God created the heavens and the earth.*

Genesis 1: 1

In the very first words of the book of Genesis, in its original Hebrew, we have many hidden secrets. The initial term, BERESHIS (בראשית), customarily translated as *"In the beginning"* suffers with the translations into Western languages.

In order for us to have a defined beginning, as "THE beginning", the term that should have been used in Hebrew is BARESHIS, but the word that appears, instead of BARESHIS, is BERESHIS, showing us that this is not actually "in THE beginning" but rather "in **A** beginning ". A beginning that took plabce in a completely indeterminate set of time.

It may seem irrelevant, but such an affirmation reveals that in the beginning of all things, as reported by the bible, was not a single "beginning" nor the first "beginning", it was just one more "beginning" among others. Everything that was created in this "beginning" is very well described by the Torah, the heavens, the earth, the animals, the nature, the human being and so on. But, all over the Tanakh, there are things that appear there that were not reported during the moment of creation, as described in Genesis, things that simply already existed and were not revealed to us when, or how, they were created. This proves that the "in the beginning" of the book of Genesis, in fact, is not quite the beginning of all things, but rather a "beginning" that comes after other "beginnings".

The sages tell us that before the creation of the reality where we are inserted into, there were seven other "beginnings", that is, God created seven other things before what is reported in the book of Genesis. These things appear out of nowhere in the Tanakh, which reveals to us that they already existed before all things we know. The understanding about some of them may bring us a light concerning where the name Yehoshua came from.

## 1st BEGINNING - KISEH HAKAVOD (כסא הכבוד)

*Kiseh HaKavod*, the "Throne of God's Glory", appears many times throughout the bible, but its creation is not reported, for it already existed before the Genesis's "beginning".

The Throne of Glory was created before the creation of the world. It is through it that the People of Israel can recognize the true God and can distinguish the true prophet from the false prophet.

There is a long debate in the *Midrash Bereshit Rabbah* if indeed the throne was the first creation, the conclusion comes through a Psalm:

*Your throne is established of old: it is from everlasting.*

Psalms 93:2

The above verse states that the Throne exists from all eternity, its creation preceded all that the human being has knowledge of and only the name of the Creator is above its importance.

*Kiseh HaKavod* concentrates all the glory, power, sovereignty, control, royalty, and strength of the Creator. It will be through it that all people will see how great is the One who created all things.

## 2nd BEGINNING - TORAH (תורה)

The sages say that God is like an engineer, an architect, who developed and created the whole universe. Every project has basically three steps, the first is the idealization, the second is the planning and, finally, the realization.

The Torah has three moments in history, the first is precisely the moment we are addressing. Like every good builder, God first idealizes all his work, so he makes a "plant". He sets up a project establishing how all things will work and it is at that moment that He creates the Torah, so that through it, He can create all things.

The Torah is not just a book, but it is the will and idealization of God, all creation, such as nature, animals and stars, behave according to the will of God. This will was born in that act. When God creates the Torah, He establishes how His whole creation would behave and obey Him. If He created all things without establishing these rules, the creation would have been a total mess.

*Adonai created me (Torah) at the beginning of His*
*course, as the first fruits of His works in antiquity.*
Proverbs 8:22

The second moment of the Torah occurs at the end of the creation of all things as reported in the book of Genesis:

*And Adonai blessed the seventh day and hallowed it,*
*for in it God finished what He had made to do.*
Genesis 2:3

This translation is a little different from the ones we have in English, I tried to keep the most of its original form, but it stills very strange. What does it mean "God finished what He had made to do"? It doesn't make much sense. But with a closer look, the thing He "made to do" refers to the Torah, because He made it to do His creation. When it says that He finished, it means that He finished establishing His Torah in this world in the seventh day. The Sabbath was the day in which God brought the Torah to the earthly realm, it was when He established His rules over all the creations.

Shabbat is not only the day of rest, but it is also the day that represents the Torah, because it was on that day that

God established the *modus operandi* of this world, that is why that day was sanctified.

Finally, we have the materialization of the Torah as reported in the book of Exodus. Moses goes up to Mount Sinai and God gives him the Torah. It is interesting to note that it does not say that God created the Torah in the Torah, but rather that God gives it. If God gives it, it means that it already existed, and since the Torah does not report its own creation, it means that it was created even before the "in the beginning" in the book of Genesis.

## 3rd BEGINNING - BEIT HAMIKDASH (בית המקדש)

The *Beit HaMikdash*, the "Holy Temple", is already revealed in its entirety to King Solomon at the moment he decided to build it. The design, the idea and the idealization in the spiritual spheres had already been established by God. All he needed was to get the "plant" of the Temple and deliver it into the hands of Solomon.

The Temple represents the Throne of Glory in this realm, it is the place where the people will be prepared for the fulfillment of the Laws of God and the summit of holiness. So that the human being could have a minimum of understanding about God's holiness, the Temple had to be created.

*Oh! Throne of Glory, from the antiquity is the place of Mikdash.*
Jeremiah 17:12

The Holy Temple is where the holiness and glory of the Throne of God rests, so it was created after the Throne.

## 4th BEGINNING - TSHUVAH (תשובה)

*Tshuvah*, poorly understood as repentance, has a very different concept from what Western Christian culture teaches. The repentance that is taught refers to an internal and particular feeling of guilt over something practiced or some decision made, which can be an eye opener on how future decisions should be taken from that moment on.

Repentance is, in reality, only a feeling of remorse and is not necessarily connected to God or sin. For example, an individual buys something and ends up taking on a debt for many years, and upon arriving home he realizes what he has done and feels a very strong repentance, even if he has committed no sin. If buying something is not wrong, and making debts is not something condemned by God, then sentimental repentance is not necessarily connected with holy things. However, this feeling is very valid, because it is through it that the real *Tshuvah* begins.

The *Tshuvah*, which in a direct translation means "answer", is an action and not just a feeling, just as "answering" is an action and not just a feeling. The true *Tshuvah*, or repentance, is to take the ways of the Torah, it is a life-changing decision before the Creator. It is not defined as a simple "remorse", but it represents all the sins that a person commits in life and as an answer to them, one gives up everything that is abominable before God and resolves to change his life, leaving the old customs behind and following a life according to the will of God.

*Tshuvah* was created by God to walk in parallel with the Torah, for without one, the other does not exist, there is no repentance without Torah. The creation of *Tshuvah* was so that man would always have an open door to access the Throne of Glory.

## 5th BEGINNING - GAN EDEN (גן אדן)

The Garden of Eden represents the land of Israel, the restored Jerusalem, the age of Mashiach. The moment when the whole creation of God will be directly under His rule, when peace will reign, when everyone will have eternal life and it will be as God's first idealization to His creation.

The creation of the Age of Mashiach (i.e. Garden of Eden) is God's final plan for humanity, it is the apex and goal of all who believe in God. This concept was created because it represents the idealization of the Creator in relation to the crown of his creation, the human being.

## 6th BEGINNING - GEHINAM (גהנום)

What we know as hell is not quite the God-created Gehinam. Gehinam is a place of punishment, it is the place where the souls of those who have lived a life far from the paths of Adonai will be placed, is the counter-part of the Gan Eden seen above. While some will be resurrected and will live the age of Mashiach, most will be cast into the Gehinam.

We cannot understand Gehinam in the way Dante Alighieri imagined, but rather as a place created by God and administered by angels that He determined to stay there. These angels are not enemies of God, they are not there because they revolted against the Creator, but they were placed in the Gehinam to take care of it and to manage this place. For them (angels), being in the Gehinam is not a punishment.

The bible says that, at the end of time, satan will be thrown there. This claim is due to the fact that this cherub was created to take care of this place, just as others were created to stand near the Throne, each with its own function.

Gehinam became necessary before the creation of the world, for it represents the "scale" of God. The Creator is not only good, but also righteous, and justice exists only when there are two opposing sides. If there was only goodness in the world, how would God judge His creation? How would we know that God is really good if we do not know the counterpart of goodness? Why would a human being need God if there was no Gehinam?

**7th BEGINNING - SHMO SHEL MASHIACH (שמו של משיח)**
Finally, before all things, Adonai creates the name of Mashiach.

*His name (of Mashiach) is eternal ...*
Psalm 72:17a

*The name of Mashiach was contemplated, for it
is written, his name precedes the sun.*
Midrash Bereshit Rabbah 1:4

The name of Mashiach is so important that it is precisely his name that defines him as "the anointed one". The anointing he receives to be what he is, is due to the name he received. Many of the Christians who have jesus as the messiah do not care if his name was jesus or not, and claim that as God knows the heart of each one, He understands what each one refers to. I believe in this definition, but the understanding of the name of the one who they call Mashiach will make a total difference in the life and relationship with the Creator of each one of them.

**THE BEGINNING - BERESHIS (ברשית)**
Now we finally have the beginning reported by the Torah, the creation of the heavens and the earth by Elohim. But in this *Bereshis*, the beginning we are used to, there was also an "expansion". According to the *Zohar HaKadosh*, at the time of the eighth *Bereshis*, six things were also created, for if we read Bereshis in Aramaic, we will have BARA - *created* + SHIS - *six*.

*Bereshis is formed by the segment BaraShis (created six),
because from the end of one heaven to another, there are six
columns that extend from the secret of Bara (created) ... ... The
pillars are Chesed, Gvurah, Tiferet, Netzach, Hod and Yesod.*
Zohar HaKadosh, 1:15b

While creating the heavens and the earth, Adonai created six pillars so that they could sustain His work. The Zohar is a very mystical and difficult to understand book, it uses terms of difficult understanding to explain God's hand work. Let's see each term that is presented to us:

### Chesed

*Chesed* is known as grace, but unlike Christian grace, the *chesed* (grace) that is vastly presented to us throughout the Tanakh, can be translated in two ways, both as "goodness" and as "mercy".

Biblical grace is totally tied to God's commandments, for they determine how that "grace" will reach someone's life. If a person obeys the Creator's will, he will receive *chesed* (goodness), if he does not obey the commandments and do Tshuvah, he will have *chesed* (mercy), two things no man deserves.

Before creating the heavens and the earth, Adonai brings to this reality His goodness and His mercy.

### Gvurah

*Gvurah* is the opposite of *chesed*, it is the severity of God. He brings this to the human reality so that it can serve as a punishment at the time of His judgment. The wicked ones, those who do not serve Him, will not receive His *chesed*, but rather His *Gvurah*.

### Tiferet

*Tiferet* is the point of balance in life, it is the column that separates the earthly from the spiritual. Because it is a balancing point, a middle ground, something in mediation. This "column" and its understanding served as the basis for the mystical author of the book of Hebrews to claim that Yehoshua is the "mediator", for in that moment, God created the concept of sacrifice, both the one that used to happen at the Temple, and also the one that would happen to Yehoshua.

The sacrifice is what connects the human being with the Creator, it is what mediates both, not only the animal's sacrifice at the Temple, but also a personal sacrifice, such as fasting for instance.

### Netzach

*Netzach* represents spiritual understanding, the capacity that God created and gave to men to be able to understand Him within the earthly reality. Hence we have the creation of *Emunah*, of faith.

Whenever Yehoshua spoke of those who possessed little faith, it was precisely the *Netzach* that lacked these people, for it is only through the understanding of the spiritual world that man is able to create faith within him.

### Hod

*Hod* represents man's intelligence and the capacity given to him so that he can understand creation and thus develop himself in it. Science, development, engineering, all come from this concept. *Hod* is vital for a minimal understanding of the word of God and the work of His hands.

### Yesod

It is man's ability to accomplish attributes that are unique to the Creator. *Yesod* is the human being's ability to become a tool of blessings in the hands of God when He works miracles through them.

This includes the ability of prophecy, healing through prayer, visions, dreams, and so on. Every form that God manifests through man.

After all of this, the heavens, the earth, and all that is in it, were ready to be created, for everything that would sustain all the work of God was set and ready.

### --DISCLAIMER--

I want to make very clear here that a self-study
of these terms cited here is extremely risky. Such
"columns" here cited have been used as a basis for
various forms of occultism, witchcraft, magic and
illusionism, as well as divination and foresight.
Things Totally FORBIDDEN BY TORAH.
Seeking knowledge of this through the internet,
books by unknown authors, commercial kabbalah
and dubious sources can bring unnecessary
weight to the lives of those who do this.
The teachings of true Kabbalah cannot be disconnected
from the Torah and applied to other areas of life, as many
teach around. Such knowledge can only be passed by
tzadikim sages to people with at least 40 years old of age.
I reaffirm, if you do not know someone who is
fearful to the Torah to learn those things from,
do NOT seek information on this subject.

## SECTION II
**THE NAME**

*And she will give birth to a son and he will be called* **Yeshua,**
*for he will save* **my** *people from their* **iniquities.**
Matthew 1:21

*And she shall bring forth a son, and you shall call his name*
**JESUS:** *for he shall save* **his** *people from their* **sins.**
Matthew 1:21 KJV

First of all, I believe that it is very important to know
the real name of the one who is the main subject of the
book of Matthew. Names, throughout the bible, are very important, their meanings reveal a lot about the person who's
named after them. By having an understanding about them
brings another perspective on our object of study and its
mission on this earth. So I believe it is necessary, before
starting the study of the book of Matthew, to make an approach on the true name of Yeshua and what "message" that
name wants to pass on, and in the first chapter we have all
the revelation we need.

Looking at the passage above, we will see an apparent
simple verse that contains much information hidden from
the eyes. Both the church's theology and the traditional
Christian understanding about the essence and the person
of Yeshua, were altered because of the misinterpretation of
these simple words.

I have placed both translations side by side in order
to analyze three inconsistencies between them that, despite
the simple appearance, make all the difference to understand what the real meaning of his name is and its connection to his work.

**Jesus**
First, it is vital that we know that the name "jesus" is

nothing more than a Latin/Greek translation of a diminutive form of his true name. Jesus never been his name, but rather the name of a pagan god created by the church, which has a very close semblance to the real Yeshua.

There are many theories around the word "jesus". Some claim that it refers to two Greek gods, IE + SOUS - IE, beloved of zeus and SOUS, the zeus itself, others say that it comes from Aramaic YE + SUS - YE, divinity and SUS, horse, alluding to some sort of false god in a shape of a horse.

Despite all of these ideas circulating around this word, the truth is that jesus is a word transliterated from an erroneous form of his name. Jesus is such a relative word in Western languages that, depending on the spoken language, its writing and pronunciation change.

Many claim that it doesn't matter what his real name was, what matters is that when they use the name jesus, God knows the intentions in their heart and will heed their supplications. Whether that is fact or not, what I do know is that the name is so important throughout the Bible that all we know about the Creator God is HIS NAME, everything that comes from Him is linked to that name and this was the most profound revelation that He gave about His own Being.

For this reason, I believe, we should not deny the need to know his true name and the dimension it possesses. It does not make sense for someone to declare him as Mashiach and not even know his real name. When Jews speak about Mashiach, the first thing they debate is precisely what his name will be, for it is through his name that he will be recognized. The church, for having created a jesus, lost all understanding about the real Yeshua, for it has been disengaged from his name.

**THE NAME**

There are some revelations that are lost when we do not read the bible in its original language. One of them is the word pun used by the angel when he told Yosef what his son's name should be, I'll put the verse one more time and leave some terms in the original form:

*And she shall give birth to a son and he will be called YESHUA, for YOSHIA my people from their iniquities.*

Matthew 1:21

Here we see something very common in Hebrew texts, this type of word pun appears in numerous passages throughout the Tanakh and the Talmud. This is a further proof that the book of Matthew was originally written in Hebrew.

YOSHIA means "He Will Save", as it appears in Western translations, but the great problem is that we have the impression that the one who is going to save is jesus, or Yeshua, and that is where the problem is in not understanding his true name.

Yeshua is a variant of the name Yehoshua, just like the name Daniel stands Dani or the name Thomas stands Tom. There are reports of this variant in the Tanakh:

*The Israelites had not done so since the days of Yeshua Ben Nun to this day.*

Nehemiah 8:17

*Then Yeshua, the son of Yozadak ...*

Ezra 3:2a

The Yeshua of the book of Ezra was the high priest at the time of the construction of the second temple, if we look in the English translation, his name will be Joshua. Just as in the first verse, Yeshua Ben Nun is none other than Joshua, Moses' servant, who led the people into the promised land. That is, in English, the name of jesus is actually Joshua, for Joshua in Hebrew is Yeshua, a short nickname from Yehoshua. It is worth remembering that this is not the original name of Joshua, his name was Hoshea, but was changed by God at a certain point in his life, just as it happened with

Abraham, Sarah and Yaakov.

Now that we know what his real name is, we must find out what weight that name has and what it can reveal to us about Yehoshua's mission.

Yehoshua is a junction of a name and a verb, as well as the name Rafael (Rafa - heals + EL - God). The name that is used in in the word Yehoshua is precisely THE NAME ABOVE ALL NAMES, the Tetragram (יהוה) – *YEHOxxx* – in connection with the verb LEHOSHIA (להושיע) – *to save* - conjugated in the future tense of the third-person singular YOSHIA (יושיע).

**YEHOxxx (יהוה) + yoSHIA (יושיע) = YEHOSHUA (יהושע)**

The name Yehoshua is the junction of the true and deepest name of the Creator to the verb "to save", so we will have ADONAI WILL SAVE, unlike the word jesus, which means nothing. In the book of Matthew, his name appears in the contracted form of Yeshua, but in other books, in its originals versions, such as the book of Luke and the book of Yohanan, his full name appears as Yehoshua Ben Yosef.

As mentioned above, people called Yehoshua ended up receiving the "nickname" of Yeshua, something very customary until the first century. In some cases, people called Yehoshua were called Yeshu and I believe it is precisely from that word, yeshu, that the word jesus arose. This is another reason we must be careful, because yeshu is a pejorative acronym in the Hebrew language:

Yeshu (ישו) - "**Yimach SH**emo **U**ezikro" (may his name and memory be erased).

If indeed the name jesus came from the word yeshu, which is quite likely, in an indirect way, the use of the name jesus makes a negative reference to Yehoshua Ben Yosef.

## INIQUITIES
Unlike the Western translation, in which the word

"sin" appears, in the original we have "iniquities". A person who practices iniquities is a person who transgresses laws and regulations.

For sure, the transgression of some law of God can be directly related to sin, but in this case, salvation does not come to take the people out of sin, but to remove the people from a lawless life, a life without Torah, the Law of God.

Matthew uses this description to prove that Yehoshua is Mashiach, for the first mission of Mashiach is to reveal how the Torah is to be lived and the last is to rule all nations through the Laws of the Torah. To say that he came to end iniquity through the Torah makes much more sense in the Jewish mentality than one who comes to save from sin, for that does not make a tangible sense, besides in the Christian mystical mentality.

With that in mind, I am going to re-introduce verse 21 by making some changes in the word pun and I believe the words of the angel will be much clearer in this way:

*And she will give birth to a son and he will be called "Adonai Saves," for Adonai will save His people from a Torah-free life.*
Matthew 1:21

Although many believe that only jesus saves, the Bible says quite the opposite:

*I alone am ADONAI, the ONLY one who can save you.*
Isaiah 43:11

The mission of Mashiach is to bring forth how the Torah is to be followed and observed. Through a walk in holiness before the Creator, we will be on the path to salvation, which is given only by Elohim and the name Yehoshua represents this.

This name makes complete sense with his mission, for he came to bring the interpretation of the Torah, all of his preaching was based on the Torah, his death opened the doors for the Gentiles to know God and His Word, he brought the knowledge of the Laws of God to the entire world, thus giving the chance for all to have a life without iniquities.

**Interesting fact**

The famous modern rabbi Yitzhak Kaduri, who died in 2007 at the age of 106, was a famous religious master in Israel, considered one of the greatest connoisseurs of Jewish mysticism and a strong influencer on political and social causes of the State of Israel.

Rabbi Kaduri was considered the supreme authority of Kabbalah and his predictions were very accurate, his prophecies were always seen as warnings and his counsels as true blessings.

A few months before his death, Rabbi Kaduri wrote the name of Mashiach on a small piece of paper as revealed to him by God and asked that it only be opened seven months after his death. According to the Israel Today newspaper, the note reads as follows:

*As for the letters of the abbreviation of the*
*name of Mashiach, he will raise the people and*
*prove that his words and laws are true.*

*This one I signed in the month of chessed,*
*Yitzhak Kaduri*

Many were disappointed at first with this note, for they were waiting for the revelation of the name of Mashiach, and it was at that moment that they realized something which is only possible to see by the way it was written in Hebrew:

ירים העם ויוכיח שדברו עומדים
*Yarim HaAm VeYokhiakh SheDbaro VeTorato Omdim*

From right to left, if we get the first letters of each

word we will have (יהושע), transliterating, YEHOSHUA.

## THE NAME AND JERUSALEM

I firmly believe that the name of Mashiach that will rule over all nations is Yehoshua, and I say this because of the many missions Mashiach will have, one of them is the rebuilding of Jerusalem and its Temple.

Such feats will not be exclusive to Mashiach, since two other people have already done so, one of them was Ezra by rebuilding the Temple that was destroyed by the Babylonians and the second one is Nehemiah, who rebuilt the walls of Jerusalem, which in an indirect way, represents the reconstruction of the City. But the question is, what does all of this have to do with the name Yehoshua? Everything!

If we make a mystical analysis of their names using Gematria, many things can be revealed and we will be able to see something very deep.

NEHEMIAH (נחמיה) - 5 ה + 10 י + 40 מ + 8 ח + 50 נ

= **133**

ESDRAS (עזרא) - 1 א + 200 ר + 7 ז + 70 ע

= **278**

YEHOSHUA (יהושע) - 70 ע + 300 ש + 6 ו + 5 ה + 10 י

= **391**

Well, we have the value for the name of Ezra 278, of Nehemiah 113, and of Yehoshua 391. Apparently there is no connection between the three, but if we think that Nehemiah rebuilt the wall and the city, Ezra rebuilt the Temple and Yehoshua, as Mashiach, will do the work of both of them by rebuilding the wall (city) and the Temple, we would have:

278 (Ezra) + 113 (Nehemiah) = 391 (Yehoshua)

Now we have another proof that the name of Mashiach is Yehoshua, for as Ezra and Nehemiah rebuilt the wall, the city and the Temple, Mashiach will restore the holy city, will protected it and will rebuild the Holy Temple.

The name Yehoshua shows that Mashiach will bring the revelation of the Living God and His Torah, by which, Adonai will save. It also shows his mission to rebuild the holy city and the Temple and finally, as Joshua (also Yehoshua) led the people to the land of Israel, Mashiach will also lead his people back to the holy land.

Knowing the true name of Mashiach makes all the difference.

*May Hashem grant us the gift of being able to study
and teach for all the days of our lives, so that we have
the merit of the final redemption, when Mashiach
Ben David comes to rebuild the Temple.*
Rav. Moshe Feinstein, Iggeros Moshe, V I 17


*The definitive result will be when Mashiach comes and
the Holy City will descend from the heavens.*
Kav HaYashar 102

*He will bring Israel from all parts to his holy city, the nation that
will build His Temple. The TZADIK will gather around Mashiach
and those who study the Torah will be able to study it with him.*
Metsudah Chumash, Bereshit 49:11

# SECTION III
## YOHANAN AND THE MIKVEH

Talking about the famous Yohanan (John, the Baptist) can be a bit tricky. Yohanan had involvement with not well known groups around the land of Israel. The little that the Bible speaks about him, and his teachings, shows how radical he was in relation to his beliefs and attitudes.

According to David Flusser, in his book *The Sage From Galilee*, Yohanan's words closely resembled the teachings of the Essene community, and it is very likely that he was part of some of these communities. By the time Yehoshua comes to him, it is possible that Yohanan had already separated himself from these groups, for the Essenes had a mentality of separation from the rest of the Jewish people, and Yohanan wanted to offer an opportunity for all Israel of repentance and forgiveness, contradicting some of the Essene's core beliefs.

**THE BAPTISM**

The thing that most attracted people to Yohanan was precisely what Christianity calls today as "baptism". Such a custom was very common in the Jewish milieu since the departure of the Hebrew people from Egypt and it is also a commandment found in the Torah, called "Mikveh". In order for us to understand the mysterious Yohanan, it is vital that we understand what a Mikveh is, how the Torah defines it and how the sages deal with it.

*Bring Aharon and his sons to the entrance of the*
*Tent and immerse them in the Mikveh.*

Exodus 40:12

*Then I will sprinkle the pure water (mikveh) upon*
*you, and you will be purified; I will purify yourselves*
*from all your filthiness and from all your idols.*

Ezekiel 36:25

*Adonai, mikveh of Israel, all those who forsake*
*you will be ashamed...*
Jeremiah 17:13

Before the beginning of the work in the Tent, God commanded Aharon and his sons to be immersed in the Mikveh, a ritual of purification, which symbolized the beginning of their ministries. All of the members of the tribe of Levi who had some work at the Temple, before they could begin, they should go through an immersion in the waters according to what is determined by the Torah. With Yehoshua was no different, he came to Yohanan just before beginning his mission effectively, the fact that he was "baptized" was not to receive salvation or forgiveness of sins, but as a purification ritual before beginning his teachings, so obeying the Torah.

Interesting that in the book of the prophet Jeremiah, the term Mikveh was translated as "hope" in several bibles that I've checked, but what the prophet is saying is that the true purifier of Israel is God Himself. The famous baptism was something that had been done long before the coming of Yehoshua. The Mikveh was not only done before the beginning of one's ministry, but also as a purification ritual if certain things established by the Torah happen, such as touching a corpse or after the monthly flow of the woman , these people should be submerged in the waters of Mikveh.

Many believe that baptism was created by Yohanan and disclosed by jesus, others think that they were ideas created and imposed by the church and also, there are those who say that the baptism of jesus was to rescue him from the old practices of the Torah in his life.

None of this is true and what few people know is that, such "baptism", exists as a ritual of purification since the creation of man. The *Midrash* says that shortly after Adam was banished from the Garden of Eden, he sat by a river that flows from the garden of Eden in order to reflect on what he had done and as a process of *tshuvah* (repentance) he dives and washes himself in a symbolic way, an attempt to return to its original perfect form.

What Christians call baptism, Yehoshua called Mikveh, which is nothing more than a ritualistic submersion determined by the Torah, and unlike Christianity, which imposes baptism as a prerequisite to go to heaven, the true baptism determined by God possesses different purposes.

The Mikveh, which Yohanan used to do and for which Yehoshua passed through, had nothing to do with the intention of guaranteeing salvation to anybody, since salvation is tied to *tshuvah* (repentance) and not to Mikveh. The intention of the Mikveh was precisely to purify the one who was submerged , in other words, to override the previous state. Imagine a seed that is planted on deep soil, before it begins to take root, it must first disintegrate, cease to exist in the form of a seed in order to be born in the form of a tree. For one to attain a higher spiritual level, one must first undo his present state and this happens through the Mikveh.

At Mount Sinai, prior to the delivery of the Torah, God commanded to all people to enter the Mikveh, so they get purified from the Egyptian paganism's impurities and to be prepared to receive the Torah. During the forty years the people wandered in the desert, the famous "fountain of Miriam" became the Mikveh that Aharon used to prepare new priests. At the time of the Temple, every Jew who wanted to enter the house of God, should first pass through the Mikveh.

On the day of Yom Kippur, when the High Priest used to enter the Holy of Holies, where no other living being could enter, he immerses first in the Mikveh as a preparatory ritual to stand before the Creator. Such a ritual is biblically very important, it serves to remove the impurities of the woman after menstruation, serves to immerse the new convert and serves to purify someone who had some contact with corpse. So, in the Torah, this so called "baptism" is not meant to be done just once, but something constant, that can be done whenever the person deems necessary.

Some sages make a lovely comparison of Mikveh with Noach's story. Why did God decide to end the world? For they were following paths abominable to God. So why was through a flood and not through fire? For by the flood we do not have a punishment but an act of purification, the waters have submerged the world totally, just as the body of man is totally covered in the Mikveh, removing the impurities and returning this earth to its purified state. But why forty days and forty nights? For forty *se'ah* is the minimum required measure of water to fill a Mikveh.

Unlike what is set by the church, Yehoshua was not baptized to be saved, he entered the Mikveh as a preparatory act of purification for the beginning of his ministry. Yohanan, when he was in the Yordan baptizing, he did not baptize people for them to become Christians, nor to ensure that they were saved, nor was it something he did only once in one's life. Yohanan was very clear, he baptized those who wanted to do *tshuvah*. *Tshuvah* is nothing more than repentance, is to quit sin and to have a life according to the Torah. From the moment one makes that decision for himself, one goes to the Mikveh to purify himself and be "reborn" to this new life.

The Mikveh personifies both the uterus and the grave, the portals of life and death.

It is important that this concept is clear, baptism was not an invention of the New Testament, neither from Yehoshua nor from Yohanan, but a Torah's commandment. Baptism was not linked directly to salvation, but to obedience to a commandment, which brings salvation. Unfortunately Christian baptism is used as a gateway to conversion to a religion or as a guarantee of eternal life, but that is not quite what we see throughout the Torah. Yohanan did not speak to the people to baptize and everything would be settled, he taught first for the people to do *Tshuvah* and then get "baptized", that is, first they repented, they decided to return to the path of the obedience to God, of the Torah, and then they were submerged to be purified, becoming thus cleansed to follow this new life that they resolved to have through *Tshuvah*. When one converts to Judaism and decides to follow the path of the Torah, one is also submerged in the Mikveh, but not because he has entered into a new religion, but to be ready and clean before God in order to be sanctified by His commandments.

Baptism is certainly of vital importance, but it must be used in the right way. As we saw above, in the verses of the Tanakh, the Mikveh serves to prepare the person before God in a purified state, let's see what the sages say about it:

### Preparation

*For this reason, halachah determines that one who has*
*not yet immersed himself in the mikveh is not ready.*
Kol Dodi Dofek, Immersion 3

### Purification

*If one is buried in the land of Israel, their sins will*
*be transferred to the ground, the land of Israel*
*will act as the Mikveh, purifying it.*
Rabbeinu Bahya, Devarim 32:43:3

*As the Mikveh purifies the unclean, so also the*
*Holy One, Blessed Be He, purifies Israel.*
Talmud of Babylon, Tractate of Yoma 85b

The three rabbinical commentaries perfectly match the verses quoted above. No one will be ready for a life of holiness, nor ministerial, without what the Christian calls baptism, as I mentioned above, it is also linked to salvation, but not as a final solution to achieve it, instead, it is part of a process that prepares the person for a life that, depending on how it is lived, will lead this person to true eternal life.

Yohanan had an Essene point of view in some cases, the Essenes exhorted the Jews differently from the Pharisees, they focused much more on justice and piety toward their neighbors. According to their view, if this was not part of the person's behavior, that is, a life according to what the Torah determines as "love one's neighbor as oneself," the Mikveh would not be valid before God. They should not seek forgiveness of sins through the Mikveh, but only a physical purification, for the soul would be cleansed only after the tshuvah.

This was exactly what Yohanan preached, first *tshuvah*, back to the ways of the Creator and then they would be ready to purify the body. Water only purifies the body of the one who already has a purified soul.

The Essenes also linked baptism with the Holy Spirit, for as the Spirit serves to write the Torah in the heart of man, after baptism, one will be ready to follow the Laws of God with the help of the Holy Spirit.

## YEHOSHUA AND YOHANAN

A very little discussed subject is the relationship between Yehoshua and Yohanan after the baptism ritual, if we look at the book of Matthew we will see that there are two stories involving them both, that if we place those stories side by side, we will have a very strange conclusion about their relationship.

*And Yohanan answered them all: behold, here I am, trully submerging you in the water of Tshuvah, and then a mightier one than I, who am not worthy to untie the sandals of his feet, will purify you with the fire of the Holy Spirit.*
*The winnowing fork is in his hands to fan his threshing floor, he will gather the grains in his barns and the straw (it will be burned in fire, which is not useful).*

*Then came Yeshua from Galil to the Yordan,*
*at the mikveh of Yohanan.*
*And Yohanan was in doubt about submerging him*
*and said: Is it more propitious that I be submerged*
*by your hands and you are coming to me?*
Matthew 3:11-14

*And heard Yohanan while in prison about the deeds*
*of Yeshua and he sent two of his talmidim.*
*Telling him: are you the one who was to come*
*or should we hope for another?*
*And Yeshua answered them: Go and tell Yohanan about*
*the things you saw and about the things you heard.*
*The blind see, and the lame walk, and the lepers are pure, and the*
*deaf hear, and the dead are revived, and the poor are committed.*
Matthew 11:2-5

How Yohanan, at the time of the baptism, recognizes Ye-hoshua as Mashiach, the one who comes to bring judgment, the one who he is not worthy to untie the sandals of his feet and suddenly, after his arrest, he sends his students to go to ask him if he was the one they were waiting for? It does not make sense, unless Yohanan went crazy in prison or something serious happened that has not been reported.

Since working with such hypotheses would be just speculation, let's try to find a solution by looking at it from another point of view, a point of view according to the teachings of the Essenes.

For this group, which possessed a much more Kabbalistic mentality than the Pharisees themselves, a group with a mentality more involved in mysticism and spiritual mysteries, the Kingdom of Heaven dealt with the post-judgmental moment, the reign of Mashiach, the new Jerusalem. Yohanan certainly followed and believed in this line of thought and it was quite possible that Yohanan himself believed that he was the prophet who would come before the end of time to announce the coming of Mashiach Ben David. Many called him Elijah, the prophet who was to precede the messianic age. For this reason he preached and taught that soon would come one after him who would bring the judgment of God and inaugurate the era of Mashiach.

As he saw himself as the embodiment of this prophecy, he hastened to call the people to do *tshuvah*, to repent, for he knew that it was a matter of a short time for the one with the fork in his hand to come and finish everything that was evil.

However, as we all know, this was not exactly what happened, the coming of Yehoshua did not come to bring the final judgment. The great catastrophes and wars, as the Essenes foretold, wasn't happening, Jerusalem was not beeing restored, the Temple was still standing and the time was passing while Yohanan was imprisoned. He was not seeing what he believed that was going to happen, happening. This was the breaking point between Yehoshua and Yohanan, for he comes to the conclusion that perhaps he was not Mashiach, he started to have doubts in his head, for the Kingdom of Heaven did not present itself concretely as he believed. Due to this, he sent two of his students to question Yehoshua about the truthfulness of who he really was.

Clearly their view point concerning the Kingdom of Heavens diverged at some vital points. For Yohanan, the Kingdom of Heaven was the Messianic era, which, according to his belief, was eminent in his time. For Yehoshua, the Kingdom of Heaven is the fulfillment of the first prophecy given to the people of Israel, which is said that they will be a blessing to all nations, it was a time to open the doors, the doors by which all nations would get to know the Torah, who God is, His strength and His sovereign. The doors of salvation would be finally opened to everyone, and the prophecy of the People of Israel to be a bless for all nations would be fulfilled. This is something that must happened before the actual arrival of the messianic age.

The Tanakh speaks about the coming of Yohanan, so for him, the arrival of the Kingdom of Heavens, as the messianic age, in his time made perfect sense. He probably did not believe that it would be a time period between the end of the Tanakh and the messianic era. In the other hand, the Kingdom of Heavens, as preached by Yehoshua, is exactly the time period we are living now, the era that God has established for all the nations to get knowledge about Him.

Knowing this, Yehoshua brings a parable in response to Yohanan:

*And he set before them another allegory (parable). The Kingdom of Heaven is like the a man who sows good seed. And it is when the men are sleeping, that their enemy comes and sows tares, in the foreign language beriyagah, over the wheat, and goes away. And when the herb grew up to bear fruit, he sees the tares. And the servants approach the lord of the field, and say unto him, O our lord, did you not sow good seeds? Where did this weed come from? And he said unto them, My enemy did this, and the servants have said unto him, Let us pluck up the tares. And he said unto them, No, unless you also pluck up the wheat But let both grow together until the harvest, and at the time of harvest I will say to the reapers: First gather the tares and bind them into individual bundles to be burned and the wheat put into the granary.*
Matthew 13:24-30

For Yohanan, in the Kingdom of Heaven, the *tzadikim* shall be saved and the tares shall be cut off. For Yehoshua, in the Kingdom of Heaven, both of them will coexist, this separation will only take place during the harvest, after what Yehoshua defines as Kingdom of Heaven.

In short, the theological vision of both came into conflict, one totally Essene, while the other, despite some influences from the Essenes, typical Pharisaic. The Kingdom of Heaven is this "in between era" that we see ourselves now, a preparation for the messianic age. Whoever does not live and behave in conformity with what the Kingdom of Heaven requires, will not enter the messianic era. In fact, the Kingdom of Heaven is the fulfillment of a prophecy given to Abraham.

## THE PROPHECY TO ABRAHAM

What is the true blessing that the Gentiles received through Abraham? Is it faith? But faith is something very subjective, no one has faith equal to anyone, the faith Abraham had, only he had. Is it the Torah? But not everyone believes that the Torah still has validity. Is it the Jewish people? What would this prophecy really be?

*I will bless those who bless you, and I will curse those who curse you; and through you all the peoples of the earth will be blessed.*
Genesis 12:3

In order to understand this, we must make an analysis of the Hebrew grammatical structure used in this verse. The Torah is almost entirely written in the passive form, when reading it in the original language, it may end up being a little weird sometimes, but when it comes to prophecy, the verb is always conjugated in the future form. In the case of this promise to Abraham, the verb is VENIBRECHU, conjugated in the passive form in a very unusual way, for it deals with a promise for the future. If we make an analysis of this verb, in its root, it leads us to a Hebrew word widely used in the *Mishnah*, which is MABRICH, which means "to engraft". Then we would have the following:

*I will bless those who bless you, and I will curse those who curse you; and through you all the peoples of the earth will be **grafted in**.*
Genesis 12:3

That is, the true blessing that God promises to Abraham is that all nations may be grafted into his faith, his people. The greatest blessing God can give to anyone is the opportunity to make him a member of His people, member of the people of Abraham.

So, the real promise that God made to Abraham is that through him, all those who believe and obey as he believed and obeyed, will be blessed with the opportunity to be engrafted onto the People of Israel.

This is what Yehoshua defines as the Kingdom of Heaven. We just have to stop and think for a moment, it was only after the coming and death of Yehoshua that all the nations of the world had a chance to know the real God, the book that existed only inside the Temple of one of the world's smallest nations, became the best-selling book in the history of mankind, most countries have laws, whether direct or indirect, based on God's word, laws about family, marriage, theft, murder. Most of the laws practiced by the western nations did not existent among foreigner nations at the time of Yehoshua. Even though many people do not believe in One God, everyone knows what monotheism is, something rare among the nations of the first century. The whole world knows about the existence of Israel, of its faith, of its people, of its history, something that was only known by the nations that lived near the land of Israel. Everything has changed, the knowledge to which the whole world has access today is like never before. One way or another, at least one Torah commandment everyone observes now a days, even by those who doesn't believe in it. The mindset and education that many countries have, are based on the bible. The opportunity that have been given to every man on earth to be grafted onto the People of Israel is what Yehoshua defined as the Kingdom of Heaven. It is incredible how he knew it, that's why he taught that both wheat and tares, good and evil, would be together in this Kingdom, differently from the messianic era, when those who are not in conformity with what that Kingdom demands, will be cut off, as he explains in the following parable:

*And the servants went out into the ways, and invited*
*all who were found, good and evil, and CHUPAH*
*was filled with those who were eating.*
*And the king came to see those who was eating and saw*
*there a man who was not clothed in CHUPAH's clothes.*
*And he said to him: my beloved, how did you come here*
*without CHUPAH's clothes? And he was silent.*
*And the king said unto his servants: bind the hands and*
*the feet of this man, and cast him into the lowest SHAOL,*
*and there shall be weeping and gnashing of teeth.*
*Many are called, but few are chosen.*

Matthew 22:10-14

*Chupah* is the Kingdom of Heaven, everyone were there, the good and the wicked, for there was one who, even being there, did not behave according to the Kingdom of Heaven, which in the end is thrown into *shaol*. And he ends saying that "many are called, but few are chosen" and that means that even the one who is given the opportunity to know God and His Word, it doesn't mean he will be accepted in the Messianic age, unless he behaves properly, according to the Torah.

There are many people who still hold to the view point that the Kingdom of Heaven is really the Messianic era, as Yohanan believed, for this reason we must look at what Yehonan said in comparison to the words of Yehoshua:

*And he said: Make Tshuvah, for the Kingdom*
*of Heaven **is approaching**.*

Matthew 3:2

Yehoshua uses similar words to refer to the Kingdom of Heaven, but with a different verbal conjugation:

*From now on Yeshua began to preach and speak about returning to Tshuvah, for the Kingdom of Heaven **had come.***

Matthew 4:17

Yehoshua claims that the Kingdom of Heaven **had already come**. If the Kingdom of Heaven really were the time of redemption, the Messianic age, which is yet to come, Yehoshua would have made a mistake there because we are clearly not in this era yet. The point in common of both is precisely the Tshuvah, that is, the repentance and the return to the ways of the Torah.

This was the greatest clash between them, how each one defined the term "Kingdom of Heaven". But in spite of the discords, Yehoshua knew the importance of Yohanan and also knew that he could not diminish what he represented, for if that were the case, Yehoshua could not affirm that he was Mashiach, because Yohanan should precede his coming. Knowing this, Yehoshua claims the following:

*Yeshua said again to his talmidim: I tell you that among all those born of woman, none arisen greater than Yohanan, the immerser.*
*From his days until now, the Kingdom of Heaven has been oppressed.*
*For all the prophets and the Torah spoke of Yohanan.*
*If you receive it, he is Eliahu, who was yet to come.*
*He who has ears, let him hear!*

Matthew 11:11-15

If we compare those passages with the translations into Western languages that we have at home, we will see a huge difference between them where Yehoshua claims that the least in the Kingdom of Heaven is greater than Yohanan, such claim does not appear in the original and it is completely incoherent.

# THE OAK AND THE REED

*And after that, Yeshua went and began to speak*
*about Yohanan to the crowd: what did you see*
*out in the desert? Moshlechet Baruach?*

Matthew 11:7

*And as they departed, Jesus began to say to the*
*multitudes concerning John, What went you out into the*
*wilderness to see? A reed shaken with the wind?*

Matthew 11:7 KJV

A final topic in relation to Yohanan, which I would like to address, concerns precisely a local term. If we compare the original with the western translations, both are difficult to understand, especially the translation of the original if the reader is not fully aware about the popular mentality of the time of Yehoshua. On the other hand, we also have a Western translation so bad that is almost hilarious sometimes, which leaves the reader completely oblivious to what is written in the text.

For centuries, Israel came under the rule of the Greeks, in that time, a very strong absorption of various aspects of the Hellenistic mentality and lifestyle happened among the Jews. Those new "ideas" completely changed the daily lifestyle in the land of Israel. This fact was so deep and serious that many rabbis wrote various commentaries and texts about this time, it was a time of strong assimilation of the People of Israel by a culture of pagan practices.

Along with these practices, also came art, history and culture as well as their tales, fables, teachings and methodologies. Among them, there was a very well-known tale, which spread very quickly among the Jewish people. By the time of Yehoshua, there was a tale known by absolutely everyone, as some kind of folklore thing. Such a tale was known by *Moshleceht Baruach* and in English, "the tale of the oak and the reed":

*A majestic and unique oak, after being pulled out*
*from the ground by the force of the wind, is hurled*
*downstream and dragged by the current of the river.*
*When crossing with some reeds, in a tone of lamentation, it says:*
*"I would like to be like you who, for being so fragile,*
*are in no way affected by this wind."*
*And they respond:*
*"You fought with the wind and so you succumbed.*
*We, on the contrary, bow before the slightest*
*breeze and thus we remain saved. "*

Yehoshua confronts the people, who thought that a majestic Yohanan, strong as an oak, would be found in the wilderness, but upon arriving there, they saw a simple guy, something more like a reed than like an oak. Then he brings up this popular tale, teaching that although he looks like a fragile reed and without strength, he stood, because he knew to bow to whom he should bow and was not an arrogant as an oak. And he continues:

*Or what did you go out to see? Did you think Yohanan*
*was a person who wore noble clothes? Those who dress*
*in noble clothes are in the palaces (not in the desert).*
*So, what did you go to see? A Prophet? Truly, I*
*say to you, he is greater than a prophet.*
*It is written upon him that is written for my good: Behold! I*
*am commanding my messenger to open the way before me.*
Matthew 11:8-10

*A voice crying out from the wilderness: Prepare the way of*
*Adonai, lift up a way in the wilderness for our Elohim.*
Isaiah 40:3

*"Prepare", this word is addressed to all nations.*
Ibn Ezra, Isaiah 40:3:2

*When the Holy One, Blessed Be He, redeems Israel, three days before the coming of Mashiach, Elijah will come and will be upon the mountains of Israel. At that time, the Holy One, Blessed Be He, will show His glory and His kingdom to all the inhabitants of the world.*

Peshikta Rabbati 35

# SECTION IV
## TEMPTATION

*Then Yeshua was led by the Holy Spirit into the
wilderness to be tempted by satan.
And Yeshua fasted for forty days and forty
nights, and after that he was hungry.
The tempter came and said to him, "If you are the
son of Elohim, tell this stone to become bread.
And Yeshua answered and said unto him: It is written,
that not by bread alone, and so forth.
Then satan took him to the holy city and stood on
the highest place, above all the Temple
And he said unto him, If thou be Elohim, jump
down, for it is written, He commanded his angels
to keep thee in all his ways, and so forth.
And Yeshua answered him the second time: you
shall not tempt Adonai your Elohim.
And satan carried him to a very high mountain and showed
him all the kingdoms of the earth and their glories.
And he said unto him, All this I will give
thee, if thou surrender unto me.
Then Yeshua answered him: Go satan, that is satanas, for it is
written that only to Hashem will I pray and only Him will I serve.
Then satan left him and behold, angels approached
him and served him (ministered him).*

Matthew 4:1-11

Every religion, every belief, every religious community, has its own means of resisting and expelling satan. Many use prayer, fasting, the name of jesus, the shouting, the interview (bizarre, but it happens) and so on. But something I never saw, it's someone resisting or casting away the spirit of satan in the same way Yehoshua did while in the wilderness.

Yehoshua battles satan by using the Torah, not only by quoting it, but by teaching that living the lifestyle determined by the Laws of God is what will keep the adversary away from the life of a man. He did not have to expel him, or to pray, or do exorcism or whatever, all he did was to show that by his lifestyle, Torah-like lifestyle, was enough to keep the adversary and his traps safely away, however much satan tries.

In the three encounters that Yehoshua had with satan, he uses four simple, but profound passages from the Torah to get rid of his presence and to show how his temptations are to be overcome.

## LIVING BY BREAD

*...But man shall not live by bread alone, but of all things found in the mouth of Adonai.*
Deuteronomy 8:3b

When the scriptures present terms such as "life", "death", "will live" and "will die", they do not refer only to physical life and death, but to eternal life and eternal damnation. See Adam himself for instance, when he ate the fruit, even if God said he would die that very same day, he lived more than nine hundred years. So, according to the biblical milieu, the terms "life", "will live", "will have life" and so on. are all referring to eternal life.

The concept of eternal life became very strong in the New Testament, for it is a terminology widely used by the Pharisees and by the Jews of the first century, this is why this idea of eternal life was an intrinsic part of the preaching of Yehoshua. For this reason, in order to understand what he refers to by quoting this passage from the book of Deuteronomy, we must look at what he based himself on.

*For a man to live, he must not place his trust in the bread, but only in that which is found in the mouth of the Lord. By the Laws that come out of His mouth will man*

*live and will be safeguarded by them and they will give*
*him life in this world and in the world to come.*
Bekhor Shor, Devarim VIII:III

According to the commentary in *Bekhor Shor*, the man who seeks eternal life should not seek bread, for bread only guarantees a momentary life, a life on this earth. Instead, man must go after what proceeds from the mouth of Adonai, which not only guarantees the life in the flesh, but also the eternal life. It also affirms that those things that are foung in the mouth of God, that guarantee the life, are His commandments.

We can connect some dots here. It is written that faith is generated inside those who hear the Word of God, it is also known that this Word of God is precisely what comes from the mouth of Adonai. Therefore, as faith is generated by the Word that proceeds from the mouth of Adonai and that same Word is what gives the eternal life, we come to the conclusion that "a man shall live by faith". Out of the mouth of God comes the word, which is heard by man, thus generating faith inside of him and consequently he will inherit eternal life.

This is a biblical concept known to both Jews and Christians, the prophet Habakkuk is the one who makes this affirmation:

*Behold, his soul is puffed up, not upright;*
*but the tzadik shall live by faith.*
Habakkuk 2:4

Although it is a statement that everyone knows, the interpretation that is usually given to those words from the prophet is not very consistent with the message he is passing. Many use this prophecy, especially Christians, to justify that having faith alone, that is, believing in something or in some event, is enough for them to achieve the eternal life. Unfortunately, this interpretation is not from the same root that formed the knowledge basis of Habakkuk, of Yehoshua and of the People of Israel, to whom this prophecy was given. This term "faith", that Habakkuk uses, does not refer to "*believing*" nor to "*emunah*", instead, there is another meaning behind it.

*God gave Israel 613 commandments, by which eternal life would be obtained. If a man observes them, he will live by them. But 613 are too many to remember, King David simplified them, from 613 to only 11 commandments in Psalms 15. But 11 are still too many to remember. Then the prophet Isaiah simplified them, from 11 to 6 commandments in Isaiah 33:13-14. But 6 are still too many to remember. Then in Micah 6:8 we have: "1) do justice, 2) love goodness, 3) walk humbly before God." But even 3 things are a bit heavy. Then Isaiah simplifies them once more, summarizing the entire Torah in just 2 principles in Isaiah 56:1: "Keep justice and do the right thing." And then Habakkuk comes and simplifies the whole Torah in only one principle: "The tzadik shall live by faith."*
Talmud of Babylon, Tractate Makkot 24a

According to the Talmud and the Jewish understanding of the words from Habakkuk, this "faith" is precisely the summation of the commandments of God. The "faith" for which man shall live is the Torah itself and the commandments of God. The Bible speaks a few things about it.

*Therefore keep my statutes and my judgments; which if a man observes, **he shall live by them**. I am Adonai.*
Leviticus 18:5

*"Shall live by them" refers to eternal life. For if you think that this verse refers to this life, is not the man doomed to die in the flesh?*
Rashi Chamisha Chomashi Torah, Leviticus 18:5

*And you shall keep my statutes and my judgments, which if a man follows them, he shall have the life through them, the eternal life.*

Targum Onkelos (Aramaic translation), Leviticus 18:5

*And you shall keep my statutes and the ordinances of my judgments, which if a man observes them, his standing in eternal life shall be among the righteous.*
Targum Yonatan, Leviticus18:5

I believe this makes very clear that the "faith", which Habakkuk speaks of, is not the "faith" taught by the Christian milieu. In this case, "faith" represents the Torah and the commandments that, according to God Himself, those who follow them will live by them, that is, they will have eternal life.

The final proof is precisely what Habakkuk speaks, *"the tzadik shall live by faith"*, what we have as *tzadik*, in English is "righteous". The Tzadik is the one who has the life according to the Torah and the true will of the true God. Thus, we could re-read this verse as follows:

*"He who observes the commandments of God and has a life according to the Torah, shall have his life in this world, and in the world to come".*

**Bread**

It is a mistake to believe that man's ability, his creative power, and his own strength are sufficient to keep him alive on the face of the earth. The primary factor that holds all this earthly existence is the divine providence alone. Those who believe in their own ability to get their daily bread are yet just another victim of the most dangerous disillusionment a human being can have, sooner or later, this foolish believe will come to charge its price.

The bread has a very interesting biblical representation, not only is it the most basic and simple among all kind of foods, it also represents the achievement that every man wants to obtain while on this earth. The word bread in Hebrew is LECHEM (לחם), from the same root of the word

MILCHAMAH (מלחמה), which means war. This gives us a pro-found revelation, for it teaches us that when this "bread" (i.e. whatever a person achieves) DOES NOT come from God, man will enter into a "war" in order to obtain it, a war against his own relatives, against his friends, against himself and for many times, against God. Even if there are some vic-tories in the path of conquering this "bread", the price that comes along with this "achievement" may be unjustifiable and in many cases, too painful. It doesn't worth it.

Now the hidden reason behind Yehoshua's answer to satan is clear. The bread, which represents earthly life and its needs, offered by satan, may be momentarily good, because if it were REALLY GOOD, man would never have hunger again after eating it, for it is only good on that day, at that moment. Just as the promises from satan, or from reli-gions and from practices forbidden by the Torah, they may appear to be good, but it is something momentary, futile and empty, and since this "looking good bread" has the same root as war, and war is something painful, this momentary "good," at some point, will bring pains like war.

*Futile, futility about futility, it's all futile.*
*What is the true value of what man gains by himself*
*through what he does under the sun?*
Ecclesiastes 1:1

On the other hand, for those who do not care about earthly things and live according to God's will, they will have bread every day at the table, without effort, without wars, without pains, and on top of that, they will have a bread that will not allow them to feel hunger ever again, the bread of eternal life.

**TO TEMPT ADONAI**
*Do not tempt (תנסו) Adonai, your Elohim, as you did in Massah.*

Deuteronomy 6:16

This passage mentioned by Yehoshua only makes real sense if studied in Hebrew. The word used as "tempt" is T'NASU (תנסו). The "to tempt" verb - LENASOT (לנסות) - has the same root as the word "miracle" - NAS (נס). What the Torah teaches us here is not to tempt God to do a miracle or to prove His existence through miracles. His existence is already proven by the perfection we see all over His creation and miracles, it is up to Him alone to decide to do them or not. Following God only because of His miracles is the real prohibition that this passage refers to.

Interesting how Yehoshua rebukes satan with this passage. Perhaps it is because of the impressive amount of religions that exist now a days, which survive through promises that God will work miracles in the lives of those who associate themselves with those religions. Intriguing, for it seems to me that satan likes to "offer" or to "try to call forth miracles" from God, something clearly forbidden to men by the Torah, and I see just that in many Christian strands.

## ONLY TO HASHEM I WILL PRAY AND ONLY HIM I WILL SERVE

Yehoshua, in his last temptation, mentions two passages from the book of Deuteronomy, the first is *"only to Hashem I will pray"* and the second *"only Adonai shall I serve"*.

In the first one, something that is only seen in the original book of Matthew, Yehoshua says that he will pray only to HASHEM. I believe that the person who believes that he is Mashiach, should do as he did and taught, and should only pray to Adonai, just as he says he did. This automatically excludes prayers made to Yehoshua himself, to jesus, to angels, to saints, to the holy spirit, to the dead, to aliens, to prophets, to buddha, to Mohammed, to virgins, and all the everything else that can cross the human mind.

*I will pray (אתפלל) to Hashem...*
Deuteronomy 9:26a

I really do not understand the reasons that lead a person to pray to someone other than the True Creator. I see in Christianity, many prayers beginning with *"my beloved jesus"* or *"my jesus"*, I get the impression that these people serve more a religion and its sick theology than they serve the word of God, who Is and always will Be. But every one knows what is the best for himself.

Now, in the second quote, we have a problem. Yehoshua reaffirms a Torah commandment, ONLY TO ADONAI is to be given worship. In Western versions also appears this claim of Yehoshua in relation to worshiping only Adonai.

Let's look from where Yehoshua takes this quotation from, it says:

*Only Adonai you shall fear (תירא) your Elohim
and only Him you WILL worship (תעבד) and only
in His name you shall swear (תשבע).*
Deuteronomy 6:13

-You shall fear (תירא) - Subordination of our mind and our will to God.
-You shall worship (תעבד) - Total subordination of one's existence to God.
-You shall swear (תשבע) - Subordination of all of one's acts to God.

It cannot be clearer, Yehoshua clearly states that only **Adonai Eloheinu** should be served and worshiped, no one else.

This is the life-style that will prevent satan on one's life, obedience, faith, prayer and worship only to Adonai

Whoever has understanding, let him understand.

❖ ❖ ❖

# SECTION V
## THE KINGDOM OF ISRAEL

*And days have passed and Yeshua heard that Yohanan*
*was taken to prison and then he went to Gilgal.*
*And he passed through Nazarael and dwelt in Kafar*
*Nahum Raitah, which in foreign language is Maritima,*
*on the outskirts of the lands of Zevulum.*
*To fulfill what the prophet Isaiah said:*
*Land of Zevulum and land of Naftali, way of the*
*sea, beyond the Yordan, Galil of the nations.*
*The people who walked in darkness saw a great*
*light, those who dwelt in a land of tremendous*
*darkness saw light shining upon them.*

Matthew 4:12-16

*For if there were to be any break of day for that which is in*
*straits, only the former would have brought abasement to*
*the land of Zevulum and the land of Naphtali – while the*
*later one would have brought honor to the Way of the sea,*
*the other side of the Yordan, and Galilee of the nations.*

Isaiah 8:23 **

*The people that walked in darkness have seen a*
*great light: they that dwell in the land of the shadow*
*of death, on them has the light shined.*

Isaiah 9:1 **

** These verses, in the Western bibles, correspond to Isaiah 9:1-2

Throughout all rabbinical literature, there are very few connections about this prophecy of Isaiah with Mashiach. For this reason, I was curious to know why the author of the book of Matthew made a point of quoting this prophecy from Isaiah, associating it with Mashiach and then, something was revealed to me.

With a very simple interpretation, we are able to

understand one of the reasons why Matthew made this connection, for Yehoshua moved out of Yehudah to the lands of the ancient Kingdom of Israel. Kafar Nahum was a land that once belonged to the tribes of Zevulum and Naphtali, and his presence there brought light to its inhabitants. This is the simple interpretation normally made by those who read this passage carefully, it is a valid one like any other rabbinical analysis. But to fully understand the deep meaning behind the reason that took the author of the book of Matthew to explain, through the prophecy of Isaiah, the motives that took Yehoshua to these lands, is of uttermost importance, and for this, we must make a careful analyses on the words prophesized by Isaiah.

So, if we want to understand all of this, we must find out what would be the "light" that was brought to the Galilee of the nations and what was the real reason why Yehoshua went there.

## THE KINGDOM OF ISRAEL

After king Solomon's death around 922 BCE, Israel was divided into two parts, the northern kingdom, called the Kingdom of Israel, which comprised the tribes of Reuven, Dan, Naphtali, Gad, Asher, Simeon, Issachar, Zevulum, Ephraim and Menasseh, and the kingdom of the south, called Yehudah, formed by the tribes of Judah and Benjamin and the Levites circulating between both kingdoms.

In the year 722 BCE, after many warnings from God, the Assyrian empire invaded Israel and the northern kingdom was conquered because of the evil ways of its kings. The great majority of the people of Israel were exiled, the Assyrian empire displaced almost all the inhabitants of the northern kingdom and dispersed them throughout the world, most of them were taken to Media and Aram-Naharaim and, in their places, people were brought from several other regions of the empire to inhabit these lands.

The lost tribes of the Kingdom of Israel is one of the

greatest mysteries in Jewish history. Multiple theories have been created on top of that, there are those who say that some are in India, others in Nigeria and there are some others who dare to say that the descendants of these tribes are the native Indians of North America.

Numerous archaeological evidences prove that the people of the Kingdom of Israel were eventually absorbed and assimilated into gentile societies and therefore, the people of these tribes were lost and disappeared altogether. Now a days nobody knows what really happened to them, the only thing left was a prophecy about the descendants of these tribes:

> *And you, O mortal, take a stick and write on it, "Of Judah*
> *and the Israelites associated with him"; and take another*
> *stick and write on it, "Of Joseph—the stick of Ephraim*
> *—and all the House of Israel associated with him."*
> *Bring them close to each other, so that they become*
> *one stick, joined together in your hand.*
> *And when any of your people ask you, "Won't you*
> *tell us what these actions of yours mean?"*
> *answer them, "Thus said the Lord GOD: I am going to take*
> *the stick of Joseph—which is in the hand of Ephraim*
> *—and of the tribes of Israel associated with him, and*
> *I will place the stick of Judah upon it and make them*
> *into one stick; they shall be joined in My hand."*
> Ezekiel 37:16-19

Many rabbis teach that in the age of Mashiach, the descendants of these tribes will be reunited in the land of Israel by the hands of the Creator Himself. There is something within each individual of the People of Israel that sets him apart from all other nations, except the Torah, all the descendants of Yaakov have a divine spark within their souls, a spark that is passed on from generation to generation. The descendants of these tribes, now scattered throughout the four corners of the world, do not know that they are part of God's chosen People. Those unknown chosen people, scattered all around the world, among various nationalities and creeds, will be called back through this divine spark that they have in their interiors, in their souls. These people, even without knowing or understanding why, they will quickly accept this divine call that will be made through Mashiach.

*Rabbi Eliezer says: Just as the day is followed by darkness and then the light returns, then also, even if it becomes darkness for the lost tribes, God will definitely bring them back to light.*
Talmud of Babylon, Tractate Sanhedrim 110b

The redemptive work of Mashiach is precisely to gather God´s people, he will bring back all the descendants of Yaakov to serve The Almighty. Rabbi Eliezer's statement is a slight allusion about what the Talmud states about Isaiah's prophecy, this rabbinic understanding is the probable reason why Matthew makes a point of quoting Isaiah in his book. The fact that Yehoshua had a connection with this region and some of the people who lived there, makes a lot of sense concerning his claim to be Mashiach, for this attitude demonstrates, even for a moment and only in a symbolic way, his connection with the northern kingdom. When Yehoshua went to these regions outside the land of Yehudah, he did not go after the Samaritans or the Gentiles, nor did he do "evangelism." He went after the remnants of these tribes, already showing one of his purposes. In one of these trips he states:

*And Yeshua said to him, I was not sent except to the lost sheep of the house of Israel.*
Matthew 15:24

Many Christians believe that these "lost sheep of Israel" are Jews who are under the curse of the law or they teach that those sheep represent the Gentiles who will accept jesus or even that these sheep show how the Jewish people are a lost people.

But leaving all these vicious Christians interpretations aside, this claim actually shows that he came after the lost sheep of the house of Israel, these sheep which he refers to are not the Jews, not the inhabitants of the Kingdom of Yehudah, but the lost descendants of the Kingdom of Israel, those people who were scattered, lost and who belonged to the other ten tribes of Israel. As well as teaching the Torah, redeeming the people and ruling over all nations, another work of Mashiach is precisely to gather the lost descendants of Yaakov, who was also called Israel. This attitude on the part of Yehoshua corroborated with the claim that he later made to be Mashiach.

Another rabbi comments the passage from Isaiah 9, relating the "light" to the end of the work made by the Assyrians, that is, the end of the dispersion of the sheep of Israel:

*After the fall of what the Assyrians did, there will be no one left of Israel who will remain in the dark and they will see the great light.*

Malbim, Isaiah 9:1

## HYPOTHESIS

Recently, a strong and unexplainable interest for the Torah in the Gentile world has taken place. In many parts of the world, many Christians are casting aside the common teachings and dogmas of the church in order to seek answers in the divine Torah. The thirst for knowledge about Adonai grows in the Western world in an unprecedented way, many people are putting aside the typical Christian mentality and are associated themselves with the commandments given by God.

Such a phenomenon, never seen before, tends to grow more and more as the age of Mashiach approaches. Perhaps these people, who's casting the religion aside, in order to take the yoke of Torah, are the people once lost, are the people who have a divine spark within their souls, the very same spark that was found in the children of the tribes of Israel and perhaps, these people are the descendants of the lost sheep of the House of Israel.

If we make some connections with the work of Yehoshua, this hypothesis may be plausible, for he himself declares that he came to gather the lost sheep of Israel. Whether one accepts it or not, it was through his life that the knowledge about the One God and about the Bible came to the Gentiles, it was not through a Jew knocking door to door teaching the "good news". For this reason, the statement that he does in relation to his mission, began to be fulfilled after his death and is becoming concrete in the present day.

I do also believe that it is not because one belongs to some Christian temple or any Christian congregation that he is a descendant of the House of Israel, for many of those, who find themselves in these religions, are strongly attached to them, to their theories, theologies, and dogmas. At the same time that Christianity has placed many people under a yoke, it was through Christianity itself that God kept those lost sheep close to Him and now, the time has come to separate them from the Western religions by bringing them back to the true will of the Creator.

It was said that the signs of the coming of Mashiach will be perceived as we look at Israel, perhaps, this Israel is not the State of Israel, instead it is the Kingdom of Israel. I believe that this spark that exists within many people, which shows that they are the descendants of these lost tribes, will serve as a beacon that will prelude the coming of Mashiach. This spark serves as some sort of radar, for this movement that has taken place all over the world, where people are increasingly seeking the Torah rather than the teachings of men, clearly shows that God is gathering their people for the messianic age. Perhaps, this is the Israel to which we must look at, many Gentiles approaching without a reason to Israel and in a miraculous way, placing themselves under the yoke of the Torah, this is not normal.

Thus, the "light" reported by Matthew and prophesied by Isaiah is now coming into the lives of those who are starting to understand the idolatry practiced by Christianity, the lies that have been taught for years by the church and they begin to identify themselves and to connect themselves to the only truth, the Word of the Creator.

SO MAY IT BE IN OUR DAYS!

# SECTION VI
## ASHREI

*And he opened his mouth and spoke with them saying,*
*Ashrei the one who has the humble spirit,*
*for his is the Kingdom of Heaven*
*Ashrei those who wait, for they will rest*
*Ashrei the meek, for they shall inherit the earth.*
*Ashrei those of heart and innocent hopes,*
*for they will see Elohim*
*Ashrei those who seek peace, for they will*
*be called sons of Elohim*
*Ashrei those persecuted for being tzaddikim,*
*for theirs is the Kingdom of Heaven.*
*Ashrei will be you when you are persecuted and rebuked*
*and when they tell you many bad things because*
*the Torah, all falsely spoken.*
*Rejoice, your reward will be great in the heavens, because*
*they persecuted the prophets.*
Matthew 5:2-12

*And he opened his mouth, and taught them, saying,*
*Blessed are the poor in spirit: for theirs is the kingdom of heaven.*
*Blessed are they that mourn: for they shall be comforted.*
*Blessed are the meek: for they shall inherit the earth.*
*Blessed are they which do hunger and thirst after*
*righteousness: for they shall be filled.*
*Blessed are the merciful: for they shall obtain mercy.*
*Blessed are the pure in heart: for they shall see God.*
*Blessed are the peacemakers: for they shall*
*be called the children of God.*
*Blessed are they which are persecuted for righteousness' sake:*
*for theirs is the kingdom of heaven.*
*Blessed are you, when men shall revile you, and persecute you,*
*and shall say all manner of evil against you falsely, for my sake.*

*Rejoice, and be exceeding glad: for great is your reward in heaven:*
*for so persecuted they the prophets which were before you.*
Matthew 5:2-12 KJV

The classic "beatitudes", widely known and preached by the Christian world, are nothing more than ancient precepts within the Jewish mentality and are dated long before the construction of the first Temple. When we compare the translations, as shown above, we can perceive strong discrepancies, both concerning the subject that is the same in both, as in the parts of the KJV that do not exist in the original, showing us the very likely manipulation made by the old church of some parts.

In the original, the verses 6 and 7 found in western translations, are not in the original version. My analysis will only be done according to the original, leaving the "extra" verses out, for those "adds" are subjects that are not in accordance with the Jewish mentality.

## ASHREI

What we have as "blessed", in Hebrew appears the term ASHREI (אשרי), which is of very common use in the rabbinical environment up to this day. Certainly, Yehoshua did not invent such jargon, for he, in addition to using a language that everyone knew, essentially taught using YVRIT TANAKHI (biblical Hebrew).

The *Siddur* (book of Jewish prayers) and the book of *Tehillim* (Psalms) are filled with the term ASHREI refering to those who are blessed according to their walk. The term ASHREI does not refer to someone who is blessed by God, but to someone who becomes blessed by the way he lives. Both concepts, although close, deal with two totally different kind of people. Yehoshua, by beginning his teaching with this term, refers to the walk and the behavior of his talmidim.

*ASHREI the man who does not walk according*
*to the counsel of the wicked...*

Psalms 1:1

The word ASHREI also refers to the name of a prayer, already well known in the time of Yehoshua, which is recited three times a day and which was composed of excerpts from Psalms 84, 115, 144 and 145.

**BLESSED**

**1-** The first ASHREI refers to a humble spirit, which is commonly taught as financial humility, implying that the poor will receive the Kingdom of Heaven, but the humble that he refers to here, is the humble of spirit. This means that our spirit must be free from pride and arrogance. We must have the understanding that everything that happens in the life of the one who really seeks the Creator is thanks to Him and not to one's own attributes and merits. It may seem simple, but for any human being, self-control of one's own ego, especially when God accomplishes something great through him, is very difficult. Not to receive the glory of men and to have the full knowledge of it, is truly to become an ASHREI. As the master of Yehoshua said:

*Be humble in spirit before all men.*
Rabbi Hillel, Pirkei Avot 4:10

*The same Yosef who took care of his father's lambs is the*
*same Joseph who was in Egypt and became a leader there, he*
*kept himself right and tzadik, because of his humble spirit.*
Rashi, Exodus 1:5:1

In addition to the resemblance between Yehoshua and Rabbi Hillel, Yehoshua teaches according to the Jewish mentality. In Rashi's commentary on the book of Exodus, he claims that Yosef became a leader, and even as a leader, he remained humble in the same way he was when he shepherded his father's sheep.

2- The second ASHREI addresses those who "wait". Israel has a long history of "waiting", a story of perseverance that we see up to this day, they waited for a land, waited for a Temple, waited for a king, waited for the return from the exile, waited for victories over their enemies and still wait, wait for the end of the diaspora and wait for the Mashiach's government.

When Yehoshua brings these words to those who hear him, he says that all of this "waiting" will come to an end. The "rest" he mentions at the end, refers to the redemption of the People of Israel under the wings of Mashiach. He confirms that all the hopes and promises made to Israel, after all the "waitings", will be fulfilled.

Also, one of the Talmudic titles given to Mashiach is Menachem, which means one who brings rest.

*What is his name? Some say Menachem is his name, as it is written: "For he that brings rest (Menachem) that will relieve my soul, is far from me" (Lamentations 1:16).*
Talmud of Babylon, Tractate Sanhedrin 98b

3- The third ASHREI deals with the meek. Some understand that a simple hearted person or a meek person is a weak one who bows down his head to anything, maybe this is truth in the Western mindset, but that's certainly not what Yehoshua was referring to.

The Hebrew word used for "meek" is ANAVIM, plural of ANAV, which actually symbolizes a power under control. Imagine a sport car that can reach 100 km/h in less than 8 seconds, but the driver, due to the traffic laws, does not drive at speeds above 60 km/h, despite having great power, this power is maintained under control. Such a teaching refers to all who has some sort of authority, from religious to political. When someone in charge knows how control his "power", by not becoming arrogant nor an abusive person.

Those will "inherit the earth", for they know how to properly lead.

This is something very rare to be seen these days, we have the famous saying that says: *"Want to get to know someone? Just give him some power".*

*As we have seen, ANAV (meek) is one of these names. So, where the greatness of Hashem is found, his humility will also be found there through the word ANAV (meek).*
Kav HaYashar 66:1

In this passage of a great Jewish sage, we see that God himself is ANAV, he keeps his power under control to not destroy everything, being one of the greatest greatness and mercies of the Creator, so we must imitate Him and also be ANAVIM (meeks).

**4-** The fourth ASHREI shows how it is getting more and more difficult to follow the Torah of Yehoshua. Having a pure heart seems an almost impossible task to achieve and maintain. We tend to fail in the ways of God and of the Torah, even with the best of intentions, our actions and thoughts do not even come close to what we need to do to achieve this ASHREI.

This idea of a pure heart ends up tied to other intentions, for in order to attain a pure heart, we need the help of God Himself and to do so, we must become *tzaddikim*, which is obtained only through the observance of His Holy Laws. By linking one point to another, life according to what God wants is what will enable man to see Him.

*David called his heart impure, as it is written, "Create for me a pure heart, oh God!"; for the heart is unclean because of the evil inclination.*
Talmud of Babylon, Tractate Sukkah 52a

*Incline my heart to His testimonies (to the Torah), and give me a pure heart so that I may see Him and serve Him in truth.*

Tikkun HaKlali 12

If King David himself needed God's help, imagine us?! Another *Tikkun's* sage asks for a pure heart to see and to serve God, following the same mentality of the teachings of Yehoshua. He also connects the need for this new and pure heart with the Torah. Impressive!

**5**- The fifth ASHREI deals with peace, with Shalom, but here we must draw a line between these two words (peace and shalom), for although peace is the direct translation of the Hebrew word Shalom, both have very different essences.

Peace, for the Western mindset, is the absence of conflicts, both external and internal. However, the word Shalom (שלום) has the same root as LEHASHLIM (להשלים), which means "to complete".

In order for us to attain Shalom we must attain completeness, over which we have:

*His merits - Therefore it will be discovered that he occupies himself and thus will have his completeness (LEHISHLEM - SHALOM) and when he attains it, he will gain the benefit of his own hand and receive his portion.*

Da'at Tevunot 14

We are told that through Shalom we will receive our portion from the hands of God Himself and Yehoshua reveals to us what that portion would be, to be called sons of God, the Most High. But what would this completeness be? How to achieve it?

*Mercy and truth meet each other; TZEDEK (tzadikim) and SHALOM kiss each other.*

Psalms 85:11

Completion to be called the son of Elohim? It will only be possible by the Tzaddikim! That is, only those who observe the Torah will be complete and will receive the merit of being called sons of Elohim.

**6** - The sixth ASHREI deals precisely with what we have said in the previous one, with the tzaddikim and with the suffering that they may go through due to the fact that they are obeying the precepts of Hashem.

Such things happen as much in Judaism as in Christianity, many of the Jews who end up leaving aside the rabbinic laws to follow exclusively the Torah are frowned upon, mainly within the Orthodox community, they end up not having the faith recognized and undergo several criticisms, losing much of prestige within the community in which that individual is a part of.

The same happens within Christianity, pejorative terms such as "Judaizing," "legalistic," or "under a curse" are extremely common to those who truly follow God through His Torah. Yehoshua says that if this happens to those who follow the Torah, they should rejoice, for it will be theirs the Kingdom of Heaven.

This is a very deep bond that Yehoshua makes between the Torah and attaining a blessed life. As he himself said: *let him that hath understanding understand.*

**7-** The seventh and last ASHREI refers to those who suffer false testimony because of the Torah, a sequence of the previous ASHREI's thought. But there is one conclusion we can draw from it, is it not for the Torah's sake that the Jewish people are so persecuted? And maybe that's why there are so many truly blessed Jews out there. Interesting, is it not?!

Yehoshua, in his beatitudes, preached nothing new, he

only preached Torah, he preached ancient Jewish concepts, he brought forth his Pharisaic origin, and he expounded in an illuminating manner the importance and the outcome of certain actions and behaviors. These teachings were not for the foreign hearers, but for those from the House of Israel and Yehudah.

AHSREI should not be interpreted through a Western Christian mentality, so that will be no mistakes.

# SECTION VII
## SALT AND LIGHT

*At that time Yeshua said to his talmidim: You are*
*salt in the world, if the salt loses its flavor, with what*
*will it be salted? It will have no use for anything, it*
*will be thrown out to be trampled under feet.*
*You are the light of the world, a city built*
*upon a hill cannot be hidden.*
*A lamp is not lit to be placed in a hidden place where*
*it cannot shine. But one should put it on a Menorah,*
*to illuminate everyone in the house.*
*Therefore let your light shine before all men, that*
*they may see your good deeds, so that glory and honor*
*may be given to your Father who is in heaven.*

Matthew 5:13-16

Yehoshua teaches in those verses the way his talmidim should behave, he uses two extremely common examples within Jewish and Torah culture. Both salt and light play a strong role in many spheres in the rabbinic mentality, which was how Yehoshua's understood these two items.

**THE SALT**

Salt has many facets. In the ancient world, having salt was a status of power and wealth, the Talmud mentions the relation between the salt and the world:

*The world can not exist without salt.*

Talmud of Babylon, Tractate Soferim 15:8

Salt was also an important commodity of exchange, but above all, salt has two great meanings in the Torah. The first one, salt is a vital item for innumerable kinds of offerings at the time of the Temple:

*...This must be an everlasting covenant of salt before*
*Adonai, for you and for your generations.*
Numbers 18:19b

*A covenant of salt means that He made a covenant*
*with Aaron of something that is holy and enduring,*
*for salt keeps the holy things enduring.*
Rashi, Numbers 18:19

*You must season all your meat offerings with salt; you must*
*not omit the salt of your covenant with your Elohim from your*
*meat offering; with all the offerings, you must offer salt.*
Leviticus 2:13

*The government of the Kingdom of Hashem will come as the*
*salt, which gives flavor to all food, for salt is like a holy alliance.*
Ramban, Leviticus 2:13

Both Rashi and Ramban affirm what Yehoshua had in mind, the analogy of salt with holiness. And holiness, in turn, is obtained only through obedience. Salt, which keeps things lasting, represents the eternal life and the Kingdom of Heaven, for they are everlasting things.

Up to this day, before the Shabbat's *kiddush*, it is customary for Jewish families to throw a little salt above the *Challah* (Shabbat's bread) as a memorial of the time that the Temple existed.

The second purpose of salt is precisely its use for the removal of blood from the red meat. For a meat to be kasher, i.e. according to the rules established by Torah, one of the vital points is that no blood at all is found in it, and for that, the raw meat must be placed in the salt, so the salt may absorb all of its blood, removing the "impurities" from the flesh.

The term "Kasher" is not for food only, but it refers to everything that is in accordance with the Laws of God, for example, a divorce letter when according to the Torah, is considered a Kasher divorce letter. *"Kasherization"* is the removal of impurities from certain things, whatever it may be, and making them in conformity to the Torah, by turning them "Kasher things". Because of this, salt, in addition to the representation of holiness, also represents *"kasherization"*, which is "to become according to the Torah".

Yehoshua, by using salt as an example, teaches that those who follow him have two main missions, the first is to remove impurities from oneself through sanctification, and this is possible only through obedience, obedience to the Laws of God. The second mission is to *"kasherize"* the world, which means to make the world conform to the Torah by teaching its Laws and precepts to men. Living and teaching Torah is the only true way for one to be "salt of the world", for it is the Torah who sanctifies and it is the Torah that *"kasherizes"*. If one does not fit in this pattern, he will be thrown out and trumbled under feet, for one becomes useless.

*The salt should be placed on the meat until no piece of meat is left without salt. It has to be salted enough, so that it is not possible to eat it with that amount of salt (until total removal of the impurities).*
Shulchan Arukh, Yoreh De'ah 69:4

*In any case, both Beit Shammai and Beit Hillel agree that becoming salt requires a change, it cannot be in an ordinary and regular way.*
Talmud of Babylon, Tractate Beitzah 14a

The book *Shulchan Arukh* describes how salt is important for the removal of impurities and for the ***"kasherization"*** of food. In the Talmud, both Rabbi Shammai and Rabbi Hillel agree that "to become" salt (doing the same analogy that Yehoshua does) requires a change, and for sure, this change is behavioral and cannot be in an ordinary way, it is a change that is made in a profound and unique way.

> *He entered the study room, and asked: is this item a Kasher item or a non-Kasher item? And the sages answered: surely Kasher, for a non-Kasher item is not bound to the heavens.*
> Talmud of Babylon, Tractate Sanhedrin 59b

We also see that a Kasher item is not necessarily a food, it can be any item, or even a person. According to the sages, for a man to be bound to heaven, he must be and have a Kasher life and as the salt, he must remove the impurities of this world through his walk.

**THE LIGHT**

The second example given by Yehoshua is the light. This term is not new in the knowledge of his hearers. The prophet Isaiah already said that his people were chosen to be the light to the nations, spreading the salvation of the One God.

> *And he said, You are my very small servant, so I will raise the tribes of Yaakov and restore the survivors of Israel: I will also make them a light to the nations, that my salvation may reach the end of the earth.*
> Isaiah 49:6

What is very difficult for the Christian world to understand is that the promise to be a light to the nations was made to the People of Israel, not to the church, not to the Gentile. If the gentile is being blessed today by the Word of God, it is because the light that came from this people has illuminated his life. In order for one to become light to the nations, he must first become a part of the People of Israel (I do NOT mean Judaism) and for this, he must live according to what defines man as God's People, the Torah.

How can one show his light, the one that Yehoshua

says it has to shine? It can only shine through the good deeds that each of us can do that are observed by other people. This always been a very strong point in his teachings. Our beliefs and actions must always walk together, holding hands. How can one become salt and light of the world if one's actions are not seen by the people around him? That is why James wrote:

*Even so faith, if it hath not works, is dead, being alone.*

James 2:17 KJV

The term "works" refers to obedience to what God has determined and does not refer to Puritanism or works inside a church, as taught by many Christian strands. No one will see Elohim with a "dead faith". However strong it may be, if it is not accompanied by obedience, it is dead!

# SECTION VII
## TORAH'S ABOLITION

*At that time Yeshua said to his talmidim: do not think that I came to* **violate** *the Torah, but to observe it in its completeness. Truly, I say to you that even if the heavens and the earth (depart), a yud or a nekudah will not be abolished from the Torah or from the prophets and everything will be fulfilled. And whoever fails to perform some Torah Mitzvot, however small it is and teaches it to others to do so, will be called HAVEL (futile) in the Kingdom of Heaven and whoever observes and teaches Mitzvot of the Torah, great will be called in the Kingdom of Heaven.*
Matthew 5:17-19

Yehoshua was part of a rabbinic circle, of a society led by rabbis, of a rabbinic-minded reality. In a rabbinic environment, daily conversations are often focused on discussions about the Torah interpretations and its Laws, by doing so, the rabbis might have a better understanding on how to apply it in daily life. Often, Yehoshua uses traditional terminologies which were used in those kinds of discussions, and most of them are not well understood by the Western Christian world. Knowing these terms will bring the truth behind on what he was talking about.

The verses presented above have always generated much confusion in the Christian milieu, for they, quite directly, go against the maxim of Christianity, that the Torah has been abolished. Many say that jesus fulfilled the law so that no one else has to fulfill it, others say that the Torah reached its completeness in christ and for this reason, it was replaced by something called the "law of christ", but all of those teachings are used as excuses for people who want to induce others away from the truth. Teaching the abolition of the Torah is comparable to hiding a lot of dust under the carpet, forgetting that half of it ends up in sight, and so, they elaborate absurd ideas to explain the inexplicable.

The first thing we should pay attention to is the way he starts talking, it already reveals his main goal. The term "I came"- *halakhti* (הלכתי) - within biblical terminology, is used to define a purpose, an intention, so, when Yehoshua begins saying "*I came to fulfill the Torah*" he reveals that his purpose in life is to live Torah and he also came with this mission.

## TO VIOLATE, TO ABOLISH AND TO FULFILL

Another point that we should pay attention to is the form that he affirms this, one of the terms that appears in the original and that I have not found in any translation into western languages, is the verb "to violate". The verb used in Hebrew is *lehafil* (להפיל), commonly translated as "to violate", but there is another rabbinic meaning for this verb and that may have been the real message for the people who were going to study his words in the future. In rabbinic terminology, the verb *lehafil* is used for what in English would be "to overthrow", which is "*to forcibly remove from power or from a prominent position*". Thus, Yehoshua, by using the term *lehafil* - "to overthrow" - affirms that in no way he did come to remove the Torah from its position. The Torah has not been replaced by the "law of christ", neither by faith *per se*, nor by absolutely nothing, and that's not all, he also clearly states that his aim is to observe it completely. Yehoshua lived, preached and breathed Torah all his life and he makes it very clear through his words.

Yehoshua then states that not a *yud* (the smallest letter of the Hebrew alphabet) nor a *nekudah* of the Torah will be abolished. A *nekudah*, or various *nekudot*, are those small dots that are placed beneath the Hebrew words of the Torah, for as the written Hebrew has occult vowels, the *nekudot* help the pronunciation of the Hebrew words, showing how each word should be read. The verb he uses for the term "to abolish" is *levatel* (לבטל), the literal meaning is actually "to abolish", but such a term has a special connotation within the orthodox language, when someone misinterprets the Torah, it is said that this someone is *levatel* - "*abolishing*" - the Torah. By saying this, he affirms that his interpretation of the Torah is valid and not a misleading one.

The Torah will never be abolished, but that term is merely an expression to refers to some misunderstanding of some commandment from the Law. In other words, Yehoshua states that, besides the Torah will never lose its validity, the interpretation he makes is not a misinterpretation, instead a valid one. Finally, he says that everything will be fulfilled, the verb used in this case is *lekayem* (לקים), its meaning is precisely "to fulfill", but, as the previous verbs, it aso has a rabbinic counter-part, which is "*to preserve*". Heaven and earth may pass, God may one day end everything, absolutely everything, but the Torah will be preserved, that's what Yehoshua says.

This kind of affirmation, in the form that Yehoshua expos it, is very common among the teachings of the rabbis, both Pharisees and Orthodox. His words are very close to many things taught by Rabbi Hillel.

*AND THE HEAVENS AND THE EARTH WERE READY -*
*everything has a measure (for it has an end), heavens and*
*earth have measures (both have ends), only one thing has*
*no measures: what would that thing be? The Torah, upon*
*which it is written: its measure is longer than the earth ...*
Genesis Rabbah X:I

*No letter will ever be abolished from the Torah.*
Exodus Rabbah VI:I

*Even if all the nations of the world unite to tear out a single*
*word from the Torah, they will not be able to do so.*
Leviticus Rabbah XIX:II

## THE MITZVOT

Finally, Yehoshua makes a parallel of "small mitzvot" with "big mitzvot", citing that whoever disobeys a small commandment and thus teaches it, will be a "nothing" in the Kingdom of Heaven.

Well, such an ideology comes from several rabbinical literatures, the concept that was used by him is just what the rabbis call *Mitzvot Kalot* (light commandments) and *Mitzvot HaMurot* (heavy or serious commandments). As a clarification of what both mean and what defines them both, I will make use of some examples:

*When you see a bird's nest on a tree, or on the ground,*
*and the mother is laying on the brood, or on the eggs,*
*you shall not take the mother with the young.*
*You shall first let the mother go freely, and then you may*
*take the brood; so that all things may go well with you,*
*and that your days on earth may be prolonged.*
Deuteronomy 22:6-7

*Honor thy father and thy mother, that thy days may be*
*prolonged in the land which Adonai thy Elohim giveth thee.*
Exodus 20:12

Here we have two examples of what the rabbis classify as "light commandment" and "heavy commandment." The command to not remove the mother when she is near her brood is considered a light commandment, simple thing, because many people, never in life, will have the opportunity to remove some animal from its mother while she is around, making this commandment quite improbable to happen. In other hand, honoring father and mother is something that demands much more attention from everyone, since everyone has a father and a mother, thus making it a heavy one. The interesting thing is that both deal with kinship and extension of days on earth.

The problem that can occur here is the contempt of the light commandment, which is a very common thing among many communities that observe the Torah, so giving more importance in what they call heavy commandments. In fact, this distinction, heavy and light, was made by the rabbis not to disparage small commandments, but to over-value the heavy ones, showing that a special attention to them is mandatory.

What Yehoshua does here is just that, he is treating the Torah as a whole, showing that he came not only to fulfill the heavy commandments, but also to fulfill the light ones, which are also very important, so important that Yehoshua uses them as a base to teach how can someone be called "great" in the Kingdom of Heaven.

He brings this theme to the fore, for many of his days, just as in the present day, believes that Torah's observance should be first by doing the heavy commandments and thus the light ones are left behind. What Yehoshua says here is that ALL commandments are HEAVY, so HEAVY that the even the so called light commandments have the same kind of reward as the heavy ones.

Another very curious thing is the term Yehoshua uses to call those who make others stumble, *HAVEL*.

*Havel* is the name of Abel in Hebrew, son of Adam. *Havel* can also be defined as that little "steam" that comes out of one's mouth on cold days, something that lasts less than a second. Another interesting meaning for *havel* is the way that King Shlomo uses that word:

> *Havel Havalim (vanity of vanities), says Kohelet, Haval Havalim (vanity of vanities), all is Havel (vanity)*
> Ecclesiastes 1:2

What we learn from these verses is that Yehoshua, in addition to not abolish the Torah, to affirm that the Torah is eternal and that he observes the Torah, he makes a rabbinical comparison on the commandments contained therein and claims that all of them, light and heavy, should be fulfilled and taught by any man. The reward is the Kingdom of Heaven itself and the status that this person, who does that, will have in it.

## SECTION IX
### LIGHT AND HEAVY

At that time Yeshua said to his talmidim, truly I say to you,
if you are not tzaddikim greater than the Pharisees and
the sages, you will not enter the Kingdom of Heaven.
Have you not heard what the ancients said? Thou shalt not
murder, and he who murders shall be guilty of death penalty.
And I tell you that he who is angry with his friend will
be judged by the court; and he who calls his brother
inferior will be judged by the Kohel and those who call
him a fool will be judged by the fire of Gehinam.
And as you approach near the altar and you remember
that you have a quarrel with your friend and
he is complaining to you about it.
Leave your offering there before the altar, and go and
please him first. Then offer your offering.
And Yeshua said to his talmidim, See that you hasten to
calm your enemies while walking with them, before they
deliver you to the judge, and this judge hand you over
to the servant who will put you into the prison.
Truly, I tell you, you will not come out until
you pay all the money you owe.
And he said unto them, you hearken to the words of
the ancients, you shall not commit adultery.
And I say unto you that whosoever looks upon a woman, and
desires her, yet commits adultery with her in the heart.
And if your right (eye) seduces you, take it
out and throw it away before you.
And if your hand seduces you, cut it off. Better for you to
lose a member than your whole body in Gehinam.
And Yeshua said to his talmidim: they heard what was
said by the ancients, whoever leaves his wife and sends
her (away), shall give her a letter of divorce (Get Kritot),
which in a foreign language is Libeila Repudiation.

*And I tell you that everyone who leaves their wives, give them*
*Get Kritot. But concerning adultery, he is the one who becomes*
*adulterous, and the one who takes her commits adultery.*
Matthew 5:20-32

In the following verses, Yehoshua, in order to expound his interpretation of the Torah, uses a very common rabbinical way of teaching, but in an inverse way. Continuing what he was teaching about light and heavy commandments, he quotes a serious commandment alongside a light commandment and then places the two of them side by side, as if they were in the same level of seriousness.

Unfortunately, many understands the words "*truly I tell you*" as a proof that Yehoshua abrogated the Torah and introduced new laws in its place, for this kind of speaking shows the replacement of what the Torah says. Such an understanding cannot be more erroneous, Yehoshua, by saying "*truly I tell you*", instead of abolishing the Torah, he actually compares the heavy commandments with the light commandments, thus raising the difficulty of following God's Law and this has nothing to do with abolishing or replacing anything in the Torah, as many believe.

**TO MURDER**

The Yehoshua's teaching on the Torah is much harder to be observed than the written Law itself, in other words, to those who claim that following the Torah is difficult, to follow the way it was exposed by him is much more arduous than just following the literal form of what is written. Let's see:

*You shall not murder...*
Exodus 20:13a

He mentions a basic Torah's commandment, which has a high degree of seriousness but easy to follow, and then

137

he compares it to hatred of one's neighbor, which, according to some people, is a light commandment. So he compares the light one to the heavy one, putting the one who is seemingly smaller on a level above a more serious commandment. Such an idea that murder is not only something physical, but it also covers the psychological side too and that begins with one's inner feeling, is not new in rabbinical teachings.

Although many theologians believe that Yehoshua replaces the Torah with new rules, as in this case, replacing the prohibition of murder by prohibiting hatred, they forget that both are in the Torah, what he really does is to place both commandments side by side.

*You should not take revenge or hate your brethren,*
*love your neighbor as yourself. I am Adonai.*

Leviticus 19:18

The feeling of hatred against the neighbor having a weight comparable to murder, was also addressed by another sage:

*Thou shalt not kill with your hand; nor with your tongue, one*
*who witness falsely already commits murder; or by a gossip;*
*or by giving a bad advice; or if you discover a secret that can*
*save someone's life and do not share it, you're like a murder.*

Ibn Ezra, Exodus 20:13

We see here in Rabbi Ibn Ezra's commentary that a bad feeling or a bad attitude towards someone, which is seen by many as something "normal", "light", is actually as serious as murdering.

Another point that we should pay attention to is that, when there is a sin that refers to the relationship "man X man", the simple sense of forgiveness does not resolve the situation unless the case is settled between the two. This is a type of sin that requires corrective action and not only a feeling of regret before God.

There is a story of a certain Jewish mayor in a ukranian city during the 16th century, that story tells that he stole a lot during his administration, after a few years that he left the office, he repented of what he did and went to his rabbi to know what to do. The rabbi explained him that in this case, only the feeling of repentance was not enough and so he should do something to portray himself before the population of that city. This ex mayor then decides to construct a bridge that the city so much needed, with the money of his own pocket, thus repairing the error that he had once made. Only then would his fasting of Yom Kippur be accepted as a sacrifice of forgiveness before God.

Another story deals with two Jewish partners in a business partnership, one of them diverts a large amount of money and the society is undone, years later, the one who stole, repents and to obtain forgiveness before the Creator, he then seeks for his former partner to repair the error. Unfortunately he discovers that his colleague had died and decides to return the stolen money to his children.

What we see here is a deep Torah's teaching, which says that when a man sins against another man, it takes more than a request for forgiveness, but an attitude that somehow repairs the damage done. These are the kinds of sins we must be more careful not to commit.

The same is true about the light commandments, for it is with them that we must be more careful, it is precisely these that lead us to break the heavy commandments. Let's take a closer look at this:

*He who violates a light commandment will inevitably violate a heavy one; he who violates "love your brother as yourself" (Leviticus 19:18), will surely violate "You must not hate your brother in your heart (Leviticus 19:17)" and "You shall not take vengeance nor bear hatred" (Leviticus 25 :35)" and also " He shall abide with you (Leviticus*

*25:35)," and in the end, he shall shed blood.*
Sifrei Devarim, Shoftim 187

Summing up, Yehoshua claims that murder begins with a feeling of hatred, if that feeling does not exist, the possibility of someone taking the life of the neighbor for awkward reasons decreases a lot. To do so, he compares hatred to murder, for if one thing leads to another, one must cut off evil at its root. Such a thought, that a transgression of a light commandment could be the path to a transgression of a heavy commandment is a common sense among the sages.

*He who publicly mocks his neighbor acts as if shedding his blood.*
Midrash Bava Metzia 58b

The verb used by the Torah in the commandment *"Thou shalt not murder"* is *tachmod* (תחמד), which does not simply mean "to take one's life", for if that were the case, we would have a strong contradiction with other commandments that deal with death penalties, or when God sends his people the war. *Tachmod* (תחמד) implies taking a life for awkward reasons. If one is at risk of life, or if his family is at risk of life, this person has the right to protection, even at the cost of the life of the aggressor. The prohibition only refers to killing someone in the role of aggressor.

## ADULTERY

We have the same case here, first he cites a heavy commandment about adultery, then he compares it to something common among many men, which is to look at other women and desire them. This is something so routine for many people that goes completely unnoticed, for this reason, we tend to end up defining such an act as a supposedly light commandment, because it is a very common thing. But Yehoshua compares this light commandment to be more serious than the forbidden act of adultery itself, elevating obedience to a level far above the literal meaning of the commandment, which would be to lie with a married person.

*Sexual immorality exists on many levels, from a look of desire to the unlawful relationship with a virgin or a widow.*
Rabbi Saadia Gaon, Deuteronomy 23

Rabbi Gaon follows the same opinion as Yehoshua in his commentary about immorality found in Deuteronomy 23, as do other Rabbis from the Midrash:

*"To Commit adultery"* (תנאף) *consists of four letters, to remind us that it can be done with the hand, the foot, the eye or the heart.*
Midrash HaGadol, Exodus 20:13

The commandment that we might consider light in this case is that of desire through the eye, because it takes place in one's heart, very personal and very common. However it is something that should be seen in a more serious way, as in many cases, it is not demonstrated outside one's heart, so it can remain hidden for years within the person, without anyone knowing it, maybe not even he does realize it . Yehoshua focused his teachings on the commandments that address more than simple attitudes, address inner attitudes, thus showing that, to follow Torah, it must begin within each one.

*Thou shalt not covet thy neighbor's house: thou shalt not covet thy neighbor's wife, nor his manservant, nor his maidservant, nor his ox, nor his ass, nor any of his neighbor's.*
Exodus 20:17

*You shall not commit adultery.*
Exodus 20:14

These are the two commandments that Yehoshua places side by side. He who covets, before God, commits the same sin as if he had committed adultery. Pharisaic Judaism followed this same line of thought, drawing the same parallel:

*He who looks covetously at the little finger of a married woman acts as if he had already committed adultery with her.*
Kalah 1

*It is not only the one who sins with his body who is called an adulterer, but he who sins with his eye is also called adulterer.*
Leviticus Rabbah, XXIII: XII

## DIVORCE

Marriage has always been something very important within Judaism, the rabbis have always given many directions on how to maintain a blessed relationship. God's perfect plan for a man and a woman is to enjoy marriage until death do them apart. Because the marriage was something settled between two individuals of fallen nature and divorce is a reality, the Torah took some provisions for a limited cases of divorces. If in case this occurs, the man is bound to give his wife a certificate of divorce called *"get"* by the rabbis and in the Torah, appears as *sefer kritot*, which literally means "book of splitting". When divorce occurs within Judaism, it has to be judged by a group of rabbis, who often take months to come up with some decision on it, due to the fact that they believe that with the delay, there may be a possibility for the couple to change their mind.

*Rabbi Eliezer says: For anyone who divorces his first wife, even the altar sheds tears for him...*
Talmud of Babylon, Tractate Sanhedrin 22a

The biggest problem we have here is a false contradiction between Yehoshua and the Torah, for many believe that the Torah allowed divorce, and Yehoshua changed that by forbidding it, except in the case of adultery. This is mainly due to what occurs in Matthew 19:

*And the Pharisees came to him, to tempt him. And they*
*asked him, saying, Is it lawful to leave your wife for any*
*reason, and give her a letter of divorce? (LEAH GAT)*
*And he answered them, have you not read that they*
*were made in old times male and female?*
*And he said, Therefore let man leave his father and his*
*mother, and join his wife, and they shall be one flesh.*
*Therefore, they are not two, for they are one flesh.*
*And what joins the Creator, man cannot break.*
*And they said to him: If so, why did command Moshe to*
*give the letter (GAT KRITOT) and to send her away?*
*And he said to them: Moshe, because of the obstinacy of your*
*hearts, told them to leave their wives. But in eternity it is not so.*
*I say unto you, that whosoever leaves his wife and takes*
*another, if not for adultery, commits adultery. And he*
*that takes a divorced wife commits adultery.*

Matthew 19:3-9

Some of the Pharisees approached Yehoshua saying that
the divorce was authorized by the Torah, which is true, as
follows:

*A man takes a woman and owns her. If she fails to*
*please him because he has found some immorality*
*in her, and he writes her a divorce letter, he shall give*
*it to her and send her away from his house.*

Deuteronomy 24:1

Yehoshua does not create new rules, but he explains,
through the Torah, the divorce that the Torah allows. First
he states that in the beginning, man and woman were created and that both would be one flesh, that is, there was
no case of divorce. He then explains that Moses allowed the
divorce because of the stubbornness of the people due to
their fallen nature, but Moses makes it clear that this is only

allowed if the woman does something offensive, which according to Yehoshua and Beit Shammai, would be some sort of immorality. Finally, he presents precisely his interpretation, which agrees with Moses, who only allowed it in the case of adultery. His interpretation is entirely patterned on the Torah and matches well with interpretations of other sages.

## THE RABBIS AND THE DIVORCE

The *get* is such an important document that there is a whole Tractate in the Talmud, Tractate Gittin, focused only on this subject. Many other Tractates also mention things about divorce, apart from the various rabbinic commentaries spread out various sources.

The interesting thing is how many disagreements there are over the reasons that can lead to divorce. Let's look at the statements made by the masters of the three greatest Pharisaic schools of the time of Yehoshua, Beit Hillel, Beit Shammai and Beit Akiva. With this, we can see what was taught at that time and how Yehoshua saw these ideas:

*And Beit Hillel says: He can divorce her even if there is a small problem, for example, if she burns his food or salts it too much.*
Talmud of Babylon, tractate Gittin, 90a

*Rabbi Akiva says: He can divorce her even if he finds another woman who is more beautiful than her.*
Mishnah Gittin 9:10

*Beit Shammai says: No man should divorce his wife unless he finds in her an immoral behavior as written in Deuteronomy 24.*
Mishnah Gittin 9:10

Beit Hillel and Beit Akiva support divorce for the most banal reasons, one claims that just because the food burns is already a good reason for divorce, Akiva claims that finding a more beautiful woman is enough.

Interestingly, Yehoshua is a Rabbi from Beit Hillel's

school and, I believe, this is the only time that he disagrees with his former master. At this time, we see a rare situation where Yehoshua agrees with some interpretation from Rabbi Shammai, for his major discussions with the Pharisees of his time were precisely with those from Beit Shammai, since both schools had several divergences, which in some cases, generated violent attitudes among the students from both schools.

Both Shammai and Yehoshua believe that the only motive for divorce is any immoral attitude, that normally concerns adultery, and this is the only plausible reason for a divorce letter to be delivered. And it does not stop there, besides the woman becoming an adulteress, the one who takes her, also becomes adulterous.

In short, what Yehoshua teaches here is precisely against such customs of using poor motives for divorce, so he begins teaching with *"you **heard** what was said .."* and not with *"your have **seen** what is written ..."*, for what has been said refers to the traditions and the Oral Torah, while what was written refers only to the Torah of Moses. It goes against what most rabbis of that time used to say, aligning himself with Rabbi Shammai and always using the Torah as the basis of all that he speaks.

The second part of what Yehoshua teaches addresses the person who marries someone who has divorced for reasons other than adultery, if that is the case, according to Yehoshua, both become adulterers when they take someone else, even though the adultery did not occur while they were still married. Yehoshua raises the Torah's standards to a higher level, for nowadays it is common to see people getting divorced. What he says is that whoever gets involved with these divorced people, will become adulterers if the divorce wasn't because of adultery.

Other schools have other viewpoints on this, as in the case of Rabbi Gamliel. His mentality is exposed by one of his best known students, Paul of Tarsus:

> *But separate himself from him that believeth not, let him be parted. For both man and woman shall not be under error. God has called us to live in peace.*
> 1 Corinthians 7:15

According to Paul and Gamliel, if one of the two decides to enter the ways of the Torah and the other does not, then the divorce is valid and makes the person free as in the case of adultery.

To close this teaching, note in verse 20, where Yehoshua states that to inherit the Kingdom of Heaven we must be more Tzaddikim than the sages and the Pharisees, people who dedicate their lives to the ways of the Torah. Just observe the degree of difficulty of Yehoshua's teaching, are we up to the task?

> *Rabbi [Yehuda haNasi] said: which is the straight path that a man should choose for himself? One which is an honor to the person adopting it, and [on account of which] honor [accrues] to him from others. And be careful with a light commandment as with a grave one, for you did know not the reward for the fulfillment of the commandments. Also, reckon the loss [that may be sustained through the fulfillment] of a commandment against the reward [accruing] thereby, and the gain [that may be obtained through the committing] of a transgression against the loss [entailed] thereby. Apply your mind to three things and you will not come into the clutches of sin: Know what there is above you: an eye that sees, an ear that hears, and all your deeds are written in a book.*
> Pirkei Avot 2:1

# SECTION X
## LOVE

*And Yeshua said to his talmidim: you have heard*
*what was spoken by the ancients, and you shall love*
*those who love you and hate those who hate you.*
*And I say to you: you shall love your enemies and*
*do good to those who hate you and make you angry, you*
*shall pray for those who persecute and oppress you.*
*So you be the children of your Father in heaven,*
*who makes the sun shine on the good and on the bad,*
*and brings rain to the wicked and to the Tzaddikim.*
*If you love those who love you, what is the gain to*
*you? Even these impudent ones love those who love them.*

Matthew 5:43-46

I have seen countless people claiming that the Torah preached love to the neighbor and hatred to the enemies and jesus came and ended this, for he was only love. It is a good thing that they are mistaken, for the Torah has never preached love only to one's neighbor, on the contrary, the love ordained by the Torah encompasses friends and foes.

We should always pay close attention to the way Yehoshua begins his teachings and in this case, he begins with *"you heard what was said..."* referring not to the Torah, but to what was taught by men.

*You should not hate your neighbor in your heart.*
*Reprove your neighbor but do not blame him.*
*You should not take revenge or hate your brother,*
*love your neighbor as yourself. I am Adonai.*

Leviticus 19:17-18

*And to the stranger who dwells in your midst as a citizen,*
*you shall love him as yourself, for you were a stranger*
*in the land of Egypt. I am Adonai, your Elohim.*

Leviticus 19:34

This proves that Yehoshua remained faithful to the Torah, without adding or removing anything. His instruction on love closely resembles that of his rabbi and teacher, Rabbi Hillel, who taught everyone should be loved, whoever one is:

*Hillel says: seek to be like the disciples of Aharon, love peace, seek peace, love all people and bring them closer to the Torah.*

Pirkei Avot 1:12

It is clear here that Yehoshua debated the teachings of some individuals, who were leading the people astray from the Torah. Certainly, such teachings did not come from the truly Tzadikim Pharisees, but they came from those with the appearance of Tzadikim, people who is rotten inside. This kind of people can lead those who follow they, straight to the abyss. The Torah always starts from within.

*Shmuel, the young says: when your enemy falls, do not rejoice, and when he succumbs, do not celebrate. For God will see this and it will be evil in His eyes and He will remove His fury from your enemy.*

Pirkei Avot 4:19

As seen above, let God take care of our enemies and do not rejoice over it, ever.

**CONCLUSION**

The Sermon of the Mount is nothing more than teachings from the Torah, rabbinic teachings concerning observance of commandments. The basis of these teachings, was by making comparisons of light commandments with the heavy ones and also the idea that the commandment must be fulfilled first in the heart, so the fulfillment outside will be valid before God.

This makes perfect sense in what Yehoshua, Paul and

the other talmidim taught, for the deed to be valid, there must also be faith, which is nothing more than following the Torah from the heart.

Yehoshua claims to have brought the Holy Spirit and therefore, these teachings of his are what really prove this, for the true function of the Spirit of God is that the Torah begins within the heart:

*And I will put my Spirit within you, and cause you to walk in my statutes, and you shall keep my judgments, and do them.*
Ezekiel 36:27

# SECTION XI
## SOLOMON'S MISTAKE

*Truly, I tell you that even if the heavens and the earth (depart),*
*a YUD or a nekudah will not be abolished from the Torah*
*or form the prophets and **everything will be fulfilled.***
Matthew 5:18

*For truly I say to you, Till heaven and earth pass,*
*one stroke or one pronunciation mark shall in no*
*wise pass from the law, **till** all be fulfilled.*
Matthew 5:18 KJV

This affirmation of Yeshua is very clear and direct to the point, but very misinterpreted by the Christians and by the Jews who study the New Testament. On the Christian side, the understanding is that this sentence is valid only **till** all be fulfilled and as jesus "fulfilled" the Torah, it means that it came to an end, because it would be UNTIL someone fulfilled everything. This error of interpretation is due to poor translation in Western languages, which states *"till all be ful-filled"* whereas in the original the word "till" does not appear. It may sound small, but it changes everything.

In the case of Jewish scholars, however, they see this as a good thing, but later they fall into the same misinterpretation that many Christians fall into, when jesus implies that he changes the Laws of the Torah by laws he apparently creates, which is NOT true.

What got most of my attention in this verse, are some small details on how Yehoshua makes this statement, he uses two words to assert that absolutely nothing from the Torah will cease to be valid, they are the *nekudah*, which are those small dots placed under the Hebrew letters to help the word's pronunciation and the Hebrew letter YUD ('), which is the smallest letter of them all.

Within rabbinic literature, the letter YUD (') has several references, always in a very mystical way; The rabbis use it as analogies to their parables and stories. There is a very interesting one that tells how this very small letter caused the bigget misfortune in the life of King Solomon. Such a story was already well known in the first century and has always been a lesson to many. Maybe, this story was in Yehoshua's mind at the moment he makes that statement.

## THE YUD AND THE KING

It was good enough for Yehoshua to say that the Torah would never be abolished, but instead of that, he uses two terms to explain where he wants to get. As nothing is by chance, the use of these words serves to reveal something between the lines.

There is a Torah's commandment that requires from every king of Israel to write for himself a hand copy of the scrolls of the Law. According to Rashi, it should be two copies, one large to stand by his throne and one small, so the king may carry it in his pocket wherever he goes.

*When he is seated on his throne, he should have a copy written by him in scrolls before the Levitical priests.*
Deuteronomy 17:18

So, every man who becomes kings should sit down and write the whole Torah with his own hands before the priests, and keep these scrolls always by his throne to help him at the time of making decisions. It also shows how no king will ever be above the Laws of God.

Everyone knows that King Solomon was a king of many women (more than seven hundred wives, according to the bible) and I wonder how was the day that King Solomon made his copy, more precisely, when he wrote down the following verse:

*He (king) shall not multiply for himself many women, for this will divert his heart, nor shall he gather silver and gold in excess.*
Deuteronomy 17:17

It is interesting to imagine what happened to Solomon at this moment. Is it true that the wisest man in the history of mankind has forgotten what he himself wrote, or has something happened that we do not see? A midrash tells a little more about that day:

> When God gave the Torah to Israel, He gave positive and negative commandments and also commandments to a king, saying, "The king must not multiply wealth for himself, he must not multiply women for himself or his heart will go astray". But Solomon arose and went to study this commandment, saying: Why did God say not to multiply women? Was it just so as not to divert my heart? Well, by my wisdom I will multiply women for myself, and I will not turn away my heart. "
>
> Shemot Rabbah 6

According to this midrash, Solomon challenges God by placing his abilities above the commandments of the Torah, and for sure, such things do not work out well at the end. But we must look at two other things, what happened to Solomon and what did he do to "circumvent" this Law.

> King Solomon loved many foreign women in addition to Pharaoh's daughter—Moabite, Ammonite, Edomite, Phoenician, and Hittite women, from the nations of which the LORD had said to the Israelites, "None of you shall join them and none of them shall join you, lest they turn your heart away to follow their gods." Such Solomon clung to and loved. He had seven hundred royal wives and three hundred concubines; and his wives turned his heart away. In his old age, his wives turned away Solomon's heart after other gods, and he was not as wholeheartedly devoted to Adonai his Elohim as his father David had been.
>
> 1 Kings 11:1-4

From what we can see here, Solomon's plan failed, his willingness to defy God by placing his wisdom and understanding above the commandments, led him to idolatry and paganism, which are two things abominable to God. What happened was very serious, both the attitude of Solomon and the result of it. It is amazing how even the wisest and richest man in all history is absolutely nothing before a small Torah commandment. A rabbi makes a very striking comment about these verses:

*It would have been better for Solomon to have spent his life cleaning up sewers than to have a verse like that written about himself.*
Rabbi Bar Yochai, 1 Kings 11:4

We do not know whether Solomon repented or not, but the disgrace that fell upon his life is unacceptable in Scripture. Solomon had no intention of deflecting his heart and serving false gods, that is a certain; His intention was to obey the commandments until the end. The problem is that he wanted to do it in his own way, something like "*the ends justifying the means*". He intended to reach the target, but the way he thought it would have been the best, was different from the way that Adonai stipulated.

Now we need to look at how Solomon did this and with that, we will have our connection with the words of Yehoshua.

The sages say that those who read the Torah written by Solomon found a tiny error, they do not know if this error was purposeful or was for du to lack of attention. In either case, I will bring up the right version according to the Torah and the version they found in the Torah of Solomon for comparison:

וְלֹא יַרְבֶּה לוֹ נָשִׁים, וְלֹא יָסוּר לְבָבוֹ.

> *He shall not gather many women unto himself,*
> *for this will divert his heart...*
> Deuteronomy 17:17a

**א**ְרבה-לוֹ נָשִׁים, לֹא יָסוּר לְבָבוֹ.
*I will gather many women to myself and not turn my heart...*
Deuteronomy of Solomon 17:17a

Interesting that the passage he makes a mistake is precisely the one that deals with the sin he will commit in the future. If we look carefully, the error appears in the verb "to multiply" (ירבה) - YARBEH. Instead of Solomon writing it correctly, with the initial letter YUD (י), he begins this word with the letter ALEF (א), writing ARBEH (ארבה) instead of YARBEH (ירבה). This change the verb "to multiply"'s conjugation to the future form of the first person in singular.

Solomon removes the smallest letter of the Torah, the YUD, and places another in its place, causing a unique confusion, which ends up in one of the worst transgressions before the Creator. In a mystical way, a Kabbalistic rabbi tells us what happened at that moment:

> *Chazal said: When King Solomon married the daughter of*
> *Pharaoh, transgressing Deuteronomy 17:17 by removing a*
> *YUD from the Torah, that YUD went up before the Blessed Lord*
> *and said to him: Something that is partially annulled is fully*
> *annulled, if Solomon is abolishing me, who will fulfill me?*
> *The Holy One, Blessed Be He, answered: Solomon,*
> *as millions like him, will be abolished, but not even*
> *a YUD of my Torah will ever be abolished.*
> Talmud of Jerusalem, Tractate Sanhedrin 2:6

*At this moment the YUD stands before Adonai and says: King*
*of the universe, did you not say that the least letter would*
*ever come out of the Torah? Now, look, Solomon stood up and*

*abolished me, will he not abolish the whole Torah tomorrow?*
*And Adonai replies: I will abolish Solomon and all like*
*him who abolishes a single YUD of the Torah.*
Shemot Rabbah 6

It's incredible what's happening. According to the sages, Solomon makes a mistake while writing the Torah, by changing the letter YUD to the letter ALEF in Deuteronomy 17:17, and thus completely changing everything. By this change, Solomon, in all his wisdom, pays a price: he falls into idolatry. This was the way God abolished him for changing a very little letter in the Torah.

This is confirmed by the words of Solomon himself years later, when he realizes what he has done and where he went wrong:

*For how will the man who tries to succeed the One (GOD) who is*
*ruling through that (Torah), that was built a while ago? I went*
*from the contemplation of wisdom to madness and foolishness.*
Ecclesiastes 2:12

Solomon, at the end of his life, recognizes his mistake. He asserts that the one who tries "to help" God through a different way that He has already determined, that is, the Torah, will fall into the same mistake that he has fallen into and will cease to be a wise person to become a foolish one.

This is a very complicated and serious matter. Nowadays, it is common things like "*do according to what one feel in the heart*", or "*what matters is that I love God*", those ideas are nothing more than justifications for one to do the willing of oneself, in the same way Solomon did. The bible is clear in stating that the heart is deceitful and to love God must be in the way He has determined. Those beliefs may end up leading people to the same fate Solomon had - idolatry.

This is a very common thing now a days, rabbis putting their laws above the Torah's Laws, priests creating new laws as if they were divine, pastors annulling the Torah completely and leaders guiding millions by teaching cheap ideologies created by themselves. They are all idolaters, all of them! Just as they nullify or modify the word of God, they will be annulled by HaKadosh, Barukh Hu.

Yeshua not only affirms that he came to fulfill the Torah, but also leaves an implied message: woe to the one who removes or changes a YUD in the Torah, may be the wisest, the richest, or the most powerful person in the world, if this person abolish anything in the word of God, he will be annulled by God Himself. It would have better for him to be cleaning sewers than that.

> *You should not add anything to what I command you,*
> *nor remove anything. But observe the commandments*
> *of Adonai, your Elohim, which I lay upon you.*
>
> Deuteronomy 4:2

# SECTION XII
## TO SWEAR

*And you have heard what was spoken by the ancients:*
*"Do not swear falsely in my name, for you must answer*
*before Adonai your promises.*
*And I say unto you, Swear not in vain for anything, nor*
*by the heavens which is the throne of Elohim.*
*And not by the earth which is the footstool of His feet, nor by the*
*city of the heavens (Yerushalayim), for it is the city of Elohim.*
*And not by your head because you cannot*
*make your hair white or black.*
*But let your words be yes, yes and no, no. Anything*
*added to this is bad.*
Matthew 5:33-37

*Again, you have heard that it has been said by*
*them of old time, You shall not forswear yourself,*
*but shall perform to the Lord your oaths:*
*But I say to you, Swear not at all; neither by*
*heaven; for it is God' throne:*
*Nor by the earth; for it is his footstool: neither by*
*Jerusalem; for it is the city of the great King.*
*Neither shall you swear by your head, because you*
*can not make one hair white or black.*
*But let your communication be, Yes, yes; No, no: for*
*whatever is more than these comes of evil.*
Matthew 5:33-37 KJV

This is a teaching that I wanted to place both translations side by side, so we see a small difference. KJV says not to swear falsely and then says to fulfill all the promises, in the original, Yehoshua says something else, he says that just by swearing falsely is enough to have to answer before Adonai. It may look more or less the same, but from the original we see that just by making a false promise, it's enough to make us guilty.

The topic of oath, as it was approached by Yehoshua, has always been something very sensitive to me and until some time ago, totally incomprehensible. The reason that led him to address such a theme, at a particular moment in his ministry, has always been somewhat confusing to me.

Of course, he brought this up for some reason that is not revealed to us by the book of Matthew and that "reason" was probably happening in his days. The oath theme is approached both by the Torah and the Tanakh, but in a somewhat different way from what we see in his words. The most sensitive point we have here is the famous *"you have heard that it has been spoken..."*, giving a false impression that Yehoshua was replacing the Torah with the famous Christian jargon "law of christ". If we look roughly at the way he speaks, we may have that understanding which, at the very least, I may call it erroneous, for in order for Yehoshua to be worthy of the title of Mashiach, which he himself claimed to be, he had must to teach only and exclusively the Torah.

Before going any deeper, let's take a look at what the One-God's teaching is about this theme:

> *To Adonai, your Elohim, you shall fear, only Him you shall serve, and by his name you shall swear.*
>
> Deuteronomy 6:13

> *And King Solomon swore by Adonai ...*
>
> 1 Kings 2:23a

> *And David swore again ...*
>
> 1 Samuel 2:3a

> *And it shall come to pass, if they shall learn the ways of my people, swearing by my LIVING NAME, as they have taught my people to swear by the name of Baal, they shall be grafted in the midst of MY PEOPLE.*

Jeremiah 12:16

The depth of these passages impresses me. First, if we take a close look at the passage of Deuteronomy, "to swear" is not only a permission, but actually a commandment. It is a commandment that the oath should be made by the Tetragrammatons' Name of God. This is so profound that in the book of Jeremiah, the prophet tells the Gentiles that, if they learn the ways of His people (i.e. Torah) and swear by His Living Name, they will be grafted onto the People of Israel.

Two other people of extreme weight before Adonai, David and his son Solomon, also swore in the name of Adonai.

So how could Yehoshua have abolished such a commandment? He who believes that Yehoshua abolished the Torah, the work of the One who he called "my father", makes him as a rebellious and undisciplined son, incoherent with the people of Israel and unable to be called Mashiach, so it is time to revise his own concepts. Other than that, Yehoshua would be also nullifying Jeremiah's prophecy about the adoption of the Gentiles, which would be inconceivable. Anyone who believes in a jesus who has done this, believes in a mythological figure, created by the church, who has some similarities with the real Yehoshua, but definitely not the same.

First we must pay attention to the words of Yehoshua, he, at no time, forbids to make an oath or abolish the commandment concerning the oath, which he affirms is that we should NOT SWEAR FALSELY. And he quotes this in reference to another passage from the Torah:

> You shall not swear falsely by my name, for you shall profane the name of your Elohim, I am Adonai.
> Leviticus 19:12

Now we see the meaning in his teaching, he did not abolish the oath, he did not deny the Torah, but he placed two commandments in parallel once again, stating that if one is to swear falsely, it is better not to swear at all.

The problem that existed in his day, as it still exists, were some interpretations of certain Pharisaic schools in relation to this verse. Some Pharisees used this passage to justify themselves to be able to swear falsely as long as it was not by the name of Adonai. They swore by the name of the Temple, by Yerushalayim, by the heavens, by the earth, and so forth. If it were not by the name of Adonai, they were not obliged to fulfill what they swore.

> *To swear by his name and not on behalf of other gods. In other words, you should not swear by the names of other gods, but by the name of Adonai. But if it is not by the names of other gods, an oath may be made to affirm a testimony or make a contract, even if it is not by His Name.*
>
> Ibn Ezra, Deuteronomy 6:13

One of the great sages and commentators of the Torah, Ibn Ezra, claims that we can by no means swear by false gods names, but he also states that if an oath is not made in the name of false gods, the person is free to swear by behalf of anything.

Unfortunately, many did not understand that the prohibition of Leviticus was not only to swear falsely in the name of Adonai, but it simply was NOT to swear falsely at all. Yehoshua was exhorting some Pharisees saying that if they swear, by whatever it is, they should fulfilled it. It is not because they have not sworn specifically by Adonai's name that they are exempt to fulfill the vow, if not, it is better not to swear by absolutely nothing.

Other rabbis fully agree with the teaching of Yehoshua, as well as many other Pharisaic schools:

> *If you have all the characteristics mentioned here, if you worship His name and if you serve Him, then you have the right to take an oath by His name. But be very careful with*

*any oath, otherwise, it is better not to swear by anything.*
Rashi, Deuteronomy 6:13

The great sage Rashi fully agrees with the teaching of Yehoshua. It is better to be very careful when it comes to oaths, otherwise it is better not to swear by anything.

I did not find anything related to the Pharisaic permission about swearing falsely since it is not by the name of Adonai, many other historians have done this research and according to some Israeli scholars, such teachings were found in part of the Jerusalem Talmud, which had great part of its work destroyed many years ago.

To end his exhortation, he cites *"all added to this is bad"*, though many have the understanding that this "bad" refers to swearing or refers to adding something to what Yehoshua spoke, in fact, such a quote is a typical Orthodox/Pharisaic jargon concerning something very serious in the Law, thus bringing another passage from the Torah:

*Thou shalt not add anything to the Torah which I command you, neither shall ye diminish from it, that ye may keep the commandments of Adonai, your Elohim, which I command you.*
Deuteronomy 4:2

He is reaffirming the basic topic of the Torah principles, probably to silence anyone who might be thinking that he is adding or removing something from the Law. What he speaks about the oath is in full accordance with the book of Leviticus, when he made clear about FALSE oaths. In the end, through a rabbinic language, he says that teaching other things that are not in the Torah, as if they were God's laws, is the real "bad" thing, for they would be adding things to it. He clarifies to his Talmidim that adding or removing anything from the Torah is what is really "bad".

What happened here was a ban on an apparent custom of some rabbinical schools to swear falsely as long as it was not by the name of Adonai. Yehoshua then uses the verse in

Leviticus 19:12, which should serve as a basis for them to make such oaths, and on top of that, he declares that a false oath is not to be made under any hypothesis. He also says that nothing should be added to the Torah, showing that the rabbinic laws that add things to God's Law are bad and for that, he was not, under any hypothesis, removing anything from the Torah.

I believe such a topic was so serious and so intrinsic in the mentality of some people that, a few chapters later, Yehoshua addresses the same topic again.

*Woe to you, blind in the chair, who say that he who swears by the Temple is not bound (to fulfill), but he who swears by whatever is consecrated to the Temple is bound to pay. Men who are mad and blind, which is greater, the Temple or that which is consecrated to the Temple? He who swears by the altar is not bound to do, but whoever swears to bring an offering is bound to do? What is greater, the offering or the altar, the Temple or the offering? He who swears by the altar swears by all that is in it. He who swears by the throne of Elohim, swears by it and by the One sited on the throne.*

Matthew 23:16-20

*Woe to you, you blind guides, which say, Whoever shall swear by the temple, it is nothing; but whoever shall swear by the gold of the temple, he is a debtor! You fools and blind: for whether is greater, the gold, or the temple that sanctifies the gold? And, Whoever shall swear by the altar, it is nothing; but whoever swears by the gift that is on it, he is guilty. You fools and blind: for whether is greater, the gift, or the altar that sanctifies the gift? Whoever therefore shall swear by the altar,*

*swears by it, and by all things thereon.*
*And whoever shall swear by the temple, swears*
*by it, and by him that dwells therein.*
*And he that shall swear by heaven, swears by the*
*throne of God, and by him that sits thereon.*
Matthew 23:16-**22** (????) KJV

In this passage, Yehoshua speaks directly to some Pharisees who, according to him, are sitting on the seat of Moses, for we have these strange term "blind in the chair", because they refer to some leaders who were making decisions concerning the Jewish laws that, according to Yehoshua, were teaching things contrary to the Torah, blind people leading blind people.

Yehoshua criticizes them for saying that if a person swear by the Temple, or by the altar, or by the throne of God, he is not obliged to keep the vow. In both cases, Yehoshua says that vows and oaths are valid regardless of what they are made by. Yehoshua gives no "hint" that he is contrary to taking an oath, nor does he imply that he who swears by the altar or throne is a wicked or a sinful person, but he sticks himself with the Torah's principle concerning the false oath.

Here we have, once again, Yehoshua trying to bring the people back to Torah, after many Pharisees having them led astray. Nowadays, the topic of the false oath has become so important that on the holiest day of the biblical calendar, the Yom Kipur, a prayer is made by all who celebrate it. The name of this prayer is KOL NIDREI, which in Aramaic means "all promises" and however intriguing it may be, it is not a prayer purely of repentance or forgiveness, but a prayer of annulment of promises made and not fulfilled. For modern Judaism, vows and oaths are of the utmost importance and are strongly addressed by the Torah and the Orthodox schools of the present day. Many passages of the Talmud advise against any kind of oath or promise. Something that Yehoshua taught two thousand years ago, we see today within orthodox Judaism.

# SECTION XIII
## EYE FOR AN EYE

*And you have heard what is said in the Torah:*
*eye for eye and tooth for tooth.*
*And I say to you, do not pay evil for evil, but whoever*
*smites on your right cheek, do also give him the left.*
*And whoever wants to oppose you in the trial*
*and steal your shirt, leave your coat too.*
*And whoever asks you to walk with him a thousand*
*steps, walk with him two thousand.*
*He who asks you, give it and he who wants to borrow,*
*do not avoid.*

Matthew 5:38-42

*Eye for eye, tooth for tooth, hand for hand, foot for foot.*

Exodus 21:24

This is a crucial topic in the teachings of Yehoshua that has caused, and still causes, a huge misunderstanding among many Christians about his relationship with the Torah. Many say that the Torah makes an apology for the right of revenge according to its teaching of "eye for an eye", for that rule allows the victim to take revenge on his aggressor. Then, jesus came, and he put an end to this, teaching that, instead of revenge, we must turn the other cheek, proving again the substitution of the Torah for the "law of christ".

But such interpretation would prove to be very problematic, for how would God, Creator of all things, Good, Benevolent, Love, create a rule that would propagate revenge? If this were indeed the case and Yehoshua was against Adonai's determination on this topic, he would no longer be worthy to claim that he was Mashiach, he wouldn't be more than a christian jesus, thus losing all his morals. The misunderstanding of this Torah's passage, which could give an impression that it allows revenge, was one of the main basis for many fathers of the church to teach, in a very subtle way, that the god of the New Testament is not the same God of the Old Testament, because the old one, was a bad one and not convenient for them.

The misunderstanding of Yehoshua's words is due to many Christian leader's lack of knowledge about the depth of God's commandments and also a sick and flawed theology created by Rome. The "eye for an eye", in fact, is a commandment that seeks to avoid revenge. Let us look at two examples, imagine if a person A stabs the leg of a person B (who recovers after a few days), thus giving the person B the right to stab the leg of the person A. When the person B stabs the person A's leg and the stab involuntarily ends up causing a rupture of a vein, which makes impossible to the person A to walk again, the damage caused by the person B's revenge was much more serious than the first damage caused by the person A, thus not being an "eye for an eye ".

Another example is that a certain person A pulls out the eye of a certain person B, who gets blind in one eye, but the person B continues to see, at the time of the revenge, the person B perceives that the person A has only one eye and if he pull it out, the person A will be totally blind, thus causing a much greater suffering.

What I want to show here is that the Torah only allows revenge that would be done in the exactly same way as the aggression, in the same manner, in the same degree, in the same intensity, in the same severity, so it causes exactly the same harm as the first act caused.

However, such conditions are impossible for a human being to attain, and so, the one who would take the revenge, by doing so, would end up causing much more or much less damage, since it is impossible to meet all these conditions. In this case it is better not to take revenge, for if the revenge does a bigger damage, the avenger would become a transgressor. That is, the Torah "allows" vengeance, but under its conditions, which are humanly impossible to attain, so the one who takes revenge will inevitably end up transgressing the Torah.

No Pharisaic school supported the act of revenge based on this Torah's passage as many think. In fact, they proposed a different interpretation:

> *If someone blinds his neighbor, he will have to*
> *financially pay the value of his eye.*
> Rashi, Exodus 21:24

> *If we were to apply a punishment equal to the crime, in all its*
> *severities, it would be improper. However, according to tradition,*
> *only financial compensation would be valid, as it is difficult*
> *to accurately measure how to apply the "eye for an eye."*
> Sforno, Exodus 21:24

The common understanding was that the inflicted damage should be financially compensated, if someone harms his neighbor, a harm that would disable him from working for the rest of his life, the one who caused the damage should support him and all those who would benefit from his work, for life.

Sforno agrees with Rashi, since it is difficult to measure a revenge, it is better to give a financial compensation.

Yehoshua uses of this understanding, as human beings will never achieve a 100% equal degree of revenge, it is better to give the other cheek, for this kind of humiliation is way better than becoming a transgressor by not achieving the exact revenge as commanded by the Torah.

We must notice that "to give the other cheek" is only an allegory, not that we should do it, it's a rabbinic expression to say "let it go, forget it" and not actually to be a nice guy with those who harm us. We can notice it through the acts of Yehoshua himself, in John 18:23, during the dialogue with the high priest, Yehoshua did NOT turn the other cheek.

As revenge deals with a relationship between two

people, Yehoshua, in the last verses, ends his teaching with a challenge, a test "to love the neighbor", by saying to his hearers that when one has his shirt taken, one should also give the coat, or to walk twice as much as requested by one's fellow, or not to deny a request or loan, thus showing how should be one's relationship with one's neighbor, for one who does that to someone else, does it for the Creator Himself, for it is a part of God's desire that His people know how to share and be generous.

Another thing concerning "to give the other cheek" is that many people cite this as a teaching from Yehoshua, saying that he was the one who brought that up, but in fact, " to give the other cheek", as quoted by Yehoshua, is actually from the Tanakh, as it was said by the prophet Jeremiah:

> *Let him offer his cheek to the smiter; Let*
> *him be surfeited with mockery.*
>
> Lamentations 3:30

## EYE, TOOTH, HAND, FOOT

This commandment in the Torah comes in a very strange way, it quotes body parts, such as eye, tooth, hand and foot. If we go a little bit further and set the idea of revenge aside, we can draw from here a very profound teaching from God.

The eye, the tooth, the hand and the foot, are representatives of the true wealth, for the eye symbolizes the window of understanding, it is mainly through the sight that man receives almost all the knowledge he absorbs. The tooth represents the power of speech as well as the tongue, for without them, spoken words would be incomprehensible. The hand represents the creative capacity of the human being, while the feet symbolize his ability to move.

It may sound kind kinda crazy, but it's precisely these four things that the Torah must represent in one's life. The

Eye to learn the Torah, the teeth to be able to speak and teach the Torah, the hand to keep its commandments and the feet to carry it to all men. This is the true wealth of a man, for to achieve this, is to attain his true purpose of his creation, this is the maxim that God seeks from a man.

To prove this, let's look at these four terms in Hebrew:

EYE (AIN) - עין
TOOTH (SHIN) - שין
HAND (YAD) - יד
FOOT (REGEL) - רגל

When we get the first letters of each word (remembering that the in Hebrew we read from right to left), we will have the word ASHIR (עשיר), which means RICH.

The lesson we can draw from here is that, he who is truly rich is not the one who has money, nor possessions, nor fame, but the one who has the ability to study and learn the Torah, to go wherever it takes to teach it and to fulfill its commandments , this is the true wealth and the lesson we can draw from it. Learn it, Live it, then Go and Teach it!

# SECTION XIV
## TZEDAKAH

*Beware lest you be tzadik only before men for them
to praise you. And if you do it, there will be no
merit for you from your Father in heaven.
Yet Yeshua said: When you do tzedakah, do not proclaim
or sound a trumpet before you like the hypocrites, in a
foreign language Yipokratis. Who do their tzedakot in
the streets and markets where they are seen by men. But I
tell you that they have already received their merits.
And when you do tzedakah, that your left hand
does not know what the right does
So that is your offering is a secret offering and your
Father, who secretly sees, completes you (rewards).*
Matthew 6:1-4

*Shimon HaTzadik said: on three things the world stands:
on the Torah, on the service to God and on the Tzedakah.*
Pirkei Avot 1:2

Much of the Yehoshua´s Torah addresses the need for the person to become a *tzadik*, and it wouldn't be possible if he did not address such an important subject as *tzedakah*. The word *tzedakah* (צדקה) has the same Hebrew root of the word *tzadik* (צדיק) - *righteous*, for one does not exist without the other. *Tzedakah,* in a direct translation, would be "righteousness" or "justice", however this is a term used for "charity".

*Tzedakah* is something vital in the life of the Jew and in the Jewish society, it is not only about charities or alms, but it has a much deeper meaning than just giving money to others, the real *tzedakah* tries to reach out to a neighbor, even if an unknown one, to give him support in whatever he needs, whatever! Of course, the easiest way to do it, is through money and material goods, but the real *tzedakah* also demands moments of solidarity with a lonely person, to visit the elderly, widows, to comfort the one who cries, to teach about God to a lost person, to guide the blind and all that a person can do for others. Without this kind of attitude within each one of us, even if we follow the Torah from A to Z, we will never be able to become real *tzadikim*, for *tzedakah* must walk holding hands with the Torah in one's life, so that he becomes a Tzaddik worthy of the Kingdom of Heaven. What Yehoshua teaches is according to the Talmud:

*He who does tzedakah has the merit of eternal life.*
Talmud of Babylon, Tractate Rosh Hashanah 4a

It is customary during the holidays for the Jews to do three things, *Tshuvah* (to repent and to return to God's will), *Tefilah* (prayer) and *Tzedakah* (charity), to avoid divine judgment.

Rabbi Maimonides compiled a list of ten items that should be observed for the practice of *tzedakah*, from helping one's own family up to making anonymous contributions. All Jews should do *tzedakah*, even the poor Jews.

For this reason, perhaps the teaching of Yehoshua on *tzedakah* may be unnecessary, for it is something that everyone there grew up doing, but if we look closely, he does not teach about *tzedakah* or even that it should be done, but he talks about something much more delicate, the intentions with which the *tzedakah* is made and this is a very complicated matter, for now he is not disagreeing with others rabbinic schools of his time, but rather he disagrees with the "MYSELF" inside of every one who was there listening to him.

In order for us to better understand what he was saying, we need to address some common "slangs" of his day, "slangs" that he mentioned in these verses.

**SOUNDS OF TRUMPETS**

Here is a strange term, the impression that it passes is that after a donation, the person who has just done it, would start announcing what he just did by telling everyone. In fact, this is not quite the case. During the first century, tall over the Temple's courtyard, thirteen containers made of bronze were placed, they were wide at the bottom and narrow at the top, remembering a Shofar, a trumpet.

When the bronze metal were strucked by the coins, due to the shape of a trumpet, it used to produce a very loud and peculiar sound. It was a habit among some people to carry several coins of little value instead of a single coin of a greater value, because when they thrown them in this container, they would make a lot more noise, like a trumpet sound, giving the impression to those around him that he was making a great donation.

> *There were thirteen SHOFAROT (trumpet shape*
> *collect chests), thirteen tables and thirteen*
> *places to prostrate inside the Temple...*
> Mishnah Shekalim 6:1

That is why Yehoshua called hypocrites those who "sound the trumpets", for they were there throwing a lot of pennies to show to others how "tzadik" they were. Who does so, clearly has no true intention of performing a *tzedakah* for love. Yehoshua was totally against this kind of practice.

**STREETS AND MARKETS**

Markets were commonplaces for *tzedakah*, not only because many needed to be there, but because of the high visibility the donator would have. The Talmud reports various discussions among the sages in the city's markets, which leads us to understand that many important people gathered in these places.

*If a collector of tzedakah finds money in the market,*

*he cannot put it in his pocket as it may seem like*
*theft. He should put it in a bag of tzedakah.*

Mishneh Torah, Giving to the Poor 9:9

As reported on innumerous occasions throughout the book of Matthew, the great "problem" that Yehoshua had with other Pharisees was precisely the hypocrisy, and this does not encompass only the Pharisees, but all human beings, without exception. I believe that almost all of his teachings, somehow, approached precisely the subject of hypocrisy.

Although all of his teachings were based on the Torah, he did not come to teach the Torah itself, it was already been taught in schools all over Israel. He came to interpret it and to teach how essential it is that a life according to the Torah begins from inside out, with no hypocrisy.

According to Judaism, the best donation is the one made anonymous. There are many Jewish communities where donations are made to a rabbi or to the synagogue and the synagogue is in charge of helping the needy, serving as an intermediary, so neither the donor nor the one who receives it, knows one another. So that the one who gives does not boast himself and the one who receives it, is not grateful to the wrong person.

*There are four kinds of people who do tzedakah, the*
*one who wants to give, but does not want others to*
*give, this one has an evil eye towards others.*
*Those who do not wish to give, but want others to*
*give, this one has a poor eye towards himself.*
*Those who wish to give and desire that others also*
*give, not having merit, this is the tzadik.*
*And those who do not want to give and do not want*
*anyone to give, that is the bad person.*

Pirkei Avot 5:13

*And he believed in Adonai, and it was*

173

*credited to him as tzedakah.*

Genesis 15:6

*It's great to give tzedakah before you pray.*

Shulchan Arukh, Orach Chayim 92:10

# SECTION XV
## THE LORD'S PRAYER

*At that time, Yeshua said to his talmidim: "Don't raise your voice*
*by the moment you pray, and do not be like those loose branches*
*that pray in the synagogues and in the corners of the courtyard,*
*praying with a loud speech that they may be praised by men.*
*And in your prayers, come to your bed and close the doors*
*behind you and pray to your Father in secret and your*
*Father, who sees in secret, will complete (reward) you.*
*And when you pray, do not multiply words like the*
*heretics, who think that they will be heard.*
*Do you not see that your Father in heaven knows the things*
*(that you ask for) before they are even asked by you?*
*And so shalt thou pray: Our Father, Holy is Your name*
*Blessed be Your kingdom, may Your will be*
*done in heaven and on earth.*
*And give us our bread always*
*And forgive us our sins when we forgive*
*those who sins against us.*
*And do not bring us next to temptation and*
*keep us from all that is evil, amen.*

Matthew 6:5-13

The famous "Lord's Prayer" is seen by many Christians as a model of prayer so unique that even became some kind of "mantra", it is almost the only way of prayer that many Christians do. What Yehoshua teaches here is not a prayer *per se* to be copied, but rather a summary of the basic concept of the Jewish prayer.

In order to be clear where this prayer came from, we should take a look at the style of rabbinical prayer. The central prayer in the Jewish liturgy is known by the number of blessings that it contains, its name is *Shmoneh Eisreh*, which means "eighteen", since it consists of eighteen topics that a prayer must composed of.

The *Shmoneh Eisreh* is also known as **Amidah** and is normally prayed standing while facing *Yerushalayim*. The Amidah is recited during Shabbat, holy days and daily service in the synagogue, being recited three times a day by some more religious Jews, in the morning, in the afternoon and in the night.

The first three blessings deal with the absolute Oneness of God and the fundamental faith that He is the Creator of all things. From the fourth untill the ninth, they deal with petitions of a personal nature. From the tenth to the fifteenth they deal with petitions of a common character and the last three deal with the service to Adonai.

Every Jew is obliged, taught, and indoctrinated to perform the Amidah at least once a day, but in times of emergency or lack of time, this obligation can be fulfilled with an Amidah in a reduced form, which is a summarization of the eighteen blessings, which is clearly what appears to have occurred when Yehoshua taught the "Lord´s Prayer", just a reduced form of the Amidah.

All rabbinic schools, especially during the first century, formulated and discussed how should those summarized forms be and how they would be taught. Each rabbi decided the parts that he believed to be more essential and taught them to his students, and through this prayer, it was possible to determine from which rabbinic school a person was, for it was something different from school to school. Such prayers were widely discussed in the Talmud:

*He who is walking in a place where there are groups of wild beasts and thieves, should recite the abbreviated Amidah. What would be the abbreviated Amidah? Rabbi Eliezer said, "May His will be done in the heavens above, and give peace of mind to those who fear Him down here, and do whatever is good before His eyes. Blessed are You, Adonai, who hears the prayers".*
Talmud of Babylon, Tractate Brakhot 29b

*Rabbi Yehoshua ben Levi says that he recites: "Listen to the*
*cry of Your nation, Israel, and quickly fulfill his request.*
*Blessed are You, Adonai, who hears the prayers".*
Talmud of Babylon, Tractate Brakhot 29b

*Rabbi Eliezer, the son of Rabbi Tzadok, says that he recites:*
*"Listen to the cry of Your people, Israel and fulfill their request*
*without delay. Blessed are You, Adonai, who listens to prayers.*
Talmud of Babylon, Tractate Brakhot 29b

We can see here that it is something very common among the rabbis a formulation of what should be prayed to God when a more short form of the Amidah is needed. It was no different with Yehoshua, what he did at that time is precisely to teach a summed up Amidah to his talmidim, something that every rabbi does. For certain, Yehoshua and his talmidim, prayed the *Shmoneh Eisreh* at least once a day.

• **OUR FATHER, HALLOWED BE YOUR NAME** - In the first part of his brief prayer, Yehoshua teaches that we should always bless what is the most intimate and the profound thing about Adonai, His Name.

• **BLESSED BE YOUR KINGDOM. YOUR WILL BE DONE IN HEAVEN AND IN EARTH** - In the second part he teaches to bless the God Creator, owner of all things and the sovereignty of His will.

• **BREAD, SIN, DELIVERANCE** - The last three topics deal with personal requests for both the physical and the soul. But here we see a typical characteristic of Yehoshua and how he hardens the "following God". The condition for us to be forgiven is first to forgive, so that we may receive God's forgiveness, an attitude required from our part, thus showing that repentance is not just a feeling but requires action.

It is of utmost importance for the Christian to understand the Jewish prayer, for apart from being the basis of the faith of the one who they call Mashiach, it teaches much about their mentality. This prayer is very ancient, much older than Yehoshua himself, perhaps some 430 years before his birth. The prayer is beautiful, full of mentions and allusions to the scriptures, as we see as follows:

## THE AMIDAH
### 1- PATRIARCHS

Blessed are you, O Adonai our Elohim and Elohim of our fathers, the God of Abraham, the God of Isaac and the God of Jacob, the great, mighty and revered God, the Most High God who bestows loving kindnesses, the creator of all things, who remembers the good deeds of the patriarchs and in love will bring a redeemer to their children's children for his name's sake. O king, helper, savior and shield.

Blessed are you, Adonai, the shield of Abraham.

### 2- DIVINE POWER

You, O Adonai, are mighty forever, you revive the dead, you have the power to save. You cause the wind to blow and the rain to fall. You sustain the living with loving-kindness, you revive the dead with great mercy, you support the falling, heal the sick, set free the bound and keep faith with those who sleep in the dust. Who is like you, O doer of mighty acts? Who resembles you, a king who puts to death and restores to life, and causes salvation to flourish? And you are certain to revive the dead.

Blessed are you, Adonai, who revives the dead.

### 3- K'DUSHAH (HOLINESS)

We will sanctify your name in this world just as it is sanctified in the highest heavens, as it is written by your prophet: And they call out to one another and say: Holy, holy, holy is the LORD of hosts; the whole earth is full of his glory.

Blessed be the Presence of Adonai in his place. And in

your Holy Words it is written, saying, Adonai reigns forever, your God, O Zion, throughout all generations. Hallelujah.

Throughout all generations we will declare your greatness, and to all eternity we will proclaim your holiness. Your praise, O our God, shall never depart from our mouth, for you are a great and holy God and King. Blessed are you, O Adonai, the holy God. You are holy, and your name is holy, and holy beings praise you daily.

Blessed are you, Adonai, the holy God.

### 4- KNOWLEDGE

You favor men with knowledge, and teach mortals understanding. O favor us with the knowledge, the understanding and the insight that come from you.

Blessed are you, Adonai, the gracious giver of knowledge.

### 5- REPENTANCE

Bring us back, O our father, to your Instruction; draw us near, O our King, to your service; and cause us to return to you in perfect repentance.

Blessed are you, Adonai, who delights in repentance.

### 6- FORGIVENESS

Forgive us, O our Father, for we have sinned; pardon us, O our King, for we have transgressed; for you pardon and forgive.

Blessed are you, Adonai, who is merciful and always ready to forgive.

### 7- AFFLICTIONS DELIVERANCE

Look upon our affliction and plead our cause, and redeem us speedily for your name's sake, for you are a mighty redeemer.

Blessed are you, Adonai, the redeemer of Israel.

### 8- HEALING

Heal us, O Lord, and we will be healed; save us and we will be saved, for you are our praise. O grant a perfect healing to all our ailments, for you, almighty King, are a faithful and merciful healer.

Blessed are you, Adonai, the healer of the sick of his people Israel.

## 9- FOR WHAT IS NECESSARY

Bless this year for us, O Adonai our God,
together with all the varieties of its produce, for our welfare. Bestow a blessing upon the face of the earth. O satisfy us with your goodness, and bless our year
like the best of years.

Blessed are you, Adonai, who blesses the years.

## 10- FOR THE EXILED

Sound the great shofar for our freedom, raise the ensign to gather our exiles, and gather us from the four corners of the earth.

Blessed are you, Adonai, who gathers the dispersed of his people Israel.

## 11- FOR ADONAI'S JUSTICE

Restore our judges as in former times, and our counselors as at the beginning; and remove from us sorrow and sighing. Reign over us, you alone, O Lord, with lovingkindness and compassion, and clear us in judgment.

Blessed are you, Adonai, the King who loves righteousness and justice.

## 12- DESTRUCTION OF GOD'S ENEMIES

Let there be no hope for slanderers, and let all wickedness perish in an instant. May all your enemies quickly be cut down, and may you soon in our day uproot, crush, cast down and humble the dominion of arrogance.

Blessed are you, Adonai, who smashes enemies and humbles the arrogant.

## 13- FOR JUSTICE AND PROSELYTES

May your compassion be stirred, O Lord our God, towards the righteous, the pious, the elders of your people the house of Israel, the remnant of their scholars, towards proselytes, and towards us also. Grant a good reward to all who truly trust in your name. Set our lot with them forever so that we may never be put to shame, for we have put our trust in you.

Blessed are you, Adonai, the support and stay of the Tzadik.

## 14- FOR JERUSALEM

Return in mercy to Jerusalem your city, and dwell in it as you have promised. Rebuild it soon in our day as an eternal structure, and quickly set up in it the throne of David.

Blessed are you, Adonai, who rebuilds Jerusalem.

## 15- FOR KING MASHIACH

Speedily cause the offspring of your servant David to flourish, and let him be exalted by your saving power, for we wait all day long for your salvation.

Blessed are you, Adonai, who causes salvation to flourish.

## 16- FOR PRAYER'S ANSWERS

Hear our voice, O Lord our God; spare us and have pity on us. Accept our prayer in mercy and with favor, for you are a God who hears prayers and supplications. O our King, do not turn us away from your presence empty-handed, for you hear the prayers of your people Israel with compassion.

Blessed are you, Adonai, who hears prayer.

## 17- FOR THE TEMPLE RESTORATION

Be pleased, O Lord our God, with your people Israel and with their prayers. Restore the service to the inner sanctuary of your Temple, and receive in love and with favor both the fire-offerings of Israel and their prayers. May the worship of your people Israel always be acceptable to you.

And let our eyes behold your return in mercy to Zion.

Blessed are you, Adonai, who restores his divine presence to Zion.

## 18- FOR ACKNOWLEDGMENT OF GOD'S MERCY.

We thank You, for You are our Elohim and Elohim of our fathers forever and ever. Through every generation you have been the rock of our lives, the shield of our salvation. We will give you thanks and declare your praise for our lives that are committed into your hands, for our souls that are entrusted to you, for your miracles that are daily with us, and for your wonders and your benefits that are with us at all times, evening, morning and noon. O beneficent one, your mercies never fail; O merciful one, your lovingkindnesses never cease. We have always put our hope in you.

For all these acts may your name be blessed and exalted continually, O our King, forever and ever. Let every living thing give thanks to you and praise your name in truth, O God, our salvation and our help.

Blessed are you, Adonai, whose Name is the Beneficent One, and to whom it is fitting to give thanks.

This is the complete Amidah that Yehoshua probably used to recite. We can see in his short prayer, the "Lord's Prayer", that he addresses the most important items, 2, 3, 5, 6, 7, 9, 18 from the Amidah.

A powerful prayer that has been re-presented by Yehoshua. By having an awareness and knowledge that this kind of thing was part of his education, mentality and daily life is vital for us to comprehend him, and with that we will be able to understand much of what he preached and taught.

*Rabban Gamliel said, "Everybody should say the eighteen every day." Rabbi Yehoshua says: "or*

*an abbreviated form of the eighteen."*
Midrash Brakhot 4:3

## HEART AND FAITH

Another thing that Yehoshua teaches, just as the *tzedakah*, prayer must be done from the heart, with pure intentions and with faith. Many Jewish prayers insist on the repetition of certain words, as some sort of mantra, by doing so they believe that whatever they ask, will be delivered. Clearly Yehoshua was against this idea, calling them heretics, because they do this and they forget that with God, mantras do not work.

Some of Yehoshua's contemporaries discuss some interesting things about prayer, faith, and the intention behind them, things that give us some info concerning what Yehoshua was talking about.

*Rabbi Eliezer is talking to Rabbi Yehoshua. How can Rabbi Yehoshua respond to Rabbi Eliezer about the powerful argument that anyone can praise God at any time of the year? Rabbi Yehoshua says: Anyone who prays for the resurrection of the dead daily, even if it does not occur daily, shows the faith that any day is a propitious day for that to occur.*
Talmud of Babylon, Tractate Taanit 2b

Here we have the faith behind prayer, Rabbi Yehoshua Ben Levi prayed every day for the resurrection of the dead and even if it did not happen, he kept praying for it, because he believed that any day is a good day for that to happen. He did not look at the circumstances, he did not look for and immediate answer, he just looked at the certainty that he had in the miracle.

This matches Yehoshua's teaching when he affirms that prayer will be rewarded by God when it is made with faith and not like the repetitions made by the heretics. He also affirms that God already knows everything we need even before we ask, it proves that our prayer must gave a different focus than our needs only.

*What is the God's service made inside the heart?*
*Is the service of prayer, for sure.*
Talmud of Babylon, Tractate Taanit 2a

*May the words of my mouth and the prayer of my heart be*
*acceptable to You, O Adonai, my Rock and my Redeemer.*
Psalms 19:15

One last thing, the intention of the heart during prayer. The only way for a prayer to be fulfilled and accepted by God is to do it with fully heart, with true intentions before the Creator. If it is made for others to see how beautiful the prayers are, or how eloquent one is, then it will be for no good.

# SECTION XVI
## AIYIN TOVAH

*Yet he said to them: Do not keep on heaping up earthly treasures*
*that decay and the grub devour it or it is stolen by thieves.*
*Make for yourselves treasures in heaven, where rust and*
*grub do not devour them, and where thieves do not steal.*
*In this place shall be your treasure.*
*And the light of your body is your eyes, if your eyes*
*look forward, your body (path) will not darken.*
*And if your light darkens, all your ways will be darkened.*
*At this time Yeshua said to his talmidim, no man can*
*work (serve) for two masters unless he loves one and*
*hates the other or honors one and dishonors the other.*
*You cannot work (serve) to EL and to the world.*
*Therefore I tell you, do not worry for the food for your souls*
*and also for the clothes for your bodies. The soul is more*
*valuable than the food and the body more than the garments.*
*Look at the birds in the sky, they do not plant, they do not harvest*
*(from the ground) nor gather in barns, but your exalted Father*
*who feeds them. Are not you more important than they?*
Matthew 6:19-26

If we take a close look, there are two topics in the same teaching that, in the Western mentality, do not make much sense when presented together; the topic that deals with material wealth and the topic about the eyes being the light of the body.

What we have here is something idiomatic, those are rabbinical terms, terms that connect the eyes with material goods. Good eyes (aiyin tovah) and evil eyes (aiyin ra'ah) are orthodox terminologies that refer to generous people and to selfish people, concerning the material goods they possess.

When Yehoshua teaches about material goods, it makes perfect sense to bring up this ideology about the "eyes", for he teaches that he who heaps treasures in heavens has *"aiyin tovah"* and by doing so, his whole body and his walk will be illuminated, in other words, the one who does it, will have a blessed life by God in every aspect. The one who holds fast to material possessions, by being selfish and greedy, possesses *"aiyin ra'ah"* and thus will have all his ways darkened, which is nothing more that a life far away from God's will.

To better understand this terminology, let's look at some rabbinical teachings on this subject. Yehoshua is not very clear about these "eyes," for all his listeners were already accustomed to this subject.

We should observe what we should do to obtain the *"aiyin tovah"* and how we should behave so we never lose them:

> *If a person does a tzedakah, he should do it with aiyin tovah.*
> Midrash Bava Batra 14:4

We can see here that the *"aiyin tovah"* is linked to *tzedakah*, charity, and it could not make more sense, because he who financially supports his neighbor, cleary does not place his heart on whatever he can accumulate on this earth.

Beit Hillel makes some comments about it, which in my point of view, are the most radical comments I have found throughout the Talmud:

> *The amount of Terumah (bestowal): Beit Hillel says: a generous amount is one-fourth. Beit Shammai says: one third. The common quantity is one-fifth. A sixth is an aiyin ra'ah.*
> Mishnah Terumot 4:3

Everyone knows that the bible commands to tithe one-tenth of everything we make, but look how interesting this is, the Rabbi of Yehoshua establishes a quarter, 25% of everything that one receives and still claims that if one gives one is sixth or less, that person does not have *"aiyin tovah"*.

In other words, in order to truly have an *"aiyin tovah"* that illuminates our path, we must go beyond the ten percent, we must reach one fourth. This shows a total detachment from material goods, just as Yehoshua is explaining. Let's look at where Yehoshua took this from:

> *He who has aiyin tovah will be blessed, for*
> *he gives of his bread to the poor.*

Proverbs 22:9

> *Do not eat the bread of the one who possesses*
> *aiyin ra'ah, nor covet his goods.*

Proverbs 23:6

There is a clear parallel between the physical and the spiritual in all of this, just as the eyes bring the concept of clarity to the mind, the detachment of material goods brings clarity to the spirit.

We must understand that neither the Torah nor Yehoshua were against the possession of material goods, what they are against is the love to these things; the value that man puts on them and how stingy he becomes, are the real problems. For this reason, Yeshoshua continues his teaching by quoting that no man can serve two masters, one cannot serve God and mammon (money in Aramaic).

Such a conception of serving two masters is something from the Torah, but it is not quite clear there, so we must do a grammatical analysis in the book of Genesis.

## YETZER

Both *"aiyin tovah"* and *"aiyin ra'ah"* are results of the two instincts that have been placed by God within every human being. They are the good instinct (Yetzer Tovah) and the evil instinct (Yetzer Ra'ah), both are the main factors that lead the life of every human being. The real struggle that each one of us goes through every day, is precisely concerning these two *"Yetzer"*. As we look into the Torah, the very moment that God creates the human being, something interesting is reported to us:

וייצר יהוה אלהים את האדם עפר מן האדמה ויפח
באפיו נשמת חיים ויהי האדם לנפש חיה

*And the LORD God formed the man of the dust
of the ground, and breathed into his nostrils the
breath of life; and man became a living soul.*

Genesis 2:7

In this verse we have an apparent grammatical error, a writing mistake, but as we are talking about the Torah, what seems like a error, is actually a message, it is something we should pay attention to.

The term "formed" in Hebrew is *Yitzer* (יצר) and it is used when God formed the animals and the mankind on the sixth day, also in Adam's creation the same term is used, however its writing comes in a different and unique way throughout the Hebrew literature; In this case, we have the same word *Yitzer* (וייצר), but with an abnormal repetition of the initial letter YUD (י); This hidden fact reveals that Adam already knew very well what was good and what was bad, because each YUD (י) of this "wrongly" written word *Yitzer* (וייצר), stands for both *Yetzer HaTov* (יצר יטוב) and *Yetzer Hara'ah* (יצר הרע).

This is because there is another word that is written in exactly the same way as the word *Yitzer* (יצר), which is the word *Yetzer* (יצר). This already changes everything, for *Yetzer* is the name of man's intrinsic inclination. Within each human being there are the *Yetzer HaTov* (good inclination) and the *Yetzer HaRa'ah* (evil inclination), and everything we do and decide in life is influenced by one of these inclinations.

*Rav Nahman bar Rav Hisda interprets: what does it
mean from what is written: "Then Adonai Elohim*

*formed (vayyitzer) the man" with two Yud? These two*
*Yud allude to the fact that the Holy One, blessed be He,*
*has created two inclinations, one good and one bad.*
Talmud of Babylon, Tractate Brakhot 61a

Yehoshua speaks in a very similar way, and certainly possessed this understanding concerning the creation of man. When he teaches about serving two masters, he refers precisely to these two inclinations, it is impossible for a person to be good while being evil, it is impossible to observe the Torah and to live in sin, for it means that the Torah is not being observed within the heart (as already taught in section 5), for if it is observed within the heart, sin is not even an option.

Beit Hillel used to teach something very similar and much replicated by Yehoshua in reference to the accumulation of treasures in heaven and the damage they may suffer if they are accumulated on earth.

Some years after Yehoshua's death, a king in Arabia named Izates received a visit from a Jew named Ananias from the Gamliel school, a school originated from the Hillel's school. Ananias taught Torah to that king until a few years later, the king ends up submitting himself to the God of Israel. What intrigues me most is how this king was taught, how his language closely resembled the teaching of Yehoshua, even though they never met each other. I will bring up here a short story about this king as told by the greatest Jewish historian of the first century, Flavivs Josefvs:

*Concerning King Izates, who exhausted all his treasures and the*
*reserves of his forefathers during the years of famine to help*
*the land of Israel. His brothers and his father's house brought a*
*delegation before him and told him, "Your father kept gold and increased the treasury of your forefathers and you are wasting it."*
*The king replies, "The truth flows from the earth like water from*
*a fountain and charity looks down from above"(Psalm 85:11).*

*My forefathers have put their treasures in a place vulnerable to rust and corrosion, but I place my treasuress in a place that is invulnerable to rust and corrosion, as it is written, "charity and judgment are the foundation of His throne"(Psalm 97:2).). My forefathers gathered something that does not bring forth fruit, but I have gathered something that bears fruit, as it is written, "Tell him that receiveth charity that all shall be well with him, for he shall eat of the fruits of his doings"(Isaiah 3:10). My forefathers have gathered treasures in the form of gold, but I have gathered my treasures in the form of souls, as it is written, "The fruit of charity is the Tree of Life, and whosoever obtaineth a soul is wise"(Proverbs 11:30). My forefathers gathered to others and I gathered to myself, as it is written, "And charity shall be for you"(Deuteronomy 24:13). My forefathers have gathered to this world, but I have gathered unto eternal life, for it is written, "Your charity shall walk before thee"(Isaiah 58:8).*

I believe that this history can make very clear about what Yehoshua was referring to, *"aiyin tovah"*, generosity, non-attachment to earthly things and especially, a life according to the *"yetzer tovah"* ruled by the Torah. This is what every human being needs, the rest is the rest , it will be given by God, for even if the birds do not have to care about the things of this earthly life, why then, he who understands these things and follows them, must worry?

## CONCERN AND PROVIDENCE

In a very profound way, Yehoshua delivers the solution to those who follow what he says about material goods.

If even the birds in the sky do not worry, because they receive divine providence daily, why do human beings should worry, since they are far more important than mere birds?

This is a very clear teaching, "Do not worry". However, we must always look at rabbinical teachings knowing that there is always something behind them, especially those of

Western origin and without knowledge of the Jewish faith.

In order for us to better understand this example, we must have knowledge of something called "the seven principles of Hillel", which are seven ways of how teaching should be passed on, seven rules that should be used to bring up about any deep interpretation on Torah's themes. Yehoshua had mastery of these seven principles, for such were written by his own master, and he, Hillel, should have passed them on exhaustively to his students. Today, such principles are widely used by the orthodox Jews. Knowing and understanding them will greatly help to better understand the words of Yehoshua in all the books about him and also the Tanakh itself.

## THE 7 PRINCIPLES OF RABBI HILLEL

Such principles already existed even before Rabbi Hillel, but they were compiled for the first time by him, because of his excessive use of them. Hillel used analogy and allegory to adapt the Torah to what he wanted to teach, allowing every one to easily understand the word of God, both the most intelligent and the dumbest.

### 1- KAL VACHOMER (LIGHT AND HEAVY)

If something is true for something of lesser importance, as in the case of a light commandment, this something also takes on greater importance for something more serious.

We observe the use of this concept throughout the Sermon of the Mount, when Yehoshua puts the heavy and light commandments side by side, teaching that by breaking a small commandment will surely lead to a break of a serious one.

### 2- GEZERAH SHAVAH (VERBAL EQUIVALENCE)

If a word appears in two different passages of the Torah, one can assume a connection between the two.

### 3- BINYAN AB MIKATUB ECHAD (GUESS THROUGH A RULE)

Application of a norm found in a certain passage in other

passages related by the same theme, but the same pattern are not directly found in them.

## 4- BINYAN AB MISHENE KETUVIM (DEDUCTION FROM VARIOUS RULES)

A principle is established by relating two texts together: The principle can then be applied to other passages.

This method is especially useful in identifying biblical principles and applying them to real life situations. In this way Scripture is recontextualized so that it remains relevant for all generations.

## 5- KEAL U'PERAT - PERAT 'KELAL (FROM THE GENERAL TO THE PARTICULAR - FROM THE PARTICULAR TO THE GENERAL)

A general principle may be restricted by a particularization of it in another verse or, conversely, a particular rule may be extended into a general principle.

## 6- KAYOTZE BO MIMAKOM ACHER (ANALOGY FROM ANOTHER PASSAGE)

When two passages conflict, use a third passage for resolution.

## 7- DABAR HILMAD MEANINO (INTERPRETATION THROUGH THE CONTEXT)

The passage is explained by some norm before or after it.

Now I believe it is simpler to understand where the example given by Yehoshua came from. Just as in the Sermon of the Mount, where he vastly uses KAL VACHOMER, at this moment he uses KEAL U'PERAT, exposing something common, which is the care of God with all His creation, but in an individual and particular way. In other words, he says that the same care that the Creator has with all that He has created, He will have a much bigger one and a much more personal one to those who serves Him. That is wonderful!

## CONSIDERATIONS

*If EL thinks of you, do not worry about what*
*you shall eat or what you shall drink.*
*All that the body needs, your Father knows.*
*He knows all the things you need.*
*Seek rather the kingdom of Elohim and be tzaddikim*
*and all these things will be given to you.*
*Do not worry about tomorrow, for tomorrow will worry about*
*itself. It is enough for you the day of today and its problems.*

Matthew 6:31-34

To bring an end to this study, Yehoshua points out something very harsh and, to some extent, radical. The way he starts verse 31, which is wrongly translated into English, begins with "IF EL", this shows something very complicated, since he makes it clear that there is a possibility that EL (God) does not think about someone. If we do not find a "way" for God to think about us, then yes, we will have to worry about everything. We must always pay a lot of attention in some simple terms that Yehoshua uses, the God's providence IS CONDITIONAL!

Second thing, which human being does not have the habit of praying with a lot of petition? I believe the vast majority does, but he says that God already knows these things, and that our prayer should be focused on the pursuit of the Kingdom of Heaven, and such an idea is strongly tied to the quest for how to perfect the commandments in our lives, this is why the AMIDAH was developed.

And finally, only one kind of person will actually receive all that is needy from God, the *tzadik*, who is nothing more than the Torah keeper person, that is, by the words of Yehoshua, only those who follow the Law of God will have all that they need given by God Himself. Again, ALL and not some.

Do not create a false Yehoshua, do not believe in the Roman jesus, which only serves to pretend that he gives what man asks, do not waste time with gods created by men. Follow the Real God, learn from His true words, tear down previous concepts and have a life full of God, of truth, of joy, full of all forms of grace and with always an eye in the Kingdom of Heaven.

Whoever has understanding, let him understand.

# SECTION XVII
## JUDGMENT

*Do not judge lest you be judged.*
*With this judgment you will be judged and with*
*this measure you will be measured.*
*And why do you see the straw in the eye of your neighbor*
*and not see the beam that is in your eyes?*
*And how will you speak to your neighbor: wait a little*
*and I will cast the straw out of your eyes and behold,*
*the beam is in your eyes ?!*
*Hypocrite! cast your beam out first of your eyes, and*
*afterwards cast the straw out of your neighbor's eyes.*

Matthew 7:1-5

I believe that none of the teachings of the Sermon of the Mount has been so misunderstood as the subject addressed at the beginning of chapter seven. Many understand this teaching as a prohibition to make a judgment, but such an idea is not consistent with what Yehoshua has been teaching.

We can observe from other passages that judgment is essential to man and he must always do it somehow. To judge between right and wrong and between light and darkness, are necessary attitudes for the life of any human being who decides to follow God. The interesting thing is, in this case above, which deals with judging the neighbor, Yehoshua does not bring up any prohibition, what he does is actually to encourage the judgment. However, is not any kind of judgment, he talks about a personal judgment, an introspective attitude towards our behaviors. By doing so, if we realize that we are in accordance with the God's Word, then we will have authority to judge our neighbor.

It may seem strange, but that is precisely what he teaches.

But, and there is always a "but", due to our fallen nature, we have the propensity to make bad judgments, both concerning ourselves and others, we have a tendency to use different rules when it comes to judge, being very light on us, taking us to a certain hypocrisy, and much harder with our neighbor. And in that case, we'd better be quiet.

We must be very careful when we try to "remove something from the eyes of our neighbor" when we have something much bigger in our own. We should have great discernment if we are to have a life according to the Torah.

If we fall into this error, the same will happen to us. When we are unfair to others, others will eventually be unfair to us. The one who feels always wronged before the judgments of others, must begin to analyze hos "ownself", because this could be a result of his own bad judgments toward others.

> *Do not be dishonest in judgment, or in length,*
> *or in weight, or in capacity.*
> Leviticus 19:35

> *The beginning for a man to judge is that he judges through*
> *his study of the Torah, what comes next is rest.*
> Mishneh Torah, Studies of the Torah 3:5

Two very interesting things, the first is the Torah's teaching about judgment, it does not prohibit it, just as Yehoshua did not prohibit it, but both impose the same condition of not being dishonest, and this could be complicated.

The Mishneh Torah states that, in order for us to judge a little better, this judgment must be elaborated through the study of the Torah, that is, it must be the basis taken into account at the time of a judgment.

Finally let's look at where Yehoshua took such teaching and interpretation from:

לא תשנא את אחיך בלבבך הוכח תוכיח
את עמיתך ולא תשא עליו חטא

*You should not hate your neighbor in your heart, reprove and
reprove your neighbor, but do not be condemned because of him.*
Leviticus 19:17

In this passage in Leviticus, in Hebrew, the term "reprove"
appears twice in succession (הוכח תוכיח). According to Rabbi
Baal Shem Tov, this repetition is due to the way the person
should approach his brother when it comes to judging or reproving him, the first "reprove" refers to oneself, who must
first correct himself and then, the second "reprove" means
that he will be able to correct others. I believe that is exactly
the same interpretation of Yehoshua.

## SWINES AND DOGS

Yehoshua then uses a very interesting example, which
addresses a number of things related to impurities. This a
strange explanation about his teaching on judgment, for it is
an example that can only be made clear if we understand the
terms used by him.

*Again he said to them: Do not give kosher meat to
dogs, nor throw (sacred things) before swine, lest they
chew them before you and turn to rend you.
Ask EL and it will be given to you, ask and you
will find, knock and it will open for you.
Whatever you ask you will be given and to who asks, he will
receive and will find, and to the one who calls, will be opened.
Who in the midst of you, that the son asks of
you a piece of bread, gives him a stone?
Or if you ask for fish, does it give you a snake?
And you who are an evil people, come and give good gifts
before you, then much more your Father in Heaven,
who gives His good Spirit to those who ask for it.*

Matthew 7:6-11

In order to understand this, we must first understand some terms used in the original that, unfortunately, were omitted in the Western translations.

### Kasher Meat

Within the laws of Kashrut (dietary laws of the Torah), the biggest prohibitions deal mostly about protein foods, i.e. food of animal origin, such as all kind of red meat, fish, seashell, etc. and the way they should be consumed.

Today, without a doubt, the most expensive kosher food is the red meat, the process it must go through to be kosher is somewhat laborious. Everything begins in the way the animal is slaughtered, the mashguiach has to slaughter the animal by cutting it's throat without having the animal to see the knife, then he must wait until all the blood has drained out and only then, the corpse may be cut. The meat must then be placed in salt so that, all excess of blood is removed, and then they are ready for sale. All of this process makes the cost of the kosher meat very high, thus making it a very valuable object.

A meal with kosher meat is inevitably a high-cost meal. Just as the term "kosher meat" could symbolize something expensive, the term "kosher meat" also represents the kashrut itself and the word kashrut can also be used as a representation of the Torah, for all who observes the Laws of God, irrevocably practices the law of kashrut.

Within rabbinical terminology, all those who practice any form of paganism or idolatry are called dogs. And also according to the rabbis, the idolaters are precisely those who do not follow or deny the Torah:

*From here we understand that whoever denies the Torah admits idolatry.*

Rashi, Deuteronomy 11:28:1

If we connect both of them, the commandments of God represented by the terminology "kosher meat" and "dogs" the idolaters, those who deny the Torah, we can understand that Yehoshua's affirmation is that one should not teach the commandments of God to those who do not seek to know more about them, do not follow them or believe they have been abolished.

This is very plausible, if we take Christianity for example, any kind of teaching that addresses the obedience to the Laws of God is very unwelcomed, the one who teaches such things is accused of blasphemy, judaizer, legalistic and under the curse of the law. For such people no teaching toward God should be passed on, for these dogs are already judged by themselves.

Just as "kosher meat" is a representation of kashrut, pork, a food vehemently forbidden by the bible, is a symbolism used to represent impurity. And the teaching now goes little harsher. As every teaching related to God is holy and should not be passed on to impure people, represented by the term "dogs" as seen above, the "swine" represents the people who not only deny the Torah, but live a life contrary to it, people who do evil , idolatry, violence, sexual immorality and all sort of impurity things.     With this kind of people, we shouldn't waste our time under any circumstances, specially with any teaching about God and His Torah. Unless these people are really willing to change their lives, insisting on these things will only harm our faith.

# SECTION XVIII
## LIFE

*At that time Yeshua said to his talmidim:* **come**
*through the narrow gate, for the gate of doom is*
*wide and deep and* **many go through it.**
*How narrow is the gate and grievous the path that leads*
*to life and how few are those who find them.*
Matthew 7:13-14

I have already heard many religious leaders using this passage to induce people to go to their religious temples, for it is those places, according to those leaders, that represent this "grievous and narrow path" that Yehoshua speaks of, for much of Christian literature says that this "grievous and narrow path" is the church itself and the Christian faith. There are also other sources who claim that this path is jesus himself, which make the interpretation of this verse something very mystical, almost magical.

According to my understanding, these interpretations do not define what Yehoshua was talking about. For so, let's focus only on the real focus of this teaching, THE LIFE, because if we discover what that "life" would be, we would have a better glimpse on what that "path" would be and what would that "gate" be. But we have a problem, is this life, which Yehoshua was referring to, the eternal life or the life lived in this world? As this is not clear in this verse, let's look at both, through the Torah and some rabbinical teachings.

### LIFE IN THE FLESH

What is to find the path that leads to true life in this world? According to the Torah, it is to find the purpose by which God chooses someone. Of course, not every human being has one, for many are nothing but numbers under the heavens, but he who is a chosen, the moment he finds his purpose, he finds real life.

Every purpose comes with a high price to pay, for this reason, Yehoshua uses words as "narrow" and "heavy", for few can bear to serve God. Only by finding God's plans in our lives, we will be able to achieve the purpose for which we are here, for that is the true meaning of having a life. Whoever finds his own purpose, finds the life.

We will see two cases in the Torah that confirms this and we will also see what these people have gone through to get there, both physically and mentally. This analysis will be done through Gematria as reported in the introduction of this book.

## 1) SARAH

ויהיו חיי שרה מאה שנה

*And it was Sarah's one hundred and twenty-seven years...*

Genesis 23:1a

This passage talks about Sarah's LIFE time. If we take the very first word of these verse, VAICHIU (ויהיו) - *and it was*- and we make the calculation of its letters by Gematria, we will have:

$$37 = (6)ו + (10)י + (5)ה + (10)י + (6)ו$$

To make sense out of this number, we must compare the passage above with another that speaks of an event in Sarah's life:

*...can Sarah give birth to a child at ninety years of age?*

Genesis 17:17b

Sarah died at age 127, her son, Itzhak, was born when she was ninety, meaning Sarah died 37 years after the birth of her greatest dream. The purpose in Sarah's life was not to marry Abraham, it was not to leave Ur to go to Canaan, not to expel Ishmael from home, but to have a child, God's greatest plan in her life was for her to have Itzhak and through him, God would rise a promised and chosen people.

The last 37 years of Sarah's life were the years she actually lived, felt alive, understood the true reason for being on this earth and she trully knew the Creator in a more practical way, as she herself said:

> *Sarah said: God brought me smile, everyone who*
> *hears this story will smile with me.*
>
> Genesis 21:6

Sarah found her purpose and so she rejoiced and lived for real.

## 2) YAAKOV

ויחי יעקב בארץ מצרים
*And lived Yaakov seventeen years in the land of Egypt...*
Genesis 47:28a

We will do the same thing that was done in the previous example, let's use the first word of this verse VAICHI (ויחי) - *and lived* - to calculate its value in Gematria:

$$34 = (6)ו + (10)י + (8)ח + (10)י$$

Again, for this value to make any sense, some details about Yaakov's life are needed. The patriarch had a favorite son, Yosef, who was sold to Egypt when he was only 17 years old. Years later, his is reunited with his brothers as leader of all the land of Egypt and so, his family moved over to these lands. When his father, Yaakov, arrived, he lived in peace, near his beloved son, for another 17 years.

Yosef lived with his father for the first 17 years of his life, before he was sold, and then for another 17 years in Egypt, thus 17 + 17 = 34. The purpose of Yaakov's life was precisely to have this son, to have Yosef, for through him the Hebrew people descended to Egypt to carry out the whole plan of God as reported in Exodus.

It was after Yosef's birth that Yaakov decided to get rid of all the yoke that was upon him in the house of Laban, it was because of Yosef that he decided to go to the promised land and it was because of Yosef that Yaakov decided to leave places with heavy influence of paganism. Yosef was the true purpose in Yaakov's life and his greatest joy.

*After Rachel gave birth to Yosef, Yaakov said*
*to Laban: Let me go to my homeland.*

Genesis 30:25

At that moment, a journey of a people begins, Egypt, desert, Sinai and ends with Joshua, entering and conquering the land of Israel.

The life that God promises throughout the Scriptures is not restricted only to an eternal life in *Olam Habah*, but often refers to our earthly life in *Olam Hazeh*. It's a life of blessing, joy and closeness to the Creator. For all of this to be possible, each one of us must discover and attain the purpose for which we were created. This is how to truly live life!

**The price**

Getting to the her purpose was not easy for Sarah, much less for Yakoov. Sarah lived years of her life as a nomad, for many years she had no land, she had no home and as she was getting older, she suffered more and more with her sterility, because she knew that getting pregnant would become more and more difficult.

Yakoov, in addition for having to run away from home, for having to work for his uncle Laban for years, for having to get married to a woman he did not love, for being deceived several times, for having to face his own brother, for having to fight an angel, after all of this, he received the news of the loss of his beloved son.

The purposes of God require preparation, which is often painful. This is the "narrow gate" and the "grievous path" of God that Yehoshua talks about, as many don't have what it takes, the purposes of God are for very few people.

## THE ETERNAL LIFE

If we look at this verse as referring to eternal life instead of an earthly life, we will need the Scriptures to have a basis on what that "gate" and what that "path" would be.

The concept of eternal life is something very strong in the New Testament, for it is a terminology widely used by the Pharisees at the time the New Testament was written, this is why the idea of eternal life was part of the preaching of Paul, the Apostles, and especially Yehoshua's. For this reason, to understand what they refer to when they mention the term "eternal life", we should look at what they were based on. I believe that in this case, we can look at two verses in the Tanakh. After exposing each one of them, I will bring Rabbinical, Talmudic and Aramaic commentaries of both of them that, of course, were part of the knowledge of Yehoshua and all his listeners.

*Therefore keep my statutes and my judgments; by the*
*pursuit of which man shall live by them. I am Adonai.*
Leviticus 18:5

*"Shall live by them" refers to eternal life. For if*
*you think that this verse refers to this life, is not*
*the man condemned to die in the flesh?*
Rashi, Leviticus 18:5

*And you shall keep my statutes and my judgments,*
*which, if a man follows them, he shall have*
*life through them, the **eternal life**.*
Targum Onkelos, Leviticus 18:5

*And you shall keep my statutes and the ordinances of*
*my judgments, which, if a man observes them, his place*
*in **eternal life** shall be among the righteous.*
Targum Yonatan, Leviticus18:5

*Rabbi Meir used to say, "How will we know when a Gentile,*
*who studies Torah, will be compared to the High Priest*
*himself?" From Leviticus 18:5, where it says, "If a man*
*does so, he shall live by them". Meir says: "It does not say*
*if a priest, a Levite or an Israelite does them, the verse says*
*if **a man does them.**" One learns here that even a Gentile*
*who studies the Torah is equivalent to the high priest.*
Talmud of Babylon, Tractate Sanhedrin 59a

According to the Torah, the Talmud, the Aramaic versions and the rabbis, following the Torah, or more than that, obeying God, is what guarantees one in eternal life and this is something available to all men, Jews or Gentiles.

However, obedience without faith is not enough, the new testament in several passages, is emphatic in relating them both. Today there are many rabbis who teach that regardless of whether the Jew has faith or not, he must follow the commandments, for this will be sufficient for him to enter into eternal life. But, not everyone thinks like that, apart from the new testament, the Tanakh and rabbinical commentaries also corroborate with the idea of faith linked to obedience, thus leading to eternal life:

*Behold, his soul is proud, it is not upright in him;*
*but the righteous shall live by faith.*
Habakkuk 2:4

*God gave Israel 613 commandments, by which eternal life would*
*be obtained. If the man observes them, he will live by them. But*
*613 are too many to remember, King David simplified them*
*from 613 to only 11 commandments in Psalms 15. But 11 are*
*still too many to remember. Then the prophet Isaiah simplified*
*them from 11 to 6 commandments in Isaiah 33:13-14.*
*But 6 are still too many to remember. Then in Micah 6:8 we*
*have: "1) do justice, 2) love goodness, 3) walk humbly before*

*God." But even 3 things are a bit heavy. So Isaiah simplifies them once again, summarizing the entire Torah in only 2 principles in Isaiah 56:1: "Keep justice and do the right thing." And then Habakkuk comes and simplifies the whole Torah in only one principle: "The righteous shall live by faith."*

Talmud of Babylon, Tractate Makkot 24a

"To live by faith" is the very summation of the whole Torah, the Laws of God and the ways of God for a man who wants to follow Him. But faith is something very subjective, very personal, for the faith of one individual will never be equal or comparable with his neighbor, on the other hand, the commandments, when followed by a group of people, these people will follow them in a similar way, all behaving alike before God.

Yehoshua, when he teaches about "life" in the verse we are studying, he does in a rather strange way, something that is only possible to see in the Hebrew original version of the book of Matthew. He begins by saying: *"COME (singular), through the narrow gate..."*. The word "come" is conjugated in the singular form, as if he were speaking to a single person, but he ends his sentence in the following way: *"... many go through it"*, referring not anymore to a single person, rather to a group of people. He begins using the singular form and ends using the plural form. It may seem only a way of speaking, but actually this manner of expressing something remotes to something that appears in the Torah, which is expressed in the very same way:

*SEE (singular), on this day, I place before YOU (plural) life and death.*

Deuteronomy 30:15

If we make a grammatical connection of Yehoshua's words with the above Torah's passage, we may understand that Yehoshua is referring to life and death that were placed by God before men.

This also makes an allusion to the concept of faith and obedience. Faith is very unique and singular, for this reason, he stars with the singular form, addressing a singular person, showing that everything must start with faith. Then, it turns from singular to plural, revealing that the next step must be obedience, for obedience is not something that is done individually. When a group of people follow the Torah, their behavior will be alike. Those are the reasons that Yehoshua uses this grammar form, because it makes an connection with Deuteronomy 30:15, which is a passage that talks about eternal life, widely know by every Jew. And by doing so, he indirectly connects faith and obedience to eternal life.

## LIFE AND LIFE

I believe that both interpretations fit here, both earthly life and eternal life present the same challenges mentioned.

If we understand Yehoshua's words as life on this earth, the "narrow gate", in this case, would be God's purpose, which represents the lapidation that is made with those who are chosen by Him, thus preparing them for the divine plans. The "grievous path" would be precisely to walk in His purpose, we just have to look at the lives of the patriarchs and of the great men in the Tanakh, that even after reaching their goals, life has not become easy on them, but despite difficulties, joy, pleasure and true reason of life overcame all that they went through.

On the other hand, if he means the eternal life, the "narrow gate" would be faith, the first step to be taken, something that, although very particular, having faith in the True God is a challenge. This is because God is not palpable nor visible, His works do not make logical sense and He likes to confuse the sages. The "grievous path" would be the next step to be taken, the commandments, the Torah, a life of obedience that guides the human being to eternal life.

Many understand that jesus is the way, or the gate,

or whatever, but this kind of interpretation would make everything very mystical, magical and difficult to access. Yehoshua states in other books that he is the way, the gate, and so on. This claim does not refer to his person itself, but to his deeds and teachings, this type of terminology is very common within Judaism to refer to great masters and sages, the Talmud has numerous examples in this regard, some rabbis are called columns, in reference to the pillars of the Temple, for it is through their teachings that the Torah is sustained.

In my point of view, what Yehoshua says here is that following his teachings will be difficult and cumbersome, but it is through them that his followers will find the purpose in this life and at the end of it, eternal life, through faith and obedience.

## THE HEBREW LETTER HEI - ה

The idea of a "grievous path" that leads to life and the "wide gate of doom" that leads to perdition is a very old rabbinic concept, it is possible to find mentions with similar contents already in the first books that were compiled by the sages. The rabbis teach that this idea is represented by the Hebrew letter HEI (ה), because the bottom is wide open, representing the wide path that leads to bad things, things from down below. However, at the top, there is also an opening, much narrower and smaller than the one below, representing the path that leads to *Olam Habah*, which is above. This opening in the letter HEI, besides narrow, is difficult to access, because it goes against gravity by being at the top.

Yehoshua's words did not surprise his listeners, for this concept was already commonly known by the Jews. What they understood through it is that his teachings and having faith in them, represent the gate and the path that, though is grievous and narrow , they lead to the true life, both earthly and eternal.

To conclude, I will leave two passages, one from the book of Psalms and another from the Talmud, both talks about this theme. The first refers to life on earth, the second to eternal life and both make a connection with the Torah:

*I will never deny your precepts (Torah), for You preserve*
*my life through them.*

Psalms 119:93


*But He also prepared Gehinam for the wicked, which is like a*
*sharp sword that consumes, and in the middle of it, He created*
*flakes of fire and burning coals for the judgment of the evil*
*ones who rebelled in life against the doctrines of the Torah.*
*Serving the Torah is better than the very fruit of the tree of life.*
*The Torah is the Word of Adonai, which, if a man observes it,*
*he will walk in the path of life, which leads to eternal life*

Targum Jonathan Ben Uzziel, Genesis 3

# SECTION XIX
## DEVAREI TORAH

*Again he told them: Everyone who listens to these
things* **(Devarim Torah)** *and does them is similar to the
man who builds the house on the top of a rock.
The rain falls on it and the wind hits it and it does
not fall, because its foundation is the rock.
And all who hear "these things"* **(Eile HaDevarim)**
*and do not do them is similar to the man who is
foolish, who builds a house on the sand.
The rains fall and the flood comes and the
house falls apart with a great fall.
While Yeshua was saying these words* **(Devarim)**, *all
the people were impressed with his conduct.
For he was preaching before the people with
great power, and not as the sages.*
Matthew 7:24-29

We have very deep words of Yehoshua before us in
these passages. There are, in these few verses, some amazing
Jewish technical terms which, if we understand them, they
can clarify many things about what was going on. These
terms are easily translated, but their meanings will only
make sense under a Jewish perspective and in their original
language.

For three times, Yehoshua quotes the term DEVARIM
(דברים), this term can be translated both as "things" or
"words". If we use either of these two terms to make a translation into English, both will make full sense, for we would
have "*Everyone who listens to these things...*" or "*Everyone who
listens to these words...*", both translations are consistent.
When we look at the translated bibles that we have in hand
now a days, we will see that one of these two terms, "things"
or "words", appears in it.

Although a direct translation like this is valid, it ends up taking away much of the essence of the meaning of the word DEVARIM. Yehoshua says that he who listens to these "things" or "words" and does them, is like the man who builds the house on the rock and who listens to these "things" or "words" and does not do them, is like the man who builds the house on the sand. A very profound, but to a certain extent, relative teaching, for I ask, what are these "things"? What are these "words"? One can answer that these "things" and "words" are the teachings of Yehoshua and I can even agree with that, but then I ask again, what teachings? And we would enter into a looping, for each answer would generate a new question, unless we can get to the source of his teaching.

DEVARIM means much more than "things" or "words", DEVARIM is the name of the last book of the Torah, the book of Deuteronomy, the book that is the repetition of all the Laws of God, the "grand summary" of what the Creator wants from His people. Perhaps, the "things" and "words" that Yehoshua says that we should listen to and do, are just those things and words that are found in the book of Deuteronomy. But to be sure, we should look more deeply into some details.

**PROOF 1**

The Hebrew word for "those" or "these" is EILE (אלה). Although it is a simple word of a very common usage, there are some things in it that can lead us to a new understanding about this teaching.

What I am going to pass on here I've learned in a Torah class with a rabbi from Tel Aviv, in the synagogue Binyan Olam, many years ago. This class was based on a book called *Sifsei Chachomim Chumash*.

This rabbi taught that there are several instances where a *"parashah"* or a verse begins with the word EILE (אלה). In the vast majority of times, the verse that begins with this term, is connected somehow with the Laws of God. Some of them are:

These (אלה) are the commandments ... - Leviticus 27:34
These (אלה) are the commandments and the Laws ... - Numbers 36:13
These (אלה) are the statutes ... - Numbers 30:17
These (אלה) are the words of the covenant ... - Deuteronomy 28:69
These (אלה) are the holy dates ... - Leviticus 23: 4
These (אלה) are the Laws and the ordinances ... - Deuteronomy 12: 1

The term EILE (אלה), in the Torah, has a mystical association with the commandments and the Laws of God, for whenever the Laws are presented or re-presented in the Torah, the term EILE (אלה) precedes them.

Now, when Yehoshua speaks in verse 26, *"Everyone who listens these things..."* in its original, he calls *"these things"* as EILE HADEVARIM (אלה הדברים). Just as in the verses mentioned above. So, we are being presented here with something that is being preceded by the word EILE. From what we have seen so far, I believe we can now begin to connect a few loose ends.

Because HaDEVARIM is preceded by the word EILE, we can then define that the word HaDEVARIM used by Yehoshua, in this case, cannot be translated as "things" or "words", for this HaDEVARIM, which comes after the term EILE (אלה) refers precisely to the Laws, to the commandments and ordinances of God, that is, the TORAH.

*We cannot disqualify EILE (אלה), for it proceeds from Deuteronomy (דברים), which has the purpose of repeating the Torah.*
Sifsei Chachomim Chumash, Exodus 21:1

*Sifsei Chachomim's* own sages teach us that we cannot disqualify this term, however ordinary it may be, it reveals many mystical things to us. We must understand that little details make a lot of difference, the rabbinical wisdom that Yehoshua had really impresses me. But let's look for more evidence on this.

## PROOF 2

If we were in Israel today, having a conversation in Hebrew with an Israeli, and if we wanted to say "these things" or "these words", we would say HaDEVARIM HaEILE (הדברים האלה).

Interestingly, for when Yehoshua says "these things" in verse 26, he does not say HaDEVARIM HaEILE (הדברים האלה), rather EILE HADEVARIM (אלה הדברים), he reverses the order of the usual way to say "these things".

This caught my attention, because if we look at the book of Deuteronomy, exactly the one called DEVARIM, in its very first words, we have something very interesting:

*These are the words (אלה הדברים) that Moses told Israel ....*
Deuteronomy 1:1

Amazing! Yehoshua, by using the term EILE HaDEVARIM, is just making a mention of the book of Deuteronomy, quoting its exact first words. This book is the repetition of all the Torah Laws and it also shows that these "things" and "words", that we should listen to and do, are just the Laws that are in the Torah!

I believe we can now re-read the above verses in a more direct way:

*Again he told them: Everyone who listens to the **Laws of the Torah** and does them is similar to the man who builds the house on the top of a rock.*
*The rain falls on it and the wind hits it and it does not fall, because its foundation is the rock.*
*And all who hear the **Laws of the Torah** and do*

*not do them is similar to the man who is foolish,*
*who builds a house on the sand.*
*The rains fall and the flood comes and the*
*house falls apart with a great fall.*
*While Yeshua was teaching **Deuteronomy** (Devarim),*
*all the people were impressed with his conduct.*
*For he was preaching before the people with*
*great power, and not as the sages.*

Matthew 7:24-29, author

I think it is now very clear what are those *"things"* that we should listen to and do, so we can build the house on the rock. The only thing solid enough, in which we can build our faith and rest our spirit, is in the Word of God and there is nothing else besides it.

## ROCK

*Wisdom has built its house ...*

Proverbs 9:1

*"Wisdom has built its house": this is the Torah, that*
*teaches how to build and it also has built all the worlds.*

Midrash Mishlei 9

*I'll tell Adonai, My rock...*

Psalms 42:10a

Throughout the book of Psalms we find that Adonai is THE ROCK, the rock upon which we must build our houses, our lives, our faith, our hopes, and our plans. Many think that the rock is Yehoshua, or the Mashiach, or the Torah, or the Bible, or jesus, but the rock itself is Adonai ONLY, the One who created all things.

The Torah, in the other turn, instructs us on how to build our house over this rock, it teaches us about the properties of the Rock, how to excavate IT, how to establish a foundation and how to let IT become the support of everything in our lives. It is the Torah that gives us this wisdom, he who does not know it, will never be able to build a house on THE ROCK, for all he knows is sand.

The teaching of Yehoshua is about how we should put everything that is relative to our lives in Adonai, how everything we plan and dream should be built upon the rock that He is and that is only possible through the "instruction booklet" that He delivered to His people.

# SECTION XX
## THE DEAD BURYING THE DEAD

*One of his talmidim told him, allow me to go and bury my father.*
*And Yeshua said, follow me and let the dead bury the dead.*
Matthew 8:21-22

These short words of Yeshoshua, if not well inter-preted, may give a negative and contrary idea concern-ing family relationship established by the Torah, especially concerning parenthood.

Many Jews, who study the life of Yehoshua, use this passage, among many others, to prove how he was against the Torah's principles, specially agaisnt the most important one, the one that shapes the society, which is the family.

The biggest problem, that prevents the real under-standing, is precisely the answer he gives to his *talmid*, *"led the dead bury the dead"*. Those harsh words that Yehoshua uses, that brings an anti-Torah feeling, actually, appear in the Oral Torah as a strange Hebrew term called METIM METEIHEM (מתים מתיהם) and encompasses precisely a com-mandment set aside in modern judaism.

*When the flesh decomposes, the bones should be collected*
*and placed in small ossuaries and taken to an appropriate*
*place. Once the bones are taken to the ossuary,*
*then the son may come out of mourning.*
Talmud of Jerusalem, Tractate Moed Katan 1:5

The transfer of the bones from the tomb to an ossuary was known as the second funeral, or *Metim Meteihem*, which, in a direct translation, gives an impression that the dead man was burying another dead man.

The *Metim Meteihem* was a ritual, it was established by the rabbis that all this ritual should be done by the eld-est son. After a year of burial, he should remove the bones from the tomb and take them to the city of Jerusalem or to the mausoleum that belongs to the family. This ritual was a common practice in first-century Judaism. For lack of this understanding, mainly by the original translator of this text, the impression that we are given here is that Yehoshua disagreed with the obligation to bury the relatives, but the real problem that he had was in relation to this Talmudic custom and with its true meaning.

Rabbi Yose said that the reason for such a ritual is, as the flesh decomposes between the first and second burial, the dead person becomes justified of his sins. Only after the second burial could the son come out of mourning. For as the flesh is sinful and it no longer existed, the sin over the spirit of the dead also no longer existed, so he could bring the "justified" bones together to his ancestors.

Of course, contrary to what many think, Yehoshua was not encouraging the young man to break the fifth commandment and dishonor his father, but he was clearly against the *Metim Meteihem*, for it gives a false impression that there might be some kind of way to receive pardon from one's sins besides through repentance before the Almighty God.

Another thing to take into consideration in this respect is the fact that this *talmid* comes to Yeshoshua, showing that he was no longer effectively in mourning. And not only had his mourning ended, but his father had died for about a year or so, because according to what was determine by the rabbis, one could not be studying Torah together to a master during that one year of mourning, in this case, with Yehoshua. This proves that the death of his father happened at least a year before and the burial that this boy was referring to was taking his father's bones to a mausoleum.

Some historians claim that this case happened just before the Sukkot's feast and Yeshoshua was on his way to Jerusalem for this celebration, which may have seemed a good opportunity for this boy to take the ossuary of his father there. This idea of using of the feasts to take the ossuary to the holy city appears in some debates in the Talmud, in the same Tractate quoted above, where Rabbi Yose and Rabbi Meir discuss whether or not there is a ban on carrying an ossuary or digging a grave at times of feasting.

# SECTION XXI
## TZITZIT

*And, behold, a woman with a flow of blood for twelve years,
came up behind him and touched the Tzitzit of his Talit.
She said in her heart: If I touch his talit, I
will be healed immediately.
He turned his face and said to her: Be strong my
daughter, the **fear** for Adonai, blessed be He (Baruch
hu) healed you. At that very hour she was healed.*
Matthew 9:20-22

### THE HEALING THROUGH THE TZITZIT
The New Testament, though many people do not
understand, makes very clear how observant of the Torah
Yehoshua was. For this reason, there is no doubt that he wore
his tzitzit all the time, just as commanded by the Torah.

*And the LORD spoke unto Moses, saying, Speak unto the
children of Israel, and tell them to make fringes on the edges
of their garments for their generations; and in the fringes
of the borders they shall add a blue cord. And it shall be in
the fringes, that ye may see it, and that ye remember all the
commandments of the Lord, and do them; and you shall not
follow after your heart nor after your eyes, by which you
have been committing adultery. That ye may remember all
my commandments, and do them, and be holy before your
God. I am Adonai your Elohim, who brought you out of the
land of Egypt, to be your God; . I am Adonai your Elohim.*
Numbers 15:37-41

*Fringes you shall put on the four corners of your
garment, with which you will cover yourself.*
Deuteronomy 22:12

According to the Torah, the garments were created
and given to man because of the Adam's sin, who, by having

consumed the fruit of the Tree of the Knowledge of Good and Evil, became aware of his evil inclination that he had within himself, thus perceiving that certain parts of his body were associated with physical pleasures. For this reason, the Creator decided to make him clothes and such an idea of "getting dressed" never left the human reality. I believe it is for this reason that the Torah commands tzitzit to be bound to the garments, for garments was created due to sin. The tzitzit has two purposes: The tzitzit reminds us to be always on guard against our evil inclinations and to resist them by following the commandments. The garments also serve as a memorial of the price to be paid if we do not pay attention to what God wants from us.

The tzitzit is part of the daily clothing of the People of Israel, it has always been present in the daily garments so that they constantly remember the commandments of the One God. This commandment has a unique symbolism and creates an exclusive approach to God. One interesting thing about the tzitzit is when a person dies, one of the four Tzitzit of the garment is cut off, for it represents the end of his obligations to the Torah. It is for this reason that in 1 Samuel 24, David cuts off the "fringes" of King Shaul's robes, in fact, he cuts off his tzitzit, representing the death of his reign.

The tzitzit is a fringe attached to the garments, but without being part of them. There are 5 interwoven cotton threads with 8 knots, giving a total of 13 different stitches. If we use the Gematria to calculate the numerical value of the word "tzitzit" in Hebrew, we will have the value of 600 and its numerical value plus the number of stitches a tzitzit has, we will have the sum of 613. 613 is precisely the number of commandments in the Torah, 613 mitzvot. That is why God commands us about the use of the tzitzit as a memorial of His commandments, for they both is connected by the numerical value of 613.

In first-century Israel, it was customary for men to

wear a simple tunic called *haluk*, both at home and on the street. When in public places, it was customary to use over the *haluk* another quadrangular tunic, called Talit, which covered the body from the shoulders to the feet and served as a climatic protection. At each of the four corners of the Talit, the tzitzit were placed in obedience to the biblical command.

There is an immeasurable power and spiritual secrets behind this commandment, so strong that Rabbi Shimon Bar Yochai says that he who puts tzitzit in his prayers receives the *Shekhinah* above him. Such power, which many do not understand, was well known to this woman with the blood flow problem. If we analyze the Tanakh, we can see from where Rabbi Shimon brought that up. In the passage from Numbers above, the Hebrew word for "borders" is *"knafeiah"*, which can also be translated as "wings", such a term appears throughout the Tanakh seventy-six times, by adding seven to six, we will again have 13, which represents the five strings and the eight knots. Of all these passages, the most interesting one is the one which appears in the book of the prophet Malachi:

> *But to you who fear my name, the sun of tzadik will*
> *rise with healing under its **wings**; and you shall*
> *rise and grow like the calves from the stall.*
>
> Malachi 4:2

The prophet says that Mashiach (sun of tzadik) will come and bring healing under his **wings**, underneath his *"knafeiah"*, which is nothing more than another word to mean his tzitzit. Malachi states that only those who fear the name of Adonai (the tetragram) will receive healing. Yehoshua, when he realizes what was happening, he turns to the woman and says that her **fear** for Adonai (referring to the tetragram) had healed her, thus confirming what the prophet had said.

With this understanding in mind, a passage in psalms becomes much clearer and more coherent:

*In the secret place of the Most High and under His wings*
Psalm 91:1-4

The healing was due a Torah command, the Living Word of the Living God, by a prophecy, by the fear of God, and by the obedience that Yehoshua had.

## HYPOCRISY BY THE TZITZIT

*And all theirs MA'ASSOT are made by them to be seen.*
*They wear expensive Talitot and long Tzitzit.*
*They love to be the first in the festive houses and to*
*be seated in the first places in the synagogues.*
Matthew 23:5-6

At times I hear some Christian teachings about the abolition of the use of Tzitzit using this passage as the excuse, further reaffirming that jesus came to abolish the Law of God. Perhaps they are right, perhaps their jesus did indeed abolish the Torah, but the true Yehoshua not only came to confirm it, but also came to fulfill it, to teach it and to propagate it. Therefore, we should not look at this verse at all as an abolition of God's command.

Yehoshua, as a good Torah observant, embraced the use of tzitzit and in no way condemned its use, rather he denounced its use as a symbol of one's spiritual state. The tzitizit only fulfills its role if the heart of whom wears it is pure.

The Torah does not establish a fixed size for the tzitzit, for that reason there were those who wear long stripes that drag on the ground, such a custom is not only reported by the words of Yehoshua, but it is also found in the Jewish sources.

*At that time, existed in Jerusalem three rich men:*
*Nakdymon Ben Gurion, Ben Kalba Savua and Ben*

*Tzitzit HaKesat ... ... Ben Tzitzit HaKesat was called by that name because he was known for his long tzitzit that was dragged through the streets on his feet.*
Talmud of Babylon, Tractate Gittin 56a

Clearly Yehoshua was not opposed to the use of the Talit and even less of the tzitzit, for if that were the case, he would be a hypocrite. He actually opposed the exaggerated use of God's commandments as a way of showing false holiness before men, many Jews use long tzitzit and huge tefilim only to appear more spiritually higher before other men, clearly showing just how empty they are. As he taught many times, everything must be in secret, so that the Father, who sees in secret, may bless. Such a concept was not just for prayers, but for everything. Discretion at its highest.

This "competition" for holiness exists even today. Over and over again, during the feast of Yom Kippur, for an abusive amount of money, wealthy families reserve the first seats in the synagogues for the Kol Nidrei's prayer and do not even appear for the celebration. This happens only so that their names are placed on the chairs so that everyone sees their financial powers. By doing so, they prevent many people, who attend the prayer, to be closer to the tribune. Yehoshua condemned these mediocre attitudes on the part of many.

One thing is certain, Yehoshua used tzitzit, tefilim, and talit, and would never abolish these commandments.

**THE TZITZIT'S STRING**

A curious fact, the yarn used for the making of tzitzit, when fabricated, is wrapped around itself 39 times. If we compare this fabrication process with the most important Torah's Mitvah, we will find a somewhat deep connection.

The most important commandment of the Torah is concerning the existence of the One Living God and the recognition of Him as such. In Hebrew, this God, who is One, is treated as ADONAI ECHAD ('י-ה-ו-ה אחד). If we make an analysis through the Gematria of these words, we will again find the symbolism of tzitzit:

**39** = 4 ד + 8 ח + 1 א + 5 ה + 6 ו + 5 ה + 10 י
(equal to the number of times a yarn of tzitzit
is wrapped during its production)

I see in the present day that many Christian strands have sought the use of Talit and tzitzit in a very frequent way. Unfortunately, many do not understand the motives of this mantle and believe that Talit itself is the "holy item" rather than the tzitzit.

Another big problem that I see a lot is the "misuse" of this ordinance. The real meaning of it is for its user to remember the commandments, in the case that a person does not follow them, or believes that they have been abolished, what is the function of wearing the tzitzit? None, it becomes hypocrisy. However they are taught that using it will be a way to receive blessings from God. This bothers me greatly, not the people who use it, but the leaders who, instead of teaching what should be taught, claim that Talit, tzitzit or any other "accessory" from the Torah is a source of blessings, making their use as something for own benefit and somewhat selfish.

It is not the Talit, or tzitzit, that guarantees true blessings, but a righteous life before the eyes of the Creator, through His Torah as a whole and not just parts of it.

**Nothing from the Torah should become a talisman**
**for blessings.**

# SECTION XXII
## DISCIPLESHIP

*I have come to separate the son of his father*
*and the daughter of her mother.*
*The enemy must be loved.*
*He who loves father and mother more than*
*me, I am not suitable to him.*

Matthew 10:35-37

At certain moment we see Yehoshua claiming that honoring father and mother is a Torah's commandment and must be observed. However, now he makes a very strange statement, he says that he will separate the childrens from their parents, for the love that the childrens must have for him must be greater than the love they should have for their parents.

This is a complicated passage to be explained, due to the strong apparent contradiction it has in relation to other teachings of Yehoshua and with the moral and family values taught by the bible, hindering its understanding. To bring it to light, a brief custom of the first-century rabbinate must be understood.

### FOLLOWERS

In first-century Judaism, many rabbis had an itinerant life, going from city to city to teach the Torah. Many people ended up following these rabbis, others became talmidim and ended up living a life like of their masters, wandering, traveling and learning alongside him. This type of ministry was common, it was standard among those who taught the Torah, and with Yehoshua was no different. The life of an itinerant rabbi in the land of Israel was not an easy one, the rabbis were forbidden to charge for their teachings, they could not accept any kind of monetary value as offering and should only accept food and accommodation by those who received their teachings. It was a hard life of total devotion to God, many students followed great rabbis for a certain period and after having acquired enough knowledge, they used to return to their home cities in order to found schools according to the line of thought of their former masters, however, even owning their own school, their financial gain was still coming from their profession.

> *Anyone who benefits from the words of the*
> *Torah removes his life from this world.*
>
> Pirkei Avot 4:5

Such was the life of Yehoshua, he was an itinerant rabbi who traveled throughout the land of Israel teaching, healing and preaching. Many listened to him, some left their life to follow him and his group counted on the charity from the people who learned from him. Yehoshua makes some comments about this practice that he had:

> *And Yeshua answered him: the foxes have holes*
> *and the birds nests, but the son of man, the virgin's*
> *son, has no place to enter (rest) his head.*
>
> Matthew 8:20

In this verse, Yehoshua speaks of his life as a traveling rabbi, where he had no comfort, no fixed income and no material good that could not be carried with him. It was a life totally dedicated to the study and to the learning of the Torah.

> *He who gives a vessel of fresh water to one of my little*
> *talmidim, by the name of the talmid, Amen (trully)*
> *I tell you that you will not lose the merit.*
>
> Matthew 10:42

In this other passage, Yeshohua refers to the charity that an itinerant rabbi and his students needed, he taught that whoever offers anything to them will receive merits before the Creator.

Such a lifestyle defines the typical first-century rabbi, the typical Torah teacher and master. The life of a sage was of teachings in cities, towns, farms, temples and synagogues. Hundreds of rabbis wandered throughout Israel in the time of Yehoshua, they did not hesitate to go to a remote, hard-to-reach place in the diaspora to obtain a new follower, a new talmid. It was very common for the teachings of these rabbis to be in family houses, or in the countryside, or under a tree, or in a boat if there were many people around.

*Raise up many disciples.*

Pirkei Avot 1:1

Discipleship was not something created by Yehoshua, it was a tradition among the rabbis of the time. Raising followers was the highest goal of anyone who taught the Torah. The Talmud relates that Rabbi Gamliel had more than a thousand talmidim. Yehoshua also had several followers, apart from the twelve already known, there were many others whom he called along the way and followed him. After his death, only in the city of Jerusalem, there were around one hundred and twenty disciples of him. The talmud tells of some cases where these disciples appear at random:

*Once I was walking through the market of the city of Tzippori and I came across a disciple of Yeshua named Yaakov of Kefar-Sekaniah who told me....*
Talmud of Babylon, Tractate Avodah Zarah 17a

The vast majority of people who followed Yehoshua were forgotten by history, but somehow, their works after the death of their master bear fruit up to this day. These men went out all over the land of Israel teaching the Torah according to the interpretation of their master, teaching that no Law of the Oral Torah should be above what is written and in no way should hypocrisy be accepted among the people.

## THE FATHER, THE MOTHER AND THE DISCIPLE

Returning to the verse, in order for we to have a better comprehension, it is necessary an analysis in the term used by Yehoshua. The verb that I have translated as "to separate" in Hebrew is LEHAFRID (להפריד), but this same verb can also be used to denote "to isolate" or "to lead away".

When a person becomes a talmid of some rabbi, this talmid should move away from his family in order to have an itinerant life with his new master. When Yehoshua states that he came to "separate" the son from his father and from his mother, he was simply saying that he would take the children with him, for he was making disciples for himself, to follow him, to have an itinerant life with him, and to learn his Torah, thus, in a certain way, physically removing the children from their parents by the time they are walking alongside him. That simple.

This is connected with what it was said in the sequence " *He who loves father and mother more than me, I am not suitable to him*". The verb "to love" in Hebrew is LE'EHOV (לאהוב), which can also be used as "to prefer". What Yehoshua was saying is that the person who prefers his parents instead of learning Torah with him, it is better for this person to stay with his parents, for he does not fit with what Yehoshua defines as a disciple. In this passage, he does not refer "to love" in a literal sense, but rather to a choice that must be made by the person who decides to follow him, for he who accepts his yoke should not look back, should not stay with his heart and mind in the past and accept the life that he chose from that moment on. That is, the son should prefer to stay with Yehoshua than to stay with the parents.

This matches very well with the Talmud:

*Just as it is important to honor father and mother, leaving*

*home to study Torah is even more important.*
*The master has precedents in comparison to the father,*
*for the father has brought him to this world, but is the*
*master who will take him to the world to come.*

Mishnah Bava Metzia 2:11

## ENEMIES

Interesting that, in the middle of two related passages, appears one that is a little out of the context, to say the least. To love the enemy, the reason the author of the book of Matthew put it there is not clear to us, but such teaching, concerning the enemies, is more a criticism to the rabbinical mentality and to some teachings from the Oral Torah.

*Concerning the enemy, you are exempt from the*
*commandment: "You shall love your neighbor as yourself".*

Chizkuni, Exodus 23: 5:1

Many teach that *"love for one's neighbor"* referred only to the "Jew". Enemies, foreigners, and those who did not observe the Torah, should not be loved. There are several mentions in this regard in various parts of ancient and modern Jewish literature. But not all of them think and teach this way, like Yehoshua, many rabbis taught quite the opposite. Hillel was one of them, who made no distinction of people by teaching the Torah to anyone who wished to learn it. A more modern Jewish book, which covers various topics on how to lead a Tzadik-style life, speaks one very interesting thing:

*One of the sages said: "The best plan anyone can make*
*against an enemy is to give him a lot of love".*

Orchot Tzadikim 6:10

Yehoshua then teaches that he seeks followers, followers who gives Torah a greater importance than to family, money, and business, for following the Torah of Yehoshua will separate him from all these things.

Whoever decides to follow this path, should never look back, because it is a decision without return. He who takes up the yoke of the Torah just to change the mind later, is of no use, this one does not serve for Yahshua, does not serve for God, does not serve for himself.

Lastly, we saw yet another Yehoshua critique of a rabbinic commandments that held hatred of the enemy. Clearly "loving" an enemy is humanly impossible, but we can apply this "love" by not seeking revenge, not causing evil, not seeking destruction and letting him to live his life in peace.

To finish, a teaching from the Tanakh:

*If your enemy is hungry, give him bread to eat.*

Proverbs 25:21

# SECTION XXIII
## YOKE

*Come unto me all the weak and those who endure labor,
and I will help you to bear the injustice upon you.
Take my yoke as your yoke and learn from my
Torah, for I am humble, I am good and pure in
heart and you will find rest in your souls.*
Matthew 11:28-29

A classical Christian interpretation of this passage is Yehoshua's comparison of the heavy burden given by the Torah with the easy going laws he was creating, the comparison of the dead Judaism with the life of Christianity, the comparison of a life of legalism with a life of grace. But all those terms used by Christians to explain this passage, such as Christianity, Christian grace, new religion, laws of christ and so on, were totally out of his reality. There were no such a things.

The question is: how did the audience, who heard those words, understood them? A relationship between a student and his rabbi begins when the student comes under the tutelage of his master, it is in that moment that the student takes the yoke of his new master through obedience, dedication and following the philosophy of this rabbi. The student's desire should always be to become like his master and according to the Jewish mentality, this is precisely what "to take a rabbi's yoke" means.

The term "yoke" brings to our mind something painful, attached to one's neck and heavy on the shoulders, which only serves to bring unnecessary difficulties to life. But in fact, the yoke, in this case, is a piece of wood that connects two oxen side by side, so that both can walk in the same compass, alongside, without one turning to the left and the other to the right. The yoke did not have a negative connotation, on the contrary, the yoke represented the union of a student with his master, walking side by side, living the same kind of life.

But Yehoshua's words can still be a bit difficult, terms like "yoke" and "injustice" never give a good impression, and we can hardly associate them with positive teachings.

There is a book written by some Jews called *Apocrypha*, this book is pre-dated to Yehoshua in at least 100 years. One of its authors, Ben Sira, makes some comments that are very similar to those affirmed by Yehoshua:

> *And put your necks under its yoke (Torah) and let*
> *your soul carry its burden. The Torah is near and it*
> *is not heavy for those who seek it and whoever gives*
> *his soul for it (the Torah), will find it (the soul).*
>
> Apocrypha, Ben Sira 51:26

This is a little-known book, but it is a compilation of ancient teachings that were widely known in first-century Judaism, many of these teachings are still followed up to this day.

There is a strong similarity between both, both Yehoshua as well as Ben Sira, talk about the Torah's yoke. Both use the term "yoke", thus giving a good insight into the rabbinic mentality of the first century and how the words of Yehoshua were easily understood among the people who listened to him.

Yehoshua did not compare the burden of his teachings with the burden of the teachings of the Pharisees, for the term yoke automatically represents the teaching of Torah and Torah is one, so its teaching. However, he refers to the cost of being his disciple, the lifestyle he has because of Torah, the traveling, the approach on other people and the practice of God's Law.

Yehoshua, by saying that he is pure-hearted and humble, he presents how his interpretation of Torah is, especially in reference to the "man X man" commandments. This type of statement is very important because it gives to a possible new student, a guidance what would be, more or less, the form of interpretation of the Torah he has. We have two very good examples in this regard, Rabbi Hillel and Rabbi Shammai, one was patient and loving, so he taught a lenient law, the other temperamental, which resulted in a more intolerant teaching. Yehoshua here reveals how his approach to the Torah would be, which very much resembles Rabbi Hillel's approaching.

Like other contemporary rabbis, Yehoshua makes it clear that following him is a yoke, even if it is a light one, it stills a yoke. The life of the talmid who decides to learn Torah with him, will be a life of a great sacrifices and strict rules. Such a lifestyle is always characterized by an extreme dedication to the duties and to the master.

With these words, Yehoshua makes a call to new followers. The Torah is not a yoke, but its study is, because studying Torah requires a lot of dedication. However, according to Yehoshua, studying with him will be so fantastic that students would not even realize the weight of the yoke that this study would bring.

## Torah's Yoke

An analysis of the Torah commandments can give us the impression that the Torah is a yoke. This is understandable and, to a certain extent, a reality, for any rule or law that demands from someone some kind of change or a behavioral style other than the usual one a person has, it becomes a burden that must be dealt with by the one who decides to follow it. However, on the other hand, laws are only painful when it points out some flaw in the character of the human being, such as the prohibition of drinking and driving, for someone who does not have the habit of drinking, it will not be a problem, it will not be a yoke, it will be something that is already a behavioral style of that person, however if drinking is a common habit, then yes, following this law becomes a yoke, because it shows a behavioral failure that must be changed.

When some Torah's commandment becomes a yoke, it shows that there is a flaw in that person's life. To use the Torah to reveal these behavioral flaws is to take the person out of his comfort zone. When the law of God becomes a yoke, it is a good sign, for it shows that God is revealing Himself and showing what He wants from us, that He cares, and that the gates of heaven are still open.

The negative thing about this is that no man likes this, many religious leaders, instead of teaching the truth, offer a faith that fits into everyone's comfort zone, for that, the annulment of the Torah is necessary. We see those seeker friendly leaders all over.

Any leader who offers a truth that instead of confronting, only comforts, his concepts should be reviewed, because as Yehoshua said, THERE IS a yoke when following him, he said it is a light one, but what may be light for him, may be heavy for us.

Contrary to what many teach, the real function of the Holy Spirit is to make the acceptance of Torah's Law a natural thing inside those who seeks the real God of Israel, as it was said by God through the prophet:

*I will put my Spirit within you. And it will cause you to follow my Laws and to faithfully keep my commandments.*

Ezekiel 36:27

# SECTION XXIV
## SHABBAT

*At that time crossed Yeshua through the standing
grain on a Shabbat day and his talmidim were hungry
and began to pluck out the grains and crushed
the grains in their hands and ate them.
And the Pharisees saw it, and said unto him, Behold, your
talmidim do things which they could not do on a Shabbat day.
And Yeshua said to them, Did you not read what
David did when he was hungry and his men?
In the house of Elohim they ate the Lechem Bela`az,
which in foreign language is Paan Sagrah, which
could not be eat except by the priests alone?
And also in the Torah did you not read that the priests of the
Temple violate the Shabbatot and they are without sin?
Amen (trully) I tell you that the Temple is greater than this.
If you knew what that is: I desire grace (chessed) and not
sacrifice, you would not have convinced the innocent.
For the Son of Man is Lord of the Shabbat.*
Matthew 12:1-8

Speaking of Shabbat is perhaps one of the most difficult themes of all that Yehoshua has been through and taught, for there are almost infinite *halachot* (Jewish laws) regarding to what is allowed and forbidden on a Shabbat day. At the verses we have above, we find a simple teaching of Yehoshua concerning Shabbat that will address various Mishnaic commentaries and Jewish *halachot*, both positively and negatively.

## IN THE BEGINNING THERE WAS THE SHABBAT

*But on the seventh day is the Shabbat of Adonai your
Elohim; you should not do any work, you, your son
or daughter, your slave male or slave female, or your
animals, or the foreigner who dwells among you.*

Exodus 20:10

The book of Genesis tells that God created the world in six days and rested in the seventh, for this reason, the literal meaning of the word Shabbat is "he rested". The etiology of Shabbat is given in the first two chapters of the book of Genesis, although the name itself does not appear. The special status of that day, as well as its name, Shabbat, was revealed to the Hebrew people during the episode of *Manah*, where God gave the daily provision for five days and in the sixth the provision was doubled. According to the book of Exodus, the work should not be performed during the Shabbat so that the workers, slaves and animals are to be given rest. When God commanded the building of the tabernacle, the first order given to the people was exactly concerning that work should NOT be performed on that day, showing the extreme importance that the Shabbat has for the Creator.

The instruction about the observance of this day came after God took the People of Israel out of Egypt in the year 2448. He taught them about the Shabbat: work for six days and rest in the seventh. The Shabbat is also one of the ten commandments that God transmitted at Sinai a few weeks later. Therefore, the Shabbat celebrates both creation, a Creator God, and divine intervention in our earthly lives.

However, the Torah is very succinct about the observance of the Shabbat, for it merely forbids working. How could be possible to bring this observance to modern day? To answer this question, the rabbinate created numerous rules based on some passages from the Torah, then came others rabbis and created more rules based in the first rules and so on until infinite rules were created.

The biblical essence of the observance of Shabbat is not a strict observance, but rather a day of great joy awaited all week long, a day for all the worries of life to be set aside and a day of devotion to really important things, such as family, friends, prayer and joy.

*This whole day should be devoted to spiritual things. This involves the study of the Torah, the teaching of the Torah, the fulfillment of the associated commandments, and the appreciation of nature. That day in which, instead of serving someone, one can focus on serving the Master, the provider of life and spiritual inspiration.*

Sforno, Exodus 20:10

### The Orthodox Shabbat

The way the Shabbat is observed in the present day, it is as stipulated by the Jewish *halachot*. Because the Torah only forbids work during that day without specifying what these "works" would be, the sages had to seek an understanding of what would actually mean this God-given restriction in the Torah and thus, they did a survey of the work that occurred at the time of the Torah's deliverance, which focused precisely on the construction of the *Mishkan* (tabernacle) and all the tasks related to its maintenance. By doing so, they were able to define what kind of work is prohibited on Shabbat. According to the sages there are thirty-nine prohibitions in the Torah concerning the Shabbat:

### FIELD
1- Sowing
2- Plowing
3- Reaping
4- Binding Sheaves
5- Threshing
6- Winnowing
7- Selecting
8- Grinding

9- Sifting
10- Kneading
11- Baking

## MATERIAL PRODUCTION
12- Shearing wool
13- Cleaning
14- Combing
15- Dyeing
16- Spinning
17- Stretching the Threads
18- Making Loops
19- Weaving Threads
20- Separating the Threads
21- Tying a Knot
22- Untying a Knot
23- Sewing
24- Tearing

## WORK ON LEATHER
25- Trapping
26- Slaughtering
27- Skinning
28- Tanning
29- Smoothing
30- Ruling lines
31- Cutting

## WOOD WORK
32- Writing
33- Erasing

## BUILDING
34- Building
35- Breaking down

## EXTRAS
36- Extinguishing fire

37- Kindling a fire
38- Striking the final hammer blow
39- Carrying

From these thirty-nine prohibitions, the sages and the rabbis began to develop "fences" around these laws, which, over time, multiplied the prohibitions related to Shabbat, up to the point of making the observance of the Shabbat somewhat painful and a burden. The day created to serve man began to demand so much of him that he who observes it according to the Jewish *halachah*, ends up becoming a slave of that day, precisely because of the obscene quantity of human laws created by the ancients.

There is a Tractate on the Talmud of Babylon called the *Tractate Shabbat*, which is focused mainly on the laws concerning observance of that day. After centuries and centuries of rabbinical debates on these thirty-nine laws from the Torah and due to each rabbi's personal interpretations, they ended up creating endless laws.

Unfortunately, many people now a days believe that observance according to the Torah is the one observed in the behavior of the orthodox Jews, which is not actually true. Shabbat should be a day of pleasure and not a day to follow what was stipulated by men. Christian theology, by a weak understanding of this and a strong need for control, states that Yehoshua abolished the Shabbat by claiming that the son of man is the lord of the Shabbat.

One of the verses used as a basis is the one found in the book of Mark:

> *And he said to them: The Shabbat was made because of the man, and not the man because of the Shabbat.*
>
> Mark 2:27

But a similar allegation is also made by Paul, let's compare them both:

> *The woman was made because of the man, and*
> *not the man because of the woman.*
>
> 1 Corinthians 11:9

Those who believe in the abolition of Shabbat using this passage as a basis, as well as a few others, when we read Paul in his letter to the Corinthians, which makes a claim very similar to the teaching of Yehoshua, should also believe in the abolition of the importance of woman due to the similarity of the language used by both of them, and this would be absurd.

The statement that Yehoshua makes is actually found in the Talmud, a book that would never abolish the Shabbat:

> *Rabbi Yonatan ben Yosef says that it is written, "for it is*
> *sacred unto you" (Exodus 31:14). This shows that the*
> *Shabbat was given into your hands and not you into the*
> *hands of the Shabbat, so you don't die in its hands.*
>
> Talmud of Babylon, Tractate Yoma 85b

Yehoshua, nor his talmidim, in no way, abolished the Shabbat, just as he did not abolish or break a single Torah commandment. The abolition of the Shabbat was the work of the church, the abolition of the Torah was done by a false Roman jesus widely worshiped by the religion formed in Rome and its branches.

### Pharisees and Pharisees

Unfortunately, the neo-testamentary narrative treats the Pharisees as a single, homogeneous group. We must always keep in mind that the Pharisee is characterized by which Pharisaic school one follows and within Pharisaism, as well as within modern orthodoxism, there are innumerable lines of thought and doctrines, for this reason, there may exist, as they already existed in the time of Yehoshua, very diverse pharisaic thoughts and beliefs. This is the main reason of the existence of so many debates regarding certain Torah laws in the Talmud.

Yehoshua was from the Beit Hillel school. Rabbi Hillel was known for his patience and teaching of a law consistent with the daily life of Israeli society. Another very famous school of their time is Beit Shammai, which was much harder in law enforcement, both Rabbi Shammai and Rabbi Hillel had a very opposite mentality and disagreed over almost all forms of Torah observance.

Hillel's sensitivity to human life was truly unique, what is the reason of following the commandments that supposed to bring life to a man, at the expense of man's life? It really does not make sense. Shammai used to say quite the opposite, for him, the observance of the law is above any conditions.

*Rabbi Aha said in the name of Rabbi Akiva: The commandments were given to Israel so that they may live by them, as it is written, "Which shall a man observe to live by them" - he must be kept alive because of them (commandments) and not to die because of them. Nothing precedes life except idolatry, sexual sins, and murder.*
Tosefta Shabbat 16:14

Rabbi Akiva clarifies in this text what every Jew knows very well, the Torah is life and not death. This verse mentioned in this part of the Talmud is found in Leviticus 18:5 and reveals the strong bond that the commandments of God have with the maintenance of life on earth and above. According to the sages, only three sins are to be avoided at all costs, even at the cost of one's own life, which are idolatry, sexual immorality and murder, in those cases death is better.

There are others who agree with the interpretation given by Yehoshua, as follows:

*Rabbi Yosei, son of Rabbi Yehudah, says: "But observe my*

*Shabbatot" (Exodus 31:13). One may think this applies*
*to all under any circumstances, but the verse states "but",*
*a term that restricts and qualifies. This shows that there*
*are circumstances where one must observe the Shabbat*
*and circumstances where one can break the Shabbat.*

Talmud of Babylon, Tractate Yoma 85b

## THE GRAINS OF SHABBAT

Matthew continues his account of Yehoshua passing near a field of grain on a Shabbat, and in an unexpected way there is a certain uneasiness between Yehoshua and some Pharisees about what is permitted and forbidden to do on that day.

We must keep in mind that the attitude the talmidim of Yehoshua had is completely in accordance with the commandments of the Torah, the great problem was precisely the day that this fact occurred:

*When you enter a grain field from another man,*
*you can pluck it with your hands; but you cannot*
*use tools on your neighbor's field.*

Deuteronomy 23:26

It is interesting how Matthew makes clear that the grains were hand plucked and not cut with tools, this proves an observance to the Torah referring to small details that few people know. Another sensitive point of this permission given by the Torah, is that it is a permission that does not quote the Shabbat, that is, the permission is open to any day.

Many schools, following the thirty-nine Rabbinical prohibitions of the Shabbat, vehemently forbid any kind of harvest on that day, but according to some rabbis the Torah was given for the maintenance of life and in no way can the commandments deprive it of someone who follows them. Therefore, any commandment can be broken if life or health is at stake, if it is not about commandments on idolatry, murder or sexual immorality, any other cannot be above the maintenance of life.

As we do not know the condition in which they were and the fact that they consumed raw grains, it is very likely that they were very hungry, to the point that they really needed some food. Since the ministry of Yehoshua was maintained by donations of those who hear from him, the access to food could be punctual at times. By this fact, I believe that the consumption of the grains by his talmidim were justified with this principle of maintenance of health and life. The following comment addresses these conditions:

> *Rabbi Mathias ben Harash says, "If a person has a sore throat, it is permissible to put medicines in his mouth on a Shabbat, because the disease can put his life at risk and anything that endangers lives exceeds the observance of Shabbat".*
> Mishnah Yoma 8:6

I believe it is very clear that the value of life, whether it be the risk of illness or even hunger, is above the observance of Shabbat for many rabbis. This attitude on the part of Yehoshua is understandable, since this way of thinking came precisely from the school in which he most resembles:

> *Beit Shammai says: He who reaps profanes the Shabbat, Beit Hillel says: he who reaps for himself does not profane the Shabbat.*
> Talmud of Babylon, Tractate Shabbat 135b

Clearly, what happens in this passage is just a clash between these schools. It is very difficult to know what was the situation of Yehoshua's talmidim at this time, but for someone to harvest some raw grain and eat it, they were indeed very hungry. It was very likely that this Pharisee, who makes the approach, came from some school contrary to the Pharisaic school of Nazareth, since he does not even question the condition of his talmidim and the reason that led them to harvest the grains.

Yehoshua only observed the Shabbat according to what he was taught in the school in which he was educated and using of his rabbinical authority, he confirms this interpretation, therefore there was no breaking of Shabbat's observance nor its abolition.

Unfortunately, we observe many Christians today who, in addition to not observing the Shabbat, abhor those who observe it. Some say that it was abolished, others say that God is not on the Sabbath and some others still claim that it is idolatry, without looking at themselves when they do their worship on Sunday, the day of a pagan god.

## DAVID, THE KOHANIM AND THE SHABBAT

Within this confrontation, Yehoshua's talmidim are accused of breaking the observance of Shabbat. To respond to such strong accusation, Yehoshua uses the source of everything, the Scriptures. In a very rabbinical way, he rebuffs an affront with a question, knowing full well that the Pharisees who accuse him, knew what he was talking about.

If we pay attention to the two things that Yehoshua brings up to confront the Pharisees we will have all the answers to what happened at that moment, the first is about David eating from the sacred bread and the second about the priests breaking the Shabbat's observance.

*And the priest said to David, I have no bread in my hand; only consecrated bread provided for the young men who is abstained from women.*
*In reply to the priest, David said: I assure you that women were kept away from us, as always. Whenever I go on a mission, even if the journey is a common one, the vessels of young men remain consecrated; so consecrated food can be placed in these vessels today.*

1 Samuel 21:5-6

*And the bread, once removed from the table and burned with incense, becomes common, for it is removed from it the prohibition of sacrilege as soon as it becomes permitted to the priest.*

Rashi, 1 Samuel 21:6

David received an order from King Shaul and goes on a mission with some men, at a certain moment he arrives at Nob, at the priest Ahimelech and asks him some loaves for him and his men. The priest says that he did not have ordinary bread, only the bread consecrated according to Leviticus:

*He (priest) must prepare them (bread) before Adonai regularly, every day of Shabbat, this is an everlasting commitment on the part of the Israelites.*

Leviticus 24:8

It was clear that the bread that was above the propitiatory was not for consumption, it should stay there representing a sacrifice to Adonai, but something happens at that moment, something very serious, that becomes even more important than the very commandment from the book of Leviticus, something which we can only see in a few places, as in the translation of the Tanakh called *Targum Yohanan* from the book of 1 Samuel:

*What is under your hands, five pieces of bread? Give them to me for we are hungry – or whatever is available.*

Targum Yonahan, Alef Shmuel 21:4

What we have here is the breaking of a very important ordinance before Adonai due to the maintenance of the life and the health of David and his men, because they were hungry. When Yehoshua approaches this theme, the Pharisees certainly understood immediately the message about what was going on there, it was because of the hunger of their talmidim.

The second point is precisely this bread being prepared and organized on a Shabbat, that is, in an indirect way, Yehoshua claims that if the priests can do such things it is because they were authorized by Adonai and if Adonai authorizes, who are the rabbis to prohibit it? Yehoshua used exceptions of the Oral Torah several times, going against the religious teachings of men and never regarding the teaching of the Writing Torah.

He addresses precisely the two points thus far exposed, the maintenance of life as the main motive of the Torah's existence and a critic on the rabbinical *halachot* that made the Shabbat a burden.

## SACRIFICE

> *I want grace (chessed), not sacrifice; Obedience*
> *to God, instead of burnt offerings.*
>
> Hosea 6:6

> *Because I have desired goodness (chessed) and not sacrifice,*
> *and the knowledge of God is great. It is possible to delineate*
> *the act of kindness (chessed) and the thoughts that arise*
> *to atone the thought. Those who do not practice goodness*
> *(chessed) do not know the Adonai, but if they do kindness*
> *(chessed) they will see the goodness (chessed) of Adonai.*
>
> Sefer Oshea from Chomat Anakh

We cannot understand this point if we do not conceptualize the term chessed that is widely used, today we know this word as "grace" and we must look at the real definition of that term.

## GRACE

This is a very delicate subject, but of vital importance, for it is the misunderstanding of grace that drives away many of those who seek God from His true ways. The grace, in the lives of many Christians, serves as an excuse, because it makes faith and to serve God all very relative and convenient.

A clear example of this is the famous "to feel in the heart", today many people think that to serve God is to follow what comes in one's heart, that all that God wants from someone comes through "feeling in the heart", leaving a huge margin for justification when one does not want to serve the Creator.

I believe, and I am sure that God speaks and reveals Himself in various ways, one of them is precisely the feeling that comes in our hearts, but we can not define this way as the only way which God speaks to us, as we cannot define the Torah as the only way that God speaks to us either. The difference between the Word of God and the feelings in the heart is the relativity that both present. The Torah is the clear method of obedience to God, while the feeling, though very valid, can sometimes be somewhat foggy, for such perception requires an advanced spiritual level, which is obtained through obedience and closeness to God.

Grace, contrary to what many believe, was not something invented by the church, nor anything invented by Yehoshua or Paul, but it is a very old concept that is found in the Torah itself. Let us address the main differences of Christian grace and the real biblical grace.

### Christian Grace

Basically, Christianity defines the grace of God in a very simple way, is to receive something one does not deserve. It is the way that God shows His love to us. When we deserve punishment for our sins, God sends jesus to pay the price and offers us salvation, so that through him we may have eternal life.

In Christianity, grace is a free gift from God to man, it is the encounter that transforms and restores the human being, through it, God makes the christian his adopted son. Grace, because it is gratuitous, no one receives because one's merit.

Grace takes the life of the Christian and makes him fit for salvation from the moment this person begins to be part of that religion and believes in certain events, such as, jesus' death.

According to the theory of the dispensation, after the death of jesus, there was the abolition of the law and the end of the Torah, then grace takes its place. The laws of God, that made the people "slave", was replaced by a grace that makes the one who believes in jesus free and fit to receive eternal life, which, by the way, only comes through his inclusion in Christianity and by having faith in jesus, which is very relative, since faith is very subjective.

Such a theory is somewhat problematic, first of all by what Yehoshua himself stated in Matthew 5, saying that he did not come to abolish the Law, but to fulfill it and even if heavens and earth were to pass, nothing from the Law would be abolished. Second, the God of Israel is not a god who changes his mind, is not a god who does something to undo after, His words and His Laws are eternal. Third, for someone to abolish a law, that one has to be greater than the one who created the law and because no one is greater than God, no one can abolish anything. Fourth, if grace depends on faith and faith without works is dead (i.e. Torah), then without the Law of God it is impossible to attain grace.

Grace is a great scapegoat, because it serves as an excuse to make life easier for all who rely exclusively on it. Imagine a church that wants to get expanded by teaching the Laws of God? How likely is a church like this to grow? Very unlikely, because the true God is for few people. Unfortunately, it is very common now a days, people looking for a god for the favors he can do for them, the easier and less demanding is a church, the more it grows, the further away from the Word of God and more wrapped in mystical and relative things, like Christian grace, the more the church fills.

The path is narrow and the gate small. Most people,

even those who serve God, are not of God. They know God, but God does not know them, so when a change of life, habits and customs to follow the Word of God are demanded, they run away, claiming that such things have been abolished, or are cursed or in some cases, that is the devil himself teaching such ideas.

## Biblical grace

Contrary to what many Christians think, when they believe that grace was something that came with jesus, the Torah already had this concept many years before:

> *Then he prayed, Lord, God of my Lord Abraham,*
> *give me this day a good success and have **kindness***
> ***(chessed)** over my Lord Abraham.*
>
> Genesis 24:12

> *Make thy face shine upon thy servant; save*
> *me by your **mercies (chessed)**.*
>
> Psalm 31:16

The Hebrew word for grace is CHESSED (חסד). If we look at these two passages, one from the Torah and another from Psalm, we will see that the term "grace" appears in both, but in their respective translations we have other terms, kindness and mercy.

Yehoshua was not a Christian theologian, but an orthodox Jew, an expert in the Torah and in the Talmud, so let's look at more sources that formed the basis of his teachings.

> *Rav Ben Yehuda in the name of Rav Pinchas says: it is 613*
> *mitzvot (commandments) of Hashem, His holy commandments*
> *are basically two laws. 365 are negative, that by performing*
> *them, we will be in sin before the One Who Is, Blessed Be*
> *He, and thus we will need His CHESSED (Mercy).*
> *Other 257 mitzvot (commandments) are positive, that by*

*performing them, we will have His CHESSED (kindness),*
*where we will have the favor of the One Who Is, Blessed Be*
*He, that we may live the glory of Adonai upon the Earth.*
Talmud of Babylon, Tractate Brakhot 2b

According to the sages, the Talmud, the Torah and the Tanakh, grace can be understood as two things, the kindness of God and the mercy of God, both are free gifts from God and certainly no man deserves them.

At the same time that the word CHESSED in Hebrew is associated with two distinct things, they also end up being close, obedience and disobedience. When we perform a positive Torah commandment, those that God commands us to do, then we will receive the CHESSED (kindness) from God in our lives. If, on the other hand, we carry out a negative commandment, that is, if we do what God tells us not to do and repent of such an act, we will have the CHESSED (mercy) of God in our lives. This is the true grace of God.

Grace is something totally and exclusively connected with the Word of God and His Laws, true grace does not exist without the Torah. Unlike Christian grace, biblical grace demands obedience to the Creator, demands to seek Him, demands to follow His ways and is not something relative, that exists only within the human's mind, but is something that goes beyond the heart of man, it becomes palpable and visible to everyone who truly follows God. Grace has existed even before the Torah was delivered. The Laws of God and grace walk and will always walk holding hands, any grace that is not bound to the Torah is a false and manipulative grace.

Now we can understand the comment of *Sefer Oshea Chomat Anakh* exposed above. The performance of any sacrifice was an act of obedience to God, obedience to the Laws of God that creates *chessed* in the form of kindness. Sacrifice was not the only form of obedience that creates *chesed,* others are the Laws relating to man's relationship with man, on which the Torah proves to be a beautiful code of ethics. Another thing that can generate *chessed* is what is written in Deuteronomy 4:2, where it forbids to add or to remove anything from the Laws of God.

Interesting, because when Yehoshua says that God wants grace instead of sacrifice, he is nudging the Pharisees who were trapped in the *halachah*, for first, the sacrifice was a simple command to obey, even if one did not believe or did not agree with it, one could very well go to the Temple and offer it. Now, the hard thing concerns the relationship between someone and his neighbor, for when there is some disagreement between them, to follow some Torah's command concerning that person becomes much more difficult than to burn an offering, that was said due to the constant attack Yehoshua suffered from his own brothers, who were not giving him peace to keep going with his ministry. And the last thing that Yehoshua was saying is about the *chessed* that they would fail to receive by adding things to the Laws of God through their *halachot*. This is a very subtle critique and a very misunderstood thing by Christian theology.

## HEALING ON THE SHABBAT

*And a few days went by and Yeshua passed from*
*there and entered in their synagogue.*
*And there was a man with a withered hand and they asked*
*him saying, Is it permissible to heal him on the Shabbat?*
*And he said to them, who among you who has a sheep that*
*falls into a pit in a Shabbat and does not raise it up?*
*So much the more is man better than that. Therefore it is*
*permissible and necessary for man to act better on the Shabbat.*
*Then he said to the man, stretch out your hand, and he*
*stretched out his hand and it became like the other.*
*And then the Pharisees took counsel and plotted to kill him.*
Matthew 12:9-14

Soon after, Matthew continues his approach on the controversies of the Shabbat, but now the story leaves a grain field and goes into a synagogue. It was during a Shabbat service that some leaders seized the opportunity to test Yeshoshua's authority by bringing to him a man with a dry hand and questioning him about whether it was lawful to heal on Shabbat. This clarifies a few things, first we see that the act of "healing" was something common within the synagogues and well accepted by the Jewish community. Second, they believed that such miracles were rabbi's deeds, for this reason many of the sick people sought for Rabbi Yehoshua seeking healing. Yehoshua clearly was not in his usual synagogue in which he was raised, for the impasse he had with the local Pharisees is clearly linked to the differences of interpretations of the Torah that used to be taught in different synagogues.

First let's see the opinion of two of the greatest rabbis of the time of Yehoshua, that was eternalized in the Talmud:

*Comforting those who are mourning and visiting the sick on Shabbat is forbidden by Beit Shammai, for such things are activities for weekdays and not for Shabbat. Beit Hillel allows to do all these activities on Shabbat, for they are mitzvot.*
Talmud of Babylon, Tractate Shabbat 12a

Here we have a typical disagreement between Rabbi Shammai and Rabbi Hillel. The first one says that all the kindness we can do for someone should be done during weekdays, because the Shabbat is not the right day for it, on the other hand, Rabbi Hillel defines the commandments at different levels of importance, putting what refers to one's neighbor and to one's life above the Sabbath's own observance, for Rabbi Hillel, like Yehoshua, believed that Shabbat would be the most propitious day for performing the mitzvot of the Torah.

We see here a complete conformity of Yehoshua with

Rabbi Hillel and clearly the same does not occur in that synagogue where he was, which leads me to believe that this place was of students attached to Rabbi Shammai or some other rabbi of a more radical vision. The most important thing to note here is that Yehoshua was not against the Torah and not even against the Talmud, he was only against the interpretation of some rabbis.

As in the previous case, Yehoshua acts in a typical rabbinical way, he answers the provocation with a question, but unlike what happened in the field of grain, this time the approach he makes is not biblical but rather talmudic:

> *Rabbi Eliezer and Rabbi Yehoshua\*\* disagreed in a dispute over some lamb that fell into a pit during a Shabbat ....*
> Talmud of Babylon, Tractate Shabbat 177b
> \*\* This Yehoshua is not the same Yehoshua from the book of Matthew

Yehoshua addresses a subject well known and approached by the Tractate Shabbat. In that part, two rabbis enter into a debate about what to do when a lamb falls into a pit during a Shabbat or a holiday, whether to remove the animal and kill it, or whether to remove it and leave it alive. Regardless of the conclusion reached by the rabbis at the end of that discussion, the fact is, after all the argumentation, they ended up removing the animal from the pit, which led to a lot of work. If human lives had a financial value as the lambs possess, Yehoshua certainly would not have said to them to act better on Shabbat, because all that lamb's discussion was more about financial value of the animal than about the well being of it.

Even the famous medieval commentator Maimonides, also known as Rambam, claims that it is a religious obligation to break the Shabbat to offer help to someone in need.

To put it very simply, he who teaches and advocates the abolition of the Shabbat is clearly a person who is not worthy of your trust concerning God's things.

# SECTION XXV
## RUACH ELOHIM

*Whoever is not with me is against me. Whoever*
*does not join me denies this work.*
*Therefore I tell you that all sins and blasphemies*
*will be forgiven the sons of man, but blasphemy to*
*the spirit of Elohim will not be forgiven.*
*Everyone who says a word against the Son of man shall*
*be forgiven. And all things spoken against the deeds*
*of Ruach Elohim (Holy Spirit) will not be forgiven,*
*neither in this world nor in the world to come.*
*Make the good tree according to good fruit and*
*the bad tree according to bad fruit, for indeed*
*by the fruit you shall know the tree.*
*Family of vipers, how can you speak good things while*
*being evil? When the mouth awakens, the heart speaks.*
*A good man, from the treasure of the heart brings forth good*
*and the evil man, from the treasure of an heart brings evil.*
*I tell you that of all things a man shall say, he shall*
*give an account at the day of judgment.*
*By the words of one's mouths he will be judged*
*and by one's deeds, he will be condemned.*

Matthew 12:30-37

I believe to be vital, for the sake of an understanding of Yehoshua's words on this occasion, a Jewish point of view rather than the usual Christian understanding of what *Ruach Elohim* is, also called *Ruach HaKadosh*, and in English, Holy Spirit. For this reason, it is necessary first to enter into the concept that was created by the church concerning the Holy Spirit and to undo some preconceived ideas, so that we can understand it without certain vices.

## CHRISTIAN HOLY SPIRIT x BIBLICAL RUACH HAKODESH

In Christianity, the Holy Spirit represents the third person of the trinity, along with the father and the jesus. The Holy Spirit was sent to sanctify and give life to the church. It also brings, through its manifestation, some things known as "manifestation of the Spirit", "baptism by the spirit", among others. The Holy Spirit, as being part of the trinity, is some sort of god, possessing the same characteristics of the god father and the god son, and there is no distinction between the three.

However, this Christian definition is logically, theologically and biblically problematic for a number of reasons. According to the Christian theology, as defined by Thomas Aquino in his book *Dio Triuno*, the Holy Spirit is the son, who is also the father, for the three are one and indeed they all are the Holy Spirit.

Such a definition, over the years, has taken different forms, but always with the same idolatry essence, an idolatrous mess that was created from a concept created by human minds. We cannot deny that if the three really were one, they would have to be one in every single way, essence, power, will and manifestation. If that was the case, when the Holy Spirit makes Miriam (Mary) pregnant with Yehoshua, he actually made her pregnant of himself. And when Yehoshua promises the coming of the Holy Spirit, saying that after he goes to the Father a comforter will come, what he was actually saying is that he would go to the Father, but when he arrives there the Father would have come as a form of the Holy Spirit and that in fact, it was he who came, even saying that he was going to leave. We could go on with this crazy line of thinking of Thomas Aquino for hours, because it's a huge mess.

That is why we should look at the Ruach Elohim in the way and in the place where it was conceptualized. The Ruach Elohim is a Jewish concept and not a Christian one, for it was a revelation given to the People of Israel and clearly not to the fathers of the church.

According to the sages of the Jewish Kabbalah, by using a very mystical language, they say that, before creating the world, Adonai had to "shrink" a little of His holiness to open a "space" and in this "space" He created all things, so that the world would not be destroyed by His holiness. However, in order to the world not be without His holiness, Adonai then creates some "particles" of His essence that come into our reality, this being the way He works, acts and speaks in this earthly realm.

These particles have no life *per se*, for they are not part of a Relative One, nor they are independent beings, but some sort of spirit detached from God Himself, used as a kind of "tool" so the human being can have contact with Him without being destroyed by His holiness. It would be like a glass of juice, the man is the one who drinks it, the juice would be the essence of God, meaning an intimate contact with Him and the straw he uses to drink from this juice is precisely the Holy Spirit, who is nothing more than a "connection bridge" created by God so that we can, from a world full of impurities, have a connection with Him.

Never, in any part of the Bible, did anyone pray to the Holy Spirit, no one in the bible had a dialogue with the Holy Spirit, and the Holy Spirit never received any veneration from anyone. Everything we see about the Spirit happens "through" the Spirit, God spoke through the Spirit, healed through the Spirit, manifested through the Spirit, that is, this "tool" is nothing more than the very connection between God and man and not an independent being.

> *The Ruach Elohim is the will of Adonai, His power and His providence...*
>
> Shadal, Genesis 1:2

The Ruach is the very act of God on earth, for it is connected to His will, His power and His providence. There is no act of God that is not based on at least one of three things. Every time the sages mention the Ruach (Holy Spirit) it is always due to something done by God.

*They were informed of all things through the Holy Spirit.*
Likutei Moharan 19:3:6

*One of the levels of divine revelation is precisely through the Ruach Hakodesh, Holy Spirit.*
Rabbeinu Bahya, Shemot 28:30:1

*Then "the Ruach of God", which is the Ruach Hakodesh, hovered (over the waters) and stretched itself over it, and He (God) brought life through it (Holy Spirit).*
Likutei Moharan 78:3:2

*The Ruach Hakodesh was the prophetic spirit operating...*
Bereshit Rabbah 85:9

It is clear here that the concept of Ruach Hakodesh is much older than the church, much older than the prophets and much older than the promise of the coming of a comforter. When the talmidim of Yehoshua heard this from the mouth of their master, they were not really surprised, for this concept was already very common in first-century Judaism. When they received the spirit as reported in the book of Acts, what happened was a closer and more intimate contact with the Creator in a way they never had before. The connection that God has with the earth through the Holy Spirit has become a more personal connection than it used to be, but this does not makes Ruach a god, or part of the trinity, Ruach HaKodesh is the term used to "God's manifestation and will" in our reality.

This is demonstrated by the very words of Yehoshua, who affirms that blasphemies against him and against the Father will be forgiven. In this case, if the Holy Spirit were part of the trinity and if there were any difference between the three, as in the case, to blaspheme one would automatically also blaspheme the other. When Yehoshua separated this, by saying that something done to one is not done to the other, there is a breakdown of the concept of unity, since it becomes relative and God is absolute.

The Ruach HaKodesh, in short terms, represents the manifestation and the will of God on this earth. If we look at the Spirit in this way, we will see that the blasphemy that has no forgiveness is not a blasphemy against to Who God Is, but rather to the way He works, manifests, decides, judges, promises, reveals, and all other forms that God acts in this reality.

This makes things much more complicated, as it is not an offense to God as a being that has no forgiveness, rather the unforgivable blasphemy is when one thinks that he has the authority to judge what is right or wrong concerning God's decisions and deeds, which are represented by the Holy Spirit. Let me give two more practical examples:

God created man to marry woman, this is God's decision on this earth, which was manifested and revealed to us through the Holy Spirit. When someone acts in a different way, it is as if this one says that what has been determined by God is not the right thing, so he feels he has the right to go against what was revealed and delivered through the Holy Spirit.

To go against what is determined by God is the real sin without forgiveness and has no return, for if we look closely, how many ex-homosexuals do we know? How many diseases are currently killing them? Just think for a little while. It is as if they say that God has decided wrongly, thus committing a blasphemy against the Holy Spirit, because they go against what God has decided when He said that a man should be with a woman.

Another thing is to believe that the Torah was abolished, the most important work of Adonai for this realm.

Simply abolished, because some father of the church decided so. It is like saying to God that what He decided for this earth through the Spirit, His Laws and Rules, are simply over, because it is not convenient or perhaps very difficult to follow. Something to think about.

Finally, I want to place here the true function of the coming of the Holy Spirit within each human being, as said by God Himself:

*And I will put within you my Ruach (Ruach Elohim) and it will cause you to walk in My statutes, and you will keep my judgments, and you will observe them.*

Ezekiel 36:27

Adonai Himself, through the Ruach HaKadesh speaking with the prophet Ezekiel, reveals the true function of the Holy Spirit to us. The promise that Yehoshua makes on the coming of the comforter was an internalization of the Spirit so that it would begin to operate within the heart of each one of us, so that according to the promise of Adonai we may live the Torah in a natural and in the manner stipulated by Him and by doing so, we would never commit blasphemy against the Holy Spirit.

## WORDS FROM THE MOUTH

"Judged by words, condemned by deeds," a strong statement that seems easy to interpret, but what would Yehoshua wanted to teach by claiming this, what would those words be and what would those deeds be?

In order to understand it well, we must fit this warning into the context in which it was used. Yehoshua was saying that the words against the Holy Spirit would not have forgiveness, we know that the Holy Spirit is a term that represents the manifestation, the decisions, the will and the method by which God acts and forms all things, that is, to blaspheme the Spirit is the same as telling God that He is wrong in what He decides to be right. To act against the Spirit is to make decisions that are contrary to what was determined by the Creator simply because there is no agreement with what He has stipulated, thus showing that the one who acts against His Word "knows" more what is better for himself than the One who created him.

> As Rav. Hamnuna said, The beginning of a man's
> judgment is through his words about the Torah.
> Talmud of Babylon, Tractate Kiddushin 40b

The Oral Torah further explains Yehoshua's words and confirms what has been seen so far, the Torah, besides representing the Laws of God, it is also the manual on how to please the Creator and how He works. When we use our words against the Torah, not just as a criticism of the book *per se*, but in a way that is contrary to the content presented by it, it is the same as criticizing what was determined by God, it is to criticize the Holy Spirit himself. The Torah is the true representation of God's will, violating it by acting contrary to what is determined there or criticizing it by words, is precisely the beginning of the judgment that man will suffer. Those who teach anything against the Torah, or ideologies that attempt to complete it, such as rabbinic laws for example, it is like if they were telling God that His work is not complete and needs the help of men. This is the greatest blasphemy against the Holy Spirit.

After all judgment comes condemnation, and in this case, it will come according to one's deeds, if in addition to a teaching that is contrary to what was stipulated by God, if the one who teaches it, also lives a life by acting against what God has determined, the condemnation will be certain. If we think coldly, what one teaches is reflected in his deeds, for he who teaches something, such as the abolition of the Law of God, certainly, doesn't live a life according to it, for someone who follows the Torah, would in no way teach or speak anything contrary to what is determined by it.

Yehoshua strongly criticizes some rabbinical laws, showing that they are blasphemies to the Holy Spirit, for they try to complete the Torah. By stating that, those who teach them will be judged and those who follow them will be condemned. We must not forget that these laws only exist in Judaism for it is no more than a religion, just like Christianity, which has innumerable non-biblical laws and theologies, and this reproof from Yehoshua is valid for both sides.

# SECTION XXVI
## YONAH

*At that time some of the Pharisees and some of the sages came
to Yeshua saying: we want to see a sign of heaven by you.
And he said to them: A wicked and blasphemous generation seeks
a sign, but a sign will not be given except the sign of Yonah.
For as he was in the fish (Dagah) for three days and for
three nights, so will be the son of man inside the earth
(buried) for three days and for three nights.
The people of Nineveh will rise to judge this generation
and condemn it because they made Tshuvah by the
words of Yonah and I am greater than Yonah.
Queen Sheba, in the foreign language Reizina of Ishtiriah,
will rise to judge this generation and condemn it, for
she came from the end of the earth to hear the wisdom
of Shlomo and here I am, greater than Shlomo.
When the unclean spirit goes out of the man, in dry
places he seeks rest, but he does not find it.
Then he says: I will return to my home from which I
left, and he goes and finds it empty, safe and ready.
Then he takes seven spirits more evil than him and they go with
him and there they dwell. And the new state of the man is worse
than his former. So shall it be with this wicked generation.*
Matthew 12:38-45

## THE SIGN OF YONAH
*Yonah prayed to Adonai, his God, from
the belly of the fish (Dagah)...*
Jonah 2:2

There is something very hidden in these words of Yehoshua. Interesting how he chooses some mystical terms to
pass his message on. The Hebrew word for fish is DAG (דג), a
masculine word, but in this case, he called fish DAGAH (דגה),

which is a female term and grammatically incorrect in Hebrew, as if he was calling it "fisha".

The term *dagah* appears a few times throughout the Tanakh and it is subject of many speculations and commentaries in rabbinical literature. As the Torah does not directly explain what this term would be and the reasons for its use, we should look to the Oral Torah to understand Yehoshua's reasons for exposing his teaching by using this strange term.

## LEVIATAN

Leviatan is a sea monster quoted in the Tanakh and his image is first portrayed in the book of Job, in chapters 40 and 41, through a brief description given by God. During the middle ages, Giordano Bruno in his book *Svmma Daemoniaca* describes Leviatan as a demon representing one of the five tips of the *baphomet*, such a theory was quickly absorbed by the Catholic church and passed on to all Christian strands.

Many of the sages claim that the *dagah* that swallowed Yonah was the Leviathan described in the book of Job. They teach that this monster was created by God on the fifth day of creation, as reported in the first chapter of Genesis, precisely for the purpose of swallowing him and taking him to Niniveh, being imprisoned by God soon after it.

On the other hand, some Kabbalists sages make a very interesting comment on a passage from the book of Numbers, where the *dagah* term also appears:

*We remember the fish (dagah) we ate for free in Egypt, the cucumbers, the melons, the leeks, the onions and the garlic.*
Numbers 11:5

*It has been said that: Dagah in this verse refers to the sexual immoralities that the Torah had not yet forbidden.*
Talmud of Babylon, Tractate Yoma 75a

In this passage, according to the sages, the term *dagah* is not referring to fish as a kind of food, nor as the monster

Leviatan, but rather as a term that characterizes the sin of sexual immorality, incest, orgy and all sorts of sodomy. This is interesting , because it shows one of the sins that made God decide to destroy Niniveh if they did not repent.

A second case is found in the book of the prophet Amos:

> Adonai my Lord swears by His Holiness: See, days
> will come upon you in which you will be carried in
> baskets, up to the last, in baskets of fish (dagah).
>
> Amos 4:2

> Carried in baskets of fish, baskets of idolatrous lands (dagah).
>
> Radak, Amos 4:2

Now we have a different case, the famous commentator Radak makes an analogy between the term dagah with idolatry, for the promise that God makes about the Babylonian Exile is that the people would be taken to a place where idolatry was practiced and where the God of Israel was not known.

Now the third case where we find this term in the Torah:

> And the fish (dagah) of the Nile died. The Nile smelled
> badly until the Egyptians could no longer drink from its
> water; there was blood all over the land of Egypt.
>
> Exodus 7:21

> The Gemara answers: The baraita is difficult according to
> the following verse: "And the fish (dagah) that was in the
> river died..." ...the Gemara answers that dagah refers to
> the large and the small taken by the blood of violence.
>
> Talmud of Babylon, Tractate Nedarim 51b

Now the Gemara makes an allusion between *dagah* and violence, because the Nile has turned red, looking like blood. If we join all the three, we will see that *dagah* can be sexual immorality, violence and idolatry, leading us to another teaching in the Oral Torah:

*Rabbi Yohanan says in the name of Rabbi Shimon ben Yehotzadak: If you say to anyone: transgress this commandment and you will not be killed, he must transgress to not be killed, unless it is idolatry, sexual immorality and bloodshed.*
Talmud of Babylon, Tractate Sanhedrin 74a

This is a teaching strongly emphasized by all the rabbis, by both the Pharisees and the modern Orthodox. It is almost a Jewish maxim so that the Jew knows how far he can go with his disobedience to the Torah for the preservation of his life.

This reveals to us the motives that led God to decide to destroy the city of Nineveh, violence, idolatry and sexual immorality, just as it was with Sodom and Gomorrah.

The challenge is to connect this study with the words of Yehoshua. He says that the sign that will be given to those who question him would be only the sign of Yonah, and he makes a comparison of Yonah inside the fish with him being inside the earth. By this comparison, we can have a direct and simple understanding in this case, just as Yonah remained three days in the belly of a fish and left alive, Yehoshua would also stay three days under the earth and leave alive. But if we stop at what meets the eyes, we will lose all the secrecy behind the terminology used by him.

The Talmudic teachings raised so far are well known to any religious scholar of the Torah. Yehoshua, by mentioning the term *dagah*, brings up these three points, immorality, violence, and idolatry. The easiest way to understand it, is by looking at the real motives behind all these debates between Yehoshua and some of the Pharisees, the Jewish laws.

## IDOLATRY

When someone has something in life that is greater than God and His Word, that person takes the serious risk of falling into idolatry, whether it is his job, status, fame, power, money, possessions, family, or anything else connected with this earthly life. If any of these things has a greater importance than the importance of the Torah, this individual becomes an idolater.

Idolatry is not only the worship of false gods, but is everything that takes the place that God should have in man's life, if God's commandments are no longer observed for reasons quoted above, these motives become more important than what God wants from this person and this can be characterized as idolatry.

If we think coldly, the rabbis and Pharisees, as well as the present orthodox and countless Christians, put human laws and the observance of rules created by men above what is stipulated by God. Many laws are created as "protecting fences" around the Torah's commandments, but some of them end up replacing what God has determined and from the moment one follows a law that is not explicit in the Torah and teaches it as if it were from God, the person ends up committing idolatry, for these laws take the place of the real ones, thus replacing the Torah.

The greatest discussions between Yehoshua and the Pharisees dealt fairly concerning the rabbinic laws, and it happens in all the Gospels. The discussions were always about the Oral Torah and the Jewish customs and never had nothing to do with the Torah itself. For this reason, Yehoshua uses the term *dagah*, as he accuses the Pharisees of being idolaters by place the rabbinical laws, which they follow, above the real observance of the Torah. Anything that takes God's place, or the place of His Word, is idolatry, even Rashi agrees with it:

> *It follows that whoever denies the Torah admits idolatry.*
>
> Rashi, Deuteronomy 11:28:1

## VIOLENCE

267

This may seem a little weird, for how could be the Pharisees murderous people? In order to answer that, a commentary from the Talmud might help us:

> *He who publicly speaks evil about his neighbor,*
> *acts as if shedding his blood.*
> Talmud of Babylon, Tractate Bava Metzia 58b

The Pharisees and Yehoshua were not only close, but they were from the same people, from the same land, from the same faith, and yet, a few verses earlier, these "brethren" of Yehoshua conspired against him and openly criticized his teachings.

With this, we have another clear reason for the use of the term *dagah*, for the evil-speaking of some of the Pharisees and the Sadducees made them as murderers, made them as people who shed blood due to their tongs.

## SEXUAL IMMORALITY

Did the Pharisees, religious, righteous and right in their ways, used to practice acts of sexual immorality, such as sodomy or incest? What proof did Yehoshua have of this?

> *Rabbi Shimom says: We can understand this in the*
> *very context in which it is found, as it says: "They*
> *(who practice incest and immorality) will have*
> *their souls cut off," for it is like **blasphemy**.*
> Mishnah Makkot 3:15

Rabbi Shimom makes a very interesting statement, he says that sexual immorality is like blasphemy. Whoever knows the Torah knows that there are different kinds of sins that, before God's eyes, have the same weight, as if one were the other and the other the one.

If we look at sexual immorality as a sin comparable to the sin of blasphemy, we can go back to the teaching of sin against the Holy Spirit, which is nothing more than the denial of God's decisions and to act contrary to what God has determined, this is what we can call blasphemy.

So I believe that, the charge that came from Yehoshua on the Pharisees is about the sin of blasphemy they committed against God by placing the laws of *halachah* more prominently than the Divine Laws and their authority above of the authority of the Almighty.

Here we have a heavy teaching from Yehoshua, which is not a teaching, but an indirect accusation using the most reprehensible sins of the Torah. But the human being does not change and such teaching may well be embedded in the present life, for who does not put anything related to this earthly life above God's things? Or who never spoke evil of anyone? Or what about those who end up committing sexual immorality, which has become very common and well accepted in our society? What would Yehoshua say to us if he were here today? Would it be *dagah*?

Yehoshua says that if the people of Nineveh, who practiced all these things, converted (made *tshuvah*) only by hearing a very bad preach from Yonah, the rabbis should also do *tshuvah* by listening to Yehoshua, for he declares that he is much greater than a prophet, therefore, the Ninevites will have the moral to judge them in the world to come.

## TSHUVAH

The term that appears in English as "repentance", in this case, as in many others throughout the book of Matthew, is just a Hebrew word called *tshuvah*. This term, in a literal translation, means "answer," but it is a widely used term in the rabbinical milieu to refer to repentance, quite common among both Pharisees and modern Orthodox Jews.

When someone states that he will "*do tshuvah*", he is saying that he will not only repent but he will also change his life according to the Torah's ordinances. The repentance that Yehoshua teaches throughout the book of Matthew is not the same that is taught by Christianity, which is no more than a feeling of remorse mixed up with repentance. However, the repentance that Yehoshua talks about is one that goes beyond a feeling, is an attitude, is something that becomes palpable, *Tshuvah* is to forsake everything that is wrong, to literally have a life according to the Torah. *Tshuvah* is not only to avoid doing what God forbids, but it is also to do what He commands to do. Without Torah, there is no *Tshuvah*!

When Yehoshua claims that the people of Nineveh did *Tshuvah*, he does not just say that they have given up immoral acts, but he claims that they laid their lives before God through the Torah. According to Yehoshua's mentality, without Torah, true repentance becomes something relative, for it is not something that can be seen through one's behavior.

## THE QUEEN OF SHEBA

The bible presents a never-before-mentioned queen, who, on a certain day, decides to leave her lands and to travel to Jerusalem to hear the wisdom of King Solomon. Accompanied by many servants and camels, she brings to the king a large quantity of spices, gold, and precious stones as reported in 1 Kings 10 and Chronicles 9.

Even if the biblical account of this strange queen ends there, others Jewish sources have stories about who she was and add more details about her visit to Jerusalem. In the 14th century, documents were found in Ethiopia about a queen who had gone to the holy city of Jerusalem, it is written that this queen "knew" the king of that place and conceived him a son, named Menelik.

Menelik, by the age of 22, decided to go to Israel to meet the king, his father. King Solomon was enchanted by his presence and did everything he could to make him to stay in Jerusalem, so he could take over the reign after his death, but the boy resisted and returned to his homeland. His father, then sends with him some guards, sages to guide him in the Torah and the ark of the covenant, so that he could have protection in the way back. That story created a theory about the presumed whereabouts of the ark now a days, it claims that it is in the city of Aksum, Ethiopia.

Stories aside, the distance between Aksum and Jerusalem is exactly 3,409 km, which takes 26 days traveling non stop, with stops for rest, it takes an average of 41 days, 82 days if we count the way back. According to Yehoshua, only for this reason, by going to learn from Solomon, this queen already has the merit of judging those Pharisees who were face to face with him and are reluctant to listen to his words.

## UNCLEAN SPIRIT

Finally, we see how interesting is the way that Yehoshua calls these "evil spirits". Not as demons, nor as evil spirits, but as unclean spirits. The term "impure" or "unclean" is something very singular throughout the Torah and it is at it's definition that we should look at.

### Impurity

One of the most misunderstood concepts of the Torah is contained in the words *Tum'ah* and *Tahara*, translated as Unclean and Clean. The two biggest mistakes I see, are the confusions made between impurity and sin and the idea that impurity is something related to this earthly world and not to the spiritual world.

The laws of purity and impurity of the Torah are within a category of commandments called *chukkim*, which are divine commandments without a reason given by God, they are not rationally understandable, unlike laws such as "Thou shalt not kill" or "Thou shalt not steal" and it is precisely for this reason that a high spiritual level is necessary to fully understand them.

The sages explain that *tum'ah*, spiritual impurity, can be defined as "absence of holiness". Unlike sin, which leads to death, spiritual impurity leads to a distancing from God, even if life continues, it will be an empty life without peace within.

According to Kabbalistic terminology, the forces of evil are called the "other side", for they are what is "outside" from God's will, they are far from the presence and holiness of God. These forces flourish in a reality where the presence of God is more "absent", "hidden", places where there is more room for "opposition" to the Creator.

Spiritual impurity happens when one sets God aside, moves away from His presence and ends up creating an emptiness, a vacuum, and the place where His presence should be, becomes empty. This can happen to anyone, with people who serve God, worship God and live a life away from sin, but for some reason, inside of them, they are empty. This is due to the fact that they do not use what serves to purify them, that is, the Torah. The Torah serves not only to teach what sin is, but it is also the manual of how to become holy, by closing the door to all spiritual impurity.

*And you must observe my statutes and do them,*
*I am Adonai who sanctifies you.*

Leviticus 20:8

Maybe now we can understand why Yehoshua talks specifically about "unclean spirits" right after he talks about *dagah*. This accusation was precisely because the Pharisees were placing the rabbinical laws above the Laws of the Torah and teaching them as if they were given by God Himself. By doing so, they cease to follow the Torah *per se*, which really sanctifies, to follow human laws, which do not sanctify, thus generating a certain kind of impurity inside of them, making the interior of each one of them a great emptiness of the sanctity of God and conducive to the proliferation of unclean spirits.

So, when one's has things in life that has a bigger meaning than God and His word, this person is not only an idolater, but also a nice place for the proliferation of unclean spirits.

◆ ◆ ◆

# SECTION XXVII
## NETILAT YADAYIM

*Then the sages and the Pharisees came to Yeshua saying to him,*
*Why don't your talmidim respect the TAKANOT of the*
*ancients concerning NETILAT YADAYIM before they eat?*
*And Yeshua said to them: Why do you not respect*
*the Torah of EL because of your TAKANOT?*

Matthew 15:1-3

*Then came to Jesus scribes and Pharisees,*
*which were of Jerusalem, saying,*
*Why do your disciples transgress the tradition of the elders?*
*for they wash not their hands when they eat bread.*
*But he answered and said to them, Why do you also*
*transgress the commandment of God by your tradition?*

Matthew 15:1-3 KJV

Some time ago, a Christian friend of mine told me that jesus had abolished the Torah and the proof of that was just the verse above. He stated that even the smallest details and most basic commandments were abolished, such as a simple washing of hands before eating for example, as the Torah of the Jews commanded.

The interesting thing is that this Christian friend of mine, was not able to show me where in the Torah this commandment concerning the washing of hands is found and even by trying as hard as he could, he wasn't able to find it, because such a command is not found in the Torah.

Today, in Orthodox Judaism, as in Pharisaic Judaism, the washing of hands, despite the appearance of a commandment, is nothing more than a ritual created by the ancient rabbis. And like all rabbinical rituals, the *Netilat Yadayim*, or the washing of the hands, is full of details that must be carefully observed.

The *Netilat Yadayim* was defined by concepts called

*tum'ah* (unclean) and *Taharah* (clean). The laws concerning these two terms are considered supra-rational laws, that is, they do not need explanations, for they are above reason because of their high spiritual level. The *tum'ah* is defined as the absence of *Kedushah*, which is the source from which all the life and God Himself emanate from.

The Torah is very detailed regarding impurities, it covers certain foods, the menstruation of the women, the contact with corpses and so on. Impurity is something that should be very much observed, since, of course, it is a big deal for God.

> *If the rolls (Torah) did not concern about things related to impurity and purity, as well as what is forbidden and permitted, why then is it written about therein?*
> Midrash Ruth Rabbah 2:14

> *Laws, the service of sacrifices, purity and impurity and illicit relationships are the essences of the Torah.*
> Mishnah Chagigah 1:8

The consensus of the importance of purity before the Creator is enormous. However, impurity is not treated as a sin or as a transgression by the Torah, but when the person, for some reason becomes impure, Adonai turns His face in the opposite direction to that person's prayers until the end of the day and I don't know what is worse. For all this reason, this hand washing ritual was born due to the high concern from the sages concerning the possibility of becoming impure.

The *Netilat Yadayim*, according to the rabbinic laws, is mainly mandatory in two moments, when one wakes up and before meals.

### By the Awakening

During sleep, the rabbis believe that the spirit rises from the body, leaving it "half-empty" and this vacuum caused by the absence of the divine, allows the impure elements to enter in the body. When the soul returns, these impure elements totally leave the body, except the tip of the fingers of one's hands. According to rabbinic laws, the only way to remove these traces of impurity is through the ritual of hands washing.

Usually, a more religious Jew has a small basin of water under his bed, so when he wakes up, before he even gets out of the bed, he already does washes his hands, for they believe that the morning blessing cannot be recited if there is some kind of impurity on the body, so may God listen to him.

### By the Meals

The ritual washing before meals is not in order to simply clean the hands, for hygiene is a common sense, but its purpose is to purify the hands so that they do not make the food impure. In other words, hands may not only contaminate the food, but also, according to he rabbis, hands may make it unclean.

Other cases where the *Netilat Yadayim* is mandatory: after cutting the hair, the nails, after physiological needs, blood work, sexual relations, putting on the shoes, touching covered parts of the body and returning from a funeral.

If the food is touched, after those above mentioned situations, the food will become unclean.

### THE RITUAL

Before the ritual, the hands should be already clean, any accessory, such as rings and watches, should be removed. A specific container for this should be held with the right hand as filled with exact 86ml of water. Once full, it is passed to the left hand and the water is poured over the right arm, washing the entire hand, wrist and part of the forearm. Then the container is filled again and the same process is done in the left hand, this is repeated three times on each arm.

There are many other details concerning water quality, the source of the water, the container to be used, the force in which the water is poured, varying amounts of water and so on.

Another very important thing is the blessing that must be recited during the ritual:

*"Blessed are You, Adonai our Elohim, King of the universe, who sanctified us with Your commandments and commanded us to wash our hands."*

Brachat Netilat Yadayim

We have to make a very careful analysis here, because there are truths mixed with half truths. As explained above, the purity and ritual of purity, as outlined by the Torah, is of utmost importance and should be taken very seriously by anyone who wants to follow the Laws of God. Yehoshua, by no chance, would oppose such rules, this is proven when he seeks Yohanan, the immerser, for what Christians know as baptism. He was actually doing what the Torah describes as *Mikveh*, which is a biblical ritual of purification.

There are two very serious things here in which Yehoshua was against, the first is relative to *Netilat Yadayim's* need before meals. From the moment a food is considered kasher, that is, if the food is determined by God as pure for consumption (Leviticus 11), nothing that any man can do will render that food impure. From the moment a word comes out of the mouth of the Creator, determining that the food is pure, no dirt or impurity attached to the body of a man can be stronger than the words from the Creator Himself, this is a heretical thought.

Yehoshua, by denying this tradition, makes it clear that something declared by God cannot be nullified or modified by concepts created by men, if food is kasher according to the Torah, no impurity can alter it. That is, why would Yehoshua be concerned with the ritualistic washing of hands, for the bread which he was eating was already purified according to the Torah itself?

The second problem is the very *brachah* (blessing) to be recited, where it states that this ordinance came from God, which is not true. Such ordinance came from rabbis, who usurped the authority of God for their own benefit.

Yehoshua at no time was against the Torah, he was against certain rabbinical laws which, even if indirectly, go against the Laws of God.

# SECTION XXVIII
## A SMALL DISHONOR

*For EL said, Honor your father and your mother, and he who
smites his mother and his father must be put to death.
And you say that any* **word that is said** *by a man to
his father and to his mother in regard to any* **charity**
*to be given, he might give for him as a sinner. But
this iniquity will be made void to him.
So he does not honor his father and his mother and
you despise EL's word by your TAKANOT.*

Matthew 15:4-6

Certain things have very strange appearances. In the
Western translations of these verses, the used words are
completely meaningless. However, in the original, a great
difficulty is also presented in the words of Yehoshua. If we
look at some of the terms used by him, it may be possible to
connect some loose ends.

First thing to take into account, something that few
people realize, is how Yehoshua maintains the death punishment as ordained by the Torah, many people believe that
the New Testament wiped out the death sentences given by
an ancient and outdated god, who gave his people a book
of cruel laws, a book that was completely abolished by the
compassion of christ. But by his own words, no compassion
should be given to those who smite father and mother.

*If a man have a stubborn and rebellious son, which will not
obey the voice of his father, or the voice of his mother, and
that, when they have chastened him, will not listen to them:
Then shall his father and his mother lay hold on him, and bring
him out to the elders of his city, and to the gate of his place;
And they shall say to the elders of his city, This our
son is stubborn and rebellious, he will not obey
our voice; he is a glutton, and a drunkard.*

> *And all the men of his city shall stone him with*
> *stones, that he die: so shall you put evil away from*
> *among you; and all Israel shall hear, and fear.*
>
> Deuteronomy 21:18-21 KJV

Yehoshua did not abolish a single comma from the Law, not even the heaviest sentences that were imposed on the disobedient ones.

Continuing the analysis, in order to better understand what he was talking about, we should look at two relevant terms he used, "*charity*" and "*words that is said*".

According to the *takanot* of the rabbis, that is, their customs and teachings, every student who comes under the supervision and tutelage of a rabbi, it was customary that all the goods that this student possessed become part of the school to which he was now a part. This was so common that even the messianic group, led by James, the brother of Yehoshua, had such a custom, for this reason they were called the *evyonim*, for every person who affiliated with this movement, donated all their goods to the group. Because of this, a number of Catholic groups emerged acting in the very same way, the person affiliated with these groups donated all their assets to the church.

So far so good, the problem begins when some schools demanded the goods that wasn't in the possession of the student yet, the goods that will be given to him as an inheritance, even without having yet received it and with their parents still alive. Many began to donate their parents' lands and assets to the rabbinic schools, as a future promise, and this generated a strong local commotion. The Talmud, in a very subtle way, talks about this custom:

> *And Beit Shammai agrees with his line of thought:*
> *One cannot ask a halakhic authority to dissolve*
> *a vow of consecration of property.*
>
> Talmud of Babylon, Tractate Nazir 9a

*The owner told him: I swear by the temple service that*
*it was so. I had no money available at that time, for I*
*vowed to consecrate all my property because of Hyrcanus,*
*my son, who did enter into the studies of the Torah and*
*did not want to leave any inheritance for him.*
Talmud of Babylon, Tractate Shabbat 127b

This story told in the *Tractate Shabbat* tells about a worker who worked on a person's land for three years and in the end, he did not receive his wage. After a while, the owner gathers the money, pays that worker and then justifies himself by saying that he had sworn (*in original: word that is said*) his possessions (*in original: charity*) because of the son's behavior. Such a procedure can be done by the father when he does not want to leave inheritance to the children or can be done by the son, when he wants to compromise the inheritance as a guarantee payment to the school to which he enters.

In some cases, after the son's oath of consecration (charity) concerning his future inheritance, the "new owners" ended up taking over the land even before the parents died, before the property properly becomes an inheritance. This clearly irritated Yehoshua, as well as the teachings of the Beit Shammai's Pharisees, who taught that from the moment the vow is made, it could no longer be annulled. This false "charity" would harm the parents of this student and that would dishonor father and mother. A *takanot* that was against a direct and clear command from the Torah. This transgression, according to Yehoshua, will not fall on the shoulders of the student, for it will be void for him, but on those who teach laws that go against the Laws of God.

# SECTION XXIX
## THE CANAANITE

*And after he said this, Yeshua went from*
*Galili to Tzot (Tyro) and Sodom.*
*And a certain Canaanite woman came to him from the lands*
*of the east, crying out to him, My lord, son of David, have*
*mercy on me, for my daughter is possessed by demons.*
*And Yeshua did not answer. And his talmidim approached*
*him and said to him: Our Lord, why do you abandon*
*this woman who cries after us?*
*And Yeshua said to them, I was not sent except*
*to the lost sheep of the house of Israel.*
*And the woman fell down and said, My Lord, help me.*
*And Yeshua said to her, It is not good for a man to take*
*the bread from his children and give it to the dogs.*
*And the woman said, for many times the dogs eat*
*the pieces that fall from their master's table.*
*And Yeshua replied to her: woman of great faith,*
*your faith done to you what you wanted. And at*
*that moment her daughter was healed.*
Matthew 15:21-28

At that time, Yehoshua traveled with his talmidim out of the land of Israel and they went to the cities of *Tzot* and *Sodom*, two cities in the region of modern day Lebanon. It is interesting to look at some stories about Yehoshua's various journeys out of Israel and how he behaved there.

In the story above, it is very difficult not to interpret that an extremely racist attitude from his part did not take place, for he did not even want to speak to this woman and was reluctant to answer her just because she was a Gentile. This is to some extent understandable, for the promise of the coming of Mashiach was given first to the People of Israel and only later it should reach the Gentile people. But this woman, calling Yehoshua as "son of David", shows that she possessed some knowledge of the Scriptures, and she knew that the promised Mashiach would also come to the non-Jewish people. Due to her spoken words, she should've known about the promise made to Abraham that said that through his seed, all the nations of the earth would be blessed and it was probably with those words in mind that she had the courage, and faith, to approach him.

This shows two things. She did not only believe that Yehoshua was Mashiach, or someone able to work miracles, but more than that, it shows that she believed in the Torah, for if it were not for her faith in the Word of God, she wouldn't be able to know what to be Mashiach means. If she didn't know the Torah, and believe it, to be or not to be Mashiach, would be irrelevant to her and therefore, she would have no reason to approach Yehoshua, for she wouldn't know what he was. So, that is the faith that saved her daughter, the faith which Yehoshua praised her for. This passage clearly shows a bigger faith in the Tanakh, in God's Word, than in the person of Yehoshua itself, for if it wasn't for her belief in Torah, she wouldn't be able to recognize him, by no chance.

Something totally comprehensible from a Jewish point of view, as Ramban says:

> The greatest signs and wonders comes by the
> faith in the Creator and in all the Torah.
> Ramban, Exodus 13:16:1

According to the Jewish perception of faith, the faith that this woman had and which Yehoshua referred to, is precisely a faith in God and in the Torah, for it was through it that this Canaanite was able to acquire knowledge to recognize him, and that happened by believing in what is written. Of course, the faith in Mashiach is important, but this faith has no basis unless there is faith in what speaks about him and teaches about him, that is, the Scriptures. I particularly believe that it was this faith in the Tanakh and in the One God that saved her daughter, rather than a simple faith in Yehoshua by itself, as many believe and teach.

However, what has not been yet clear is the reason that lead Yehoshua to be so harsh on her, giving a racist and a cold idea when it comes to Gentiles. If we understand that Yehoshua was a rabbi, educated according to the Torah and according to the Jewish traditions, it will be much easier to see why he acted in this way.

Within the rabbinate there is a very strong custom about the treatment that should be given to Gentiles, who somehow, try to approach Judaism, both for conversion or for simple things, such as study or explanations of something related to the Torah. This is taught by the Oral Torah:

*Proselytes are as hard on Israel as a wound.*
Talmud of Babylon, Tractate Yevamot 47b

*The judges must tell him: What motivated you to come to the People of Israel?... ...Do you not know how much the Jewish People are persecuted?... ...Do you accept the yoke of the Torah?*
Talmud of Babylon, Tractate Yevamot 47b

This chapter from the Tractate Yevamot deals with the inclusion of Gentiles within the Jewish people and their conversions, Judaism is not against proselytism, but strongly discourages it, for there are many rules to be observed. So the Talmud stipulates three questions that must be made in order to make the Gentile change his mind, for if the person converts and sets aside the Torah, by forsaking it, according to the Talmud, this proselyte becomes like a "wound to Israel".

It is usual for many rabbis to reject any Gentile who tries to approach them for three times. Usually, in the first one, the rabbi does not even pay any attention to the Gentile, rejecting him completely. In the second attempt, the rabbi tends to question his reasons and then criticizes them. In the third, he will refute the motives presented by the Gentile. If this gentile gives the rabbi satisfactory answers, then this rabbi must accept what he asks for, as this proves that there is a real intention in what the Gentile is seeking for.

This custom does not encompass only conversion, but everything that involves a Gentile and a Jew, from conversion as to the possibility of attending a synagogue, of learning Torah and everything that concerns them.

In this context, Yehoshua's encounter with this Gentile woman reflects a natural response from a rabbi to a potential new Gentile follower. Like a good rabbi, Yehoshua rejects the woman three times. The first one by not even looking at her, the second by saying that he came only to the people of Israel and the third by saying that the bread should not be given to the dogs. When he realized that this woman remained faithful to her belief, he accepted her request.

Yehoshua's attitude was not a racist attitude, but it was according to what was established by rabbinic customs. When the woman first approached him, he certainly did not intend not to help her. Therefore, he tested not only her faith, but as well as her true intentions and understanding of the Scriptures.

Here we have a clear example of how Yehoshua was a rabbi, his mercy fell upon a person who had faith in the God of Israel and had knowledge of the Holy Torah. For this two reasons, this woman had her daughter freed from the demonic possession in which she was.

This example is very useful, for it shows us how we can attain the mercy and kindness from God, the true grace.

# SECTION XXX
## TO BIND AND TO LOOSE

*And I tell you that you are a stone (אבן) and I will*
*build (אבנה) upon you my BEIT TEFILAH. And the*
*gates of Gehinam will not prevail over IT.*
*For I give you the keys of the Kingdom of Heaven. And*
*whatever you bind on earth will be connected in heaven and*
*whatever you loose on earth, will be disconnected in heaven.*
Matthew 16:18-19

**STONE**

When we read the versions translated from the Greek, we will see an almost poetic pun with the words "Peter" and "stone", but as shown in the original, it was not quite what was said. It is commonly agreed that these words of Yehoshua "gave" the church of Rome the authority to claim and to teach that it was at this specific moment that Yehoshua created the church, which is clearly not true.

When Yehoshua declares that Peter would be the "stone", he declares something that was instantly understood by his talmid, for such words are nothing more than a rabbinic terminology much used when one becomes responsible for something before God, such as a synagogue or a group of studies.

*When the Blessed One created the world, He passed through the*
*generations of Enoch and the Flood, but when He saw that Abra-*
*ham was coming, He said, "Look, I found the stone on which I can*
*establish the world." Therefore, He called Abraham "the stone".*
Yalkut, Numbers 23:9

The habit that the rabbis have, to call someone as "stone", is very old and it is always in reference to those who create a "line of thought" or led a Torah school. The language used by Yehoshua here, simply defined that, the new messianic community to be created, would be led by Peter. It was not a terminology to make a word pun with the name *Petrvs*, nor new words for the foundation of something new, in this case, the church.

One current example is precisely one of the greatest orthodox Jewish movements in the world today, called the *Chabad-Lubavitch*. This movement was founded on the "stone" called Rabbi Menachem Mendel Schneerson, also known as Rebbe of Lubavitch, because the members of Chabad follow his Torah's teachings and his vision concerning Judaism and secular life.

## BEIT TEFILAH

Another crucial point is, what Yehoshua really establishes, is not a church, but a *Beit Tefilah*, which obviously is something completely different.

A common *Beit Knesset* (Synagogue) is basically the junction of a *Beit Tefilah* (house of prayer) and a *Beit Midrash* (house of study). A *Beit Tefilah* has two functions; the first one is to define the line of thought of the synagogue, whether it is Orthodox, reformist, liberal and so on. Through that definition, its prayers are established. The line that the synagogue follows is what defines the form of prayer, for prayer is the way in which the people of this community will approach and will relate to God.

What Yehoshua establishes through Peter is exactly the ideology to which his synagogue would follow, in other words, a messianic synagogue, a community that would make prayers according to the teachings of Yehoshua rather than the prayers already defined by other rabbis of his day or earlier.

What intrigues me most is that Yehoshua does not cite anything about *Beit Midrash*, which clearly shows that the studies that are performed in a synagogue should be kept, that is, the teachings of the Written Torah and of what the Oral Torah teaches when it does not replace the Written Torah. The teaching os both would be the same as in any other synagogue. These studies should be kept as they were already done in his time, for it is through the Torah that God becomes known, it is in the Tanakh that the Mashiach is prophesied and it is in the Oral Torah that many explanations are found about the Written Torah.

Yehoshua did not found a church nor any other religion, rather a Jewish community that would follow a messianic vision through the teachings he brought up. Everything that used to be already taught according to the *Torahs* was maintained.

Unfortunately, this kind of teaching is rarely seen in temples that claim to follow the true Yehoshua and that is why we see so many churches being swallowed up by the *gehinam*. Becoming a follower of Yehoshua first requires an understanding of these things.

## TO BIND AND TO LOOSE

For years, this text has been a victim of many misinterpretations. As Peter was considered by the Catholic Church as the first pope, the church uses much of this text to prove the authority that the descendants in his position hold, for, according to the church, this authority was passed on to the popes and through this "authority", they did what everyone know very well in the last one thousand eight hundred years.

Looking at the verbs Yehoshua uses in that phrase, within the Jewish mentality, such terms were very common. In this case, what we have as a "to bind" is LIKSHOR (לקשור), which can also be translated as "to tie", "to link" or "to connect". In the case of "to loose", Yehoshua uses the verb LEHATIR (להתיר), which can also be understood as "to disconnect" or "to unplug".

These terms are widely used by the Oral Torah when it comes to legal decisions, both *likshor* and *lehatir* were used to determine what was permitted and what was forbidden in relation to the Laws of the Torah and that is what we should look into.

*The one who makes a vow of abstinence to milk is allowed (verb lehatir used) to eat rennet. But Rabbi Yose forbids. Abba Shaul says: "One who makes a vow of abstinence to cheese, then this is also forbidden (verb likshor used), both salty and unsalted.*
Mishnah Nedarim 6:5

Throughout history, one of the most essential functions of the rabbinate within a community is the scriptural interpretation of both the Written Torah and the Oral Torah. We can use as example the *kashrut*, the Torah determines what may and may not be eaten, there are also several other determinations related to it that are in the Oral Torah, but if there is a kind of food that is not clearly treated in neither case, it is up to the rabbis to decide whether its consumption is permitted or prohibited.

On their shoulders was the authority to bind, or to connect, by forbidding something and to loose, or to disconnect, by allowing something, for the "keys" was given to them by the community in which they were part of. That is, such terms and such authority is only about the interpretation of the Torah, the authority that was given to Peter was about how certain Torah's Laws should be followed, it was he who gave the final word on any doubt that might have existed within the Scriptures and this same authority could not be used for secular decisions, for in this case, the leadership was in Yaakov's hand, Yehoshua's brother.

This authority is not with the Pope, it is not with the priests, nor with the pastors, nor with the bishops, nor with the modern "apostles", and with no one connected to the church, for they have abolished the Torah. For this reason, the power of this kind of decision is inconsistent with the faith they profess. Whoever doesn't follow the Torah and claims this authority, is a cheater.

Yehoshua promised Peter this authority and did not say that it would be inherited by those who would substitute him some day.

# SECTION XXXI
## YOM KIPPUR

*At that time said Yeshua to Simon, named Pietros, if your
brother sins against you by disobeying the Torah, rebuke him
privately. If he hears you, you will have merit for your brother.
And if he does not listen to you, rebuke him before another,
and if by all oath he does not hear you, you add one or two
more before you, being three witnesses, for with two or
three witnesses, the word will be established (Torah)
And if by all this, he does not hear, take him to the congregation,
and if the congregation he does not hear, he will be banished as
one who does not respect the Torah, an enemy and a cruel one.
Amen (trully) I tell you that every promise you make on earth
will be connected in heaven and every promise that is loosen
on earth will be disconnected in heaven (KOL NIDREI)
And I also say to you that if two of you wish to
bring **LASIM SHALIM** into this land, whatever
you ask will be yours from the heavens.
And everywhere, if two or three are gathered
under my name, I will be among them.
Then Pietros approached, saying: my lord, if my brother
sins against me, I must forgive him up to seven times
And Yeshua said to him, I do not tell you until
seven, but until seventy-seven.*

Matthew 18:15-22

I've decided to make a comment on this part because,
according to my particular understanding, this teaching occurred in a time of Yom Kippur, for Yehoshua deals with typical topics of that day, such as forgiveness, rebukes, promises, and a hidden term in translations, *lasim shalim*. I will
raise one by one:

**REBUKES**

The way Yehoshua approaches Yom Kippur is exactly as it is done by any rabbi around the world, they deal with corrections, breaking of promises, offering and forgiveness, just as it appears in these verses from the book of Matthew.

The first issue is precisely the most delicate, because rebuking the neighbor is something that many love to do, but it is a very dangerous thing if we do not know how to correctly make an approach. Yehoshua is very clear about people's attitudes and shows that there is a limit to everything in this life, including God's forgiveness. One is to be rebuked up to three times, the first in particular, the second with two or three witnesses, and finally, before all the community. If that person chooses to keep himself in the error, he should be cast out, banished, and so, the doors to the Creator will be shut, something very serious.

There are several rabbinical laws regarding how this correction should be made and they were all formulated having as a base the following verse from the Torah:

*You shall not hate your brother in your heart; thou shalt not fail to rebuke thy neighbor, and for his sake thou shalt not suffer sin.*
Leviticus 19:17

*"Because of him you shall not suffer sin", for if you do not correct him, you may be punished because of him.*
Ibn Ezra, Leviticus 19:17

*Regarding the mitzvah of rebuke, the Gemara understands that because there is a repetition of the verb "hokhe'ah tokhiah" it is derived by the sages that one should rebuke the neighbor several times if necessary. One of the sages told Rava that "hokhe'ah" is the particular correction that must be made once, and "tokhiah" is the obligation to make a public correction with witnesses and then with the community, and after that, there will be no further obligation.*
Talmud of Babylon, Tractate Bava Metzia 31a

Look how fantastic, Yehoshua teaches two things that are common things among the rabbis. The first is the need for rebuke, lest we be punished for not correcting our neighbor as determined by the Torah, and the second is the very interpretation of that verse (which must be read in Hebrew), in which the term "rebuke" appears twice in a row, the first representing the private rebuke, and the second the public rebuke, with witnesses and before the community, giving a total of three rebukes, after which "*we shall not suffer sin for his sake anymore*" and Yehoshua teaches just that, the Torah according to a totally rabbinical interpretation.

## YOM KIPPUR

The Torah tells that, after the sin of the golden calf, Moses prayed and God bestows pardon to the people, that happened on the tenth day of the seventh biblical month called *Tishrei*. That is why this date has become the MOST IMPORTANT date of the entire Torah calendar.

*And this must be an eternal statute for you: In the seventh month, on the tenth day of that month, you must afflict your soul. And no work shall be done by the citizen and by the foreigner that dwells among you.*
Leviticus 16:30

*Only on the tenth day of the seventh month is the day of forgiveness (Yom Kippur) (only those who repent will be granted pardon). A holy calling should it be for you. And you must afflict your soul and present Adonai with a burnt offering.*
Leviticus 23:27

About the Yom Kippur, the great Rabbi Maimonides, also known as Rambam, writes: "*It is the day of repentance for all, for the individual and for society, it is the time of forgiveness for Israel. That is why everyone is obliged to repent and confess the wrong doings in Yom Kippur*".

The forgiveness received on the day of Yom Kippur is much deeper and higher than an ordinary forgiveness, for it is on that day that Adonai and His people become as one and that is an union that cannot be touched by sin. The rabbis teach that the person must first repent and then offer to God an offering.

At the time of the second Temple, this offering, that was presented before God during Yom Kippur, had a proper name, it was called *"peace offer"*. In the first century, due to many different reasons, it was very difficult for many of the Jews, from all over Israel and the diaspora, to go to the holy city to provide this sacrifice at the Temple, in addition to the long distances and very high expenses, for many times, the Temple itself could not attend to all, therefore, the sages had the understanding of another possibility of "peace offer" and called it *Lasim Shalim*, being the word *"Shalim"* derived from the word *"Shalom"* (peace), and that could be done when the person had no access to the Temple, which fits perfectly in the present day, for the Temple no longer exists.

*Beit Shammai says: they bring Lasim Shalim on Yom Kippur and do not lay their hands on it, but they do not need to bring burnt offerings. Beit Hillel says: they can bring both Lasim Shalim and the burnt offering and they can put their hands on them.*
Mishanah Chagigah 2

Both Beit Shammai and Beit Hillel agree with *Lasim Shalim*, of course, under their own specific terms, but both know how important it is for all people to observe such a sacred day, so the two rabbis agree about an unburnt sacrifice when the Temple is not accessible.

Yehoshua clearly had knowledge of this other kind of offering, and not only knew it, but also confirmed its observance and gave it a level of importance far above of what is found throughout all rabbinical literature, saying that he who in Yom Kippur presents Adonai with a *Lasim Shalim*, will receive from heaven <u>all</u> that he asks for, and this is definitely something else.

But what would a *Lasim Shalim* be? Just look at the Torah, it says that it must be an offering that afflicts us and the most common form of afflicting oneself is by fasting. Nowadays, all who follows the Torah and believes in the Creator, observes that day in full fasting and repentance, and that is exactly what Yehoshua stipulates as a condition for us to be heeded by the heavens.

## KOL NIDREI

Another point that we should take into consideration is Yehoshua's approach to promises, in a very strange way, between two themes that are not related to promises, correction and offerings, he brings the "promises" idea up. Yom Kippur is not just a day about forgiveness and repentance, this holy day has a third facet that few know, which is precisely about the promises we make throughout the year.

In all synagogues, on the night of Yom Kippur, at the beginning of the services, a statement called *Kol Nidrei* (from Aramaic - "All Promises") is recited by all present therein, by doing so they annul all the vows, promises and oaths that were taken and have not been fulfilled the past year.

The statement used nowadays was composed around 590 CE during the Spanish Inquisition, where King Richard of Spain forced all Jews to convert to Christianity and thus, they used the *Kol Nidrei* to break the promise they made at the moment they converted. Although the text that is read is more modern than Yehoshua, the concept which it represents precedes him.

Within Judaism, both promises and oaths are of the utmost importance and the Torah is very explicit on this point. It affirms that a promise made on earth should not be broken, therefore, before receiving the pardon of Yom Kippur, every man should disconnect in heavens all the unfulfilled promises made and all unfulfilled oaths taken.

Yehoshua rightly addresses this topic since they are talking about Yom Kippur, about forgiveness and about offering. It would not be a surprise to talk also about promises. According to what I understand from his words, a prayer for "disconnection" of unfulfilled promises, it's not only necessary, but also valid and functional, for he warns that everything we promise will be bound in the heavens; by unbinding them in Yom Kippur, it means that it will also be unbide in the heavens. This is of the utmost importance.

Here is the Kol Nidrei as follows:

*"All vows, promises, oaths, consecrations, compromises that we may vow, swear, consecrate, or prohibit upon ourselves - from this Yom Kippur until the next Yom Kippur, may it come upon us for good - regarding them all, we regret them henceforth. They are all declared without value, abandoned, cancelled, null and void, without power and without standing. Our vows shall not be valid vows; our prohibitions shall not be valid prohibitions; and our oaths shall not be valid oaths".*

Finally, the approach to forgiveness is clear, when Peter asks Yehoshua how often we should forgive, unlike the translations in English where he says seventy times seven, he replies that it is up to seventy-seven, which is still a lot.

We must always keep in mind that Yehoshua was a Jew, never ceased to be a Jew, he did not found religions, he was not a hippie, he was not a pacifist and above all, he never abolished the Torah, on the contrary, he followed it faithfully, observing and teaching everything contained therein, such as the Yom Kippur.

# SECTION XXXII
## ANOKHI

*And in everywhere, if two or three are gathered under my name, ANOKHI (אנוכי) will be among you (בתוככם).*

Matthew 18:20

One of the biggest problems I encounter when translating texts from the *Yvrit Tanakhi* (biblical Hebrew) is the lack that this language has of punctuation. Texts from the Tanakh, the Talmud, the Midrash, and other contemporaries, do not use commas, quotation marks, colon, etc. This causes some problems, because the translator needs a good perception when there is a change of subject or when a quote from a third party is made. It is quite true that some modern versions of the Torah have some punctuation that were placed there by the rabbis, but in other ancient sources, which rarely undergo revisions, this "facilitator" of understanding is not found.

And it is no different with the book of Matthew in its Hebrew version, the text suffers strongly for lack of punctuation, the only one that this manuscript possesses is the final dot, which was added by the person who made its copy. This causes enormous problems for anyone who translates it, because a single comma, or lack thereof, can completely change the interpretation of what is written.

This passage that we have above suffers precisely from this problem, the translator who translated this book into Greek and then into Latin, seems to have had some difficulties on this when translating the words of Yehoshua. If we look at the Western versions, we will have the impression that this is a statement, implying that if two, or more, are gathered together in the name of Yehoshua, he will be among them, but in truth, what we have here is not a statement, but actually a quote from what has already been said before. That is, the "colon" and the "quotation marks" were missing, so verse 20 is simply a continuation of "I tell you" of verse 19.

What I'm trying to say is this:

*And I tell you: "And in everywhere, if two or three are gathered under my name, ANOKHI (I) will be among you."*

Yehoshua does not say that he will be among any-one, but he makes a citation of something that was said by "*anokhi*", he claims that this "*anokhi*" will be among those who are united under the name of the one who claims to be "*anokhi*".

## ANOKHI

The word "I" in Hebrew is ANI (אני), both in the ancient and in the modern Hebrew, as seen in both the Tanakh and the Talmud. This term is always the same and has always been used in the same way, referring to the first person singular.

But in the Torah, when God says "I", He doesn't only uses the word ANI (אני), but he also uses the word ANOKHI (אנכי), especially when He speaks that He is God or when He speaks about some of His attributes. This is a term much used by Adonai when He speaks something in the first person singular. There are some cases where other people in the Torah also use *anokhi* when saying something, such as Avra-ham and Moses for example, but this term is known as some-thing almost exclusive to the Creator, because it is the first word that appears in the ten commandments.

*Anokhi (I) am your shield...*

Genesis 15:1

*Anokhi (I) am Adonai, your God, who brought you out of the land of Egypt.*

Exodus 20:2

*Anokhi (I) am Adonai, your God...*
Deuteronomy 5:6

*These commandments Anokhi (I) I command*
*today in your heart.*
Deuteronomy 6:6

*See, on that day, Anokhi (I) set before you the blessing*
*and the curse.*
Deuteronomy 11:26

*Anokhi* is a curious term, there are some comments about it in the rabbinical literature.

*Rabbi Yohanan said that the word anokhi is an abbreviation*
*of: I myself wrote and gave (ana nafshi ketivat iehavit). Others*
*say that it is an abbreviation of: a pleasurable statement*
*was written and given (amira ne'emanim ketiva iehiva).*
Talmud of Babylon, Tractate Shabbat 105a

This statement that the Talmud talks about are phrases formulated using every letter of the word *anokhi*, each letter of that word is being used as the first letter of the words that form the phrases quoted above. Using this type of thinking, we can also form another sentence, but this time using the letters inverted:

ANOKHI - *Iehiva KHetiva Ne'emamim Amareha* - "It was written, it was given, your statements are faithful."

These statements refer precisely to the commandments of the Torah. On the other hand, there is a Midrash which explains the origin and the reason for the use of the word *Anokhi* by the Torah. It says that this word is of Egyptian origin and because the Hebrew people have spent years in the land of Egypt, they accustomed to some kind of analogy between God and the word *Anokhi*, so God decided to use it, so the people would easily recognize what was going on. However, the Midrash does not explain whether the Egyptians used this word to refer in anyway to any deity they possessed.

*Rabbi Nehemiah said: What is "anokhi"? It's an Egyptian word. What is this comparable to? To a king, who had his son captured and kept for a long time with his captors.*
Midrash Tanchuma, Yitro 16:1

In any case, regardless of the origin of the word or what it means, the fact is, in the popular mindset, the use of this term automatically remotes to the Torah and words spoken directly by God. Throughout the book of Matthew, the word "I", in the ANI (אני) form appears 111 times and in only one situation, the "I" appears as ANOKHI (אנכי). This one time happens exactly in the verse we can see above. This shows that he, Yehoshua, did not speak of himself, for to do so, he would have used the word ANI (אני) in the same way he has been using it throughout the book.

When Yehoshua quotes *Anokhi*, he refers to Adonai's words, for the other word he says, " *among you* ", as it appears in Matthew, is B'TOKH'KHEM (בתוככם), this term is exactly the same as was used by God in the book of Leviticus, when He promises that He will forever be among the People of Israel:

*I will be forever present among you (B'TOKH'KHEM -*
בתוככם*), I will be your Elohim and you will be my people.*
Leviticus 26:11

If we place the punctuation and by using what we have seen so far about *Anokhi*, we can read this verse from another perspective:

*Yehoshua says that Adonai says: "Everywhere, if two or three are gathered under My name (י-ה-ו-ה), Anokhi (I, Adonai) will be among you".*

I have no intention of disqualifying any belief about the presence of Yehoshua, or jesus for some, among those who gather under his name. My intention with this study is to verify the terms he used to make such a statement.

On thing is for sure, when Yehoshua walked on this earth, in his prayers, he did not seek his own presence, for if that were the case, why would he pray? Or why would he seek God? If it was his presence that mattered, then he would be self-sufficient, without any need of Adonai. However, we see the contrary in his attitudes, for many times he withdraws and prays to God. Yehoshua teaches to pray to God seeking for His presence, at no time does he command anyone to pray for him, but rather to pray only to the Father who is in heaven. It was the presence of the Father that he sought and it was about the presence of the Father that he taught, so I believe that when he speaks about presence, it is the presence that he has always taught and sought.

That's my point.

# SECTION XXXIII
## SHALEM

*At that time Yeshua said to his talmidim: the Kingdom*
*of Heaven is like a king who sat to make a reckoning*
*with his servants and ministers.*
*And when they begin to make the reckon, comes*
*one that owes ten pieces of gold.*
*And he has nothing to give and his lord commands*
*him to be sold along with his children and with all*
*that he owns to pay (לשלם) that value.*
*And the servant falls before his master and asks him to be merci-*
*ful on him and give him time, for **he will pay** (ישלם) all the debts.*
*And then his master took pity on him and forgave*
*him all the debt.*
*And the servant went out, and found another*
*that owed him a hundred pieces of silver, and*
*grasped him, and attacked him, and said,*
*Trust me and be patient with me, **I will pay** (אשלם) everything.*
*And he was not willing to listen to him, so he took*
*him to jail until everything **was paid** (שלם).*
*And the servants of the king saw what was done, and*
*were very angry, and went and told their master.*
*Then the lord called him and said to him: cursed(ARUR) servant,*
*did not I forgive you of all the debt that you had with me?*
*So why did you not forgive the servant when*
*he pleaded you, as I forgave you?*
*And his master was angry with him and commanded*
*to afflict him until all his debts **were paid**(ישלם).*
*So will you do my Father in heaven if you do not forgive*
*each man his brother with a **complete** (שלם)heart.*

Matthew 18:23-35

These passages serve as further proof that the book of
Matthew was originally written in Hebrew, the word pun

that the author uses, as seen at the words of Yehoshua, is something very typical of the Hebrew language and we can see it through the repetition of words that possess the same root. This word-pun, with words from the root (ש-ל-ם), occurs six times throughout the text, five of them representing some conjugation of the verb "to pay" and the last one, at the conclusion of his teaching, representing the complete heart.

One of the methods of interpretating the Torah is precisely by the observance of repetitions of words or terms that have the same Hebrew root. Here we have a typical teaching that says more than meets the eyes. These passages show something that goes beyond a simple forgiveness, it teaches character, teaches that no sin committed against us is greater than those we commit every day against God, and just as He forgives our great failures, we must forgive our neighbors every little thing they do against us.

To go a little further, we must look at the terms that are repeated, so it will be possible to find a meaning beyond what we have as usual. The root (ש-ל-ם) can form several words with different meanings.

- TO PAY (לשלם)
- TO COMPLETE (להשלים)
- PEACE (שלום)

Another word from this root is the word SHALEM (שלם) and it is a word that appears in some passages throughout the Tanakh:

*And Malkitzedek, the king of Shalem, brought bread and wine ...*
Genesis 14:18a

Shalem is the ancient name of the city of Jerusalem. Malkitzedek was a person of great importance in his days, for he was a priest of the Living God, he knew the divine commandments and the laws of sacrifice many years before the Torah had been handed over to the People of Israel. Interestingly, he already knew the sanctity of his city, the city of Shalem, where he was king. The patriarchs, Avraham, Yaakov and Itzhak, at some point in their lives, also had some connection with this place.

> *And Yaakov came to Shalem, a city of Shekhem, which is in the land of Canaan, when he came from Padam-Aram, and pitched his tent in front of the city.*
>
> Genesis 33:18

Jerusalem, *Yerushalayim* in Hebrew, has a meaning that goes beyond "holy city", it represents the "complete heart", the " shalem heart ", as we can see:

> *The whole heart is called YeRuSHaLaiM (ירושלים) - for where there is **YRah** (ירא – FEAR), it has **SHaLeM** (שלם – COMPLETENESS).*
> *YR + SHLM (ירא + שלם) = **YRuSHaLeM** (ירושלים).*
>
> Likutey Moharan 22:10:19

If we understand the "shalem heart", the "complete heart", which Yehoshua refers to at the conclusion, as a "Yerushalaim heart", we will have the between the lines message of his words. The word *Shalem* can also be understood as Yerushalaim. Yerushalaim, in turn, means that "completeness" is only possible through "fear" of God. That is, Yehoshua claims that the forgiveness from God will only be given to the man who forgives his neighbor due the fear of God that he has in his heart, if forgiveness is given for some other reason, it will not be valid before the eyes of the Creator.

But what would that fear be? The sages teach:

> *Shalem (completeness) is in the hands of the heavens, except the Yrah (fear) of the heavens.*

This is a very profound claim, it teaches that everything is in God's control, our lives, our futures, what we will do or what we will not do, with the exception concerning the decision to fear or not to fear God by accepting Him or denying Him in our lives, everything else will be decided by Him according to that choice. This is the true free will that has been given to humankind, this is the only choice that has been given to us, a "yes" or a "no" to God.

A "shalem heart" is nothing more than a heart of one who chooses to serve and to follow God's ways. The one who forgives for fear of the heavens is the one who gives forgiveness for love, who forgets all offenses, who does not take revenge and is able to transform the old relationship into something totally new. True forgiveness is given only by those who have a heart devoted for God, for only such people can reach a spiritual level high enough to truly forgive others, for the technique of true forgiveness is not part of human characteristics, it is an attribute given by God to those who fear Him. Thus Yehoshua's message goes beyond forgiveness, he affirms the need to fear God, to follow His ways and Laws, and through this, we will receive from God the ability to truly forgive others.

A passage from the book of Psalms confirms this. Only the heart that fears the heavens can become capable of forgiving, for only this heart can be inhabited by the Most High God:

*In Shalem is his tabernacle and His dwelling place in Zion.*
                                                    Psalms 76:3

A "shalem heart" is where the tabernacle of God will rest, those who do not have a heart in this way, will *"be afflicted in this life until all the debts are paid"*. The message is: choosing to fear the heavens is the only way to have a life without afflictions, in peace, in SHALOM, because only then will man know how to forgive. It's not about forgiveness, rather about fear.

## ARUR (ארור)

There is a term in those passages that caught my attention, the word ARUR (cursed) used in reference to the servant. This is an unusual, and somewhat cumbersome, term to call someone as cursed. The word *arur* sometimes appears in the Tanakh, it is the first word that Adonai casts upon the snake in the story of the Garden of Eden. If we look at the root of the word ARUR, we will see a secret message about the fate of those who do not have a "shalom heart," who do not choose to fear the heavens.

The root of ARUR (ארור) are the letters א-ר-ר which may be related to the root ע-ר-ר, which means "desolate", "without the company of others", "without connection with the future", "without pleasure".

Yehoshua teaches that those who do not choose the ways of God, do not choose to fear Him and consequently, do not know how to truly forgive, will have a desolate life, without pleasure, without true friends, without future, that is, without a life in OLAM HABAH and at the end of everything, your name will be forgotten, just another number under the heavens. Gets born, grows up, dies and that's it. This is confirmed in verse 34, where Yehoshua says that such people will be afflicted and this is the affliction they will suffer.

It is extremely important to understand the terms used, since they indirectly explain the teaching. The teaching of forgiveness is obvious and clear to those who read the passages, but to understand that forgiveness is linked to fear of the heavens, to a righteous life according to the commandments of God and whoever does not get there will have a desolate life, is only possible when we go deeper in the knowledge of God and His Torah.

# SECTION XXXIV
## ONE FLESH

*And he answered them, have you not read that they*
*were made in old times male and female?*
*And he said, Therefore let man leave his father and his*
*mother, and join his wife, and they shall be one flesh.*
*Therefore, they are not two, for they are one flesh. And*
*what joins the Creator, man cannot separate.*
Matthew 19:4-6

*So God created man in his own image, in the image of God*
*created he him; male and female created he them.*
Genesis 1:27

This mention from the Torah that Yehoshua makes, occurs during a discussion between him and some Pharisees as to why Moses authorized man to give a divorce letter to his wife. Clearly, and as we have seen previously, Yehoshua is against divorce and his ideas in this regard walks alongside with the teachings of Beit Shammai, which is the only topic on which both of them agree.

Although it seems obvious Yehoshua's teaching about what God brings together, no man can separate, the passage from the book of Genesis that he quotes has a huge weight and meaning within the Jewish culture and mentality.

All creatures and beasts were created either male or female, these creatures, regardless of sex, are self-sufficient, they do not need the opposite part to be complete. Sexuality in the animal world occurs only for the purpose of reproduction and propagation of the species, and the male only seeks the female at the time of procreation.

According to the sages, the same does not happen with the human being. The first man was created as a hybrid being, he had in his nature both male and female. When God decides to create Eve, by taking from Adam one of his ribs,

He removes from Adam part of his essence, part of his existence and being. This makes the woman part of the man and not just an opposite sex, something very different in what we have in the animal kingdom.

This is proven in the book of Genesis, chapter 2:

ויאמר יהוה אלהים לא טוב היות האדם לבדו אעשה לו עזר כנגדו

*And the Adonai Elohim said, It is not good that the man should be alone; I will make you a helper-opponent to him.*

Genesis 2:18

I do not know if it seemed strange to you the way I translated this verse, but I kept a term that does not appear in our traditional bibles, something that we are not used to read. Thanks to our translators and millions of reviewers, we can have access to a bible that tries to be consistent, even at the cost of what it really wants to teach us.

But leaving the translators aside and focusing more on the strangeness of biblical language as in the verse above, the moment God decides to create the woman, according to the original text, He creates a helper who is also an opponent. Before we can draw any conclusions from this, Rashi will help us with one of his comments on this passage:

> "If a man is worthy, then his wife will be a AZAR
> (עזר) - helper, but if it is unworthy, then she
> will be a K'NEGDO (כנגדו) - opponent"

Rashi, Genesis 2:18

Rashi's comment is very cool, but it leaves me in doubt. If what Adam really needed was a helper, then why did God also create an opponent?
I believe this term well characterizes the role of a woman in the life of a man, for a wife is not like a Japanese *geisha* for example, someone who says amen to everything, who is always praising her husband and serving him as a trophy on his shelf. A genuine wife must know how to say "no" when ne-

cessary, thus becoming a *k'negdo* for the sake of her husband, otherwise they will be living a great illusion.

Just as "opponent", the word *k'negdo* can also mean "opposite", "other side", just as the left side is opposite of the right side and both complete the whole, the woman is the opposite of man, since she is his other side, the side that he is missing.

## THE MAN, THE WOMAN AND THE CREATOR

*Therefore a man shall leaves his father and his mother*
*to join his wife, and they shall become one flesh.*

Genesis 2:24

Yehoshua's assertion that no man can separate what God has joined together seems a little strange, for how many marriages, something that God has supposedly joined, do not end up in divorce?

In fact, I believe this statement was made according to the knowledge that Yehoshua possessed. He does not affirm that no marriage can end because it is something that God has joined together, he affirms that what God joins togheter, no man can separate, it is different. We will see:

In the Hebrew words MAN - ISH (איש) and WOMAN - ISHA (אשה), there is a small difference between them. In the word "man", we have the letter YUD ('), while in the word "woman", we have the letter HEI (ה), the remainder of both words are equal (אש). By joining the letters HEI (ה) and YUD ('), which differentiate both terms, we will have one of the God's names, HAI (הי).

If we take YUD (') from the word ISH (איש) and HEI (ה) from the word ISHA (אשה), symbolizing a removal of God from the life of a couple, both words will become the same word, ESH (אש), which means FIRE.

In other words, ISH (איש) – MAN and ISHA (אשה) – WOMAN, can only become one flesh when HAI (הי) - GOD is in their midst, otherwise the life of this couple will be just ESH

(שׁא) – FIRE, a real hell. And that is precisely what Yehoshua refers to, the marriage that no man can separate, is the marriage that has HAI in the middle of it, and not any random marriage.

## THE MYSTICAL SIDE OF MAN AND WOMAN

Yehoshua's words, when he says "*no man can separate*", referring to the union of a man and a woman, male and female, strongly reminded me of some deep and mystical teachings from the book *Zohar HaKadosh*, which also does part of the Talmud.

The Zohar is very delicate to approach and its understanding very difficult, so I will cite only a few points that make some reference to the subject we are seeing.

*"In the beginning created Adonai" is an ancient secret, called the Chochmah (wisdom) that in this case was called the "beginning". The term "created" alludes to a hidden secret, from which everything that exists has expanded. The meaning of this secret of Elohim is what holds everything below. The term heavens (which is in the plural) alludes to the union of male and female, and it is forbidden to separate them, but they must be combined, for they are the secret of the voice and emanation of YUD - HEI - VAV - HEI - ADONAI, which is ONE.*
Zohar HaKadosh 1:15b

This text is part of a book forbidden to be studied without the aid of a master. I do not want to talk about the whole text, but if we look at it, it makes the same mention of Yehoshua about the union made by God, the male and the female, and the prohibition to separate them.

When the Torah, in its beginning, teaches that God created the heavens and the earth, in a mystical way, these "heavens" do not represent the physical sky, the heaven of angels, the heaven of God's dwelling, and so on. For when God begins the creation reported in the Torah, He already possessed a "dwelling place", just like the angels. Therefore, these "heavens" that He created are not the heavens we are normally taught about.

Those heavens, in fact, is the concept of male and female, something that goes beyond the sex of each one, but a unique and very deep concept. Then, when God creates the heavens (male and female concept), He puts into this concept His Voice and the EMANATION of His deepest Name, the (י-ה-ו-ה), for if God represents true life, then it occurs through the male and the female , for it is through this concept (male and female) that all life on earth, in all kingdoms, propagates, is maintained and is generated. In other words, the life that this Name of God generates, which emanates from the "male and the female", is the power of God so that all beings can give birth and procreate, by begetting children. This represents the "heavens" created in Genesis 1:1 and one of God's power, the power of giving life, that has been placed in the "heavens", in the hands of the concept of male and female.

Then right after it, we are taught that it is forbidden to separate them, because the male and the female were created as one and always have been one, until at a certain moment in history, when God Himself decides to make a physical separation of this concept, creating the woman from the man. When the two joins together again, bringing back to their reality what was created by God and where His Real Name emanates from, God's creative work returns to its origins. On the other hand, when there is a separation, that concept where the Name emanates from, gets broken and the emanation of God ceases to exist in that reality.

Therefore, marriage must be definitive, and one who gets married thinking that if things don't work out well, there is the divorce to solve everything must keep all of this in mind. The separation brings disastrous consequences in many areas in the life of both. I believe that Yehoshua's teachings on union somehow revolved around this mentality.

❖ ❖ ❖

# SECTION XXXV
## THE POOR MAN

*And a young man came to him and bowed his*
*head, saying, Rabbi, what is good to do*
*to obtain eternal life?*
*And he answered him, Why do you ask what is good?*
*No man is good, for God only is good. And if you*
*want to enter eternal life, keep the MITZVOT.*
*And he said to him, What are they? And Yeshua*
*said, Thou shalt not kill, thou shalt not steal, shall*
*not bear false witness against thy neighbor.*
*Honor your father and your hand and love*
*your neighbor as yourself.*
*And the young man said to him: all of this I already*
*observe, but what do I lack?*
*And Yeshua said to him: If you want to be perfect, go and*
*sell everything that is yours and give it to the poor and you*
*will have treasure in the heavens and then follow me.*
*And when the youg man heard, he left. For he*
*did **NOT** possess many properties.*

Matthew 19:16-22

## GOOD

This is the famous story of "the rich man", who preferred to forsake eternal life for the sake of his supposed
wealth. The misuse of this passage strengthened the Christian belief concerning the necessity of poverty to obtain
eternal life, such deception led many people away from
what God wanted to give them and enriched the Roman
church throughout most of modern history. Neither the
bible nor God is against possessions and money, what they
are against is what money could represent for those who
have it, by being made as a god.

I think it is important to look at this passage with

different eyes, eyes more on first-century Judaism so that we can find a meaning that can be much deeper than the usual understanding from a simple reading of the text.

Let's pay attention to the young man's question, he asks what is GOOD to do to obtain the eternal life. This is a very common question in the Pharisaic milieu at the time of Yehoshua and still in some of the current Orthodox communities. This idea of asking "what is good to do" is a question that must be done within oneself, it is a personal kind of questioning developed by the rabbis based on the book of Micah, but from what we can observe in some passages of the Talmud and in Matthew's book, it was vastly popularized and ended up being used in a somewhat distorted way of what the rabbis intended it to be used.

> *He said to you, O mortal, what is good and what*
> *Adonai demands of you: do justice, kindness and*
> *walk in modesty before your Elohim.*
>
> Micah 6:8

The initial idea of this questioning was precisely a self-analysis of whether one's life is in accordance with what is good, namely, the commandments. But the popular misunderstanding of this teaching, led people to a search for commandments that would be "good enough" to ensure a direct passage into eternal life. Such people were called by the sages " the Pharisees calculators", for they were always calculating their own merits according to every commandment they performed, something like "throwing in God's face" the observance of what He tells us to observe.

We must pay close attention to Yehoshua's answer, the first point he addresses is "*Why do you ask what is good?*", Yehoshua certainly knew very well what that young man meant, and so he criticized him in a typical rabbinical way due to the way that he used the term "good". As if Yehoshua was saying: "Why do you use the word *good* like that?"

Yehoshua clearly opposed the young man's suggestion that eternal life would be obtained through certain "good commandments", that is, specific commandments that should be observed for the attainment of eternal life, as if there were a set of specific commandments for it. This mentality causes one to seek certain commandments in order to obtain eternal life, some others to obtain healing, some others to solve financial problems and so on, which, although very common, is not a biblical truth. Yehoshua, like many rabbis of his day, strongly opposed the idea that there are levels of commandments. As we have seen in other passages, light commandments are as important as heavy commandments, so we must be very careful with the little ones, lest we err in the heavy ones. There is no "good" commandment that guarantees eternal life for a man, for ALL commandments are good and are to be observed, not for an everlasting life, but for the simple fact that they are the will of the Creator.

In every religion, inevitably, there are people who follow the object of their faith by the simple fact of waiting for something in return, some reward from the divine. In both Judaism and Christianity such a mentality is no different, which is why not only Yehoshua, but several rabbis are totally against such behavior.

*Blessed is the man who greatly devotes himself*
*to His commandments.*

Psalm 112:1

*Blessed is the man who devotes himself to His commandments*
*and not to the rewards of His commandments.*
Talmud of Babylon, Tractate Avodah Zarah 19a

*Do not be like servants who serve their master to receive a reward, but be as servants who serve their master not for a reward.*
Pirkei Avot 1:3

In this Yehoshua's teaching, the greatest lesson we can draw, much more than anything that concerns money, is the importance of the mitzvot, all of the mitzvot! They should be observed by simply obedience and not as a bargaining method to acquire something from God. According to Yehoshua, even he who observes all *mitzvot* is not worthy of eternal life, observing them is only part of our obligation, eternal life is a free gift from God. Rabbi Hillel had the same point of view:

*If you have observed many mitzvot (if you have fulfilled much Torah), do not think that you have any merit (that you deserve any reward), for obeying it (Torah) is the reason for what you were created.*

Pirkei Avot 6:7

There is no commandment specifically "good" for achieving something, just as there is no good man, only EL, no one else. Fully obeying Him is the ONLY good thing we can do for ourselves, without expecting anything in return.

**RICH MAN, POOR MAN**

Undoubtedly this young man who approaches Yehoshua was a connoisseur and Torah observant, just by recognizing Yehoshua as a rabbi shows that he knew very well what he was asking, but the interesting thing is the apparent surprise that he had with the rabbi's response.

Yehoshua addresses a particular set of Torah commandments, those referring to the "man X man" commandments, which are the hardest to follow and with the worst consequences if they are broken. For the Torah, the relationship between brothers is the second main reason for its existence, the first one is for us to know who God is. To love our neighbor above all things is the representation of all the commandments concerning the relationship between men, without them, loving our neighbor is unattainable.

The young man, by being a person inserted in a Jewish environment, responds that he already observes all of them and then, Yehoshua approaches another totally different theme, he no longer speaks about *mitzvot*, but of accumulations of treasures in the Kingdom of Heaven and now is when the misunderstanding begins. As we have already discussed, the Kingdom of Heaven is not the post-life or the age of Mashiach, but rather, the era we live today, with unrestricted access to God, His word, His truth, an era in which the the whole world knows at least what the bible is. What Yehoshua is saying is, in order to be perfect, we should heed the commandments of God and not cling to material goods, by following Mashiach we will truly gather treasures, treasures well explained in Leviticus 26, treasures that we will possess and enjoy them here, in this life, so that we may rejoice and understand God's true purpose when He created us.

Finally, although the translations into the Western languages treat this young man as a rich person, in the original, this man did not possess many properties. The fact is, it is not because one is rich that he will have difficulties to enter the heavens, but anyone who has some attachment to material goods. It doesn't matter if one is rich or poor.

The approach that I present here is very different from the traditional one, Yehoshua is not against wealth and does not make an apology to poverty, but rather, he criticizes men who have attachments to material goods, doesn't matter if they are rich or poor. Eternal life is guaranteed to those who seek to obey the Torah out of love and not out of rewards, with as much care for the light commandments as for the heavy commandments. We are to serve God out of love so that we can please Him, those who seek the "good" commandment, seek only what is good for themselves.

*Tzedakah*, although it is of the utmost importance both in the Torah and in the life of the Jew, is not the main point of the teaching of Yehoshua in this case, he addresses a teaching that spread erroneously in his day and became popular in the mentality of the Jews of the first century, which is the pursuit of salvation through certain commandments.

The young man also illustrates the interior of every human being who somehow ends up getting too attached to material possessions, often neglecting the importance of obeying the Creator, this is why Yehoshua repeatedly warns about love for money and not about the possession of money. And finally, he talks about the great treasures that we will have in life, which are part of the promise of God to those who obey His Torah.

Let's take another look at the Torah and the Talmud for some examples of what was part of Yehoshua's education, knowledge, and teaching:

*And thou shalt have no other gods before me.*
Exodus 20:3

*Where the term "other gods" appears, is an incorrect translation and must be translated as "other idols", which is everything that has more importance than Adonai.*
Chizkuni, Deuteronomy 11:16

*You shall observe my Laws and my Statutes, those who seek them shall live by them; I am Adonai.*
Leviticus 18:5

*This verse explains that the Laws and Statutes bring life to those who practice them. Life in this world and in the world to come. Those who cling to the deepest things of the Torah of Adonai will enjoy eternal life and will never die.*
Ibn Ezra, Leviticus 18:5

The rabbinic commentaries make much clearer what Yehoshua has been teaching about the Torah. First of all, everything that has a more important role than Adonai in our lives, becomes a god, as in this case, the money.

The second one confirms obedience to the Torah to obtain eternal life and not to certain specific commandments or to some kind of behavioral rules that are defined by men. Simple as that.

# SECTION XXXVI
## ASHIR

*And Yeshua said to his talmidim: Amen (truly) I tell you that*
*it is hard for a rich man to enter the Kingdom of Heaven.*
*And I tell you that it is easier for a camel to enter the eye of a*
*needle than for a rich man to enter the Kingdom of Heaven.*
*And his talmidim heard and were greatly amazed,*
*and said to Yeshua, If so, who can save them?*
*He turned to them saying, all things are difficult*
*to men, but to Elohim all things are easy.*
Matthew 19:23-26

As soon as the young man leaves, Yehoshua turns to his talmidim and says that the access to the Kingdom of Heaven, for a rich man, is very difficult. Certainly, the traditional interpretation about wealth has much validity, but in order to give a continuity to the line of thought used so far, a search for more detailed meanings about this statement is important.

To do so, we must look at the Hebrew term that Yehoshua used to refer to a rich person, the word is ASHIR (עשיר), which in a direct translation, actually means "rich", but that word is used by the rabbis in the Talmud to refer to someone stingy, attached to things that money can bring. I believe that Yehoshua, for also being a rabbi, uses this terminology not referring to a financially well person, rather to those emotionally attached to material goods.

Look how interesting, Yehoshua does not claim that these people will burn in the *Gehinam*, as many teach, but rather, he says that they will not be part of the Kingdom of Heaven. This implies that people who serve money, greedy people, idolaters to work, people who need power and possessions, shall never be part of the true People of Israel, they will never be able to reconcile their lives with the eternal

Torah, they will never be able to see and experience the Creator and so, they will not be part of the Kingdom of Mashiach and that is a little deeper than simply burning in the *Gehinam*.

Unfortunately, no man can help or save anyone who is like that, only God, but God does not save everyone, He is very selective, saves only those that He wants to save, we must keep this in mind, so that it may motivate us to walk in His ways.

## EYE OF THE NEEDLE

Many things that Yehoshua says seem disconnected or sounds like new concepts that he formulates. The Catholic Church has always taught the importance of a simple life, always praised poverty, taught how poor jesus was and how important poverty is to those who seek salvation. This interpretation kinda makes sense due to the words of Yehoshua, when he makes a comparison of a rich man entering the Kingdom of Heaven with a camel passing through the eye of the needle, something impossible.

But interesting, is it really that a rich person cannot truly serve God and have a heart that loves Him? This is very strange, just as no leaf falls from the tree without the will of the Creator, no one gets rich except by His will. Here comes the question, is God condemning these people by allowing them to have money? I find it very difficult that this is the case.

Yehoshua's words apparently leave no doubt, but is this what he is saying about people who posses money and material goods? So we know the true, let's take a look at a very similar passage in the Oral Torah:

*Rava said: Know that if that is the case, one is never shown a golden palm or an elephant passing through the eye of a needle in a dream, for dreams deal with the mind of the individual.*
Talmud of Babylon, Tractate Brakhot 55b

The rabbinical custom of comparing animals passing through "the eye of a needle" was not new to any of Yehoshua's listeners, for this was already a custom.

That part of the Talmud, which speaks about an elephant passing through the eye of the needle, is addressing themes concerning the human mind and how it is affected by external factors. The mind is a very interesting thing, both in the Torah and in the rabbinical mentality, it is what many call the "heart" in the Western world. When God speaks through the heart, it is actually in the mind that He is speaking, the faith that is in the heart is something defined by the mind. The mind is actually what we call the heart, everything happens through it, and it is precisely in this concept that we should cling to understand what Yehoshua and the rabbis of his day taught when they referred to the term quoted above.

When Yehoshua speaks of the "eye of the needle", it automatically refers to the human mind in a way, that is rapidly associated with the actions of the mind that deal with the "heart". The claim that the rich will have difficulty entering the kingdoms of heaven does not refer to the rich man who owns a lot of money and many possessions, but refers to that rich man who has wealth inside his MIND, inside his HEART. People who live for money, personal gain, work, success, fame, have expensive car, own mansions, financial achievement and all things of the sort, will have real difficulty to enter, because a heart turned to these life plans, will hardly have time and willingness to serve God.

When his talmidim ask, *"who can save them?"* Yehoshua answers nothing in this regard, he only says that all things to men are difficult, but easy to God and that's it, giving an impression that salvation may never reach them.

# SECTION XXXVII
## THE FIG TREE

*And he saw a fig tree by the side of the road, and came to it, and found none on it except leaves, and said to it, may fruit never come forth from you. And the fig tree immediately dried up. And his talmidim saw it, and were amazed, and said, How did the fig tree dried up immediately? And Yeshua answered them, saying, If there were faith in you, without doubt, not only the fig tree would do it, but also if you tell this mountain to go and to go to the sea, it would go. And whatever you ask in **Tefilah** with **Emunah**, you will receive it.*

Matthew 21:19-22

The story of the fig tree reported above is well known to Christians. This happened on a day when Yehoshua was hungry and approached a tree in search of figs, when he did not find them, he curses the fig tree, immediately drying it up.

It is believed that this incident brings up a lesson about faith. His talmidim, upon seeing such an event, are astonished and ask Yehoshua how this was possible and he teaches them that, doing such things is possible to anyone from the moment one asks for those things through *Tefilah* with *Emunah*. These two terms I have deliberately left them in Hebrew, because their translations do not reveal the deep meaning that each one has and I believe, to be important to pay special an attention on both.

### Tefilah

The translation for *tefilah* is "prayer", but this definition is horribly inaccurate. A prayer deals with two distinct entities establishing a communication, one of them inferior, making a request to a superior. The word for that in Hebrew would be *bakashah*, from the verb LEVAKESH (לבקש) – *to ask for*. On the other hand, there is also the term SHEVACH (שבח), which means "worship". The *tefilah* is precisely the junction of these two concepts, a connection of an inferior being with a higher being through worship. A better word to define *tefilah* would be "communion."

Tefilah is nothing more than the awakening of a hidden love within the heart of the one who loves the Creator through a "conversation" with him, until the state of union is reached. *Tefillah* is what makes the commandments in one's life something lively and pleasurable. This differs greatly from the traditional prayer.

### Emunah

*Emunah*, translated as "faith", is something that goes far beyond that. The basic concept of faith is more or less like something one believes even without seeing it. But to understand *Emunah* as being something as something that is simply believed, is to devalue its real meaning, for as King Solomon said, "*fools also believe*".

The *Emunah* is a perception of the truth that transcends reason. This is something that only comes through three things, wisdom, understanding and knowledge, for this reason it is said that faith comes by hearing the Word of God, for without these three things that comes through the Torah, the faith is nothing more than a fool's belief. When a person has the true *Emunah*, he feels that what he believes is an intrinsic part of his own existence, to the point where, if he denies that *Emunah*, he would be denying his reason for existing. It's much deeper than believing in something one does not see.

With these definitions in mind, it becomes easier to understand how difficult are Yehoshua's teachings.

**Only the one who has an intimate communion with the Creator by Tefilah, will be able to make it the true reason for his existence on this earth through the Emunah,**

and only then, one will receive EVERYTHING asked.

## THE FIG TREE

The fig tree in this story was not by chance, for it has a very strong representation that can be associated with *tefilah* and *emunah*. In order to understand it, it is necessary to enter again into what formed the basis of the teachings and faith of Yehoshua, the Oral Torah.

In order to make a deeper association, let's look at another case where "fig tree" appears in the book of Matthew:

*From the fig tree, you learn by the mishnah, when you see the branches and the leaves above them, know that The gates are close by.*

Matthew 24:32

In Western translations, where I left the original term *mishnah*, we find words like "parable" or "lesson". If we look carefully, this is intriguing, for the "parable of the fig tree" found the book of Matthew is not reported in this chapter, nor mentioned by Yehoshua. Out of this verse above, the other case is the story we saw earlier about the fig tree that has dried up and it is not a parable. What Yehoshua speaks, in fact, is not "parable", but rather he mentions the Oral Torah, where famous *mishnot* about fig trees are reported.

There are three things that we must notice, what is the fig tree, what is the fruit of the fig tree, and what means the branches and leaves, as mentioned by him.

### The Fig

*Rabbi Hiyya Bar Abba said that Rabbi Yohanan said: what is the meaning of what is written, "He who keepss the fig tree shall eat of its fruit" (Proverbs 27:18)? Why are the things of the Torah compared to the fig? Just as a person who looks for figs to eat, he finds figs in the fig tree, for the fig tree is not dry, and so it is with the Torah. Every time a*

*person meditates upon it, he will find new secrets in it.*
Talmud of Babylon, Tractate Eruvin 54a / 54b

According to the Oral Torah, the fruit of the fig tree represents the Torah and everything that comes out of it. Just as anyone who seeks fig, finds it in a fig tree, so will the person, who seeks secrets about God in the Torah, will always find them. The Talmud makes another analogy:

*Just as the fig is a fruit that is always found, so the fruit of the Torah will always be found by the person who seeks it in it.*
Ein Yaakov, Eiruvin 5:9

Ein Yaakov is a compilation of Talmudic materials alongside with its commentaries and it teaches that, just as one who is hunger and seeks the fruit of the fig tree, which can always be found , he who seeks God will always find Him when He seeks Him in the Torah .

**The Fig tree**
*Why is the fig tree compared to those who study the Torah? For unlike other trees, in which their fruits must be harvested all at once, the figs must be harvested little by little. Just as one who studies the Torah, today he studies a little and tomorrow a little bit more, because it is not learned in a year or two.*
Midrash Tanchumah, Pinchas 11:1

Personally, I think this teaching from *Midrash Tanchumah* fantastic. It compares a person who studies the Torah with the fig tree itself, for to become a tree that always bears fruit, one must always study the Torah to always bear fruit. Just as the fig tree bears fruit little by little, the one who studies the Torah will also bear fruit gradually, for it is something that transforms one's life and walk, which are things that come one step at a time.

The Talmud confirms this with a rather mystical but impressive passage:

*He who dreams with a fig tree receives a sign
that the Torah is within him.*
Talmud of Babylon, Tractate Brakhot 57a

If we bring everything that was said in Matthew chapter 21 together, we will have two answers, the first is why the fig tree dried up and the second is how we will have our prayers answered as Yehoshua said.

The fig tree, which Yehoshua had dried up, was a tree that bore no fruit. First, as we have seen above, we must understand that in order to be a fig tree we must study the Torah, the Word of God. So, a dried fig tree can be seen just as one who knows God and His Word, but, for some reason, he doesn't bare fruits anymore, that is, he doesn't bare Torah, this happens when one leaves aside the study of God's Word and if this happens, this tree is of no use to God. Only by claiming faith in Yehoshua and reading the bible, if life does not bear fruit of Torah, one will become dry.

On the other hand, when one knows God and His Word, thus becoming a fig tree and beginning to bear fruit of Torah, that one will have fellowship with God. His life and behavior will be a true worship to HaKadosh Baruch Hu, thus performing the real *tefilah*. Then when the ways of the Torah become an essential part of one's life, one will receive the true *emunah*, reaching the promise where everything one asks for will be given.

Who are able to understand it, let him understand it.

### Leaves and Branches

Finally, on another occasion, as reported in chapter 23, by dealing with the end of times and the desolation that will come upon the world before the coming of Mashiach Ben David, Yehoshua again uses as an example the fig tree. But he does not speak of its fruit, but rather of leaf and branches, and yet he quotes it as a *mishnah*.

I believe that Yehoshua refers to a teaching from the

Oral Torah which was compiled by Rabbi Eliezer in his commentary book on the *mishnot* of the Oral Torah. Rabbi Eliezer was a great scholar and disciple of the great Rabbi Yochanan Ben Zakai.

Rabbi Eliezer explains the association that the branches and leaves of a fig tree have with the end of times, just as Yehoshua mentioned:

> *Rabbi Eliezer said: when the fruit of the fig tree is gone and only a dry tree is left, and then, when they begin to produce fresh branches and leaves, this is the sign that there will be no more evil, no more plagues, no more misfortunes, as has been said: "I create new heavens".*
>
> Pirkei Rabbi Eliezer, 51:3

This statement of Rabbi Eliezer is very deep and fits well with the words of Yehoshua. It is through this rabbi that we can have a deepening of what was taught in the book of Matthew.

Rabbi Eliezer states that when there is NO more fruit in the fig tree and when it returns to produce new leaves and branches **without mentioning fruit**, it will be a sign that soon all evil will cease to exist. This idea of evil, plagues, and misfortunes ceasing to exist, refers precisely to the era of Mashiach Ben David, the end of time.

Interpreting the words of this rabbi through what we have seen so far, the age of Mashiach, the end of time, will be preceded by people who "know" and "follow" God (fig trees), but people that don't bear fruit (Torah), either by not believing in the Torah or by thinking it has been abolished. They will be beautiful trees, full of branches and new leaves, giving the impression that they are blessed trees, while the truth is that they are of no use.

Today, we see many churches and communities that are huge, have services that look more like a show, leaders full of beautiful words, that are nothing more than pitfalls to those who learn from it. Everything they teach bares the wrong fruits, a fig tree baring apples is an abomination, because they have left the Torah aside.

This is the sign to which Yehoshua referred to, are we witnessing these fig trees full of leaves covering the branches in our days?

# SECTION XXXVIII
## MURDERS AND HARLOTS

*In that same night Yeshua said to his talmidim: what is your*
*opinion? There was a man who had two sons, he approached one*
*and said to him: go my son, today you will work in my vineyard.*
*And he replied: I do not feel like it. But after*
*that, he repented and went.*
*And he said to the other son the same thing, and he*
*said, Behold, here I am my lord, and he did not go.*
*Which one did the will of the Father? And they said*
*unto him, the first one. And Yeshua said to them, Amen*
*(truly) I tell you that the murderers and the harlots*
*have preceded you in the Kingdom of Heaven.*
*Yohanan came to teach you the Tzadik's path (Torah) and they*
*did not believe him. The murderers and the harlots believed him,*
*you saw this and did not do Tshuvah. Also, after all, they still*
*do not believe him. Whoever has ears to hear, let him hear.*

Matthew 21:28-32

This little parable has a simple teaching, the son who says "no" and then changes his mind, represents those who know the word of God, but decide not to listen to it at first, thus having a life as they think best, until a certain time comes that, they recognize the error and repent.

However, the son who says "yes" and then does not go, are those who live a "holy" life for others to see, but in the inside they are evil and they will never do a true *Tshuvah*.

But once again, if we compare the original with the Western translations, we miss some understanding that comes with certain terms. The terms that appear as "murderers and harlots" have a hidden meaning within Judaism. Because the parable quotes a vineyard, and vineyard represents Israel, I would like to propose a different interpretation to this parable.

## GENTILES

This may be the most delicate part of the entire book of Matthew to expose. In chapter 32, where Yehoshua quotes "murderers and harlots", the most common interpretation out there is that Judaism forbade conversion of people who practiced such acts. Assassins and prostitutes were forbidden to convert or even to repent and to seek *Tshuvah* for their ways.

But I believe that this was not what Yehoshua meant, I read this verse and imagine it being taught in a very ironic way, up to the point of being some sort of criticism of the ridiculous and reprehensible mentality of some rabbis and sages of his day, which, unfortunately, lasts up to modern day in some Jewish communities.

Within the milieu used by some bad rabbis, the term "murderer" refers to the gentile man and the term "harlot" to the gentile woman. In some communities it was taught that all Gentile men are murderers and all Gentile women are harlots. Such garbage thinking appears in the Talmud in some verses that have been nullified by some Jewish communities around the world, which shows extreme good sense. I do not think it is necessary to put them here, for this is not the purpose.

In modern versions of the Talmud, these passages are no longer found, they have been excluded by Jewish communities many years ago, they are poor definitions made by forgotten rabbis who do not represent Jewish mentality and faith.

In my view, Yehoshua knew this and in an indirect way, he says that those people who they diminish with pejorative nicknames, the Gentiles in the case, will be those people who will do *Tshuvah* from the heart, because they will listen to the word of God .

I see many more Gentiles looking for to God, loving

Him and seeking Him than many Orthodox Jews, who wear a mask of holiness, but on the inside are treacherous. True murderes and true harlots are those who hide behind a fake holiness, or as Yehoshua defines, the hypocrites.

By the grace of the Creator, we can find true followers of God among the Gentiles, among the Jews and among the Orthodox. We cannot judge a group of people by the words or by the attitudes of just one or two individuals.

I believe it is now easier to interpret the example Yehoshua gave. The vineyard represents Israel, the first child who says "no", are like murderers and harlots who, at first act badly, but as they have a heart turned to God despite the sorrows, they end up going to work, they end up repenting and doing Tshuvah.

Now the second son, who says "yes", is like those who wear the mask of holiness, showing a fidelity to God, saying yes to everything, but when it comes time to do something, he jumps out.

You may ask, why did I associate the murderers and the harlots with the Gentiles since in the time of Yehoshua the Torah and the knowledge of the God of Israel had not yet reached the nations, how could they have said "no" and Then they said "yes"?

*The Holy One, Blessed Be He, before giving it to Israel, offered his Torah to all nations and peoples of all tongues, but all refused.*
Talmud of Babylon, Tractate Avodah Zarah 2a

According to the Talmud, God at some point in history, offered the Torah to the Gentiles and they denied it, being accepted only by the Jewish people. Then, according to my understanding, these Gentiles, the "murderers and harlots", who once said "no" to the Torah, are now returning to it's ways and going to work in the vineyard after many years. On the other hand, many of the children of Israel, who said "yes" at mount Sinai, did not really accept the Torah.

◆ ◆ ◆

# SECTION XXXIX
## GOD OF THE LIVING

*On that day, the Sadducees and those who did not believe in
the resurrection of the dead, met him and asked him,
saying, Rabbi, Moses told us that when two brothers dwell
together and one of them dies, which has no son, the brother
must take his wife and give continuity in his seed.
And, behold, there were seven brethren in the midst of us,
and the first took a wife unto himself, and died without
seed, and his brother took his wife unto himself.
So with the second, the third and still the fourth.
And then the woman died.
Since she was of all, she will be the woman of which one?
And Yeshua answered and said unto them, your err and do
not understand the books and the power of Elohim.
On the day of the resurrection, men will not take
women for themselves, nor women men, they will be
like the angels of Elohim who are in heavens.
Did you not read concerning the resurrection of
the dead that Adonai said to you, saying,
I Am Adonai, Elohei Abraham, Elohei Itzhak
and Elohei Yaakov. Therefore there is no Elohim
of the dead, but Elohim of the living.
And the crowds heard him, and they were astonished
at his wisdom.*

Matthew 22:23-33

The classic understanding of this teaching is Yehoshua's refutation of the belief of the Sadducees, who did
not believe in the resurrection of the dead. In a somewhat
ironic way, they approached Yehoshua and asked a question
that, according to my understand, was somewhat malicious,
because what would be their interest in something they did
not believe? He who does not believe in something, shows

no Interest in it, only repudiates it.

By using the law of levirate (Deuteronomy 25) as an example, they questioned Yehoshua about the afterlife, leading him to declare that God is not the God of the dead, but the God of the living, implying that even after death, the person still lives, thus shows that there is no "eternal death" in the way they believed.

This interpretation is extremely correct in my view and could not be more accurate, since for God ,the concept of "alive and dead", does not exist, but rather the concept "incarnate and discarnate", for no soul dies nor ceases to exist, making Him the Eternal God of the eternal living.

But there is something curious about the question that Yehoshua asks in the middle of this conversation, "*Did you not read that concerning the resurrection of the dead, Adonai said to you...*" The Tanakh has various teachings about resurrection, especially through the mouths of the prophets, but none of them is related to the term "*Elohei Avraham, Elohei Itzhak, Elohei Yaakov*", and by the way in which Yehoshua presents it in his teaching, kind shows us that this association between theses two things he said, would be something "to be read".

Where did this association come from?

## ELOHIM OF THE DEAD, ELOHIM OF THE LIVING

Yehoshua might well have used a prophet's verse to speak about the resurrection and how it would proceed, so he would have been able to give the exact same message and refute the Sadducees' belief. But the Sadducees, by believing only in the Torah and not in the Tanakh, caused Yehoshua to approach this lesson using books that do not directly deal with the resurrection and therefore, he had to connect a passage from the Torah with some traditions of his time that were well known by all, for this was the only way to refute their faith, and this was only possible by using the book they believed in.

*I AM, He said, "the Elohim of your father, Elohei*
*Avraham, Elohei Itzhak, Elohei Yaakov." And Moses hid*
*his face, for he was afraid to look upon Adonai.*

Exodus 3:6

God, when he first appears to Moses in the midst of the burning bush, presented Himself in a manner as if He were showing His Resume. In many ways He could reveal Himself as God, such as presenting Himself as the Creator of all things, or the God who saved you during your childhood, instead He preferred to introduce Himself by saying first that He is the God of Amram (Moses' father) and then the God of the patriarchs.

This is a verse that has innumerable comments from the sages, among the many topics covered by them, some are very similar to what Yehoshua is talking about:

*"I Am the Elohim of your father," in saying these words,*
*God revealed to Moses that his father had already died,*
*for we have a tradition that God does not associate his*
*name with the living, since we do not know whether that*
*person will abandon the ways of God before he dies.*

Chizkuni, Exodus, 3:6

It is necessary a careful analysis here, so that we can have a coherent understanding between what happened with Moses, the words of Yehoshua and the rabbinical tradition.

Rabbi Hezekiah Ben Manoah, the Chizkuni, in one of his commentaries, mentions an age-old tradition within rabbinical teachings, which is the belief that God does not associate His Name with the living. This thesis appears in several other teachings and commentaries throughout rabbinic literature. In my point of view, when Yehoshua quotes that God is not Elohim of the dead, rather the Elohim of the living, he is referring precisely to this mentality. This idea of God not associating His Name with the living may not be good, for it could alienate many people from an intimate and true relationship with God while alive, something that would bring a great frustration to those who have a love for the Creator, for they could think that they will never be able to approach God.

But to interpret Yehoshua's word according to Chizkuni it may raise even more questions, for the three patriarchs quoted by Yehoshua, Avraham, Itzhak and Yaakov were already dead, both in his time and in the time that God appeared to Moses, which could confirm the Jewish tradition that Yehoshua was against.

Rabbi Naftali Zvi Yehuda Berlin, also in one of his commentaries, teaches us something very deep, that was also part of the knowledge of the ancients, something that supports the understanding that Yehoshua had in relation to the dilemma of the God of the dead and the God of the living.

> God was the shield of Avrahan Avinu not only in the war but everywhere, for even without a rabbi, he spent nights and days in search of the Torah, which came from his "kidneys". And with Itzhak, God was his livelihood, He blessed his work and he was an immigrant in peace, for he dedicated his life to prayer and mitzvot. And with Yaakov, thanks to his tzedakot and his studies in his tents (Torah), God took care of him and gave a new meaning to his name. This is the meaning of Elohei Avraham, Elohei Itzhak and Elohei Yaakov, for each one had a way before God and they were all taken care of by Him.
>
> HaAmek Davar, Exodus 3:6:1

This line of thinking is incredible and it is very likely that Yehoshua was associated with it. It teaches that God took care of the three patriarchs, Avraham, by being his shield during the wars, Itzhak by being his livelihood and to Yaakov, God gave a new meaning to his existence. And the most important thing is, all of this was due to obedience to God.

We do not need to study a lot to understand that all of these God's graces, that happened in the lives of these three men, came while they were alive and not dead, and for this grace that was given to them in life, they are recognized up to this day. That is, God did the great work while they were alive and not dead.

What Yehoshua says here is that God becomes known by associating His name and His Chesed (grace) with the living, for it is through them that He makes Himself known to all generations.

Another proof to refute this idea was the way God Himself speaks to the People of Israel:

*Shma Israel: Adonai is your Elohim, Adonai is One.*

Deuteronomy 6:4

In this passage, among many others, Elohim associates Himself with His listeners, the People of Israel, formed by a multitude who heard these words while alive, making them connected with God, for as He said to be the "Elohim of your father" to Moses, in this passage He says "YOUR ELOHIM" to His people.

It is fantastic, a few verses above, Yehoshua says that they err and do not understand the "books", revealing to us that his teaching, in this case, would go against some rabbinical tradition that he did not agree with. The term used by him, "books", refers to the Written Torah, for this was the only book that the Sadducees believed in, so, Yehoshua used the Torah to abolish some rabbinical teaching and mentality.

And as mentioned above, even if the person is dead, he is only dead in the flesh, for to God, either in *Olam Hazeh* or in *Olam Habah*, everyone is alive, there is no such thing as "*end after death*".

## GOD OF AVRAHAM, GOD OF ITZHAK, GOD OF YAAKOV

Another interesting thing that God does not present Himself as "Elohei Avraham, Itzhak and Yaakov", but rather as "Elohei Avraham, Elohei Itzhak and Elohei Yaakov". By doing this, our sages teach that if we could ask each one of them who God is, we would have three different answers about the same God.

The concept of the name Elohim ending with "IM" (plural of masculine words in Hebrew) could denote the personal relationship that each one of us has with God, the way each one sees Him and how each one understands Him. There will never be two people with the exact same concept about the Creator, for Elohim is unique to each one who serves Him.

On the other hand, the name Adonai (tetragrammaton) is immutable and represents the essence of the Creator, this is the way He defines Himself, surpassing any concept that the human being can create about Him.

A great care must be taken, for Christian theology falsely teaches that because the name Elohim is plural, it would represent the trinity, which is not true and cannot be proved using the bible.

## THE DOUBLE CONCLUSION

This teaching has two possible interpretations that are interconnected, one adressess the living in the *Olam Hazeh* and the other addresses the living in the *Olam Habah*.

The first one is about those who are alive in the flesh, they may have their names associated with Elohim, they may receive His grace, they may see His wonders and they may be taken care by Him, all due to the love He has for us.

The second concerns the spiritual realm, the *Olam Habah*, where everyone is also alive, for the resurrection of the dead is a reality vastly taught throughout the bible, for every soul and spirit created by God will never cease to exist.

So, from here we learn that God can only be the God of the living.

## SECTION XL
### GREATEST COMMANDMENTS

*Rabbi, tell me, what is the greatest mitzvah*
*(commandment) in the Torah?*
*And he said unto him, you shall love Adonai your*
*Elohim with all your heart, and so forth.*
*This is the first*
*The second is this, you shall love your neighbor as yourself.*
*And on these two Mitzvot (commandments)*
*all the Torah and the prophets hang.*
Matthew 22:36-40

Every time I begin to write some commentary on Yehoshua's words from the book of Matthew, the first thing that comes into my mind is "here is a dangerous verse". Unfortunately I could begin every explanation of his teachings with these words, for somehow, all of them have created strong misconceptions that enslave many people.

For several times, I asked some Christians friends why did they not follow the Laws of Torah and one of the most common answers I received was based precisely on this passage, because, according to them, christ replaced the entire Torah by these two commandments, saying that from the moment one loves God above all else and one's neighbor as oneself, he no longer needs to observe the Torah.

As already shown in several parts of this book and stated by Yehoshua himself in chapter 5, he did not abolish anything of the Torah. The teaching of this passage not only encompasses the Torah, but it is nothing more than an ancient understanding of it.

### THE COMMANDMENTS

The Torah has a total of 613 commandments, these commandments are not applicable to everyone. There are commandments applicable only for men, others for women only, others for kings, priests, judges, and so on. With the exception of the commandments concerning ethics, sexual morality and character, all commandments fit into certain groups and are not generally applicable.

The commandments of the Torah can be divided into two parts in two different ways. The first division is between the positive commandments and the negative commandments, i.e. the ones you MUST do and those you SHOULD NOT do.

There are 365 negative commandments, things that shouldn't be done, as if one says a "no" every single day for an entire year. The positives have a total of 248 commandments, which require care and attention to their observance, 248 is also the total number of bones and organs that the human body possesses, as if the whole body were willing to give a "yes" to God.

The second division is made according to the type of commandment, which may be separated as "man x God" relationship and "man x man" relationship. In the first group we have the commandments concerning Shabbat, feasts, kashrut, tzedakah and so on. In the second, we have the commandments concerning sexual immorality, murder, robbery and so forth. This division is represented by the very tablets of the Law, given by God to Moses on Mount Sinai, in the first tablet we have the commandments referring to "man x God" and in the second one, the commandments referring "man x man".

The answer Yehoshua gives in this passage deals with this second division of commandments. Doing such an approach in reference to the Torah has a well-defined meaning within the Jewish mentality.

## TO LOVE GOD

*Shma Israel, Adonai is our Elohim, Adonai IS ONE.*
*And you shall love Adonai, your Elohim, with all your*

*heart, with all your soul and with all your much.*
Deuteronomy 6:4-5

This wonderful passage from the book of Deuteronomy, known as "shma", is the highest representation of the People of Israel and the cornerstone of the Jewish faith. These verses are so powerful that they are recited three times a day by the Jews, they are written inside the *tefilim* (phylacteries) and inside the *mezuzot* placed on the doorposts in every Jewish house.

When Yehoshua quotes this verse, in addition to affirming the faith he had, due for being a Jew and as a servant of the single and indivisible God, he automatically refers to all the commandments "man x God", saying that to be able to achieve this love for God , it is necessary first to observe all of these ordinances, for only those who love God with all their "heart, soul and much" can really change the way of their life in favor of this God.

*As it is written, "And you shall love Adonai your Elohim with all your heart," it means with your evil inclination and with your good inclination, for both should be subjugated to God. "With all your soul" means that you must love God even by the cost of your soul. "With all your much" means with all your money and possessions. Another understanding: "With all your much" is to submit to the mitzvot of Adonai.*
Talmud of Babylon, Tractate Brakhot 54a

The Talmud quotes the connection between "loving God" with the mitzvot concerning the relationship "man x God". To love God above all things must be through one's inclinations, wills, dreams and feelings, for the love to God must be greater than the love one has for oneself. This love is only truly reachable through the observance of ALL the commandments of the Torah that belong to the commandments concerning "man x God" relationship.

## TO LOVE THE NEIGHBOR
Classical rabbinical affirmation. It is not only quoted by Yehoshua, but also by Paul and countless other rabbis.

Yehoshua does not refer to a feeling, for to love strangers is unnatural to the human beings, but "to love", in this case, refers to attitudes towards others and such attitudes are defined only by the Torah. Let's see where he got this concept from:

*Thou shalt not take revenge, nor bear a gruge with the sons of thy people; but you shall love your neighbor as yourself. I am Adonai.*
Leviticus 19:18

*Rabbi Akiva says: To love one's neighbor is the greatest principle of the Torah.*
Talmud of Jerusalem, Tractate Nedarim 30b

*Every morning, before your prayers, commit yourself to loving your neighbor as yourself. Then your prayers will be accepted and bear fruit.*
Rabbi Yitzchak Luria

*Do you hear what they say in the heavenly academy? That loving your neighbor means to totally love the wicked as you totally love the righteous.*
The Maguid of Mezeritch

Now I wonder, did all these sages forsake the Torah because they believed that "to love God" and "to love the neighbor" are all the commandments one needs? Or did they understand that, in order to reach these two commandments, man needs to follow the way that is taught by God in the Torah?

Being Yehoshua a Jew, who received an education based on the Torah, on the Talmud and on the sages, did he not think in the same way as the rabbis mentioned above? So why do many Christians claim that these two laws abolished the entire Torah? It does not make any sense.

By quoting "to love God" and "to love the neighbor," which represent the pinnacle of all Torah's commandments, Yehoshua says that there is no more or less important commandment, for they are all important. In order to reach a total love for God, in the way He demands, it is necessary to keep all the commandments "man x God" and to reach true love for the neighbor, something that transcends a feeling, something that deals with ethics, respect, education, compassion, affection, dedication, common sense and support, the Torah is necessary because it was through it that such concepts were revealed to mankind.

In a less rabbinical way, Yehoshua's answer is: "**All the Torah**".

## RABBINICAL CONNECTION BETWEEN THE TWO PASSAGES

*"To bear a grudge" refers to problems concerning*
*money and not to personal insults.*

Talmud of Babylon, Tractate Yoma 23a

*Revenge, when it exceeds, it will cause the soul to*
*be cut off and will not have eternal life.*

Mishneh Torah, Rep 8:5

*When we love our neighbor, we begin to love God.*

Yismach Yisrael, Haggadah Shel Pessach, Maror 1:2

*As it is written, "And you shall love Adonai your Elohim with*
*all your heart," it means with your evil inclination and with*
*your good inclination, for both should be subjugated to God.*
*"With all your soul" means that you must love God even by*
*the cost of your soul. "With all your much" means with all*
*your money and possessions. Another understanding: "With*
*all your much" is to submit to the mitzvot of Adonai.*

Talmud of Babylon, Tractate Brakhot 54a

According to the rabbinical mentality, to love God with all our "much" is when we do not bear grudge in our heart. To love God with all our "soul" is never to take revenge. To love God with all our "heart" is to love our neighbor, thus making a connection between Deuteronomy 6:4-5 and Leviticus 19:18.

The two sentences of Yehoshua are totally interconnected, you cannot do one without doing the other, you cannot love God without loving your neighbor and you cannot love your neighbor without the commandments of the Torah. It is like a ladder, first we adapt our lives according to the will of the Creator, then we will have honorable attitudes before our neighbor, for God's precepts will change our lives, attitudes and character, then we will reach the apex, loving God above all things and so fulfilling His commandments in a natural way.

*"Loving God" has its roots in the mitzvot (commandments).*
Likutei Moharan 93:1:3

Yehoshua did not substitute the whole Torah by two commandments. These commandments, in fact, represent the entire Torah and to reach them, an observance of all the commandments of God is necessary. He who declares that he follows Yehoshua must keep this in mind, for following him is much more complex than the church teaches. If the leaders were teaching the truth, the church would lose all of its appealing appearance.

## SHMA ISRAEL

*Shma Israel, Adonai is our Elohim, Adonai IS ONE.*
*And you shall love Adonai, your Elohim, with all your*
*heart, with all your soul and with all your much.*
Deuteronomy 6:4-5

I will use thus subject to go a little deeper into the two verses that represent the whole Jewish faith and the unity of the People of Israel, these two verses are recited every day and are known as SHMA ISRAEL (listen Israel).

## 1- SHMA (שמע)

The Torah does not say SEE ISRAEL, but rather, LISTEN ISRAEL. This is because our knowledge of God is based on sensory perception. During the time prior to the Torah, little was known about God, this conception of a single God reigning over the whole earth was a very abstract idea and inconsistent with human reality and the post-flooding common mentality.

God, in order to make Himself known, had to seek men, introduce Himself to them, and through these men, He accomplished great deeds. If we make a comparison of the time of Abraham, of Moses and of the prophets with the present day, the impression we will have is that, over time, God hid Himself, his "apparitions" and great miracles became more scarce. However, on the other hand, the access that every single one, whoever one is, poor or rich, white or black, Latin or Asian, has to the Word of God and to the knowledge about who He is, is unrestricted. Because of this fact, the Torah commands: HEAR! Hear who God is, hear what He has done, hear His prowess, hear His wonders, for in these days it is through this "hearing" that God becomes known by a man.

Of course, God can reveal Himself to whoever He wants, in the way He wants and not just by hearing. But this revelation does not come before we "hear" His Word, about who He is and how He works, for if He presents Himself before that, it is very difficult for the person, that receives this revelation, to have the ability to recognize its source.

## 2-ONE (אחד)

This is a statement that generates several theories, especially by those who want to create and justify false gods. The word ECHAD (אחד) - ONE – doesn't only mean that

God is one, but also represents His essence, for He is an absolute ONE and not a compound ONE. If God were a compound ONE, then, within that composition, there would be a grouping, if there is a grouping, it means that someone had to group it, that is, if God is a compound ONE, someone had to compose it, which shows us that that there is something, or somebody, greater than God, for this "greater somebody" was able to gather three in one. Faith in a triune god and faith in a god that is not absolute is a strange thing, for this triune-god's compositions had to be compounded sometime. If one creates the other, then this other does not have the same power as the one who created him has, thus breaking the equality they should have to be a ONE in balance.

If God were to be three in one, the word in this passage would not be ECHAD (אחד), but rather ACHER (אחר) - the difference is just a single Hebrew letter at the end of both words, DALET (ד) and REISH (ר).

## 3- YOU SHALL LOVE (אהבת)

The Hebrew word for love shows a much deeper meaning than those we have in Western languages. AHAVAH (אהבה) - *love* - begins with the letter ALEF (א) and every word that its root begins with this letter, deals with an individual and personal conception, something reflective. As for the rest of the word, the letters (הב), the remaining letters of the word AHAVAH, we have it means something as "to donate". Therefore, the word AHAVAH (אהבה) means something like "self-giving".

When the Torah commands us to love God, it does not refer to an internal feeling, but rather to give ourselves to God, to submit to His will and to His plans, and for this reason, following His commandments is a way to truly love Him. Now it makes sense.

## 4 – WITH ALL YOUR HEART (לבבך)

Giving ourselves to God with all our hearts is not a

simple task, precisely because of the word "ALL". This is only possible through a recognition of the absolute unity of the Creator, for it is only through this recognition that the human being can understand that "loving with all one's heart" is nothing more than giving up both the good inclination and the evil inclination, that exist within of every human being, in the hands of God.

The true nature of this mitzvah encompasses the idea that we are ready to place our desires, dreams and wills in the hands of God and, if they are not what God wants from us, we will gladly give up those things.

## 5- WITH ALL YOUR SOUL (נפשך)

The soul represents the true essence of the human being, it defines the closeness that we can have with the Creator and His designs. As the "heart" represents our dreams and desires in this earthly life, the soul represents our being, our thoughts, our character, our devotion and acceptance of God.

According to our sages, it is at this moment that the commandments enter, for it is through them that a person demonstrates true devotion to God, and that's not all, only through them that an intimate relationship with God will be established, that is, it is through the miracles that will occur in our lives, due to our obedience, that we will be able to recognize God in a irrevocably way.

To surrender one's soul to God is to follow His commandments and His Torah.

## 6- WITH ALL YOUR MUCH (מאדך)

This Hebrew commandment can be interpreted in two ways. The "much", according to the sages, represents the material possessions that an one possesses. To love God with all our much is to use our material possessions in His service and by being aware that everything belongs to Him and also, by not breaking any of the commandments to obtain those goods.

But in addition, the term MEOD (מאד) - *much* - has a deeper meaning, for represents a term for measures and quantities. This means that we must surrender to God all that we have and that can be "measured", that is, everything.

# SECTION XLI
## THE LORD OF DAVID

*And gathered together more Pharisees and Yeshua asked them.
Saying: What, in your opinion, is Mashiach? Son of
whom? And they said to him, Son of David.
And he said to them, As David by the Holy
Ghost called him, saying: Lord.
As it is written, Adonai said to my lord, Sit at my right hand
and until I make your enemies the footstool of your feet.
If David called him Lord, how could he then be his son?
And they could not answer him a word, and since
then they were afraid to ask him anything.*

Matthew 22:41-46

The New Testament is not a book that should be interpreted without the Tanakh, for it is a book written by Jews, about Jews, to Jews. By reading the teachings of rabbis like Yehoshua and Paul, it is of the utmost importance that, in addition to a good knowledge of Torah, a deeper understanding about how was their relationship with the Torah; for the teaching of both of them is strongly influenced by their personal vision about the Word of God.

One's view of the Bible is made up by two factors. The first one is something more personal, is the particular interpretation that each one of us has when reading the bible. The second involves education, background and how the Scriptures was taught to us. The Torah, without any doubt, is the central core for these two rabbis. Their Judaism exerted enormous influence on everything they did and taught, for it was the only reality they knew, the world to them, first-century rabbis, was seen through Jewish lens. Therefore, the Oral Torah and the rabbinic mentality are the major sources that we must look at in order to understand the teachings of these two men, especially those of Yehoshua, who only taught for the Jews.

In these verses we have a classic case of confrontation between Yehoshua and the sages. Yehoshua begins by asking them who, according to their point of view, would be Mashiach. Through the answer they gave, Yehoshua quotes a Psalm of David and places a question that makes them speechless.

The Psalm quoted by Yehoshua, according to the sages, is a Messianic Psalm, where King David calls Mashiach as lord. Yehoshua, clinging to that, questions the sages how could David call his descendant, as master.

*By David. A Psalm. Adonai said to my lord, "sit you at my right as I make your enemies the footstool for your feet".*
Psalms 110:1

Let's look at some points in this story from the book of Matthew. The common understanding about those verses is that he was saying that he is greater than king David. However, if we pay a closer attention to Yehoshua's words, unlike other occasions, he does NOT claim to be Mashiach, what he actually does is an indirect questioning without compromising himself. This alone already refutes the thesis that he was claiming to be greater than David, this is not what he was talking about. Claiming to be greater than David would be only understood by his talmidim, because only to them he said to be Mashiach up to that moment.

Secondly, every Jew knows very well that Mashiach is greater than David, if the purpose of Yehoshua's question was to teach this topic, no sage would have remained without an answer. And finally, Yehoshua, the way he asked the question about Mashiach, he induced the Pharisees to answer something specific, *"son of whom?"* Yehoshua did not want to know who Mashiach was for them, but he wanted to know the origin of Mashiach. Only these topics alone annul the theological interpretation that simply states that he told the Pharisees that he is greater than David.

The answer we need lies in two questions, why did Yehoshua specifically mentioned this Psalm and what was he refuting, in regard to the teachings of the sages, that left them without answer?

## DAVID BY THE HOLY SPIRIT

Yehoshua opens his speech justifying his own questioning. He speaks of how David recognized Mashiach as his lord and this had been passed to him by the Holy Spirit.

This affirmation alone could have created a lot of debates among them, since in the Tanakh, no statement appears that this recognition of Mashiach by David was given to him by the Holy Spirit. However, this was, somehow, already known by the sages. There is something in the rabbinical literature that approaches this revelation from the Holy Spirit to David in a very similar way:

*The way one talks privately with his **Lord** is an aspect of the **Holy Spirit**, as well as King **David**, of blessed memory, who had great virtues according to the book of **Psalms**.*
Likutey Moharan, Torah 156:1

David, when he affirms the words of Adonai in this psalm, with absolute certainty, they were revealed to him by the Holy Spirit, as well as all his virtues which are found in the book of Psalms.

This passage from *Likutey Moharan* fits like a glove in what Yehoshua said, for as soon as he said that David's revelation came from the Holy Spirit, he quotes a Psalm in the sequence. Yehoshua's connection to the Oral Torah and rabbinic teachings are strikingly strong, so this statement did not cause oddities among his listeners.

## A PSALM OF DAVID

Understanding why Psalm 110 is a messianic psalm can change many things about the interpretation of Yehoshua's words in this case. For this, a structural analysis of the Hebrew language used in this Psalm will be necessary, as well as some comparisons with later verses of the same chapter.

One of the methods used in rabbinic exegesis is the comparison of two verses which use similar terms or words. In some cases, when this occurs, it is customary for some rabbis to separate the verse into two parts, part A and part B. Then the same thing is done with the second verse, which was associated with the first one. Both are divided into two parts, part A and part B and then they connect the part A of the first verse with the part B of the second verse, and vice versa, and so, many hidden messages in the Tanakh are revealed.

In addition to this method, an analysis of some of the terms of this verse in its original will be required. Every Hebrew word has a root, this root usually consists of three letters, four in a few cases, and through these three letters, new words can be formed. These new words, by being from the same root as the original word, can be replaced in the verse, thus bringing a new understanding. Let's look at the word "my lord" which, according to the rabbis, refers to Mashiach:

*By David, a Psalm, Adonai said | To **my lord** (אדני): "sit you at my right as I make your enemies the footstool for your feet".*
Psalms 110:1

In this passage, the word "my lord" appears as ADONI (אדני), which is a contracted form of ADON SHELI (אדון שלי). The word ADON - *lord* - has the same root as DIN (דין) - *law* - which can also be YADIN (ידין), which is a conjugated form of the verb TO JUDGE, as it appears in Psalm 110:6:

**ידין** בגוים מלא גויות מחץ ראש על ארץ רבה
*You will judge (YADIN) the nations, heaping up bodies and crushing heads far and wide.*

Psalms 110:6

Now it is possible to divide both verses into parts A and parts B, because we found a word that connects them. The partition should be held just where the words ADONI (my lord) and YADIN (judges) appear, because they are words of the same root.

Psalm 110:1
- PART A = By David, a Psalm, Adonai said.
- PART B = Sit at my right as I make your enemies the footstool of your feet.

Psalm 110:6
- PART A = You will judge the nations.
- PART B = Heaping up bodies and crushing heads far and wide.

By crossing the first A eith the second B and the first B with the second A, we shall have:

*1- By David, a psalm. Adonai said I will heap up bodies and I will crush heads far and wide.*

*2 – You will judge the nations, sit at my right hand while I make your enemies the footstool of your feet.*

Looking at the number 1, we do not have a very weird verse, but in the case of the number 2, apparently, it completely loses its meaning. Perhaps if we look at it in Hebrew, something might appear behind this crazy definition:

ידין בגוים מלא | שב לימיני
עד-אשית איביך הדם לרגליש

This is the number 2 in Hebrew. If we take the first letters of the first three words (ידין בגוים מלא) from left to right we will have (מ - ב - י) representing:

Mashiach - מ - משיח
Ben - ב - בן
Yosef - י - יסף

Now we have something meaningful about what the Psalm says. If we take number 2 and replace the words, we will have the reason why this psalm is seen as a messianic psalm, as follows:

*Mashiach Ben Yosef sits at my right as I make his enemies the footstool of his feet.*

And verse 7 continues this subject, confirming what we have seen so far:

מנחל בדרך ישתה על-כן ירים ראש

*He shall drink from the stream on his way, and shall hold his head high.*

Psalms 110:7

Just as before, if we take the first letters of the first three words (מ - ב - י) but from right to left this time, we shall have again:

Mashiach - מ - משיח
Ben - ב - בן
Yosef - י - יסף

Likewise, if we replace the original three words by the name of Mashiach, we will have:

*Mashiach Ben Yosef shall hold his head high.*

To conclude, an interrelated reading of these three verses, 1, 6 and 7, will show the true revelation of Mashiach. It is impressive:

*By David, a Psalm. Adonai said: Mashiach Ben Yosef will judge the nations sitting at my right as I will make his enemies the footstool of his feet, by heaping up bodies and crushing heads far and wide and Mashiach Ben Yosef shall hold his head high.*

## MASHIACH BEN YOSEF

So far so good, but the above psalms speak about Mashiach Ben Yosef and the book of Matthew refers to Mashiach Ben David. Some topics on Mashiach have already been set forth at the beginning of this book, but let's look back at some things that might clarify what was happening between those sages and Yehoshua.

Looking at Mashiach Ben Yosef, the sages say that his main purpose is to prepare the People of Israel (we are not talking about Jews here) for redemption and to bring it to an appropriate spiritual level for the coming of Mashiach Ben David, and this will be done through the teaching of Torah. This redemption means repentance, which will cause the coming of Ben David. As the sages say:

*"He announces salvation". It is written in the singular because it refers to Mashiach Ben Yosef.*

Kol HaTor 2:81

*"To Bring a Redeemer" - This is the mission of Mashiach Ben Yosef*

Mashiach Ben Yosef will prepare the world for the coming of Ben David. He will perform miracles, healings and wonders, he will cause strife and many wars, and will cause Edom to strike against Israel, and for this reason they will be destroyed by Mashiach Ben David. This is an interesting claim, for the term Edom, in Jewish literature, refers to the Christian nations, which are anti-Semitic in their essences.

Another thing we must notice about Mashiach Ben Yosef is, in order for his work to be complete, he must first know death. We must keep in mind that there are no two *Mashiachim* (plural of Mashiach), but only one. The distinction of Ben Yosef and Ben David is given by the difference of his missions. While Ben Yosef will bring redemption to Israel and will pass through death, Ben David will bring the judgment upon the nations, will separate the good from the wicked and will reign in Jerusalem, bringing an era of peace to the world.

**THE TRICKY SIDE**

When Yehoshua questioned the sages, he was actually being a little tricky somehow, for he wanted to reveal, even if in a very indirect way, that his mission as Mashiach was not exactly as they expected.

When we approached the disagreements between Yehoshua and Yohanan, the immerser, we saw that the vision and expectation that Yohanan had in Mashiach were not being "realized" by Yehoshua, which generated doubts in Yohanan's mind about him, because the immerser was expecting a Ben David. This expectation did not only happen with Yohanan, but with a lot of the Jewish people, with many of the Pharisees, with many of the rabbis and with many of the sages, for to them, Mashiach Ben Yosef had already come, as Rabbi Saadiah Gaon said:

*Rabbi Gaon notes that: Joshua is Mashiach Ben Yosef, just as*
*Ezra and Nehemiah had the mission of Moshiach Ben Yosef.*

Kol HaTor 2:116

For many of the sages, Joshua Bin Nun was Mashiach Ben Yosef and therefore, the Mashiach would now have to come in the form of Ben David.

When Yehoshua mentions this Psalm, he indirectly points out an error of interpretation in some of the Jewish exegeses. The question, that the sages were not able to answer, is precisely referring to the work of Ben Yosef, a work that Yehoshua had been doing and the sages were not seeing. This is the reason his question caused great confusion in their minds.

The accounts of Yehoshua's deeds in the book of Matthew are well compatible with the rabbinical descriptions of Mashiach Ben Yosef, his teachings, the open doors to the gentiles, redemption, salvation, death, and bringing wars. And that's not all, but the full name of Yehoshua also resembles this form of Mashiach, for he was named Yehoshua Ben Yosef.

Thus we have the answers to the initial questions, he mentioned this Psalm to reveal that the rabbinical teachings, of which Mashiach Ben Yosef had already come, were mistaken and also, he wanted to show that his mission was as Ben Yosef and not as Ben David, as they expected.

**ARGUMENTS**

Psalm 110 is an aggregate of mystical verses, the study we have done about them reveals some things concerning the differences between Adonai and Mashiach, and the extent of his mission.

The Psalm tells us that Mashiach's mission will be to judge the nations and Adonai's mission is to subdue the nations under Mashiach's feet. Mashiach, if were some sort of "god," would not need God to subdue his enemies, he would do it by himself, as well as sitting at one's own right is somewhat inexplicable.

The difference between Mashiach and God is clear, surely Mashiach has a spiritually elevated soul and a divine essence, but Adonai is God and Mashiach is Mashiach.

# SECTION XLII
## TAKANOT

*Upon the seat of Moses the Pharisees and the sages sit.
And now, all that HE said to you, observe and
do, but their TAKANOT and their MA'ASSOT do
not listen to, for they say but do not do.
They demand and set forth a great burden (on the shoulders
of men) that they cannot bear, but they themselves do
not even want to move a finger (to do them).*
Matthew 23:2-4

*Saying The scribes and the Pharisees sit in Moses's seat:
All therefore whatever they bid you observe, that observe and
do; but do not you after their works: for they say, and do not.
For they bind heavy burdens and grievous to be borne,
and lay them on men' shoulders; but they themselves
will not move them with one of their fingers.*
Matthew 23:2-4 KJV

The chapter 23 of the book of Matthew is replete with teachings directed to the talmidim of Yehoshua. At its very beginning, he already states, in a few words, how his instruction would be like. Unfortunately, the translator who translated this book into Greek had some problems concerning some small details of the Hebrew language, which affected generations of people by making a huge mess in the Yehoshua's words above.

Some English Bibles have subtitles between verses to facilitate the understanding of what will be addressed in the following verses. In the case of this part, the subtitle that I found in several bibles refers to the teaching of Yehoshua on hypocrisy. However, if we read very carefully the translation we have in English, this teaching about hypocrisy is a bit obscure, for, Yehoshua by saying: *"whatever they say to you, do and observe, but don't do as they do."*, in fact, he is not teaching against hypocrisy, but he is making an apology to hypocrisy, that is, he teaches his talmidim to be hypocrites, by doing what the Pharisees say, but not doing as they do. All we need is a little common sense and a good interpretation of the text so we can see the absurdity that a bad translation caused and many of the Christians never realized.

In order to understand the origin of the error, we must look at the verse 3 in Hebrew:

כל אשר יומר לכם

*KOL ASHER **YOMAR** LACHEM*
*All that **HE** said to you...*

and what the translator wrote:

כל אשר יומרו לכם

*KOL ASHER **YOMRU** LACHEM*
*All that **THEY** said to you...*

The difference is in a small Hebrew letter, the letter VAV (ו), which is one of the smallest letters in Hebrew. This makes a huge difference, for YOMAR (יומר) means HE SAID, third person singular and YOMRU(יומרו) means THEY SAID, third person plural.

Yehoshua, at no moment, did teach that the Pharisee's traditions are to be followed or about hypocrisy. What we must look at, is his quotation on Moses' seat, for this is an representation of authority within pharisaism, within the synagogue and within the Torah's interpretation. However, Yehoshua claims that, even if the Pharisees were sitting on the seat of Moses, he (Moses) still had authority, so, his teaching is what his listeners should do and observe, all that he (MOSES) said and not what the Pharisees say.

For this to become clearer, we must understand more about the terms used by Yehoshua in this part, terms that were poorly translated by someone who clearly did not know first-century Judaism.

## TAKANOT x MA'ASSIM

After instructing his talmidim to do and to observe what Moses said, Yehoshua goes on and says that they should not do the *Takanot* and *Ma'assim* of the Pharisees. Although these terms have been translated as "works", their original versions are full of meanings that cannot be translated, this again shows how the translator had very poor knowledge about the society in which Yehoshua was inserted and how damaging this was on Christian theology.

In Pharisaic jargon, the term TAKANOT means "decrees, reforms" and more specifically "reforms on biblical laws". As we all know, any reform seeks some kind of change and with the TAKANOT are no different, they are changes proposed by the rabbis to adapt certain laws to the daily life in societies where they are inserted.

The rabbis distinguish very well the laws of Torah and the laws that they invent, I will use a very good example of a man made law that is very common within the orthodox Judaism of the present day.

> *...You shall not boil a kid in its mother's milk.*
> Deuteronomy 14:21b

> *The Torah does not only prohibit cooking meat in the milk.*
> *However, it is forbidden to eat both together, even if eating*
> *both without salting is prohibited by rabbinic law, in*
> *addition, one must wait between eating meat and milk.*
> Shulchan Arukh, Yoreh De'ah 87:4b

In orthodox Judaism it is expressly forbidden to eat meat with any kind of food derived from milk. In order to a kitchen be totally kasher, according to the Jewish law, one should have two different refrigerators, one for meat and one for dairy products, as well as two different sinks, the contact with one another already makes the food unfit for consumption.

Such a rule was based on the verse above, where Adonai forbids cooking the lamb's meat in its mother's milk (see also Exodus 23:19 and Exodus 34:26), and from there, the rabbis created extremely strict laws regarding consumption and even the contact of meat with milk, being any type of meat, including poultry, which are not even mammals.

Such customs, among many others, known as TAKANOT, are the first things that Yehoshua goes against, modifications of Torah's laws by human hands. He did not teach against the Torah, as many think, but he was against some topics of the Jewish theology, laws and theories created by men. We must keep in mind that this occurs in every religions, especially in Christianity, which is why there are several very different Christian branches, due to the TAKANOT of Christianity.

The TAKANOT word appears in another passage in the book of Matthew and Yehoshua brings another opinion regarding this TAKANOT:

> *But he answered and said to them, Why do you also transgress the commandment of God by your tradition?*
> Matthew 15:3 KJV

> *And Yeshua said to them: Why do you not respect the Torah of EL because of your TAKANOT?*
> Matthew 15:3

Yehoshua accuses whoever follows men made laws, theologies, biblical theories and all that is not explicit in the Torah of EL, as people that do not respect His Word. But once again, we are all victims of bad translations done by people who are clearly unprepared.

Another term quoted by Yehoshua is the word MA'AS-SIM, such a term was very common in first-century Judaism and means something like "precedent" or "traditions". This term is unique and profound, it does not surprise me that whoever translated into Greek did not have the slightest idea of what was being translated, for using the generic term "works" already proves that. But when Yehoshua mentions this, he is talking about something very specific.

In order for us to understand what *Ma'asseh* is, we must look at some examples. When a Pharisee encounters a situation in which he does not know how the law should be applied, he will seek an answer through the attitudes of his predecessors, it could be a sage from the Oral Torah or some of his teachers. For supposing that the sages and the teachers are sinless people, they seek moments in their lives where they went through the same situation in which this Pharisee is going through now, so he tries to act in the same way that the sage acted.

Let's look at some examples in the Talmud:

*Ma'asseh Rabi - Ma'asseh is a teacher*
Talmud of Babylon, Tractate Sabbath 21a

A slightly more practical example. In Shabbat, in addition to the Torah's prohibition to work, it is also forbidden to make others to work, whether Jews or Gentiles.

Let's suppose that this Pharisee needs to get off a boat on a Shabbat, so a Gentile places a ramp between the boat and the shore, so everyone could disembark. This gentile works by putting down the ramp and if the Jew uses, he could be committing a sin, in this case, what should he do?

*If a Gentile places a ramp on a Shabbat to disembark from a ship, let the Jew disembark only after him. If the ramp was placed specifically for the Jew, then it is forbidden. There was an incident in which Rabbi Gamliel and the elders were traveling and a gentile placed a ramp on a Shabbat for disembarking and Rabbi Gamliel disembarked by it.*
Talmud of Babylon, Tractate Shabbat 122a

Problem solved, it is good enough to this Pharisee, who is in doubt on how to act in a certain situation, to look at other men. Rabbi Gamliel really was a Tzadik in his time, he was the teacher of Paul and his name is mentioned in the book of Acts.

Now we have a better idea of the term MA'ASSIM used by Yehoshua. It is the habit of looking at other men, who were considered righteous, in order to know what to do when it comes to the Jewish laws and TAKANOT.

## EINAM OSSIM

In the last words of verse 3, some particularly interesting words appear.

*"For they say but do not"*

What did Yehoshua mean by that? What do they say? What do they do not? The feeling that I have when I read this in Hebrew is that something is missing, some information was already implicit in what Yehoshua was talking about.

As I have said before, beyond the problems of translation, it is impossible to understand it without a broad knowledge of the Tanakh. Yehoshua makes a very subtle quotation, but widely known by the Jewish people. If we look at the book of Kings, we will understand the message that Yehoshua wants to teach. An indirect, but very strong message.

*Even to this day, they do according to their former practices;*
*they do not fear Adonai and "do not" (einam ossim);*
*such as the laws, the ordinances, and the Torah...*

2 Kings 17:34a

By the time this book was composed, the tribes of the Kingdom of Israel had already been exiled and in its place, the Assyrian empire brought people from different parts of Babylon, people with a completely pagan background, who eventually absorbed various Jewish customs and knowledge of the God of Israel and of the Torah, such people later became known as the Samaritans.

The problem is, for an idolatrous mindset, worshiping different gods is commonplace. Then, while they worshiped the God of Israel during the day, they worshiped their ancient gods at night, and this brought a lot of rebukes from the Jews and from God Himself, one of then is the one we just read in the passage quoted above. By not fearing Adonai, many of the Samaritans continued doing their pagan practices that they possessed before they knew the true God.

However, what I want to address here is how this verse was written in its original. EINAM OSSIM that we have in the book of Kings, is exactly the same term used by Yehoshua at the end of verse 3, the literal translation of it from Hebrew looks a bit strange, but this EINAM OSSIM (do not), this thing that "they do not", refers to the Torah.

Such term was commonly used in first-century Judaism to subtly refer to someone who does not respect and does not observe the Torah. Yehoshua was saying that, just like the Samaritans of old with their own customs, certain Pharisees had their own laws and statutes to which they followed and taught. The same time that they used to speak about the Torah, they "do not" the Torah, for they "do not" fear Adonai.

What Yehoshua teaches is that, in order to someone to follow him, one must follow what Moses said and not any kind of TAKANOT and MA'ASSIM. The same is also true in Christianity, that suffers from the Christian theology, Christian customs and doctrinal theories, for whoever does them, besides not following Torah, shows a lack of fear of Adonai.

Verse 4 is now clear. Such a verse was widely used by many Christian theologians to claim that the Torah was a burden, which was put on a man's shoulders and no one could carry it. In fact, what Yehoshua called to be a burden was precisely the rabbinic laws, which really are a burden, there are so many, but so many, that the person who seeks to follow them all cannot do anything else in life, that is why so many Orthodox Jews, from places as *Meah Shearim* and *Bnei Brakh* do not work, because they have no time.

A law, or rule, only becomes a burden on someone's life when this law somehow bothers him by prohibitions that inhibits something that this person likes to do. If the Torah Laws represent a burden on one's life, one urgently needs to revise their behavioral life before the Creator, for the law rightly points to our flaws and this is something that bothers many people.

# SECTION XLIII
## TEVILAH

*Woe to them, sages and Pharisees, who tithe mint, dill and
pomegranate. But who commit robberies. It is better to
honor the Torah sentences, which are: Chesed, truth and
faith. The Torah is worth of following, never forget that.
Seeds of blind leaders, who walks in the narrow
path like a gnat and can swallow a camel.
Shame on you Pharisees and sages, who submerge the cups and
the dishes on the outside and inside is full of evil and impurities.
Hypocrites, first cleanse inside of you and
then be pure in the outside.*
Matthew 23:23-26

What we have here is a commandment from the
Torah, much practiced by every Jew, being used as an example for a criticism of the behavior of some people around
Yehoshua. The commandment he mentions is called TEVI-
LAH and deals with the *"kasherization"* of household utensils. Before any utensil can be used in a kitchen, it needs to attain a certain level of "holiness" and to do so, it must undergo
a ritual of immersion as determined by the Torah:

*Any utensil that can withstand fire, those you must pass
through fire and they will be purified except when they need
to be purified with water of lustration, and anything that
cannot pass through fire you must pass it through water.*
Numbers 31:23

The *halachah* determines several rules concerning the
immersion of utensils. The place where the submersion is
made, also called *Mikveh*, must be constructed according to
the measures stipulated by the rabbis, the water that is used,
must be water from a natural source, as water from rain for
example. The purification of household utensils is a ritual

called TEVILAH, a name that comes from the Hebrew word TOVEL - *to immerse*.

Also according to the *halachah*, not all utensils should go through the *tevilah*, only those that are not made by Jews or if they already belonged to some Gentile. *Tevilah* is not meant to wash or to clean the item, it is just a ritual for the purification of it, thus making the kitchen kasher.

*He also points out that utensils from some non-Jew are subject to immersion according to rabbinical decrees.*
Contemporary Halakhic Problems, Vol. V, Chapter XII

The Torah does indeed command that every acquired utensil must undergo immersion, but that is all, it does not determine anything else beyond that. Based on this mitzvah, the rabbis created numerous laws and rules regarding this ritual. However, if it is full of rabbinical laws or not, Yehoshua expresses no opinion in this regard, but by citing such a Torah commandment, we have yet another proof of the importance he gave even to the smallest and simplest commandments of the Law, as already stated above.

Yehoshua uses *tevilah* as an example to attack the Pharisees, who have the appearance of a righteous person but are rotten on the inside. Such criticism, unfortunately, covers all religions and creeds, for many use the mask of religion and its rules to hide one's true face. Any religion, whatever it may be, is a fertile ground for one to hide his true nature by using rules, theories, and theologies created by man, for this reason, so many of them have spread so rapidly all over the world.

The Torah is not a book that only serves to be followed, but it is a book that serves to be followed from the moment in which one has total faith in it, so that the observer can be purified from within through its teachings.

**MINT, DILL AND POMEGRANATE**
Pomegranate is a fruit widely found all over Israel, the

sages say that the pomegranate represents the Torah itself, for just as the Torah has 613 commandments, every pomegranate has 613 seeds. King Solomon had a pomegranate tree in the backyard of his palace, also the carvings on top of the Temple's columns were pomegranates, a symbol widely used within Judaism.

Dill in Hebrew is *shevet*. *Shevet* was a plant with a good economic value, it was the income of many families in Israel, as reported by the Talmud:

> *He told him: we have a type of seasoning called dill (shevet),*
> *which can be placed on cooked dishes and its fragrance*
> *diffuses. The emperor said: give us some of that.*
> Talmud of Babylon, Tractate Shabbat 119a

The mint, in this case, appears in Hebrew as (נמנע) which also means *abstention*. It is a bit obscure for Yehoshua's actual intention to use this term, but mint is still a type of grass in the field, which is directly quoted by the Torah:

> *You must separate every tenth of every*
> *herb that is sowed in the field.*
> Deuteronomy 14:22

What we should note is why Yehoshua specifically quotes these items, he could have said silver, or coins, or figs, or anything else.

> *These are those we are lenient with Demai (products from*
> *which tithes should be taken): wild fig, pomegranate,*
> *apple, white fig, sycamore fruit, mint, dill and capers.*
> Mishnah Demai 1

This passage from the Mishnah, which deals with tithing, highlights some items that require care, to make sure that the tithe has been taken. This study in this Mishnah continues in a very long way and tells the reason for each of these items to be so important and their meaning. The tithing of the pomegranate represents the 10% that must be given to God through the study of the Torah, the mint represents the 10% that must be given to God through material goods, such as money, and the dill represents the 10% that must be given to God through abstention from the pleasures of the flesh, even if they are not forbidden by the Torah, such as fasting.

Yehoshua raises an interesting theme, although he is not speaking specifically about this, he cites such items because it was a common knowledge and easily associated with tithes to God and the symbology that each one had, Torah, money and pleasures.

## CHESSED, TRUTH AND FAITH

First of all, the definition of the Hebrew word *Chessed* is necessary. This topic has already been seen in this bood, but I will place it here once again.

### Chessed, grace

In a direct translation, the word *chessed* is exactly what we have today as "grace", but the biblical grace is not the one defined by the church.

This is a very delicate subject, but of vital importance, for it is the misunderstanding of grace that drives away many of those who seek God from His true ways. The grace in the lives of many Christians serves as an excuse, because it makes faith and to serve God all very relative.

Grace, contrary to what many believe, was not something invented by the church, nor something invented by Yehoshua, rather it is an age-old concept found in the Torah itself. Let us address the main differences of the Christian grace and the biblical grace.

Contrary to what many Christians think, when they believe that grace was something that came with jesus, the Torah already had this concept many years before:

*Then he prayed, "Lord, God of my master Abraham,*
*grant me success this day and that Your kindness*
*(chessed) stays with my master Abraham.*

Genesis 24:12

*Make thy face to shine upon thy servant; save*
*me for your mercies (chessed).*

Psalm 31:16

The Hebrew word for grace is CHESSED (חסד). If we look at these two passages, one from the Torah and another from the Tanakh, we will see that the term grace appears in both, but in their respective translations we have other terms, kindness and mercy.

*Rav Ben Yehuda in the name of Rav Pinchas says: it is 613*
*mitzvot (commandments) of Hashem, His holy commandments*
*being basically two laws. 365 are negative, that by performing*
*them, we will be in sin before the One Who Is, Blessed Be He,*
*and thus we will need His CHESSED (Mercy). Other 257*
*mitzvot (commandments) are positive, that by performing*
*them, we will have His CHESSED (kindness), by which*
*we will have the favor of the One Who Is, Blessed Be He,*
*that we may live the glory of Adonai upon the Earth.*
Talmud of Babylon, tractate Brakhot 2b

According to the sages, the Talmud, the Torah and the Tanakh, grace can be understood as two things, the kindness of God and the mercy of God, both are free attributes from God and certainly no man deserves them. At the same time that the word CHESSED in Hebrew is associated with two distinct things, they also end up being close, obedience and disobedience.

When we perform a positive Torah's commandment, those that God commands us to do, then we will receive the CHESSED (kindness) from God in our lives. If, on the other hand, we carry out a negative commandment, that is, if we do what God tells us not to do and repent of such an act, we will have the CHESSED (mercy) of God in our lives. This is the true God's grace.

Grace is something totally and exclusively connected with the Word of God and His Laws, true grace does not exist without the Torah. Unlike Christian grace, biblical grace demands obedience to the Creator, demands to seek Him, demands to follow His ways and is not something relative, that exists only within the human being, but is something that goes beyond the heart of man, it becomes palpable and visible to everyone when biblical grace is given to a man. Grace has existed since the Torah was delivered. The Laws of God and grace walk and will always walk side by side, any grace that is not linked to the Word of God is a lying and manipulative grace.

### Truth

The word for "truth" in Hebrew is EMET (אמת) and is one of the few words without plural in the Hebrew language, because truth, is unique and singular, the Word of God.

### Faith

And lastly, we have faith, which is totally linked to the Word of God:

> *The Torah represents absolute faith in the Creator*
> *and the acceptance of His righteousness.*
> Talmud of Babylon, Tractate Pesachim 113b

His words make it very clear that no matter how hard we do the commandments of God, if we do not do it with our hearts, with true faith in the Creator, it's of no use.

Yehoshua has raised the greatest representations of the Torah: the kindness and the mercy of God, the only truth above all human theology and the faith in the Almighty. Those are the highest honors of the Torah. Therefore, according to Yehoshua, the Torah is worthy to be followed, that we may never forget that.

❖ ❖ ❖

# SECTION XLIV
## BLIND LEADERS

*Seeds of blind leaders, who walks in the narrow
path like a gnat and can swallow a camel.*
Matthew 23:24

*You blind guides, which strain at a gnat, and swallow a camel.*
Matthew 23:24 KJV

I placed the original translation side by side with the most common translation in English, so we can see one almost imperceptible difference. In the first part, according to the KJV, Yehoshua calls his listeners "blind guides", people who do not see and who tend to lead others in a tortuous path. In the original, however, Yehoshua does not call them "blind guides", but rather "seeds of blind leaders", that is, he attacks not his audience, but rather the sages who educated the most who were there, thus attacking not the person, but the pharisaical line of thought in which they belonged to. It may not seem a big deal, but it is interesting to understand this difference and what, according to the Jewish mentality, is the problem of having a "blind" leader.

According to Kabbalah and the book *Zohar HaKadosh*, there are 50 gates of impurities that represent extremely mundane attitudes, which take the person to lowers levels of impurities. The deepest level of this impurity is directly connected with idolatry, pagan sacrifice, and murder. The sages of the Zohar also tell that whoever reaches the 50th gate of impurity will have no return and his condemnation will be eternal.

The Zohar states that the Hebrew people, when they were in Egypt, reached the 49th portal, and for this reason the redemption and the deliverance of the Torah did not take place on those lands. In order for God to not "lose" His chosen ones, He took them out of there at the right moment.

The people of Israel have reached this level, for they had no able spiritual leaders after Yosef, the son of Yaakov, and therefore, among them remained only those who had little knowledge about God, who, according to the Zohar, were "blind leaders". This term is not a creation of this book, but the Zohar brings back this "saying" from the Jewish milieu and gave it a more mystical explanation.

The evil that a blind person (read sinful person) cause, is mystically explained by the Torah, in the book of Deuteronomy:

וירעו **אותנו** המצרים

*The Egyptians have made evil to us and oppressed us ...*

Deuteronomy 26:6a

When we read this passage, we soon understand that Egypt did very bad things to the Hebrew people, by causing great pain and suffering among the descendants of Yaakov. But this is not quite what is literally written in the Torah.

We have in the passage the term (אותנו) - *otanu* - translated as "to us". If this translation were correct, we should have the word (לנו) - *lanu* - instead of *otanu*. The meaning with the use of *otanu* changes a bit, the Torah does not say that "*the Egyptians made evil to us*", but rather "*the Egyptians have made us evil*" and that changes everything.

What the Torah is revealing here is that the Egyptians not only did evil to the people, but also made this people evil, far from God and His ways. But the question is: how did the Egyptians make the people evil? The Torah also responds. The word used in this passage translated as "evil" is (וירעו) - *yar'u* – and through the root of that word, we will have the term (רעות) which means "company", "influence".

The way that the Egyptians wronged the Hebrew people is very clear and detailed in the Torah. It was through the influence they exerted on the people that made them evil, leading them to the lowest degrees of impurities.

Returning to Yehoshua, when he calls some people "seeds of blind leaders", he claims that their masters were blind and therefore, those who hear from them, were made blind and those who were made blind, in the future, will also make their followers blind. According to the Torah, by being in the company of the "blinds", will turn the people around them also blinds, as happened to the Hebrew people while in Egypt.

This is a lesson we must take for life in relation to friendships, relationships, leaders, church, synagogue, whatever, for they will have enormous influence on whoever lies beneath their wings. Therefore, a knowledge of Torah is essential, because it is through it that we will be able to see if the place we attend to really serves God or only has an appearance of holiness.

## GNAT AND CAMELS

The difference between the two is obvious, the gnat is a tiny insect, while the camel is a huge animal. But Yehoshua, by using these terms, says that these leaders are so strict and demanding that they do not let even a gnat to pass their strictness, but on the other hand, they live a life so unrestricted that even camels can pass.

But I was struck by this comparison that Yehoshua made, of so many opposites examples that he could have used, he precisely mentioned the gnat and the camel. This reminded me of a little teaching in a Jewish compilation called *Yalkut Shimoni*:

> *The soil will be cursed because of you if you*
> *change a gnat in the Torah. And this will bring you*
> *condemnations in the size of a camel...*
>
> Yalkut Shimoni Torah 32

Well, Yehoshua first says that, those who come from schools of the blind leaders, are not only blind, but they will teach others to be blind. Then he criticizes their hypocrisy, saying that from the outside they are so restricted that they do not even let a gnat to pass, but in the inside, they are so liberal that a huge camel can pass. I see this a lot in our days, there are many pseudo-religious leaders, who have an all-orthodox pomp and anyone who sees from the outside, has the impression that they live a life in conformities with the Torah. These people end up becoming examples to those around them and they teach about the whole demand of the Jewish law in a very restricted way. But on the other hand, when problems come, especially financial or when too much power is put into their hands, they completely forget the Torah that they teach, they become greedy, selfish, and arrogant.

This is not something exclusive in Judaism, we can see in every religion, people showing reverence and restraint over religious rules, but inside they are dirty and vile, up to the point where all such restrictions become so unrestricted in their acts, that even a camel can pass through.

According to my personal interpretation, he uses these two examples, because both already had this analogy with the human behavior. This analogy is not only about restrictions and hypocrisy, but also about the size of the sin in comparison to the size of the price to be paid due to that sin. Those terms also mean that, if one changes a gnat in the Law, the price one will pay is the size of a camel, something that people do a lot.

Using a typical rabbinic language, he manages to give a more intimate message about their hypocrisy and blindness, which is nothing more than to place human laws upon the Laws of God, altering them in various ways and thus cursing the land and condemning those who listen to them.

Despite a simple teaching, when we look at Western translations that we have now a days, it is very difficult to understand the basics. And Again:

*The soil will be cursed because of you if you*
*change a gnat in the Torah. And this will bring you*
*condemnations in the size of a camel...*
Yalkut Shimoni Torah 32

# SECTION XLV
## FROM THE EAST TO THE WEST

*And Yehoshua said to them: as the lightning comes from the east*
*and is seen in the west, so will the coming of the Son of Man.*

Matthew 24:27

Nothing is by chance, chance is something that only exists in the dictionary and in people's mind. Yehoshua could have used several examples to speak that the coming of the Son of Man will be seen throughout the earth, however, as he always talks in mystery, we must mystically look at the Torah in order to understand his mystical teaching.

What struck me most was when he said that it would be like a lightning, which will come from the east in direction to the west. This idea of "from east" and "to the west" have deep connection with some things about God.

## GOD'S VOICE

*And they heard the voice of Adonai Elohim, walking*
*in the garden at the breezy time of the day; and*
*Adam and his wife hid from the presence of Adonai*
*Elohim among the trees of the garden.*

Genesis 3:8

This is a verse full of mysteries, if we do a literal translation, we shall have a very weird meaning when compared to what we are accustomed to read. I will put the literal translation and I want to be able to analyze some of the terms used.

*And they heard the voice of Adonai Elohim, withdrawing in*
*direction of the **wind of the day**, and they hid themselves,*
*the man and his wife, from before the face of Adonai*
*Elohim in the midst of the trees of the garden.*

Genesis 3:8

Although it seems like something totally meaning-less, we actually have great mysteries hidden in this passage. Unfortunately, due to translations, we lose the access to it. If we pay close attention, we have a completely new idea of what was happening, Adam and Eve did not simply hear the voice of God echoing throughout the garden, but they felt the voice of God echoing out of the garden, as if it were re-treating. I ask, is this thing that the Torah calls "voice", really a voice in the literal meaning of the word?

The verb used for movement in Hebrew is LALECHET (ללכת), but in this passage, we have the word MITCHALEKH (מתהלך) being used as the verb for movement, which is an unusual thing. The difference between one and the other is that, in the case of *mitchalekh*, the space where the move-ment happens is limited within a certain area. We can thus understand that the movement made by God's "voice" moves in a way as if it were to withdraw from a certain area where it already "dwelt".

Another interesting term is LERUACH HAYIOM (לרוח היום) - *wind of the day* - this term can only mean two things, "the direction where the sun rises, East" or "the direction where the sun sets, West." According to the Aramaic transla-tion of Onkelos, this term refers to the place where the sun sets. Then, the "voice" of God, that moved in retreat from the predetermined place where it already was, moved toward the West. If we look at the Temple of Solomon, the only thing that we have today is a wall that was part of the Tem-ple, this wall is so important because, according to the sages, the presence of God is still there, for when it left the Tem-ple, it moved toward this wall and, as this wall was the last place of the Temple that God's presence touched (because the wall was the "edge" of the sacred area of the Temple), there remained part of His presence. And this wall is exactly the WEST WALL. In short terms, the voice is nothing else than God's *Shekhinah*, His presence, which left the garden by moving towards west just as it did at the Temple.

I like to remember a story I once heard, it tells that, by the time of the evening prayer held in the Temple of Jerusalem, the inclination of the solar rays, that came from the West, when they hit the bronze columns of the Temple, the sun light reflection used to give the impression that the columns were burning like fire, remembering God's *Shekhinah* in the form of a pillar of fire while the people were in the wilderness.

Another thing that we must always remember is the standard that God acts on. God acts in cycles, the life created by God is defined into cycles in every aspect. We have nights and days, weeks, months, years, everything repeats itself. Bible stories repeat themselves, God's move always follows a pattern. Today we are underneath, tomorrow we will be on top, everything is a circle, if something ends on the left side, when it restarts, it will start again on the right side. Being more direct, if indeed God's *Shekhinah* went away towards West, I believe, that it will return from the East, as well as the sunrise and sunset.

Let's see what the scripture says about it:

*Those who were to set their tents before the tabernacle, to the east, before the tabernacle of the congregation, to the east side...*
Numbers 3:38a

*Then he led me to the gate, to the gate that faces the east.*
*And, behold, the glory of the God of Israel comes*
*from the east with a roar like a roar of many waters,*
*and the earth shone by his Presence.*
Ezekiel 43:1-2

*He brought me back to the entrance of the Temple, and, behold,*
*there came out waters under the threshold of the Temple; for*
*the Temple faces east, and the waters came from below, from*
*the right side of the Temple, from the south side of the altar.*

Ezekiel 47:1

The tabernacle and the Temple were facing east expecting the coming of the *Shekhinah*, we also have Ezekiel claiming that the *Shekhinah* of God will come from the East. That is why many sages prays toward East, for they wait the return of God's *Shekhinah*.

So, I understand that the moving direction established by God is from East to West, as well as the earth's motion around the sun. And see how cool that is, we have some passages that talk about going east, that is, in the opposite direction of the *Shekhinah's* movement of the Creator, making an allusion of going against God:

> *And when he had cast out man, he put cherubim*
> *in the east of the garden of Eden...*
>
> Genesis 3:24a

Adam was cast out of the garden toward East. When the people of Israel were taken into Babylonian exile, they also headed east. That is, when we go in the opposite direction of what God determines, it will always end up in exile, or being casted out and separated from the real blessing. This was all set by God at that very moment, so his "voice" went west and Adam's expulsion was toward east, opposite directions.

Maybe Yehoshua was making an association between the coming of the son of man with the returning of God's *Shekhinah*.

# SECTION XLVI
## ZODIAC

*At that time, after those days, the sun will darken, the moon will not give forth its light, the stars will fall from the heavens and all **hosts** (**chail**) of the heavens will tremble. And then the sign of the son of man will appear in heaven and all the families of the earth will weep and will see the son of man among the clouds of heaven with a great **host** (**chail**) and with a dreadful appearance. And he will send his angels with a trumpet and with a loud voice to gather all his chosen ones from the four winds of the heavens, from one end of heaven unto the other.*

Matthew 24:29-31

Every study that is made concerning unfulfilled prophecies, both from the Tanakh and from the New Testament, is nothing more than speculation. If we do a search on those prophetic verses, we will find millions of different interpretations, and every one of them will end up making the words of Yehoshua even more nebulous.

I believe, instead of looking at the future in pursuit of an answer to the prophecy, we better look back, at the source of it.

At that time, Yehoshua makes a quotation from the prophet Isaiah, who is dealing with a future moment. The mysticism that surrounds any prophecy found in the Tanakh makes its interpretation only possible when the prophesied fact has already occurred. For this reason, getting into that subject is very difficult.

However, something caught my attention in the Isaiah´s verses quoted by Yehoshua. This prophecy from Isaiah served as a base for the old kabbalistic rabbinical segment to testify the concept of the existence of the zodiac and how it influences the man's life.

First of all, I would like to make clear that I am not an astrologer, I am not interested in this subject and for this reason, I know just a little of it. This little I know, comes from teachings and conceptions formed by the rabbis. Such ideas may differ a little, or a lot, from the Western modern astrology, those found on the internet or in books that address this theme.

## THE JEWISH ZODIAC

The sages say that the conception of the zodiac, which exerts influence on the behavioral character of the human being, was developed by the Jews through revelations of the secrets found in the book of Genesis. Such revelations are known as *Sefer Yetsirah* and although it has never been written, it is the fifth oldest "book" of the Jews.

Throughout the Tanakh we find descriptions of how God imposes His power and His divine will in our world through celestial bodies, causing a strong influence on man's behavior. Such a concept, within Judaism, is not just a way of knowing ourselves, as astrologers do, but it is a knowledge about obstacles that man must overcome. For through the observance of the Torah we will be plugged with the supernatural, with the true divine will, which will help us to overcome the influences of the astrological forces.

Just as there are 12 signs defined by Judaism, there are 12 yearly months, 12 roots of the soul, 12 tribes of Israel, and so on. The sign indicates a force and characteristics hidden within each individual that must be overcome and not accepted.

## THE ZODIAC IN THE PROPHECIES

Now I can bring the passage of Isaiah mentioned by Yehoshua and we will see that it has a very bizarre term.

כי כוכבי השמים ו**כסיל**יהם לא יהלו אורם חשך
השמש בצאתו וירח לא יגיה אורו
*The stars and the **constellations** of the heavens shall*

*not give their light, the sun will darken when it rises*
*and the moon shall not diffuse its brightness.*

Isaiah 13:10

Yehoshua quotes the Isaiah's prophecy almost in its entirety, except for a term added by him, translated as "hosts" in verses 29 and 30 (see above). The added word CHAIL (חיל) has some meanings, such as "strength", "hosts", "a strength holding something united". However, its meaning in Aramaic is the collective noun for stars, in other words, it means "constellation", which leads us to understand that, like Isaiah, Yehoshua is also speaking of something mysterious.

In the verse from Isaiah, the word translated as "constellations", in Hebrew, is KSILIM (כסילים), plural of KSIL (כסיל) and not CHAIL (חיל) as used by Yehoshua.

KSIL does not mean "constellation", but it is the name of a specific star, located in the South Pole. This star is known as *"the sign that the camels will die"*, because it only becomes visible in the northern hemisphere during summer, when camels are exposed to extreme high temperatures and die from the heat.

As in the verse of Isaiah, names of stars associated with constellations are mentioned three other times by the Tanakh:

*The stars and **Ksilim** of the heavens shall not give*
*their light, the sun will darken when it rises and*
*the moon shall not diffuse its brightness.*

Isaiah 13:10

*The one who made **Kimah** and **Ksil**. He who transforms*
*the deepest darkness into dawn and the dark day into*
*night. He who invokes the waters of the seas and pours*
*them over the earth - His name is Adonai.*

Amos 5:8

*The one who made **AS, Ksil, Kimah** and **Chadrei Teman.***
Job 9:9

*Can you tie strings on the **Kimah** or undo the realms of **Ksil?***
Job 38:31

In these four mentions, there are four strange names that have been translated at random because the translators did not know their true meanings, these terms are: *Ksil, Kimah, AS* and *Chadrei Teman.*

These hidden terms can only be understood through the mystique and astrological knowledge of the ancient sages. The associations they have with the zodiac reveal deep things:

**STARS AND SIGNS**

**KSIL**

*Ksil* is a star in the heart of the constellation of *Scorpio*, equinoctial point of South. For a long time, the constellation of *Libra* was considered as being part of the constellation of *Scorpio,* as it's central area. According to the great Kabbalistic, rabbi Ibn Ezra, *Ksil* used to be the star at the heart of Scorpio, representing the center of this constellation and now it belongs to the constellation of Libra.

**LIBRA (month: TISHREI)** - The Libra period is the most delicate, it is the time that has two important appointed times, the Rosh Hashanah (new year) and ten days later, the Yom Kippur (day of forgiveness). Our sages teach that these ten days between one feast and another is precisely the time when the heavens will be opened, so that we may reflect upon our sins and ask for real forgiveness for them, when the day of Yom Kippur comes, God will give the sentence. For this reason, the symbol of this sign is a scale.

## AS

Close to Ursa Major, in North Pole. *AS* can be understood as a star called *"eta geminorum"* and is close to the constellation of *Taurus*. Its most exact position places *AS* within the constellation represented by the sign of *Gemini*, which can be seen from both hemispheres.

**GEMINI (month: SIVAN)** - This is the month considered the month that represents the learning to walk on the paths of the Torah. In this period, we have the celebration of the feast of Shavuot. The symbol of the "twins" is given by the two tablets of the law, for it was at this time that the Torah was delivered at Sinai.

## KIMAH

Star also known as *Ari*, equinoctial point North. This star is located within a constellation called by the name of Aries.

**ARIES (month: NISSAN)** - The first month of the Jewish calendar and during this period we have the Passover celebration. God defined this month as the first month of months (Ex. 12:2) and by that fact, it became the first sign of the zodiac. Its symbol is a lamb, a symbol which is the representation of Passover itself (Ex. 12:3-5).

## CHADREI TEMAN

A star also known as *Spica*, South Pole. The most important star within the constellation of Virgo.

**VIRGO (month: ELUL)** - The time before Libra, in which our sentence will be given. So in this period, we should behave humbly and innocently to prepare ourselves for the day of forgiveness. The symbol of a virgin represents just that, purity and innocence before the Creator.

This idea is shown by King Solomon himself, when he wrote - *ani ledodi Vedodi li* - giving the name of the month of

*Elul* (אלול), seeing by the first letter of each word in this verse:

אני **ל**דודי **ו**לדודי **ל**י

*I am my beloved's and my beloved is for me.*

Song of Songs 6:3

In this preparatory time is when we should have a life totally devoted to God, so He will be for us.

## KSIL AND YOM KIPPUR

Yom Kippur is the most important appointed time of the Torah, it is an ordinance represented by the sacrifices that were taken to the Temple. The star of *Ksil* has a symbology associated with Yom Kippur, as it is part of the constellation which is represented by a scale, thus making a reference to the day of God's judgment.

The word *Ksil* appears in another place in the Torah, but this time not as a star or constellation, but in reference to the *korban*, to the sacrifice:

*The two kidneys and the fat that are upon them, that is the loins (**Ksilim**); and the protuberance on the liver, which he shall remove with the kidneys.*

Leviticus 3:4

In this passage we have the association of *Ksil* with the sacrifice to be taken to the Temple, remembering that these Torah's rules were used in both Pessach and in Yom Kippur.

## SOME CARES

The Jewish zodiac is very different from the one practiced by modern mysticism. Care is very important, because it is like a double-edged sword, as it may be interesting to get to know more about the man's character definitions they represent, which may be accurate to a certain extent, the use them to forecast the future, such as astral map or even to know how the day will be like, is divination, something forbidden by the Torah.

The intention of this study is not to explain how this prophecy will be fulfilled, because if anyone explains it, one will be doing nothing but speculation. Only those who will witness it, will know how it will be fulfilled. But it is interesting how Yehoshua's mystical teaching develops and how his teachings are connected with the Jewish mysticism.

No one truly knows about the end of days, only God knows. However, there is something we can learn from it. Yehoshua first quotes a prophecy that talks about *KSIL*, a star that is part of the constellation of Libra and then, he claims that angels will come blowing trumpets, blowing the *shofar*. The most important appointed time that is found within the Libra's period, and when the *shofar* is blown, is precisely the Rosh Hashanah and the ten days period before the Yom Kippur. Perhaps, this is a hint of the time of year that all of this will take place, for the end times that Yehoshua refers to, is nothing more than the day of God's judgment.

## THE SIGN OF YEHOSHUA BIN NUN

As mentioned earlier, knowledge regarding the signs serves only to know how not to be doomed by the stars definition on us. The rabbis teach that, by observing the Torah and consequently obtaining a high spiritual level, we will no longer be subjugated to the constellations, nor to fate and nor to chance. We will not be people who get born, grow and die, but we will be people greatly used by God, contrary to everything that the human being determines as "natural".

A good example of this is Joshua Ben Nun and the way Moses instructed him on how to select some men to go with him to war:

> *Moses said to Joshua, "Choose for us some men and go out and fight against Amalek. Tomorrow I will be at the top of the hill, with the rod of Adonai in my hands.*

Exodus 17:9

*"Choose for us some men". Moses was referring to men*
*born in the second month of Adar, for people born*
*this month were not afraid of sorcerers and witches.*
*Such persons were not influenced by negative forces*
*of the twelve constellations of the zodiac.*

Chizkuni, Exodus 17:9:1

Here is a very strange comment on this passage from Exodus. Chizkuni claims that Moses wanted men born in the second month of Adar, because they would not be influenced by the zodiac nor by fear of witchcraft.

The Jewish calendar, unlike the Western calendar, is not solar but rather lunar. The day begins and ends as the moon appears and disappears in the sky, which causes a mismatch with the months of the solar calendar, for the lunar months have twenty-nine and a half days. For this to be corrected, a month called Second Adar, which would be the thirteenth month, is added to the annual calendar every three years. A month in which, as claim the sages, Joshua was born.

Because there are only twelve signs, those born in the month of Second Adar are not under any of kind of influence from the zodiac and so are brave men, for their spirits are not under astrological determinations. So must be those, who were not born in this month, to achieve the prowess by following God's will as Joshua was and to be changed and elevated by that.

This is the reason why zodiac was taken into consideration, so that, through God's Laws, every men may free himself from a pre-destined life.

## SECTION XLVII
### THE RAPTOR ACCORDING TO YEHOSHUA

Rapture is an eschatological concept created by Christianity to define how the end of those, who accept this faith, will be. According to this idea, jesus would come from the heavens to gather the church in order to take the Christians out of this earthly reality. The church would go with him to some sort of heavenly Jerusalem, where everything is perfect. There would be the new dwelling place of the church, alongside with its jesus.

Meanwhile, on earth, tribulation would occur, where the anti-christ would bring suffering to those who did not accept jesus as savior, especially to the Jews. After seven years, jesus would return to earth to bring judgment upon the wicked people here and condemn satan.

There are many passages that served as basis for the formation of this theological idea, but just as it was possible to develop this concept through them, it is also possible to refute this concept using the same passages, since they are verses out of context, interpreted by minds that little know about the true faith of those who wrote those verses.

Anyways. Yehoshua speaks a few things about this great moment and for what it seems to me, it actually does not agree with this Christian concept.

*And Yeshua said to his talmidim: as in the days of*
*Noach, so it will be in the days of the Son of man.*
*Before the flood, they ate and drank, were fruitful and*
*multiplied until the day that Noach entered the ark.*
*And they did not know until the flood came upon them and took*
*away the **non-Tzadikim**, so will be the coming of the Son of Man.*
*If there are two ploughing a field, the one who is **Tzadik***
*will stay and the one who is evil will be taken away.*
*Two women are working on a mill, one will be taken and*

*the other left. This is because the angels, at the end of*
*the world, will take the stumbling blocks away from the*
*world, and will separate the good from the evil.*

Matthew 24:37-41

*This is the genealogy of Noach, Noach a **tzadik** man; for*
*he was blameless in his day; Noach walked with God.*

Genesis 6:9

*God said to Noach, I have decided to put an end to*
*all flesh, for the world is full of iniquities because*
*of it, I will destroy it with the earth.*

Genesis 6:13

**TZADIK (TZADIKIM, plural)** - Hebrew word usually translated into English as "righteous". Such a term is widely used throughout the Tanakh in reference to the person who follows the Torah and observes the God's will. The more time given to the understanding and the observance of the Laws of God, according to the Creator Himself, a greater **Tzadik** will that person be.

I have heard many explanations and studies regarding what the church calls as rapture. Despite small differences regarding some statements in those theological studies, the summary is that jesus will come out of the blue, will get the church and will take it to live in a Jerusalem that is somewhere in space.

But what makes me most indignant is how such a theology, which is clearly against the words of the one who was supposed to come to take them, can stand so strongly in the minds of millions of Christians. I do not think we need to do a very deep analysis of what is written to see that.

Yehoshua uses the story of Noach as an example. Although the church interpreted this teaching as a comparison between the days of Noach and the present day, it was not quite what Yeshohua meant. Noach lived in an age when iniquity and sin prevailed, God resolved to destroy everything and to start over, then He sends a flood **to take away** those who live in sin. On the other hand, Noach, the **Tzadik**, remained alive and continued on this earth, for he was a person who followed the Laws of God.

In the same way, Yehoshua affirms that it will be so in the days of the Son of Man, which is nothing more than another term referring to the end of time. Those who **will be taken** will be the **sinners** and the **tzadikim** will stay, something totally contrary to the idea of the Christian rapture. Yehoshua speaks this in a very clear and direct way.

The last verse has a huge difference from the Western translations, Yehoshua says that the *"stumbling blocks"* will be taken away in order to separate the good from the evil. A simple and straightforward teaching. I do not understand how the theology of rapture holds up against the words of Yehoshua, who, by the way, supposed to be the main character of this theory. Besides all of this, is God going to take someone to live in heaven? Is that what the bible truly claims?

### To Dwell in Heaven

I would like to approach on this Christian concept of "dwelling in heaven", and for that matter, let's look at some verses from the Tanakh and from the new testament:

*There are many abodes where my Father lives, and I will prepare them for your arrival. When everything is ready, then I will come to take you, so that you can always be with me wherever I am. If it were not so, I myself would have told you plainly.*

John 14:2

This is the golden Christian text to defend the doctrine of "dwelling in heaven". But there are two things that we must take into consideration when analyzing this passage. These words were spoken by Yehoshua himself to his followers, if the mission of Mashiach is to reign on this earth for a thousand years, having his government established in Jerusalem and if there is a promise that he and his followers will be together, it becomes somewhat obvious that No follower of his will dwell in heaven, but in this earth under his rule. For how can he be on earth and his followers in heaven? It makes no sense.

Another thing to note is the reason why Yehoshua had used these words as a form of comfort to his disciples. Every time he used the expression "my Father's house", he did not refer to heaven, but to the Temple in Jerusalem and this is made clear in innumerable Scripture's passages. When Yehoshua says that " *There are many abodes where my Father lives*", he addresses an ancient desire of the Jewish People to dwell in the Temple of God:

> *One thing I have asked of the Lord, and I will seek it, that I may dwell in the house of the Lord all the days of my life, to behold the beauty of the Lord, and to dwell in His Temple.*
>
> Psalms 27:4

The comfort that Yehoshua brings through these words is precisely the possibility to those who follow God, of dwelling in the Temple, in other words, in the New Jerusalem, for it is the place where the Temple will be rebuilt. Once in new Jerusalem, saved will be.

The concept of "dwelling in heaven" was not born in Christianity, it comes from much older cultures such as Nimrod for example, who built a tower so that he could reach the heavens and dwell there. This necessity of dwelling in heaven, that exists within the human being, kind suppresses a certain disregard for the situation of life in this earthly realm, for how better would dwelling in heaven be? It is certainly the solution of all the problems present here. However, people who seek this, forget that the mission of the man, who serves God, is to perfect this world, by establishing in it the Kingdom of God through his obedience to

His commandments. God's plan was never to take man out of the earth in order to place him somewhere else, for the earth was created by God thinking of man.

Here are some other passages about this topic:

> *The heavens are the heavens of the Lord; but the earth was given to the sons of men.*
> Psalm 115:16

> *The **Tzadikim** will inherit the earth and dwell therein forever.*
> Psalm 37:29

> *And I will bring forth seed unto Jacob, and to Judah an heir that will posses my hills; and my chosen ones shall inherit the land, and my servants shall dwell there.*
> Isaiah 65:9

We have to be very careful about some concepts rooted in our religious upbringing, not because we've heard them all our lives, it means they are the true. If in this, case the rapture theory was correct, the Psalms would be a lie, everything would be a lie, the Torah, the Tanakh, the teachings of Yehoshua, the prophets, everything.

## "RAPTURE" ACCORDING TO JUDAISM

Every time the new testament dealt with the subject of "rapture", it was indeed a very old concept within the Jewish faith, a concept that was somehow misinterpreted by the church. This concept that we shall see, makes all the difference, for it is upon it that Yehoshua was basing his teaching, it is in it that all of his talmidim believed and it is upon it that the book of Revelation was written.

> *Purity leads to separation, separation leads to holiness, holiness leads to modesty, modesty leads to fear of sin, fear of sin leads to pity and pity leads to the Holy Spirit. The Holy Spirit leads to resurrection and resurrection will begin when Elijah comes, of blessed memory, Amen.*

Mishnah Sotah 9:15

This *mishnah* shows how one's behavior leads to the Holy Spirit, the Holy Spirit leads to resurrection and the resurrection will begin when Elijah comes, as Elijah is the precursor of Mashiach, it means that the resurrection will occur in the Messianic era.

*HaKadosh Baruch Hu, as a punishment for Adam having eaten of the fruit of the tree, declared that every man should pass through death until when Mashiach comes and the resurrection of the dead occurs.*
Rav Moshe Feinstein, Choshen Mishpat II 73 32

This phenomenon is nothing more than the resurrection of the dead, according to the Jewish faith, when Mashiach comes to judge the nations, all the dead will return to be judged. They will meet Mashiach in the heavens, for they will receive the sentence before than the living and those who are considered tzadikim, will be resurrected and will dwell in this earth with Mashiach. Then Mashiach will judge the living, the wicked will be cast out, and the Tzadikim will receive the same physical form as those who have risen again and everyone will reign with Mashiach for a thousand years.

*These will have no place in the world to come: Those who say that the resurrection of the dead is not from the Torah.*
Mishnah Sanhedrin 10:1

Making an approach on concepts is never an easy task, especially when they are connected with people's faith. Unfortunately, every human being has the habit of following the easiest way, it is much easier to learn by listening than by studying. We all have a tendency to go into places where the word of God is taught, we hear the message and for some reason, we end up accepting this interpretation we just heard as absolute truth, especially when we hear the same thing for years.

Some concepts must be undone, especially when they are against the bible. Look at Yehoshua's own teachings, what else did he do? He was refuting many of the teachings, customs, theologies and theories of the Jewish faith, that were against the bible.

Imagine if Yehoshua would come today as a Christian, would he not be against this bunch of theological ideas created by men? Would he not be against this plethora of priests, reverend, and pastors, who cling to the church more than to the Bible? All of those problems that Yehoshua had with the Pharisees of his time are just the same problems he would have with Christianity today. Today's hypocrites Pharisees are the priests, the pastors, and all community leaders who teach the abolition of the Torah, replacement theology, dispensation theology, and everything created by a misinterpretation of the Bible. It's always good to think about that.

# SECTION XLVIII
## PESSACH

*Do you not know that in two days will be Pessach, and the son of man will be delivered into the hands of the Jews to be hanged?*
Matthew 26:2

Pessach is a biblical feast that represents the departure of the People of Israel from Egypt as reported in the book of Exodus. There is a lot of confusion between Pessach and Easter, for they supposed to be the same thing, but Easter is nothing related to the Biblical Pessach. The celebration of Pessach is so important and intrinsic into the Jewish people that, according to a survey in Israel, 98% of the population celebrates Pessach in some way, both Jews and non-Jews that reside in this country.

The roots that the Pessach has, are very deep, it is a time of celebration of the exit from the "house of slavery", "the end of the yoke" and "freedom". Everything around it's celebration is symbolic and always related to the Torah, from the ten plagues that devastated Egypt until the crossing of the sea of reeds by the People of Israel.

*Adonai said to Moses and Aharon in the land of Egypt. This month should be for you the beginning of the months. It must be the first of the months of the year for you. Speak to every community of Israel and say that on the tenth of this month, each one should take one lamb per family, one lamb per household.*
Exodus 12:1-3

The redemption of Egypt and the delivery of the Torah established the identity of the People of Israel as "servants of Adonai" and not "servants of servants." A great sage, named Maharal of Prague, explained in his lectures that, the departure from Egypt transformed the nature of the People of Israel and this transformation is reaffirmed in every Pessach. Despite the many achievements and enslavement that the People of Israel has passed through, the nature of free men they possess, has never been altered.

Pessach, more than an act of liberation, represents the nature of a free people in order to serve the True God, for God sets free His people from Egypt every single day. The miracle of Pessach is not a celebration of something that happened, but it is a celebration of something that constantly happens in our lives.

In the time of Yehoshua, the Passover celebration, with all its Jewish customs, was already very popular and well established. Flavius Josefvs estimated that in the Pessach of the year 29 CE, which is very likely to be the same year that Yehoshua entered Jerusalem to celebrate the feast, there were more than three million people in the city in order to celebrate Pessach. The Talmud also reports an interesting fact about this year.

*The sages teach that King Agrippa wanted to set his eyes on the multitude of Israel. He told the high priest to keep an eye on the Passover lambs and to count how many animals would be brought. The high priest made the account through the pairs of kidneys before they were burned and counted six million kidneys, as each animal has two kidneys, the population there was three million people, double the number of those who left Egypt.*
Talmud of Babylon, Tractate Pesachim 64b

Yehoshua enters Jerusalem in this same time for the observance of this feast. The famous holy supper was not a supper, but rather a *"Passover seder"* (Passover Jewish celebration), the famous bread that represented his body, wasn't a bread, but a *matzah*, the reunion of Yehoshua with his talmidim did not was a farewell occasion before his death, but rather an observance of a Torah commandment.

Therefore, I think it is important a few clarification

regarding some terms and customs described in the book of Matthew.

## SEDER SHEL PESSACH

*And on the first day of the Feast of Unleavened Bread came the talmidim of Yeshua, saying, Where should we prepare the place for the SEDER of PESSACH?*

Matthew 26:17

The *Seder Shel Pessach* (Pesach celebration) is the established form for the celebration of this feast. For centuries, this celebration had no defined rules regarding what was to be done on that day, until King Josiah instituted the reforms, as reported in 2 Kings 23, and determined how the celebration should be held, the Seder, as we know it today, began to be developed. During the second Temple, the way the feast was observed was already well defined and regulated, both by the Oral Torah and by the rabbinic schools. Yehoshua irrefutably follows these rules as we shall see later.

The *seder* is too long to be described, but it determines the types of symbolic foods that must be eaten, interspersed with the reading of the passages where these symbologies lie. During the Seder, a book called *Hagadah Shel Pessach* is also read.

The *Hagadah* is a book that was introduced by the great assembly almost two thousand five hundred years ago and it tells the story of the departure from Egypt and all the miracles, some psalms and songs to be recited during the feast and it also determines the order that each food should be eaten with its symbolic representation.

In this passage, Yehoshua's talmidim question him where he would like to perform the Seder Shel Pessach. Certainly, in addition to what was reported in the book of Matthew, they sang the Psalms, blessed God, read the Hagadah, ate the symbolic foods and studied the book of Exodus. No one ate a chocolate egg there.

## FOODS OF PESSACH

*And he answered to them: he who shall dip the Karpas in the salted water with me, is the one who passes the information on me. And no one could recognize him, for if they had recognized him, they would have destroyed him.*

Matthew 26:23

The symbolic foods that are eaten in a *Seder Shel Pessach* are: *Matzah* (unleavened bread), *Maror* (bitter herb), *Charosset* (mashed apple with walnuts), *Zeroah* (bone-in meat), *Beitzah* (boiled egg) and *Karpas* (boiled vegetable). In the center of the table is placed a bowl with salted water that is used to dip the *Karpas*.

The salted water symbolizes the tears shed by the People of Israel in their years of slavery, a symbol of sadness.

Among so many ways to prove who the traitor was, Yehoshua decides to use specifically the salted water, perhaps to show his sadness and his cry for being betrayed.

## MATZAH

*As they ate, Yeshua took the MATZAH, blessed God and departed it, handing it to the talmidim and said: take and eat, this is my body.*

Matthew 26:26

Matzah is a type of unleavened bread, more like a biscuit, and it is produced under strict rabbinic supervision. This type of bread is consumed during Pessach in observance of a Torah commandment:

*Seven days thou shalt eat unleavened bread, because thou hast come out of Egypt, that it may be remembered in the day of thy coming out of the land of Egypt, all the days of thy life.*

Deuteronomy 16:3

We see here a very strict Torah observance by Yehoshua, for the author of Matthew does not affirm that he ate bread, for if that were so, he would be breaking a commandment of the Torah, but Matthew makes clear that Yehoshua ate *matzah*, as ordained by God. Such a comparison may be interesting, the new testament states that Yehoshua became the perfect lamb because no sin was found on him, the yeast is biblically associated with sin, as *matzah* has no yeast, it would be "a sinless bread", so it fits with his words when he said that the *matzah* "is his body".

To finish about Pessach, I want to leave a teaching from Rabbi Gamliel, the Rabbi of Paul of Tarsus.

*Rabbi Gamliei used to say: anyone who does not mention these three things on a Passover has not fulfilled his obligation, and they are the sacrifice of Pessach, the matzah and the bitter herbs. The sacrifice, for the Omnipresent passed over the houses of the People of Israel. Matzah, for the people were redeemed from slavery and bitter herbs, for God delivered them from the bitterness of the Egyptians. We are bound to thank, pray, praise, glorify, exalt, magnify, bless, and worship HIM who does all these miracles. It brings us from bondage to freedom, from sorrow to joy, from darkness to light, from bondage to redemption. That is why we must say before Him, Halleluyah!*
Mishnah Pesachim 10

Interesting thing, the same three things that must be mentioned on a Pessach, are mentioned by the author of Matthew in his book, matzah, bitter herb and the sacrifice of pessach. Did this happen by chance.

## SECTION XLIX
### THE NEW COVENANT

*And he took the cup, and gave thanks unto his Father, and*
*gave unto them, saying, drink from this, all of you.*
*This is my blood, and **the new part of the covenant**, which*
*shall be poured out upon many for the justification of sins.*
Matthew 26:27-28

According to the church, we are no longer under the Law, but under grace. The covenant made with Moses fulfilled its role and thus lost its purpose, being replaced by a higher covenant through the ministry of jesus. Under this new covenant, we have salvation as a free gift, that is, without having to obtain any merit before God, our only responsibility is to have faith. Through the Holy Spirit we share the heritage of christ and his laws have become superior to the Laws of the ancient people of God, who lost their position by not accepting and killing christ.

All of this theological nonsense is based on an anti-Semitic interpretation of some fathers of the church and sadly, this theology became as an absolute "truth" in all Christian strands. Yehoshua does not speak of "a new covenant", but rather he speaks of the "NEW PART OF THE COVENANT," for a covenant, specially those made by God, cannot be broken or replaced.

Knowing the birth place of this theology is important for the understanding of these words of Yehoshua:

*Behold, the days are coming, said Adonai, that I will make a new*
*covenant with the house of Israel, and with the house of Judah.*
*Not according to the covenant that I made with their fathers,*
*in the day that I took them by the hand, to bring them out*
*of the land of Egypt; because they have broken my covenant*
*even though I have married them, says the Lord.*

> *But this is the covenant that I will make with the house*
> *of Israel after those days, said the Lord: I will put my*
> *law within them, and write it in their heart; and I*
> *will be their God, and they shall be my people.*
> Jeremiah 31:30-32

This is God's promise about the "new covenant" that serves as one of the main foundations for the formation of this Christian theory. In order for us to not fall into theological sophistry anymore, let us examine this passage very carefully.

**1)**

Something very important in the Bible is about the "differentiation" that it teaches. On one side we have the house of Israel, blood descendants of Abraham. On the other side, the Gentiles, who approach God and enter the People of Israel, even though the two groups are part of the same people, within that people, there are and will always be a differentiation between them, each one with different goals and responsibilities inside this People, one not being better than the other one.

God, by making this promise through the prophet Jeremiah, makes it very clear that this "new covenant" would be made with the house of Israel and with the house of Judah, and NOT with the Gentiles directly, not with the church and not even a little bit with anyone who is not part of the People of Israel. In other words, if a Gentile wants to be part of this "new covenant", he must first be grafted onto the olive tree according to Romans 11, it is imperative that he joins the People of Israel (I do not mean Judaism) and be part of the House of Israel, and then, he will be included in this promise.

**2)**

God states that the covenant was broken, but by the People of Israel only, because they did not obey Him. God, by no chance, says that He has invalidated or will invalidate the covenant. Although they have broken the covenant, God marries his people and this is eternal. I doubt that God, by being married to the People of Israel, will have some other bride.

**3)**

This passage holds hand with Ezekiel 36, where the prophet says that the coming of the Holy Spirit will be to place the Torah inside the heart of the people of God.

I am sick of hearing that following the Laws of God is placing oneself under a burden, for the Torah is a very painful thing to follow. Actually, the Law reveals what is wrong within us, if a particular law is difficult to follow, it means that it directly affects a side of us that must be fixed.

We must be aware that the real function of the Holy Spirit is precisely to make possible this new covenant, and this new covenant is to place what is determined by the Torah inside of each one of His people, so the Law will be followed naturally, ceasing to be a yoke and becoming a pleasure. In this way, the Holy Spirit will transform our inner thoughts and attitudes totally in accordance with what God wants from us.

The death of Yehoshua assured the Gentiles the knowledge about the Torah and the possibility to be engrafted unto the People of Israel and then, only then, making them heirs of the promise of the new covenant.

Before I finish, I will bring the same passage from Jeremiah 31, but in Hebrew, and so we shall see some differences that were lost with the terrible translation that we have nowadays:

נתתי את תורתי בקרבם ועל לבם אכתבנה
והייתי להם לאלהים והמה יהיו לי לעם

Jeremiah 31:33b

407

I gave - נתתי
My TORAH- את תורתי
Next to them - בקרבם
And above their heart - ועל לבם
I'll write it down - אכתבנה
And I will be to them by God - והייתי להם לאלהים
And he will be to me by people - והמה יהיו לי לעם

There is the passage in its original with the translation of each word, which makes it even clearer that the new covenant that God promises is to have the Torah within the heart, making it something natural within our daily life and behavior, thus forming the true People of Israel. People who are open to the Gentiles thanks to the sacrifice of Yehoshua.

This understanding differs greatly from the common Christian mentality, which preaches only faith. Faith is something totally relative by itself, that is why faith without works is dead, not works that are done in a temple, but rather works of the Laws of God, the Torah.

Being part of the new covenant is the possibility for a Gentile to enter the People of Israel through the Torah, which came to him thanks to the death of Yehoshua.

## JUSTIFIED

We have a huge problem here, many claim that no one is justified by the works of the law, this led many to the understanding that the Word of God, i.e. the Torah, does not justify man and so it was abolished from the life of the Christian. Perhaps in that case, such a statement is right, but perhaps not right in a way we imagine it to be.

To understand what it means to be "justified" I would like to propose two passages from the Torah:

*If there be contention among some, and they come to be judged, the innocent shall be justified, and the guilty shall be condemned.*
Deuteronomy 25:1

*A single witness shall not rise against any person for
any kind of iniquity, or for any kind of sin, whatever
the committed sin would be; by the mouth of two or
three witnesses the fact will be established.*

Deuteronomy 19:15

According to the Torah, in order for someone to be brought to trial and condemned, at least two witnesses were required to prove one's sin, if only one were present, the charged person would be acquitted and justified.

Let's imagine the following situation, Dany Boy kills a person in Israel and such fact is seen by a person. When he was brought before the judge, because there was only one witness, he is acquitted, that is, Dany Boy is justified, even though he committed the crime and was guilty. So, what the Torah defines as "being justified" is when someone, even though he committed a sin, is declared innocent and free from punishment even without merit.

Now, we must understand something else that is usually confused with "being justified", which is "being sanctified". According to the Torah, to be holy and to sanctify oneself, is to follow the Laws contained therein, as God himself says:

*Therefore sanctify yourselves, and be holy,
for I am Adonai your God.
And keep my statutes and fulfilled them. I
am Adonai who sanctifies you.*

Leviticus 20:7-8

*Sanctification* and *justification* are completely different things, and none of them abolishes the Torah, quite the contrary.

## SECTION L
### THE IGNORANTS

*Behold, one of those who were with Yeshua stretched
out his hand, drew his own sword, and attacked
one of the priests, cutting off his ear.*
Matthew 26:51

There are some things that, no matter how hard I try,
I cannot understand. Many of the Christian teachings and
commentaries, especially those from Catholic priests, treat
Yehoshua's students in a very pejorative way, every time
I read them, they give me the impression that they were
ignorant people, who could not read nor write, with a little
notion about life and no clue about the Torah and the Jewish traditions. By knowing Jesus, they learned about God, received the Holy Spirit and became prodigal, for that reason
they have earned the right to become saints and worthy of
worship.

But Catholic theology aside, none of Yehoshua's
talmidim was ignorant, although a good part of the population did not know how to read, they knew the Torah and the
Oral Torah very well, because the method of learning was
the memorization of what was taught orally. Even a fishermen was an expert about the culture of his people and things
related to his God.

The proof of this comes from the verse above, for cutting the priest's ear was not accidental.

*Moses then brought forward the sons of Aharon and put
some of the blood on the tip of their right ears...*
Leviticus 8:24a

*No man among the descendants of Aharon, the
priest who has a physical defect shall be qualified
to offer the Adonai's offering by fire.*

Leviticus 21:21

*This ordinance is intended to include all those who have other physical defects that were not included in verse 18.*
Rashi, Leviticus 21:21:1

*Rava says: Why did the Merciful One have to write that physical defects would cause disqualification from the Temple services if such defects appear in a priest? For a defect would also disqualify an animal for sacrifice.*
Talmud of Babylon, Tractate Bekhorot 43a

Well, if we make a connection between these three passages, we will see that the priests were anointed in their ears, in some chapters later, God forbade any priest to render any service in the Temple if he had any physical defects.

Rashi then explains verse 21, which in addition to the defects reported in verses 18 to 20, 21 includes all others defects that were not listed therein, and finally, the Oral Torah teaches that the defect is not the one the person has before becoming a priest, but if that defect appears during his years of service, that priest must be disqualified.

This person, who is identified as Peter elsewhere, knew very well where to attack the priest. The position of this man, who had his ear cut off, was as assistant to the high priest, which used to bring him enormous prestige among the community. The loss of his ear would cause him an instant disqualification and a huge humiliation that could be even worse than death.

An ignorant fisherman, without study and without knowledge, could never know this and be so precise in his action. None who followed Yehoshua, or any other rabbi, were ignorant concerning the Laws of God, they knew and observed the Torah very well.

# SECTION LI
## TWO WITNESSES

*But they have not found even one, even though they*
*have provided many false witnesses against Yeshua.*
*Finally two false witnesses presented themselves.*
Matthew 26:60

Matthew reports that two witnesses were arranged for the judgment of Yehoshua, for, according to the Torah, no man can be put to death if there are not at least two witnesses.

*A person shall be put to death only on the testimony*
*from the mouth of two or three witnesses, one must not*
*be put to death on the testimony of one witness.*
Deuteronomy 17:6

*Rabbi Shimon witnessed a man chasing his friend to the*
*ruins. He ran after him and found his friend dead, while*
*the pursuer was close to the body holding a sword full of*
*blood. Rabbi Shimon said, "O wicked man, who killed this*
*man? Either it was me or it was you. But what can I do? Your*
*blood was not delivered into my hands, because the Torah*
*says: 'Based on two witnesses, he will be put to death.'"*
Talmud of Babylon, Tractate Sanhedrin 37b

The book of Matthew, just as the whole New Testament, has a very strong connection with the Tanakh and the Talmud. The interpretation of these books without prior preparation, led to the creation of countless different religion sects and Christian's branches based on a misunderstanding of the teachings of Jesus and Paul.

Here, we see that the author of the book of Matthew makes a report concerning the need for two witnesses during Yehoshua's judgment, this shows the connection that he had with the Torah's commandments. But the interesting thing here is not the connection he makes with the Torah, but rather with the *halachah*, that is, the Jewish law. It was through the *halachah* that the author of the book of Matthew was able to classify the witnesses as "false witnesses", and that was what made me more curious on the account of the judgment of Yehoshua, because the author of Matthew did not present clear evidences concerning this accusation.

So, how did the author of the book of Matthew came to the conclusion that these witnesses were indeed "false", since Yehoshua had a public life, he was seen and heard by all? Anyone who did not agree with him could be a witness, without necessarily being a "false" witness, for although this someone testifies against Yehoshua in a partial way, he testifies something he has seen and heard, thus not being a "false witness".

Although Yehoshua had only declared that the Temple would be destroyed and the witnesses said that he would destroy it, according to the Torah, the witnesses would not be "false" (עד חמס), but rather "vain" (עד שוא). The Torah has two terms to refer to witnesses that are invalid. The "vain", are those who lie or distort the facts and the "false", are those who do not have the minimum requirements to testify. In Matthew's case, the author calls them as "false", that is, he does not refer to the incoherent statements of these witnesses as reported in chapter 26, but to other things.

To clarify what happened at that time, an understanding of some *halachah's* rules is needed.

Within *halachah*, there are several rules that concern capital punishment. The purpose of these rules, which were created by the rabbis using the Torah's commandments as basis, was to avoid as much as possible the application of these penalties.

## CAPITAL PUNISHMENT

### RULE 1

Two witnesses are greater than a circumstantial evidence. That is, the word of two witnesses carries more weight than any concrete evidence.

### RULE 2

There are minimum requirements for witnesses, i.e. witnesses must be "kasher". This means that they cannot be related to each other or have any relationship with the perpetrator. In addition, the Talmud still imposes a variety of reasons for declassifying a witness, making the sentence even more difficult.

### RULE 3

The warning. No one could be sentenced to death for a crime unless he has been previously warned. This means that the witnesses, when witnessing the crime, should at least yell at the person who commits it, in order to warn him that what he is doing is wrong.

### RULE 4

The acceptance. Among all the rules, this is the most absurd, for he who commits the crime, after having been warned about the penalty, he should shake his head to show that he understood the warning before committing the crime, so then, the court may sentence him to death .

Contrary to what many people think, that God's Law is punitive, and the punitive appearance of the Torah, what we have here is just the opposite, even though there are death sentences, in order to apply them, exist a lot of rules in order to make harder its application, which made the death sentence very rare.

Based on these rules, we can now try to suppose the motive that made these witnesses as "false witnesses". They are not false because they have not seen or heard Yehoshua, as many understand. For he himself declares:

*After this Yeshua said to the multitude: as if we were thieves you came to get us with whips and swords?* **Have I not been with you,**

*teaching in the Temple every day, and I have not posed a threat?*
Matthew 26:55

Since these witnesses would probably have heard and seen Yehoshua, they were not false. So we must look at other points that served to make them "false witnesses". What seems most likely to me, in this case, are the rules 3 and 4, for I do not particularly believe that the hearers of Yehoshua, by learning Torah with him, warned him of a possible condemnation if he kept his teachings, therefore, if a witness, even if he had witnessed the case, if he did not warn the accused of the error he was committing, he could not become a valid witness and therefore, for this reason, I believe that the witnesses against Yehoshua were called as "false witnesses".

Yehoshua was not condemned and killed by the Jewsish people in general, but by the Sadducees, who were the targets of his criticisms, that also includes the elders, the priests, the leaders and the high priest. Apart from the Sadducees, some groups of Pharisees also suffered attacks for being hypocrites and placing human laws above the Torah, which made them to agree with his death.

*Rabbi Elazar Ben Azarya says: every court that condemns a person to death every seven years, is a murderous court.*
Talmud of Babylon, Tractate Makkot 7a

# SECTION LII
## LAST WORDS

The last two verses of the book of Matthew caused me some impact when I translated them from the original and compared them with the Western translations.

*Go!*
*And observe (SHAMRU) all things (DEVARIM)*
*as I have commanded you, forever.*
Matthew 28:19-20

**X**

*Go you therefore, and teach all nations, baptizing them in the*
*name of the Father, and of the Son, and of the Holy Ghost:*
*Teaching them to observe all things whatever I have*
*commanded you: and, see, I am with you always,*
*even to the end of the world. Amen.*
Matthew 28:19-20 KJV

It's frightening the difference found in two small verses. We must notice various problems when we deal with these kinds of problems, from translations of translations, difficulties presented in the translation of slangs and local habits and re-adaptations for a more modern language.

But in this case, we do not have any of these kind of problems, for these two passages have been altered by the Catholic church at some point in history. This is not my statement, but it is as published by the *Biblioteca Apostòlica Vaticana* a few years ago, under the command of John Paul II, along with some other altered verses. Some Bible versions bring in their footnote what would be these changes made by the church.

This talk of father, son and holy spirit is completely alien to Jews, especially in the first century. Such terms do not appear in any of the <u>original</u> books of the New Testament that I've seen so far, they are not part of the teachings of Yehoshua, as well as not part of the teachings of his followers. This concept was created a few years later by Ignatius of Antioch and Tertullianvs, later confirmed by Martyr Justus, John Chrysostom and arriving at its total conception through the writings of Thomas Aquino, men who, despite a biblical appearance, had nothing to do with the True God's Word.

Regarding the baptism, certainly, it is important for Christianity. However, the way it was used, especially by the Catholic church, was as a way to bring as many people as possible under the control of Rome. It is very interesting and profitable for Rome to make its followers to go to other peoples and nations in order to baptize this people, because by doing so, the baptized one would be under the authority of the Vatican. Unfortunately, baptism is no longer a purifying ritual, as we see in the bible, for it has become a method of conversion to Christianity.

But I want to look at the original text and explain two important terms that appear in the last verse. The first of them is the word SHAMRU which is a conjugated form of the verb LISHMOR (לשמור).

*Lishmor* may be translated as "to observe", "to maintain", "to preserve". The most common usage of this verb is in reference to the Torah, for a person who obeys the Laws of God is called SHOMER TORAH (שומר שבת). The rabbis use this verb with everything related to Torah, SHOMER SHABBAT (observant of Shabbat), SHOMER CHAGIM (who celebrates the feasts) and so on.

The second word we have is DEVARIM. In a direct translation it means "things". But within Jewish terminology, this term has a somewhat deeper meaning, as seen before in this book. DEVARIM TORAH, or "things of the Torah", is another term for the commandments that are found there.

DEVARIM is also the Hebrew name for the book of Deuteronomy, which is nothing more than a repetition of the most important Laws which were given in the four previous books.

Bringing together both things, when Yehoshua commands SHAMRU DEVARIM, he is commanding that "the things of the Torah", i.e. the Laws of the Torah, should be observed and followed. However, he makes something very clear, "as I have commanded", that is, according to his rabbinical teachings.

The last command of Yehoshua in the book of Matthew, is for his talmidim to follow the Torah according to the rabbinic interpretation given by him.

I believe that such advice may serve to the true followers of Yehoshua in the present day.

# PART III
# PARABLES

# SECTION I
## THE SOWER

*And he spoke to them many things in allegories*
*(parables) and said to them: A man left his house*
*in the morning to sow his seeds.*
*Some of it fell from on the road, and were eaten by the birds.*
*And some fell on the rocks, where the soil has no density and*
*when they grew, they withered, because the soil was shallow*
*And the sun came and it became warm and burned*
*it and dried it up, for there were no root*
*And some of it fell among the thorns, and the*
*thorns grew up, and they stood above it*
*And some of it fell on the good soil, and brought forth fruit and*
*produce, the first a hundred, the second sixty and the third thirty.*
*Whoever has ears to hear, let him hear.*

Matthew 13:3-9

The usage of parables to pass on some teachings, is something very usual among the rabbis, in the Talmud itself, we can find several examples. The parable is a small narrative based on symbolism with the intention of passing a life lesson or a moral lesson, which is often a criticism of the society or the common mentality of the time. Yehoshua, when he made use of such teaching methods, was actually criticizing teachings and thoughts that were common in his days. In an indirect way, the parable is a harsh teaching about the vices and habits of the society in which this parable is inserted.

The parable of the sower is one of the best known among Christians, it is used in various preaching and teachings, always with a different focus. In order for us to have a full understanding of what is taught through this parable, we need to understand that it is a small story with two facets, the main one has a corrective purpose, that is, a heavy criticism and the other one is the solution that must be adopted, so this correction can be effective.

## REVELATIONS FROM THE SCRIPTURE

In order for us to have a clear and complete understanding of a parable, it is necessary to study it according to what the Scriptures teach. We must understand the way it was elaborated, who was the target audience and especially, what was the knowledge that the people who heard it, possessed.

The sages teach that there are four levels for understanding any passage in the Scriptures, these levels are known as PaRDeS, which in Aramaic means "*garden*". Understanding these concepts and using them for Biblical studies makes a lot of difference in order to achieve a complete understanding of the text.

The word PARDES is the junction of 4 words, **PaRDeS:**
**1 - Pshat**
**2 - Remetz**
**3 - Drash**
**4 - Sod**

I will use this methodology to make a different approach to this parable. At each level, we will have different revelations, but always connected in some way, revealing hidden secrets in the teachings of Yehoshua.

**1- Pshat = "The simple meaning or the literal meaning";** So it is taught to children and adults who are not yet familiar with the Torah's Literature. The literal teaching is the most appropriate in this case and the most superficial of all, it sticks only to what is written.

If we look at a few verses later, we will see Yehoshua explaining to his talmidim the meaning of this parable, in a simple and direct way, in PSHAT:

*But hear the parable of the sower.*
*The sower is the son of man, and the seed that fell on the way*
*is everyone who hears about the Kingdom of Heaven, but does*
*not understand it. Satan comes and snatches from the heart*
*all that was sown. This is the seed which fell on the road.*
*That which fell upon the rock is the one who hears the*
*word (the teaching) of EL and rejoices immediately.*
*And as it has no roots because is confusing one, when a*
*little trouble and distractions come to hem, satan uses*
*this to make him forget what is in his heart.*
*That which fell among the thorns are those who hear the*
*word (the teaching) for their own gain, satan makes him*
*forget the teaching of EL and he does not bear fruit.*
*That which fell on good soil are those who hear the word*
*(the teaching) and understand it and bear fruit, which are*
*the Ma`assim Tovim. And he brings forth from the first*
*a hundred, and from the second sixty, and from the third*
*thirty. The one hundred is the one who purifies the heart*
*and sanctifies the body (Torah). The second is the one who*
*separates from woman (Lev 19) and the third is the one*
*who is sanctified in matrimony, in body and in heart.*

Matthew 13:18-23

I have already heard many teachings about this parable, always with the same content. A shallow form of interpretation with different embellishments around it. If we confine ourselves to the simple explanation that Yehoshua gave, though very valid, we will only have the superficial understanding of it. This can be compared to a fruit that is eaten by someone, and this someone, only eats its peel. This is the Pshat form of this parable, the superficial interpretation, the peel that surrounds it.

**2- Remetz** = A brief allusion to the meaning of the passage through allegories. It is a deeper teaching than just the literal meaning. This level is reached by people with a better cultural level and a broad knowledge of the Torah.

The scholars who traced a chronology of the Gospels, state that this parable came about a year before Yehoshua's triumphal entry into Jerusalem, as this entry was more or less in the time of Pessach, so this parable was also taught in a time close to Pessach and it is for Pessach that we need to look at.

During Pessach's celebration, in every synagogues throughout the world, a book called *Hagadah Shel Pessach* is read. In this book, we have the whole narrative of the departure of the Hebrew people from Egypt, addressing various commandments that are in the Torah that are related to this celebration, the *Hagadah* serves as a guide for the whole celebration's ritual. Among some customs, there is one that says that we should encourage the children to ask about the reasons for this feast. The book directs the children to ask their parents four questions, symbolizing the four types of people that exist within the People of God. This parable is strongly attached to Pessach, for apart from the time in which they were, the manner in which the *Hagadah* presents the four types of children, is just the same order that Yehoshua presents the types of soils in these parable.

**1st SON - She'eino Yodea Lishol** *(the one who does not know how to ask)*

According to the *Hagadah*, this is the worst kind of son, he does not know how to ask, for he has no interest in asking, he does not care about God's things, about the Torah, about the teachings, about the prayers. For him, it's all a big lie and a waste of time.

He is like the seed that falls by the road, it is a lost seed. He listens to the Word of God, but do not even bother to understand it. This type of person is the one who should receive the hardest treatment, the Talmud makes two interesting comments about this type of person:

*Do not give the words of the Law to a pagan...*
*Do not put holy things in unclean places...*
Talmud of Babylon, Tractate Brakhot 20b

People with closed hearts to God and people who see His Word as a waste of time, have no solution, it is better if they are carried away by birds, for as far as they are, as better.

## 2nd SON -Tam *(naive)*

The naive son, due to his lack of capacity, the teachings never generate roots. He learns, he is taught, but due to a certain lack of interest, this knowledge does not change his life, for he is like a rock, that has no deep soil and almost does not bear fruit, and those few that he bears, end up being dried up by the sun.

This is one needs examples of how to live, how to obey, how to study. That is, he has knowledge, but soon discourages.

The Talmud instructs to teach him about the mysteries of the Torah, to always talk to him, and to discover what attracts him to God at most and then to teach him how to apply it.

He needs love, patience, and perseverance.

## 3rd SON - Rashah *(wicked)*

The wicked son is the one who mocks and causes confusion. The interesting thing is, in order to be someone who causes problems, one needs knowledge about what he mocks, that is, the wicked son knows the word of God, knows who God is and is very likely that, at some point in his life, he was a person who sought the Creator. But due to external problems, he ended up distancing himself and losing his faith, thus becoming a critic person who uses of his previous knowledge to cause trouble.

The wicked one is like a seed that has generated root, but was suffocated by what was externally. The Talmudic orientation is to *"break his teeth"*, but in a metaphorical way, where the intention is to force him to drop off the bad habits.

Unlike the first son, and despite being labeled as the "wicked son", this one has a solution, even if in a harsh way.

### 4th SON - Adamah Tovah *(good soil)*

This is the *Chacham* - the wise son. He asks: *"What are the Testimonies (Edot), the decrees (Chukim) and the Laws (Mishpatim) which Adonai, our God, has commanded us?"* The *Haggadah* instructs us to give him the following answer: *"According to the laws of Passover, we are not allowed to eat anything after the Corban shel Pessach, the Passover's sacrifice"*.

This is the person who takes an interest in all aspects of God, His Word, a righteous life, prayer, faith and even self-sacrifice for what he believes.

Now we know who are the "sons of Pessach", the representation of four kinds of people, the four kinds of soil that Yehoshua was referring to. Those who do not want to know about God, those who have learned from God but who have become disillusioned and critical, those who want to know about God but are easily influenced by the outside world and lastly, those who truly seek Him.

But there is something we should pay attention to, just as all the seeds were in the same bag, these four types of people are under the same "roof", that is, they are all part of Israel. Yehoshua does not speak about the pagans or about the impious, rather he only uses, as examples, the people who are supposedly already serving God.

**3- Drash = "interpretation"**; to discover the meaning through a *Midrash* (exegesis), by analyzing the words, their placements inside the context, the formats of the Letters, comparisons of words, grammatical forms and by similar occurrences in other passages. This level is available to people of great knowledge of the Torah, in this case, highlighting them from others!

There is a book that has teachings long before Yehoshua, dating back to the time of the return of the Jewish people from the Babylonian exile. It is a Biblical commentary book with deep knowledge and has never been translated in its entirety into any other language. The teachings of this book are sometimes commented in the Talmud by Rabbi Hillel, who was the teacher of Yehoshua. Rabbi Hillel certainly did not only comment this, but also teach it in his *Yeshivot* (Torah's school), which leads me to believe that Yehoshua had full knowledge about what is addressed in this book.

For our third analysis of the parable in question, I will use this book by which we shall have a much greater depth in what has been taught. For a better understanding, I will separate the teachings of this Midrash according to each son of Pessach, who represent the soils.

Just as REMETZ has revealed to us the four kinds of people, DRASH will reveal to us what their real problems are, how they actually act to get to where they are. Now it becomes very interesting.

In its beginning, the *Midrash Tanchumah* speaks about four kinds of people, three for whom God would destroy the world, but because of the fourth kind of people, He decided to keep His creation.

### 1st SOIL - She'eino Yodea Lishol *(the one who does not know how to ask)*

We have already seen that the seed that falls on the ground is that seed that represents the person who does not care about God or anything related to Him, despises everything about Him and repudiates those who follow Him. The *Midrash* comments on a type of person for whom God would destroy the world, interesting that the term "bird" also appears in this passage, which shows us a connection with what Yehoshua said.

*And to all the **birds**, what would you do? If it were for*
*them, You would destroy the world, for YOU SHALL NOT*
*PROSTRATE YOURSELF BEFORE OTHER GODS.*
Midrash Tanchumah, 1 Bereshit Barah

The seed that falls on the road and is carried away by the birds, are those people who repudiate God and now we know why. They are people who serve other gods, god money, god success, god work, god physical appearance, god fame, god power, god alcohol, god drugs and so on.

They do not serve The God, for they are extremely mundane people, putting all things connected with this poor existence over what really matters, making all of these nonsense the real gods that they serve.

All of those who have something in their life that is above God or His Word is like the seed that falls on the road, it is like the son who does not know how to ask, is the one that is better to be taken away, because his idolatrous way of life might end up influencing others. People who have jobs, family, money, dreams or anything else that stands above the Creator, is no different than any pagan.

For this kind of person, God would destroy the world!

## 2nd SOIL - Tam *(naive)*

*And what about the mountains of **rocks**? They*
*would not be made as <u>servants</u>, For these people You*
*would destroy the world, for SHMA ISRAEL.*
Midrash Tanchumah, 1 Bereshit Barah

By the citation of rocks in this passage, we can associate it with the naive son, who represents the seed that falls upon the rock. If we pay attention, the *Midrash* answers the reason that this son is easily influenced by the outside world and why he needs better instructions. This answer is precisely in the quote SHMA ISRAEL.

The SHMA is the maxim of the Jewish faith and the two most important verses of the bible, it is in Deuteronomy 6:4-5 and basically states two things, loving God above all things and recognizing that He is ONE. This shows us that the naive is easily influenced by not recognizing this maxim, he does not recognize the absolute oneness of the Creator, and does not serve Him with all his soul and heart.

This happens because, when they learn the Word, they learn from dubious sources, thus falling into human theologies, into theories created by men, and they take this as absolute truth. They live a total misunderstanding of what the Bible teaches.

People like this believe in concepts such as replacement theology, dispersion theology, trinity, etc.

With these people we must have patience in teaching and if possible, teach the hidden secrets of the Torah.

For this kind of person, God would destroy the world!

### 3rd SOIL - Rashah *(wicked)*

The wicked son, the seed among the thorns. It is a seed that took root, somehow grew a little, but the thorns of life ended up killing this bloom and he ends up becoming a rebel, a frustrated and for this reason, blame the faith he once had, he blames God for everything that went through in his life.

The *Midrash* reports exactly this type of person, who, due to frustrations in life, ends up defiling the Holy Name of God.

> For everything that is twisted (adulterated knowledge) will be like piles of **thorns**, for YOU SHOULD NOT DEFILE MY HOLY NAME. For these people You would destroy the world.
> Midrash Tanchumah, 1 Bereshit Barah

True wickedness are attitudes that defile the name of God, by using His Word with awkward and twisted teachings. Today, it is very common to see people taking random and disconnected passages to create false theologies, theories and concepts to get what they want for personal gain, as Yehoshua quotes in his later explanation.

Let's remember something, these people are all part of God's people, not everyone who revolts, moves away, often they stay infiltrated and end up causing great destruction. There are many leaders like these these days. People who say that they serve God, but actually, "use" Him for their own benefit, which, normally, is a financial gain.

For this kind of person, God would destroy the world!

## 4th SOIL - Adamah Tovah *(good soil)*

Regarding the good soil, the wise son, the Midrash brings forth a fantastic teaching:

> *And all the acts of creation will say, just as it has been said, I will trust in Him. They will be like the **good soil** and because of them, You will NOT destroy the world.*
> Midrash Tanchumah, 1 Bereshit Barah

The good soil, the true wise one, is the one who knows how to put his trust in the Lord, it will be through them that the world will be sustained, it will be through them that the world will know the Creator, it will be through them that God will reveal Himself to all nations.

And it does not stop there, Yehoshua quotes something weird, by relating the good soil with some numbers. The *Midrash* will explain to us what makes these people truly wise:

> *And his merits shall be thirty for His testimonies, sixty for His statutes, and a hundred for His Torah.*
> Midrash Tanchumah, 1:2 Bereshit Barah

Incredible, the 30, 60, 100 that no Christian has ever been able to explain, is now clear. The numbers show the step by step of wisdom. First the 30, which represents the testimonies of God, which is to believe in what He speaks, it is to have faith. Then comes the 60, His statutes, that represent the "limits", to know how far they can and cannot go to commit no sin. 100 represents the Torah, when the person truly becomes involved with the Creator, it is when one becomes the true good soil, the true sage.

*Love Adonai, your Elohim, and keep His testimonies, His statutes, His judgments, and His mitzvot (TORAH) every day.*
Deuteronomy 11:1

**4- Sod ="secret"**; represents the mystical and metaphysical meaning of a passage. It is a secret knowledge, it is usually more for people who have a very advanced level of Torah knowledge and with a deep relationship with the Creator. *Sod* is only attained by those who are gifted by God with this unique and precious gift.

To go even deeper, let's look at some details before. According to some scholars, this happened on a Pessach. Pessach is unfortunately remembered by Christians as Easter, but Pessach is an iconic date, it's a representation of the true power and plan of God. Apart from the death of Yehoshua, Pessach has several other stories, such as the exit from Egypt and the sacrifice of Itzhak. But I would like to look at the first Pessach ever reported by the Torah, the one that happened in the book of Genesis. It was at this time of the year, that God appeared to Avraham, demands of him a sacrifice and then, the patriarch fell asleep. This was the first sacrifice of Pessach, the source, the first fruit of all the Pessach, for it was through it that God rectified what he had promised to Abraham, the promise to create a people and to make these people the blessing for all nations.

But what all of this have to do with the parable of Yehoshua? EVERYTHING! Let's take a look at the promise made to Abraham:

*I will bless those who bless you, and I will curse those who curse* *you; and by you all the peoples of the earth **will be blessed.***

Genesis 12:3

In order to make it clear, we must make an analysis of the Hebrew grammatical structure used in this verse. The Torah is almost all written in the passive form, when reading it in its original, it ends up being very strange sometimes, but when it comes to prophecy, the verb is always conjugated in the future. In the case of this promise made to Abraham, the verb to *"will be blessed"* is NIVRKHU, but conjugated in the passive form, in an unusual way, for it is a promise for the future. This already shows us that there is something behind it. Every Hebrew word has a *shoresh*, a root, which is composed of three to four letters, every word that uses the same root has a certain sharing of meanings. If we make an analysis of this verb in its root, it leads us to another Hebrew word commonly used in many *Midrashim*, which is MAB-RIKH, which means *"to engraft"*, so we could also read this promise as follows:

*I will bless those who bless you, and I will curse those who curse you; and by you all the peoples of the earth **will be engrafted in**.*

Genesis 12:3

This is it, the true blessing that God promises to Abraham is that all nations may be engrafted into the faith of Abraham. The greatest blessing that God can give to someone, is the opportunity to make him a part of His people, part of the people of Abraham.

So God promises Abraham that due to his faith, all those who believe and obey, as he believed and obeyed, may be blessed with the opportunity to be grafted onto the People of Israel. No conversion to Judaism, no human laws, no rabbinical laws, no religion, for all this happened at the time when Abraham was uncircumcised, there was no Judaism, no church, only obedience to God and faith in Him.

In my view, the Kingdom of Heaven is not the afterlife, it is not the messianic era, but the era we are living now, where the whole world has free access to the true God. But I see the Kingdom of Heaven as something deeper than this, I see it as the true People of Israel, and I do not mean Judaism, I do not mean Christianity, for Adonai did not create any of that. He created a people and He determined what He would do with these people, He would make them the People of God, the People of Israel.

I, particularly, interpret the first seed as the heathen, who will suffer eternal damnation. The seed that falls on the rock, are the Christians, because their teachings have no roots and are nothing but vanities. Those suffocated by the thorns, I see as the synagogues, for the rabbinic teachings and laws suffocate all those who want to truly serve God and finally, the good soil, the true People of Israel, who have no religion, have no human doctrines and has a life according to the will of the Creator, according to the Torah.

*Midrash Tanchumah* ends the study reported above with a very interesting phrase:

> *David looked up and said, How great is your goodness, which*
> *you hid for those who will come to the olive tree of Yaakov.*
> Midrash Tanchumah, 1:3 Bereshit Barah

Yaakov is Israel and this olive tree represents the People of Israel, he claims that "those" will come to this " olive tree". There are the natural ones, who may be cut off if they fall into dogmas and there are those who will be the grafted ones, after they truly understand what that is. This idea was so common that even Rabbi Paul makes a similar quotation in one of his books, Romans chapter 11.

> *And if some of the branches be broken off, and you, being*
> *a wild olive tree, were grafted in among them, and with*

*them partake of the root and fatness of the **olive tree.***

Romans 11:17 KJV

## UNDERSTANDING A DIFFICULT PARABLE

Yehoshua teaches that there are four kinds of people within the People of God, the first is the idolater, who has worldly things as his gods, they are the seeds that fall on the road and are carried away by the birds, these are already doomed.

The second refers to people who learn the Torah, but are weak and end up falling into the worldly influences. For they have no roots, they end up being burned by the sun. With these people we must have patience and teach with care about the love and the ONESS of the Creator.

The third is the one who blames God for bad things that happened to him, everything he learned is suffocated by thorns, so he ends up blaspheming God and creating false dogmas by distorting what is taught in the Scriptures. These people have a solution, but not through a sweet and delicate approach.

The last ones are those who truly follow God, obey his Torah, seek a life far from sin, have faith in Him and always seek correction in their ways, it is the part of the People that sustains the world.

Many are already a natural part of this people, others, the Gentiles, must be grafted in to take part. Unfortunately, many churches teach that being part of the People of Israel is to be under a curse, it is to be enslaved and disobedient to God, because jesus already solved all of these problems for them. I see this theory worse than the son who does not know how to ask.

Well, after all of this, the question is, how to get into this people?

*And for the foreigners, who attach themselves to Adonai, to serve Him, and to love the **name of Adonai (RASHAH***

*– **wicked**), and to be His **servants (TAM - naive)**, all that keep the Sabbath, by not profaning it, all who embrace my **Torah (ADAMAH TOVAH – good soil)**,*
*And I will bring them to my holy mountain, and they will rejoice in my house of prayer; their burnt offerings and their sacrifices shall be accepted upon my altar; for my house shall be called a house of prayer for all peoples.*

Isaiah 56:6-7

Look at this, Isaiah quotes exactly the three sons. First the RASHAH, who instead of desecrating the name of the Lord, will love It. The TAM, who did not serve Him with all his heart, with all his soul and with all his much (SHMA), now becomes His servant and finally, the one who is the good soil, the one who embraces the Torah. This shows the foreigners how to be part of it.

Gentle, Jew, it does not matter, he who embraces the Word of the Creator with love, faith and righteousness, is the true People of Israel.

# SECTION II
## THE GOOD SEED

*And he set before them another allegory (parable). The*
*Kingdom of Heaven is like the a man who sows good seed.*
*And it is when the men are sleeping, that their*
*enemy comes and sows tares, in the foreign language*
*beriyagah, over the wheat, and goes away.*
*And when the herb grew up to bear fruit, he sees the tares.*
*And the servants approach the lord of the field,*
*and say unto him, O our lord, did you not sow good*
*seeds? Where did this weed come from?*
*And he said unto them, My enemy did this, and the*
*servants have said unto him, Let us pluck up the tares.*
*And he said unto them, No, unless you also pluck up the wheat*
*But let both grow together until the harvest, and at the*
*time of harvest I will say to the reapers: First gather*
*the tares and bind them into individual bundles to be*
*burned and the wheat put into the granary.*
                                        Matthew 13:24-30

This is an easy-to-understand parable, also, a few
verses ahead, Yehoshua himself explains it to his talmidim.
The real function of a parable is to pass a hidden message
behind allegories and with this one is no different. The interesting thing to note, in this case, is not the message that the
parable wants to pass, but to whom it was addressed.

Some terms that Yehoshua uses may give us this hint,
words like "wheat", "tares to be burned", and "granary" were
part of the language that Yohanan, the immerser, used when
referring to Mashiach:

*The winnowing fork is in his hands to fan his threshing*
*floor, he will gather the grains in his granary and the*
*straw (will be burned in fire, which is not useful).*
                                        Matthew 3:12

Yehoshua formulates a parable using the same language and the same theme as Yohanan did, in order to send him a message. In an indirect way, Yehoshua reformulates the teaching of Yohanan in order to correct some misleading teachings that the immerser planted within the people who heard him.

This idea may seem strange, but there was a very strong point in the teachings and beliefs of Yehoshua that were not conforming to what Yohanan taught, to which, he indirectly addresses in this specific parable.

## THE ERA OF MASHIACH

Yohanan, the immerser, like every good Jew, even in modern days, possessed an apocalyptic vision regarding the beginning of the era of Mashiach. He believed that he would destroy the enemies of Israel, restore the sanctity of the Temple and rule the whole world from the city of Jerusalem. For Yohanan, the coming of Mashiach represented an immediate revolution in the history of the Jews and of the humanity:

*And the ax has reached the root of the tree, the one which does not bear good fruit, will be cut down and thrown into the fire.*
Matthew 3:10a

Yohanan's concept concerning the Kingdom of Heaven was very different from the concept of the Kingdom of Heaven that Yehoshua preached. The arrival of this time, for Yohanan, represented the moment of Gog and Magog, the great battle, the great redemption.

For Yehoshua, the Kingdom of Heaven is a transitory era, in which we are today, an era that prepares the Age of Mashiach. It is at this time, in the Kingdom of Heaven, that the word of God would reach out all Gentiles, the world would recognize God as the One God, the gateway to the People of Israel would be open to all and the knowledge about the One God would become vast.

These are two very different definitions, Yohanan believed in an immediate judgment, Yehoshua proclaimed that it was still necessary for the world to recognize God. Therefore, this parable was taught by Yehoshua to break certain vices that probably some of Yehoshua's followers had, since many of them were former students of Yohanan. But despite the big difference, there is something that connects them, something that makes both Yehoshua and Yohanan correct, the concept of Mashiach Ben Yosef and Mashiach Ben David.

## YOSEF AND DAVID

*Rav. Hana Bar Bizna said that Rabbi Shimon Hasida said: there is Mashiach Ben David and Mashiach Ben Yosef.*
Talmud of Babylon, Tractate Sukkah 52b

According to Judaism, there are no more than one Mashiach, but Mashiach will have two facets, two different missions, the first will define him as Mashiach Ben Yosef and the second will define him as Mashiach Ben David.

The concepts about Mashiach are strongly addressed in the Talmud and in Jewish literature and once again, it is at this literature that we need to look at.

*The dialogue between Rabbi Nachman and Rabbi Yitzchak begins as follows: Rabbi Nachman asks Rabbi Yitzchak: Listen, when will this Bar Nafleh (son of the fallen) come? Rabbi Yitzchak: who is this son of the fallen? Rabbi Nachman: it's Mashiach! Rabbi Yitzchak: Do you call Mashiach as Bar Nafleh? Rabbi Nachman: Yes, because it is written in a passuk "I will raise David's fallen tent".*
Talmud of Babylon, Tractate Sanhedrin 96b

In this passage from the Tractate Sanhedrin, Rabbi Nachman teaches that Mashiach will have to fall so he can raise as Ben David. Yehoshua knew this line of thought, for it resembled his death and return as one who fell and raised, revealing to his talmidim that his mission, at that particular time, was as Mashiach Ben Yosef.

*(Psalm 126:6) "The one of the precious seed will go weeping and will come back, without doubt, with joy."*
*- According to Gaon's comment, this verse refers to the two types of Mashiach. The first refers to Mashiach Ben Yosef and the second to Mashiach Ben David.*

Kol HaTor 2:13

According to Gaon's interpretation of Psalm 126:6, the verbs *coming* and *going* presented together in this passage, show that Mashiach Ben Yosef will come and will go away weeping in sorrow and then he will return in joy as Mashiach Ben David. This concept also agrees when Yehoshua taught that he would die and return.

*There is unity between Mashiach Ben Yosef and Mashiach Ben David.*

Kol HaTor 1:35

In this verse we have the proof that there are not and there will not be two Mashiachim, but Ben Yosef and Ben David will be the same person, but with different objectives.

*Mashiach Ben Yosef and Mashiach Ben David, the first will bring redemption and the second will separate the people "by his hands".*

Kol HaTor 2:101

Now we have the definition of his mission. Mashiach Ben Yosef will come first, bringing redemption, this redemption will be the spreading of the knowledge about the God of Israel to the Gentiles and consequently, opening the doors for their adoption within the People of Israel.

Mashiach Ben David will come to separate people, this

concept also fits in this parable when Yehoshua affirms that he will come to separate the tares from the wheat.

## YOHANAN'S VISION

The belief in Mashiach differs greatly among the Jews, for the Orthodox Judaism, as for most Jews, Mashiach is the redeemer yet to come. However, there are many others who have their own conception of Mashiach. I have already met some who claimed that Mashiach Ben Yosef was Moses, others claim that Mashiach Ben Yosef was the rebbe Lubavitch and there are still others who believe that Mashiach Ben Yosef would not be a person, but a reality, being the existence of the State of Israel itself.

Regardless of how each Jew defines Mashiach, the exactly same thing could be happening precisely with Yohanan, it is unclear to us who Mashiach Ben Yosef was to him, but according to his relationship with Yehoshua, he strongly believed that he came as Mashiach Ben David, the one who would bring the separation between the tzadik and the wicked.

For Yehoshua, however, this was not the case, by teaching this parable, he gives Yohanan the message that he would be Mashiach Ben Yosef and instead of bringing "separation", he should first bring "redemption", which would serve to reach the whole world. This "redemption" era was defined by Yehoshua as the Kingdom of Heaven.

Going back to the parable, everything is very clear now. First comes the sower, Mashiach Ben Yosef, plants the seed, teachs his Torah, leaves this knowledge at everyone's disposal and then goes away. Many will know about him, recognize him and will get to know the word of God, but many among these will be nothing more than a "satan seed", they will be the tares that will coexist alongside the tzadikim.

Then the sower will return to the field, but this time

as Mashiach Ben David and this time to bring the separation, he will save the tzadikim (observers of the Torah) and will throw in the fire the ungodly.

Interesting is that this passage refers to two types of people who are together, have grown up in the same field, side by side and this shows that both have the same access and knowledge of God. This reminds me of another passage from Yehoshua:

> *Many will say to me in that day, lord, lord, did we not*
> *prophesy in your name, and in your name we have cast out*
> *demons, and have not done many signs in your name?*
> *And then I will say to them: I never knew you, depart*
> *from, all who do not practice the Law (Torah).*
>
> Matthew 7:22-23

According to Yehoshua, the tares will do wonders, cast out demons, prophesy and make many signs, but because they do not practice the Torah, they will be casted out from his presence. Yehoshua's words, not mine.

# SECTION III
## THE GRAIN OF MUSTARD

*And he set before them another allegory (parable).*
*The Kingdom of Heaven is a grain of mustard,*
*which a man takes and sows in the field.*
*And it is the **smallest** of all the seeds in the field, and when*
*it grows, it is greater than all herbs and becomes a great tree*
*until the birds of the heavens hide within (in its branches).*
Matthew 13:31-32

The Parable of the Grain of Mustard is widely known in the Christian milieu, at least once in a lifetime, every Christian has heard some preaching based on it, and in the vast majority of cases, it is linked to some kind of teaching about faith. However, "faith" is not actually mentioned by Yehoshua.

Therefore, this parable becomes very dangerous, because it presents a false simplicity, which ends up generating a great contradiction and misunderstanding of the real purpose it has. Three things should be taken into account, the purpose of the parable, the reason for using mustard as an example, and what this mustard tree and seed would really be.

## THE USAGE OF THE MUSTARD
### The Representation of Mustard

Mustard has a strong Talmudic representation, it is quoted in several Tractates, addressing various types of things, from a comparison due to the size of its seed, to its handling on a Shabbat, the interesting thing is, mustard is embedded in some of the customs of the Jews and this may have a connection with this parable:

*And Rav. Mari sai that Rav. Yohanan said: He who*
*is accustomed to eating mustard once a month, will*

*prevent diseases from plaguing his home.*
Talmud of Babylon, Tractate Brakhot 40a

Rabbi Yohanan made a very interesting statement, although it is unclear what led him to this conclusion, it is reported in one of the most famous Tractates of the Talmud, that the consumption of mustard avoids disease, not to the one who eats it, but to his whole House. Such a statement has not a physical but a spiritual character, for how can the consumption of mustard by someone could free his entire house from diseases? This shows the mystical symbolism that mustard has.

### The Value of Mustard
*In this incident, it was possible for Rava to eat his
meat even with mustard, for Rava was not poor.*
Talmud of Babylon, Tractate Chullin 133a

The mustard, once ready for seasoning, was expensive and a luxury item. As reported in the above incident, Rava could consume it because he was not poor.

The use of mustard as an example in this passage, because of its financial value, may also mean something.

### The Characteristics of Mustard
*The baskets were filled with mustard seeds,
which were extremely small.*
Talmud of Babylon, Tractate Nazir 8a

This is a common consensus statement, the mustard seed, if not the smallest seed, is one of the smallest among all seeds. That is why Yehoshua compares it to faith in some chapters ahead.

If we gather the three Talmudic references, we will have something very small, of extreme high value and with important spiritual characteristics. Observing these three things, only one thing comes to my mind, the People of Israel. Israel has one of the smallest countries in the world, a small country that accounts for a total of 0.2% of the world's population. The People of Israel, being a people that serves the one true God, is a spiritual people, every conception of miracles, angels, wonders, creation, eternal life, salvation, etc., comes from the spirituality of this people, which makes it the most spiritual people among all others and consequently, by being hand-picked by the Creator of all things, they are a people of immeasurable value.

In an indirect way, the mustard is nothing more than the representation of the chosen people itself, it represents the main characteristics that distinguish it from the rest of the world.

*It is not because you are the most numerous of peoples that Adonai has placed His heart upon you and chose you - indeed, you are the **smallest** of peoples.*

Deuteronomy 7:7

*The name Israel reflects the high **spirituality**.*
Or HaChaim, Genesis 47:28

*The love of Israel and its **value** is great and not just emotional, for they are great masters of the Torah.*
Orot Israel 1:1

## THE TREE AND THE SEED

Both the tree and the seed must be taken into account, the seed really is one of the smallest among all the other seeds, but the relevant factor of being small is linked to the type of tree it becomes.

If we do an on-line research on mustard tree, we will find a huge tree, with very green leaves and a broad trunk. This tree is called _Brasica Alba_, also known as a yellow mustard tree and, incredible as it may seem, this tree is typical European, differing greatly from that tree found in the Middle East, which Yehoshua certainly based on this passage. The mustard tree of Israel is called _Sinapis Alba,_ or white mustard tree, and it is not a tree but a shrub.

Despite being a large shrub, larger than most shrubs, it is not large enough to become a large tree, let alone enough foliage for birds to hide under it. Through an allusion of a small and weak tree as being large and strong, Yehoshua shows us the miracle that Israel is, despite his weak and small appearance, Israel is able to hide birds under it branches and to spiritually become a huge tree.

## THE PURPOSE OF THE PARABLE

_On the high hill I will plant Israel, and bring forth branches, and bring forth fruit, and into a noble cedar shall grow; and birds of all kinds shall take shelter under it, in the shade of their branches they shall dwell._

Ezekiel 17:23

The parable of the mustard seed, in fact, is not a parable, but a _midrash_ done by Yehoshua in reference to chapter 17 of the book of the prophet Ezekiel.

The smallest among of all peoples, spiritual because they have been chosen by God and of great value, for having kept His ways, will become a great and strong tree and under it, all nations will be able to hide.

The Kingdom of Heaven, for Yehoshua, is the moment in which we now live, it is the moment when the gates of the heavens are open to all Gentiles and the Word of God is accessible to them. The faith of Israel, the spirituality of Israel and the God of Israel have become known to the whole world. At that time, Israel became a solid cedar, as both Christianity and Islam drank from its waters, thanks to its existence, the whole world has access to the Living God.

But we must look at Yehoshua's motives in bringing such teaching. Someone who clearly understood this part quite well was another rabbi, known as Paul, when he wrote his letter to the Romans:

> *For if you were cut out of the olive tree which is wild*
> *by nature, and were grafted contrary to nature into a*
> *good olive tree: how much more shall these, which be the*
> *natural branches, be grafted into their own olive tree?*
> *For I would not, brothers, that you should be ignorant*
> *of this mystery, lest you should be wise in your own*
> *conceits; that blindness in part is happened to Israel,*
> *until the fullness of the Gentiles be come in.*

Romans 11:24-25 KJV

Yehoshua explains that the prophecy contained in Ezekiel does not refer to the sovereignty of the State of Israel, nor to the Jewish people, but refers to the sovereignty of the faith and of the book of this people. He explains that through knowledge and observance of the Torah, everyone can be grafted onto the olive tree, everyone can be part of the true People of Israel, dwelling under its branches.

This answers our question about what this tree would be. It represents precisely the spiritual strength of Israel, for even being a small shrub, it becomes as if it were the largest tree in the field, able to hide the birds under its branches. This *midrash* of Yehoshua is confirmed by another prophet

> *In the days to come, the mount of Adonai's House shall*
> *stand firm above the mountains and tower above the*
> *hills, and all nations shall gaze on it with joy.*
> *And many peoples shall go and say: come, let us go up to*
> *the mount of Adonai, to the House of the God of Yaakov,*
> *that He may instruct us in His ways, and that we may*
> *walk in His Paths. For instruction shall come forth*
> *from Zion, The word of Adonai from Jerusalem.*

Isaiah 2:2-3

Amazing! Yehoshua teaches that there will be a time where truth will be given to all nations (who does not know the Bible today?) And then the nations will run to learn the Torah of Adonai (that time is now) and those who understand this, will become part of the People of Israel and that is the true salvation. To be part of the people is to be part of the Kingdom of Heaven which Yehoshua talks so much about, because it was through his death that the Torah came to the Gentiles.

# SECTION IV
## THREE SHORT PARABLES

*Again Yeshua said to his talmidim: the Kingdom of Heaven is*
*like a man who finds a hidden treasure and in joy over the value*
*(found), he sells everything he has and buys the field for himself.*
*And yet the Kingdom of Heaven is like a merchant*
*seeking precious stones.*
*And when he finds a good one, he sells everything*
*he owns and buy it.*
*The Kingdom of Heaven is like a net in the middle*
*of the sea in which all kinds of fish gather.*
*And when it is full, it is pulled out, and the fishermen choose*
*the kosher among them and the bad ones are thrown away.*
*Thus shall the ends of the days be, the angels shall come forth,*
*and shall distinguish the wicked from the tzaddikim.*
*And they will be cast into the pyre of fire and there*
*will be weeping and gnashing of teeth.*

Matthew 13:44-50

## HIDDEN TREASURE

The first parable that is presented to us is a comparison between the Kingdom of Heaven and a hidden treasure that is found. It is very clear and self-explanatory how Yehoshua exposes the value of things that concern God.

But this parable has a loose end, which must be connected to its origin. Yehoshua does not tell us the reason that this treasure was hidden, but he states that the person who found it, hid it again, until he could acquire the field for himself. This is odd, for why didn't he simply take the treasure and went away?

The Talmud tells a number of anecdotes about hidden treasures that are found, one of them is about a person who has inherited an ugly field, because he was too lazy to fix it, he ends up selling it for a minimal amount. The person who bought it, when cleaning it, found a chest with a sufficient amount of gold to build a huge palace. The person who sold the field, when he learned of this, regretted being lazy. Another case involves a buyer and a seller of a field where a treasure was found, while they were arguing about the ownership of the treasure, Alexander, the great, passes by and they decide to ask him, so Alexander decides to marry one's daughter with the other's son and so the treasure would be of both.

The Tractate Bava Metzia has a long rabbinic debate about how to proceed when someone decides to hide something of value. They stablish from the place where it must be hidden to the depth that the hole should have if the person decides to bury it. At some point, an argument about theft, loss of that treasure and if it is found by someone else, begins. A rabbi named Shmuel claims that if the treasure is found on a public place, one has the right to keep the treasure for himself. However, if it is found on a private filed, if he wants to keep the treasure for himself, he should buy the field first.

I am struck by Yehoshua's familiarity with the Oral Torah and how he used it. The basis of his teaching is the Torah, but he never left the Talmud aside and he uses what is determined in those books to formulate his teachings and debates. Regardless of how he developed this parable, it teaches us about a person who has had so much joy in finding a treasure that he resolves to restructure all his priorities to get that field, for the Kingdom of Heaven has a greater value than anything he had.

## PRECIOUS STONES

Following the same line of thought as the previous parable, Yehoshua makes another comparison between the Kingdoms of the Heavens and earthly things of high value. It is about a merchant who is impressed by some precious stones that he finds, just as in the previous parable, he decides to sell everything he has to acquire them.

Perhaps the difference between the two parable is that the man of the first, because he is digging holes, is not rich, and the second man, certainly, had a better financial condition. This shows that the Kingdom of Heaven is open to all kinds of people and the sacrifice to acquire it, is equal for all, for it must have a greater value than anything else that anyone can have in life.

This is another parable that suffers with translation, in most Western bibles, instead of "precious stones", "pearls" appear, and this causes a slight disconnection of a very interesting Talmudic teaching.

*The Torah is like a chest full of precious stones.*
Talmud of Babylon, Tractate Taanit 21a

I do not believe that the Kingdom of Heaven is the Torah *per se*, but it is certain that it takes us and keeps us in that kingdom.

## NET AT THE SEA

In the last one, things become interesting, precisely because of the terms used by Yehoshua that no translation has maintained. He compares people who will enter the Kingdom of Heaven with fish, more specifically, with Kasher fish and non-kasher fish.

According to the Jewish mentality, there are two things that represent one's observance of the Torah. The first one is when the person says that he is *shomer Shabbat*, in a direct translation, "observant of Shabbat", which is a maxim of obedience to Torah, such a term is synonymous to orthodox Jews, for they are called *"shomrim Shabbat"*.

Another is the "kasher" term, this term does not only represent the biblical diet, but it also represents all that is according to the Torah.

*Rabban Gamliel said to them: My servant Tavi was not like*

*the other servants, he was kasher (according to the Torah).*
Mishnah Brakhot 2:7

*If someone builds a sukkah among the trees, with
them serving as a wall, that sukkah is kasher.*
Mishnah Sukkah 2:4

In the first example we have Rabbi Gamliel calling his servant as kasher, this teaches us that such a term fits for people, showing that this people have a life of observance to the Torah, for they are according to what it stipulates.

The second one talks about a regulation concerning the construction of *sukkah* (sukkot's huts), it says that if it is between the trees, this sukkah is kasher, that is, it is in accordance with what the Torah demands concerning the construction of these huts.

The fish in this parable are the people, and the term "kasher" determines their behavior and the required for them to be chosen. In more direct words, Yeshohua clearly states that the chosen one is the one who is kasher, one who has a life as determined by the Torah. This is confirmed at the end, where he states that the angels will differentiate the wicked from the tzadikim and tzadik is a biblical Hebrew term that means the one who observes the commandments of the Torah.

Yehoshua could never make such an assertion if he really had abolished the Torah. Yehoshua, without the Torah, loses his meaning, for both his teachings and his existence were directly connect to it. Unfortunately the church did not understand that.

# SECTION V
## REWARD

*After this Yeshua said to his talmidim: the Kingdom
of Heaven is like the man who is lord in his house
and rises in the morning to hire servants.
And he hires them for one dinar a day and
sends them to his vineyard.
And he goes out in the third hour of the day and
sees others standing in the market
And he said unto them, Come you also into my vineyard,
and I will give you what is suitable for you.
And they went. Then he went out again at noon
and at the ninth hour and did the same.
And in the eleventh hour, he went out again and
saw others standing and told them: Why are
you standing in the market all day?
And they answered him: no one hired us. And he said
unto them, Go you also unto my vineyard.
And that night, said the lord of the vineyard to the supervisor
of the laborers: call them so that I may give them their salary.
And he started with the last and finished with the first.
The latter received a dinar.
And the first thought he would receive more, but
he gave nothing to anyone but a dinar.
And the first murmured upon the lord of the vineyard
And told him: the last ones worked only for an hour and
you made them like us, who worked all day in the heat.
And he answered one of them, saying, I did you
no wrong, did I not call you for a dinar?
Take it and go. If I want to give it to the last one like you.
May I not do according to my desire? Is there something
wrong in your eyes when I'm being good?
Then the first will be the last and the last will be the first.
Many will be called but few will be the chosen.*

Matthew 20:1-16

This is a parable that deals with reward, but more important than the reward itself, are the reasons why these rewards are given, as well as the characters and the setting found in this parable.

The first information we have is that of a lord hiring servants to work in his vineyard. In the vast majority of cases, when vineyard appears in the Tanakh, it is automatically associated with the People of Israel, as it appears in the book of the prophet Isaiah:

*Let me sing a song to my beloved about his vineyard,*
*my beloved had a vineyard on a fruitful hill.*
*He dug the soil, removed the stones, and planted selected vines.*
*He built a watchtower in its midst, he even built a wine press, for*
*he believed that grapes would yield. Instead, it yield wild grapes.*
*Now, inhabitants of Jerusalem and men of Judah,*
*be the judges between me and my vineyard.*
*What else could I have done for my vineyard*
*that I failed to do? Why, when I thought I would*
*yield grapes, did it wield wild grapes?*
*...For the vineyard of the Lord of Hosts is the People of Israel...*
Isaiah 5:1-4 + 7

God didn't create for himself a religion, but a people. When He took the Hebrew people out of Egypt and gave the Torah into their hands, they officially became the People of Israel, the servants of the Living God. The vineyard represents these people. The construction of the vineyard, as the prophet Isaiah talks about, refers precisely to the formation of this people by God.

In this parable, the lord goes after servants to work in his vineyard. The first ones that he finds are the only ones that a promise of reward is made, are the only ones to which the owner of the vineyard promises to pay a dinar. I believe it is possible to make an association with these early workers with the Hebrew people, who have received the Torah and all the promises that are therein, and by so, officially becoming the "vineyard".

The other workers, however, represent the Gentiles, who were later called in to enter into the People of Israel. The interesting thing about them is, unlike the Hebrews, no rewards were promised to them. They simply had a disposition, which to some extent is weird, for they agreed to enter the vineyard without an agreement on payment.

Today it is very difficult, but very difficult indeed, to see a Gentile approaching or seeking the Creator God without a secular reason that leads one to Him. Every time I witnessed someone who starts seeking God, this mainly happened for "selfish" reasons. Some because of illnesses, some because of financial problems, and also those who seek a solution to a family problem. The reality is that I have never witnessed anyone, who never had any kind of relationship with God, seeking Him without any "second intentions". A person with an excellent life, without problems or any concern, to take such an attitude, is really out of the ordinary.

But apparently this is exactly what happens to these workers that this lord calls over the course of the day, they simply said "yes" and went to serve the new master without any agreement. This shows a very rare willingness to serve, as if, more than seeking for blessings, simply serving God for them, is the ONLY thing that matters.

This is something that is commented on in the Talmud. To serve God only because He is God the Creator. Even if one shall never be physically blessed by doing so, only by serving Him is good enough:

> Do not be servants who serve the master to receive
> a reward, but be servants who serve the master not
> for the reward, but for fear of heavens.

Pirkei Avot 1:3

Fear of heavens, whoever has it, is trully blessed. Fear of heavens is better than health, money, fame, power, influence and everything one can imagine; It is the sign of a heart according to the heart of God. But what intrigues me is: what makes a person with such a disposition, without interest in bargaining with God? Thinking about it, a story came to my mind:

> *Therefore said Adonai the God of Israel, I am about to pluck the kingdom out of the hands of Solomon, and I will give you ten tribes.*
>
> 1 Kings 11:31

After the death of King Solomon, because of the incessant sins of idolatry practiced by the people, God allows the Assyrian empire to invade the Kingdom of Israel, where ten of the twelve tribes were found, and destroy it. The people of the kingdom of Israel are taken captive and scattered throughout the gentile world. In its place, Assyrian Gentiles were established. Up to this day, no one knows what happened to the people of these ten tribes. They completely disappeared from the map, being totally absorbed by other cultures and, over time, "became" Gentiles.

The rabbis state that with the coming of Mashiach, the descendants of these ten tribes will be found and restored into the vineyard, into the People of Israel.

> *Rabbi Eliezer says: Just as this day grows dark and then becomes clear again, so it will be with the ten tribes. Even if they have fallen into darkness, in the future they will be brought back into the light.*
>
> Mishnah Sanhedrin 10:3

The sages teach that all of those who belong to the House of Israel, possess in their souls a divine spark, which is passed down from generation to generation. This spark, which comes from God, is what helps the Jews to follow the

Torah, to serve the One God and to stand in His ways. Even when a Jew falls into idolatry or converts to idolatrous religions, at some point in his life, he will return to the Living God because of the spark that has been given to him.

Now, surely these people from the lost tribes also had this divine spark, and that spark was passed on to all their generations. Even if they are lost all over the world, their souls are still intertwined with God. So, some people, who have a natural ease of accepting the Living God, even without ever having known Him or served Him, because of this spark, may be a descendants of one of these lost tribes.

What I am saying here could be just a hypothesis. However, this idea can be fully compatible, for lately I have seen many Gentiles seeking the True God for pure love and not for the blessings, they are submitting themselves to the yoke of the Torah for no apparently reason. When they hear about God and His Laws, in an unexpected way, they are filled with joy and willingness to serve Him, without even worrying about what He can give. This is fantastic, because it can be the true sign of the end of times. This is God restoring His true people, He is awakening the lost tribes in various parts of the world to follow His ways and His Torah.

It is not because the individual is in a church or in a synagogue that he has this love, this willingness, this spark inside his soul. What we see most out there are people who serve false gods, who abolish the Torah, who practice only religion's dogmas, and when they are confronted about these things, they become really aggressive.

So, the first ones called are the Jews, the rest are the Gentiles who have a divine spark within themselves, who seek to serve God and to enter His People, without promises, without rewards, without contracts, without nothing, only for the pleasure to serve the living God.

(this theme is covered elsewhere in this book).

## REASONS FOR THE REWARD

We have already discussed the subject of this parable, but I have not yet dealt with the reason why the lord of the vineyard paid the same wage for workers who worked for different hours.

In the *Midrash Shir HaShirim Rabbah*, a collection of rabbinical teachings on the book of Song of Songs of Solomon, there is a tale very similar to this parable that Yehoshua made. It is very likely that this tale is older than Yehoshua himself and it's popularly widespread among the most scholars. This tale is later associated with Rabbi Bon, as it appears in some parts of the Jerusalem Talmud.

Despite the similarities, the parable of Yehoshua and that *Midrash* are used with different intentions of teaching, but they may be associated. Yehoshua, when he teaches this parable, relies on the prior knowledge of this older *Midrash* from his hearers and, in order not to teach "more of the same", he adds his vision in this parable, without explaining what this tale refers to, for people probably already knew that.

Because they are very ancient, the texts are difficult to translate and are in Aramaic. It follows the most logical way I could translate it:

*It is similar to a king who owned a vineyard, and hired
many laborers to work in his vineyard. This king had
a worker who was extremely skilled in his work, more
than all other workers. What did the king do? He gave
to this worker long breaks in order to rest.
The night has come and the workers came to receive
their wages and this worker went with them and the
king gave him the full salary. The other workers began
to proclaim, saying: We work all day and this one only
for two hours and the king pays him a full salary!
The king says to them, "Why do you complain? This worker
worked in a qualified way. What hurts you about working
all day? Just like Rabbi Bon son of Rabbi Chiyya who had*

*a spiritual qualification for having learned Torah in eighteen years, while the others took a hundred years.*
Shir HaShirim Rabbah 6:2

This *Midrash* does not specifically deal with reward, though it addresses it. The purpose of this teaching is to show the spiritual advantage that the study of Torah gives to those who study it, thus reflecting on the material world by bringing enormous rewards (blessings). The example is Rabbi Bon himself, who by studying Torah, was so skilled in his work that he could do in eighteen years what others would take a hundred to do.

We can understand this skilled worker as one who used to study the Torah. The blessings that came upon him, as recorded in Leviticus 26, were reflected in the material world, making him a good professional, with recognition from the king, with the possibility of rest for study and yet, receiving the entire salary.

In the case of Yehoshua, in addition to teaching this parable, he adds that "the last shall be the first". According to my understanding from this parable, the "last" are the people who will surpass those who have high secular qualifications. That is, a person spends his life studying; He has a college degree, a master's degree, a doctorate's degree, and in the end, he ends up earning the same, or even less, than another individual who is not as skilled as someone with all this studying, but is a person who is a God-fearing and has a life according to the Creator's will. This takes him from a position of inferiority, when compared to the one who studied, and places this God-fearing person above all of those who have all those degrees.

This is something we can see these days when we look at the State of Israel, which, despite being a "new" country, holds half of all the world's Nobel Prize winners, people with no qualifications becoming millionaires, a place that does not have the best universities in the world, but the technological development that happens there surpasses many countries that have the best scientists in the world. It is a country that could be one of the last, but because of the Torah, they are the best in many areas.

Thus follows the true "dinar" of the parable of Yehoshua:

*And when it all happens, if you will obey the voice of
Adonai, your Elohim, to observe and to perform His
Mitzvot, which I have commanded upon you this day, your
Elohim will set you over all the nations of the earth.
And these blessings will come upon you and will take
you, if you will hearken to the voice of Adonai.
Blessed shall you be in the city and in the field, blessed shall
be the fruit of your womb, and the fruit of your land, and the
fruit of your flock, and your cattle and your flock shall grow.
Blessed shall be his basket. Blessed shall you be upon entering
and going out. Adonai will put to rout the enemies that rise up
against you and in seven ways they will flee from you. Adonai
will ordain blessing upon your barns and upon all that you put
your hands and He will bless you in the land where He gives
you... ...Adonai will open the treasures of the heavens, giving
rain to your land in the right time and will bless all the works of
your hands, and you will be creditor to many, but debtor to none.*

Deuteronomy 28:1-12

## TO BE CALLED x TO BE CHOSEN

Many teach that those who are called are those who are far from the church, who have had the opportunity to hear about jesus and have not accepted him, while those within a temple would be the true chosen ones. But in truth, Yehoshua was referring exclusively to Israel and he based himself on a passage found in the book of Isaiah:

*Adonai Elohim, who created His People, says: "Do
not be afraid, for I will save you, I will call you
by your name, FOR YOU ARE MINE!*

Isaiah 43:1

Whoever God really called was the People of Israel, He called them to serve Him and to be His. Theology disseminates deception through the Christian replacement theology, of how the church took the place of Israel, and how this prophecy now refers to the church, for the Jews denied jesus. But God does not speak things only to change His mind later, when He said this through the prophet Isaiah, God already knew of the rejection that Yehoshua would have. Yet, he still made this claim in reference to the People of Israel, the church will never, ever, take the place of the People of Israel before the Lord. Those prophetic words of Isaiah show that God will call Israel by its name, that Israel will be saved by the Creator Himself, they will be taken by the hand, for they are HIS. However, the Gentile who becomes adopted and engrafted unto God's People, may also be included in that promise.

Those who are called and are not chosen, to which Yehoshua refers, are also found within the People of Israel, will be those whom Paul mentions in Romans 11, when he claims that many branches will be cut off from the "olive tree" so others may be grafted. In other words, by combining the passage of Isaiah with this from the book of Romans, when the Gentile is adopted as a son and enters into the People of Israel, it indirectly says that this gentile will be saved by God, he will become His alone and he will be redeemed through his obedience to the Almighty. We must always keep in mind that Yehoshua preached to the House of Israel and to the House of Yehudah, all that he spoke was based on the Torah, the prophets and with his people in mind. If we do not seek the understanding of his words with these two things in mind, we will make a great mess of interpretation.

*May the Gentile, who enters the People of Israel, never say, "Adonai will keep me apart from His People" ... ... The foreigner who Worships Him, who loves His name, to be his servant, all those who observe the Shabbat, by not profaning it and who hold fast to my covenant. I will bring him to my holy mountain and he will rejoice in my house of prayer. His burnt offerings and sacrifices shall be accepted at my altar, for my house shall be called the house of prayer for all people.*

Isaiah 56:3 + 6-7

One last observation: to enter the People of Israel is to accept the Torah and the God's covenant, and NOT TO BE-COME A JEW. Judaism is a religion, the People of Israel is a people. Let's make no confusion.

# SECTION VI
## THE VINEYARD

*At that time, Yeshua said to his talmidim and to a company
of the Jews: listen to the parable of the sower. A certain
honorable man planted a vineyard and walled it up all around,
built a tower in the middle, also dug a vat in it and entrusted
it to the hands of his servants and went on his way.
It came to pass, at the time of the harvest of the produce, he
sent his servants to the tenants to receive his produce.
And the tenants took his servants, and smote the first, and
slew the second, and stoned the third with stones.
And he sent many more servants after the
first, and they did the same to them.
Finally he decided to send his son, saying: perhaps
they will see my son.
And the tenants saw his son, and said one to another, This
is the heir; let us kill him, and inherit his inheritance.
And they took him, and cast him out of the vineyard,
and killed him.
And now when the lord of the vineyard comes,
what will he do with them?
And they answered him, saying, The wicked shall be
destroyed, and his vineyard shall be given to other tenants,
who shall immediately give him his share of his produce.
And Yeshua said to them, have you not read what is written?
The stone rejected by the builders will become the head of the
corner. This is from Adonai (tetragram), it is marvel in our eyes.
Therefore I tell you that the Kingdom of Heaven will be torn
before you and given to the Gentiles who bear fruit. (tear
of the veil, opening of the place where the Torah was)
He who falls upon this stone will be cast down. He
who falls upon it will be broken apart.
And the leaders of the sages and the Pharisees heard this
parable, and understood that he was speaking about them.*

*And they sought to kill him, but they feared the*
*multitude, to whom he was a prophet.*

Matthew 21:33-46

According to my point of view, from all the parables found in the book of Matthew, this is the most dangerous. The false impression of simplicity that it passes, served as the basis for the church's fathers to create a false Christian theology called "replacement theology".

Alongside with this theology came the anti-Semitism, because the feeling created inside the Christians, who believe in this theology, is that of a certain superiority towards the People of Israel. A misinterpretation of texts from the Bible is a risk without equal, because all misinterpretations create lies, lies create heresies, heresies create theologies and theologies create sects and pagans religions.

## Replacement Theology

This theology, also known as *supersessionism*, suggests that the old covenant of Sinai was replaced by a new covenant made by christ. This "substitution" was due to the non-acceptance of jesus by the Jews and therefore, God transferred all the promises He had given the Jewish people to the church, making it the true Israel of God.

Church's Fathers, such as John Chrysostom, Justyn Martyr, Augustine of Hippo, Origen and Martin Luther teach that all the promises, that once belonged to Israel, was taken away from them and given to the church, for God punished them for not having accepted and having killed the jesus. For this reason, some of them, like Luther and Chrysostom, strongly encouraged their followers to persecute and punish the Jews, for they became a race wretched by God.

In one way or another, directly or indirectly, many churches follow this theology, which generates a huge distance between the church and the divine will. Christian theologians, as many arrogant leaders from various denominations, believe that they are the owners of the truth, they are indoctrinated into fouls theologies, and they end up teaching and defending such concepts up to the point of becoming incredibly resistant to any idea that the Torah represents.

This is a fetid theology, in addition to the enormous misfortune it has brought to the Jewish people, it goes against what God Himself says:

> *Thus said Adonai, Who stablishdd the sun for light by day, who had decreed that the moon and the stars for light by night, who stirs up the sea into roaring waves, whose name is the Lord of hosts. When these things cease to exist, Adonai says, also the descendants of Israel shall cease to be a nation before me, for they shall be it for ever.*
>
> Jeremiah 31:35-36

## THE PARABLE

If we follow the "obvious", we will understand that the vineyard from this parable is God's promise, the bad tenants are the Jews, the king's son is jesus, who was killed by the Jews and the alleged new tenants, those who will receive the vineyard (promise), are the church. I cannot deny that a reading without a "baggage" of necessary knowledge about Judaism and the social context of Yehoshua, leads precisely to this understanding. However, because this interpretation has generated theological lies, it already provides enough reason to look at this parable in search for other interpretations.

God will never replace the People of Israel. It is inconsistent with the promises made by Him, if such an idea were taught by Yehoshua, we would have a great heretic who really deserved to be killed because of it. But this is not the case, Yehoshua kept himself in accordance with the Word of God in all his teachings, the idea of a church was not part of his reality, the People of Israel has always been the goal of his mission.

## The Targets

Due to these reasons, we must look at this parable with a new mindset and without vices, we must understand what would be this vineyard, the tenants, the son and the new tenants. First of all, it is vital to understand the context in which Yehoshua was inserted at the moment of this passage and who were the targets of it.

*And he went to Mikdash to teach Torah and there came to him the sages and the priests and leaders of the people...*
Matthew 21:23a

A few verses above, Matthew reports that Yehoshua was in Jerusalem, he was teaching near the *Mikdash* (Temple) and among the many *talmidim*, the author is categorical in affirming that the sages, the priests and the leaders were also there. Only with this information, it already reveals for whom it was this message.

As mentioned earlier, Yehoshua had two enemies, some of the Pharisees who placed their authorities above the Torah and the Sadducees. At the time of the second Temple, all politics, Templar services and judiciary were in the hands of this group, its members had full control over Israel and the Jewish people, they decided who was guilty or innocent, they decided how the relationship with the Roman Empire should be, they decided how Judaism should be observed, they chose who the priests would be, whether they were from the tribe of Levi or not, and they decided which Torah laws were to be observed. They were people who grew rich and possessed great power and influence. Yehoshua's death was "carried out" when he began to attack the Sadducees, by causing revolt among the people due to the Sadducee's doctrines and manipulations that went against those determined by God.

## The Vineyard

Within Jewish literature, for many times, the vineyard is used as a symbol for the People of Israel. In both the Torah and the Talmud, many associations are made between the two. But there are a few cases that, due to the context where the teaching is inserted, the vineyard has other representations besides Israel.

In that case, Yehoshua was inside Israel, talking to people of Israel on matters concerning Israel. Using the symbology of the vineyard in reference to this land would be inconsistent, for talking about Israel in the midst of Israelis is not a risk and therefore, the use of a parable would be unnecessary. For this reason, we must see this "vineyard" as a representation other than Israel.

A very unusual term is used by Yehoshua in this parable, it is brought up when he initially calls the people who took care of the vineyard as "servants" and in the following verse, he begins to call them as "tenants". The Hebrew term for tenants is EIRISIM (עריסים) and it appears in a *Midrash*, by making a connection with "*receiving something*", just as these "*tenants*" received the vineyard:

*When God revealed Himself to Moses on Mount Sinai in order to give the Torah to Israel, He taught it to Moses in the following order: Torah, Mishnah, Talmud and Aggadah. Moses said to God, "God, should I write them down?" And God said, "I do not want you to give them to Israel in writing, for I know that in the future the nations will reign over them and take their Torah and it will be degraded by the nations, therefore I will give you the Scriptures in writing, but the Mishnah, Talmud and Aggadah, I will give them to you orally ... ... For I gave the nations (**EIRISIM-tenants**) a portion of my commandments and they degraded it, then I gave another portion of my commandments again and again and they degraded them, then came my son, Israel, who took the commandments* *from them, but the nations decided to kill Israel, my son.*

Shemot Rabbah 47

Just as in the parable of Yehoshua, where the tenants received something, according to this *Midrash*, the tenants also received something. *Shemot Rabbah* tells us that God gave commandments to some tenants to guard them, but they despised and disobeyed them, then God again gave his commandments to other nations, to serve as tenants of the Creator's will, and once again, the nations disrespected them, and finally God decides to give them to Israel and for this reason, because they became the tenats of the Torah of God, the Jews have always been a persecuted people.

When Yehoshua associates *"receiving something"* with *"becoming a tenant"* by the usage of the Hebrew word EIRISIM (עריסים), the crowd who heard him quickly understood that the "vineyard", which Yehoshua referred to, was the Torah itself. For such association was only possible by the *midrashic* terms used by Yehoshua, otherwise the vineyard would be understood as Israel itself.

### The Son

Lastly, we should look at the figure of the son. It would not make sense to believe that Yehoshua would be the son in this case, for it would not be logic with what we have raised so far.

There is another well-known *Midrash* that tells a very similar story to the one told by Yehoshua:

*A king had a field and gave it to his servants, who began to steal from him - then it was passed to their sons, who were even worse than the first ones. When a son was born to the king, the son said to them, "Get out of my place" ... ... You, Israel, were chosen by your God to be His son, His people.*

Sifrei Devarim 312:1

The similarity of both parables is undeniable, so this

connection between the two can be useful. In *Sifrei Devarim* we have the revelation of who this son would be and it is precisely the People of Israel.

## Conclusion

Yehoshua, in his enormous knowledge of Oral Torah, uses it in his teachings, so his teachings speak for themselves. He sent a message gathering various stories from the *Midrash*. First he set up a scenario according to *Sifrei Devarim* in order to show that he was speaking about Israel, the son. Then he presents the vineyard and the tenants through the *Midrash* of *Shemot Rabbah*, which makes an allusion of the vineyard with the Torah and of the tenants with the nations. In this way, he is able to send a subtle, but straightforward message, to the Sadducees.

*And the leaders of the sages and the Pharisees heard this parable, and understood that he was speaking about them.*
Matthew 21:45

According to Yehoshua, the power of decision that concerns the Law's of God, i.e. the Torah, was given to the Sadducees (who were servants at the beginning) by God, just as the vineyard was given to the tenants (who were called servants at the beginning), but they became evil, illicitly enriched, created concepts that were contrary to God's commandments and all of this was killing the People of Israel, a spiritual death that was taking place because they were in control and this was also bringing physical death to the people. Therefore, the king would come and take them out of power, passing this power to new tenants, who are the tenants up to this day, the orthodox Pharisees.

After the fall of the Temple and the destruction of Israel by the Romans, the Sadducees completely disappeared, it is a group that little is known about and its existence represents absolutely nothing in the history of the Jews, just a memory in the past. On the other hand, everything fell into the hands of the Pharisees, nowadays, everything is regulated by the Orthodox, the synagogues are led by them, the studies are passed down by them, the marriages, the conversion, the Beit Din (house of law) are controlled by them, as well as how it must be the relationship between the people and the Torah. This parable, which was actually a prophecy, came to pass.

It is not about the church, it is not about replacements, it is not about Christians, it is not about anything that Christian theology insists to teach.

### The Rejected Stone

*The stone that the builders rejected, has become the main cornerstone*

Psalm 118:22

*All Israel will be the main building of the world, for the commandments of Adonai, which have been rejected by the nations, are its cornerstone.*

Radak, Psalms 118:22

The Mention of this passage in Psalms makes total sense, as it can be seen from the explanation of the great sage Rabbi David Kimchi, RaDaK.

It would be obvious to say that this cornerstone would be Yehoshua, for he was rejected, as many interpret this passage. But if that were the case, we would have two problems. First, he would become the cornerstone of what, of the church? If this understanding were correct, then we would fall into the theological interpretation described above, we would again have an anti-Semitic and a pro replacement theology understanding.

The second problem is about the rejection he suffers. As we study closely, we will see that Yehoshua had many followers and *talmidim*, which shows clearly that he did not suffer rejection on the part of the people, his rejection was on the part of the Sadducees, the leaders, the priests and the judges, as well as from some Pharisee's and sage's schools, who felt offended when Yehoshua criticized them for being hypocrites and for placing their authority above the Torah. The Jewish people, in general, did not reject him, the idea of a Mashiach was very well accepted among the Jews and we see it by Paul himself, who was always well received in the synagogues throughout the Diaspora when he taught about Yehoshua.

Yehoshua's rejection by the Jews came much later when the church made them "swallow" a jesus created by it, who had nothing to do with Yehoshua Ben Yosef, besides the two thousand years of suffering that these people suffered "in the name of jesus".

Even if Yehoshua does not represent the cornerstone in this case, his teaching is not disqualified or made less valued, for his words, his revelation given through the parable, have been fulfilled. The cornerstone, mentioned in the book of Psalms and by Yehoshua, is the Torah.

### The Gentiles

*Therefore I tell you that the Kingdom of Heaven will be torn before you and given to the Gentiles who bear fruit. (tear of the veil, opening of the place where the Torah was) He who falls upon this stone will be cast down. He who falls upon it will be broken apart.*

Matthew 21:43

Yehoshua makes another allusion, he says that the Kingdom of Heaven will be torn, just as the curtains were torn in the temple at the moment of his death. This curtain is what separated the Holy of Holies from the rest of the Temple, it was behind that curtain that *Aron HaKadosh* (the ark of the covenant) was placed. With this statement, Yehoshua says that in the Kingdom of Heaven (the time that we are now) the curtains that separate the ark from the people would be torn before the Gentiles, which means a direct access to the Scriptures, for inside the ark is where the Torah's Scrolls were.

This message that Yehoshua passed on also materialized, since every Gentile has easy access to the Torah now a days.

But let us pay attention to one small detail, Yehoshua does not say that the Torah (the understanding of it) will be given to the Gentiles "in order to bear fruit", not to the Gentiles who "will bear fruit", but rather to the Gentiles who "BEAR FRUITS" (the verb is in the present sentence), that is, he mentions those Gentiles who already know the Torah and through it, already bear fruit. The "tear of the curtains" does not only represents access to the Torah, but also the revelation and understanding of the secrets of the Torah and about God will be given only to those who already practice it.

## Stone

*He who falls upon this **stone** will be cast down. He who falls upon it will **be broken apart**.*
Matthew 21:44

The confirmation of all this comes from the last words of Yehoshua when he connects two passages from the Tanakh:

*In that day I will make Jerusalem a heavy **stone** for all peoples, all who try to move it will be greatly wounded. All the nations of the earth will unite to fight against it.*
Zechariah 12:3

*Many of them will stumble, fall and be **broken apart**...*
Isaiah 8:15a

The first verse talks about the "stone" and the second about "being broken apart". The stone is Israel, which is the son of the king, which one all the nations will try to *move* (destroy it). In the second one, it refers to the stumbling of the Sadducees and to all those who try to, somehow, cause any harm to Israel.

### Moral

This passage fits very well in our days. It is very common to see leaders, pastors, priests, rabbis and so on, using God's word for self-enrichment, to gather followers, to gain power and influence. God has delivered His word into the hands of these men, and they use it in a selfish, materialistic, self-winning way.

Like the evil tenants and the Sadducees, they will be destroyed by the hands of God Himself, for they guide people by using misleading and vicious teachings. They will all be blamed for it.

# SECTION VII
## THE TEN VIRGINS

*Yeshua said to his talmidim: the kingdom of heaven is like ten
virgins who took their lamps and went out to meet the bride-
groom and the bride. (IN THE ORIGINAL THERE IS THE BRIDE).
Five of them were lazy and foolish, and five
of them were alert and wise.
The five fools brought their lamps, but did not bring the oil.
And the wise brought the vessels of oil together with their lamps.
And the bridegroom was late and behold they all lingered
and fell asleep.
Then at midnight, behold a voice was heard: behold, the
bride and the groom have come, come and meet them.
Then all the virgins came and trimmed their lamps.
The foolish ones said to the wise: Give us some of
your oils, for our lamps have gone out.
And the wise answered, saying, Please go to the vendors
and buy from them, for we have not enough for
ourselves and for you, we fear to run out of it.
And it was when they went to buy, the bridegroom arrived, and
the virgins went with him to CHUPAH and closed the gates.
Afterwards, the foolish ones came and shouted
from the gates, saying: Our Lord, open to us.
And he answered to them, trully I say to
you, I do not know who you are.
So, be careful, because you do not know the
day nor the hour of CHUPAH.*

Matthew 25:1-13

I remember one day, when a Christian friend of mine, explained to me this parable for the first time. According to him, this allegory talks about the end of times, about what he defined as "tribulation", by which the Jews and those who do not serve God will pass through.

He defined the bridegroom as being the christ, his bride would be the church and while both would be inside the hall (paradise) enjoying the feast, the virgins who stood outside represent the Jews during the *"tribulation"* as defined by the Christian eschatology. Half of this group of Jews, the wise ones, would recognize jesus as the savior god, while the other group, the fools, would not bow to such an idea and therefore would be destined for the eternal fire.

I see this interpretation as something very problematic. First, it was based on unscriptural eschatological concepts and secondly for the simple fact of teaching a very anti-Semitic idea. Two questions came to my mind when I heard this interpretation given by my acquaintance. First, why the church would be all special and the God's chosen people completely diminished? And second, why would Yehoshua speak about church, something totally out of his reality? The impression is that of an arrogant church, which believes and teaches that its faith is above other beliefs, other peoples, Torah, God, everything.

A second interpretation that I have been told is that the ten virgins represent the Christians, the wises are those who attend church, who live a life conforming to Christianity, who follow human puritanism as God's law and preach the gospel, while the foolish are those who have accepted jesus but they strayed from the church. Okay, less problematic than the previous one, but I still wonder, was Yehoshua really talking about a Christian life, a life according to what was created and defined by human hands in Rome? Perhaps because of my limitations, I cannot find anywhere in the Bible a teaching that says that a Christian life is what brings one to eternal life. I also can't find nothing about the knowledge that Yehoshua had about what would "a church" be.

I believe that each one should stick to whatever one believes, if one agrees with the above interpretations, amen, may one go and live according to it. But for those who seek something beyond the ordinary, I would like to present an interpretation in conformity to first-century Judaism, through the Torah and the Talmud, which form the basis of knowledge and the person of Yehoshua.

## THE MESSAGE

This parable deals with a specific matter, "*precaution*". The two kinds of people, reported as *"virgins"*, are differentiated according to the type of preparation they had and how that preparation would make them always ready for an emergency, which in this case, is the arrival of the bride and the groom.

Every good Jew eagerly awaits the coming of Mashiach and as the time is unknown, precaution is vastly addressed in the Talmud in various ways, for everyone must be prepared for this special day and thus be able to recognize and be accepted by Mashiach. The Oral Torah relates another parable of a very famous rabbi, Rabbi Akiva, who speaks about the same theme as Yehoshua in this parable. Remembering that both parables are not from such distant periods.

*Rabbi Akiva answered him: I will relate a parable. What can this be compared to? It is like a fox walking alongside a river and sees a group of fish fast swimming from one side to another. The fox told them: What are you running away from? And they said: we are running away from the nets that people cast at us. The fox said to them: don't you want to come here in dry lands, we can live together, just as my ancestors lived together with their ancestors? One fish said to the fox: are you not the one who is said to be the **wisest** among the animals? You are certainly not wise, you are **foolish**. If we are already scared in the water, in our natural habitat that gives us life, just imagine in an environment that would cause us certain death. The moral is: so as we, Israel, even by having **precaution** by sitting and studying Torah, we are still at great risk,*

*just imagine if we were **fools** and we did not study it?*
*It would be like to abandon our natural habitat.*
Talmud of Babylon, Tractate Brakhot 61b

This parable speaks about precaution and what it would be. Rabbi Akiva uses as an example a dialogue between a fox and a fish to show that, what keeps the People of Israel alive and prepared is to hold on to what connects them to the Living God, the Torah. Just as it is better for the fish to stay in the water, even at the risk of falling into the net, it is much better for the whoever serves God to maintain himself in the ways of the Torah, even if it risky.

*Preparation in the Torah is the **precaution** of keeping*
*away the possibility of sinning.*
Rashi in reference to Brakhot 2a

## TERMINOLOGY

Before we reach a final conclusion, we must also note some very specific terms used in this parable.

### Chupah

In modern Judaism, this word is most commonly used in reference to the small hut, where the bride and the groom stays below during the wedding ceremony. But more generally, this term refers to the wedding itself. Weddings in first-century Judaism, from the beginning of the first ceremony, up to the nuptial night, lasted seven days.

Before the wedding, it was customary to set a contract between the bride's family and the groom's family, which was signed a year earlier before the ceremony and during that time, the groom should prepare the house and the way to financially support it. The bride, however, should prepare herself to be a good wife to her husband. All this process, from the contract until the end of the seven days of celebrations, can be called CHUPAH.

Something interesting happens in this parable, something that does not appear in other translations, the groom arrives with the bride, that is, he is already married, this is proven by the fact that they arrive at night. No Jewish wedding celebration is held overnight, meaning whoever represents these virgins, they are not the bride and they play another part in this story.

## Oil

Oil has a very specific connotation throughout Jewish literature. There were several types of oils in the first century, the two most important are the olive oil (שמן זית - *shemen zait*), which had several functions, not only to light a lamp, and a cheaper oil, called *shemen* (שמן), that was produced from animal's fat. This second one, for it was a cheaper oil, was used to light lamps. This oil that Yehoshua quotes is used exclusively to illuminate, so, it is a great representative of the idea of "light".

*Your Word is a lamp to my feet and a light for my path.*
Psalms 119:105

*Oil (shemen), that is, the Torah.*
Bamidbar Rabbah 13:16

The Oil (*shemen*) represents the Torah itself, just as the oil lights our path, so the Torah lights our lives. Unlike the olive oil, which has other functions besides illuminating, the *shemen* has a unique function, thus making it as a better representation of the Torah, whose sole purpose is to bring Adonai's light upon our lives.

## To Carry Oil Vessels

Finally, Yehoshua also reports that the wises carried oil vessels. Just as oil represents the Torah, because it generates light, the *"to carry oil"*, according to the Oral Torah, is the study of the Torah:

*It was taught in a baraita that Rabbi Yehuda HaNasi said:*

*when we study Torah, it is like if we were carrying oils.*
Talmud of Babylon, Tractate Shabbat 147b

## THE BRIDE

According to Christianity, the church is the bride of the lamb. One day jesus will return to this earthly realm in order to take his bride to dwell with him on a different planet, or whatever. The idea of "bride" is nothing more than a symbology that refers to the people who are chosen by God in order to serve Him and to receive eternal life.

I know that Christian theology has several theses to prove such a concept, but I would like to look at something very simple in the Bible:

*It will not be like the covenant that I made with their fathers, when I took them by the hand and brought them out of the land of Egypt, a covenant which they broke, **but I still married them** - declares Adonai.*
Jeremiah 31:32

We all know that there were several kings, such as David and Solomon, who possessed several women, but looking at the norms of the Torah, at the teachings of Yehoshua, and for the rabbinical approach concerning marriage, polygamy does not seem to be what God has determined. God can really do whatever He wants to, but by self-determination, He has decided to restrict Himself to His Word, that is, God acts according to what says the Scriptures. Now, if the Word determines monogamy, why then, God, would take the church as bride, since He is married to the People of Israel, His eternal bride?

I find church's theory, that claims the church to be the bride, quite disturbing, but as I said before, each one has to keep whatever one believes. If God is already "married" to His people and Mashiach comes to take care of this people, then, Mashiach comes to the People of Israel, as Yehoshua himself has already said that he came to the lost sheep of the

House of Israel. It is not because many have not accepted the messianic message of Yehoshua, that God has divorced this people to take other people for Himself, for if that were the case, God would be a liar.

**THE PARABLE**

I believe we now have everything we need to *"connect the loose ends"* and to better understand what Yehoshua said from a more Jewish perspective.

First we have the groom, who is Mashiach, who arrives with his bride, the People of Israel (I do not mean Judaism or members of the Jewish religion) and ten virgins go to greet them.

All ten knew who Mashiach was and knew the Torah, for they all knew the need for oil and recognized him. Unlike the foolish, the wise made precautions, in addition to recognizing Mashiach and knowing the Torah, they studied it and used its light to illuminate their ways, that is, they used the Torah to determine the way of life they should follow, by following its Laws and Ordinances, just as it was ordained by God. By doing so, they would be ready for the coming of Mashiach. The other five, although they knew the Torah, this knowledge was not sufficient for a life change according to God's will. This happens for a variety of reasons, from little concern about God and His will, up to a belief in the abolition of the Torah.

Finally, when the ten virgins are presented before the bridegroom, the first five are invited to enter and to join the people of Israel, and the last five, Mashiach looks at them and does not recognize them, because they did not have a behavior according to what God has determined.

The bride, the People of Israel, represents those who are already part of the people whom God has chosen for Himself and will be recognized by Mashiach, and the 10 virgins represent the Gentiles, who will be recognized, or not, through the lifestyle they have and according to how enlighten are their ways. If this path is illuminated by THE "oil", they will enter.

# PART IV
# FINAL CONCEPTS

# SECTION I
## JOHN'S MYSTICISM

*In the beginning was the Word, and the Word*
*was with God, and the Word was God.*
*The same was in the beginning with God.*
*All things were made by him; and without him*
*was not any thing made that was made.*
*In him was life; and the life was the light of men.*
*And the light shines in darkness; and the darkness*
*comprehended it not.*
*There was a man sent from God, whose name was John.*
*The same came for a witness, to bear witness of the*
*Light, that all men through him might believe.*
*He was not that Light, but was sent to bear witness of that Light.*
*That was the true Light, which lights every*
*man that comes into the world.*
*He was in the world, and the world was made*
*by him, and the world knew him not.*
*He came to his own, and his own received him not.*
*But as many as received him, to them gave he power to become*
*the sons of God, even to them that believe on his name:*
*Which were born, not of blood, nor of the will of*
*the flesh, nor of the will of man, but of God.*
*And the Word was made flesh, and dwelled among*
*us, (and we beheld his glory, the glory as of the only*
*begotten of the Father), full of grace and truth.*

John 1:1-14 KJV

John really is an intriguing person. Among the four authors of the four gospels, he is the only one who makes an approach that does not address the deeds of Yehoshua itself. The book of John works on a singular concept, the very person of the one he called master, John presents a more human side, rather than the rabbi side of Yehoshua.

This is because John has a different spirituality from the other followers, he has a more human side, he is more connected to what don't meet the eyes, this is a kind of sensitivity proves the mysticism on which he based his faith on. This mysticism is not only proven by the way he makes his approache, but also by the language that, in a cabalistic way, he writes his book.

Just as the book of Matthew was written in Hebrew, contrary to the teaching of the church, the book of John was also written in Hebrew, I can affirm that, because the *Biblioteca Apostòlica Vaticana*, without knowing what it was, placed among its digital files, the copy of the first page of John's original book and incredible as it may seem, it is in Hebrew. Below, I will put the translation from the original that I made myself, it should be compared with the western version above, so we can see a few, but extremely important changes and using the translation from the original, I will raise some studies about it:

*In the beginning of the Word, the Word was with*
*Elohim, and Adonai (tetragram) was the Word.*
*It was in the beginning with Elohim.*
*All things were made through IT (the word), and without*
*IT (the word) nothing that was made, would be made.*
*In IT (the word) was the light of life, and*
*the life was the light of men.*
*And the light shines in the darkness, and by those from*
*the darkness, IT (the word) is not understood.*
*There was a man sent from Adonai, called Yohanan.*
*He came as a witness, that he might testify about the*
*light, that all might believe through IT (the word).*
*He was not the light, but one to testify through the light.*
*There was the true light, which enlightens*
*every man that comes into the world.*
*IT (the word) was in the world, and the world was made through*
*IT (the word), and the world did not know IT (the word).*

*And Then (only after all above) one came to those
who were his, and his own received him not.
But all who received him, it has been given to them he power to
be made children of Elohim, those who understood his teaching;
Who were born not of blood, nor of the will of the
flesh, nor of the will of man, but of Adonai.
And the Word was made as flesh, and dwelt among us, and
we beheld ITS glory (of the Word), as the glory of the
the only begotten son of the Father, full of grace and truth.*
John 1:1-14, from the original in Hebrew

Now, from the original translation, we are going to raise some biblical verses considered mystical in the Kabbalah, and do some comparisons of them with John's words.

## IN THE BEGINNING

*In the beginning God created the heavens and the earth.*
Genesis 1:1

*In the beginning of the Word, the Word was with
Elohim, and Adonai (tetragram) was the Word.*
John 1:1

As already seen in the beginning of this book, this "beginning" that John quotes, is not the same "beginning" as reported in Genesis 1:1, but rather it is a "beginning" that represents the creation of the Laws of God, the creation of the Torah, for he says that in this "beginning" was *"the beginnig of the Word"*, thus revealing what has already been studied previously.

Then he claims that Adonai (ה-ו-ה-י) was the Word, he does not say that Elohim was the Word, but rather Adonai (ה-ו-ה-י). He makes a comparison of the Torah with the name above all names, the tetragrammaton. This is something that can only be understood through Gematria:

## TORAH (תורה)

ת 400 + 6ו + 200 ר + ה5
$= 611 = 6+1+1 = 8$

## ADONAI (י-ה-ו-ה)

י10 + ה5 + 6ו + ה5
$= 26 = 2 + 6 = 8$

Gematria reveals us that the absolute value of the name of God is the same absolute value of the word Torah. John, in asserting that Adonai was the Word, does not claim that the Torah is a god, but he demonstrates mystically that the essence that the Torah possesses is the same essence found in the name above all names, the essence From the One who created it.

Many believe that the Word, as mentioned by John, is Yehoshua himself, but such an idea is not true, this is a concept formulated by Western minds without prior knowledge of the Jewish mentality. The book of John begins with the statement that the Torah represents the essence of the Creator on this earth.

## YEHOSHUA x THE WORD

*Through the Torah, heavens and earth were created.*
Likutei Moharan 54:6:2

*All things were made through IT (the word), and without IT (the word) nothing that was made, would be made.*
John 1:3

*IT (the word) was in the world, and the world was made through IT (the word), and the world did not know IT (the word).*
John 1:10

The book *Likutei Moharan* is a Kabbalistic book that has a collection of mystical Jewish teachings, which come from more than two thousand years ago, but it was compiled only two hundred years ago. As we can see in John's words, he is in accordance with the Jewish mystical mentality and belief.

He states that the Word, the Torah, was in the world, for it was brought to us through Moses, then he claims what we have already seen above, that the world was created through it and lastly, he says that the world did not know it, which is clearly true, for the knowledge of the Torah until the first century was almost exclusive to the Jews.

Unlike the partial translation of the church, instead of the word "IT", we find the word "HE". That changes everything, for John has not yet begun to speak about Yehoshua. If we keep the "HE", we will have the impression that John talks about Yehoshua, which takes away the essence of the text. In this verse, John is still in his argument about the Torah, for it is necessary to prove that Yehoshua is Mashiach.

## LIFE AND LIGHT

> *In IT (the word) was the light of life, and*
> *the life was the light of men.*

John 1:4

> *Your Word is a lamp to my feet and a light to my path.*

Psalms 119:105

> *I will never forget Your Torah, for through it, You gave me life*

Psalms 119:93

John, in his argument about the Word of God, quotes two psalms. He associates the Word with light and with life, as we see in the mentioned verses above.

Unlike the translations we have, he has not yet presented Yehoshua in his book.

## DARKNESS

> *And the light shines in the darkness, and by those from*
> *the darkness, IT (the word) is not understood.*

John 1:5

*I ponder Your Torah, therefore I hate every false way.*

Psalms 119:104

This is a statement we see a lot these days in places where worship services are provided, places where many people do not understand the Word of God. It is very common for leaders to take advantage of loose and disconnected verses, using them with totally erroneous, manipulative, and poor interpretations, in order to deceive those who hear them.

The statement that John makes is the same as that taught by the Psalm. Those who do such things, do because they have no understanding, they are from the darkness and they like the false ways. This is a very strong claim, for it seems that he already knew what would happen to his book for the next two thousand years. Many, in the name of "God", use John's writings for his own benefit and personal gain. Those are from the real darkness.

## THOSE WHO WERE HIS

*And Then one came to those who were his,*
*and his own received him not.*

John 1:11

In verse 11 we have the first mention about Yehoshua, that is when he finally comes into the scene. John affirms what we all know. He came to those who were the People of God, but this People of God did not receive him, as prophesied by the prophet Isaiah.

## WORD MADE FLESH

*And the Word was made as flesh, and dwelt among us, and*
*we beheld ITS glory (of the Word), as the glory of the*
*the only begotten son of the Father, full of grace and truth.*

John 1:14

Now that all the Christian Trinitarian confused idea

begins. They claim that John says that the word is "god" and then says that the word became flesh, it automatically associates the idea of a jesus that is a god, or that god is jesus. This interpretation made through the writings of John is completely incoherent and heretical if we read the original with a previous knowledge of the Word of God and the Jewish mystique.

First, let's look at some Jewish customs:

*And when James, Cephas, and John, who seemed to be pillars, perceived the grace that was given to me, they gave to me and Barnabas the right hands of fellowship; that we should go to the heathen, and they to the circumcision.*

Galatians 2:9 KJV

This passage in Galatians relates the moment in which Paul finally gets to know and submits himself under the apostles' authority in Jerusalem. One thing that few notice here is the way Paul refers to the apostles, he calls them "*pillars*".

All over the Talmud, it is very common to find some "nicknames" given to some illustrious figures of Jewish history, when the one had a high spiritual level, there was the custom of nick naming him with parts of the Holy Temple or holy things.

*When the patriarchs came and showed themselves righteous. God said, "In them I will establish My world"; As it is written (1 Samuel 2: 8): "For the pillars of the earth belong unto the Lord, and over them, He upholds the world"*

Midrash Exodus Rabbah 15:7

Another Talmudic passage also shows the students of Rabbi Yochanan Ben Zakkai referring to him as "the right-hand column", in reference to the pillar on the right side of the Temple's Gate.

Paul, as a good Jew and a profound connoisseur of the

Talmud, addresses the apostles as *"pillars"* in reference to the columns at the entry of the Holy Temple, which represented the Temple's function of "sustaining" the world.

Yehoshua uses the same kind of terminology when he said to be the "gate", for he was precisely referring to the gate of the Saints of Saints, within the Sacred Temple, where the Torah and the *Shekhinah* of God were found, thus making an analogy to what his teaching represented. A rabbinical custom on the part of Paul and Yehoshua.

As alleged elsewhere, Yehoshua had no sin, and since what defines sin is the Torah, it reveals to us that he had a life 100% according to the Laws of God. When this occurs in one's life, this person is automatically called "The Torah" or "The Living Torah" in the Jewish milieu. It is very common to see students of certain sages calling their masters with these nicknames.

With John it was no different, as for him, Yehoshua had a life according to the commandments of God, interpreted it and taught Torah it, for this reason it would be common to call him "The Torah", or "The Word", or "The Living Word of God" or anything similar.

Another point to consider is the term "**AS** flesh", this term is used in a comparative way. John does not claim that the Torah itself became flesh, but he says that Yehoshua lived the Torah so intensely that it was AS if the Torah had been made flesh, for it was possible to see it through one's life, in this case, of Yehoshua's.

Yehoshua makes use of this kind of custom elsewhere in the book of John:

> *Jesus said to him, I am the **way**, the **truth**, and the **life**: no man comes to the Father, but by me.*
>
> John 14:6 KJV

> *And I am the **way** to the **truth** that gives **life**. No one comes to the Father except through this.*

John 14:6, from the original Hebrew

It is amazing the discrepancy that this passage has in its translations in comparison to the original. In western languages, we have three different types of adjectives that are not given to people, only to things. This shows us that Yehoshua uses this custom of "nicknames" to refer to himself. The interesting thing is that he does not nickname himself three times, but rather only one, by claiming that he is the way, the terms "truth" and "life" do not refer to him, but rather to what he, as a way, leads to.

Let's look at these three terms through the Jewish lens:

*The **way** to be chosen is the one where the Holy One, Blessed Be He, is made worthy in that way. The way to be chosen is that when the commandments are performed in the proper way.*
Rabbeinu Yonah on Pikei Avot 2:1:1

*And **truth** (EMET) refers only to the Torah, as it is written: buy the truth and do not sale it, as well as wisdom, guidance and understanding.*
Talmud of Babylon, Tractate Brakhot 5b

*You shall keep my Laws and ordinances, by which, man shall have eternal **life**. I am Adonai.*
Leviticus 18:5

First, we see *Rabbeinu Yonah's* commentary on the passage found in Pirkei Avot 2:1, which talks about which ways one should choose. He claims that it must be the one who dignifies God, he also claims that the way is where the commandments are performed in the right way.

This brings some meaning to Yehoshua's claim about being "the way", for by the Jewish cliché, when a rabbi is recognized as the "way", it is not he who is the way, but rather his teachings on how to observe the commandments of the

Torah. When Yehoshua makes such a statement, he says that the way he has been teaching Torah, is the way it should be followed and observed and not according to other rabbis.

So he claims that his teaching on Torah is what will lead the person who follows him to the true truth, the EMET (truth in Hebrew) and that means the Torah itself. The word EMET (truth) is one of the very few words in Hebrew that has no plural form, for truth only exists one.

Finally, he says that this truth gives life. As promised by God in the book of Leviticus, every man who observes His Law, will have eternal life.

So, we might try a new approach:

*I am the **way**, for my teachings of Torah are what really will lead one to the understanding of the **truth**, to the true understanding of the Torah and the man who observes them as I teach, will have eternal **life**. And no one will come to the father except through the observance of the Torah, as I teach.*

John 14:6 repaginated

# SECTION II
## SIX HUNDRED SIXTY-SIX

A study about John was necessary in order for us to understand some of the things he wrote in the book of Revelations. Such a book, about the end of time is clearly a mystical and extremely Kabbalistic book. Concepts such as future's forecast, divine revelation, prophecy, usage of numbers and terms like stars and beasts, may not be interpreted without prior knowledge of the Jewish mysticism.

How John's faith was, is expressed in the words of this book. John didn't only deal with some of the revelations that he had, but he also uses his kabbalistic knowledge to pass on certain "messages", one of these method is seeing by the usage of the number six hundred and sixty six.

*Here is wisdom. Let him who has understanding count the number of the beast; for it is the number of a man, and his number is six hundred and sixty-six.*
Revelation 13:18 KJV

Many speculations were born from this passage, the number six hundred and sixty-six has always been a representation of satan himself in all cultures of the Western world. Theology teaches that this number is what represents the anti-christ and John was talking about the time of Messianic redemption.

In my point of view, this period that John refers to, is not the Messianic Era, but a period of time that already has been happening for many years now and we are still living it, although many people do not realize it, this many people are an effective part of this prophecy that is taking place in our time. In order for us to understand better John's book, let us analyze it using a mystic Jewish perspective on the number mentioned by him.

**BEFORE WE BEGIN THIS STUDY, <u>PLEASE NOTICE THAT I AM NOT NOT REFERRING TO YEHOSHUA BEN YOSEF</u>, THE ONE REPORTED IN THE ORIGINAL BOOK OF MATTHEW. FROM NOW ON, I WILL TALK ABOUT ANOTHER INDIVIDUAL WHO, DESPITE SOME SIMILARITIES, <u>IS NOT YEHOSHUA</u>.**

## THE 666

The book of Revelation is not the first one to quote this number, and by using those other verses, in a very hidden way, John also mentions this number, so, through hidden teachings from the Tanakh, his message can be demystified. There are many Kabbalistic analysis used to break the Torah's code, one of them is by the comparison of verses. This comparison is made when verses have unusual terms in common. Within these verses, where these common terms appear, one must find another term that, in a hidden way, composes the message that the first verse wants to teach.

To explain in a more practical way, let's look at the 666. Throughout the bible, this number appears three times in three different passages, within these three passages, we must look for other terms that allude to this number and by these new terms, we will have the hidden message that we are looking for.

### 1st 666

*The sons of Adonikam, six hundred and sixty six.*

Ezra 2:13

A seemingly innocent passage that calls for no attention, but within it, there is an important term for Christians.

The first 666 we are looking for is rightly related to the name of Adonikam, which means ADONI (my lord) + KAM (arose).

KAM (קם) is the past form of the verb LAKUM (לקום) - *to raise* - and it can also be used for "to resurrect" or "to rise from the dead". In other words, this verse claims that the "sons" of this "666" will claim that their master raised from the dead.

But, who actually raised from the dead? Well, Yehoshua did, but there is someone else who also claims that he also raised from the dead, jesus.

## 2nd 666

*The gold that Solomon received every year weighed six hundred and sixty six talents.*

2 Chronicles 9:13

The only person presented in this second passage is the King Solomon. Solomon was the son of King David, a genealogy by which Mashiach will be recognized, Mashiach Ben David. Just as Solomon was the one who inherited his father's throne, so Mashiach will inherit this throne.

The connection we have now is with regard to Mashiach. In another language, may also be called as christ.

## 3rd 666

When we connect these two passages, one talking about a person who has "risen", something that was done by Yehoshua and by jesus as some claim, with the second one, that shows King Solomon, a Ben David, just as the Mashiach is Ben David, who was also called christ, we find that they might be talking about Yehoshua HaMashiach as well as about jesus the christ.

In order for us to know whom the 666 refers to, we must look at the last passage where this number is found, and this answer comes from John, when he closes this cycle in the book of Revelations, in the passage quoted in the opening of this section:

*Here is wisdom. Let him who has understanding count the number of the beast; for it is the number of a man, and his number is six hundred and sixty-six.*

In order to understand what defines this 666 of John, we must understand to whom this message was. The cycle of this message closes itself precisely by pointing at a man in Rome, that is, a Roman, a word that, in Hebrew, would be ROMITI (). An analysis of this word will give us the answer and a final term concerning the person to which that number refers to:

## ROMITI (רומיתי)
10י + 400ת + 10י + 40מ + 6ו + 200ר
= **666**

If we bring all of the 3 "666's" together, we will unveil the hidden message. Well, the real one, YEHOSHUA BEN YOSEF, WAS NOT ROMAN, so, this 666 is NOT talking about him, which leads us to understand that 666 is about another figure, a roman one, "jesus christ, the ROMAN".

Although many people think that the Roman jesus, created by the church in Rome, is the same than Yehoshua, who lived and taught in Israel two thousands years ago, they are definitely not the same! This is revealed to us through the mystical words of John in the book of Revelation. To make this clear, let's look at the differences between the two:

## YEHOSHUA BEN YOSEF, MASHIACH
• WAS JEW;
• SON OF GOD;
• WAS A RABBI;
• CONFIRMED AND TAUGHT TORAH;
• WAS A PHARISEE;
• DID NOT FOUND RELIGION, PREACHED FAITH IN GOD THROUGH THE TORAH;
• PERFORMED MIRACLES THROUGH THE POWER OF GOD IN

HIM;
• TAUGHT THAT ONLY ADONAI SALVES;
• OPENED THE GATES TO THE GENTILES;
• OBEYED THE FATHER;
• NEVER SAID HE SHOULD BE WORSHIPED;
• HIS ANOINTING IS REPRESENTED BY HIS NAME;
• WAS HUNG;
• PREACHED OBEDIENCE;

## <u>JESUS CHRIST, THE ROMAN</u>

• EUROPEAN;
• SON OF ROME;
• CHRISTIAN;
• ABOLISHED THE TORAH;
• WAS AN ENEMY OF THE PHARISEES AND OF THE JEWS;
• FOUNDED CHRISTIANITY IN OPPOSITION TO JUDAISM;
• WAS A MIRACLE WORKER, SELLS HIS IMAGE WITH PROMISES OF MIRACLES;
• TEACHES THAT SALVATION COMES THROUGH BELIEVING IN HIM AND IN THE CHURCH;
• CLOSED THE DOORS TO THE JEWS;
• DID NOT OBEY THE FATHER, FOR HATH ABOLISHED HIS WORD;
• REQUIRES WORSHIP, FOR HIS DECLARES TO BE A gOD;
• HAD A NAME THAT MEANS NOTHING;
• WASN'T HUNG;
• PREACHED PURITANISM;

On the one hand we have Yehoshua Ben Yosef, the one who is related by the four gospels, the one who appears in vision to Paul, the one who died as a sacrifice, the one who brought to the Gentile's world the opportunity to know the true God, who taught true salvation, who revealed the mysteries of the Torah, who was against hypocrisy, who shed its blood for the justification of those who believed in his work.

On the other hand, we have a mythical figure, an idea,

a pagan concept that never truly existed, a being created by minds that came from pagan cradles, minds who founded the church. This being, the roman jesus christ, who has nothing to do with the one who truly existed, is a being who declares himself to be a god, who serves as a "helper" in exchange for devotion, one who does not require obedience, does not require sacrifice, can be stored in a box when he is not needed, for some, he is a hippie, for others, a revolutionary, for others an anarchist. A being with many representations, a confused being who came to confuse. This false messiah created by the church is the true beast that has been plaguing the Western world for centuries. The interesting thing is that John reports how far would his power go:

> *And the name of the star is called wormwood, and the third part of the waters became wormwood, and many men died of the waters because they were made bitter.*
>
> Revelation 8:11 KJV

According to the census conducted in 2017, Christianity has 2.3 billion adherents worldwide, representing a total of 33% of the world's population, that is, a third of all men on earth have faith in this roman jesus and they are drinking from the water he offers, thinking that it is the same offered by the true Yehoshua.

According to John, the roman jesus christ will take the place of God's commandments. As we have seen previously, the maxim of the representation of the Torah is Deuteronomy 6:4-5. These verses are so important that they are written in small rolls and placed inside the Tefilim (phylacteries), the interesting thing is the way the Tefillim's commandment is given to us:

> *Bind them as a sign in your right hand and let them serve as a symbol on your forehead.*
>
> Deuteronomy 6:8

Why do we put them on the right hand and on the forehead? For the hand represents the work and the forehead represents the mind, which is where faith is established. The commandment is a representation that faith and the works of our hands should only be to the One God, as reported in Deuteronomy 6:4.

*And he causes all, both small and great, rich and*
*poor, free and bond, to be given a mark in their*
*right hand and in their foreheads,*
*So that no one might buy or sell, except he who has the sign,*
*or the name of the beast, or the number of his name.*

Revelation 13:16-17 KJV

This roman jesus wants to take the commandment's place and wants to divert people's faith from the One God to him. By placing himself in people's hands, making them "to work" for him, he was able to scatter his church and his figure Worldwide and by being placed in the forehead, he will make blind everyone who has faith in him. He is completely opposed to Yehoshua. it is amazing how this jesus teaches things completely different from the real one and whoever believes in him, do not understand the words of Yehoshua.

Even a great theory was created by the church in this regard, in order to mislead more and more people from the true understanding of God. The idea of a chip that will be implanted in people right hand or forehead, as seen in many Christian movies and documentaries. This only serves to draw people's attention far from the truth, for this sign has been in the hands and foreheads of many for many years already.

Lastly, John states that anyone who does not have his mark will not be able to sell or buy, well, that already happened and happens a lot. Looking at a more recent event, the Holocaust, we see that during many years it was forbidden, throughout Germany, to buy or to sell anything to or from the Jews, for the simple fact that they were Jews and non-Christians, they did not serve the roman jesus christ, just as it was during the Inquisition and the Russian pogrom.

John tells us that a "man" would rise, a "man" who will claim to be a messiah, to have died on the cross, to have saved mankind, but he didn't do none of that, instead, he enslaved many people in the darkness of ignorance, far from the true God and demanded worship from this men. A murderous being, for how many people died in his name? Inquisition, pogrom, holocaust, crusades, Christian populace in Antioch, condemnation of the Jews by the reform leaders and so on, all in the name of jesus christ, the roman. This is the real beast John talks about.

Churches today, in all parts of the world, worship and serve this roman jesus, specially for the "miracles" he performs in exchange for people's belief in him, since, as John reports, he was given this power, so that he may deceive many.

## 666 x 999
*(Isaiah 60:22) "the smallest will become a thousand" this verse is equal to 999, which is in the sefira Yesod. This represents the beginning of redemption and redemption means the secrets concerning the steps of Mashiach Ben Yosef.*
Kol HaTor 1

*The 999 is the highest level of Mashiach Ben Yosef.*
Gaon of Vilna

*The verse "by which they shall be saved" is equal to 999.*
Kol HaTor 2

*The redemption will gradually proceed, by the 999 steps of Mashiach Ben Yosef.*
Gaon of Vilna

Within the rabbinic mentality, Mashiach Ben Yosef, who Yehoshua declared to be, is represented by the numerical value of 999. This number represents the redemption and salvation that Mashiach Ben Yosef will bring, or brought.

According to the great sage Gaon of Vilna, 999 represents the footsteps of Mashiach Ben Yosef and this value lies within the *sefira Yesod*, which, according to Kabbalah, represents the knowledge of what is spiritual, of what is hidden. This is also associated with Mashiach Ben Yosef, for he is the one who will bring the spiritual revelation of the Torah.

The 999 has the same shape, the same format and the same design as the 666, but they are opposite, completely inverse. Interesting how John, author of the book of Revelations, writes a book full of Kabbalistic messages. By this we can see that, when John speaks of 666, he speaks about someone who is very similar, but completely opposite to Mashiach Ben Yosef.

If Yehoshua is Mashiach Ben Yosef, represented by the number 999 and the roman jesus by the 666, this confirms to us that John already warned us that there would come someone with the same shape, same format and same design as Yehoshua, however, completely opposite to him.

## THE AUTHORITY JESUS DOES NOT HAVE

והיה האיש אשר אבחר **בו מטהו יפרח** ...
*And it shall come to pass that the man's staff
that, whom I choose, shall blossom...*
Numbers 17:20 (17: 5 in the Western versions)

This is a passage that tells how the choice of Aharon, brother of Moses, as high priest took place. Just as it is a story full of mysteries, so too, the verse that relates it, is full of mysteries. Although it is a verse that talks about Aharon, it also talks about Mashiach, for it is a verse that deals with leadership.

If we look at the terms MATEHU IPHRAKH (מטהו יפרח) - *his staff shall blossom* - and make its Gematria, we shall have the following:

## MATEHU IPHRAKH (מטהו יפרח)

מ40 + ט9 + ה5 + ו6 + י10 + פ80 + ר200 + ח8

## = **358**

## MASHIACH (משיח)

מ40 + ש300 + י10 + ח8

## = **358**

The *"his staff shall blossom"* is Mashiach himself, but which Mashiach, Ben David or Ben Yosef? Let us look at the first letters of this Hebrew term:

בו מטהו יפרח = *his staff shall blossom*

(מ)MASHIACH - (ב)BEN - (י)YOSEF

We can draw two lessons from this single verse, the first is the relation that Mashiach Ben Yosef has with the staff of Aharon, which represented the office of high priest. Along side with the Order of Melekhtzadik, this is another plausible proof of the authority that Yehoshua had as a high priest, even though he was from the tribe of Judah and not from Levi. It is through his connection with Aharon's priestly authority, as mystically showed by this verse, that many of the authors of the New Testament called him as priest.

The second lesson is the representation of authority that the "staff" has and how it is connected, not only with Mashiach Ben Yosef, but also, according to John, with Mashiach Ben David:

*And shall rule the nations with a **staff** of iron...*
Revelation 2:27a KJV

According to my understanding, both verses speak of the SAME STAFF.

# SECTION III
## TRINITY

*Hear Israel, Adonai is our Elohim, Adonai is **ONE**.*
Deuteronomy 6:4

*Thus said Adonai the king of Israel, Their redeemer,
Adonai of hosts: I am the first and the I am the
last, And there is **NO** other god but ME.*
Isaiah 44:6

*And this is the eternal life, that they might know You, as the
**ONLY TRUE GOD**, and to Yehoshua, whom You have sent.*
John 17:3

*Yet for us there is **ONE GOD**, the Father, of who is
everything and for Whom we live; and one master,
Yehoshua, by whom are all things, and we by him.*
1 Corinthians 8:6

One thing is a fact, and many people turn a blind eye to it, the trinity is not a term, a concept or a biblical definition. Nowhere in the bible, in both the Tanakh and the New Testament, there is this idea of three gods into one. Quite the contrary, if the trinity were valid, the rest of the Tanakh would be wrong. God, throughout the bible, both by the prophets and by other men reported in the Tanakh, never said that He would become man and would come down to the earth, such an idea is one of the greatest biblical heresies and an intrinsic misconception within most Christians.

## THE ROOT OF THE TRINITY

The church, just as all its theology and theories, was born in Rome, conceptualized by men's minds, who came from pagan cradles; minds far from knowing the true faith of Yehoshua, the Torah and the People of Israel. It is humanly impossible, for people with such mentalities, to create a concept that is consistent with the One True God.

The Roman Empire, when created Christianity, sought a way to unite people again in a time that the empire was declining. The emperor then meets with some men, known as fathers of the church, and through some councils, defines how this way to unite the empire would be, a new faith. In order for it to be easily accessible and simply understandable by all, they transformed the ancient Roman pagan religion into what we know today as a Catholic church. This transformation, in fact, was only a name's change of the ancient Roman pantheon. Everything else, the idolatry, the lies, the manipulations, the deceptions, the heresies and so on, remained exactly the same.

One of those changes was precisely in relation to what they had as the "capitoline triad". The triad, ancient Roman faith, deals with the worship of three supreme divine beings in the Capitol. The first would be the main god, the father, the creator, called jupiter, a Roman retelling of the Greek god zeus. The second, called mars, was considered the god son, because it was the son of the main god, jupiter. Finally, the god qvirinvs, which represented the realization of the will of the god jupiter on earth.

The resemblance they have to the Christian trinity is clear; first we have the father, jupiter, the creator. Secondly, we have his son, mars, who is considered the protector of those who believe in him, making an intermediary between humanity and the punitive force of jupiter and Qvirinvs, who fulfills the will of jupiter on earth, a form of messenger, he also was in charge of giving divine powers to men. According to the trinity, there is the father, creator of earth and men, the son jesus who is the intermediary and the holy spirit, who manifests the power of God among men.

There is no denying the similarity between the *capitoline triad* and the Christian trinity. If we make a deeper analysis on the second figure of each, we will see how jesus and mars are similar. Mars was known as the god of carnage, just as jesus caused the carnage in the inquisition, in the holocaust, in the pogrom, in the persecutions and so on. Perhaps, the roman jesus of many churches, is just mars in disguise, for many have died and many will die in the name of this jesus.

## TRINITY'S IDEALIZERS

As already said, the bible is not the basis that was used for the creation of trinity, but rather human minds, sick and misguided minds that have been able to propagate Roman paganism to millions of people with a mask of a true god.

The concept of jesus being a god did not come from the councils, but from older church fathers. Let's see what they claim in this regard.

> *Christ is both god and the lord of all hosts.*
> Justin Martyr, Dialogue with Trypho, c.36

> *Isaiah proves that god was born of a virgin.*
> Justin Martyr, LXVI

> *For who will say that god is one? For he is manifest in three.*
> Hippolytus, Against the Heresy of the One

> *For christ is god above all.*
> Hippolytus, Refutations, Book X

> *None of the trinity can be considered larger*
> *or smaller than the other.*
> Origen, De Principis, Book I

*We have a doctor who heals us, the lord our god, jesus christ.*
Ignatius of Antioch, Letter to the Ephesians.

*But our god, jesus christ, was conceived by the virgin Mary.*
Ignatius of Antioch, Letters to Ephesians 18:2

*We believe in a god, the almighty father, creator of heavens and earth, of all things that are visible and invisible. We believe in our lord jesus christ, the only son of god, who*

*is the substance of god. jesus is the god of the god, light of*
*light, the true god of the true god, born and not made.*
The Nicene Creed, The Base of All Christianity – 325CE

These are some statements, among many others, from the idealizers of the Trinity concept, which was later adapted by Rome. I am astonished at how god was born of a woman, or how god died, or how jesus is the god of hosts, taking for himself a statement made by the One God in the book of Isaiah. The true essence of a single God, according to the Christian faith, has always been something obscure, something that is so clear throughout the bible, was lost because of the lack of knowledge and the paganism that these church fathers had. How can the basic concept of the Christian faith, idealized in 325CE in Nicaea, claim that jesus is the god of god? That does not make any sense according to the Scriptures.

But what can we notice in common among all this trinitarian idealizers? They all come from a pagan religions, none of them were a Jew, nor a messianic Jew, nor were somehow attached to any of the apostles, they are all from doubtful origin.

But these commentaries, as mentioned above, deal with truly ancient trinitarian ideas, this concept of trinity has been readapted and reformulated by Catholic priests over the years. In the twelfth century, a famous priest named Thomas Aquinos "modernized" the whole Christian concept of the trinity and made it very close to what we see today in many churches. In his book *Dio Uno e Triuno*, he claims the following (the following citations were translated by the author of this book from latin):

*In fact Augustine says, the son did not create the father*
*because it wasn't convenient for him. For in god there is*
*no difference between "being" and "power", nor about*
*eternity. So, the son begot another son, and thus, there are*

*two sons in god. Therefore, there are more than three.*
Thomas Aquinos, Dio Uno e Triuno, Article 9:1

*Moreover, the father generates the son by nature. However, it is the same nature of father and son. Therefore, as the father begets, so does the son. Therefore there are many sons in god, so there are more than three.*
Thomas Aquinos, Dio Uno e Triuno, Article 9:10

*Moreover, for the perfection of divine goodness, happiness and glory, it is required to be true charity in god. However, true charity requires, in god, three people. In fact, the love for which one loves oneself is a private love and not true love. However, God cannot love another who is not extremely lovable. So, it is clear that true charity in god cannot be summed up if there is only one person in him, nor if there are two, that is why there are three.*
Thomas Aquinos, Dio Uno e Triuno, Question 9:2

*Moreover, three things are required in love, namely, the one who loves, and the one who is also loved with the same love. However, the two who love each other are the father and the son, this love is bonded by the holy spirit. So god is three.*
Thomas Aquinos, Dio Uno e Triuno, Question 9:4

In my view, Thomas Aquinos has gone too far, he uses human, rather than biblical concepts to prove the existence of the trinity. He goes so far as to say that the son could have created the father if he wanted to. If we look at this, what would this god that has been created be? Everything that is created, besides having an end, has someone greater than it, since it was created by someone, then this created god is a false god.

Other mentions he makes is of the multiplurality of god, how can there be several gods in god? This is what happens when pagan minds, linked to idolatrous religions, without knowledge of the truth, try to define God. Unfortunately, this is not unique among the church fathers, such "phenomena" still occur today in various temples, through various leaders.

All these statements, besides not being biblical, are against the bible, this is the truth essence of the man created roman jesus christ, a god that is born and dies, is totally incoherent and illusive.

## THE TRINITY AND THE BEHAVIOR OF YEHOSHUA

It is enough for us to look at how Yehoshua behaved, it is clear the distinction he had between himself and God. He declared himself to be Mashiach through the Jewish conception of Mashiach, for this was the conception he believed and the only one valid. According to this Jewish conception, Mashiach is not God. Yehoshua as a Jew, as a follower of the Torah and as Mashiach, could never state that he was a god. This is incoherent with his faith, his teachings, and his behavior.

For this fact, true Christian faith relies heavily on Paul's teachings, for as Yehoshua became god, the chair of Mashiach became vacant, being taken by Paul. This is the biggest problem, because Paul was a person that wrote using only a rabbinic language, which cannot be understood by those who do not know the Oral Torah. For this reason, so many heresies were created through Paul's teachings. If the church were based on the true teachings of Yehoshua, its faith would be totally different.

Let's look at some of Yehoshua's attitudes toward God:

> *And he answered him, Why do you ask what is good?*
> *No man is good, for EL only is good. And if you want*
> *to enter eternal life, keep the MITZVOT.*
>
> Matthew 19:17

In this verse we see a clear distinction made by Yehoshua himself between him and God. He makes it clear that ONLY God is good, the "only" automatically excludes all other beings, whoever they are, and that also excludes himself, thus proving that there was a distinction between the two.

Any kind of distinction annuls the theory of the trinity, because the basis of it is the total equality between the beings that compose it.

> *And then he will say to those to his right: welcome blessed of my Father, enter the Kingdom of Heaven that has been prepared for you since the creation of the world until now.*
> Matthew 25:34

Why *"blessed of my Father"* and not *"my blessed ones"*? Perhaps it is because only the Father blesses, even though through his envoys, like Yehoshua for example, the blessing has only one source, God.

This is another factor that distinguishes the two, going against the equality that trinity members should have.

> *Then he went forward very slowly and fell on his face and prayed and said: if it is possible, may this cup be removed from me, please. But in fact, it may not be as I want it to be, but according to Your will.*
> Matthew 26:39

By the prayer of Yehoshua, it is clear that he did not want to die, it is clear that he did not want to give himself as sacrifice, but he gave himself to the will of God and God, gave him over as a sacrifice. This is a very different point of view, because the honor for such a deed, Yehoshua's sacrifice, must be given to God, with acknowledgment of the merit of Yehoshua for having obeyed the Father, his obedience is what must be observed here.

This also proves that he was clearly under the divine power and the divine will, which proves even more his declaration as being the Mashiach.

*Yeshua shouted aloud, in the holy language (Hebrew):*
*ELI ELI, why did you forsake me?*
Matthew 27:46

If the trinity were a reality, we would have the saddest monologue in history in this passage.

Yehoshua was a Jew, a rabbi, a Pharisee, a connoisseur of the Oral Torah, an observer of the Written Torah, a servant of the One God, a master in what he taught, and God manifested on this earth through him. It was also through his death that the knowledge about the Word of God and of the One God came to all nations, that is why all of those who do not come from a Jewish cradle, should see him as Mashiach and believe in him as Mashiach, for it was through him that salvation has reached the Gentiles.

Yehoshua was an elevated person, the holiness and the obedience to God that he had, has never been seen before in any human being. However, to believe in Yehoshua as Mashiach is not by worshiping him, not by seeing him as a god, but by believing in his work and by following his teachings, it is to live the Torah in the way he interpreted it. He must be the rabbi of those who believe in him.

## YEHOSHUA AS ELOHIM

There is a brief mention that associates Yehoshua as being Elohim. Although many believe that Elohim is one of God's names, it is actually a "title", as well as the word "God" is.

*Behold, the young woman is pregnant and will bear a son*
*and will call his name Ym'Anu'El, that is, Elohim with us.*
Matthew 1:23

This verse in Matthew, among others, was also used as basis for the conception of the idea of a jesus god, for many understand this *"Elohim with us"* as if God became man and came down to earth.

The term Elohim is somewhat confusing and has already generated much speculation among the Christian milieu. Elohim, for being a word in the plural form, for words that end with ~IM is plural masculine in Hebrew, many claim that this refers to the trinity. But as I said before, Elohim is not one of God's names. If being called Elohim would make anyone a "god", we would have some problems, let's see:

> *Then said Adonai unto Moshe, behold, I make*
> *thee Elohim over Pharaoh...*
>
> Exodus 7:1a

> *I have said, you are Elohim, and all of you are children*
> *of the Most High.*
>
> Psalms 82:6

If by being called Elohim one becomes a god, or part of the trinity, the trinity would not be a trinity, but a pantheon full of gods, because according to the bible, Moses would also be a god, just as all the judges of Israel, who were reported in Psalm 82 as "Elohim". Just as Moses, even made as Elohim, is not a god, Yehoshua by being called Elohim is also not a god, even though he was made as Elohim.

The word Elohim is not a name, but a kind of nickname in reference to the God of Israel. Elohim is a plural word, for it refers to the sum of all attributes that God possesses, such as goodness, mercy, healing, judgment, salvation, love, power, glory, honor, and so forth. When God gives authority to some man to accomplish something that is only up to Him to accomplish, this man is made as Elohim.

Let us look at Moses, Moses performed many miracles, something that only God can do, he somehow saved the people of Egypt, something that only God can do, he prophesied, something that only God can do, that is, Moses performed "things" unique to God, for God "lended" His power to him, thus making him as Elohim.

The same is true concerning the judges of Israel, for only God can judge, so when men judge, by doing something that only God can do, they are made as Elohim.

Yehoshua, by performing healings, by casting out demons, by revealing the Torah, among other things, performed deeds unique to God, therefore, was made as Elohim.

## SACRIFICE AND TRINITY

*But this man, after he had offered one sacrifice for sins for ever, sat down on the right hand of God.*

Hebrews 10:12

Every sacrifice rendered, in every religion or sect, is always made to some higher authority. In this passage in Hebrews, the author claims that he was a sacrifice for sins, but before whom he was a sacrifice? If he were a god, would he be sacrificing himself before himself? This is weird, for in Matthew 26:39, he asks God to take away this "cup" from him, because he did not want to sacrifice himself. Certainly, if it depended on him and if he was a god, he would have found another for what he did. But as he was obedient to God, he placed himself under God's will and he sacrificed himself in order to do the Creator's will.

The trinity is nothing more than dichotomy and blasphemy.

# SECTION IV
## SHKUTZ SHOMEM

*And that BESSORAH will be TEDARESH to all the earth so that*
*all the Gentiles will hear of me and then the end will come.*
*And these will be the anti-Maschiach, this is SHKUTZ*
*SHOMEM spoken by Daniel's mouth while standing in*
*the holy place. May whoever reads it, understands it.*
Matthew 24:14-15

*Shkutz Shomem* is a term that appears only three times throughout the Tanakh and many speculations have been created around it, both rabbis and Christians seek an understanding, often mystically, of what Daniel was talking about.

*Shkutz Shomem* is translated in the western languages as "abomination of desolation" and is a term which I find particularly weird, it does not make a concrete sense and is something difficult to mentally visualize. That is why I believe that innumerable mystical interpretations have been created around this term. Both rabbis and Christians have different interpretations in this regard, let's look at both of them and see if any agrees with what Yehoshua is talking about.

First, the three verses of the book of Daniel where this term appears:

*For a week he will make a firm alliance with many. For half*
*a week he will put an end to the sacrifices and offerings of*
*food. In the corner of the altar will SHKUTZ MESHOMEM*
*until the destruction decreed is poured on the SHOMEM.*
Daniel 9:27

*Forces will be guided by him; they will defile the temple,*
*the fortress. They will abolish the regular offer and*
*will establish the HASHKUTZ MESHOMEM.*

Daniel 11:31

*From the time that the regular offering is abolished,*
*and SHKUTZ SHOMEM is established, it shall be*
*one thousand and two hundred and ninety days.*

Daniel 12:11

## THE CHRISTIAN UNDERSTANDING

There are basically two Christian interpretations of these verses in Daniel. On the one hand we have the understanding of Rome and on the other an apocalyptic vision according to the Christianity that comes from the reform.

The Roman church clings to the understanding of the teachings of the ancient fathers of the church. John Chrysostom, in his book *Homilies in the Gospel of Matthew*, states that these prophecies of Daniel refer to the destruction of the city of Jerusalem that took place around 70 CE and the *shkutz shomem* represents the army that sieged the city.

Another famous father of the church also agrees with this interpretation, Augustine of Hippo makes a comment in one of his books about these verses of the book of Daniel:

*Luke was a living witness that the prophecy of Daniel*
*was fulfilled when Jerusalem was destroyed.*

Father of the Church Augustine of Hippo, vol. 6

On the other hand, the mysticism that surrounds the mentality and faith of many reformed churches, such as Protestants, Adventists, Baptists, etc., cling to a more apocalyptic interpretation. It is said that the *shkutz shomem* is the antichrist himself, who will be a messenger of satan to rule the world for a thousand two hundred and ninety days in peace and a thousand two hundred and ninety days in war. He will deceive the Jews, who will see him as a messiah, but in the last three and a half years of his rule, he will demand worship from the Jews, and this is the turning point, it is when they will have their eyes opened.

This idea of a false Messiah deceiving Jews while the church is rapted and all the tribulation that the "left behind" will have to endure under the rule of some antichrist, was elaborated by two Jesuit priests. The first was Francesco Ribera (1537-1591) and Manuel Lacunza (1731-1801) who continued the work of the first one.

These apocalyptic interpretations they created were quickly rejected by the Catholic Church, but years later, in the nineteenth century, they were adopted by the reformed churches. Within this theology, we have few variations on how each one believes, some say that the church will be taken before the tribulation, others in the middle and others at the end of it. The truth is that such theology is nothing more than a human interpretation of books that the mind of men cannot understand without the revelation from God. These theologies have a strong appealing character, for apocalyptic ideas attract much curiosity and the fear that they creat inside people, brings many to the church, not out of love but out of fear.

This interpretation from the priests may even make sense when some verses, scattered throughout the book of apocalypse, come together. The real thing is that this is not biblical and contrary to the rabbinic and Yehoshua's teachings, as we have already discussed.

## THE RABBIN UNDERSTANDING

*Rabbi Akiva told him: it is a mitzvah to give nicknames to idols.*
Talmud of Babylon, Tractate Avodah Zarah 46a

*Then the temple will burn and on the altar the*
*wing of shkutz shomem will be placed.*
R. Joseph Ibn Yahya, Daniel 9:27

The rabbis teach that nicknames should be assigned to idols so that their name is not pronounced, thus dishonoring their meaning. Idols and false gods are nothing more than abominations before the Creator.

There was a god within the Roman pantheon called jupiter, this god is the Roman version of the Greek god zeus. Some scholars say that jupiter was known as the *baal shamem* (lord of heaven) and the term *shkutz shomem* is a distortion of this name, a negative nickname. This interpretation makes sense, since Daniel states that after the sacrifices are abolished, the *shkutz shomem* would be established in its place, and so it was. With the destruction of the Temple, the sacrifices ceased and in its place, it was erected a statue of the god jupiter, which was treated as *shkutz shomem*. Another interesting thing is that this fact only occurred after the "good news" was taken to the Gentile world, exactly as Yehoshua stated.

If we take this historical fact into account, the warning that Yehoshua gave was precisely about the destruction of the Temple and paganism taking its place, a prophecy that lasts until the present day and will only end with the coming of Mashiach.

This is the typical rabbinic interpretation of Daniel's prophecy, which makes perfect sense. Daniel referred to the destruction of the temple, to the end of the sacrifices and false gods that would be erected in its place. Unlike the Christian interpretation, this prophecy does not deal with an apocalyptic age. But they have something in common. SHKUTZ SHOMEM will only come to an end in the messianic age.

## GEMATRIA

The only way to understand a mystical message is by analyzing it through mystical tools. Calculating the Gematria of some terms may reveal a very interesting thing about this *shkutz shomem*.

Let's do two analyzes by summing the values of their letters, the first is the absolute value that is the sum of each number of the total value and the reduced value is the sum of the sum, until it reaches a value between 1-9.

## שקוץ שמם (shkutz shomem)

2246 = 600ם + 40מ + 300ש + 900ץ + 6ו + 100ק + 300ש

2+2+4+6 = **14** (absolute) | 1+4 = **5** (reduced)

*shkutz shomem* has an absolute value of 14 and a reduced value of 5. Let´s now look to the greek name of the roman jesus:

## ישו קריסטוס (yeshu kristos)

761 = 600ס + 6ו + 9ט + 600ס + 10י + 200ר + 100ק + 6ו + 300ש + 10י

7+6+1 = **14** (absolute) | 1+4 = **5** (reduced)

Interesting! We have the same absolute value of 14 and the same reduced value of 5 and I believe, this is sufficient proof that there is a hidden connection between the two. If we look closely, it is the jesus christ created by Rome that is on the altar of the lives of many people today, he took the place of the Temple, the place of Elohim, is worshiped by Christians, many pray for him, do things in his name. Two things are undeniable, whether or not he is the *shkutz shomem*, he sits on the corner of the altar and the Temple was destroyed by those who established him as god, the Romans.

> *Forces (ROME) will be led by him (jesus); they (ROME)*
> *will defile the temple, the fortress. They (ROME) will*
> *abolish the regular offering and will establish the*
> *HASHKUTZ MESHOMEM (jesus, the god).*
>
> Daniel 11:31

We got into this matter by a quotation made by Yehoshua. But, what else does he think about this? Let's look at a verse from the original alongside with the most well-known english translation:

> *For many will come **with** my name saying, I am*
> *the Messiah, and they will turn you away.*

Matthew 24:5

*Many will come in my name, saying, I am the*
*Christ, and they will turn away many.*

Matthew 24: 5 KJV

One word that changes everything, Yehoshua does not state that they will come in his name, as if someone representing him. He says that they will come by using his name, that is, by claiming that he is himself.

Jesus christ came affirming that he is Yehoshua Ben Yosef, but they are not the same person. jesus is the one upon whom Yehoshua warned, they will come with my name and will divert many. Whoever has faith in Yehoshua as Mashiach should begin to pay attention to some things.

### BESSORAH TEDARESH

Two terms I kept untranslated, *bessorah* and *tedaresh*. *Bessorah* means "good news" in Hebrew, a word that has been translated as "gospel", but this translation diminishes the value the word *Bessorah* has.

*Bessorah* (בשורה) has the same root as the word "flesh" - BASSAR (בשר) - for a good news from God does not come freely, does not come without someone suffering in the flesh, whatever this good news is. All the great men in the Bible, who received something from God and took this good news to humanity, suffered and suffered a lot in the flesh. So, when the good news comes without a price to pay in the flesh, this good news may not be so good.

The word *Tedaresh* (תדרש), translated as "preach", has the same root as MIDRASH (מדרש) and it changes everything.

A Midrash is an interpretation, an exegesis, an understanding of passages from the TORAH. It is the study that seeks to reveal and to understand the hidden teachings of the Word of God. Therefore, when Yehoshua says that his good news should be TEDARESH, a MIDRAH, he refers to his teachings, that they should be seen as a midrash, that is, as the interpretation of the Torah.

This confirms everything we are seeing so far, for he now asserts that his interpretation of the Torah is to be taught, the true good news he brought is precisely how he taught the Torah and how it should be lived through his midrash, through his interpretation of it.

The Torah is what is to be taught to the Gentiles and according to the teachings of Yehoshua, it must be in conformity to his interpretation. The sign of the end of time is precisely the strong movement of the Christian world towards the Torah, as it has been seen for some years now, in an unprecedented way.

No Torah, No Bessorah!

## SECTION V
### A FEW PROPHECIES

#### BEIT LECHEM OF EFRATAH

*And you Beit Lechem of Yehudah, Ephratah, land of Yehudah, you are the smallest in the land of Yehudah, from you will come forth to me to be the ruler in Israel.*

Matthew 2:6

*And you Bethlehem, in the land of Juda, are not the least among the princes of Juda: for out of you shall come a Governor, that shall rule my people Israel.*

Matthew 2:6 KJV

*And you, O Beit Lechem of Efratah, the smallest among the clans of Yehudah, from you will come forth to rule Israel for Me. One whose origin is of old, from ancient times.*

Micah 5:1

One of the prophecies that Matthew quotes in order to prove Yehoshua's messianism, is found in the book of Micah, where the prophet states that he who will reign over Israel, shall come from Beit Lehem, in the region of Ephratah. However, if we compare the book of Micah with the Western translations of Matthew, it might give an impression that Matthew made a mistake, for he does not mention Ephratah as stated by the prophet, thus giving the impression of two different Beit Lechem.

But what made me mention this slight error is, by mentioning that word, a word left aside by the KJV, is of extreme importance as we shall see next.

First of all, so that we may have an aid to understand it, let us look at a comment made by Rabbi Malbim about Micah's prophecy, the same one that Matthew quotes in his book:

*And you, Beit Lechem, in order to awaken the*

*ten scattered tribes of Israel, your king, Mashiach*
*Ben Yosef, will be made brave for you, until the total*
*restoration of Yehudah by Mashiach Ben David.*

Rabbi Malbim, Micah 5:1

Malbim explains that this prophecy is not simply about Mashiach, but about a very specific mission of Mashiach, the mission of awakening the lost tribes of Israel. As we have already seen in this book, *PART 2, SECTION V, THE KINGDOM OF ISRAEL*, the mission of gathering the lost tribes of Israel concerns Mashiach Ben Yosef and in order to understand what is going on here, it is at him that we must look at.

When Matthew associates this prophecy with Yehoshua, he automatically declares that he is Mashiach Ben Yosef, and thus is also confirmed by Yehoshua himself:

*And Yeshua said to him, I was not sent **except** to*
*the lost sheep of the House of Israel.*

Matthew 15:24

But the question is, how can we prove that this prophecy of Micah really deals with Mashiach Ben Yosef and, what is the connection that Beit Lechem, the city where Yehoshua was born, has with Mashiach Ben Yosef?

In order that we may understand the message, we should not look at the prophecy of Micah, but rather at another passage found in the Tanakh:

*These were the sons of Chur, the firstborn of Ephratah*
*and the father of Beit Lechem.*

1 Chronicles 4:4b

This passage changes everything, Beit Lechem and Efratah are not just two locations, but also two people. According to the book of I Chronicles, Efratah was the father of Chur who was the father of Beit Lechem. And it is precisely this passage that reveals to us what is happening in the book of Matthew and the connection he makes of Yehoshua with Mashiach Ben Yosef.

As prophecies are mystical revelations, we must analyze them mystically. The passage in 1 Chronicles reveals that Beit Lechem is the son of Chur, who is the first-born of Efratah. The prophet however, makes a direct connection between the grandson and the grandfather, which is a very common thing in the Tanakh, as if he called Beit Lechem the son of EFRATAH, without mentioning Chur.

With all of this in mind, let's analyze these people using the Gematria and we shall see the message that it deliveries to us:

### BEIT LECHEM BEN EFRATAH (בית לחם בן אפרתה)

ב2 + י'10 + ת400 + ל30 + ח8 + ם600 + ב2 +

700ן + 1א + 80פ + 200ר + ת400 + ה5

= 2438 = 2 + 4 + 3 + 8 = **17**

*Gematria with sofit

### MASHIACH BEN YOSEF (משיח בן יוסף)

מ40 + ש300 + י'10 + ח8 + ב2 + ן50 + י'10 + ו6 + ס600 + ף80

= 566 = 5 + 6 + 6 = **17**

*Gematria without sofit

Both have the Gematria's value of 17, which, according to my point of view, confirms many things. Matthew is able to use this prophecy to show that Yehoshua was Mashiach Ben Yosef, for he came from Beit Lechem, just as Rabbi Malbim teaches that Mashiach Ben Yosef would come from there. Matthew also confirms that his mission is exclusively for the house of Israel, as mentioned by Malbim in his commentary, as prophesied by Micah, when he quotes that he came to Israel and again, by Yehoshua himself, when he said:

*And Yeshua said to him, I was not sent except to*
*the lost sheep of the House of Israel.*

Matthew 15:24

This has a very deep and delicate meaning. Many believe that Yehoshua came to save the Gentiles, in fact, this is not his main mission. It is true that many Gentiles had access to the Bible and to the knowledge of the God of Israel through his death, but that was only a "blessing that overflowed the cup".

Because the descendants of the Kingdom of Israel, the lost tribes, were scattered throughout the world and assimilated by foreign cultures, they became "Gentiles" in a certain way. The mission of Mashiach Ben Yosef, in this case, Yehoshua's, is precisely to bring these people back to the God of Israel and to the Torah. As they are among the Gentiles, it was to the Gentiles that the work of Yehoshua intended, but with the real intention of reaching out these lost tribes.

We do not know who the descendants of these tribes are, but as already discussed in this book, these people have a "spark" within themselves, a "spark" given to all members of the People of Israel in their earliest days. When the knowledge of the true Yehoshua, the Torah, and the will of the One God are revealed to them, they will automatically feel something burning inside of them, which will lead them back to the Creator.

This will not happen to everyone who knows God or His Word or is part of a church, for simply knowing God doesn't make one His servant. These people, despite having been given this chance, as a reflection of the search for the lost tribes, will never accept the God of Israel in the way that as He wants to be accepted, that is, Torah for these people is an absurd thing. This is why there is a roman jesus, for he serves this people who wants no connection with the true God and His Torah.

Many will never accept a Maschiach who is not in conformity with Christian theology, many will never accept a God other than the roman jesus, many will never accept the yoke of the Torah, even those inside temples, hearing and learning about the God of Israel and His Word. On the other hand, others under the same yoke, by hearing about these things, will have an awaken as never seen before and quickly, without knowing the motives and without someone having to convince them, they will accept all these things and will have their lives immediately transformed. These are the descendants of the lost tribes of Israel and the targets of the work of Mashiach Ben Yosef.

The prophecy from Micah also reveals why Yehoshua was not accepted by the Jews, for Jews, as we know them today and as they were in the first century, are not from the House of Israel, but rather from the House of Yehudah, and to the House of Yehudah, the Mashiach will be the Messiah Ben David, as Gematria reveals to us:

### YEHUDA (יהודה)

$$5ה + 4ד + 6ו + 5ה + 10י$$
$$= 30 = 3 + 0 = \mathbf{3}$$

### MASHIACH BEN DAVID (משיח בן דוד)

MASHIACH (משיח)
$$40מ + 300ש + 10י + 8ח$$
$$= 358 = 3 + 5 + 8 = 16 = 1 + 6 = 7$$

BEN (בן)
$$2ב + 50ן$$
$$= 702 = 7 + 2 = 9$$

DAVID (דוד)
$$4ד + 6ו + 4ד$$
$$= 14 = 1 + 4 = 5$$

## TOTAL = 7 + 9 + 5 = 21 = 2 + 1 = 3

*Gematria with sofit

From what we can see, for the House of Yehudah, for the Jews, the Mashiach will be at his coming as Mashiach Ben David, and for the House of Israel, because they are among the Gentiles, he will come as Mashiach Ben Yosef. His work will reach all the nations with the intention of lighting the "spark" within the descendants of the lost tribes, if anyone understands it, even if they are not descendants of these tribes, one can also be grafted unto the olive tree of Israel.

Certainly, both Maschiach Ben Yosef and Mashiach Ben David are the same, only two different missions. This is confirmed in another passage of the Tanakh:

> *David was the son of a certain Ephratite of Beit Lehem in Yehudah, named Yessi. He had eight children, and in Shaul's day, this man was old, advanced in age.*
> I Samuel 17:12

In a single passage we have a connection of Efratah and Beit Lechem with King David. Efratah and Beit Lechem allude to Mashiach Ben Yosef and king David to the Mashiach Ben David himself, thus showing that both are intertwined, both are the same.

## A VOICE FROM RAMAH

> *Then was fulfilled what the prophet Yrmiahu said. A voice is heard in Ramah, lamentations and bitter weeping, Rachel weeping for her son and so on.*
> Matthew 2:17-18

> *Thus said Adonai: a voice is heard in Ramah, wailing, bitter weeping, Rachel weeping her children. She does not want to be comforted, for they are gone.*
> Jeremiah 31:15

Matthew quotes this prophecy shortly after the account of the massacre caused by Horodos, when, in search of Yehoshua, he orders a slaughtering of all the male newborns.

The fact that Yrmiahu's prophecy deals with "weeping" and "death" of children, it gives us a simple impression that Matthew mention was made because of the act of this murderer.

But if we look closely at the prophecy, it does not make much sense with that simple fact, for what does the matriarch Rachel have to do with that slaughter, since she was not even present at that moment?

Well, Rachel was the wife of Yaakov, the mother of Yosef and Benjamin. The Torah tells us that when Yaakov's favorite son, Yosef, was taken into captivity, his brothers told his father that he was killed and for years, Yaakov wept for the loss of his son. Many years later, his brothers found him alive in Egypt and as the story develops, Benjamin, for being the youngest, ended up serving as a rescue tool to rid Yaakov's family from hunger and death.

If we make a simple connection with what has been seen until now, the two tribes from the sons of Yosef belonged to the Kingdom of Israel, they are two of the tribes lost in the world. In contrast, the tribe of Benjamin, as the tribe of Judah, were part of the Kingdom of South, the Kingdom of Yehudah, which was not dispersed and assimilated by the nations.

With this in mind, we can understand that just as one day Yaakov cried for having lost Yosef, Rachel's cry has the same symbology, the loss of her son Yosef to the nations of the world. But Benjamin, who represents the Kingdom of Yehudah, from which Mashiach Ben Yosef comes from, will serve as a ransom for Yosef and for his brothers, as we have seen so far.

This idea is confirmed by the prophet Yrmiyahu himself in the following two verses:

*Thus said Adonai, restrain your voice from weeping, your eyes from shedding the tears, for there is a reward for your labor, Adonai says, for they shall return from the lands of the enemy. And there will be hope at the end. Says*

*Adonai, for your children will return to their country.*
Jeremiah 31:16-17

Yrmiahu, by continuing his prophecy, says that Adonai will return the sons of Rachel from the lands of the enemy, that is, those who have been assimilated by the nations, will return. Prophesying that Adonai says that they will return to their country, to the land of Israel. Another interesting point is the word Ramah; there is a city in the territory of Benjamin called Ramah, which was right on the border with the tribe of Manasseh, one of the sons of Yosef. This city, after the separation of Israel in two kingdoms, ended up being annexed to the territory of the north, thus being part of the tribe of Manasseh. This is the city that made the connection between the two tribes that represented the two sons, Manasseh of Yosef and Benjamin, and is a city that ended up being lost along with the rest of the Kingdom of Israel.

The use of this prophecy by Matthew goes far beyond the atrocity caused by Horodos at that time, it shows that Mashiach Ben Yosef, who will come from the Kingdom of South, will bring back the lost son of Rachel, that is, he will serve as a rescue tool in order to save the lost tribes.

** *Both Moshiach Ben Yosef and Mashiach Ben David are from the tribe of Yehudah. Benjamin, in this case, is only a representation of the Kingdom of South, it doesn't mean that Mashiach is from the tribe of Benjamin.*

## VOICE FROM THE WILDERNESS

*In those days came Yohanan, the immerser, preaching
in the wilderness of Yehudah.
And he said: Do Tshuvah, for the Kingdom
of Heaven is approaching.
Fulfilling what was said by Isaiah, the prophet, a
voice calls from the desert to return to the ways of
Hashem and straighten the way of our Elohim.*

Matthew 3:1-3

This prophecy quoted by Matthew, which is found in the book of Isaiah, also refers to the coming of Yohanan, the immerser. The author of the book of Matthew makes a connection of the prophet's mystical words with the ministry and lifestyle of the Immerser, who wandered around the wilderness of Yehudah, preaching Tshuvah and the return to the ways stipulated by Adonai.

The prophecy to which he refers to is as follows:

*A voice cries out in the wilderness: Make way for Adonai.*
*They will **set a path in the plains** for our Elohim.*

Isaiah 40:3

There is a Midrash about this prophecy and this Midrash is consistent with the way Matthew interpreted the words of the prophet, revealing the common understanding of these words of Isaiah:

*What does he say?* **When he sees Israel engaging in Torah,** *he says: A voice that cries out in the desert, cries out the way of Adonai, prepare a path for your Elohim in the wilderness (Isaiah 40: 3). And the reality of His ways through Tshuvah says: "Blessed is the man who trusts in God and the Lord is in His trust.*

Otzar Midrashim, Perek Shirah 1:58

Both the Midrash and Matthew understand that the voice that cries out in the wilderness and seeks to set a path for Adonai is precisely the Tshuvah, repentance and involvement of the people with the Torah.

This was precisely what Yohanan preached, besides being a voice from the desert, he taught Tshuvah's need for his Mikveh to be valid. Tshuvah is nothing more than a form of repentance that goes beyond the sentimental, beyond remorse, but a palpable repentance, it is a return to the Laws of God. The Tshuvah that Yohanan preached, according to the

Jewish understanding, which we see in these Midrash, occurs only by a true involvement with the Torah.

## THE BROKEN MASHIACH

*In order to fulfill what was spoken by Isaiah,*
*Behold my servant whom I have selected, my chosen one*
*with whom my soul is pleased, I will put my spirit upon*
*him, and he will declare justice to the nations.*
*He will not fear nor will he run nor shall*
*one hear him in the street.*
*A crushed reed he will not break and a dim wick he will*
*not quench until he establishes justice forever*
*And in his name, the gentile hope.*

Matthew 12:17-21

*This is my servant, whom I uphold, My chosen one,*
*in whom I delight. I have put My spirit upon him,*
*He shall teach the true way to the nations.*
*He shall not cry out or shout aloud, Or make*
*his voice heard in the streets.*
*He shall not break even a bruised reed, Or snuff out even*
*a dim wick. He shall bring forth the true way.*
*He shall not grow dim or be bruised Till he has established the*
*true way on earth; And the coastlands shall await his TORAH.*

Isaiah 42:1-4

The mention of this prophecy by the author of the book of Matthew has already caused much debate and discord between Jews and Christians. The Jews claim that this is a very big mistake in the book of Matthew, because this prophecy was not fulfilled by jesus. According to the prophecy, the servant chosen by God could not be broken without establishing peace first. As we know, this is not the case, because the world is not and never been in peace, according to the Jewish argument related to this prophecy, jesus could not be Mashiach.

On the Christian side, they affirm that jesus did establish peace, but not a world peace, as the Jews expected. The peace they claim that has been established, would not be a "peace" in its literal meaning, but rather the unification of the Gentiles with the Jews into one people, for all would be children of God through jesus.

In my view, none of the explanations are satisfactory. On the side of the Jews, they are right, jesus did not fulfill this prophecy, as he did not fulfill a single one related to Mashiach, for he is not and never been Mashiach, for jesus was born from an erroneous interpretation, an interpretation that does not address Yehoshua, but the mythical figure created through him. On the other hand, Christians tend to think that they will be like the Jews, or even better than them, but the reality is not quite this, the Christians are those who will have to be more like the Jews and not the Jews more like the Christians, it may seem the same thing, but it is not.

Not that Judaism is a religion to be followed, but the Torah that represents them is what allows the Jews a more intimate connection with the Creator. Another point to consider is that Yehoshua did not come to every Gentile, but to a very specific group that is scattered among the Gentiles and no one knows who they are. Obviously, all of those who doesn't make part of this group, can be accepted into the People of Israel.

In order for us to understand what happens in this prophecy and the motives that the author of the book of Matthew had to quote it, we must ask two questions. First, does this prophecy really speak of Mashiach? Second, if so, which Mashiach?

To answer the first one, let's look at what some sages say in the Talmud, something that no Jew bring up when discussing the book of Matthew:

*One who sees a reed in a dream should rise early*

*and recites: "A bruised reed he will not break" (Is*
*42:3), in praise of the Mashiach.*
Talmud of Babylon, Tractate Brakhot 56b

*Rabbi Ḥiyya said to him: No; this referred to a different*
*verse, one that deals with the Mashiach, as they said to*
*you as follows: "A bruised reed he shall not break and*
*the dimly burning wick he shall not quench; according*
*to truth he shall bring forth justice" (Is 42:3).*
Talmud of Babylon, Tractate Yevamot 93b

The sages answer the first question and confirm what many deny, these verses speak about Mashiach and not about any prophet or anything. Now, in order for us to understand exactly what the prophet Isaiah refers to in his words, we must look at these verses in a somewhat more mystical way.

In the first verse, in its original language, we have the following:

# הן עבדי אתמך בו בחירי רצתה נפשי
# נתתי רוחי עליו משפט לגוים יוציא

*This is my servant, whom I uphold, My chosen one,*
*in whom I delight. I have put My spirit upon him,*
*He shall teach the true way to the nations.*
Isaiah 42:1

If we take the first 3 words that appear in this verse and look for its numerical value, we will have:

**(this is my servant) הן עבדי אתמך**
ה5 + 50נ + 70ע + 2ב + 4ד + 10י + 1א + 400ת + 40מ + 20ך

$$= 602 = 6 + 2 = \mathbf{8}$$

Interesting, its absolute value is the same value as the

word MASHIACH BEN YOSEF, as shown below:

**MASHIACH BEN YOSEF (משיח בן יוסף)**

80ף + 600ס + 6ו + 10י + 50ן + 2ב + 8ח + 10י + 300ש + 40מ

= 566 = 5 + 6 + 6 = 17 = 1 + 7 = **8**

This reveals to us that this verse deals with Mashiach Ben Yosef, not only the first verse, but also the second verse, for as we look at the third verse through Gematria, in the same way as the previous one, we will see that Isaiah's prophecy changes its object:

## קנה רצוץ לא ישבור ופשתה כהה
### לא יכבנה לאמת יוציא משפט

*He shall not break even a bruised reed, Or snuff out even a dim wick. He shall bring forth the true way.*

Isaiah 42:3

קנה רצוץ לא ישבור

100ק +50 נ+ 5ה + 200ר +90צ+ 6ו + 90ץ + 30ל

+ 1א + 10י + 300ש + 2ב + 6ו + 200ר

= 1090 = 1 + 9 = **10**

**MASHIACH BEN DAVID (משיח בן דוד)**

4ד + 6ו + 4ד + 50ן + 2ב + 8ח + 10י + 300ש + 40מ

= 424 = 4 + 2 + 4 = **10**

From verse three on, Isaiah no longer deals with Mashiach Ben Yosef, but with Mashiach Ben David. As the author of the book of Matthew quotes only the first four verses of Isaiah 42, we understand that the first two deal with Mashiach Ben Yosef and the third and fourth with Mashiach Ben David, and perhaps this is why it exists in the middle of this enigmatic prophecy some things that Yehoshua really did not fulfill, for they are meant to Mashiach Ben David.

But first, we will seek confirmation of what was said above through some *Midrashim* and Rabbinic comments:

### Mashiach Ben Yosef (v. 1 e 2)

*Let us not be ashamed of the generation of Mashiach and this time, the Holy One, Blessed Be He, said to him, **Ephraim, Mashiach**, my **tzadik**, I have already received you from the six days of creation. Now my sorrow will be upon you.*

Midrash Psikta Rabbati 36:1

This Midrash talks about some rather mystical things. First, it is directly related to the passage we are analyzing, for it directly mentions Isaiah 42:1. Then he quotes both the word "Mashiach" and the name "Ephraim".

Ephraim was the firstborn of Yosef and it is through this name that many *Midrashim* refer to Mashiach Ben Yosef, Ephraim became a second term in reference to this facet of Mashiach. Thus revealing to us that this verse speaks precisely of Mashiach Ben Yosef.

Another thing that we must observe is when the author speaks of a "sorrow" that God will have in relation to this Mashiach, for it concerns his suffering.

*"He shall teach the true way to the nations" (Is 42:1), this is the Torah that everyone will eager to listen to, his Torah.*

Rashi, Isaiah 42:1

As we have seen before, two of Mashiach Ben Yosef's main missions are to take the Torah to the Gentile world and to teach how it should be lived, Mashiach's interpretation of Torah is the interpretation that "all will eager to listen to".

Through Rabbi Rashi, we have another confirmation that this verse deals specifically about Mashiach Ben Yosef.

Now it is clear, as we read the first two verses again, we will see that the servant chosen by Adonai is clearly Mashiach, but Mashiach Ben Yosef in this case, for it is his mission to teach the true ways to the nations, to reveal and to teach the Torah. If we look at Yehoshua and see him as Mashiach Ben Yosef, the second verse makes sense, for as much as he preached and taught, in the end he was not heard by the Jews and was not understood by the Christians.

### Mashiach Ben David (v. 3 e 4)

*"nor will be broken" uses the word* ירוץ. *This term took me to* ירון *as we can see in Proverbs 29:6 and the meaning of this "joyously" found there is that he will not die nor will be beaten by men's violence.*

Ibn Ezra, Isaiah 42:4

In this fantastic comment, Rabbi Ibn Ezra takes the word YARUTZ (ירוץ) - *broken* - and compares it with another word YARUN (ירון) – *sing out* - which appears in the book of Proverbs, thus making an analogy about this form of Mashiach through comparing both verses.

לא יכהה ולא **ירוץ** עד ישים בארץ משפט **ולתורתו** איים ייחילו

*He shall not grow dim or be bruised Till he has established the true way on earth; And the coastlands shall await his TORAH.*

Isaiah 42:4

בפשע איש רע מוקש וצדיק **ירון** ושמח

*An evil man's offenses are a trap for himself, But the righteous sing out joyously.*

Proverbs 29:6

Ibn Ezra confirms Mashiach Ben David using the obvious, he will not be the facet of Mashiach who will suffer, but he is the one who will rejoice, as we see in the book of Proverbs. He will not die and will not be overcome by the violence of men (war of Gog and Magog that will precede Mashiach Ben David, he will not be defeated by it).

*He will not be darkened, for he is the real Mashiach. The Laws of Adonai and the leadership of Mashiach will be imposed*

*up to the most distant islands in the world and the Torah*
*and the worship to the true God will be spread all over.*

Malbim, Isaías 42:4

Also according to Malbim, in his commentary on verse four, we see that it deals precisely with the Age of Mashiach, which will be ruled by Mashiach Ben David.

However, among all these things we have seen, I believe that the author of the book of Matthew had one more reason to cite this prophecy, and this motive is self-explained right at the very beginning of the prophet's words:

*This **IS** My servant....*

Adonai does not speak of two servants, even if the text does speak about Mashiach Ben Yosef and Moshiach Ben David, God calls him using the singular form, thus showing that both Ben Yosef and Ben David are one and the same person. However, with different facets, missions and eras.

The intention of this study was not to explain the prophecy itself, rather to explain the reason that the author of the book of Matthew used it.

# SECTION VI
## YEHOSHUA AND THE JEWS

Everyone knows quite well that jesus was not accepted by the Jews; He wasn't only accepted, but he never will be. Missionaries, who go after the Jews in order to convert them into Christianity, are truly a big problem, because they have the ability to divert the true people of God from the ways He has determined.

An American group called *"Jews for Jesus"* insistently sends Christian missionaries to Israel, so they convince it's people that they must accept their jesus in order to go to heaven, and by doing so, they end up removing the Torah from the lives of those who hear them. Those who hear them, inevitably end up falling into idolatry, just as it happened when the Greeks invaded Israel and induced many of the Jews to convert to the gods of the Greek pantheon. Such attitudes represent a burden that the Jews have to bear. I hope, with God's help, they will never listen to such people.

On the other hand, if we set the mythical figure of jesus christ aside, the one that was created by the church and serves as an object of idolatry for many people, and look only at Yehoshua Ben Yosef, the one who declared to be Mashiach Ben Yosef – a rabbi, a Pharisee, the one who was hung on the tree and has revolutionized the history of mankind - we may discover that there is a relationship between him and the Jewish people that no Westerner knows.

In order to the Christian world never find out, so that the church would not be given a false idea of jesus' acceptance by the Jews, Yehoshua, or Yeshua, is secretly quoted in some Jewish books, but not by his real name, rather by some "nicknames" that he has, so that he is not easily recognized. Obviously, many of the Jews and rabbis do not believe that Yehoshua Ben Yosef was some form of Mashiach. But there are several others, including many among Orthodox Jews and rabbis, who recognize him as Mashiach, or at least as a Jewish brother, who would have to come and die so that Mashiach Ben David could rise. Those Orthodox will never recognize this openly.

Before we look into some rabbinic texts, we must know how Yeshua (contraction of the name of Yehoshua) is called. The first "nickname" is found in the Talmud itself:

> *About Mashiach, the Gemarah asks: What is his name?*
> *The school of Rabbi Yannai says: YNNON is his name,*
> *for it is written: that his name may endure forever,*
> *that his name may exist as long as the sun.*
> Talmud of Babylon, Tractate Sanhedrin 98b

According to the school of Rabbi Yannai, the name of Mashiach is YNNON. This name, although strange, is a Kabbalistic name to refer to the name Yeshua, for by Gematria, we have the following:

### YESHUA (ישוע)
70ע + 6ו + 300ש + 10י
= 386 = 3 + 8 + 6 = 17 = 1 + 7 = **8**

### YNNON (ינון)
50 + 6ו + 50נ + 10י
116 = 1 + 1 + 6 = **8**

Both YESHUA and YNNON have the same numerical value, as it is a codified way of referring to him.

> *May his name be eternal, just as the sun, may YNNON also endure forever. And he will bless all the Gentiles and all will be happy.*
> Psalms 72:17

This passage from the book of Psalms, when translated more literally, shows that YNNON will bless all the Gentiles and "coincidentally" is what Yeshua did, because, whether one likes it or not, it was through him that the knowledge of the Torah and about the God of Israel spread throughout the Gentile world.

During the celebration of the Rosh Hashanah (Jewish New Year) it is customary to read a book called *Machzor Rabah Rosh Hashanah.* This book is a guide for the celebration of that feast. In it, are found the customs, prayers, shofar's blows, and so on.

But there is something very interesting about this book: there is a *brakhah* (blessing) that must be recited between the first and the second shofar's blow, as follows:

> *May His will, through the shofar that we have just blew,*
> *be interwoven into the veil by the angel appointed by You.*
> *Just as You were with Eliahu (Elijah), of blessed memory*
> *and with Yeshua, the Sar HaPanim (minister of the*
> *face), so we also may be worthy of Your compassion. For*
> *You are Adonai, the only One worthy of worship.*
> Machzor Rabah Rosh Hashanah, TaSHRaT

I will not lie, when I studied this, I was really surprised, because this is a prayer between the first and second shofar's blow during a very important feast, in which Yeshua is mentioned. And not only mentioned, he is also called *Sar HaPanim*, which literally means *"Minister of the face"*. This is an ancient terminology among the rabbis to say that Yeshua represented the "face" of God, that is, he represented His true will in relation to His people and in relation to the Torah's observance.

Do not think that because the Jews know about Yeshua, and even possess knowledge that goes far beyond those I have exposed here, they are Christians, for they are not. Since Judaism and Christianity have very few things in common, both should not be confused. This example I brought is not meant to show to the Christian world that the

Jews believe in jesus, because they do not believe and will never believe, with the help of God. I have brought this study to those who are open-minded about the true Yehoshua Ben Yosef, for it is precisely this one that the Jews know and refer to.

# SECTION VII
## CONFIRMING THE HYPOTHESIS

As seen previously, in *Part II, section V - The Kingdom of Israel*, the Kingdom of Israel, also known as the Northern Kingdom, due to various sins of idolatry, was invaded and destroyed by the Assyrian empire. Its population, which was formed by ten tribes, was taken into exile and dispersed throughout the Gentile world. These people, over the years, ended up being assimilated by the Gentile cultures and completely disappeared, this is the greatest mystery concerning the tribes of Israel.

In this section of the book, a hypothesis has been presented, a hypothesis referring to an awakening, as never seen before all over the world that has been taking place in the lives of many people. Those people are leaving the Christian faith aside, in order to seek a life according to the Torah. This section also presents the three missions of Mashiach Ben Yosef, who, Yehoshua declared to be. One of these missions is regarding the gathering of these lost tribes, that is, the descendants of the tribes that have been scattered and assimilated by pagan cultures and religions; they will be identified and brought back into the bosom of the People of God.

As a proof, it is enough for us to look at the life and teachings of Yehoshua. Undeniably, it was through his life and death that the knowledge about the God of Israel, about the prophets and about the Torah was taken to all nations. Today, in any part of the world, everyone has at least an awareness about a book called "the bible". This "miracle", though it is taught in Christian circles that it was to save the Gentiles, in fact, it was not. This feat came to the Gentile world, because the lost tribes of the House of Israel are in those places. Due to the unawareness of the descendants of those tribes about who they really are, the Torah and the knowledge of God have been brought into the world, and so opening a possibility to these people to begin to return to the ways of the Creator.

The sages say that each one of the six hundred thousand men, who stood at the foot of Mount Sinai, at the moment when the Torah was delivered and they said "yes" to it, they received a "spark" inside of their souls, something that differentiated them as The Chosen People from the rest of the nations. Also, according to the sages, this "spark" is handed down from generation to generation. In other words, the dispersed descendants of these lost tribes, even after many centuries, still have this inner "spark" that connects them, somehow, to the True God and His Torah.

When Mashiach Ben David comes, he will only gather these tribes under his wings, but identifying them is not his mission, for when he comes, all these people will have already established, in a way only God knows how, a real and rational connection with the Torah, with the One God and with Israel. This phenomenon that we witness in modern times, where many people of the Gentile world are accepting the "yoke" of the Torah, by abolishing the Christian practices and concepts and by connecting themselves to the biblical commandments, is something never seen before, this is the sign of the approach of the coming of Mashiach Ben David. This only happens because of this "spark" that exists within each of these people.

This "spark" is the beacon of the coming of Mashiach, when these people shall awake, and they will awake, to the ways of the Torah, then the prophecies of the Tanakh will be fulfilled and they will be brought back to Israel to serve Mashiach personally. This was the real reason for Yehoshua's death and the knowledge of the God of Israel to have come to the Gentiles. Not because of them, but because of God´s seek for His people, the descendants of Yaakov, the tribes of Israel, those who once said YES to Him at the foot of a mountain.

On the other hand, it is well known that the God's

blessings always overflow, for these reason the gates to the Gentiles, who are not part of these tribes, will also be open, for there will be those who will understand and accept all of these things; as described by Paul, in the book of Romans, chapter 11, where he states that many will be grafted onto the olive tree. This olive tree is precisely the People of Israel, the grafting takes place through the Torah and the recognition of the One God of Israel, being this only possible to them due to the death of Yehoshua. Many, even if they do not the have the "spark", will be grafted unto this People and they will receive from Mashiach the same "spark" that those, who stood at the foot of Mount Sinai, have. A "spark" which will also be passed down by all generations of those people, who shall cease to be Gentiles, in order to become chosen. That is why it has been said that many will be called, but few will be chosen, for many will hear these things, but will still stick to the dogmas of religions.

Many of the Gentiles blindly believe that church and Christianity are the only absolute truths, they do not believe in the Hebrew originality of the gospel, except what was affirmed by the fathers of the church, they do not accept a God who is One Absolut, they live under human doctrines and dogmas created by vicious and pagan minds and they are indoctrinated through fear of an eternal condemnation or a life without the "blessings" that they seek so much. The Torah for them is something forgotten in the past, dead, abolished, they follow a messiah who they consider to be a god, they condemn those who follow the Laws, they live in a non-biblical puritanism and they seek more someone who performs miracles than a messiah itself. I am no one to state what God's judgment will be about it, but I am certain that these people are not from the lost tribes, they are not part of the true chosen people. For these, this book will be like an abomination, because they believe in the mythical jesus, that has nothing to do with Yehoshua Ben Yosef.

I reaffirm, Yehoshua came to the House of Israel and

not to the Gentiles who has nothing to do with the Chosen People, but as far as no one knows who these people are, it could be anyone.

He himself states this in a very clear way:

*And Yeshua said to him, I was not sent **except** to the lost sheep of **the house of Israel**.*

Matthew 15:24

If one who hears about these things and feels a restlessness, a calling voice from inside, an attraction to the true God, to Israel, to the Torah and to the Laws of God, then it is very likely that this one has this "spark" within himself and God, through Mashiach, is finally calling this person to return back home, to return to be under His wings, for the time has come. If not, if this person continues to believe in the Christian faith, then may he stay in what he already believes.

Now, let's look at all of this through the Word of God, let's see what the Tanakh reveals about the tribes of Israel and the mission of Mashiach Ben Yosef in this regard.

## 1- THE CONCEALED MATTER

כבד אלהים **הסתר דבר** וכבד מלכים חקר דבר

*It is the glory of God to **conceal a matter**, and the glory of a king to plumb a matter.*

Proverbs 25:2

Solomon claims that the glory of God is in *"to conceal a matter"*, the way it is expressed in its original, is something we do not see in Western translations. In Hebrew, this passage has a great mystery, for it doesn't clearly explain what this "matter that God has concealed" would be.

The term we have in English as *"to conceal a matter"*, in its original, is HASTER DAVAR (הסתר דבר) and this is what we should analyze:

## HASTER DAVAR (הסתר דבר)

ה5 + ס60 + ת400 + ר200 + ד4 + ב2 + ר200

## = **871**

The Tanakh also tells us that Joshua, Yehoshua in Hebrew, "brought" the tribes into the land of Israel, the Hebrew term for this statement is ALIAT SHVATIM (עלית שבטים) - *bring the tribes* - and this is one of the missions of Mashiach Ben Yosef , "to Bring the tribes" back to Israel. How do we know that?

### ALIAT SHVATIM (עלית שבטים)

ע70 + י10 + ל30 + ת400 + ש300 + ב2 + ט9 + י10 + ם40

## = **871**

Look how interesting, according to Solomon, the Glory of God is the return of the lost tribes of Israel to the Holy Land. This phenomenon discussed above, which has become commonplace today, is what the true Glory of God is. This confirms that this return is part of God's plans, another point is the name of both who had this mission, Yehoshua, coincidence?

## 2- THE LOST TRIBES

והיה כל אשר יקרא בשם יהוה ימלט כי בהר ציון ובירושלים תהיה

פליטה כאשר אמר יהוה ו**בשרידים** אשר יהוה קרא

*But everyone who invokes the name of Adonai*
*shall escape, for there shall be a remnant in Zion*
*and in Jerusalem, as Adonai promised. Anyone who*
*invokes Adonai will be among the **survivors**.*

Joel 3:5

This is a very strong passage, a prophecy given by the prophet Joel regarding the end of times. Through the mouth of the prophet, God affirms that ONLY those who invoke His Name shall escape and survive.

In order to understand the secret of these words, we

must first ask two questions. For whom this prophecy was made and who, exactly, would those "survivors" be.

Before we continue, let's look for whom this prophecy was made. According to the text, the prophecy is for the people of Zion, as well as for the people of Jerusalem. Jerusalem as everyone knows, is the capital of the Kingdom of Yehudah, it represents the Jews. But, what does the prophet mean by mentioning Zion? Who are the ones in Zion, since the Jews are represented by Jerusalem?

Let's make some comparisons before we draw any conclusions:

### ZION (ציון)

50ן + 6ן + 10י + 90צ

### = **156**

The value of the word Zion led me to make an association with another name, which revealed to me who this prophecy is referring to:

### YOSEF (יוסף)

80ף + 60ס + 6ן + 10י

### = **156**

Look, both YOSEF and ZION have a connection, for they represent each other. Yosef is also a term that represents the Mashiach, in this case, Mashich Ben Yosef, just as David represents Mashiach Ben David.

This answers one of the questions, just as Jerusalem represents the Jews, the people from the Southern Kingdom. Zion represents the Northern Kingdom, the lost tribes of Israel, the people scattered throughout the Gentile world. Hence the prophecy quotes two different places, Zion and Jerusalem, for it speaks to the two peoples who form the twelve tribes of Israel, the true Chosen People.

So that we can continue, let's look at the Gematria of Mashiach Ben Yosef, since he represents Zion:

**MASHIACH BEN YOSEF (משיח בן יוסף)**
80ף + 600ס + 6ו + 10י + 50ן + 2ב + 8ח + 10י + 300ש + 40מ
= **566**

The term for *"survivors"* that appears in this passage, in Hebrew, is BASRIDIM (בשרידים), which may also mean "the rest". This is a curious term, for it reveals something that goes far beyond what meet the eyes:

**BASRIDIM (בשרידים)**
40ם + 10י + 4ד + 10י + 200ר + 300ש + 2ב
= **566**

Look at that! Now the passage is clear, let's try a re-reading:

*But everyone who invokes the name of Adonai shall escape, for there shall be a remnant among the tribes of Israel and among the Jews, as Adonai promised. Anyone who invokes Adonai will be among those of Mashiach Ben Yosef.*

And to confirm the association of Zion with the Northern Kingdom, a Psalm:

*Joy of all the earth, Mount **Zion**, in the lands of the **north**, the city of the great King.*

Psalms 48:3

The mission of Mashiach Ben David will be to reign over Jerusalem in Yehudah. Mashiach Ben Yosef's mission will be to reign over Zion in Israel, as Ben David and Ben Yosef are the same person, just with different facets, he is the "great King", in the singular, of that verse. Mashiach will rule over the House of Israel and over the House of Yehudah.

## 3- HOW AND BY WHOM

עור ופסח הרה וילדת יחדו קהל גדול ישובו הנה בבכי יבאו
ובתחנונים אובילם אוליכם אל נחלי מים בדרך ישר לא יכשלו

בה כי הייתי לישראל לאב ו**אפרים** בכרי הוא

*I will bring them out of the land of the north, and
gather them from the ends of the earth, the blind and
the lame among them, those with child, and those in
labor; A large congregation shall return here.*

**They shall come with weeping and supplication**, *and I will lead
them to the streams of water, by a level road where they will not
stumble, for I am a Father to Israel, and* **Ephraim** *is My firstborn.*
Jeremiah 31:8-9

In these two verses we have many important infor-
mations, the first thing we should pay attention to is the
prophecy that comes from the mouth of God concerning the
return of the tribes. He does not refer, in this case, to the return of the Babylonian exile, for to this exile only the Jews,
the tribes of Yehudah and Benjamin, were taken. However, in
this case, God presents Himself as a Father to Israel, and this
shows who is this message for.

A second information is found at the end of verse nine,
where God refers to His firstborn Ephraim. Ephraim, in fact,
was the firstborn of Yosef, thus making a connection between "Ephraim, My firstborn" with Yosef, and by looking at
Yosef, we have the information we need, for God refers precisely to Mashiach, in this case, presented as Ben Yosef. This
is why He mentioned Ephraim.

According to the Gematria of the one represented by
Ephraim:

**MASHIACH BEN YOSEF (משיח נן יוסף)**

80ף + 600ס + 6ו + 10י + 50ן + 2ב + 8ח + 10י + 300ש + 40מ

## = 566

This proves, once again, that this mission of "gathering the tribes" will be done by Mashiach Ben Yosef.

A third piece of information can be taken from the phrase *"They shall come with weeping and supplication"*, for it is this how the lost tribes will be when they realize and understand who they really are.

According to the great sage, Gaon of Vilna, the "weeping" and "supplication" presented in this verse are linked to Mashiach Ben Yosef, as we can see below:

> *"They shall come with weeping and supplication" - this phrase has the numerical value of (566), thus referring to Mashiach Ben Yosef, as when He said "Ephraim is My firstborn."*
>
> Gaon of Vilna

"With weeping" refers to the joy of returning to Israel, "with supplication" refers to the forgiveness of past sins. This will be done through the work of Mashiach Ben Yosef.

If we look at the work of Yehoshua, it makes perfect sense, besides what was discussed above, about the knowledge of God reaching the Gentile world, Yehoshua speaks often about the forgiveness of sins through his death and the enjoyment they will have in him.

## 4- FROM WHERE

עורי צפון ובואי תימן הפיחי גני יזלו בשמיו
יבא דודי לגנו ויאכל פרי מגדיו

*Wake up, O **North** wind, for from the **South** wind something will blow in my garden to scatter its scent again. Let my beloved come to this garden and enjoy its fruits.*

Song of Songs 4:16

The terms "north" and "south" in this passage refer to the kingdoms of Israel (north) and Yehudah (south). Solomon says that "something" comes from the south toward the north, this "something" will cause the garden to spread its scent again and this "something" will enjoy the fruits of that garden. The "something" from this passage is revealed to us by the passage itself.

When we get the first letters of the first four words in Hebrew, we will have:

$$400ת + 5י + 90צ + 70ע$$

$$= 566$$

566, as seen above, is the Gematria of Mashiach Ben Yosef. What this verse tells us is that he will come from the south (Yehudah, a Jew) toward north (Israel, lost tribes) and he will restore that "garden" (the tribes), he will make its scent (glory) spread again and he, Mashiach, will rejoice over the fruits (to serve Mashiach) generated by these tribes.

*The Mashiach will go to the north, and thus will begin the gathering of the northern exiles.*
Midrash Rabbah

*And after saying this, Yeshua went from Galili to Tzot (Tyro) and Sodom (cities in the region where the Kingdom of North was located).*
Matthew 15:21

*For the days are coming, where the guardian (MASHIACH) will proclaim to those from Mount Ephraim (Ephraim - BEN YOSEF): Come, let us go to Zion (Israel), to Adonai, to your GOD.*
Jeremiah 31:6

## 5- BEN YOSEF ACCORDING TO THE BOOK OF MATTHEW
*Fulfilling what was said by Isaiah the prophet, a voice calls from the desert to return to the ways of Hashem and straighten the way of our Elohim.*
Matthew 3:3

קל קורא במדבר פנו דרך יהוה **ישרו בערבה מסלה** לאלהינו

*A voice cries out in the wilderness: Make **way** for Adonai.*
*They will **set a path in the plains** for our Elohim.*

Isaiah 40:3

If we take the original version of the prophecy quoted by Matthew, concerning the words of the prophet Isaiah, and look at the words *"set a path in the plains"* (ישרו בערבה מסלה), we will have something very interesting.

To do so, we must use the first letters of each of the three words, from left to right:

מ - ב - י

מ - משיח - Mashiach
ב - בן - Ben
י - יוסף - Yosef

Although this prophecy, as presented by Matthew, appears to refer to Yohanan, in fact, it deals with Mashiach Ben Yosef, for it is he who will prepare a way for Adonai.

Unlike the Western versions, where the word "desert" (or wilderness) appears twice, in the original, the second word translates as "desert", is actually "plain".

In the geological map of Israel, basically, we will see that in the southern region is where the Negev desert is located, inside the territory of Yehudah, and most of the Israeli plains are located where the Kingdom of Israel was.

Now, if we reread the verse of Isaiah again, it will become easier to figure what the author of the book of Matthew is saying:

*A voice that will come from Yehudah will open the*
***way** to (Adonai). (Mashiach Ben Yosef) will set a **path***
*in the north (lost tribes) towards Adonai.*

*Preparing the **way** and the paving a **path** for the redemption*
*of the exiles is part of the mission of Mashiach Ben Yosef.*

Gaon of Vilna

## 6- YEHOSHUA SEEN ON YOSEF

*(Ge 48:2) Yosef recognized his brethren, but his brethren did
not recognize him - This is one of the proofs that Mashiach
Ben Yosef will recognize his brethren, but his brethren will
not recognize him. This is the work of satan, who hides the
characteristics of Mashiach Ben Yosef, so that his steps
and teachings are not recognized because of idolatry.
When the House of Israel recognizes Yosef, we
will have the complete redemption.*

Gaon of Vilna

Rabbi Gaon of Vilna makes a very curious statement.
He states that just as Yosef recognized his brothers, his
brothers did not recognize him.

This could be understood as if he were talking about
the relationship between the Jews and Yehoshua, who
wasn't recognize by them. However, there is a small detail
that we should note, he mentions HOUSE OF ISRAEL, this
prophecy does not refer to the Jews from the House of Yehudah, but to those who belong to the House of Israel, the
lost tribes.

Yehoshua's death brought the knowledge about the
God of Israel to the Gentile world, but, as we have seen, not
because the Gentiles, but because the descendants of these
tribes, who are mixed within the Gentiles. However, something is for sure, if a Gentile understands this mystery, he
will be grafted onto Israel.

For almost 2000 years, these descendants did not recognize Mashiach Ben Yosef, for they could only see jesus and
that was because of satan, due to their sin of idolatry. For
some years now, a mysterious phenomenon has been leading
many Christians toward the Torah, and thus making them
forsaking Christianity and its theology. This is the glory of
God and the true divine call.

This phenomenon, by which many people are getting

to know the Torah, will culminate in the recognition, by these people that Yehoshua is Mashiach Ben Yosef and not jesus, these people will acknowledge the oneness of God and will automatically accept of the "yoke" of the Torah. At the moment this takes place in all over the world, the House of Israel will no longer be an exiled nation. May it be in our days!

## 7- YEHOSHUA AND GABRIEL, THE ANGEL

The book of Matthew does not mention the angel's name that came to Miriam and Yosef, Yehoshua's parents. However, it can be found who this angel was in other books that address the same topic.

I was once intrigued by the reason that God specifically sent the angel Gabriel and not some other angel, and it was by doing this research that I discovered that the angel Gabriel is a being directly linked to Mashiach Ben Yosef, through Yosef, Yaakov's son.

First of all, I would like to present some passages found in the Tanakh in order to understand this angel's connection with Yosef:

> While I was in my prayers, the man Gabriel, whom I
> had seen before in vision, was sent and came flying
> to me well at the time of the evening offering.

Daniel 9:21

The way Daniel talks about this angel is very unique, he refers to him as "the man Gabriel". Although no other prophet treats an angel in this way, the Torah uses the exact same terms, though not quoting the word Gabriel, to tell another apparition of this "man".

> And the man found him wandering in the fields, and
> the man said unto him, What are you looking for?

Genesis 37:15

This passage relates the moment when Yaakov orders

his son, Yosef, to look for his brethren who were shepherding in the field, just before he was sold as a slave to Egypt. This "man" is presented to us in the same way as the "man" in the book of Daniel. Although the book of Genesis does not tell us who he was, through biblical exegesis, we can define who this "man", who talked with Yosef, was, by looking at the words of Daniel.

Gabriel came to Yosef at that moment, because a bond between both was established by God. Our sages tell us that the revelations about dreams that Yosef possessed, were brought to him directly from the Throne of God by the angel Gabriel himself, and it was also this angel who taught him the language of the Egyptians.

In order to confirm this connection, it is enough to look at their names:

YOSEF (יוסף)

80ף + 600ס + 6ו + 10י

156 = 1 + 5 + 6 = **12**

GABRIEL (גבריאל)

30ל + 1א + 10י + 200ר + 2ב + 3ג

246 = 2 + 4 + 6 = **12**

The connection between Yosef and the angel Gabriel is well known among Jewish scholars. This also creates a connection between Mashiach Ben Yosef and this same angel. As Yehoshua claimed to be Mashiach Ben Yosef, to prove a connection with this angel is of utmost importance, this is why some New Testament authors have decided to be emphatic about who this angel was.

Another point to note is the reason for the appearance of this "man Gabriel" to Daniel, he comes to the prophet just to bring the revelation about SHKUTZ SHOMEM, something already seen in this book and somehow, has a connection with Yehoshua, for it's the fake yehoshua created by man.

## A FEW MORE OF YEHOSHUA'S WORDS

Before concluding this topic, I shall raise two more short statements made by Yehoshua, which were omitted in the Western translations, as follows:

> *Go and learn that which is written, I desire kindness and not sacrifice, I have no come for the Tzadikim, but for those who forgot the Law.*

Matthew 9:13

Yehoshua, once again, makes it very clear to whom he really came, to those *"who forgot the Law"*. I believe it is easy enough to understand that he refers to the Torah by the usage of the term "Law". In other words, he especially came to the people "who forgot the Torah".

If someone forgets something, it is because that someone knew, learned and understood that something. If Yehoshua's target people are the ones who have forgotten the Torah, it means that these people once knew it, learned it and followed it.

Everything that is related to God, once learned, can never be forgotten, even if it is never practiced. Thus, this *"forgot"* does not refer to an individual act, but rather to an event that caused a disconnection between this people and the Laws of God, thus leading them away and denying them access to the word of the Creator. What we can understand in this case, concerns precisely to the lost tribes of Israel, because, by being assimilated, they lost contact and the knowledge about the existence of the One God of Israel. Through this statement from Yehoshua, we can understand that he did not come to the Tzadikim, those who follow and know the Torah (Jews), but rather to those who have lost contact with the Torah and therefore have forgotten it over the years (Israel).

> *Go, search for those who have been lost*
> *from the House of Israel.*
>
> Matthew 10:6

This verse from the book of Matthew tells of the time when Yehoshua sends his talmidim to the other cities to teach, heal, and cast out demons. What is interesting about it, is whom should be their main targets and it is exactly the people who are somehow linked to the lost tribes of the House of Israel.

Now we have sufficient evidence to understand Mashiach Ben Yosef, his mission, the lost tribes of Israel, and how much Mashiach Ben Yosef we can see in the life, in the teachings and in the attitudes of Yehoshua, as reported in the book of Matthew. Something irrefutable.

I hope that through this book many may find this spark and have it lighten. That they may understand the true Yehoshua and bind themselves to the God of Israel and His Torah. May this reading bring us merit before the Creator.

Amen!

# PART V
# MATTHEW'S BOOK ENGLISH

## THE HOLY GOSPEL OF YEHOSHUA, THE MASHIACH, ACCORDING TO MATATYAH

# Chapter 1

Part 1

1- These are the generations of Yeshua, the son of David the son of Avraham.

2- Avraham begot Ytzhak and Ytzhak begot Yaakov, Yaakov begot Yehudah and his brothers.

3- Yehudah begot Peretz and Zerah from Tamar, Peretz begot Hezron, Hezron begot Ram.

4- Ram begot Aminadab, Aminadab begot Nachshon, Nachshon begot Shalmon.

5- Shalmon begot Boaz from Rahab, the harlot. Boaz begot Obed from Ruth and Obed begot Yesse.

6- Yesse begot David, David begot (Shlomo) from the woman of Uriah.

7- Shlomo begot Rehoboam, Rehoboam begot Abia, Abia begot Asa.

8- Asa begot Yehoshafat, Yehoshafat begot Yoram, Yoram begot Uziah.

9- Uziah begot – Yotam, who begot Ahaz, who begot – Hezekiah.

10- Hezekiah begot Manasseh, Manasseh begot Amon, Amon begot Yishiah.

11- Yishiah begot Yechoniah and his brothers in the Babylonian exile.

12- Yechoniah begot Shaaltiel, Shaaltiel begot Zeruvavel – after the exile.

13- Zeruvavel begot Avihud, Avihud begot – Eliahim, who begot Azor

14- Azor begot Zadok, who begot – Achim, Achim begot Elihud.

15- Elihud begot Eleazar, Elezar begot Matan, Matan begot Yaakov.

16- Yaakov begot Yosef. This Yosef was the husband of

Miriam – the mother of Yeshua – who is called Mashi-ach.

17- (All the generations from Avraham unto David were fourteen generations and from David unto the Babylonian exile were fourteen generations and from the Babylonian exile unto Yeshua were fourteen generations.

**Part 2**

18- The birth of Yeshua was in this way) It came to pass when his mother was betrothed to Yosef, before he knew her, she was found pregnant by the Holy Spirit.

19- Yosef was a Tzadik man and did not wish to live with her nor to expose her by bringing her to shame or to bind her over to death. Instead, he concealed her.

20- While he thought on this matter in his heart, an angel came to him in a dream and said, Yosef, son of David, do not fear to take your wife Miriam, because she is pregnant by the Holy Spirit.

21- And she will give birth to a son and he will be called Yeshua, for he will save my people from their iniquities.

22- All this was to fulfill what was written by the prophet according to Adonai

23- The young woman is conceiving and will bear a son and you will call him Ym'Anu'El, that is, Elohim with us.

24- Then Yosef awoke from his sleep, did according to all which the angel from Adonai said, and took his wife.

25- But he did not know her until she bore her first son and he called his name Yeshua.

## Chapter 2

**Part 3**

1- It came to pass when Yeshua was born in Beit Lechem of Yehudah in the days of Horodos, the king, behold astrologers came from the East to Jerusalem

2- Saying, where is the king of the Jews who has been born. We have seen (stars) in the East and we have come with important gifts to honor him.

3- Horodos the king heard and was dismayed and all the inhabitants of Jerusalem with him.

4- So he gathered all his ministers and inquire from them if they knew where Mashiach would be born.

5- They answered him, in Beit Lechem, Yehudah, as it is written according to the prophet.

6- And you Beit Lechem of Yehudah, Ephratah, land of Yehudah, you are the smallest in the land of Yehudah, from you will come forth to me one to be the ruler in Israel.

7- The king Horodos calles the magicians in secret and asked them well concerning the time the star came to them.

8- He sent them to Beit Lechem and said unto them, go and inquire well concerning the child and when you find him inform me. I also will go to honor him.

9- They harkened unto the king and went, and behold the star which they saw in the East was going before them until they came to the place. When they arrived in Beit Lechem, they stood in the front of the place where the child was.

10- When they saw the star they rejoiced with exceedingly great joy.

11- They went into the house, found him and his mother Miriam, knelt before him, honored him, opened their sacks and brought to him gifts of gold, frankincense and myrrh, that is, mira.

12- Then they were commanded in a dream by the angel who spoke to them not to return to Horodos, so they returned to their land by another route.

Part 4

13- As they were going, behold the angel of Adonai appeared unto Yosef, arise, take the boy and his mother, flee to Egypt and stay there until I tell you, because Horodos will seek the boy to kill him.

14- So he took the boy and his mother

15- And was there until Horodos died, to fulfill what was spoken by the prophet, out of Egypt I called my son.

Part 5

16- Then Horodos saw that the magicians mocked him and was very sad. Being grieved at heart, he commanded that word be sent to all his ministers to kill all the male children who were in Beit Lechem and its borders who had been born from the time when the magicians spoke to him concerning the birth of the boy.

17- Then was fulfilled what the prophet Yrmiahu said.

18- A voice is heard in Ramah, lamentations and bitter weeping, Rachel weeping for her son and so on.

19- It came to pass when king Horodos died, the angel of Adonai appeared in a dream to Yosef in Egypt.

20- Saying, arise, take the boy and his mother and go to the land of Israel, because those who were seeking the boy to kill him are dead.

21- So he arose, took the boy and his mother, and they returned to the land os Israel.

22- Then he heard that Horcanus, his name is Argelaus, reigned in Yehudah in the place of Horodos his father, and he feared to go there. The angel urged him in a dream that he should turn unto the land of Gilgal.

23- He came an dwelt in a city called Notzrit, in order to fulfill what the prophet said, he shall be called Notzeret.

## Chapter 3

Part 6

1- In those days came Yohanan, the purifier, preaching in

the wilderness of Yehudah.

2- And he said: Do Tshuvah, for the Kingdom of Heaven is approaching.

3- Fulfilling what was said by Isaiah, the prophet, a voice calls from the desert to return to the ways of Hashem and straighten the way of our Elohim.

4- Behold Yohanan was clothed with the hair of camels and black leather girded his loins and his food was locust and the honey of the forest.

5- Then they came out to him from Jerusalem, from all Yehudah, and from all the kingdom around the Yordan,

6- And at that time were confessing their sin and were baptizing in the Yordan because of his word.

Part 7

7- He saw that many Pharisees, that is, Farizei, and Sadducees came to his Mikveh and he said to them, in order to flee from the fury of EL, they should

8- bear the fruit of the perfect Tshuvah.

9- Do not say in your heart, Abraham is our father. Truly I say to you that Elohim is able to raise up his son Avraham from these stones.

10- (Already the axe has reached the root of the tree, the one which does not produce good fruits will be cut down and burned in the fire. The crowds asked him, if so what shall we do? Yohanan answered them, he who has two shirts let him give one to him who has none. So the people emerged in his Mikveh) Many asked him, what shall we do? And he answered them, be anxious for no man and do not chastise them, and be pleased with you lot. And all the people were thinking and reckoning in their circumcised heart, Yohanan is Yeshua.

11- And Yohanan answered them all: behold, here I am, trully submerging you in the water of Tshuvah, and then a mightier one than I, who am not worthy to untie the sandals of his feet, will purify you with the fire of the Holy Spirit .

12- The winnowing fork is in his hands to fan his threshing floor, he will gather the grains in his barns and the straw (it will be burned in fire, which is not useful).

Part 8

13- Then came Yeshua from Galil to the Yordan, at the mikvah of Yohanan.

14- And Yohanan was in doubt about submerging him and said: Is it more propitious that I be submerged by your hands and you are coming to me?

15- Yeshua answered and said to him, permit it, because we are obliged to fulfill all that makes one a tzadik, them Yohanan submersed him.

16- Immediately when he came up from the water, the heavens were opened to him and he saw the Spirit of Elohim coming down like a dove and it dwelt upon him.

17- Then behold a voice from heaven was saying, this is my son, my beloved, he is lover very very much and my pleasure is in him.

## Chapter 4
Part 9

1- Then Yeshua was led by the Holy Spirit into the wilderness to be tempted by satan.

2- And Yeshua fasted for forty days and forty nights, and after that he was hungry.

3- The tempter came and said to him, "If you are the son of Elohim, tell this stone to become bread.

4- And Yeshua answered and said unto him: It is written, that not by bread alone, and so forth.

5- Then satan took him to the holy city and stood on the highest place, above all the Temple

6- And he said unto him, If thou be Elohim, jump down,

for it is written, He commanded his angels to keep thee in all his ways, and so forth.

7- And Yeshua answered him the second time: you shall not tempt Adonai your Elohim.

8- And satan carried him to a very high mountain and showed him all the kingdoms of the earth and their glories.

9- And he said unto him, All this I will give thee, if thou surrender unto me.

10- Then Yeshua answered him: Go satan, that is satanas, for it is written that only to Hashem will I pray and only Him will I serve.

11- Then satan left him and behold, angels approached him and served him (ministered him).

Part 10

12- And days have passed and Yeshua heard that Yohanan was taken to prison and then he went to Gilgal.

13- And he passed through Nazarael and dwelt in Kafar Nahum Raitah, which in foreign language is Maritima, on the outskirts of the lands of Zevulum.

14- To fulfill what the prophet Isaiah said:

15- Land of Zevulum and land of Naftali, way of the sea, beyond the Yordan, Galil of the nations.

16- The people who walked in darkness saw a great light, those who dwelt in a land of tremendous darkness saw light shining upon them.

Part 11

17- From now on Yeshua began to preach and speak about returning to Tshuvah, for the Kingdom of Heaven had come.

18- Yeshua went along the shore o the sea of Galil and saw two brothers, Shimon, who is called Simon, also called Pietros and Andireah his brother casting their nets into the sea because they were fishermen.

19- He said to them come after me and I will make you fish for men.

20- So they left their nets in that moment and went after him.

21- He turned from there and saw two other brothers, Yaakov and Yohanan, brothers sons of Zevadiel, that is, Zavaadahm and their father in a boat setting up their nets and he called them.

22- They hastened and left their nets and their father and followed after him.

## Part 12

23- The Yeshua went around the land of Galil teaching their assemblies and preaching to them the good gift, that is, mavangeilio, of the kingdom of heaven and healing all the sick and every disease among the people.

24- So a report about him went into all the land Syria and they brought unto him all those who were sick from various kinds of diseases, those possessed by demons, those who were terrified by an evil spirit and those who shook, and he healed them.

25- Many followed him from Kapoli and Galil, from Jerusalem, Yehudah, and across the Yordan.

## Chapter 5

Part 13

1- It came to pass after this when he saw the crowds that he went upon the mountain and sat down. Then his talmidim approached him.

2- And he opened his mouth and spoke with them saying,

3- Ashrei the one who has the humble spirit, for his is the Kingdom of Heaven

4- Ashrei those who wait, for they will rest

5- Ashrei the meek, for they shall inherit the earth.

6- OMISS

7- OMISS

8- Ashrei those of heart and innocent hopes, for they will see Elohim

9- Ashrei those who seek peace, for they will be called sons of Elohim

10- Ashrei those persecuted for being tzaddikim, for theirs is the Kingdom of Heaven.

11- Ashrei will be you when you are persecuted and rebuked and when they tell you many bad things because the Torah, all falsely spoken.

12- Rejoice, your reward will be great in the heavens, because they persecuted the prophets.

13- At that time Yeshua said to his talmidim: You are salt in the world, if the salt loses its flavor, with what will it be salted? It will have no use for anything, it will be thrown out to be trampled under feet.

Part 14

14- You are the light of the world, a city built upon a hill cannot be hidden.

15- A lamp is not lit to be placed in a hidden place where it can not shine. But one should put it on a Menorah, to illuminate everyone in the house.

16- Therefore let your light shine before all men, that they may see your good deeds, so that glory and honor may be given to your Father who is in heaven.

17- At that time Yeshua said to his talmidim: do not think that I came to violate the Torah, but to observe it in its completeness.

18- Truly, I say to you that even if the heavens and the earth (depart), a yud or a nekudah will not be abolished from the Torah or the prophets and everything will be fulfilled.

19- And whoever fails to perform some Torah Mitzvot, however small it is and teaches it to others to do so, will be called HAVEL (futile) in the Kingdom of Heaven and whoever observes and teaches Mitzvot of the Torah, great will be called in the Kingdom of Heaven.

## Part 15

20- At that time Yeshua said to his talmidim, truly I say to you, if you are not tzaddikim greater than the Pharisees and the sages, you will not enter the Kingdom of Heaven.

21- Have you not heard what the ancients said? Thou shalt not murder, and he who murders shall be guilty of death penalty.

22- And I tell you that he who is angry with his friend will be judged by the court; and he who calls his brother inferior will be judged by the Kohel and those who call him a fool will be judged by the fire of Gehinam.

23- And as you approach near the altar and you remember that you have a quarrel with your friend and he is complaining to you about it.

24- Leave your offering there before the altar, and go and please him first. Then offer your offering.

## Part 16

25- And Yeshua said to his talmidim, See that you hasten to calm your enemies while walking with them, before they deliver you to the judge, and this judge hand you over to the servant who will put you into the prison.

26- Truly, I tell you, you will not come out until you pay all the money you owe.

## Part 17

27- And he said unto them, you hearken to the words of the ancients, you shall not commit adultery.

28- And I say unto you that whosoever looks upon a woman, and desires her, yet commits adultery with her in the heart.

29- And if your right (eye) seduces you, take it out and throw it away before you.

30- And if your hand seduces you, cut it off. Better for you to lose a member than your whole body in Gehinam.

## Part 18

31- And Yeshua said to his talmidim: they heard what was said by the ancients, whoever leaves his wife and sends her (away), shall give her a letter of divorce (Get Kritot), which in a foreign language is Libeila Repudiation.

32- And I tell you that everyone who leaves their wives, give them Get Kritot. But concerning adultery, he is the one who becomes adulterous, and the one who takes her commits adultery.

## Part 19

33- And you have heard what was spoken by the ancients: "Do not swear falsely in my name, for you must answer before Adonai your promises.

34- And I say unto you, Swear not in vain for anything, nor by the heavens which is the throne of Elohim.

35- And not by the earth which is the footstool of His feet, nor by the city of the heavens (Yerushalayim), for it is the city of Elohim.

36- And not by your head because you cannot make your hair white or black.

37- But let your words be yes, yes and no, no. Anything added to this is bad.

38- And you have heard what is said in the Torah: eye for eye and tooth for tooth.

39- And I say to you, do not pay evil for evil, but whoever smites on your right cheek, do also give him the left.

40- And whoever wants to oppose you in the trial and steal your shirt, leave your coat too.

41- And whoever asks you to walk with him a thousand steps, walk with him two thousand.

42- He who asks you, give it and he who wants to borrow, do not avoid.

Part 20

43- And Yeshua said to his talmidim: you have heard what was spoken by the ancients, and you shall love those who love you and hate those who hate you.

44- And I say to you: you shall love your enemies and do good to those who hate you and make you angry, you shall pray for those who persecute and oppress you.

45- So you be the children of your Father in heaven, who makes the sun shine on the good and on the bad, and brings rain to the wicked and to the Tzaddikim.

46- If you love those who love you, what is the gain to you? Even these impudent ones love those who love them.

47- OMISS

48- Be you innocent for you Father is perfect.

## Chapter 6

Part 21

1- Beware lest you be tzadik only before men for them to praise you. And if you do it, there will be no merit for you from your Father in heaven.

2- Yet Yeshua said: When you do tzedakah, do not proclaim or sound a trumpet before you like the hypocrites, in a foreign language Yipokratis. Who do their tzedakot in the streets and markets where they are seen by men. But I tell you that they have already received their merits.

3- And when you do tzedakah, that your left hand does not know what the right does

4- So that is your offering is a secret offering and your Father, who secretly sees, completes you (rewards).

Part 22

5- At that time, Yeshua said to his talmidim: "Don't raise your voice by the moment you pray, and do not be like those loose branches that pray in the synagogues and in the corners of the courtyard, praying with a loud speech that they may be praised by men.

6- And in your prayers, come to your bed and close the doors behind you and pray to your Father in secret and your Father, who sees in secret, will complete (reward) you.

7- And when you pray, do not multiply words like the heretics, who think that they will be heard.

8- Do you not see that your Father in heaven knows the things (that you ask for) before they are even asked by you?

9- And so shalt thou pray: Our Father, Holy is Your name

10- Blessed be Your kingdom, may Your will be done in heaven and on earth.

11- And give us our bread always

12- And forgive us our sins when we forgive those who sins against us.

13- And do not bring us next to temptation and keep us from all that is evil, amen.

Part 23

14- If you forgive men their sins your father who is in heaven will forgive your sins.

15- But if you do not forgive them he will not forgive you your sins.

Part 24

16- Again he said to them, when you fast do not be as the sad hypocrites who make themselves appear sad and who change their faces to show their fasting before men, truly I say to you, they have received their reward already.

17- But when you fast, wash your heads

18- That you might not appear to men to be fasting, but to your father who is in secret, and your father who is in secret will complete will.

Part 25

19- Yet he said to them: Do not keep on heaping up earthly treasures that decay and the grub devour it or it is stolen by thieves.

20- Make for yourselves treasures in heaven, where rust and grub do not devour them, and where thieves do not steal.

21- In this place shall be your treasure.

22- And the light of your body is your eyes, if your eyes look forward, your body (path) will not darken.

23- And if your light darkens, all your ways will be darkened.

Part 26

24- At this time Yeshua said to his talmidim, no man can work (serve) for two masters unless he loves one and hates the other or honors one and dishonors the other. You cannot work (serve) to EL and to the world.

25- Therefore I tell you, do not worry for the food for your souls and also for the clothes for your bodies. The soul is more valuable than the food and the body more than the garments.

26- Look at the birds in the sky, they do not plant, they do not harvest (from the ground) nor gather in barns, but your exalted Father who feeds them. Are not you more important than they?

27- Who among you of those who are anxious is able to add to his height on cubit?

28- If this is the case, why are you anxious for clothes? Behold the lilies of Sharon, that is, Gilyon.

29- But I say to you that king Shlomo in all his glory was not clothed like these.

30- If EL clothes the straw which is left in the standing grain, that is, penon, which is fresh today and dried up tomorrow and is placed in the fire, so much more you of little faith.

31- If EL thinks of you, do not worry about what you shall eat or what you shall drink.

32- All that the body needs, your Father knows. He knows all the things you need.

33- Seek rather the kingdom of Elohim and be tzaddikim and all these things will be given to you.

34- Do not worry about tomorrow, for tomorrow will worry about itself. It is enough for you the day of today and its problems.

## Chapter 7
Part 27

1- Do not judge lest you be judged.

2- With this judgment you will be judged and with this measure you will be measured.

3- And why do you see the straw in the eye of your neighbor and not see the beam that is in your eyes?

4- And how will you speak to your neighbor: wait a little and I will cast the straw out of your eyes and behold, the beam is in your eyes ?!

5- Hypocrite! cast your beam out first of your eyes, and afterwards cast the straw out of your neighbor's eyes.

Part 28

6- Again he said to them: Do not give kasher meat to dogs, nor throw (sacred things) before swine, lest they chew them before you and turn to rend you.

7- Ask EL and it will be given to you, ask and you will find, knock and it will open for you.

8- Whatever you ask you will be given and to who asks, he will receive and will find, and to the one who calls, will be opened.

9- Who in the midst of you, that the son asks of you a piece of bread, gives him a stone?

10- Or if you ask for fish, does it give you a snake?

11- And you who are an evil people, come and give good gifts before you, then much more your Father in Heaven, who gives His good Spirit to those who ask for it.

12- And whatever you want men to do to you, do to them, that's all the Torah and the prophets.

## Part 29

13- At that time Yeshua said to his talmidim: **come** through the narrow gate, for the gate of doom is wide and deep and many go through it.

14- How narrow is the gate and grievous the path that leads to life and how few are those who find them.

## Part 30

15- Again he said to them, beware of false prophets qho come to you in wool clothing like sheep, but inside are tearing wolves.

16- By their deeds you will know them. Does a man gather grapes from thorns or fig from birars?

17- Every good tree makes good fruit and every bad tree makes bad fruit.

18- The good tree cannot make bad fruit nor can the bad tree make good fruit.

19- Every tree which does nor make good fruit is burned.

20- Therefore it is according to fruits, that is, by their deeds, you will know them.

21- Because not everyone who says unto me, lord, will enter the kingdom of heaven, but the one who does the will of my father who is in heaven will enter the kingdom of heaven.

22- Many will say to me in that day, lord, lord, did we not prophesy in your name, and in your name we have cast out demons, and have not done many signs in your name?

23- And then I will say to them: I never knew you, depart

from, all who do not practice the Law (Torah).

Part 31

24- Again he told them: Everyone who listens to these things (Devarim Torah) and does them is similar to the man who builds the house on the top of a rock.

25- The rain falls on it and the wind hits it and it does not fall, because its foundation is the rock.

26- And all who hear "these things" (Eile HaDevarim) and do not do them is similar to the man who is foolish, who builds a house on the sand.

27- The rains fall and the flood comes and the house falls apart with a great fall.

28- While Yeshua was saying these words (Devarim), all the people were impressed with his conduct.

29- For he was preaching before the people with great power, and not as the sages.

## Chapter 8
Part 32

1- It came to pass when Yeshua came down from the mountain that a great crowd was after him.

2- Then behold a leper came and greet him saying, lord, are you able to heal me?

3- Yeshua stretched out his hand, touching it, and said: I desire that you be purified and at that time the leper was cleansed of his leprosy.

4- And Yeshua said to him, Be careful when you tell this to the men, go to the priest and offer an offering as ordered by the Torah of Moses.

Part 33

5- It came to pass when he entered into Kafar Nahum Hamarta that a captain of hundreds came to him and implored him,

6- Saying, lord, my son lies in my house with the sickness of contraction, that is, paralitiko, and he is weal with the illness.

7- Yeshua said, I will go and heal him.

8- The captain of hundreds answered and said to him, lord, I am not worthy that you should come under my roof, only make the decision that he might be healed.

9- I am a sinful man and I have authority on the Pharisees and horses and riders and I say to one of them go and he goes, come and he comes, and to my servants do this and they do it.

10- Yeshua heard and was amazed and said to those who were following him, truly I say to you, I have no found a great faith in Israel.

11- So that many will come from the East and from the West and will rest with Abraham, Itzhak and Yaakov in the kingdom of heavens.

12- But, the sons of the kingdom will be cast into the darkness of Gehinam. There will be weeping and gnashing of teeth

13- The Yeshua said to the captain of hundreds, go, as you have believed, it will be done to you. So the boy was immediately healed.

## Part 34

14- At that time, Yeshua went into the house of Pietros and behold his mother in law was laying sick with a fever.

15- He touched her hand and the fever left her. Then she arose and served him something.

16- At the time of evening they brought to him those seized by demons and he healed them by his word alone and he healed every sickness,

17- to complete what was said by the prophet Isaiah, of blessed memory, surely out sickness he bore and our pains he suffered.

## Part 35

18- It came to pass after this Yeshua saw many crowds around him and he commanded to go across the sea.

19- Then a sage came to him and said to him, master, I will follow you wherever you go.

20- And Yeshua answered him: the foxes have holes and the birds nests, but the son of man, the virgin's son, has no place to enter (rest) his head.

21- One of his talmidim told him, allow me to go and bury my father.

22- And Yeshua said, follow me and let the dead bury the dead.

## Part 36

23- It came to pass when Yeshua entered a boat, his talmidim followed him.

24- A great storm came on the sea, and many waves were coming on excessively, and was almost breaking up.

25- His talmidim came to him and begged him saying, o our master, save us lest we perish.

26- he said to them, why do you look at one another, you little of faith? He arose and commanded the sea and the winds that they should be quiet and immediately they became quiet.

27- When the men who were there saw, they marveled and said, who is this that the winds and the sea do his will?

## Part 37

28- It came to pass when he crossed over the sea and passed by the region beyond the sea into the realm of Gaderi, that is, Ginitraros, there met him two men possessed by demons who came out of a tomb, raging until no man could pass by that way.

29- They cried out saying to him, what is between you and us, Yeshua son of Elohim? Yeshua said to them, come out from there, evil host.

30- There near them were herds of many swine feeding.

31- So the demons asked him, since we have to go out from here, grant us authority to go into these swine.

32- He said to them, go. The demons went out from the men and entered the swine, and all the herd went in sudden haste, slipped off into the sea and died in the water.

33- Those who were feeding, feared, fled, and told everything in the city. So the whole city was frightened.

34- They went out to meet Yeshua. They saw him and entreated him no to pass over into their border.

## Chapter 9

1- Then Yeshua entered a boat, they set sail and returned to his city.

2- They brought to him one who was sick with contractions, that is, paralitico, lying upon his bed. Yeshua saw their faith and said to the sick man, have courage my son. It is by your faith of EL that your sins have been forgiven.

3- Some of the sages were saying in their heart, this one blasphemes.

4- Yeshua saw their thoughts and said to them, why do you think evil in your heart?

5- Easier to say, your sins are forgiven, or rise and walk?

6- To inform you that the son of man is able to show who has been forgiven on this earth, then he said to the sick man, arise and take your bed and walk.

7- He arose and went to his house.

8- The crowds saw, feared a lot, and praised Elohim who had given power t men to do such things.

## Part 38

9- It came to pass when Yeshua passed on from there, he saw a man sitting at the table of exchange, Matatya was his name, that is, Matyeo, and he said to him, follow me. So he arose and followed him,

10- He brought him to his house to eat. It came to pass while he was eating, that behold many violent and evil men were at the table and behold they were eating with Yeshua and his talmidim.

11- Some Pharisees saw and said to his talmidim, why does your master sit and eat with violent and evil men?

12- Yeshua heard it and said, the healthy have no need for healing, but the sick.

13- Go and learn that which is written, I desire kindness and not sacrifice, I have no come for the Tzadikim, but for those who forgot the Law.

Part 39

14- Then Yohanan's talmidim came to him and said to him, why do we and the Pharisees fast often but your talmidim does not?

15- Yeshua answered them and said, the friends of the bridegroom cannot weep and fast while he is with them. Days will come when the bridegroom will be taken from them, then they will fast.

16- No man wastes a piece of new garment on an old garment, for the force of the piece stretches the worn out garment and it tears more.

17- Nor do they put new wine into old vessel lest the vessel break, and the wine spills out and the vessel perish. The new is for new vessels and both of them are preserved.

Part 40

18- It came to pass when he had spoken to them, a captain approached and bowed his head saying, master, my daughter just died. Please come and place your hand upon her and restore her to life.

19- Yeshua arose and went, he and his talmidim with him.

20- And, behold, a woman with a flow of blood for twelve years, came up behind him and touched the Tzitzit of his Talit.

21- She said in her heart: If I touch his talit, I will be healed immediately.

22- He turned his face and said to her: Be strong my daughter, the **fear** for Adonai, blessed be He (Baruch hu) healed you. At that very hour she was healed.

23- It came to pass when he entered the house of the captain, he saw many people weeping.

24- He said to them, go outside all of you and stop weeping because the girl is asleep and not dead. But in their eyes he was as one who jests. They were saying, have we not seen that is she dead?

25- When they went outside, Yeshua went to her, touched her hand and the girl arose.

26- This report went out in all that land.

## Part 41

27- Yeshua passed on from there, and behold two blind men were running after him and crying out loud to him, have mercy on us, son of David.

28- He came to the house, and the blind men drew near him. He said,

29- Your faith will heal you.

30- The eyes of the two blind men were immediately opened and they saw. He commanded them saying, be careful for the matter not to be known.

31- As for them, they went out and made him know in all that land.

## Part 42

32- Yeshua went out from there and they brought before him a dumb man who was demon possessed.

33- He cast out the demon so that the dumb man spoke. The crowds were amazed and said, we have not seen it like this in Israel.

34- The Pharisees said, truly in the name of demons he

casts out demons.

35- He went around all the cities and towers teaching in the synagogues and preaching the good tidings and healing every illness and every sickness.

36- Yeshua saw the crowds and had pity on them because they were weary and lying like sheep without shepherd.

37- Then he said to his talmidim, the standing grain is much but the reapers are few.

38- Entreat now Adonai of the standing grain that he send many reapers to harvest his grain.

## Chapter 10
Part 43

1- Then Yeshua called his twelve talmidim and gave them power over every unclean spirit to cast them out from man and to heal every sickness and every plague.

2- These are the names of the twelve talmidim, Shimon, called Pietros, and Andireah, his brother.

3- Filipos and Bortolameios and Yaakov, called Yimi and Yohanan his brother, sons of Zevediel, Tomais and Matatya, called Mateo, which was known as lender of money, Yaakov Alufei and Tereos,

4- Shimon the Cannanite, that is, Simon Kananayos, and Yehudah Eshkarioto, who after this betrayed him.

5- These twelve Yeshua sent, he commanded them by saying, to the lands of the gentiles do not go and into the cities of the Samaritans do not enter.

6- Go, search for those who have been lost from the House of Israel.

7- Teach them that the Kingdom of Heaven will be fulfilled.

8- Heal the sick, restore life to the dead, cleanse the lepers, and cast out demons from men. Do not accept money, freely you received, freely you give.

9- Do not heap up silver and gold, nor wealth in your

purse,

10- Nor changes of clothes, nor shoes, nor a staff in your hand. The workman is worthy to receive enough for his food.

11- In every city and in every tower you enter ask who is the good man among them and there remain until you go out.

12- When you enter into the house, give to them Shalom saying, Shalom to this house, Shalom to all who dwell in it.

13- If that house is worthy, your Shalom will come upon it, but if not, your Shalom will return to you.

14- One does not receive or listen to you, you shall go out from that house and shake off your feet from the dust.

15- Truly I say unto you, it will be better for Sodom and Gomorrah in that day than for that city.

## Part 44

16- Behold I send you like sheep in the midst of wolves. Be as crafty as snakes and humbles as doves.

17- Beware of men. They will not deliver you up in their congregations and in their synagogues.

18- But to governors and kings. You will be able to bear witness on my behalf to them and to the gentiles.

19- When they seize you, do not consider what you will say, because in the hour that you are in need an answer will come to you.

20- It will not be you who speak, but the Holy Spirit of my Father will speak through you.

21- Brother will deliver up brother to death and a father his son, the sons will rise up against father and lead them unto death.

22- You will become a derision and a fright to all the nations because of my name. Whoever endures until the time of the end will be saved.

Part 45

23- Again Yeshua said to his talmidim, when they pursue you in this city flee to another, truly I say to you, you will not have completed for yourselves the cities of Israel before the son of man comes.

24- No talmid is greater than his rabbi, nor is the servant greater than his master.

25- It is enough for the talmid to be like his rabbi and for the servant to be like his master. If they call the master of the house Baal Zevuv, so much more the sons of his house.

26- Do not fear because there is nothing which will not be seen, nor hidden.

27- I say to you in secret, say it in the light.

28- Do not fear those who kill and have no power to kill souls, but fear the one who has power to destroy the soul and the body in Gehinam.

29- Are not two sparrows sold for a small coin and not one of them will fall to the earth except by the will of your Father who is in heaven?

30- Are not all the hairs of your head numbered?

31- Do not fear, because you are better than the sparrows.

32- He who compliments me before man I will compliment him before my Father, who is in heaven.

33- (NO VERSE, except for:) Those who diminishes me before the sons...

Part 46

34- At that time Yeshua said to his talmidim, do not think that I came to put in the nations (peace), but rather desolation.

35- I have come to separate the son of his father and the daughter of her mother.

36- The enemy must be loved.

37- He who loves father and mother more than me, I am

not suitable to him.

38- NO VERSE

39- He who loves his life will lose it, he who loses it for my sake, will find it.

40- He who receives you, receives me and he who receives me, receives the One who sent me.

41- He who receives a prophet in the name of a prophet, will receive the merit of a prophet, he who receives a tzadik in the name of a tzadik, will receive the merit of a tzadik.

42- He who gives a vessel of fresh water to one of my little talmidim, by the name of the talmid, Amen (trully) I tell you that you will not lose the merit.

## Chapter 11
Part 47

1-　It came to pass when Yeshua finished commanding his twelve talmidim that he passed on from there and commanded them to teach and reprove in their cities.

2-　And heard Yohanan while in prison about the deeds of Yeshua and he sent two of his talmidim.

3-　Telling him: are you the one who was to come or should we hope for another?

4-　And Yeshua answered them: Go and tell Yohanan about the things you saw and about the things you heard.

5-　The blind see, and the lame walk, and the lepers are pure, and the deaf hear, and the dead are revived, and the poor are committed.

6-　And ASHER those who are not perplexed in me.

7-　And after that, Yeshua went and began to speak about Yohanan to the crowd: what did you see out in the desert? Moshlechet Baruach?

8-　Or what did you go out to see? Did you think Yohanan was a person who wore noble clothes? Those who dress in noble clothes are in the palaces (not in the desert).

9- So, what did you go to see? A Prophet? Truly, I say to you, he is greater than a prophet.

10- It is written upon him that is written for my good: Behold! I am commanding my messenger to open the way before me.

## Part 48

11- Yeshua said again to his talmidim: I tell you that among all those born of woman, none arisen greater than Yohanan the immerser.

12- From his days until now, the Kingdom of Heaven has been oppressed.

13- For all the prophets and the Torah spoke of Yohanan.

14- If you receive it, he is Eliahu, who was yet to come.

15- He who has ears, let him hear!

## Part 49

16- Again Yeshua said, I will liken this generation to boys who sit in the market place calling to one another,

17- Saying, we sang and you did not dance, we wailed and you did not weep.

18- And when Yohanan came, he did not eat nor drink, they said of him: he is possessed by demons.

19- And the men will eat and drink and say that he is a glutton, drunkard and friend of violent and sinful men. Fools judging the wise.

## Part 50

20- Then Yeshua began to curse the cities where his signs were done and they did not do Tshuvah.

21- Woe to Corozim, and woe to Beit Saida, for if in Tyro and Sodom, the signs had been done which were done in you, they would have done Tshuvah at that moment using sack cloth and ashes.

22- Truly I say to you, it shall be easier for Tyro and Sodom.

23- You Kafar Nahum, will you ascend to heaven? From

there you will be brought down. Because if in Sodom the signs which were done in you had been done, perhaps she should have remained. Unto Sheol you will be brought down.

24- Truly I say to you that it shall be easier for the land of Sodom in the day of judgment than for you.

## Part 51

25- At that time Yeshua raised himself up and said, be praised the Creator of heaven and earth, because you have hidden these words from the wise and prudent and have revealed them to the humble.

26- Truly this is because it was upright before you, my Father.

27- All has been given to me from my Father, there is none who knows the son, but the Father alone, and the Father no one knows, but the son and to those who are revealed

28- Come unto me all the weak and those who endure labor, and I will help you to bear the injustice upon you.

29- Take my yoke as your yoke and learn from my Torah, for I am humble, I am good and pure in heart and you will find rest in your souls.

30- Because my yoke is soft and my burden easy.

## Chapter 12
Part 52

1-    At that time crossed Yeshua through the standing grain on a Shabbat day and his talmidim were hungry and began to pluck out the grains and crushed the grains in their hands and ate them.

2-    And the Pharisees saw it, and said unto him, Behold, your talmidim do things which they could not do on a Shabbat day.

3-    And Yeshua said to them, Did you not read what David

did when he was hungry and his men?

4- In the house of Elohim they ate the Lechem Bela`az, which in foreign language is Paan Sagrah, which could not be eat except by the priests alone?

5- And also in the Torah did you not read that the priests of the Temple violate the Shabbatot and they are without sin?

6- Amen (trully) I tell you that the Temple is greater than this.

7- If you knew what that is: I desire grace (chessed) and not sacrifice, you would not have convinced the innocent.

8- For the Son of Man is Lord of the Shabbat.

Part 53

9- And a few days went by and Yeshua passed from there and entered in their synagogue.

10- And there was a man with a withered hand and they asked him saying, Is it permissible to heal him on the Shabbat?

11- And he said to them, who among you who has a sheep that falls into a pit in a Shabbat and does not raise it up?

12- So much the more is man better than that. Therefore it is permissible and necessary for man to act better on the Shabbat.

13- Then he said to the man, stretch out your hand, and he stretched out his hand and it became like the other.

14- And then the Pharisees took counsel and plotted to kill him.

Part 54

15- It came to pass after this that Yeshua knew it, he turned aside from there. Many sick followed him and he healed all of them.

16- He commanded them saying not to reveal him,

17- In order to fulfill what was spoken by Isaiah,

18- Behold my servant whom I have selected, my chosen one with whom my soul is pleased, I will put my spirit upon him, and he will declare justice to the nations.

19- He will not fear nor will he run nor shall one hear him in the street.

20- A crushed reed he will not break and a dim wick he will not quench until he establishes justice forever

21- And in his name, the gentile hope.

## Part 55

22- Then there was brought to him a blind and dumb man who was demon possessed, he healed him. The crowds saw

23- And marveled and said, is this not the son of David?

24- The Pharisees were quick to hear and said, this one does not cast out demons except by Baal Zevuv, the lord of demons.

25- Yeshua knowing their thoughts and said to them in allegory, every kingdom among you divided shall be made desolate, and so every city or house upon which division shall fall shall not stand,

26- If satan casts out another satan, there will be division among them, how will his kingdom stand?

27- And if I cast out demons for Baal Zevuv, then why your sons do not expel them? They will be your judges.

28- But if I cast out demons by the Spirit of EL, truly the end of this kingdom has come.

29- How shall a man be able to enter the house of the strong man to take his goods without biding him first? Then he shall plunder his house.

## Part 56

30- Whoever is not with me is against me. Whoever does not join me denies this work.

31- Therefore I tell you that all sins and blasphemies will be forgiven the sons of man, but blasphemy to the spirit of Elohim will not be forgiven.

32- Everyone who says a word against the Son of man shall be forgiven. And all things spoken against the deeds of Ruach Elohim (Holy Spirit) will not be forgiven, neither in this world nor in the world to come.

33- Make the good tree according to good fruit and the bad tree according to bad fruit, for indeed by the fruit you shall know the tree.

34- Family of vipers, how can you speak good things while being evil? When the mouth awakens, the heart speaks.

35- A good man, from the treasure of the heart brings forth good and the evil man, from the treasure of an heart brings evil.

36- I tell you that of all things a man shall say, he shall give an account at the day of judgment.

37- By the words of one's mouths he will be judged and by one's deeds, he will be condemned.

## Part 57

38- At that time some of the Pharisees and some of the sages came to Yeshua saying: we want to see a sign of heaven by you.

39- And he said to them: A wicked and blasphemous generation seeks a sign, but a sign will not be given except the sign of Yonah.

40- For as he was in the fish (Dagah) for three days and for three nights, so will be the son of man inside the earth (buried) for three days and for three nights.

41- The people of Nineveh will rise to judge this generation and condemn it because they made Tshuvah by the words of Yonah and I am greater than Yonah.

42- Queen Sheba, in the foreign language Reizina of Ishtiriah, will rise to judge this generation and condemn it, for she came from the end of the earth to hear the wisdom of Shlomo and here I am, greater than Shlomo.

43- When the unclean spirit goes out of the man, in dry

places he seeks rest, but he does not find it.

44- Then he says: I will return to my home from which I left, and he goes and finds it empty, safe and ready.

45- Then he takes seven spirits more evil than him and they go with him and there they dwell. And the new state of the man is worse than his former. So shall it be with this wicked generation.

Part 58

46- While he was speaking to all the crowds, behold his mother and his brothers were standing outside seeking him to speak with him.

47- A man said to him, behold your mother and your brothers are seeking to see you.

48- And he answered to the Maggid, who are my brothers and who is my mother?

49- He stretched out his hand to his talmidim and said, these are my mother and brothers.

50- Everyone who does the will of my Father who is in heaven is my brothers, my sisters, and my mother.

## Chapter 13

Part 59

1- On that day Yeshua went out of the house and sat on the shore of the sea.

2- Crowds joined themselves around him until he needed to enter a boat, the whole crowd was standing on the shore.

3- And he spoke to them many things in allegories (parables) and said to them: A man left his house in the morning to sow his seeds.

4- Some of it fell from on the road, and were eaten by the birds.

5- And some fell on the rocks, where the soil has no density and when they grew, they withered, because the soil was shallow

6- And the sun came and it became warm and burned it and dried it up, for there were no root

7- And some of it fell among the thorns, and the thorns grew up, and they stood above it

8- And some of it fell on the good soil, and brought forth fruit and produce, the first a hundred, the second sixty and the third thirty.

9- Whoever has ears to hear, let him hear.

10- Then his talmidim drew near him and his talmidim said to him, why do you speak in allegories?

11- He said, to you it has been given to know the kingdom of heaven, but not to them.

12- Whoever has, it will be given more, but whoever has nothing, that which he think he has, it will be take from him.

13- For this reason I speak in allegories, for they see but do not see, hear but do not hear.

14- In order to fulfill what was said by the prophet Isaiah, go and say to this people, hear but do not comprehend, see but do not understand.

15- Make the heart of this people fat and make their ears heavy and blind their eyes, lest they should see with their eyes.

16- Ashrei are your eyes that see and your ears that hear.

17- Truly I say to you that many prophets and tzadikim desired to see what you see but did not see it, and to hear what you hear but did not hear it.

18- But hear the parable of the sower.

19- The sower is the son of man, and the seed that fell on the way is everyone who hears about the Kingdom of Heaven, but does not understand it. Satan comes and snatches from the heart all that was sown. This is the seed which fell on the road.

20- That which fell upon the rock is the one who hears the word (the teaching) of EL and rejoices immediately.

21- And as it has no roots because is confusing one, when a

little trouble and distractions come to hem, satan uses this to make him forget what is in his heart.

22- That which fell among the thorns are those who hear the word (the teaching) for their own gain, satan makes him forget the teaching of EL and he does not bear fruit.

23- That which fell on good soil are those who hear the word (the teaching) and understand it and bear fruit, which are the Ma`assim Tovim. And he brings forth from the first a hundred, and from the second sixty, and from the third thirty. The one hundred is the one who purifies the heart and sanctifies the body (Torah). The second is the one who separates from woman and the third is the one who is sanctified in matrimony, in body and in heart.

## Part 60

24- And he set before them another allegory (parable). The Kingdom of Heaven is like the a man who sows good seed.

25- And it is when the men are sleeping, that their enemy comes and sows tares, in the foreign language beriyagah, over the wheat, and goes away.

26- And when the herb grew up to bear fruit, he sees the tares.

27- And the servants approach the lord of the field, and say unto him, O our lord, did you not sow good seeds? Where did this weed come from?

28- And he said unto them, My enemy did this, and the servants have said unto him, Let us pluck up the tares.

29- And he said unto them, No, unless you also pluck up the wheat

30- But let both grow together until the harvest, and at the time of harvest I will say to the reapers: First gather the tares and bind them into individual bundles to be burned and the wheat put into the granary.

Part 61

31- And he set before them another allegory (parable). The Kingdom of Heaven is a grain of mustard, which a man takes and sows in the field.

32- And it is the smallest of all the seeds in the field, and when it grows, it is greater than all herbs and becomes a great tree until the birds of the heavens hide within (in its branches).

33- He spoke to them another allegory. The kingdom of heaven is like a leaven which it is put into three measures of flour and it leavens all of it.

34- All of those allegories Yeshua spoke to the crowds and without an allegory he did not speak to them,

35- To fulfill what was said by the prophet, I will open my mouth in allegories, I will utter riddles from ancient times.

Part 62

36- Then Yeshua was parted from the crowds and went into the house. His talmidim came to him and asked him to explain for them the allegory of the tares.

37- He answered them and said to them, the one who sows good seed is the son of man,

38- The field is this world, the good fruit is the tzadikim, and the tares are those who forsake Adonai's commandments.

39- The enemy who sowed it is satan, the standing grain ate the end is the Olam Habah, and the reapers are the angels.

40- As the reapers gather the tares to burn, so will it be at the end of the days.

41- The son of man will send his angels to uproot from his kingdom all evil and all who does not follow the Law (TORAH).

42- They will be cast into the fire pit, there will be weeping and gnashing of teeth.

43- Then the tzadikim will shine like the sun in the kingdom of their Father. Whoever has ears to hear, let him
hear.

## Part 63

44- Again Yeshua said to his talmidim: the Kingdom of
Heaven is like a man who finds a hidden treasure and
in joy over the value (found), he sells everything he has
and buys the field for himself.

45- And yet the Kingdom of Heaven is like a merchant
seeking precious stones.

46- And when he finds a good one, he sells everything he
owns and buy it.

47- The Kingdom of Heaven is like a net in the middle of
the sea in which all kinds of fish gather.

48- And when it is full, it is pulled out, and the fishermen
choose the kosher among them and the bad ones are
thrown away.

49- Thus shall the ends of the days be, the angels shall
come forth, and shall distinguish the wicked from the
tzaddikim.

50- And they will be cast into the pyre of fire and there
will be weeping and gnashing of teeth.

51- He said to them, have you understood this? They said
they did.

52- Every wise man in the kingdom of heaven, therefore,
is like a certain father of children who brings forth
from his treasure things new and old.

## Part 64

53- It came to pass after this, when Yeshua finished these
words, he left that place.

54- He came into his own country and was teaching the
people in the synagogues. The Pharisees were amazed
and said in their heart, whence came to this one the

wisdom and power to do those things?

55- Is he not the son of the blacksmith and Miriam? Do you not know all these, his mother Miriam, his three brothers, Yosef, Shimon and Yehudah,

56- And his sisters? Do you not know all these who are with us? Whence came to this one all this things?

57- So they were confused about him. Yeshua answered them, a prophet is not without honor except in his own land, city and house.

58- Then he did not wish to do there any sign for they had little faith.

## Chapter 14

Part 65

1- At that time Horodos Titrakah heard about Yeshua.

2- He said to his servants, behold I believe that Yohanan, the immerser, is doing these miracles.

3- This happened because Horodos has seized Yohanan in those days and had bound him in prison because he was reproving him that he should not take Herodias for a wife because she was the wife of his brother.

4- Yohanan was saying to him, she is not permissible to you.

5- Then behold Horodos wished to have him killed, except for fear of the people, who believed he was a prophet among them.

6- On the feast of Horodos' birthday, he called the ministers of the kingdom to eat with him, and while they were eating, his daughter danced among them and it was pleasing to Horodos.

7- he swore to give her whatever she asked from him.

8- The girl, being instructed by the mother, asked for the head of Yohanan, the immerser, in a bowl.

9- The king was very sad because of the oath which he had made before those invited. But he commanded to do so.

10- and sent to kill Yohanan in prison.

11- They brought the head of Yohanan in a bowl and gave it to the girl and the girl gave it to her mother.

12- Then Yohanan's talmidim came and took and buried it and the talmidim told the matter to Yeshua.

13- When Yeshua heard it, he departed from there in a boat and went into the wilderness of Yehudah. When the crowds heard they followed him from all the cities.

14- When they came out he saw behind him a numerous people, so he extended kindness and healed all of their diseases.

15- At the time of the end of the day his talmidim came to him and said to him, this place is limited and it is getting late. Let the crowds go into the towers that they might take the necessities for themselves.

16- Yeshua answered them, they have no need to go, give them to eat.

17- they answered, we have nothing except five loaves, two fish.

18- He said to them, bring them to me.

19- Then he commanded that the people should sit on the grass. When they sat he took the five loaves and two fish and as he looked into heaven, he said, Baruch Atah Adonai. Divided them, gave them to his talmidim and the talmidim gave to the groups.

20- All of them ate and were satisfied. They also ate the fish according to what they desired. After they had finished, they took the left over and filled twelve sacks with them.

21- The number of those eating was five thousand men apart from women and children.

## Part 66

22- After this, he commanded his talmidim to gather in a boat that they might go before him to the city to which the crowds were going.

23- After he left the crowds, he went upon a mountain and prayed alone. At the time of evening he was standing alone.

24- The boat was in the midst of the sea and its power were driving it because the wind was contrary.

25- At the fourth watch of the night Yeshua came to them walking on the sea.

26- When his talmidim saw him walking on the sea they were scared, thinking he was a demon, and from the greatness of their fear they were crying out.

27- Then Yeshua answered them and said to them, let faith be among you because it is, do not fear.

28- Pietros answered and said to him, master, if it is you, command me to come to you on the water.

29- Yeshua said to him, come. So Pietros came down from the boat, walked on the sea and came to Yeshua.

30- But when he saw the power of the wind, he feared exceedingly and as he began to sink he cried out and said, master, save me.

31- Immediately Yeshua stretched out his hand, took him, and said to him, man of little faith, why did you doubt?

32- When they went up into the boat, the wind became quiet,

33- And those in the boat honored him by saying, truly you are the son of Elohim.

34- When the people of the place recognized him they sent into all that kingdom and brought to him all who were sick with various kinds of diseases.

35- NO VERSE

36- They begged him that he might be pleased to allow them to touch the tzitzit of his tallit, and whoever touched, was healed.

## Chapter 15
Part 67

1-   Then the sages and the Pharisees came to Yeshua saying to him,

2-      Why don't your talmidim respect the TAKANOT of the ancients concerning NETILAT YADAYIM before they eat?

3-   And Yeshua said to them: Why do you not respect the Torah of EL because of your TAKANOT?

4-    For EL said, Honor your father and your mother, and he who smites his mother and his father must be put to death.

5-    And you say that any word that is said by a man to his father and to his mother in regard to any charity to be given, he might give for him as a sinner. But this iniquity will be made void to him.

6-   So he does not honor his father and his mother and you despise EL's word by your TAKANOT.

7-   Woe hypocrites, behold Isaiah prophesied concerning you and said,

8-    Thus said Adonai, because this people has come near with their mouth and has honored me with their lips, but their heart is far from me

9-   And their reverence toward me, which is taught, is the commandment of men.

10- Yeshua called to the crowds and said to them, hear and consider.

11- That which enters through the mouth does not make the man impure, but what comes out does make him impure.

12- Then his talmidim came to him and said to him, know that the Pharisee were perplexed by those words.

13- Yeshua answered them, every plant which my Father who is in heaven did not plant will be destroyed.

14- Leave them alone because the blind are leading the blind, and if a blind man leads another who is blind, both will fall into a pit.

15- Pietros answered him, lord explain to us this riddle.

16- Yeshua answered them, are you still without knowledge?

17- Do you not understand that every thing that enters through the mouth goes into the belly and all of it goes on to the natural place?

18- But that which goes out through the mouth is moved by the heart, this is what makes the man impure.

19- Because the defiled heart brings forth deceitfulness, murder, adulteries, robberies, the witness of liars and curses.

20- All these things are what makes the man impure. Indeed eating without washing the hands does not make the man impure.

Part 68

21- And after he said this, Yeshua went from Galili to Tzot (Tyro) and Sodom.

22- And a certain Canaanite woman came to him from the lands of the east, crying out to him, My lord, son of David, have mercy on me, for my daughter is possessed by demons.

23- And Yeshua did not answer. And his talmidim approached him and said to him: Our Lord, why do you abandon this woman who cries after us?

24- And Yeshua said to them, I was not sent except to the lost sheep of the house of Israel.

25- And the woman fell down and said, My Lord, help me.

26- And Yeshua said to her, It is not good for a man to take the bread from his children and give it to the dogs.

27- And the woman said, for many times the dogs eat the pieces that fall from their master's table.

28- And Yeshua replied to her: woman of great faith, your faith done to you what you wanted. And at that moment her daughter was healed.

Part 69

29- When Yeshua moved on from there, he went to the region across Galil, to a mountain, and stood there.

30- He saw many people and lames, leprous, those who limped, and many others, they fell at his feet and he healed them.

31- The people were amazed at how the dumb were speaking and the lame were walking and the blind were seeing, all of them were praising Adonai.

32- Then Yeshua said to his talmidim, I have compassion on them because they have remained with me these two days since they came across and they have nothing to eat. I do not want to lead them fasting, for they will grow faint in the way.

33- His talmidim answered him, whence will we be able to find bread in this wilderness to satisfy the people?

34- Yeshua answered and said to them, how many loaves of bread do you have? They answered, seven and some fish.

35- So Yeshua commanded the people to sit upon the grass.

36- He took the seven loaves and broke them and gave them to his talmidim and they gave to the people.

37- All of them ate and were satisfied and seven sacks (left)

38- Those who were eating were four thousand men besides women and children.

39- After this Yeshua entered a boat and went do Macedonia.

## Chapter 16
Part 70

1- Sages and Pharisees came to him, trying to make him to teach them some sign from heaven.

2- Yeshua answered them, hypocrites, you say in the evening, tomorrow will be a clear day because the sky is red.

3- Then in the morning you say, today it will rain because the sky is dark. If so, you know the law regarding the appearance of the sky, but you do not know the law regarding the times.

4-      The offspring of evil doers ask for a sign, but no sign will be given them except the sign of Yonah the prophet. Then he was separated and went away.

5-      Then Yeshua came to the sea shore he told this talmidim to prepare bread. Then he entered a boat with his talmidim, but the talmidim forgot and did not bring any bread.

6-  NO VERSE

7-  NO VERSE

8-      NO FIRST PART, EXCEPT FOR – Yeshua said to them, you have little understanding when you think you do not have bread.

9-12- Do you not remember the five loaves and four thousand men, how many sacks were left over? So, you should understand that I am not speaking of natural loaves but I am saying to you that you should watch the behavior of the Pharisees and Sadducees.

Part 71

13- Yeshua went out unto the country of Syria and in the land of Philot, and asked his talmidim saying, what do men say about me?

14- They said unto him, some say he is Yohanan, the immerser, some say he is Eliahu, and some say he is Yrmiahu, or any prophet.

15- Yeshua said to them, what do you say about me?

16- Shimon, called Pietros, answered and said, you are Mashiach, the son of the living Elohim, who has come into this world.

17- Yeshua said to him, blessed are you Shimon Bar Yonah, because flesh and blood has not revealed to you but my Father who is in heaven.

18- And I tell you that you are a stone (אבן) and I will build

(אבנה) upon you my BEIT TEFILAH. And the gates of Ge-hinam will not prevail over IT.

19- For I give you the keys of the Kingdom of Heaven. And whatever you bind on earth will be connected in heaven and whatever you loose on earth, will be dis-connected in heaven.

20- Then he commanded his talmidim not to say that he is the Mashiach.

Part 72

21- Then Yeshua began to reveal to his talmidim that it was necessary for him to go to Jerusalem and to suffer the injustice of many, from the priests and the elders of the people, until they should kill him, then on the third day he would arise.

22- Pietros took him aside privately and began to rebuke saying, far be it that it should be like this to you, lord.

23- Yeshua turned, looked at him, and said to him, do away satan, do not disobey, because you do not regard the things of EL but the things of men.

24- Then Yeshua said to his talmidim, whoever wishes to come after me let him despise himself, offer himself to death and come after me.

25- Everyone who wishes to save his soul will lose it for my sake, and he who loses his life in this world for my sake will save his soul for the life of the world to come.

26- What profit is there for a man if he should gain the whole world but lose his soul forever, what good ex-change does the man make if for present things that are spoiled he should give his soul to the judgment of Gahinam?

27- Because the son of Elohim will come in the glory of his Father who is in heaven with his angels to reward each man according to his work.

28- Truly I say to you there are some of those standing here who will not taste death until they see the son of

Elohim coming in his kingdom.

## Chapter 17
Part 73

1- After six days Yeshua took Pietros, Yaakov, that is, Jimi and Yohanan his brother and brought them to a high mountain where he might pray.

2- While he was praying he was changed before them and the skin of his face shine like the sun and his garments white like snow.

3- Moshe and Eliahu, while talking to, were revealed to them and they told Yeshua all which would happen to him in Jerusalem. Pietros and his companions were asleep. Asleep but not asleep, awake but not awake. They saw his body and the two men with him.

4- When then went away, Pietros said to Yeshua, it is good to be here. Let us make here three tabernacles, one for you, one for Moshe, and one for Eliahu, because he did know what he was saying.

5- While he was still speaking, behold a cloud covered them, and they were greatly alarmed, while they were under the cloud they heard from the midst of the cloud a voice speaking and saying, behold, this is my son, my beloved, my delight is in him, you shall obey him.

6- The talmidim heard, fell on their faces to the ground, and feared a lot.

7- When the voice ceased, Yeshua said to them, arise, do not fear.

8- They lifted up their eyes and saw no one except Yeshua alone.

Part 74

9- Yeshua came down from the mountain and commanded them saying, tell no man the vision you have seen until the son of man has risen from death.

10- His talmidim asked him saying, why do the sages say

that Eliahu will come first?

11- He answered them and said, indeed Eliahu will come and will save all the world.

12- I say to you, he has already come, they did not know him, and they did to him according to their desire. They will do to the son of man.

13- Then the talmidim understood that regarding Yohanan, the immerser, he was talking about.

Part 75

14- It came to pass when he approached the crowds, a man came to him, bowing.

15- He said, have mercy on me, lord, and pity my son because he is terrified of an evil spirit and is very sick. He grinds his teeth at his mouth, falls from his place to the ground and falls sometimes into the fire and sometimes into water.

16- I brought him to your talmidim, but they were unable to heal him.

17- Yeshua answered and said, evil generations, we to you who deny, how long will I be with you, how long will I bear your trouble? Bring him to me.

18- MARK 9:20 – 9:28

*THE TEXT FROM MARK 9:20-27 SEEMS TO ORIGINALLY BE PART OF THIS BOOK OF MATTHEW AND WAS MODIFIED FOR UNKNOWN REASONS. THUS, I WILL NOT ENUMERATE THE VERSES, RATHER I WILL PLACE THE WHOLE STORY IN A DIRECT WAY.*

They brought him and immediately when Yeshua looked at him, the satan subdued him and cast him to the ground, and he began rolling in the dust and foaming. Yeshua asked the father of the boy: How long has the satan taken him? The father answered him: From a certain time and beyond. Often he casts him into fire or water to destroy him

if possible. If, lord, you are able to help him an any
way, help him. Then the man found favor in his eyes,
and he was filled with compassion for him.
He said to him: If you can believe, you will be
able to accomplish anything, because to the
one who believes all things are easy.
Immediately the father of the boy cried out
with a shout and said: Lord, I believe, indeed
help me according to my faith.
When Yeshua saw that the people were gathering together,
he said to the demon: Hard and dumb, behold I command
you to come out from there and do not return again.
Then the satan came out screaming and inflicting
pain and the boy was left as dead so that
many were saying that he was dead.
Yeshua tool him, stood him up and he arose.
When Yeshua entered the house.

19- The talmidim came near to Yeshua secretly and said to
him, why were we unable to cast it out?

20- He said to them, because of the limitation of your
faith, truly I say to you if there be in you any faith, as
a grain of mustard, if you believe, you will say to this
mountain depart and it will depart, nothing will be
without your reach.

21- But this kind of demon does not come out except by
prayer and fasting.

Part 76

22- They were in Galil and Yeshua said, the son of man will
be delivered into the hand of men.

23- They will kill him and on the third day he will arise.

24- They came to Kafar Nahum Maritima and the tax col-
lectors drew near to Pietros and said, your teacher does
not follow the custom to pay tax.

25- Thus they spoke. He went into the house and Yeshua

anticipated him saying, Pietros, what is in your eyes, the king of the earth, from whom do they take tribute, from their sons or from foreigners?

26- He answered him, from foreigners, Yeshua said to them, if the sons are free, then he said, do not be dismayed because of this.

27- He said to Pietros, go to the sea and cast a fishing hook and fish with it because in the mouth of the one you will catch first you will find a silver coin. That you will give for both of us.

## Chapter 18
Part 77

1- At that time the talmidim drew near Yeshua and said to him, whom do you think is big in the kingdom of heaven?

2- He called a kid (small, in their midst,

3- He said, I say if you do not become like this kid, you will not enter the kingdom of heaven.

4- NO VERSE

5- He who receives a kid) like this in my name receives.

6- He who cause on the small kids who believe on me to stumble, it would be good for him to tie a stone upon his neck and be cast into the depths of the sea.

7- (Woe to he inhabitants of the world because of confusion, because confusion must come.) He also said, woe to the man who comes because of it.

8- If your hand or your foot causes you to stumble cut it off from you, it is better for you to be in the kingdom of heaven lame than having two hands and two feet for you to be given to everlasting fire.

9- If it should cause you to stumble, pick it out and cast it from you. It is better for you to enter into life with one eye than to have two eyes and to be given to Gehinam.

10- Take heed lest you judge one of the small kids. I say to you, their angels always see the sons of my Father who is in heaven.

11- And the son of man has stopped saving the enemy.

## Part 78

12- What is your view? If a man has a hundred sheep and one of them goes, will he not leave the ninety nine in the mountains and go seek the one which has strayed?

13- If he should find it, truly I say to you he will rejoice over it more than the ninety nine which did not go stray.

14- Thus my Father who is in heaven does not wish any of these kids should be lost.

## Part 79

15- At that time said Yeshua to Simon, named Pietros, if your brother sins against you by disobeying the Torah, rebuke him privately. If he hears you, you will have merit for your brother.

16- And if he does not listen to you, rebuke him before another, and if by all oath he does not hear you, you add one or two more before you, being three witnesses, for with two or three witnesses, the word will be established (Torah)

17- And if by all this, he does not hear, take him to the congregation, and if the congregation he does not hear, he will be banished as one who does not respect the Torah, an enemy and a cruel one.

18- Amen (trully) I tell you that every promise you make on earth will be connected in heaven and every promise that is loosen on earth will be disconnected in heaven (KOL NIDREI)

19- And I also say to you that if two of you wish to bring LASIM SHALIM into this land, whatever you ask will be yours from the heavens.

20- And everywhere, if two or three are gathered under my name, ANOKHI will be among you.

21- Then Pietros approached, saying: my lord, if my brother sins against me, I must forgive him up to seven times

22- And Yeshua said to him, I do not tell you until seven, but until seventy-seven.

## Part 80

23- At that time Yeshua said to his talmidim: the Kingdom of Heaven is like a king who sat to make a reckoning with his servants and ministers.

24- And when they begin to make the reckon, comes one that owes ten pieces of gold.

25- And he has nothing to give and his lord commands him to be sold along with his children and with all that he owns to pay (לשלם) that value.

26- And the servant falls before his master and asks him to be merciful on him and give him time, for he will pay (ישלם) all the debts.

27- And then his master took pity on him and forgave him all the debt.

28- And the servant went out, and found another that owed him a hundred pieces of silver, and grasped him, and attacked him, and said,

29- Trust me and be patient with me, I will pay (אשלם) everything.

30- And he was not willing to listen to him, so he took him to jail until everything was paid (שלם).

31- And the servants of the king saw what was done, and were very angry, and went and told their master.

32- Then the lord called him and said to him: cursed servant (ARUR), did not I forgive you of all the debt that you had with me?

33- So why did you not forgive the servant when he pleaded you, as I forgave you?

34- And his master was angry with him and commanded to afflict him until all his debts were paid.

35- So will you do my Father in heaven if you do not forgive each man his brother with a complete heart (שלם).

## Chapter 19
Part 81

1- It came to pass when Yeshua finished these word he passed on from Galil and came to the outskirts of the land of Yehuda across the Yordan.

2- There followed him a large crowd to tempt him. They asked him saying,

3- And the Pharisees came to him, to tempt him. And they asked him, saying, Is it lawful to leave your wife for any reason, and give her a letter of divorce? (LEAH GAT)

4- And he answered them, have you not read that they were made in old times male and female?

5- And he said, Therefore let man leave his father and his mother, and join his wife, and they shall be one flesh.

6- Therefore, they are not two, for they are one flesh. And what joins the Creator, man cannot separate.

7- And they said to him: If so, why did command Moshe to give the letter (GAT KRITOT) and to send her away?

8- And he said to them: Moshe, because of the obstinacy of your hearts, told them to leave their wives. But in eternity it is not so.

9- I say unto you, that whosoever leaves his wife and takes another, if not for adultery, commits adultery. And he that takes a divorced wife commits adultery.

10- Then his talmidim said to him, if the matter of a man with his wife is so, it is not good to take her.

11- He said to them, this matter is not for everyone but for those to whom it has been given.

12- Because there are eunuchs from their birth, these are those who have not sinned and there are self-made eunuchs who subdue their desire for the sake of the kingdom of heaven, these are into great prominence. Whoever is able to understand, let him understand.

Part 82

13- Then they brought children to him that he might lay his hand on them and pray for them, but his talmidim were sending them away.

14- Yeshua said to them, permit the kids to come to me and do not refrain them, for of them is the kingdom of heaven. Truly I say to you that one will not enter the kingdom of heaven except like these.

15- So he laid his hand on them and went from there.

16- And a young man came to him and bowed his head, saying, Rabbi, what is good to do to obtain eternal life?

17- And he answered him, Why do you ask what is good? No man is good, for EL only is good. And if you want to enter eternal life, keep the MITZVOT.

18- And he said to him, What are they? And Yeshua said, Thou shalt not kill, thou shalt not steal, shall not bear false witness against thy neighbor.

19- Honor your father and your hand and love your neighbor as yourself.

20- And the young man said to him: all of this I already observe, but what do I lack?

21- And Yeshua said to him: If you want to be perfect, go and sell everything that is yours and give it to the poor and you will have treasure in the heavens and then follow me.

22- And when the youg man heard, he left. For he did NOT possess many properties.

23- And Yeshua said to his talmidim: Amen (truly) I tell you that it is hard for a rich man to enter the Kingdom of Heaven.

24- And I tell you that it is easier for a camel to enter the eye of a needle than for a rich man to enter the Kingdom of Heaven.

25- And his talmidim heard and were greatly amazed, and

said to Yeshua, If so, who can save them?

26- He turned to them saying, all things are difficult to men, but to Elohim all things are easy.

## Part 83

27- Pietros answered and said to him, behold we have left all to follow after you, what will be ours?

28- Yeshua said, truly is say to you who follow me, in the day of judgement, when man sits upon the throne of his glory you also will sit upon the twelve thrones of the twelve tribes of Israel.

29- Everyone who leaves his house, his wife, and his children for my name, will receive more like them and will inherit the kingdom of heaven.

30- Many who are first will be last. And many who are last will be first.

## Chapter 20

Part 84

1- After this Yeshua said to his talmidim: the Kingdom of Heaven is like the man who is lord in his house and rises in the morning to hire servants.

2- And he hires them for one dinar a day and sends them to his vineyard.

3- And he goes out in the third hour of the day and sees others standing in the market

4- And he said unto them, Come you also into my vineyard, and I will give you what is suitable for you.

5- And they went. Then he went out again at noon and at the ninth hour and did the same.

6- And in the eleventh hour, he went out again and saw others standing and told them: Why are you standing in the market all day?

7- And they answered him: no one hired us. And he said unto them, Go you also unto my vineyard.

8- And that night, said the lord of the vineyard to the

supervisor of the laborers: call them so that I may give them their salary. And he started with the last and finished with the first.

9- The latter received a dinar.

10- And the first thought he would receive more, but he gave nothing to anyone but a dinar.

11- And the first murmured upon the lord of the vineyard

12- And told him: the last ones worked only for an hour and you made them like us, who worked all day in the heat.

13- And he answered one of them, saying, I did you no wrong, did I not call you for a dinar?

14- Take it and go. If I want to give it to the last one like you.

15- May I not do according to my desire? Is there something wrong in your eyes when I'm being good?

16- Then the first will be the last and the last will be the first. Many will be called but few will be the chosen.

Part 85

17- Yeshua drew near to Jerusalem and took his twelve talmidim secretly and said to them,

18- Behold we are going up to Jerusalem and the son of man will be delivered over to the leaders of the sages and priests and they will condemn him to death.

19- Also, they will deliver him to the Gentiles to smite and to destroy him, but on the third day.

20- Then came the wife of Zevediel with her sons bowing down and making a request from him.

21- He said to her, what do you wish? She said, that you command these my two sons to sit the on your right and the other on your left in your kingdom.

22- Yeshua answered them, you do not know what you are asking for. Are you able to endure the suffering and the death that I am going to endure? They said, we are able to.

23- Then he said to them, drink my cup, but on my left or my right is not for me to grant to you but to the one who is prepared before my Father.

24- The ten heard this and it was a matter of anger in their eyes in regard the two brothers.

25- Yeshua drew near them and said to them, know that the princes of the gentiles have dominion over them and their great ones seek.

26- It will not be so among you, because he who wishes to be great among you, will serve you.

27- He who among you wishes to be first ill be your servant.

28- The son of man did not come that they might serve him, but that he might serve and give himself as a ransom for many.

## Part 86

29- They entered into Yericho and a crowd followed him.

30- Behold two blind men came out beside the road. They heard the noise of the multitude and what might this be? It was said to them, the prophet Yeshua from Natza'arit is coming. Then they cried out saying, son of David, have mercy on us.

31- But the crowd rebuked them, they nevertheless were crying out and saying, lord, son of David, have mercy on us.

32- So Yeshua stopped, called them and said, what do you want me to do for you?

33- They said, lord, that our eyes might be opened.

34- Yeshua had pity on them, touched their eyes and said to them, your faith has healed you. Immediately they saw, praised Adonai, and followed him. Then all the people praised Adonai because of this.

## Chapter 21
Part 87

1- They drew near to Jerusalem and came to Beit Pa'agi on the Mount of Olives and Yeshua sent two of his talmidim.

2- He said unto them, go into the fortress which is at the opposite side of you and immediately you will find a she-ass and its colt. Untie them and bring them to me.

3- If a man should say anything to you, tell him the master has need of them and right away they will let them go.

4- All this was to fulfill the word of the prophet saying,

5- Say to the daughter of Zion, behold your king comes to you, tzadik and victorious, humble and upon a she-ass and upon a colt the foal of a she-ass.

6- Then they went and did as Yeshua commanded them.

7- They brought the she-ass and the colt, and Yeshua rode upon it while the others placed their garments and clothes upon them. Then they made the ascent.

8- Many of the crowd spread out their garments in the way, and others branches from the trees and cast them before him and behind him,

9- calling out saying, Hosheanah, savior of the world, blessed is he who comes in the name of Adonai. Hosheanah, our savior, may you be glorified in heaven and on earth.

## Part 88

10- It came to pass when Yeshua entered Jerusalem, all the city quaked saying, who is this?

11- The people said to one another, Yeshua the prophet from (Nazareth) which is Galil.

12- Yeshua entered the house of Adonai and found there those who buy and sell. He overturned the tables of the money changers and the seats of those who were selling doves.

13- He said unto them, it is written, my house will be called a house of prayer for all the nations, but you have made it a cave of violent men.

14- Then the blind and the lame came to him in the Temple and he healed them.

15- The chief sages and priests came to see the wonders which he did. The young boys were calling out in the Temple saying, let the son of Elohim be praised, The sages mocked.

16- And said to him, have you not heard what these are saying? He answered them and said, I heard them. Have you not read, from the mouth of children and babes you have established strength?

17- He left and went out to Bethany and spend there (night), and there he was explaining to them about the Kingdom of Heaven.

18- It came to pass in the morning that he returned to the city hungry.

19- And he saw a fig tree by the side of the road, and came to it, and found none on it except leaves, and said to it, may fruit never come forth from you. And the fig tree immediately dried up.

20- And his talmidim saw it, and were amazed, and said, How did the fig tree dried up immediately?

21- And Yeshua answered them, saying, If there were faith in you, without doubt, not only the fig tree would do it, but also if you tell this mountain to go and to go to the sea, it would go.

22- And whatever you ask in Tefilah with Emunah, you will receive it.

## Part 89

23- He went near the Temple to teach and there came to him the sages, the priests and the rulers of the people, saying, by what power do you do this, who gave you this strength?

24- Yeshua answered them and said to them, I also will ask you a question and if you tell me the I also will tell you by what power I do.

25- Yohanan's Mikveh whence was it, from heaven or from men? They grieved among themselves saying, what should we say? If we say from heaven, he will say to us, why did you not believe him?

26- If we say from men, we fear the crowd because all of them believed Yohanan was a prophet.

27- So they said, we do not know. He said, also I will not tell you by what power I do.

## Part 90

28- In that same night Yeshua said to his talmidim: what is your opinion? There was a man who had two sons, he approached one and said to him: go my son, today you will work in my vineyard.

29- And he replied: I do not feel like it. But after that, he repented and went.

30- And he said to the other son the same thing, and he said, Behold, here I am my lord, and he did not go.

31- Which one did the will of the Father? And they said unto him, the first one. And Yeshua said to them, Amen (truly) I tell you that the murderers and the harlots have preceded you in the Kingdom of Heaven.

32- Yohanan came to teach you the Tzadik's path (Torah) and they did not believe him. The murderers and the harlots believed him, you saw this and did not do Tshu-vah. Also, after all, they still do not believe him. Whoever has ears to hear, let him hear.

## Part 91

33- At that time, Yeshua said to his talmidim and to a company of the Jews: listen to the parable of the sower. A certain honorable man planted a vineyard and walled it up all around, built a tower in the middle, also dug a vat in it and entrusted it to the hands of his servants and went on his way.

34- It came to pass, at the time of the harvest of the produce, he sent his servants to the tenants to receive his produce.

35- And the tenants took his servants, and smote the first, and slew the second, and stoned the third with stones.

36- And he sent many more servants after the first, and they did the same to them.

37- Finally he decided to send his son, saying: perhaps they will see my son.

38- And the tenants saw his son, and said one to another, This is the heir; let us kill him, and inherit his inheritance.

39- And they took him, and cast him out of the vineyard, and killed him.

40- And now when the lord of the vineyard comes, what will he do with them?

41- And they answered him, saying, The wicked shall be destroyed, and his vineyard shall be given to other tenants, who shall immediately give him his share of his produce.

42- And Yeshua said to them, have you not read what is written? The stone rejected by the builders will become the head of the corner. This is from Adonai (tetragram), it is marvel in our eyes.

43- Therefore I tell you that the Kingdom of Heaven will be torn before you and given to the Gentiles who bear fruit. (tear of the veil, opening of the place where the Torah was)

44- He who falls upon this stone will be cast down. He who falls upon it will be broken apart.

45- And the leaders of the sages and the Pharisees heard this parable, and understood that he was speaking about them.

46- And they sought to kill him, but they feared the multitude, to whom he was a prophet.

## Chapter 22
Part 92

1- Yeshua answered and spoke to them again in the words of an allegory.

2- The kingdom of heaven is like a king who made a Chupah.

3- He sent his servant to those who had been invited to the Chupah, bu they did not wished to come.

4- He again sent other servants saying, Tell those who are invited, behold I have prepared a feast, I have killed oxen and fowl, and all is ready. Come to the Chupah.

5- But they scorned and went away, some into the city and some to their business.

6- Others abused the servants and killed them.

7- The king heard this, was angry, sent those murderes away, and burned their house with fire.

8- Then he said to his servants, the Chupah is ready, but those who were invited were unworthy.

9- Now go out unto the roads and all whom you find invite to the Chupah.

10- And the servants went out into the ways, and invited all who were found, good and evil, and Chupah was filled with those who were eating.

11- And the king came to see those who was eating and saw there a man who was not clothed in Chupah's clothes.

12- And he said to him: my beloved, how did you come here without Chupah's clothes? And he was silent.

13- And the king said unto his servants: bind the hands and the feet of this man, and cast him into the lowest shaol, and there shall be weeping and gnashing of teeth.

14- Many are called, but few are chosen.

Part 93

15- Then the Pharisees came and took counsel to take him

in speech.

16- They sent to him some of their talmidim with violent men from Horodos saying, rabbi, we know you are trustworthy, you faithfully learns Talmud and the way of Elohim, have no fear and are impartial.

17- Tell us your opinion, is it right to give tribute to Tzeizarei or not?

18- Yeshua saw their deceit and said, why do you entice me?

19- Show me a tax coin, they brought to him.

20- He said to them, whose form is this and impression?

21- They said, Tzeizarei. Then Yeshua said to them, return to Tzeizarei what is Tzeizarei's and to EL what is EL's.

22- They heard and were amazed. They left him and went away.

## Part 94

23- On that day, the Sadducees and those who did not believe in the resurrection of the dead, met him and asked him,

24- saying, Rabbi, Moses told us that when two brothers dwell together and one of them dies, which has no son, the brother must take his wife and give continuity in his seed.

25- And, behold, there were seven brethren in the midst of us, and the first took a wife unto himself, and died without seed, and his brother took his wife unto himself.

26- So with the second, the third and still the fourth.

27- And then the woman died.

28- Since she was of all, she will be the woman of which one?

29- And Yeshua answered and said unto them, your err and do not understand the books and the power of Elohim.

30- On the day of the resurrection, men will not take women for themselves, nor women men, they will be like the angels of Elohim who are in heavens.

31- Did you not read concerning the resurrection of the dead that Adonai said to you, saying,

32- I Am Adonai, Elohei Abraham, Elohei Itzhak and Elohei Yaakov. Therefore there is no Elohim of the dead, but Elohim of the living.

33- And the crowds heard him, and they were astonished at his wisdom.

Part 95

34- When the Pharisees saw that the Sadducees had no answer, they joined his servants.

35- Then a sage asked him tempting him,

36- Rabbi, tell me, what is the greatest mitzvah (commandment) in the Torah?

37- And he said unto him, you shall love Adonai your Elohim with all your heart, and so forth.

38- This is the first

39- The second is this, you shall love your neighbor as yourself.

40- And on these two Mitzvot (commandments) all the Torah and the prophets hang.

41- And gathered together more Pharisees and Yeshua asked them.

42- Saying: What, in your opinion, is Mashiach? Son of whom? And they said to him, Son of David.

43- And he said to them, As David by the Holy Ghost called him, saying: Lord.

44- As it is written, Adonai said to my lord, Sit at my right hand and until I make your enemies the footstool of your feet.

45- If David called him Lord, how could he then be his son?

46- And they could not answer him a word, and since then they were afraid to ask him anything.

## Chapter 23
Part 96

1- Then Yeshua spoke to he people and to his talmidim

2- Upon the seat of Moses the Pharisees and the sages sit.

3-   And now, all that HE said to you, observe and do, but their TAKANOT and their MA'ASSOT do not listen to, for they say but do not do.

4- They demand and set forth a great burden (on the shoulders of men) that they cannot bear, but they themselves do not even want to move a finger (to do them).

5- And all theirs MA'ASSOT are made by them to be seen. They wear expensive Talitot and long Tzitzit.

6-   They love to be the first in the festive houses and to be seated in the first places in the synagogues.

7-    To prostate to themselves in the streets and to be called rabbi.

8-   But as for you, do not desire to be called rabbi. One is your rabbi and all of you are brothers.

9- Call no man upon the earth father. One is your father who is in heaven.

10- Do not be called rabbi, because one is your rabbi, Mashiach.

11- The greatest among you will serve you.

12- He who exalts himself will be humbled, he who is humbled will be exalted.

## Part 97

13- Woe to you Pharisees and sages, hypocrites, because you close the kingdom of heaven before men, and those who wish to enter you do not allow to enter.

14- Woe to you Pharisees and sages, hypocrites, because you devour and divide the wealth of certain widows with lengthy exposition. For this, you will suffer a long punishment.

15- You encompass sea and land to bind the heart of one man to your teachings and when he is bound he is doubly worse than before.

16- Woe to you, blind in the chair, who say that he who swears by the Temple is not bound (to fulfill), but he who swears by whatever is consecrated to the Temple is bound to pay.

17- Men who are mad and blind, which is greater, the Temple or that which is consecrated to the Temple?

18- He who swears by the altar is not bound to do, but whoever swears to bring an offering is bound to do?

19- What is greater, the offering or the altar, the Temple or the offering?

13- He who swears by the altar swears by all that is in it.

20- He who swears by the throne of Elohim, swears by it and by the One sited on the throne.

21- NO VERSE

22- He who swears by the throne of Elohim.

## Part 98

23- Woe to them, sages and Pharisees, who tithe mint, dill and pomegranate. But who commit robberies. It is better to honor the Torah sentences, which are: Chesed, truth and faith. The Torah is worth of following, never forget that.

24- Seeds of blind leaders, who walks in the narrow path like a gnat and can swallow a camel.

25- Shame on you Pharisees and sages, who submerge the cups and the dishes on the outside and inside is full of evil and impurities.

26- Hypocrites, first cleanse inside of you and then be pure in the outside.

27- Woe to you sages and Pharisees, hypocrites, who are like whitened sepulchers which appear on the outside to be nice to men, but on the inside are full of bones of the dead and filthy.

28- Thus you appear on the outside to be Tzadikim, but within you are full of hypocrisy and evilness.

29- Woe, hypocrites, Pharisees and sages, because you build the tombs of the prophets and glorify the Tzadikim.

30- You say, if we had been in the days of our fathers we would not have allowed them to kill the prophets.

31- In this you bear witness against yourselves for you are the sons of those who killed the prophets.

32- You behave according to the deeds of your fathers.

33- Vipers, seed of vipers, how will you escape the judgment of Gahinam if you do not turn in repentance?

Part 99

34- At that time Yeshua said to the crowds of Jews, behold I am sending to you prophets, sages, and scribes. Some of them you will kill, some of them afflict in your synagogues and you will pursue them from city to city.

35- Upon you, the blood of every Tzadikim, one which has been poured out upon the earth, from the blood of Abel, the tzadik, unto the blood of Zechariah, the son of Barachiah, whom you killed between the Temple and the altar.

36- Truly I say to you that all these things will come upon this generation,

37- And upon Jerusalem who kills the prophets and removes those who are sent. How many times I wished to gather your children as a hen gathers her chicks under her wings and you would not.

38- Therefore you will make your house desolate.

39- Truly I say to you, you will not see me until you will say, baruch habah b'shem Adonai.

## Chapter 24

Part 100

1- It came to pass when Yeshua went out from the Tem-

ple, as he was going, his talmidim drew near to show
him the Temple.

2- He said, you see all these, truly I say to you that all will
be destroyed and there will not be left there one stone
upon another.

3- As he sat on the mount od olives in front of the Temple, Pietros, Yohanan and Andreiah asked him secretly,
when will all these things happen, and what will be the
sign when all these matters will take place, or when
will they begin and when will be the end of the world
and your coming?

4- Yeshua answered them, beware lest anyone should
lead you astray,

5- For many will come with my name saying, I am the
Messiah, and they will turn you away.

6- As for you, when you hear of wars and a company
of hosts, beware lest you get fooled, because all of this
will occur, but it is not yet the end.

7- Nations will rise up against nations and kingdoms
against kingdoms, there will be great tumults, grievous
famine, and earthquakes in places.

8- All of this are the beginning of suffering.

9- Then they will bind you over for tribulation and will
kill you, and you will become a reproach to all the nations for my name.

10- Then many will be perturbed, deal treacherously with
each other, and be enraged among themselves.

11- False prophets will arise and lead many astray.

12- When evilness multiplies, the love of many will grow
faint.

13- Whoever waits until the end will be saved.

14- And that BESSORAH will be TEDARESH to all the earth
so that all the Gentiles will hear of me and then the end
will come.

15- And these will be the anti-Maschiach, this is SHKUTZ
SHOMEM spoken by Daniel's mouth while standing in

the holy place. May whoever reads it, understands it.

16- Then those who in Yehudah, let them flee to the mountains.

17- He who is upon the house, let him not come down for anything in his house.

18- He who is in the field, let him nor turn back to take his garment.

19- Woe to those who are pregnant and to those who take care of children in those days.

20- Pray to EL that your scape will not be in Shabbat.

21- Because there will be great distress which has not been from the creation of the world unto now and as will not be.

22- Except those days were few, no flesh would be saved, but for the sake of the chosen ones, those days will be few.

23- At that time, if one should say to you, behold, the messiah is here or there, don't believe it.

24- Because false messiahs and false prophets will arise and they will give signs and great wonder so that if will lead many of the chosen astray.

INVERTED VERSES

26- If they should say to you, behold he is in the wilderness, do not go there, and, behold he is in the chambers, do not believe it.

25- Behold I tell you before it takes place.

Part 101

27- And Yehoshua said to them: as the lightning comes from the east and is seen in the west, so will the coming of the Son of Man.

28- Wherever the body is, there wil be gathered the vultures.

29- At that time, after those days, the sun will darken,

the moon will not give forth its light, the stars will fall from the heavens and all hosts (chail) of the heavens will tremble.

30- And then the sign of the son of man will appear in heaven and all the families of the earth will weep and will see the son of man among the clouds of heaven with a great host (chail) and with a dreadful appearance.

31- And he will send his angels with a trumpet and with a loud voice to gather all his chosen ones from the four winds of the heavens, from one end of heaven unto the other.

32- From the fig tree, you learn by the mishnah, when you see the branches and the leaves above them, know that

33- The gates are close by.

34- Truly I say to you, this generation will not pass away until all these things shall be done.

35- Heaven and earth will pass away

36- But of that day or that time there is none who knows, not even the angels of heaven, but the father only.

Part 102

37- And Yeshua said to his talmidim: as in the days of Noach, so it will be in the days of the Son of man.

38- Before the flood, they ate and drank, were fruitful and multiplied until the day that Noach entered the ark.

39- And they did not know until the flood came upon them and took away the non-Tzadikim, so will be the coming of the Son of Man.

40- If there are two ploughing a field, the one who is Tzadik will stay and the one who is evil will be taken away.

41- Two women are working on a mill, one will be taken and the other left. This is because the angels, at the end of the world, will take the stumbling blocks away from the world, and will separate the good from the evil.

## Part 103

42- Then Yeshua said to his talmidim, watch with me because you do not know at what hour your lord is coming.

43- This you know, if one knew at what hour the thief was coming, he would watch and not allow him into his house.

44- So you should be prepared, because you do not know at what hour the son of man is coming.

45- What do you think of the faithful and wise servant whose lord places him over his children to give food in the time?

46- Ashrei is that servant whose lord sees him doing thus when he comes.

47- Truly I say to you that he will place him over his children.

48- But if that servant should be evil and should say in his heart, my lord is late in coming.

49- And should begin to beat the servant of his lord and should eat and drink without control.

50- His lord will come in a day which he does not expect and at a time which he does not know.

51- He will divide him and place his portion with the hypocrites, there will be weeping and gnashing of teeth.

## Chapter 25
### Part 104

1- Yeshua said to his talmidim: the kingdom of heaven is like ten virgins who took their lamps and went out to meet the bridegroom and the bride.

2- Five of them were lazy and foolish, and five of them were alert and wise.

3- The five fools brought their lamps, but did not bring

the oil.

4- And the wise brought the vessels of oil together with their lamps.

5- And the bridegroom was late and behold they all lingered and fell asleep.

6- Then at midnight, behold a voice was heard: behold, the bride and the groom have come, come and meet them.

7- Then all the virgins came and trimmed their lamps.

8- The foolish ones said to the wise: Give us some of your oils, for our lamps have gone out.

9- And the wise answered, saying, Please go to the vendors and buy from them, for we have not enough for ourselves and for you, we fear to run out of it.

10- And it was when they went to buy, the bridegroom arrived, and the virgins went with him to CHUPAH and closed the gates.

11- Afterwards, the foolish ones came and shouted from the gates, saying: Our Lord, open to us.

12- And he answered to them, trully I say to you, I do not know who you are.

13- So, be careful, because you do not know the day nor the hour of CHUPAH.

## Part 105

14- Yeshua told his talmidim another example, the kingdom of heaven is like a man going on a far journey, he called his servants and dispersed to them his money.

15- To one he gave five coins of gold, to the second he gave two coins of gold and to the third, one. To each according to what was suitable for him he gave. Then he went on his journey.

16- The one who received five coins of gold went and gained other five.

17- Likewise the one who received two, went, bought, sold and gained other five.

18- But he who received the one, went, dug in the earth, and hid the money of his lord.

19- After many days, the lord of those servants came and sought from them an accounting of the money.

20- The one who received five coins of gold came near and said to him, my lord, you gave me five coins of gold and here for you are five others which I made.

21- His lord said to him, truly you are a good and faithful servant. For you have been faithful in a little, I will appoint you over much, enter and enjoy your lord.

22- Also the one who received two coins of gold drew near and said, my lord, you gave me two coins of gold, here are two others that I have made.

23- His lord said to him, truly you are a good and faithful servant. For you have been faithful in a little, I will appoint you over much, enter and enjoy your lord.

24- Then the one who received one drew near and said, my lord, I know that your are firm and hard and that you reap what you did not sow and gather what you did not scatter.

25- So in fear of you I hid your coin of gold and behold you have what is yours.

26- His lord answered him and said, wicked and lazy servant, since you know that I reap what I did not sow and gather what I did not scatter?

27- Therefore, you should have given mu wealth to my money changers so that at my coming I would have received what is mine with profit.

28- Take from him the coin of gold and give it to the one who gained five coins of gold.

29- To the one who has it will be given, but to the one who does not have that which was intended for him will be taken from him.

30- As for the lazy servant cast him into the darkness of the lowest places, there shall be for him weeping and gnashing of teeth.

Part 106

31- Yeshua said to his talmidim, when the son of man comes in his revelation with his angels, then he will sit upon the throne of his glory.

32- All the nations will be gathered before him, and he will separate them as the shepherd separates the sheep and the goats.

33- He will place the sheep on his right and the goats on his left.

34- And then he will say to those to his right: welcome blessed of my Father, enter the Kingdom of Heaven that has been prepared for you since the creation of the world until now.

35- Because I was hungry and you gave me to eat, I was thirsty and you gave me to drink, I was lost and you took me in,

36- Naked and you clothed me, sick and you visited me, I was in prison and you came to me.

37- Then the tzadikim will answer, O lord, when did we see you hungry and satisfied you, and gave you to drink,

38- Naked and clothed you,

39- Sick and visited you, in prison and came to you?

40- The king will answer and say to them, truly I say to you that every time you did it to one of the needy of my brothers, even the little ones like these, you did it to me.

41- Also he will say to those on his left, depart from you cursed and go into eternal fire, to the place prepared for you, with satan and his angels,

42- Because I was hungry and did not give me to eat, I was thirsty and you did not give me to drink,

43- I was lost and you did not take me in, naked and you did not clothe me, sick and in prison and you did not visit me.

44- Then they also will answer and say to him, then did we see you, O our lord, hungry, or lost, naked, sick, or in prison and were not with you serving you?

45- He will answer them and say, I say to you that whenever you did not do this to one of these needy, even the little ones like these, you did not do it to me.

46- Then these will go into eternal abhorrence but the Tzadik into eternal life.

## Chapter 26

Part 107

1- It came to pass when Yeshua finished speaking all the things, he said to his talmidim,

2- Do you not know that in two days will be Pessach, and the son of man will be delivered into the hands of the Jews to be hanged?

3- Then the leaders of the priests and the leaders of the people were gathered together in the court of the high priest who was called Kaiafash.

4- They took counsel together to seize Yeshua by craftiness and to murder him.

5- But they said it should not be at the feast lest there be a mess among the people.

6- It came to pass when Yeshua was in Kafar Nahum in the house of Shimon the leper,

7- A woman came near to him with a jar of expensive ointment, she poured it upon his head while he was reclining at the table.

8- But this waste was very annoying to them.

9- It would have been possible to have sold it for a great price and to have given to the poor.

10- Yeshua, who knows everything in regard to all matter, said to them, are you making accusation against this woman? Truly she has performed a good and wonderful deed to me.

11- Because the poor with you always, but I will not be

with you always.

12- Her pouring this on my body refers to my burial.

13- Truly I say do you, everything this gospel, that is, evungel, is proclaimed in all the world, that which this one has done will be said in reference to my memory.

## Part 108

14- Then one of the twelve, whose name was Yehudah Eshkarioto, went to the high priest.

15- He said, what will you give me that I should deliver Yeshua over you? They settled with him for thirty pieces of silver.

16- From then on he sought a context for delivering him over.

17- And on the first day of the Feast of Unleavened Bread came the talmidim of Yeshua, saying, Where should we prepare the place for the SEDER of PESSACH?

18- He said to them, go into the city to a certain man who will be a volunteer for the task and say to him, thus says the master, my time draws near, with you the Pessach with my talmidim. (observe).

19- NO VERSE

20- It came to pass at the time of evening, he was sitting at table with his twelve talmidim.

21- As they were eating he said to them, I say to you that one of you will pass information against me.

22- They were very sad and spoke each other to him saying, lord, is it me?

23- And he answered to them: he who shall dip the Karpas in the salted water with me, is the one who passes the information on me. And no one could recognize him, for if they had recognized him, they would have destroyed him.

24- Yeshua said to them, truly the son of man goes as it is written concerning him, woe to that man for whose sake the son of man is betrayed. Better would be for that man not to have been born.

25- Yehudah, who sold him, answered and said to him, rabbi, am I the one? He said, you have spoken.

## Part 109

26- As they ate, Yeshua took the MATZAH, blessed EL and departed it, handing it to the talmidim and said: take and eat, this is my body.

27- And he took the cup, and gave thanks unto his Father, and gave unto them, saying, drink from this, all of you.

28- This is my blood, and **the new part of the covenant**, which shall be poured out upon many for the justification of sins.

29- I say to you I will not drink from the fruit of this vine until that day when I drink it again with you in the kingdom of heaven.

30- And went out to the Mount of Olives.

## Part 110

31- Then Yeshua said to his talmidim, come, all of you, be grieved because of me tonight as it is written, smite the shepherd and the sheep will be scattered.

32- After my resurrection from death, I will be revealed to you in Galil.

33- Pietros answered and said to him, if all of them are grieved because of you, I will never be grieved.

34- Yeshua said, truly I say to you, this night before the cock crow you will deny me three times.

35- Pietros said to him, if it is arranged for me to die with you, I will not deny you. The same was said by all the talmidim.

36- Then Yeshua came with them to the village of Gie Shemanim and said, sit now until I go there and pray.

37- He took pietros and the two sons of Zevediel and began to be sad and troubled.

38- Then he said to them, my soul is grieved unto death,

support me and watch with me.

39- Then he went forward very slowly and fell on his face and prayed and said: if it is possible, may this cup be removed from me, please. But in fact, it may not be as I want it to be, but according to Your will.

40- He came to his talmidim and found them sleeping. He said to Pietros, so you are unable to watch with me one hour?

41- Watch and pray lest you fall into temptation, because truly the spirit is ready to go, the flesh is weak and sick.

42- He went again to pray saying, if you are not able to remove this cup except I should drink it, let it be according to your will.

43- Afterwards he returned and found them sleeping because their eyes were heavy.

44- He left them and went to pray a third time according to the first words.

Part 111

45- Then Yeshua came to where the disciples were and said to them, sleep and be rest, behold the time has come near when the son of man will be delivered into the hands of the sinners.

46- Arise, let us go, for behold he who will betray me is near.

47- While he was speaking, behold Yehudah Eshkarioto, one of his twelve talmidim, came. With him was a large crowd with swords and whips sent from the high priest and the princes of the people.

48- He who betrayed him had given them a sign, whom I kiss is the one whom you are to arrest.

49- Immediately he drew near Yeshua and said to him, shalom Aleikha rabbi and kissed him.

50- Yeshua said to him, my friend, what have you done? They came, stretched out their hands against Yeshua and arrested him.

51- Behold, one of those who were with Yeshua stretched out his hand, drew his own sword, and attacked one of the priests, cutting off his ear.

52- Yeshua said to him, return your sword to its sheath, for (draws) the sword will fall by the sword.

53- Do you not understand that I can meet my enemies and indeed there will be for me at once more than twelve legions of angels?

54- But how will the Scriptures be fulfilled? Because thus it is intended to be done.

55- After this Yeshua said to the multitude: as if we were thieves you came to get us with whips and swords? Have I not been with you, teaching in the Temple every day, and I have not posed a threat?

56- Surely all this was done because the writings of the prophets were being fulfilled. Then all talmidim left him and fled.

57- They led Yeshua to the house of Kaiafash the high priest. Then all the scribes and Pharisees were gathered together.

58- Pietros was following him at a distance unto the house of the high priest. He entered the house and sat near the craftsmen until he should see the end.

59- The high priest and some Pharisees wished false witnesses against Yeshua in order to put him to death.

60- But they have not found even one, even though they have provided many false witnesses against Yeshua. Finally two false witnesses presented themselves.

61- This one said I have the power to destroy the Temple of EL and after three days to rebuild it.

62- The high priest arose and said to him, do you not answer anything against the testimony that these are bearing against you?

63- But Yeshua answered not a word. The high priest said to him, I adjure you by the living EL, that you tell us if you are the Mashiach, the son of EL.

64- Yeshua answered him, you say so. But again I say to you, you have yet to see the son of EL sitting at the right of the power of Elohim coming on the clouds of heaven.

65- Than the high priest tore his garments and said, this one has "blesses" EL, what need do we have for other witnesses? Behold all of you have heard how he "blesses" EL.

66- What do you think can be done? They answered, he is guilty of death.

67- Then they spit in his face and struck him on the back, and others slapped him in the face.

68- saying, tell us Mashiach, who struck you.

69- Pietros was standing at the entrance of the courtyard, and there came near to him a maid who said to him, were you not standing with Yeshua from Gallil?

70- Pietros lied to her before all and said to her, woman I do not know what you are saying.

71- When he passed through the gate another maid saw and said to those whe were there, this man was standing with Yeshua HaNotzri.

72- Again he denied Yeshua with an oath that he did not know him.

73- After a little while, those who were standing outside drew near to Pietros and said to him, you are from this prophet's group, it is clear by your accent you are one of them.

74- Then he began to deny and to sweat that at no time had he known him. Immediately the cock crowed.

75- Pietros remembered what Yeshua had said to him, that before the crowing of the cock he would deny him three times. Then he went outside and wept with bitterness of soul.

## Chapter 27
Part 112

1- It came to pass in the morning all the head sages and

elders took counsel against Yeshua that they should surely put him to death.

2- They led him bound to the house of Poitatz Pilat who was the leader.

3- Then Yehudah Eshkarioto saw that he had been judge, he began to turn in repentance. He turned the thirty dinars to the high priest and to the elders of the people.

4- He said, I have sinned because I have shed innocent blood. But they said to him, what is this to us? This is on you.

5- He threw the coins in the Temple, went and took a rope and hanged himself.

6- When the high priest got the coins, he said, it is not allowed for us to place these coins in the Temple for they are the fruit of blood, since they were given for the blood of Yeshua.

7- So they took counsel and gave them for a field of a certain potter of clay that they might put strangers there.

8- Therefore that field is called tent of blood unto this day.

9- Then was fulfilled the words of Zechariah, the prophet, and I said to them, if it is good in your eyes, multiply my wages, but if not, forbear. So they weighed for my wages thirty pieces of silver. Then Adonai told me, cast it unto the potter. This is from the man who forms clay.

10- as Adonai commanded.

11- Yeshua was standing before Pilat who asked him, are you the king of the Jews? Yeshua said, you are saying it.

12- When Yeshua was harassed by the leaders of the priests and elders of the people in regard to some word which they spoke against him he did not reply.

13- Pilat said to him, do you not see how much testimony there is against you?

14- But Yeshua did not answer him a word and Pilat was very amazed by this.

15- On the day of the honored feast of Pessach, it was their custom for the leader of the city to give to the people one of the prisoners whom they whished.

16- Pilat had a prisoner who was almost crazy, his name was Bar Baesh. Busted for murder and placed in dungeon.

17- When they were gathered together Pilat said to them, which of these do you wish that I should release, Bar Baesh or Yeshua who is called Mashiach?

18- This is because Pilat knew that due to hatred without cause he had been taken.

19- While he was sitting upon the throne his wife sent him a word saying, I beg of you that in no matter you should speak a word against this tzadik man because in this night I have suffered many things in vision because of him.

20- The leaders of the priests and the elders of the law assembled the people so they might ask for Bar Baesh and that Yeshua might die.

21- Pilat addressed them, which of them do you wish that we should release? They said Bar Baesh.

22- Pilat said to them, if so, what shall I do with Yeshua who is called Mashiach? All of them answered that he should be hung.

23- Pilat said to them, what evil has he done? They vigorously cried out, let them hand him, let them hand him, let them hand him.

24- Pilat, when he saw he could no more make resistance and was unable to make any peace among them, before a great dispute among the people might arise because of this, took water and washed his hands before the people and said, I am innocent. Be careful with what you do.

25- All the people answered him and said, his blood will be upon us and upon our seed.

26- Then he released Bar Baesh, and delivered to them

Yeshua for beating and affliction that they might hand him.

Part 113

27- Then the horsemen of the court took Yeshua under guard and came together before a great company of many people.

28- They clothed Yeshua with silk garments and covered him with a greenish silk robe.

29- They made a crown of thorns and placed it on his head and set a reed in his right hand and were bowing down mocking him. Peace be upon you, king of the Jews.

30- They spit in his face and tool the reed and struck his head.

31- When the had mocked him, they stripped the robe from him, dressed him in his own clothes and gave orders to hang him.

32- As they were going out from the city, they met a man whose name was Shimon the Canaanite. They made him to carry the beam.

33- They came to a place called Gulgota, that is, Mount Calvary.

34- And they gave him wine mixed with MARAH (Extract from an extremely bitter plant). But when he began to drink, he noticed it and did not drink.

35- When they placed him in the beam they shared his garments by lot.

36- NO VERSE

37- After, they set for him over his head a writing which said, ZEH YEHOSHUA NA´AZERET MELEKH ISRAEL.

38- Then two thieves were hung with him, one on his right and one on his lest.

39- Those who were passing by mocked him and shook heads.

40- Saying, see, you would lay waste the Temple of Adonai and in yet three days build it. Save yourself, if you are the son of Elohim, come down from the <u>tree</u>.

41- The leader of the priests and the elders of the people mocked him saying,

42- others he saved, himself he cannot save. If he is the king of Israel let him come down from the <u>tree</u> and we will believe.

43- Since he trusted in EL, let Him save him now if He wishes, because he said he is the son of Elohim.

44- The thieves who were hung with him said to him these very same words.

45- At the sixth hour, darkness came in all the world and it remained until the ninth hour.

46- Yeshua shouted aloud, in the holy language (Hebrew): ELI ELI, why did you forsake me?

47- On of those standing there said, this one is calling for Eliahu.

48- At that moment he took a spongy bread, filled with vinegar and gave it to him to drink.

49- Others were saying, we will see if Eliahu will come to deliver him.

50- Yeshua cried another time in a loud voice and sent his spirit to his Father.

51- immediately the curtain of the temple was torn into two pieces, from the top downwards, the earth shook and the rocks were broken.

52- The graves were opened and many of those who asleep in the dust arose.

53- They came out of their graves and after, they entered the holy city and were revealed to many.

54- The captain of the hundred and those standing with him watching Yeshua saw the earthquake and the things which were done and were very scared saying, truly this was the son of Elohim.

55- Many women were standing there at a distance from among those who served Yeshua from Galil unto that time.

56- Among them were Miriam Magdaline, Miriam the mother of Yaakov and Yosef, and the mother of the sons of Zevediel.

57- At evening time, a rich man named Yosef came, a talmid of Yeshua.

58- He came to Pilat and asked him for the body of Yeshua. Pilat commanded that they should give it to him.

59- Yosef took it and wrapped it in a very fine silk garment.

60- He placed him in his own tomb which had been freshly hewn from stone and placed a large stone over the entrance of the tomb.

61- NO VERSE

62- On the morrow of Pessach, the leader od the priests and some Pharisees came to Pilat.

63- They said to him, sir, we remember that this liar said while still alive that at the end of three days he would arise and come to life.

64- Therefore command his tomb to be guarded until the third day, since perhaps one of his talmidim might come and steal him. After that, they might say to the people that he arose from death. If they should do this, the last perversion will be greater than before.

65- Pilat said to them, search out guards, guard it as well as you can.

66- So they completed the structure of the tomb, sealed it, and placed a guard there.

## Chapter 28
Part 114

1- On the first weekly day, at the turn of the day (Saturday around 18pm), Miriam Magdaline and other Miriam came to the tomb.

2- Then the earth shook because the angel of Adonai came from the heaven to the tomb, overturned the stone, and stood there without moving.

3- His appearance was like the sun and his garments like snow.

4- From the fear of him the guards passed out and remained like dead.

5- The angel answered and said to the women, fear not, for I know that you seek Yeshua who was hung.

6- He is nor here for he is already alive as he said. Come, and see the place where the lord arose.

7- Then go now and tell his talmidim that the lord has already arisen there. He will be before you and there you will see him as he told you.

8- The women went out of the tomb with fear because they had seen the angel, but with great joy because the lord come back to life. They ran to tell the talmidim.

9- As they went going Yeshua passed before them saying, may the NAME (HASHEM) deliver you. They came near to him,

1- they bowed down their heads and honored him.

10- Then Yeshua said to them, do not be afraid, tell my brothers that they should go to Galil and there they will see me.

11- While they were going some of the guards entered the city and declared to the high priest all that happened.

12- They came together for counsel with the elders of the people. Then they gave much money to the horsemen.

13- And said to them, say that his talmidim came by night and stole him while you were sleeping.

14- If this should come to the ears of Pilat, we will tell him that he should leave you alone.

15- They took the money and said thus as they commanded them. This is the word in secret among the Jews up to his day.

16- After this when his twelve talmidim came to Galil he appeared to them in the mountain where they had prayed.

17- Then they saw him they bowed before him, but there were some of them who doubted him.

18- Yeshua drew near to them and said to them,

19- Go!

20- And observe (SHAMRU) all things (DEVARIM) as I have commanded you, forever.

# PART VI
# MATTHEW'S BOOK
# HEBREW

# הבשורה הקדושה של ישוע המשיח כפי מתתיה

<u>פרק ראשון 1</u>

<sup>1</sup>אלה תולדות יש''ו בן דוד בן אברהם.

<sup>2</sup>אברהם הוליד את יצחק ויצחק הוליד את יעקב יעקב הוליד את יהודה ואחיו.

<sup>3</sup>יהודה הוליד את פרץ וזרח מתמר פרץ הוליד את חצרון חצרון הוליד את רם.

<sup>4</sup>ורם הוליד את עמינדב ועמינדב הוליד את נחשון ונחשון הוליד את שלמון.

<sup>5</sup>שלמון הוליד את בועז מרחב הזונה בועז הוליד את עובד מרות ועובד הוליד את ישי.

<sup>6</sup>ישי הוליד את דוד דוד הוליד את שלמה מאשת אוריה.

<sup>7</sup>שלמה הוליד את רחבעם רחבעם הוליד את אביה אביה הוליד את אסא.

<sup>8</sup>אסא הוליד את יהושפט יהושפט הוליד את יודם יורם הוליד את עוזיה.

<sup>9</sup>עוזיה הוליד את חזקיה.

<sup>10</sup>חזקיה הוליד את מנשה מנשה הוליד את אמון אמון הוליד את יאשיה.

<sup>11</sup>יאשיה הוליד את יכניה ואחיו בגלות בבל.

<sup>12</sup>יכניה הוליד את שאלתיאל שאלתיאל הוליד את זרובבל.

<sup>13</sup>זרובב''ל הוליד את אביהוד ואביהוד הוליד את.

<sup>14</sup>אקים ואקים הוליד את אליהוד.

<sup>15</sup>ואליהוד הוליד את אלעזר ואלעזר הוליד את מתן ומתן הוליד את יעקב.

<sup>16</sup>ויעקב הוליד את יוסף. הוא יוסף איש מר''ם הנקרא משיח ובלעז קריס''טוס.

<sup>17</sup>(וכל תולדות מאברהם עד דוד תולדות י''ד ומדוד עד גלות

בבל תולדות י''ד ומגלות בבל עד יש''ו תולדות י''ד.

## פרק שני

[18]ולידת מיש''ו היה בזה האופן) ויהי כאשר היתה אמו ארוסה ליוסף קודם שידע אותה נמצאה מעוברת מרוח הקדש.

[19]ויוסף איש צדיק היה ולא רצה לישב עמה ולא לגלותה להביאה לבושה ולא לאוסרה למות אבל היה רוצה לכסות עליה.

[20]ובחשבו בזה הדבר בלבו והנה מלאך נראה אליו בחלום ואמר יוסף בן דוד אל תירא לקחת אשתך מר''ים שמרוח הקדוש היא מעוברת.

[21]ותלד בן ותקרא שמו ישו''ע כי הוא יושיע את עמי מעונותם.

[22]כל זה לגמור מה שנכתב מאת הנביא על פי ה''.

[23]הנה העלמה הרה ותלד בן וקראת שמו עמנואל שר''ל עמנו אלקים.

[24]ויקץ יוסף משנתו ויעש ככל אשר צוה אותו מלאך ה'' ויקח את אשתו.

[25]ולא ידע אותה עד שילדה בנה הבכור ויקרא את שמו ישו''ע.

## פרק שלישי 2

[1]ויהי כאשר נולד יש''ו בבית לחם יהודה בימי הורודוס המלך והנה חוזים בכוכבים באים ממזרח לירושלים.

[2]לאמר איה מלך היהודים הנולד. ראינו סבבו במזרח ובמתנות חשובות באו להשתחוות לו.

[3]ושמע הורודוס המלך ויבהל וכל יושבי ירושלים עמו.

[4]ויקבוץ כל גדוליו ויבקש מהם אם היו יודעים באיזה מקום נולד המשיח.

[5]ויענו אליו בבית לחם יהודה ככתיב על פי הנביא.

[6]ואתה בית לחם יהודה אפרתה ארץ יהודה הן אתה צעיר באלפי יהודה ממך לי יצא להיות מושל בישראל.

[7]אז קרא המלך הורודוס לקוסמים בסתר וישאל מהם היטב זמן

ראית הכוכב להם.

⁸וישלחם לבית לחם ויאמר אליהם לכו ושאלו היטב בעד הילד ובמוצאכם אותו הגידו לי וגם אני אבא אליו להשתחוות.

⁹וישמעו אל המלך וילכו והנה הכוכב אשר ראו במזרח הולך לפניהם עד בואם אל המקום. וכאשר באו בית לחם עמד נגד המקום אשר שם הילד.

¹⁰ויהי כאשר ראו את הכוכב שמחו שמחה גדולה עד מאד.

¹¹ויביאו אל הבית וימצאהו ואת מר''ים אמו ויכרעו לפניו וישתחוו לו ויפתחו את אמתחותיהם ויביאו אליו מנחת זהב ולבונה ומור בלעז מי''רא.

¹²ויצוו בחלום לבלתי שוב אל הורודוס מהמלאך אמר להם ויפנו דרך ארצם בדרך אחרת.

## פרק רביעי

¹³המה הולכים והנה מלאך ה'' נראה אל יוסף קום וקח את הנער ואת אמו וברח למצרים ושם תעמוד עד אמרי אליך כי הורודוס יבקש את הנער להרוג.

¹⁴ויקח את הנער ואת אמו.

¹⁵ויהי שם עד מת הורוד''וס לגמור מה שנאמר על פי הנביא וממצרים קראתי לבני.

## פרק חמישי

¹⁶אז ראה הורודוס שראו אותו הקוסמים וירע אליו מאד ויתעצב אל לבו ויצו וישלח לכל שריו להרוג לכל הילדים אשר בבית לחם וגבוליה הנולדים מזמן אשר אמרו לו הקוסמים שנולד הנער.

¹⁷אז נשלם הדבר מה שאמר ירמיה הנביא.

¹⁸קול ברמה נשמע נהי בכי תמרורים רחל מבכה על בניה וכו.

¹⁹ויהי כאשר מת הורוד''וס המלך ומלאך ה'' נראה בחלום אל יוסף במצרים.

²⁰לאמר קום קח את הנער ואת אמו ולך אל א''י כי מתו המבקשים את הנער להמית.

²¹ויקם ויקח את הנער ואת אמו וישובו אל א''י.

²²וישמע כי הורקנוס שמו ארגי''לאס מלך ביהודה תחת הורודוס אביו. וירא ללכת שם ויזרזהו המלאך בחלום ויפן אל ארץ הגלגל.

²³ויבא וישכון בעיר הנקראת נאזרית לקיים מה שאמר הנביא נאזרית יקרא.

## פרק ששי 3

¹בימים ההם בא יוחנן המטביל דורש במדבר יהודה.

²ואמר חזרו בתשובה שמלכות שמים קרובה לבא.

³לקיים מה שנאמר ע'' ישעיהו הנביא קול קורא במדבר פנו דרך ה'' ישרו בערבה מסילה לאלקינו.

⁴והנה יוחנן היה לבוש מצמר הגמלים ועור שחור אזור במתניו ומזונו הארבה ודבש היערים.

⁵אז יצאו אליו מירושלם ומכל יהודה ומכל המלכות סביבות הירדן

⁶ואז מתודים חטאתם וטובלים בירדן על מאמרו.

## פרק שביעי

⁷וירא כי רבים מהפרושים בלעז פאריזיאי ומן הפרושים באו לטבילתו ויאמר להם לברוח מן הקצף לעתיד לבא מהאל.

⁸עשו פרי תשובה השלמה.

⁹ואל תאמרו בלבבכם אבינו אברהם. אמן אני אומר לכם שיוכל אלקים להקים את בנו אברהם מן האבנים האלה.

¹⁰(וכבר הגיע הגרזן לשרש העץ אשר לא יעשה פרי טוב יכרת ובאש ישרף. וישאלו לו החבורות א''כ מה נעשה. ויען להם יוחנן מי שיש לו שתי כתנות יתן הא' למי שאין לו. ויבאו העם להטביל.) וישאלוהו רבים מה נעשה ויען להם תצטערו לשום איש ולא תענשום ותשמחו בחלקיכם. וכל העם היו חושבים ומדמים בלבם נמול יוחנן הוא יש''ו.

¹¹ויוחנן ענה לכולם באמת הנני מטביל אתכם בימי תשובה ואחר יבא חזק ממני שאיני ראוי להתיר שרוך נעלו. והוא יטביל

אתכם באש רוח הקדוש.

<sup>12</sup>אשר בידו מזרה לזרות את גרנו ויאסוף הדגן לאוצרו והתבן ע''כ.

## פרק שמיני
<sup>13</sup>אז בא יש''ו מהגליל את הירדן להטביל מיוחנן.

<sup>14</sup>ויוחנן היה מספק להטבילו ויאמר אני ראוי להטביל מידך ואתה בא אלי.

<sup>15</sup>ויען יש''ו ויאמר לו הנח שכן אנו חייבים להשלים כל צדקה ואז הטבילוהו.

<sup>16</sup>ומיד שעלה מן המים נפתחו לו השמים וירא רוח אלקים יורדת כיונה ושרתה עליו.

<sup>17</sup>והנה קול מן השמים אומר זה בני אהובי מאד מאד נאהב וחפצי בו.

## פרק תשיעי 4
<sup>1</sup>אז לוקח יש''ו ברוח הקדוש למדבר להתנסות מהשטן.

<sup>2</sup>ויצום מ'' יום וארבעים לילה ואח''ב נרעב.

<sup>3</sup>מקרב המנסה ואמר לו אם בן אלקים אתה אמור שהאבנים האלה ישובו לחם.

<sup>4</sup>ויען יש''ו ויאמר לו כתוב כי לא על הלחם לבדו וגו''.

<sup>5</sup>אז לקח אותו השטן בעיר הקדוש ויעמידהו על מקום היותר גבוה שבכל המקדש

<sup>6</sup>ואמר אליו אם אלקים אתה דלג למטה וכ' כי מלאכיו יצוה לך לשמרך בכל דרכיך וגו.

<sup>7</sup>ויען אליו יש''ו שנית לא תנסה את ה'' אלקיך.

<sup>8</sup>וישא אותו השטן בהר גבוה מאד ויראהו כל ממלכות הארץ וכבודם

<sup>9</sup>ויאמר לו כל אלה אתן לך אם תפרע אלי.

<sup>10</sup>אז ענה לו יש''ו לך השטן בלעז שאטאנאס שכן כתיב את ה'' אתפלל ואותו לבדו תעבוד.

<sup>11</sup>אז עזב אותו השטן והנה מלאכים קרבו אליו וישרפוהו.

## פרק עשירי

<sup>12</sup>ויהי בימים ההם וישמע יש''ו כי נמסר יוחנן במאסר וילך אל הגלגל.

<sup>13</sup>ויעבור את נאזראל וישכון בכפר נחום ראיתה לעז מאריטמה הקצה ארץ זבולון

<sup>14</sup>לקיים מה שאמר ישעיהו הנביא

<sup>15</sup>ארצה זבולון וארצה נפתלי דרך הים עבר את הירדן גליל הגוים.

<sup>16</sup>העם ההולכים בחושך ראו אור גדול יושבי בארץ צלמות אור נגה עליהם.

## פרק י''א

<sup>17</sup>מכאן ואילך התחיל יש''ו לדרוש ולדבר חזרו בתשובה שמלכות שמים קרובה.

<sup>18</sup>וילך יש''ו על שפת הים הגליל וירא שני אחים שמעון שיקרא סימ''ון ונקרא פייט''רוס ואנדיר''יאה אחיו משליכים מכמרותיהם בים שהיו דייגים.

<sup>19</sup>ויאמר להם לכו אחרי ואעשה אתכם מדייגים אנשים.

<sup>20</sup>ויעזבו מכמרותיהם באותה שעה וילכו אחריו.

<sup>21</sup>ויט משם וירא שני אחים אחרים יעקב ויוחנן אחים בני זבדיאל בלעז זבאד''או וזאב''אדה ואביהם באניה מכינים מכמרותיהם ויקרא אותם.

<sup>22</sup>וימהרו ויניחו מכמרותיהם ואת אביהם וילכו אחריו.

## פרק י''ב

<sup>23</sup>ויסב יש''ו אל ארץ הגליל ללמד קהלותם ומבשר להם זבד טוב לעז מאוונג''''ייליו ממלכות שמים ומרפא כל חולים וכל מדוה בעם.

<sup>24</sup>וילך שמועתו בכל ארץ סור''יא וישאו אליו כל החולים מכל מיני חלאים משונים אחוזים השדים והנבעתים מרוח רעה והמתרעשים וירפא אותם.

<sup>25</sup>וילכו אחריו רבות מקפ''ולי והג''ליל מירו''שלם ויוד''א

ועבר היר''דן.

פרק י''ג 5

<sup>1</sup>ויהי אחרי זה בעת ההיא וירא החבורות ויעל ההר וישב. ויקריבו לו תלמידיו

<sup>2</sup>ויפתח פיו וידבר אליהם לאמר.

<sup>3</sup>(אשרי שפלי רוח שלהם מלכות שמים.)

<sup>4</sup>אשרי החוכים שינוחמו.

<sup>5</sup>(אשרי הענוים שהם ירשו ארץ.)

<sup>6</sup>

<sup>7</sup>

<sup>8</sup>אשרי זכי הלב והמה יראו אלקים.

<sup>9</sup>אשרי רודפי שלום שבני אלקים יקראו.

<sup>10</sup>אשרי הנרדפים לצדק שלהם מלכות שמים.

<sup>11</sup>אשריכם כאשר ירדפו ויגדפו אתכם ויאמרו אליכם כל רע בעדי ויכזבו.

<sup>12</sup>שישו ושמחו ששכרכם רב מאד בשמים שכן רדפו הנביאים

פרק י''ד

<sup>13</sup>בעת ההיא אמר יש''ו לתלמידיו מלח אתם בעולם אם המלח יבטל טעמו במה יומלח ואינו שוה כלום אלא שיושלך בחוץ להיות מרמס רגלים.

<sup>14</sup>מאור אתם בעולם. עיר בנויה על ההר לא תוכל להסתר.

<sup>15</sup>לא ידליקו נר להשים אותו במקום נסתר שלא תאיר רק משימים אותו על המנורה להאיר לכל בני הבית.

<sup>16</sup>כן יאיר מאורכם לפני כל אדם להראותם מעשיכם הטובים המשובחות ומכבדות לאביכם שבשמים.

<sup>17</sup>בעת ההיא אמר יש''ו לתלמידיו אל תחשבו שבאתי להפר תורה אלא להשלים.

<sup>18</sup>באמת אני אומר לכם כי עד שמים וארץ יוד אחת ונקודה אחת לא תבטל מהתורה או מהנביאים שהכל יתקיים.

<sup>19</sup>ואשר יעבור מאמר א'' מההמצוות אלו אשר אלמד אחרים בן

הבל יקרא
מלכות שמים והמקיים והמלמד גדול יקרא במלכות שמים.

## פרק ט''ו

20בעת ההיא אמר יש''ו לתלמידיו באמת אני אומר לכם אם לא תגדל צדקתכם יותר מהפרושים והחכמים לא תבואו במלכות שמים.

21הלא שמעתם מה שנאמר לקדמונים לא תרצח ואשר ירצח חייב הוא משפט מות.

22ואני אומר לכם שהמכעיס לחבירו חייב הוא למשפט ואשר יקרא לאחיו פחות יחייב במשפט בהקהל ואשר יקראוהו שוטה חייב לאש גהינם.

23ואם תקריב קרבנך למזבח ותזכיר שהיה לך עם חברך דין והוא מתרעם ממך מאיזה דבר

24הנה קרבניך שם לפני המזבח ולך לרצותו קודם ואחר כך הקרב קרבניך.

## פרק ט''ז

25אז אמר יש''ו לתלמידיו ראה שתמהר לרצות שונאך בלכתך עמו בדרך פן ימסור אותך לשופט וזה השופט ימסורך לעבד לתת אותך לבית הסוהר.

26באמת אומר לך לא תצא משם עד תנתן פרוטה אחרונה.

## פרק יז

27עוד אמר להם שמעתם מה שנאמר לקדמונים לא תנאף.

28ואני אומר לכם שכל הרואה אשה ויחמוד אותה כבר נאף עמה בלבה.

29ואם יסיתך עיניך הימין נקר אותה ותשליכה ממך.

30וכן אם יסיתך ידך חתוך אותה. טוב לך שתפסיד אחר מאבריך מכל גופך בגהינם.

## פרק י''ח

31עוד אמר יש''ו לתלמידיו שמעתם מה שנאמר לקדמונים

שכל העוזב אשתו ושלח לתת לה גט כריתות ובלעז ליבי''ל ריפודייו.

$^{32}$ואני אומר לכם שכל העוזב אשתו יש לו לתת לה גט כריתות כי אם על דבר נאוף הוא הנואף והלוקח אותה ינאף.

## פרק י''ט

$^{33}$עוד שמעתם מה שנאמר לקדמונים לא תשבעו בשמי לשקר ותשיב לה'' שבועתך.

$^{34}$ואני אומר לכם לבלתי השבע בשום עניין לשוא לא בשמים שכסא אלקים היא.

$^{35}$ולא בארץ שהדום רגליו הוא לא בשמים שעיר אלקים היא.

$^{36}$ולא בראשך שלא תוכל לעשות שער א'' לבן או שחור.

$^{37}$אבל יהיו דבריכם הן הן וגם לא לא. כל הנוסף על זה הוא רע.

$^{38}$ועוד שמעתם מה שנאמר בתורה עין תחת עין שן תחת שן.

$^{39}$ואני אומר לכם לבלתי שלם רע תחת רע אבל המכה בלחיך הימין הכן לו השמאל.

$^{40}$ואשר ירצה לחלוק עמך במשפט ולגזול כתניך עזוב אליו מעילך.

$^{41}$ואשר ישאל אותך לילך עמו אלף פסיעות לך עמו אלפיים.

$^{42}$השואל ממך תן לו והרוצה ללות ממך אל תמנע.

## פרק כ''

$^{43}$עוד אמר יש''ו לתלמידיו שמעתם מה שנאמר לקדמונים ואהבת לאוהבך ותשנא לשונאך.

$^{44}$ואני אומר לכם אהבו אויביכם ועשו טובה לשונאכם ומכעיסכם והתפללו בשביל רודפיכם ולוחציכם

$^{45}$למען תהיו בני אביכם שבשמים שמזריח שמשו על טובים ורעים וממטיר על רשעים וצדיקים.

$^{46}$אם תאהבו אוהביכם איזה שכר לכם? הלא עזי פנים אוהבים אוהביהם?

$^{47}$

$^{48}$היו אתם תמימים כאשר תם אביכם.

<sup>1</sup>השמרו פן תעשו צדקתכם לפני האדם להלל אתכם ואם תעשו לא יהיה לכם שכר מאת אביכם שבשמים.

## פרק כ"א 6

<sup>2</sup>עוד אמר נהם יש"ו כאשר תעשו צדקה לא תרצו להעביר כרוז וחצוצרות לפניכם כמו החנפים בלעז איפוקראטיס שעושים צדקתם ברחובות ובשווקים בעד שיראו אותם בני אדם. אמן אני אומר לכם שכבר קבלו שכרם.

<sup>3</sup>ואתם כאשר תעשה צדקה אל ידע שמאלך מה יעשה ימינך <sup>4</sup>להיות מתנך בסתר ואביך הרואה הנסתרות ישלם לך.

## פרק כ"ב

<sup>5</sup>בעת ההיא אמר יש"ו לתלמידיו השעה שתתפללו אל תרימו קול ואל תהיו כחנפים העצבים האוהבים להתפלל בבתי כנסיות ובמקצוע חצרות ומתפללים בגבהות שישמעו וישבחו בני אדם. אמן אני אומר לכם שכבר קבלו שכרם.

<sup>6</sup>ואתה בהתפללך בא למשכבך וסגור דלתיך בעדך והתפלל לאביך בסתר ואביך הרואה בסתר ישלם לך.

<sup>7</sup>ואתם כאשר תתפללו אל תרבו דברים כמו שהמינים חושבים שברוב דברים ישמעום.

<sup>8</sup>ואתם אל תראו שאביכם שבשמים יודע דבריכם קודם שתשאלו ממנו?

<sup>9</sup>וכן תתפללו אבינו יתקדש שמך

<sup>10</sup>ויתברך מלכותך רצונך יהיה עשוי בשמים ובארץ.

<sup>11</sup>ותתן לחמנו תמידית.

<sup>12</sup>ומחול לנו חטאתינו כאשר אנחנו מוחלים לחוטאים לנו <sup>13</sup>ואל תביאנו לידי נסיון ושמרינו מכל רע אמן.

<sup>14</sup>אם תמחול לבני אדם עונתיהם ימחול אביכם שבשמים עונותיכם.

<sup>15</sup>ואם לא תמחלו להם לא ימחול לכם עונותיכם לכם.

## פרק כ"ג

<sup>16</sup>עוד אמר להם וכאשר תצומו אל תהיו כחנפים העצבים

שמראים עצמם עצבים ומשנים פניהם להראות צמותם לבני
אדם אמן אני אומר לכם שכבר קבלו שכרם.
<sup>17</sup>ואתם בצומכם רחצו ראשיכם
<sup>18</sup>שלא תראו מתענים לבני אדם אלא אביך שהוא בסתר ואביך
שהוא בסתר ישלם לך.

## פרק כ"ד

<sup>19</sup>עוד אמר להם אל תרבו לצבור אוצרות בארץ כדי שיאכלנו
רקב ותולעה או יחפרו הגנבים ויגנבום.
<sup>20</sup>עשו לכם אוצרות בשמים במקום שרימה ותולעה לא יאכלם
ובמקום שהגנבים לא יחפרו ויגנבו.
<sup>21</sup>באותו מקום שיהיה אוצרך שם.
<sup>22</sup>וניר גופך עיניך אם עיניך לנוכח יביטו כל גופך יחשוך.
<sup>23</sup>ואם האור שבך מחשיך כל דרכיך יהיו חשוכים.

## פרק כ"ה

<sup>24</sup>בעת ההיא אמר יש"ו לתלמידיו לא יוכל איש לעבוד לשני
אדונים כי אם האחד ישנא והא'' יאהב או לאחד יכבד ולאחד
יבזה לא תוכלו לעבוד האל והעולם.
<sup>25</sup>לכן אני אומר לכם שלא תדאגו למאכל לנפשותיכם ולא
במלבוש לגופכם שהנפש יקרה מהמזון והגוף מהמלבוש.
<sup>26</sup>הסתכלו בעוף השמים אשר לא יזרעו ולא יקצרו ולא יאספו
אוצרות ואביכם העליון מכלכל אתכם הלא אתם יקרים מהם?
<sup>27</sup>מי בכם מהדואגים שיוכל להוסיף בקומתו אמה אחת?
<sup>28</sup>א''כ על מה תדאגו בלבוש ראו חבצלת השרון לעז גיל''יון
החומש.

<sup>29</sup>ואני אומר לכם שהמלך שלמה בכל כבודו לא היה מלובש
כמוהו.

<sup>30</sup>ואם תבן הנשאר בקמות לעז פי''נן אשר היום לחה ומחר
יבשה ומשימים אותה בתנור האל מלביש אותה כ''ש אנחנו
מקטני אמנה.

<sup>31</sup>וא''כ שהאל יחשוב מכם אל תדאגו לומר מה נאכל ומה

נשתה

<sup>32</sup>שכל אלה הגופים מבקשים. ויודע אביכם שכל אלה אתם צריכים.

<sup>33</sup>בקשו קודם מלכות אלקים וצדקתו וכל אלה הדברים ינתנו לכם.

<sup>34</sup>אל תדאגו ליום מחר שיום מחר ידאג ממנו די לו ליום בצרתו.

## פרק כ"ו 7

<sup>1</sup>אל תדינו פן תדונו

<sup>2</sup>באיזה דין תדונו ובאיזה מדה תמודו ימודד לכם.

<sup>3</sup>ולמה תראו קש בעין זולתך ולא תראה קורה שבעיניך?

<sup>4</sup>ואיך תאמר לזולתך כתר לי זעיר ואוציא קש מעיניך הנה הקרה בעיניך.

<sup>5</sup>החנף תוציא קודם הקורה מעיניך ואח"כ תוציא הקש מעין זולתך.

## פרק כ"ז

<sup>6</sup>עוד אמר להם אל תתנו בשר קדש לכלבים ואל תשימו פניכם לפני חזיר פן יכרסמנו אותה לעיניכם ויחזרו אותה לקרוע אתכם.

<sup>7</sup>שאלו מהאל וינתן לכם בקשו ותמצאו דפקו ויפתחו לכם.

<sup>8</sup>כל השואל יקבל ולאשר יבקש ימצא ולקורא יפתח.

<sup>9</sup>מי בכם שיבקש בנו ממנו לפרוס לחם ויתן לו אבן?

<sup>10</sup>או אם יבקש דג ויתן נחש?

<sup>11</sup>ואם אתם עם היותכם רעים תבואו לתת מתנות טובות לפניכם כ"ש אביכם שבשמים שיתן רוחו הטוב למבקשיו.

<sup>12</sup>וכל מה שתרצו שיעשו לכם בני אדם עשו להם זאת התורה ודברי הנביאים.

## פרק כ"ח

<sup>13</sup>בזמן ההוא אמר יש"ו לתלמידיו באו בשער הצר ששער

האבדון רחב ומצולה ורבים הולכים בה.

$^{14}$כמה השער צר וכבד הדרך המשייר לחיים ומעטים המוצאים אותה.

## פרק כ''ט

$^{15}$עוד אמר להם הזהרו מנביאי השקר הבאים לכם במלבושי צמר דומים לצאן שמתוכם זאבים טורפים.

$^{16}$ובמעשיהם תכירום הילקוט אדם מן הקוצים ענבים ומן הברקונים תאנים?

$^{17}$שכל עץ טוב יעשה פרי טוב וכל עץ רע יעשה פרי רע.

$^{18}$ועץ הטוב לא יוכל לעשות פרי רע ועץ רע לא יוכל לעשות פרי טוב.

$^{19}$וכל עץ אשר לא יעשה פרי טוב כאשר ישרף.

$^{20}$לכן כפריים ר''ל במעשיהם תכירום.

$^{21}$שכל האומר אלי אדוני לא יבא במלכות שמים אבל העושה רצון (תורת) אבי שבשמים יכנס במלכות שמים.

$^{22}$רבים אומרים אלי ביום ההוא אדוני אדוני הלא בשמך נבאנו ובשמך שדים הוצאתנו ואותות רבות על שמך עשינו?

$^{23}$ואז אמר להם מעולם לא ידעתי אתכם סורו ממני כל פועלי און.

## פרק שלושים

$^{24}$עוד אמר להם כל השומע דברים אלו ועושה אותם דומה לאיש חכם שבנה בית בסלע.

$^{25}$וירד הגשם עליו והרוחות מקישות אותו ולא יפול לפי שיסודו אבן.

$^{26}$וכל השומע אלה הדברים ולא יעשם דומה לאיש שוטה אשר בנה ביתו על החול.

$^{27}$וירדו גשמים ויבואו זרמים ויפילוהו נופל מפלה גדולה.

$^{28}$ובעוד שיש''ו היה מדבר דברים אלו כל העם היו תמהים מרוב טוב הנהגתו

$^{29}$לפי שהיה דורש להם בכח גדול שלא כשאר החכמים.

## פרק ל''א 8
<sup>1</sup>ויהי כאשר ירד יש''ו מן ההר וחבורות אחריו.

<sup>2</sup>והנה מצורע אחד בא וישתחוה לו לאמר אדו' אם תוכל לרפאת אלי.

<sup>3</sup>ויט יש''ו את ידו ויגע בו לאמר רוצה אני שתטהר ובאותה שעה נטהר המצורע מצרעתו.

<sup>4</sup>ויאמר אליו יש''ו השמר לך פן תגיד לאדם ולך לכהן להקריב קרבניך כאשר צוה משה בתורתכם.

## פרק ל''ב
<sup>5</sup>ויהי כבואו בכפר נחום המרתה ויבא אליו שר המאות ויתחנן לו

<sup>6</sup>לאמר אדוני בני שוכב בביתי מחולי הכווץ בלעז פירא''לשיזה ומתחלחל מהמחלה.

<sup>7</sup>ויאמר אלי יש''ו אני אלך וארפאהו.

<sup>8</sup>ויען שר המאות ויאמר לו אדו' אינך ראוי שתבא תחת גגי אלא שתגזור אומר וירפא.

<sup>9</sup>ואני אדם חוטא ויש לי ממשלת תחת ידי פירושים ופרשים ורוכבים ואומר אני לא'' מהם לך וילך בא ויבא ולעבדי עשו זה ויעשו.

<sup>10</sup>וישמע יש''ו ויתמה ולבאים אחריו אמר אמן אני אומר לכם לא מצאתי אמונה גדולה בישראל.

<sup>11</sup>כי האומר אני לכם שיבואו רבים ממזרח וממערב וינוחו עם אברהם ועם יצחק ועם יעקב במלכות שמים

<sup>12</sup>ובני המלכות יש לנו במחשכי גהינם ושם יהיה בכי ותחזק שנים.

<sup>13</sup>ויאמר יש''ו לשר המאות לך וכאשר האמנת יעשה לך. ונרפא הנער בעת ההיא.

## פרק ל''ג
<sup>14</sup>בעת ההיא בא יש''ו לבית פיטיירוס והנה חותנתו שוכבת מקדחת.

<sup>15</sup>ויגע לידה ויעזבה הקדחה. ותקם ותשרתהו.

<sup>16</sup>ויהי לעת הערב ויבאו אליו אחוזי השדים וירפאום במאמרו לבד וכל החולי ריפא

<sup>17</sup>לגמור מה שנאמר ע''י ישעיה הנביא ז''ל אכן חליינו הוא נשא ומכאובינו הוא סבלם.

## פרק ל''ד

<sup>18</sup>ויהי אחרי זאת וירא יש''ו חבורות רבות סביבותיו ויצוה ללכת עבר הים.

<sup>19</sup>ויקרב חכם א'' ויאמר לו אדו' אלך אחריך בכל מקום שתלך.

<sup>20</sup>ויען אליו יש''ו לשועלים חורים ולעוף קנים ולבן אדם בן הבתולה אין מקום להכניס ראשו.

<sup>21</sup>וא' מתלמדיו אמר לו עזוב אותי שאלך ואקבור את אבי.

<sup>22</sup>ויאמר לו יש''ו בא אחרי ועזוב המתים לקבור מתיהם.

## פרק ל''ה

<sup>23</sup>ויהי כאשר באו יש''ו באניה ויבואו תלמידיו אחריו.

<sup>24</sup>ויהי סער גדול בים והגלים הולכים מאד והאניה חשבה להשבר.

<sup>25</sup>ויקרבו אליו תלמידיו ויבקשו ממנו לאמר אדונינו הושיענו פן נאבד.

<sup>26</sup>ויאמר אליהם למה תתראו מקטני אמנה. ויקם ויצו לים ולרוחות שינוחו ומיד נחו.

<sup>27</sup>והאנשים אשר שם ראו תמהו ויאמרו מי הוא זה שהרוחות והים עושה רצונו.

## פרק ל''ו

<sup>28</sup>ויהי כאשר עבר הים ויעבור עבר הים במלכות גארגיזאני נקראים בלעז גיינטר''ארוס ויפגעו בו שנים אחוזי שדים יוצאים מהקברים משתגעים עד שלא יוכל איש לעבור בדרך ההיא.

<sup>29</sup>ויצעקו אליו לאמר מה לך עמנו יש''ו בן אלקים באת קודם הזמן לצערנו וגם להשמידנו? ויש''ו אמר להם צאו משם מחנות

רעות.

<sup>30</sup>ושם קרוב מהם עדרי חזירים רבים רועים.

<sup>31</sup>ויפגעו בו השדים יען יש לנו לצאת מכאן תן לנו רשות לבא באלו החזירים.

<sup>32</sup>ויאמר להם לכו. ויצאו השדים מהאנשים ויבאו בחזירים וילכו כל העדר בבהלה ונשמטו בים ומתו במים.

<sup>33</sup>ויפחדו הרועים ויברחו ויגידו בעיר הכל. ותהום כל העיר.

<sup>34</sup>ויצאו לקראת יש''ו. ויראו אותם ויחלו פניו לבלתי עבור בגבולם.

## פרק ל''ז 9

<sup>1</sup>ואז יש''ו בא באניה וישוטו וישובו לעירו.

<sup>2</sup>ויקרבו לפניו חולה א'' מכווץ בלעז פארא''לטיקו וישכב על מטתו וירא יש''ו אמונתם ויאמר לחולה תתחזק בני. באמונת האל כי נמחלו עונותיך.

<sup>3</sup>וקצת החכמים אומרים בלבם זהו מגדף.

<sup>4</sup>וירא יש''ו מחשבותם ויאמר אליהם למה תחשבו רעה בלבבכם.

<sup>5</sup>זהו קל לאמר נמחל עוניך או קום לך?

<sup>6</sup>רק להודיעכם שבן אדם יכול למחול עונות בארץ אז אמר לחולה קום וקח מיטתך ולך.

<sup>7</sup>ויקם וילך אל ביתו.

<sup>8</sup>ויראו החבורות ויראו מאד ויהללו לאל אשר נתן יכולת לבני אדם לעשות כאלה.

## פרק ל''ח

<sup>9</sup>ויהי כאשר עבר יש''ו משם וירא איש אחד יושב על שלחן החלוף מתתיה שמו בלעז מאט''יאו ויאמר לו לך אחרי ויקם וילך אחריו.

<sup>10</sup>ויוליכוהו לביתו לאכול. ויהי בעת אכלו והנה פריצים רבים ורשעים בשלחן והנה סועדים עם יש''ו ותלמידיו .

<sup>11</sup>ויראו הפרושים ויאמרו לתלמידיו למה רבכם יושב ואוכל עם

הפריצים והרשעים.

<sup>12</sup>וישמע יש''ו ויאמר בבריאים אינם צריכים רפואה כי אם החולה.

<sup>13</sup>לכו ולמדו הכתוב כי חסד חפצתי ולא זבח ולא באתי להשיב הצדיקים כי אם הרשעים.

## פרק ל''ט

<sup>14</sup>אז קרבו אליו תלמידי יוחנן ויאמרו לו למה אנו והפרושים מתענים הרבה פעמים ותלמידך אינם מתענים.

<sup>15</sup>ויען להם יש''ו ויאמר לא יוכלו חבירי החתן לבכות ולהתענות בהיותו עמהם. יבואו ימים וילקח מהם החתן ויצומו.

<sup>16</sup>לא יאבד איש חתיכת מלבוש חדש במלבוש ישן לחוזק החתיכה משוך מהמלבוש הבלויה ויקרע יותר.

<sup>17</sup>ולא ישימו יין חדש בכלים ישנים פן ישברו הכלים וישפוך היין והכלים יאבדו. רק חדש בכלי חדש ושניהם ישמרו.

## פרק ארבעים

<sup>18</sup>ויהי בדברו אליהם ויקרב שר אחד וישתחוה לו לאמר אדו' בתי אתה עתה מתה. בא נא ושים ידך עליה והחיה.

<sup>19</sup>ויקם יש''ו וילך הוא ותלמידיו עמו.

<sup>20</sup>והנה אשה אחת שופעת דם שתים עשרה שנה בא אחריו ותגע בציצית בגדו.

<sup>21</sup>ואומרת בלבבה אם אגע בלבושו לבד ארפא מיד.

<sup>22</sup>וישב פניו ויאמר אליה התחזקי בתי בש''ית שאמונתך רפאך. באותה שעה נרפאת

<sup>23</sup>ויהי בבואו בית השר וירא אנשים רבים בוכים.

<sup>24</sup>ויאמר אליהם צאו כולכם חוצה ואל תבכו שהנערה ישנה ולא מתה. ויהי כמצחק בעיניהם. ואומרים הלא אנו רואים שהיא מתה.

<sup>25</sup>ובהוציאם אותם החוצה בא אליה יש''ו ויגע בידה ותקם הנערה.

<sup>26</sup>ותצא שמועה זאת בכל הארץ ההיא.

## פרק מ''א

$^{27}$ויעבור משם יש''ו והנה שני עורים רצים אחריו וצועקים אליו חנינו בן דוד.

$^{28}$ויהי הבית ויקרבו אליו העורים. ויאמר

$^{29}$אמונתכם תרפא אתכם.

$^{30}$ותפקחנה עיני שניהם מיד ויראו. ויצום לאמר השמרו פן יודע הדבר.

$^{31}$והם יצאו ויגלוהו בכל הארץ ההיא.

## פרק מ''ב

$^{32}$ויצא משם יש''ו ויביאו לפניו איש אלם והשד בתוכו.

$^{33}$ויוציא את השד וידבר האלם. ויפלאו החבורות ויאמרו לא נראה כזה בישראל.

$^{34}$ויאמרו הפרושים באמת בשם השדים מוציא השדים.

$^{35}$ויסב כל הערים והמגדלים מלמד בבתי כנסיות ומבשר בשורות ומרפא כל חולי וכל מדוה.

$^{36}$וירא יש''ו החבורות ויחמול עליהם שהיו יגיעים ושוכבים כצאן אשר אין להם רועה.

$^{37}$אז אמר לתלמידיו הקמה מרובה והקוצרים מעטים.

$^{38}$חלו נא פני בעל הקמה וישלח הקוצרים רבים לקצור קומתו.

## פרק מ''ג 10

$^{1}$אז קרא יש''ו לי''ב תלמידיו ויתן להם יכולת על כל רוח טומאה להוציא מהאדם ולרפאת כל חולי וכל נגע.

$^{2}$ואלה שמות י''ב השלוחים נקראו אפוסט''ולוס סימ''ון נקרא פייטר''וס ואנדר''יאה אחיו

$^{3}$פיליפ''וס ובורטולאמיאוס יעקב נקרא גאי''מי ויוחנן אחיו בני זבדיאל טומא''ס ומתתיה הוא מאט''יאו מלוה בריבית בפרסום ויעקב אלופיאי וטריא''וס

$^{4}$שמעון כנעני לעז סימ''ון קאנא''נאיוס ויוד''א אסקאר''יוטה אשר אחר זה מסרהו.

$^{5}$אלה שנים עשר שלח יש''ו ויצו אליהם לאמר בארצות הגוים

אל תלכו ובערי השמרונים אל תבאו.

<sup>6</sup>לכו לצאן אשר נדחו מבית ישראל.

<sup>7</sup>ובשרו להם שתתקיים מלכות שמים.

<sup>8</sup>רפאו החולים והחיו המתים והנה טהרתם המצורעים והוציאו השדים מבני אדם. ואל תקבלו שכר. חנם קבלתם ובחנם תתנו.

<sup>9</sup>אל תצברו כסף וזהב ולא ממון בכיסכם

<sup>10</sup>ולא חליפות שמלות ולא מנעלים ולא מקל בידכם. ראוי הפועל לקבל די אכילתו.

<sup>11</sup>ובכל עיר ובכל מגדל אשר תבואו מי האיש הטוב שבתוכם ושם תנוחו עד שתצאו.

<sup>12</sup>ובבואכם אל הבית תנו להם שלום לאמר שלום בזאת הבית שלום לכל היושבים בתוכה.

<sup>13</sup>ואם תהיה הבית ההיא ראויה תבא שלומכם עליה ואם לא תהיה ראויה תשוב שלומכם לכם.

<sup>14</sup>ואשר לא יקבל אתכם ואשר לא ישמע אליכם תצאו מן הבית ההיא והעתקם רגליכם מן העפר.

<sup>15</sup>אמן אני דובר אליכם יותר טוב יהיה אל סרום ואל עמורה ביום ההוא מן העיר ההיא.

## פרק מ''ד

<sup>16</sup>הנני שולח אתכם כצאן בין הזאבים תהיו ערומים כנחשים וענוים כיונים.

<sup>17</sup>הזהרו בבני אדם. לא ימסרו אתכם בקהלותם ובבתי כנסיותם

<sup>18</sup>ולפחות ולמלכים. תוכלון בעדי להעיד להם ולגוים.

<sup>19</sup>כאשר יתפשו אתכם אם תחשבו מה שתאמרו שבשעה שתצטרכו יבא לכם מענה.

<sup>20</sup>אינכם המדברים כי אם רוח קדשו של אבי הוא הדובר בכם.

<sup>21</sup>ימסור האח את אחיו למות והאב לבנו ויקומו הבנים על האבות ויובילו אותם עד למות.

<sup>22</sup>ותהיו ללעג וזעוה לכל העמים על שמי אכן מי שיסבול עד

עת קץ יושע.

## פרק מ''ה

23עוד אמר יש''ו לתלמידיו כאשר ירדפו אתכם בעיר הזאת ברחו לאחרת אמן אני אומר לכם לא תשלימו לכם ערי ישראל עד כי יבא בן אדם.

24אין תלמיד גדול מרבו ולא העבד גדול מאדוניו.

25די לתלמיד להיות כרבו ולעבד כאדוניו. אם לבעל הבית יקראו בעל זבוב כ''ש לבני ביתו.

26אל תראו מהם שאין דבר שלא יראה ולא נעלם.

27אני אומר לכם בחשך אמרו אותו באור.

28ואל תפחדו מהורגי שאין בידם להרוג הנפשות רק פחדו לאשר יכולת בידו לאבד הנפש והגוף בגהינם.

29הלא שני צפורים אבדו בפרוטה אחת ולא תפול אחת מהם על הארץ כי אם ברצון אביכם שבשמים?

30הלא שערות ראשיכם כלם ספורים?

31אל תראו שטובים מצפורים אדם.

32המשבח אותי בפני אדם אשבחנו לפני אבי שבשמים.

## פרק מ''ו

34באותה שעה אמר יש''ו לתלמידיו אל תחשבו שבאתי לשים בארץ אלא חרב.

35באתי להפריד האדם הבן מאביו והבת מאמה.

36והאויבים להיות אהובים.

37האוהב אביו ואמו יותר ממני איני ראוי לו.

38

39האוהב את נפשו יאבדיה האובד אותי בשבילי ימצאנה.

40המקבל אתכם יקבל אותי והמקבל אותי יקבל את אשר שלחני.

41המקבל נביא לשם נביא שכר הנביא והמקבל צדיק לשם צדיק יקבל שכר הצדיק.

42והנותן כלי א'' של מים קרים לאחד מתלמידי הקטנים לשם

תלמידי אמן אני אומר לכם שלא יאבד שכרו.

## פרק מ''ז 11

<sup>1</sup>ויהי בכלות יש''ו לצוות לשנים עשר תלמידיו ויעבור משם ויצום ללמד ולהוכיח בעריהם.

<sup>2</sup>וישמע יוחנן בהיותו תפוס מעשה יש''ו וישלח שנים מתלמידיו <sup>3</sup>לאמר לו האתה הוא מי שעתיד לבא או נקוה אחר.

<sup>4</sup>ויען להם יש''ו לכו והגידו ליוחנן את אשר ראיתם ואשר שמעתם

<sup>5</sup>העורים רואים ופסחים הולכים והמצורעים נטהרים והחרשים שומעים והחיים מתים והענוים מתפשרים.

<sup>6</sup>ואשרי אשר לא יהיה נבוך בי.

<sup>7</sup>ויהי המה הולכים ויחל יש''ו לדבר אל החבורות מיוחנן. לראות מה יצאתם במדבר קנה מושלכת ברוח?

<sup>8</sup>או מה יצאתם לראות? התחשבו שיוחנן אדם לבוש בעדים רבים? הנה לובשי הבגדים רבים בבתי המלכים.

<sup>9</sup>א''כ מה יצאתם לראות נביא? באמת אני אומר לכם שזה גדול מנביא.

<sup>10</sup>זהו שנכתב בעדו הנני שולח מלאכי ופנה דרך לפני.

## פרק מ''ח

<sup>11</sup>עוד אמר יש''ו לתלמידיו באמת אני דובר לכם בכל ילדי הנשים לא קם גדול מיוחנן המטביל.

<sup>12</sup>מימיו עד עתה מלכות שמים עשוקה קורעים אותה.

<sup>13</sup>שכל הנביאים והתורה דברו על יוחנן.

<sup>14</sup>ואם תרצו לקבלו הוא אליה העתיד לבא.

<sup>15</sup>למי אזנים לשמוע ישמע.

## פרק מ''ט

<sup>16</sup>עוד אמר יש''ו זה הדור אדמהו לנערים היושבים בשוק קוראים זה לזה

<sup>17</sup>ואומרים שדנו ולא דקדקתם ספרנו לכם ולא בכיתם.

<sup>18</sup>כי בא יוחנן ואינו אוכל ושותה ואומרים עליו שהוא אחוז

משדים.

‏¹⁹וֹבן האדם בא לאכול ולשתות ואומר עליו שהוא זולל וסובא ואוהב לפריצים וחוטאים והסכלים שופטים לחכמים.

## פרק חמישים

‏²⁰אז התחיל יש''ו הנערים שנעשו מאותותיו ולא חזרו בתשובה.

‏²¹אי לך בורוזואים ואי לך בית שידה שאם בצור וסדום לעז טיראו דיטיר או סדומה נעשו האותות שנעשו בכם היו חוזרות בתשובה בזמן ההוא בשק ואפר.

‏²²אמן אני אומר לכם יותר קל יהיה לצור וסדום אכן.

‏²³ואתה כפר נחום אם לשמים תעלה? משם תורד. שאם בסדום נעשו מאותות שנעשו בך אולי תשאר. עד שאול תורד.

‏²⁴אמן אני אומר לך שיותר קל יהיה לארץ סדום ליום הדין ממך.

## פרק נ''א

‏²⁵בעת ההיא נתרומם יש''ו ואומר אני ישתבח אני בורא שמים והארץ שהסתרת דברים אלה מהחכמים והנבונים וגלית אותם לעניים.

‏²⁶אמנם כי כן ישר לפניך אבי.

‏²⁷הכל נתון לי מאת אבי. ואין מכיר את הבן אלא האב בלבד ולאב אין מכיר הבן ולאשר ירצה הבן לגלותו.

‏²⁸בואו אליו כל היגעים ונושאי העמל ואני אעזור אתכם לשאת עולכם.

‏²⁹צאו עולי עולכם ולמדו ממני ותכירו כי עני אני וטוב ובר הלבב ותמצאו מרגוע לנפשותיכם

‏³⁰רק ומשאי קל.

## פרק נ''ב 12

‏¹בעת ההיא עבר יש''ו בקמות ביום השבת ותלמידיו רעבים התחילו לעקור השבולים ולפרוך אותם בין ידיהם ולאכול אותם.

‏²ויראו הפרושים ויאמרו אליו הנה תלמידך עושים דבר שאינו נכון לעשות ביום השבת.

³ויען להם יש''ו ולא קראתם מה שעשה דוד כשהיה רעב ואנשיו

⁴בבית האלקים שאכלו מלחם הפנים בלעז פא''ן סאג''רה שאינו נאכל אלא לכהנים בלבד .

⁵וגם בתורה לא קראתם שהכהנים בבית המקדש מחללים לפעמים השבתות ואין להם חטא?

⁶אמן אני אומר לכם שמקדש גדול ממנו הוא.

⁷אילו ידעתם מהו חסד חפצתי ולא זבה לא הייתם מחייבים התמימים.

⁸שבן אדם אדון השבת.

## פרק נ''ג

⁹ויהי לקצת הימים ויעבור משם יש''ו ויבא בבתי כנסיותם.

¹⁰ושם אדם וידו יבשה וישאלוהו לאמר אם מותר בשבת לרפאתו.

¹¹ויאמר להם מי בכם שיש לו צאן אחת ותפול בשוחה ביום השבת ולא יקימנה.

¹²כ''ש האדם שהוא טוב ממנה. לפיכך מותר לעשות ויש לאדם לעשות יותר טוב בשבת.

¹³אז אמר לאיש נטה ידך. ויט ידו ותשב כמו האחרת.

¹⁴ואז נוסדו הפרושים וינכלו אליו להמיתו.

## פרק נ''ד

¹⁵ויהי אחרי זאת וידע יש''ו ויט משם וילכו אחריו חולים רבים וירפא את כולם.

¹⁶ויצום לאמר לבל יגלוהו

¹⁷לקיים מה שנאמר ע''י ישעה

¹⁸הן נערי אשר בחרתי בחירי רצתה נפשי אתן רוחי עליו ומשפט לגוים יגיד.

¹⁹ולא ירהה ולא ירוץ ולא ישמע אחד בחוץ.

²⁰קנה רצוץ לא ישבור ופשתה כהה לא יכבנה עד ישים לנצח משפט

²¹ולשמו גוים ייחלו.

## פרק נ''ה

22אז הובא לפניו אדם אחד עור ואלם והשד בתוכו וירפא אותו. וראו

23ונפלאו החבורות ויאמרו הלא זה זה בן דוד.

24וישכימו הפירושים וישמעו ויאמרו זה אינו מוציא השדים אלא בבעל זבוב בעל השדים.

25וידע מחשבותם יש''ו ויאמר אליהם במשל כל מלכות שביניכם מחלוקת תשומם וכן כל עיר ובית שתפול מחלוקת בתוכם לא יתקיים.

26ואת השטן מוציא שטן אחר מחלוקת ביניכם איך תעמוד מלכותו?

27ואם אני מוציא השדים בבעל זבוב בנים שלכם למה לא הוציאם ולזה יהיו הם שופטיכם.

28ואם אני מוציא השדים ברוח אלקים באמת בא קץ מלכות.

29ואיך יוכל איש לבא בבית גבור לקחת את כליו אם לא יקשור אותו תחילה? ואח''כ ישלול בביתו.

## פרק נ''ו

30מי שאינו עמדי לנגדי. הוא מה שלא יתחבר עמי יכפור בפועל.

31כן אני אומר לכם שכל חטא וגדוף ימחל לבני אדם וגדוף הרוח לא ימחל.

32וכל האומר דבר נגד בן האדם ימחל לו. וכל האומר דבר נגד רוח הקדוש לא ימחל לו לא בעה''ז ולא בעה''ב.

33עשו עץ טוב כפרי טוב או עץ רע כפרי רע שהאמת מן הפרי יודע העץ.

34משפחת פתנים איך תוכלו לדבר טובות בהיותכם רעים? והלא הפה מתעוררת הלב מדברת.

35אדם טוב מאוצר לב טוב יוציא טוב ואדם רע מאוצר לב רע ווציא רע.

36אומר אני לכם שמכל הדברים אשר ידבר האדם חייב לתת

חשבון ליום הדין.

<sup>37</sup>על פי דבריך תהיה נשפט ועל פי מעשיך תתחייב.

## פרק נ"ז

<sup>38</sup>בעת ההיא בא ליש"ו קצת פירושים וחכמים לאמר נרצה לראות אות מהשמים בעבורך.

<sup>39</sup>ויאמר להם דור רע וחנף מבקש אות ואות לא ינתן לו אלא האות של יונה.

<sup>40</sup>שכאשר היה במעי הדגה ג' ימים וג' לילות כן יהיה בן אדם בבטן הארץ ג' ימים וג' לילות בקבר.

<sup>41</sup>אנשי ננוה יקומו למשפט עם זה הדור וירשיעו אותו כי חזרו בתשובה לדברי יונה ואני גדול מיונה.

<sup>42</sup>מלכת שבא בלעז ריזינה "די אישטריאה תקום למשפט עם זה הדור ותרשיעם שבאה מקצות הארץ לשמוע חכמת שלמה והנני גדול משלמה.

<sup>43</sup>וכיוצא רוח טומאה מהאדם הולך בציות מבקש מנוח ולא ימצא.

<sup>44</sup>אז אומר אשיב לביתי אשר יצאתי ממנו ובא ומוצא אותו ריק בטוח ונכון.

<sup>45</sup>אז יקח שבעה רוחות יותר רעים ממנו ובאים עמו ויושבים שם ויהיה אחרית האדם רע מראשיתו. כן יהיה לדור הרע הזה.

## פרק נ"ח

<sup>46</sup>עודנו מדבר על כל החבורות והנה אמו ואחיו עומדים בחוץ מבקשים ממנו לדבר עמו.

<sup>47</sup>ויאמר לו אדם אחד הנה אמך ואחיך מבקשים לראותך.

<sup>48</sup>ויען למגיד מי אחי ומי אמי.

<sup>49</sup>ויפרוש כפיו על תלמידיו ויאמרו אלו הם אמי ואחי.

<sup>50</sup>כל העושה רצון אבי שבשמים הוא אחי ואחיותי ואמי.

## פרק נ"ט 13

<sup>1</sup>ביום ההוא יצא יש"ו מהבית וישב על שפת הים.

<sup>2</sup>ויתחברו אליו חבורות עד שנצטרך לבא באניה וכל החבורה

עומדת בחוץ.

³וידבר להם דברים רבים במשלים ויאמר להם איש יוצא מביתו בבוקר לזרוע את זרעו.

⁴ובזרעו נפל ממנו בדרך ואכל אותו העוף.

⁵וממנה נפלה באבן שאין שם עובי עפר ובצמחו נתייבש לפי שאין שם עפר לרוב.

⁶ובחום השמש עליו נשרף ונתייבש שאין לו שורש.

⁷וממנו נפל בין הקוצים ויגדלוהו הקוצים ויעמדוהו.

⁸וממנו נפל בארץ טובה ויעשה פרי ותבואה האחד מאה והשני ששים והשלישי שלשים.

⁹למי אזנים לשמוע ישמע.

¹⁰ויקרבו אליו תלמידיו ואמרו לו תלמידיו למה תדבר במשלים.

¹¹ויאמר שלכם נתן מלכות שמים להכיר ולא להם.

¹²למי שיש לו ינתן עוד ולמי שאין לו מה שהוא חושב ילקח ממנו.

¹³לזה אני מדבר במשלים שהם רואים ואינם רואים שומעים ואינו שומעים

¹⁴לגמור מה שנאמר ע׳׳י ישעיה הנביא לך ואמרת לעם הזה שמוע שמוע ולא תדעו וראו ראה ואל וכו׳.

¹⁵השמן לב העם הזה ואזניו הכבד ועיניו השע פן יראה בעיניו וכו׳.

¹⁶ואשרי עיניכם שרואות ואזניכם ששומעות.

¹⁷אמן אני דובר לכם שנביאים רבים וצדיקים התאוו לראות מה שאתם רואים ולא ראו ולשמוע מה שאתם שמעים ולא שמעו.

¹⁸ואתם שמעו משל הזורע.

¹⁹הזורע הוא בן אדם והזרע שנפל בדרך כל השומע מלכות שמים ולא יבין. יבא השטן ויחתוף מלבו כל מה שנזרע בו. וזהו הזרע שנפל על הדרך.

²⁰ואשר נפל על האבן הוא השומע דבר האל וקבלנו מיד בשמחה.

²¹והוא בלא שורש ומבוכה ובבא מעט צער וצרה להם השטן

משכחו מלבם.

22ואשר נפל בקוצים זה השומע את הדבר ובחמדתו לאסוף עושר השטן משכחו דבר האל ולא יעשה פרי.

23ואשר נפל בארץ הטובה הוא השומע את הדבר ומבין ועושה פרי ר''ל ממעשים טובים. ויוציא מן הא'' מאה ומן השני ששים ומן השלישי שלשים. הא'' מאה זהו מטהרת הלב וקדושת הגוף. ומהאחד ששים זהו מפרישות האישה. ומהשלישי שלשים זהו מקדושה בזיווג בגוף ובלב.

## פרק ששים

24וישם לפניהם משל אחר. מלכות שמים דומה לאיש הזורע כשזרעו זרע טוב.

25ויהי כאשר בני אדם ישנים בא שונאו ויזרע על החטים זון בעז ברייא''גה וילך.

26ויהי כאשר גדולה העשב לעשות פרי וראה הזון

27ויקרבו עבדי בעל השדה אליו ויאמרו לו אדונינו הלא זרע טוב זרעת. ומאין היה הזון?

28אמר להם שונאי עשו זה ויאמרו לו עבדיו נעקור הזון.

29ויאמר להם לא פן תעקרו החטה.

30אלא הניחו זה וזה ויגדל עד הקציר ובעת הקציר אמר לקוצרים לקטו הזון ראשונה וקשרו אותה חבילות חבילות לשרוף והחטה תנו באוצר.

## פרק סייא

31וישם לפניהם משל אחר. מלכות שמים דומה לגרגיר חרדל שיקח אותו אדם ויזרעהו בשדה.

32והוא דק מכל זרעונים ובגדלו יגדל על כל העשבים ונעשה עץ גדול עד שעוף השמים יצאילו באנפא.

33וידבר להם משל אחר. מלכות שמים דומה לשאור שמביא אותו האלה בשלש סאים קמח ויחמיץ את כולו.

34כל המשלים האלה דבר יש''ו לחבורות ובלי משל לא היה דובר אליהם.

³⁵לקיים מה שנאמר ע''פ הנביא אפתחה במשל פי אביעה
חדות מני קדם.

## פרק ס''ב

³⁶אז נפרד יש''ו מן החבורות ויבא אל הבית. ויקרבו אליו
תלמידיו ובקשו ממנו לפרוש להם משל הזון.

³⁷ויען להם ויאמר להם הזורע זרע טוב הוא האדם

³⁸והשדה הוא העולם הזה ופרי הטוב הם הצדיקים והזון הם
הרשעים.

³⁹והשונא שזרע אותו הוא השטן והקמה אחרית העה''ב
והקוצרים הם המלאכים.

⁴⁰וכאשר לקטו הקוצרים הזון לשרוף כן יהיה באחרית הימים.

⁴¹ישלח בן אדם את ממלאכיו לעקור ממלכותו כל רשע וכל
פועלי און.

⁴²וישליחו אותם במדורת אש ושם יהיה בכי וחריקת שינים.

⁴³אז יזהירו הצדיקים כשמש במלכות אביהם. למי אזנים
לשמוע ישמע.

## פרק ס''ג

⁴⁴עוד אמר יש''ו לתלמידיו מלכות שמים היא דומה לאדם
המוציא מטמון אשר יסתירוהו ובשמחת הממון ימכור כל אשר
לו ויקנה השדה בעדו.

⁴⁵ועוד מלכות שמים דומה לאדם סוחר המבקש אבנים יקרות.

⁴⁶וכאשר ימצא אחת טובה ימכור כל אשר לו ויקנה אותה.

⁴⁷מלכות שמים דומה לרשת בתוך הים שכל מיני דגים נאספים
בה.

⁴⁸וכאשר תמלא יוציאוה לחוץ ויוצאים הדייגים ובוחרים הטובים
בכליהם והרעים משליכים חוצה.

⁴⁹כן יהיה באחרית הימים יצאו המלאכים ויבדילו הרשעים
מתוך הצדיקים.

⁵⁰וישליכו אותם במדורות אש שם יהיה בכי וחריקת שינים.

⁵¹ויאמר להם הבנתם זה. ויאמרו כן.

⁵²לזאת כל חכם ידמה במלכות שמים לאדם אבי הטף המוציא

מאוצרו דברים חדשים גם ישנים.

## פרק ס''ד
<sup>53</sup>ויהי אחרי זאת כאשר כלה יש''ו הדברים האלה עבר משם.

<sup>54</sup>ובא לארצו והיה מלמד לאנשים בבתי כנסיות. והפרושים נפלאו ויאמרו בלבם מאין בה לזה החכמה וכח לעשות אלו הפעולות.

<sup>55</sup>אין בן זה הנפח ומרים? הלא ידעתם שכל אלו אמו מרים ואחיו ג' יוסף ושמע''ון ויהוד''ה

<sup>56</sup>ואחיותיו. הלא ידעתם שכל אלו עמנו? ומאין בא לזה כל אלה?

<sup>57</sup>והיו נבוכים בו. ויען להם יש''ו אין נביא שאין לו כבוד כ''א בארצו ועירו וביתו.

<sup>58</sup>ולא רצה לעשות שם שום אות למיעוט אמונתם.

## פרק ס''ה 14
<sup>1</sup>בעת ההיא שמע הורוד''וס טיטרא''קה שמועות יש''ו.

<sup>2</sup>ויאמר לעבדיו הנה אני מאמין שאלו הפלאות עושה יוחנן המטביל.

<sup>3</sup>שהיה לפי שהורוד''וס תפש ליוחנן בימים ההם ויאסרהו במאסר לפי שהיה מוכיחו שלא יקח לאורדיסא לאשה שהיתה אשת אחיו.

<sup>4</sup>והיה אומר לו יוחנן אינה ראויה לך.

<sup>5</sup>והנה הורוד''וס היה רוצה להורגו לולי יראת העם שלנביא היה ביניהם.

<sup>6</sup>ובמשתה יום הולד את הורודוס קרא לגדולי המלכות לאכול עמו ובעוד שהיו אוכלים היתה בתו מרקדת ביניהם וייטב להורודוס.

<sup>7</sup>וישבע לה שיתן לה את כל אשר תשאל ממנו.

<sup>8</sup>והנערה מיוסרת מיומה שאלה ראש יוחנן המטביל באגן א''.

<sup>9</sup>והמלך נעצב מאד בעד השבועה שעשה בפני הקרואים ויצו להעשות כן.

<sup>10</sup>וישלח לשחוט יוחנן בבית הסוהר.

<sup>11</sup>ויביאו ראש יוחנן באגן ויתנוהו לנערה והנערה נתנה לאמה.

<sup>12</sup>ויבאו תלמידי יוחנן וישאו הגוף ויקברוהו והתלמידים הגידו הדבר ליש''ו.

<sup>13</sup>וכשמוע יש''ו נסע משם באניה וילך למדבר יהודה. וכשמוע החבורות וילכו אחריו מכל המדינות.

<sup>14</sup>וכשיצאו ראה אחריו עם רב ויט אליו חסד וירפא כל מחלותם.

<sup>15</sup>ובעת ערב קרבו אליו תלמידיו ויאמרו לו זה המקום צר עובר. עזוב החבורות שילכו במגדלים ויקחו הצורך אליהם.

<sup>16</sup>ויען להם יש''ו אינם צריכים לילך תנו להם לאכל.

<sup>17</sup>והם ענו אין לנו בכאן כי אם חמש ככרות שני דגים.

<sup>18</sup>ויאמר להם הביאו אותם אלי.

<sup>19</sup>ויצו שישובו העם על העשבים. וכשישבו לקח החמש ככרות והשני דגים ובהיותו מביט לשמים ברך אותם ויחלקם ויתנם לתלמידיו והתלמידים חלקו לסייעות.

<sup>20</sup>ואכלו כלם וישבעו. וכן מהדגים אכלו כרצונם. ואחר שתכלו לקחו הפתיתים הנשארות וימלאו מהם שנים עשר סאים.

<sup>21</sup>ויהי מספר האוכלים חמשת אלפים אנשים מלבד הנשים והטף.

## פרק ס''ו

<sup>22</sup>ואחרי זה צוה לתלמידיו לכנס באניה וישליחו קודם ממנו בעיר שהחבורות הולכות.

<sup>23</sup>ואחר שעזב החבורות עלה להר והתפלל לבדו ויהי לעת ערב והוא לבדו עומד.

<sup>24</sup>והאניה באמצע הים וגליהם היו דוחפות אותה לפי שהרוח היה מנגד.

<sup>25</sup>למשמרה הרביעית מהלילה בא להם יש''ו הולך בים.

<sup>26</sup>וכאשר ראוהו תלמידיו הלך בים נבהלו בשר בחושבם שהיה שד ומרוב פחדם היו צועקים.

<sup>27</sup>ואז ענה להם יש''ו ויאמר להם יהיה אמונה בכם שאני הוא

ואל תיראו.

28ויען פייט''רוס ויאמר לו אדו' אם אתה הוא צוה אותי לבא אליך במים.

29ויאמר לו יש''ו בא. וירד פייט''רוס מהספינה והלך בים ובא ליש''ו.

30ובראותו חוזק הרוח הרוח פחד מאד ובהתחילו ליטבע צעק ואמר אדו'הושיעני.

31ומיד יש''ו האריך ידו ולקחו ואמר לו אדם מאמונה מעוטה למה נסתפקת.

32וכאשר עלו באינה נח הרוח

33ואשר בספינה השתחוו לו ואמרו באמת אתה הוא בן אלקים.

34

35וכאשר הכירוהו אנשי המקום שלחו בכל אותו המלכות והביאו לו כל החולים מכל מדוים.

36וחלו פניו ירצו לעוזבם יגעו בכנף מעילו וכל אשר נגע נתרפא.

## פרק ס''ז 15

1אז בא אל יש''ו החכמים והפרושים ויאמרו אליו

2למה עוברים תלמידך תקנות הראשונות שהם אינם רוחצים ידיהם קודם האכילה.

3ויאמר להם יש''ו ולמה אתם עוברים מאמרי האל בעד תקנותיכם

4שהאל אמר כבד את אביך ואת אמך ומכה אביו ואמו מות יומת.

5ואתם אומרים שאיזה דבר יאמר האדם לאביו ולאמו שבאיזה נדבה שיתן בעד אותו חטא שיכופר לו אותו עון.

6ולא יכבד אביו ואמו ואתם מבזים אמרי אל בתקנותיכם.

7היו חנפים הנה ישעיה ניבא מכם ואמר

8כה אמר ה'' יען כי נגש העם הזה בפיו ובשפתיו כבדוני ולבו רחק ממני

9ותהי יראתם אותי מצות אנשים מלומדה.

וֵישׁ"וֹ קרא לסיעות ויאמר להם שמעו והביטו.[10]

הנכנס בעד הפה אינו מכלכל האדם אבל היוצא מהפה[11] מכלכל האדם.

אז קרבו אליו תלמידיו ויאמרו לו דע שהפרושים נבוכים בעד[12] דבר זה.

ויען להם יש"וֹ כל נטיעה שלא נטעה אבי שבשמים תשחת.[13]

הניחו אותם שהעורים מדריכים לעורים ואם עור ידריך עור[14] אחר יפלו שניהם בבור.

ויען לו פייט"רוס אדוני פרוש לנו זאת החדה.[15]

ויען להם יש"וֹ עדיין אתם מבלי דעת.[16]

לא תבינו אתם שכל הנכנס בעד הפה הולך לבטן והכל הולך[17] בעד המקום הטבעי?

והיוצא בעד הפה מתנועע מהלב וזהו המכלכל האדם.[18]

לפי שמחלל הלב יוצא התרמית והרציחה והנאופים והגנבות[19] ועדות שקרים והקללות.

וכל אלה הדברים הם המבלבלים האדם. אמנם האכילה בלי[20] רחיצת ידים אינה מכלכלת האדם.

## פרק ס"ח

ואחר שאמר יש"וֹ זה הלך בגלילי צור וסדום.[21]

ותבוא לפניו אשה כנענית באה מארצות מזרח צועקת אליו[22] אדוני בן דוד חנני שבתי אחוזת השדים.

וֵישׁ"וֹ לא ענה דבר. ותלמידיו קרבו אליו ויאמרו לו אדונינו[23] למה אתה מניח לזאת האשה צועקת אחרינו.

ויען להם יש"וֹ לא שלחוני כי אם לצאן אובדות מבית ישראל.[24]

והאשה משתחוה לו ואומרת אדני עוזרני.[25]

ויאמר לה יש"וֹ לא טוב שיקח האדם הפת מבניו ויתננו[26] לכלבים.

ותען האשה פעמים רבים אוכלים הכלבים הפתיתים[27] הנופלים משלחן אדוניהם.

ויען לה יש"וֹ אשה גדולה אמונתיך יעשה לך כאשר שאלת.[28] ומהעת ההוא והלאה נרפאת בתה.

## פרק ס''ט

<sup>29</sup>וכאשר הלך יש''ו משם הלך עבר הגליל להר. בעומדו שם <sup>30</sup>ראה עם רב מביטים הרבה צולעים ומנוגעים ופסחים ורבים אחרים ויפלו לרגליו וירפאם.

<sup>31</sup>והעם היו תמהים איך האלמים היו מדברים והפסחים הולכים והעורים רואים וכלם משבחים לאל.

<sup>32</sup>אז אמר יש''ו לתלמידיו יש לי רחמנות מהם שהם מיחלים אותי זה שני ימים שעברו ואין להם מה שיאכלו. ואיני רוצה להוליכם בתענית יען לא יחלשו בדרך.

<sup>33</sup>ויענו לו תלמידיו ומאין אנו יכולים למצוא לחם במדבר הזה לשביע לעם.

<sup>34</sup>ויען יש''ו ויאמר להם כמה ככרים לחם לכם. ויענו שבעה ומעט דגים.

<sup>35</sup>ויצו יש''ו לעם לישב ע''ג העשבים.

<sup>36</sup>ולקח השבעה ככרות וישברם ונתנם לתלמידיו והם נתנו לעם.

<sup>37</sup>ויאכלו כולם וישבעו והותר שבעה סאים.

<sup>38</sup>והאוכלים היו במספר ארבעת אלפים אנשים לבד הנשים והטף.

## פרק שבעים 16

<sup>39</sup>אחר זה נכנס יש''ו בספינה ובא לארץ מאצידונייא

<sup>1</sup>ויבואו אליו החכמים והפרושים מנסים אותו וילמדם איזה אות מהשמים.

<sup>2</sup>ויען להם יש''ו חנפים אתם אומרים ערב מחר יום צח יהיה לפי שהשמים אדומים

<sup>3</sup>ובבקר אתם אומרים היום ימטיר שהשמים חשוכים. א''כ אתם יודעים משפט מראים השמים ואין אתם יודעים משפט הזמנים.

<sup>4</sup>זרע מרעים שאל אות ואות לא ינתן להם כי אם אות של יונה הנביא. ואז נפרד והלך לו.

5וכאשר יש''ו היה בשפת הים אמר לתלמידיו שיכינו לחם והוא נכנס לספינה עם תלמידיו ותלמידיו שכחו ולא הכניסו שום לחם.

6

7

8ויש''ו אמר להם אתם מעטי השכל חושבים שאין לכם לחם.

9-12ואין אתם זוכרים מהחמשה ככרות וארבע אלף איש וכמה סאים נשארו? ולכן תבינו שאיני מדבר מהחלמיש וגם מהלחמים הטבעיים אבל אני אומר לכם שתשארו מהנהגת הפרושים והצדוקים.

## פרק ע''א

13ויצא יש''ו אל ארץ סוריא''ה וארץ פיל''ופ נקרא פיליב''וס וישאל לתלמידיו לאמר מה אומרים בני אדם בשבילי.

14ויאמרו אליו מהם אומרים שהוא יוחנן המטביל ומהם אומרים שהוא אליהו ומהם ירמיהו או א'' מהנביאים.

15ויאמר להם יש''ו ואתם מה אומרים בשבילי.

16ויען שמעון נקרא פייט''רוס ויאמר אתה משיח לעז קריסט''ו בן אלקים חיים שבאתה בזה העולם.

17ויאמרו אליו יש''ו אשריך שמעון בר יונה שבשר ודם לא גלה לך כי אם אבי שבשמים.

18ואני אומר לך שאתה אבן ואני אבנה עליך בית תפלתי. ושערי גהינם לא יוכלו נגדך

19לפי שאני אתן לך מפתחות מלכות השמים. וכל אשר תקשור בארץ יהיה קשור בשמים וכל אשר תתיר בארץ יהיה מותר בשמים.

20אז צוה לתלמידיו לבל יאמרו שהוא משיח.

## פרק ע''ב

21מכאן ואילך התחיל יש''ו לגלות לתלמידיו שהוא צריך ללכת לירושלם ולשאת עול רבים מהכהנים וזקני העם עד שיהרגוהו ויום השלישי יקום.

²²ויקחוהו פייט''רוס בינו לבינו והתחיל להוכיח לאמר חלילה לך להיות לך כן אדו'.

²³וישב יש''ו ויבט אליו ויאמר לו לך השטן לא תמרה פי שאינך מכיר דבר האל כי אם דברי השדם.

²⁴אז דבר יש''ו לתלמידיו מי שירצה לבא אחרי יבזה עצמו ויקח את השתי וערב ר''ל שקרב עצמו למיתה וילך אחרי.

²⁵כל הרוצה להושיע נפשו יאבד אותה בעדי והמאבד את חייו בעה''ז בשבילי יושיע נפשו לחיי העה''ב.

²⁶מה בצע לאדם אם ירויח את כל העולם אם נפשו יאבד לעד ואיזה תמורה טובה יעשה האדם אם בעד הדברים ההווים והנפסדים יתן נפשו לדין גהינם.

²⁷כי בן האל יבא בכבד אביו שבשמים עם מלאכיו להשיב לכל איש כמפעלו.

²⁸אמן אני אומר לכם שיש מהעומדים פה שלא יטעמו מות עד שיראו בן אלוה בא במלכותו.

## פרק ע''ג 17

¹אתר ששה ימים לקח יש''ו לפייט''רוס וגם יעקב לעז גאי''מי ויוחנן אחיו ויוליכם אל הר גבוה משם להתפלל הוא.

²ובעוד שהיה מתפלל השתנה לפניהם וקרן עור פניו כשמש ומלבושיו לבנים כשלג.

³אליהם משה ואליהו מדברים עמו והגידו ליש''ו כל מה שיקראהו בירושלם. ופייט''רוס וחביריו היו נרדמים. נים ולא נים תיר ולא תיר. ראו גופו ושני אנשים עמו.

⁴וכאשר הלכו אז אמר פייט''רוס ליש''ו טוב להיות בכאן. ונעשה פה שלש משכנות לך אחד ולמשה אחד ולאליהו אחד שלא היה יודע מה היה דובר.

⁵עודנו מדבר והנה ענן שכסה אותם ויבהלו עד מאד ובעוד שהם תחת הענן שמעו מתוך הענן קול מדבר ואומר הנה זה בני יקירי וחפצי בו אליו תשמעון.

⁶וישמעו התלמידים ויפלו על פניהם ארצה וייראו מאד.

⁷וכאשר נפסק הקול ויאמר להם יש''ו קומו אל תיראו.

⁸וישאו עיניהם ולא ראו כי אם יש״ו בלבד.

## פרק ע״ד

⁹וירד יש״ו מן ההר ויצו להם לאמר אל תדברו לאיש המראה אשר ראיתם עד שיקום בן האדם מן המות

¹⁰וישאלוהו לו תלמידיו לאמר מה חכמים אומרים שאליה יבא ראשונה.

¹¹ויען להם ויאמר אמנם אליה יבא ויושיע כל העולם.

¹²אומר אני לכם שכבר בא ולא הכירוהו ועשו בו כרצונם. פן יעשו כבן אדם.

¹³אז הבינו התלמידים שבשבל יוחנן המטביל היה מדבר זה.

## פרק ע״ה

¹⁴ויהי בבואו אל החבורות ויבא לפניו איש כורע על ברכיו.

¹⁵ויאמר אדוני חנני וחוסה על בני כי נבעת מרוח רעה וחולה מאד וחורק את שיניו ומקטף בפיו ונופל מקומתו ארצה ונופל פעמים באש ופעמים במים.

¹⁶והביאותיו לתלמידך ולא יוכלו לרפאתו.

¹⁷ויען יש״ו ויאמר דור רע אוי לכם אתם הכופרים עד מתי אהיה עמכם ועד מתי אשא טרחכם. הביאוהו אלי.

## מרקוס ט:כ עד ט:כ״ה

והביאוהו אליו ומיד שיש״ו ראהו השטן מכניעו ומפילו לארץ והתחיל מתעפר ומתקצף.

ויש״ו שאל לאבי הנער כמה זמן שהשטן לקחו. והאב השיבו מזמן פלוני והלאה.

והרבה פעמים הפילו באש ובמים בעניין יוכל השמידו. ואם אתה אדו' בשום עניין תוכל לעוזרו עזרהו. וישא האיש חן בעיניו ונתמלא רחמים עליו.

ואמר לו אם תוכל להאמין כל דבר תוכל להשלים לפי שלמאמין כל הדברים קלים.

ומיד בכה בצעקה אבי הנער ואמר אדו' אני מאמין אמנם עוזרני לפי אמונתי.

וכאשר ראה יש''ו שהעם מתקבצים לזה ואמר לו חזק ואלם
הנני מצור שתצא מכאן והלאה לא תשוב כאן עוד.
והשטן יצא צועק ומכאיב והנער נשאר כמה בעניין שרבים היו
אומרים שהוא מת.
ויש''ו לקחו והעמידו וקם.
וכאשר נכנס יש''ו לבית

## מתתיה

[19] אז קרבו התלמידים ליש''ו בסתר ויאמרו אליו מדוע לא נוכל
אנחנו להוציאו.
[20] ויאמר להם למיעוט אמונתכם. אמן אני אומר לכם אם יהיה
בכם מן האמונה כגרגיר חרדל אם תאמינו להר הזה תאמרו
סורו ויסור וכל דבר לא יבצר מכם.
[21] וזה המין מן השדים לא יצא כי אם בתפילה וצום.

## פרק ע''ו

[22] המה בגליל ויאמר יש''ו בן האדם ימסר ליד בני האדם.
[23] ויהרגוהו וביום השלישי יקום.
[24] ויבואו כפר נחום מרתה ויקרבוהו מקבלי המכס לפייט''רוס
ויאמר אליהם רביכם אוני נוהג ונותן מכס.
[25] ויאמרו כן. ויבואו בבית והקדים יש''ו לאמר אליו לפייט''רוס
מה נראה לך פייט''רוס מלכי ארץ ממי לוקחים מכס מן בניהם
או מן הנכרים.
[26] ויען אליו מן הנכרים. ויאמר להם יש''ו אם כן הבנים תפשים.
ויאמר לא תהיו בעבר זה נבהלים.
[27] ויאמר לפייט''רוס לך לים והשלך חכה ואותו דג שתקח
ראשונה תמצא בפיו מטבע כסף ואותו תתן בעדינו.

## פרק ע''ז 18

[1] בעת ההיא קרבו התלמידים אל יש''ו ויאמרו אליו מי אתה
חושב שהוא גדול במלכות שמים.
[2] ויקרא נער אחד (קטן וישימהו בתוכם.
[3] ויאמר אני אומר אם לא תשובו להיות כנער הזה לא תבואו

במ''ש.

4

⁵והמקבל נער א') כזה על שמי מקבל.

⁶ואשר יכשיל אחד מהנערים הקטנים המאמינים בי טוב לו שיקשור פלח רכב על צוארו ויוטל במצולות ים.

⁷(אוי ליושבי תבל מפני המבוכות שצריכות המבוכות לבא.) ויאמר אוי לאדם שיבא בשבלו.

⁸ואם ידך ורגלך יכשילך תכריתהו ותכשילהו ממך. טוב לך לבא בחיים עוד או פסח מהיות לך ידים ורגלים לתתך באש עולמית.

⁹ואם עיניך תכשילך ותקרה ותשליכה ממך. טוב לך לבא בחיים בעין אחד מהיות לך עינים ולתתך בגהינם.

¹⁰והזהרו פן תדינו אחת מהנערים הקטנים. אומר אני לכם למלאכיהם הם רואים תמיד בני אבי שבשמים.

¹¹ובן אדם בטל להושיע האויבים.

## פרק ע''ח

¹²מה יראה לכם אם יהיה לאיש מאה צאן ופרח אחת מהן הלא יעזוב תשעים ותשעה בהרים וילך לבקש הנדחה.

¹³ואם ימצאנה אמן אני אומר לכם שישמח עליה יותר מהתשעים ותשעה אשר לא נדחו.

¹⁴כן לא ירצה אב שבשמים שיאבד א'' מהנערים.

## פרק ע''ט

¹⁵בעת ההיא אמר יש''ו לשמעון נקרא פייט''רוס אם יחטא לך אחיך הוכיחנו בינו לבינך. אם ישמע אליך קנית את אחיך.

¹⁶ואם לא ישמע אליך הוכיחנו בפני אחר ואם בכל אלה לא ישמע לך תוסיף עוד אחד או שנים לפנים שנים או שלשה עדים שעל פי שנים או שלשה עדים יקום דבר.

¹⁷ואם בכל אלה לא ישמע אמור אותו בקהל ואם לא ישמע בקהל חשוב אותו כמנודה ואויב ואכזר.

¹⁸אמן אני אומר לכם שכל אלה אשר תאסרו בארץ אסור הוא

בשמים וכל אשר תתירו בארץ מותר יהיה בשמים.

$^{19}$וגם אני אומר לכם אם ירצו שנים מכם לשים שלים בארץ כל אשר יבקשו יהיה לכם מאת שבשמים.

$^{20}$ובכל מקום שיתחברו שנים או שלשה על שמי שם אנכי בתוככם.

$^{21}$אז קרב פייט''רוס אליו לאמר אדוני אם יחטא לי אחי עד שבע פעמים אמחול לו.

$^{22}$ויאמר לו יש''ו איני אומר לך עד שבע כי אם עד שבעים ושבעה.

<u>פרק פ''</u>

$^{23}$בעת ההיא אמר יש''ו לתלמידיו מלכות שמים דומה היא לאדם מלך יושב לעשות חשבון עם עבדיו ומשרתיו.

$^{24}$וכאשר התחיל לחשוב בא א' שהוא חייב כעשרת אלפים זהובים.

$^{25}$ואין לו מה ליתן ויצו אדוניו למכור אותו ואת בניו ואת כל אשר לו לשלם הממון.

$^{26}$ויפול העבד לפני אדוניו ויתחנן לו לרחם עליו ולהמתין לו כי הכל ישלם.

$^{27}$ויחמול עליו אדוניו ומחל לו הכל.

$^{28}$ויצא העבד ההוא וימצא אחד מחביריו שהוא חייב לו מאה מעות ויחזק בו ויפגע לו לאמר

$^{29}$חוסה עלי והמתן לי והכל אשלם.

$^{30}$ולא אבה לשמוע לו ויוליכוהו לבית הסוהר עד שלם לו הכל.

$^{31}$וראו עבדי המלך את אשר עשה ויחר להם מאד ויבאו ויגידו לאדוניהם.

$^{32}$אז קרא אותו אדוניו ויאמר לו עבד ארור הלא מחלתי לך כל חוביך כאשר פייסתני.

$^{33}$ומדוע לא מחלת לעבדך בהתחננו אליך כאשר מחלתיך?

$^{34}$ויחר אף אדוניו בו ויצו לענותו עד ישלם לו כל החוב.

$^{35}$כן יעשה לכם אבי שבשמים אם לא תמחלו איש את אחיו בלב שלם.

## פרק פ''א 19

[1]ויהי כאשר כלה יש''ו הדברים האלה עבר מן הגליל ויבא לקצות ארץ יהודה אשר בעבר הירדן.

[2]וילכו אחריו חבורות רבות וירפא את כולם.

[3]ויגשו אליו את הפרושים לנסותו. וישאלוהו לאמר אם מותר לעזוב את אשתו בשום עניין וליתן לה גט.

[4]ויען להם הלא קראתם לעושיהם מקדם זכר ונקבה בראם.

[5]ואמר על כן יעזוב איש את אביו ואת אמו ודבק באשתו והיו לבשר אחד.

[6]א''כ אינם שנים כי אם בשר אחד ומה שחבר הבורא אין אדם יכול להפריד.

[7]ויאמר לו אם כן מדוע צוה משה לתת גט כריתות ושלחה מביתו.

[8]ויאמר להם משה לעקשות פה לבבכם אמר לכם לעזוב את נשיכם. ומעולם לא היה כן.

[9]אומר אני לכם שכל העוזב את אשתו ויקח אחרת אם לא בשביל ניאוף הוא נואף והלוקח הגרושה ניאף.

[10]ויאמרו אליו תלמידיו א''כ דבר אדם עם אשתו לא טוב לקחת אותה.

[11]ויאמר אליהם אין דבר זה לכל אלא למי שנתן להם.

[12]שיש סריסים מתולדותם אלו הם אשר לא חטאו. ויש סריסים מעצמם שכובשים את יצרם בשביל מלכות שמים אלו הם חכמים במעלה גדולה. מי שיוכל להבין יבין.

## פרק פ''ב

[13]אז הובאו אליו ילדים לשים ידו עליהם ולהתפלל עליהם ותלמידיו מגרשים אותם.

[14]ויאמר אליהם יש''ו הניחו הנערים לבא אלי ולא תמנעום שמהם מלכות שמים. באמת אני אומר לכם שלא יכנס במלכות שמים אם לא כאלה.

[15]וישם ידו עליהם וילך משם.

<sup>16</sup>ויגש אליו בחור א'' משתחוה לו ויאמר לו ר' איזה טוב אעשה לקנות חיי העה''ב.

<sup>17</sup>ויען אליו מה תשאל מטוב אין האדם טוב כי האל לבדו הוא טוב. ואם תרצה לבא בחיים שמור המצוות.

<sup>18</sup>ויאמר לו מה הן. ויאמר לו יש''ו לא תרצח לא תגנוב לא תענה ברעך עד שקר.

<sup>19</sup>כבד את אביך ואת אמך ואהבת לרעך כמוך.

<sup>20</sup>ויאמר לו הבחור כל אלה שמרתי ומה יחסר לי עוד.

<sup>21</sup>ויאמר אליו יש''ו אם תרצה להיות תם לך ומכור כל אשר לך ותנהו לעניים ויהיה לך אוצר בשמים ובא אחרי.

<sup>22</sup>ויהי כשמוע הבחור הלך לפי שלא היה לו קרקעות רבות.

<sup>23</sup>ויאמר יש''ו לתלמידיו אמן אני אומר לכם שכבד לעשיר לבא במלכות שמים.

<sup>24</sup>ועוד אני אומר לכם שיותר קל לבא הגמל בעין המחט מן העשיר במלכות שמים.

<sup>25</sup>וישמעו התלמידים ויתמהו מאד ויאמרו ליש''ו א''כ מי יוכל להושיע.

<sup>26</sup>ויפן אליהם ויאמר נגד בני אדם הדבר קשה ונגד האלקים הכל דבר קל להיות.

## פרק פ''ג

<sup>27</sup>ויען פייט''רוס ויאמר לו הנה עזבנו הכל לילך אחריך מה יהיה לנו.

<sup>28</sup>ויאמר יש''ו אמן אני אומר לכם שאתם ההולכים אחרי שביום הדין כאשר ישב האדם על כסא כבודו תשבו גם אתם על י''ב כסאות שנים עשר שבטי ישראל.

<sup>29</sup>וכל העוזב ביתו גם אחיותיו ואביו ואמו ואשתו ובניו על שמי יקבל כמותם ומלכות שמים ירש.

<sup>30</sup>רבים ראשונים יהיו אחרונים ורבים אחרונים יהיו ראשונים.

## פרק פ''ד 20

<sup>1</sup>אחר זה אמר יש''ו לתלמידיו מלכות שמים דומה לאדם יחיד

אדין ביתו המשכיר בבקר לשכור פועלים.

²והשכירם בדינר אחד ליום וישלחם לכרמו.

³ויצא בשלישית היום וירא אחרים עומדים בשוק בטלים.

⁴ויאמר להם לכו גם אתם לכרמי ובראוי אתן לכם.

⁵ויכלו. ויצאו עוד בצהרים וגם בשעה תשיעית ויעש כן.

⁶ובאחת עשרה שעה יצא ג''כ וימצא אחרים עומדים ויאמר להם מדוע אתם עומדים בטלים כל היום.

⁷ויענו לו שלא שכרנו אדם. ויאמר אליהם לכו גם אתם לכרמי.

⁸ויהי לעת ערב ויאמר בעל הכרם לניצב על הפועלים קרא אותם ואתן להם שכרם. ויחל באחרונים ויכל בראשונים.

⁹והאחרונים קבלו דינר אחד.

¹⁰והראשונים חשבו לקחת יותר והוא לא נתן לכולם כי אם דינר.

¹¹וילונו הראשונים על בעל הכרם

¹²לאמר אלו האחרונים עמלו שעה אחת והשוית אותם עמנו שעמלנו כל היום והחורב.

¹³ויען לאדם מהם ויאמר לו אהובי איני עושה לך עול. הלא בדינר א'' שכרתיך?

¹⁴קחנו ולך. אם אני רוצה לתת לזה האחרון כמותך

¹⁵הלא אעשה כרצוני? הידע בעיניך כאשר אני טוב?

¹⁶כן יהיה אחרונים ראשונים והראשונים אחרונים. רבים הם הקרואים ומעטים הנבחרים.

## פרק פ''ה

¹⁷ויקרב יש''ו אל ירושלם ויקח את י''ב תלמידיו בסתר ויאמר אליהם

¹⁸הנה אנחנו עולים לירושלם ובן האדם ימסר לגדולי החכמים והכהנים וייחייבוהו למות.

¹⁹וגם ימסרו אותו לגוים להכותו ולהשביתו וביום השלישי.

²⁰אז בא אשת זבדיאל עם בניה משתחוה ומבקשת בקשה ממנו.

²¹ויאמר אליה מה תרצי. ותאמר שתצוה לשבת שני בני אלה

האחד לימינך והשני לשמאלך במלכותך.

22ויען להם יש''ו לא תדעון מה תבקשון. התוכל לסבול היסורין והמיתה שאני עתיד לסבול? ויאמרו נוכל.

23ויאמר להם שתו כוסי והושיבו לשמאלי או גם לימיני אין לי לתתה לכם כי אם לאשר הוא נכון לפני אבי.

24וישמעו העשרה ויחר בעיניהם בעניין שני אחים.

25ויקרבם יש''ו אליו ויאמר להם דעו שנשיאי הגוים רודים בהם וגדוליהם מבקשים לנפשם.

26לא כן יהיה ביניכם שהרוצה להיות גדול ביניכם ישקת אתכם.

27ואשר ירצה ביניכם להיות ראשון יהיה לכם עבד.

28שאשר בן אדם לא בא שישרתוהו כי אם הוא לשרת ולתת נפשו כופר לרבים.

## פרק פ''ו 21

1וירכבו אל ירושלם ויבואו לבית פאגי להר הזתים וישלח יש''ו שנים מתלמידיו.

2ויאמר אליהם לכו אל המבצר אשר הוא נכחכם ומיד תמצאו אתון אחת ועירה אחת. והתירו אותם והביאום אלי.

3ואם יאמר לכם איש שום דבר אמרו לו שהאדון צריך להם ומיד יעזוב אתהם.

4כל זה לקיים דבר הנביא לאמר

5אמרו לבת ציון הנה מלכך יבא לך צדיק ונושע הוא עני ורוסב על אתון ועל עיר בן אתון.

6ויכלו ויעשו כאשר ציום יש''ו.

7ויביאו האתון והעיר וירכב יש''ו עליה והאחרים שמו עליהם כליהם ומלבושיהם ויעלו למעלה.

8ורבים מהחבורה פורשים מלבושיהם בדרך ואחרים הסודרנא ענפי העצים וישליכו לפניו ולאחריו

9קוראים לאמר הושענא מושיע העולם ברוך הבא בשם ה'' הושענא מושיענו תתפאר בשמים ובארץ.

## פרק פ''ח

10ויהי אחרי כן בבא יש''ו ירושלם חרדה כל העיר לאמר מי היא זה.

11ויאמר העם זה לזה יש''ו הנביא מנאזא''ריל אשר בגליל.

12ויבא יש''ו בית ה'' וימצא שם הקונים והמוכרים. ויהפוך לוחות השולחנים והמושבות מוכרי היונים.

13ויאמר אליהם כתיב כי ביתי בית תפלה יקרא לכל העמים ואתם עשיתם אותה מערת פריצים.

14ויקרבו אליו עורים ופסחים במקדש וירפאם.

15ויבואו גדולי החכמים והכהנים לראות הפלאות שעשה. והנערים קוראים במקדש ואומרים ישתבח בן האל. והחכמים ילעגו

16ויאמרו לו הלא שמעת מה אומרים אלו. ויען להם ויאמר שמעתי אלו. הלא קראתם מפי עולים ויונקים וסדת עוז?

17ויעזוב וילך חוצה אל בית חניא וילך שם ושם היה דורש להם ממלכות האל.

18ויהי בבקר וישב לעיר רעב.

19וירא תאנה אחת אצל הדרך ויגש אליה ולא מצא בה רק העלים לבד. ויאמר לה אל יצא ממך פרי לעולם. ותיבש התאנה מיד.

20ויראו התלמידים ויתמהו ויאמרו איך יבשה התאנה מיד.

21ויען יש''ו ויאמר להם אם תהיה בכם אמונה בלי ספק לא לתאנה בלבד תעשו כי אם תאמרו להר הזה שימוש ויבא בם יעשה.

22וכל אשר תשאלון בתפלה יתהיו מאמינים תקבלון.

## פרק פ''ט

23ויבא אל המקדש ללמד ויקרבו אליו החכמים והכהנים וקציני העם לאמר באיזה כח תעשה החיל הזה.

24ויען להם יש''ו ויאמר להם אשאל מכם גם אני שאלה אחת ואם תאמרו לי אותה גם אני אומר לכם באיזה כח אני עושה.

25טבילת יוחנן מאין היתה מן השמים או מן האנשים? ויתעצבו ביניהם לאמר מה נאמר. אם נאמר מהשמים יאמר לנו למה לא

תאמינו בו.

‏‎26‎‏ואם נאמר מן האנשים נירא מן החבורה שלכם מאמינים שיוחנן נביא היה.

‏‎27‎‏ויאמרו לא ידענו. ויאמר גם אני לא אומר לכם באיזה כח אני עושה.

## פרק צ''

‏‎28‎‏בערב ההיא אמר יש''ו לתלמידיו מה נראה לכם. איש א'' היו לו שני בנים ויגש האחד ויאמר לו לך בני היום לעבוד כרמי.
‏‎29‎‏ויאמר לו איני רוצה. ואח''כ נחם והלך.
‏‎30‎‏ויאמר לאחר כמו כן ויען אליו הנני אדו' ולא הלך.
‏‎31‎‏מי משניהם עשה רצון הבא? ויאמרו לו הראשון. ויאמר להם יש''ו אמן אני אומר לכם שהפריצים והקדישות יקדמו אתכם במלכות שמים.
‏‎32‎‏שבא אליכם יוחנן דרך צדקה ולא המנתם. באו הפריצים והקדישות והאמינו בו ואתם רואים ולא חזרתם בתשובה. גם אחרי כן לא נחמתם להאמין בו. למי אזנים לשמוע ישמע בחרפה.

## פרק צ''א

‏‎33‎‏(בעת ההיא אמר יש''ו לתלמידיו ולסיעת היהודים שמעו נא משל הזורע. אדם אחד נכבד נטע כרם וגדר אותו מסביב ויבן מגדל בתוכו וגם יקב חצב בו ויפקידהו לעובדים וילך לדרכו.
‏‎34‎‏ויהי לעת אסוף התבואה שלח אל עבדיו אל העובדים לקבל תבואתו.
‏‎35‎‏ויקחו העובדים את עבדיו ויכו את האחד ויהרגו את השני והשלישי סקלו באבנים.
‏‎36‎‏וישלח עוד עבדים רבים מהראשונים ויעשו להם כמו כן.
‏‎37‎‏סוף דבר שלח להם בנו לאמר אולי יראו את בני.
‏‎38‎‏ויראו העובדים את בנו ויאמרו איש אל רעהו זהו היורש. לכו ונהרגהו ונירש נחלתו.
‏‎39‎‏ויקחוהו ויוציאוהו מן הכרם ויהרגוהו.

⁴⁰ועתה כאשר יבא בעל הכרם מה יעשה להם?

⁴¹ויענו לו לאמר הרעים יאבדם ברעה וברמו יתן לעובדים אחרים שיתנו לו חלק תבואתו מיד.

⁴²ויאמר להם יש''ו הלא קראתם הכתוב אבן מאסו הבונים היתה לראש פנה מאת ה'' היתה זאת היא נפלאת בעינינו.

⁴³לזאת אני אומר לכם שתתקרע מלכות שמים מעליכם ותנתן לגוי עושה פרי.

⁴⁴והנופל על האבן הזאת ידחה ואשר יפול עליה יסדק.

⁴⁵וישמעו גדולי הכהנים והפרושים משליו ויכירו שהוא מדבר בעדם.

⁴⁶ויבקשו להמיתו ויראו מהחבורות שלנביא היה להם.)

## פרק צ''א (צ''ב) 22

¹ויען יש''ו ויאמר להם עוד בדברי משל.

²מלכות שמים דומה למלך אשר עושה חופה.

³וישלח את עבדיו בעד הקרואים לחופה ולא אבו לו.

⁴וישלח עוד עבדים אחרים לאמר אמרו לקרואים הנה הכנתי המשתה וזבחתי שורים ועופות והכל מוכן. בואו אל החופה.

⁵והם בזו וילכו מקצתם בעיר ומקצתם בעסקיהם.

⁶והאחרים (לקחו את עבדיו) והתעללו בם והרגום.

⁷וישמע המלך ויחר אפו וישלח הרוצחים ההם ואת ביתם שרף באש.

⁸אז אמר לעבריו החופה מוכנת היא רק הקרואים לא היו ראויים.

⁹ועתה צאו אל הדרכים וכל אשר תמצאו קראו לחופה.

¹⁰ויצאו עבדיו אל הדרכים ויקבצו כל הנמצאים טובים ורעים ותמלא החופה מהאוכלים.

¹¹ויבא המלך לראות האוכלים וירא שם אדם אשר לא היה מלובש בגדי החופה.

¹²ויאמר לו אהובי איך באתה לכאן בלא לבושי החופה. והוא החריש.

¹³אז אמר המלך למשרתיו אסרו ידיו ורגליו והשליכוהו בשאול

תחתית ושם יהיה בכי וחרוק שינים.

14הקרואים רבים והנבחרים מעטים.

## פרק צ''ג

15אז הלכו הפירושים ויועצו לקחתו בדבר.

16וישליחו אליו מתלמידיהם עם פרושים מהורוד''וס לאמר רבי ידענו שנאמן אתה ותלמוד באמונה דרך האלקים ואינך חושש לשום דבר ולא נושא פנים.

17אמור מה יראה לך הנכון לתת מס לציזא''רי אם אין.

18ויחרישו את נכלותם ויאמר למה תמיתוני חנפנים.

19הראו לי מטבע המס. ויביאו לו.

20ויאמר אליהם למי הצורה הזאת והרשום.

21ויאמר לציזא''רי. אז אמר אליהם יש''ו השיבו לציזא''רי את אשר לציזא''רי לציזא''רי ואשר לאלקים לאלקים.

22וישמעו ויתמהו ייעזבוהו וילכו.


## פרק צ''ד

23ביום ההוא קראו אליו הצדוקים והכופרים בתחיית המתים. וישאלוהו

24לאמר ר' אמור לנו אמר משה כי ישבו אחים יחדיו ומת אחד מהם ובן אין לו שיקח אחיו את אשתו לקיים זרע אחיו.

25והנה שבעה אתים היו בינינו ונשא הראשון אשה ומת בלא זרע ויבם אחיו את אשתו.

26וכן השני ושלישי עד השביעי.

27ואחריהם מתה האשה.

28שכבר היה לכולם אל מי מהשבעה תהיה האשה.

29ויען יש''ו ויאמר אליהם תשגו ולא תבינו הספרים ועוז האלקים.

30ביום התקומה לא יקחו האנשים נשים ולא הנשים אנשדים רק יהיו כמלאכי אלקים בשמים.

31הלא קראתם מתחיית המתים שאמר ה'' לכם שאמר

32אני ה'' אלקי אברהם אלקי יצחק ואלקי יעקב. וא''כ אינו

אלקי המתים כ׳׳א אלקי החיים.

33וישמעו החבורות ויתמהו מחכמתו.

## פרק צ׳׳ה

34וכאשר ראו הפירושים כי אין מענה לצדוקים התחברו עבדיו.

35וישאלוהו חכם א׳׳ לנסותו

36ר׳ אמור איזה היא מצוה גדולה שבתורה.

37אמר לו ואהבת את ה׳׳ אלקיך בכל לבבך וכו.

38זו היא הראשונה.

39שנית דומה אליה ואהבת לרעך כמוך.

40ועל שתי המצוות האלה התורה כולה תלויה והנביאים.

41ויאספו הפרושים וישאלם יש׳׳ו

42לאמר מה יראה לכם מן המשיח ובן מי יהיה. ויאמרו לו בן דוד.

43ויאמר להם איך קראו אותו דוד ברוח הקדש לאמר אדון

44דכתיב נאם ה׳׳ לאדוני שב לימיני עד אשית אויביך הדום לרגליך.

45אם דוד קראו אדון איך יהיה בנו?

46ולא יכלו להשיבו דבר מכאן ואילך פחדו לשאול ממנו דבר.

## פרק צ׳׳ו 23

1אז דבר יש׳׳ו אל העם ואל תלמידיו

2לאמר על כסא משה ישבו הפירושים והחכמים.

3ועתה כל אשר יאמר לכם שמרו ועשו ובתקנותיהם ומעשיהם אל תעשו שהם אומרים והם אינם עושים.

4ודורשים ונותנים משאות גדולות לא יוכלו לסובלם והם אפי׳ באצבעם אינם רוצים לנוע.

5וכל מעשיהם עושים למראה עינים ולובשים מלבושים יקרים וציציות נקראים פיב׳׳ליאוס גדולים

6אהבים להיות מסובים ראשונה בבתי משתאות ולהיות מושבם בבתי כנסיות בראשונה

7ולהשתחוות להם בחוצות ולקוראם רבנים.

⁸ואתם אל תרצו להיות נקראים רבנים. אחד הוא רבכם וכולכם אחים.

⁹ואב אל תקראו לאדם על הארץ. אחד הוא אביכם שבשמים.

¹⁰ואל תקראו רבנים שרבכם אחד הוא המשיח.

¹¹הגדול ביניכם יהיה משרת אתכם.

¹²ואשר יתרומם ישח ואשר ישח ירום.

## פרק צ''ז

¹³אוי לכם הפרושים והחכמים חנפים מלכות שמים בפני בני אדם והרוצים לבא אינכם עוזבים אותם לבא.

¹⁴אוי לכם הפרושים והחכמים חנפים שאתם אוכלים וחולקים נכסי הנשים האלמנות בדרש ארוך ובעבור זה תסבלו עונש ארך.

¹⁵סובבים הים והיבשה לקשור לב איש אחד באמונתכם וכאשר יהיה נקשר יהיה רע כפלים מקודם.

¹⁶אוי לכם מושבי העורים אשר תאמרו שהנשבע בהיכל אינו חייב ואשר ידור באיזה דבר שהוא נקדש לבניין ההיכל חייב לשלם

¹⁷משוגעים ועורים איזה יותר גדול ההיכל או דבר הנקדש להיכל

¹⁸ואשר ישבע במזבח אינו חייב והנשבע שיקריב קרבן חייב לתת.

¹⁹איזה יותר הקרבן או המזבח המקדש או הקרבן?

²⁰אשר ישבע במזבח נשבע ובכל מה שבתוכו.

21

²²ואשר ישבע בכסא אלקים נשבע בו וביושב עליו.

## פרק צ''ח

²³אוי להם לחכמים ולפרושים המעשרים הנמנע והשבת והרמון והגוזלים ענבים אשר הוא יותר נכבד זהו משפטי התורה והם החסד והאמת והאמונה. אלו המאמרים ראויים לעשות ולא לשכוח אותם.

²⁴זרע מנהיגים העורים מדקדקים בדבר היתוש ובולעים את הגמל.

²⁵אוי לכם הפרושים והחכמים שתקנחו הכוסות והקערות מבחוץ ותוכם מלא נבלה וטומאה.

²⁶רחוף נקה תחלה מה שבתוכו להיות טהור אשר מבחוץ.

²⁷אוי לכם החכמים והפרושים החנפים הדומים לקברים המלובנים שידמו מבחוץ יבין לבני אדם ובתוכן מלאות עצמות מתים ומטונפים.

²⁸כן תראו אתם מבחוץ צדיקים לבני אדם ובקרבכם מלאות חנפות ורשעות.

²⁹אוי להם החנפים והפרושים והחכמים שתבנו קברי הנביאים ותכבדו צאני הצדיקים.

³⁰ותאמרו אם היינו בימי אבותינו לא היינו מניחים בימי הנביאים.

³¹בזאת אתם מעידים על עצמכם שבנים אתם לאשר הרגו הנביאים

³²ואתם נוהגים במעשה אבותיכם.

³³נחשים זרע צפעונים איך תנוסו מדין גיהנם אם לא תשובו בתשובה.

## פרק צ׳׳ט

³⁴בעת ההיא אמר יש׳׳ו לחבורות היהודים לזאת הנני שולח לכם נביאים וחכמים וסופרים. ומהם תהרגו ומהם תכאיבו בבתי כנסיותכם ותרדפוני מעיר אל עיר.

³⁵עליבם דם כל צדיק הנשפך על הארץ מדם הבל הצדיק עד דם צכריה בן ברכיה אשר הרגתם בין ההיכל ולמזבח.

³⁶באמת אני אומר לכם שיבואו כל אלה על הדור הזה

³⁷ועל ירושלים ההורגת הנביאים ומסלקת השלוחים כמה פעמים רציתי לאסוף בניך כאשר תאסוף התרנגולת אפרוחיה תחת כנפיה ולא רצית.

³⁸לכן אתם תעזבו בתיכם חרבות.

³⁹באמת אני אומר לכם לא תראוני מכאן ואילך עד שתאמרו

ברוך מושיענו.

<u>פרק ק' 24</u>

$^1$ויהי כאשר יצא יש''ו מן המקדש וכשהיה הולך נגשו תלמידיו להראותו בניני המקדש.

$^2$ויאמר תראו כל אלה אמן אני אומר לכם שהכל יהרס ולא ישאר שם אבן על אבן.

$^3$ובשבתו על הר הזתים נגד בית המקדש שאלו לו לו פיט''רוש ויחנן ואנדריאה בסתר מתי יהיה כל אלה ומה האות שיהיה כשיהיו כל אלה הענינים או כשיתחילו ומתי יהיה תכלית העולם וביאתך.

$^4$ועין להם יש''ו השמרו פן יתעה אתכם איש

$^5$שרבים יבאו עם שמי לאמר אני הוא המשיח ויתעו אתכם.

$^6$ואתם כאשר תשמעו המלחמות וחברת הצבאות השמרו פן תהבלו שכל זה עתיד לבא אבל עדין אין התכלית.

$^7$ויקום גוי על גוי וממלכה על ממלכה ויהיו מהומות רבות ורעב כבד ורעש במקומות.

$^8$כל אלה תחלת המכאובות.

$^9$אז יאסרו אתכם לצרות ויהרגו אתכם ותהיו לחרפה לכל העמים על שמי.

$^{10}$ואז ירגזו רבים ויבגדו הם בהם ויתקצפו ביניהם.

$^{11}$ויקומו נביאי השקר ויטעו את הרבים.

$^{12}$וכאשר תרבה הרשעות תפוג אהבת רבים.

$^{13}$ואשר יחכה עד התכלית יושע.

$^{14}$ותדרש בשורה לעז או''נגילי זאת בכל הארץ לעדות עלי על כל הגוים ואז תבא התכלית.

$^{15}$זה אנטיק''ריסטוס וזהו שקוץ שמם האומר על פי דניאל עומד במקום קדוש והקורא יבין.

$^{16}$אז אשר ביודא ינוסו להרים.

$^{17}$ואשר על הבית לא ירד לקרות שום דבר מביתו.

$^{18}$ואשר בשדה לא ישוב לקחת כתנתו.

$^{19}$הוי להרות ולמניקות בימים ההם.

20התפללו לאל שלא תהיה מנוסתכם בסתו ובשבת.

21שאז תהיה צרה גדולה אשר לא נהיתה מבראה העולם עד עתה וכמוה לא תהיה.

22ולולי היות הימים ההם מעטים לא יושיע כל בשר רק בעבור הנבחרים ימעטו הימים ההם.

23ובאותו הזמן אם יאמר איש לכם הנה המשיח או לשם לא תאמינו.

24שיקומו משיחי שקרים ונבאי השקר ויתנו אותות ומופתים גדולים בענין שאם יוכל להיות יבאו בטעות את הנבחרים.

26ואם יאמרו לכם הנו במדבר אל תצאו והנו בחדרים אל תאמינו.

25הנני אומרו לכם קודם היותו.

## פרק ק''א

27עוד אמר להם יש''ו לתלמידיו כמו שהברק יוצא במזרח ונראה במערב כן תהיה ביאתו שלבן האדם.

28באיזה מקום שיהיה הגויה שם יתחברו הנשרים.

29ובאותה שעה אחרי הימים ההם יחשך השמש והירח לא יגיה אורו והככבים יפלו מהשמים וחיל השמים יתנודד.

30ואז יראה האות שלבן האדם בשמים ויבכו כל משפחות האדמה ויראו את בן האדם בעבי השמים בחיל רב ובצורה נוראה.

31וישלח מלאכיו בשופר ובקול גדול לאסוף את נבחריו מארבע רוחות השמים מקצה השמים עד קצותם.

32מעץ התאנה תלמדו המשל כאשר תראו ענפיה ועלים צומחים תדעו כי

33קרוב הוא לשערים.

34אמן אני אומר לכם שלא יעבור זה הדור עד שכל אלו הדברים יהיו עשוים.

35והשמים והארץ יעברו.

36ומהיום ההוא ומהעת ההיא אין מי שיודע ולא מלאכי השמים אלא האב בלבד.

## פרק ק"ב

<sup>37</sup>עוד אמר יש"ו לתלמידיו כאשר בימי נח כן תהיה בימינו שלבן האדם.

<sup>38</sup>כאשר היו קודם המבול אוכלים ושותים ופרים ורבים עד יום שבא נח בתיבה.

<sup>39</sup>ולא ידעו עד שבא המבול עליהם ושחיתם כן תהיה ביאתו של בן האדם.

<sup>40</sup>אז אם יהיו שנים חורשים בשדה אחד האחד צדיק והאחד רשע האחד ילקד והאחד יעזב.

<sup>41</sup>שתים נשים טוחנות בטחון אחת האחת תלקד והאחת תעזב. וזה יהיה שהמלאכים בתכלית העולם יסירו המכשולים מהעולם ויפרידו הטובים מהרעים.

## פרק ק"ג

<sup>42</sup>אז אמר יש"ו לתלמידיו לזאת שמרו עמי שלא תדעו אזו שעה אדוניכם בא.

<sup>43</sup>זאת תדעו אם היה יודע איזו שעה הגנב בא ישמור ולא יעזוב לחבור ביתו.

<sup>44</sup>כן אתם תהיו נכונים שלא תדעו איזו שעה בן אדם עתיד לבא.

<sup>45</sup>מה אתם חושבים מהעבר הנאמן והחכם ששם אותו אדוניו על טפיו לתת אכלם בעתו?

<sup>46</sup>אשרי העבד ההוא שתצווהו אדוניו בבואו עושה כן.

<sup>47</sup>אמן אני אומר לכם שעל טפיו ישימהו.

<sup>48</sup>ואם יהיה העבד ההוא רע ויאמר בלבו אדוני מתמהמה ובא

<sup>49</sup>ויתחיל להכות עבדו אדוניו ויאכל וישתה עם הזוללים

<sup>50</sup>ובא אדוניו ביום אשר לא וחכה ובעת אשר לא ידע.

<sup>51</sup>ויפרידהו וישים חלקו עם החנפים שם יהיה בכי וחרוק שינים.

## פרק ק"ד 25

<sup>1</sup>עוד אמר יש"ו לתלמידיו מלכות שמים דומה לעשר בתולות שלקחו נרותיהן ויצאו לקראת חתן וכלה.

<sup>2</sup>חמש מהן היו עצלות כסילות וחמש מהן זריזות וחכמות.

³החמש כסילות הוציאו נרותיהן ולא הוציאו שמן עמהן.

⁴והחכמות הוציאו שמן בכליהן עם נרותיהן.

⁵ויתמהמה החתן והנה כלן נתמהמהו ונשנה.

⁶ויהי בחצי הלילה והנה קול נשמע הנה החתן בא באו לקראתו.

⁷אז באו הבתולות כולנה והטיבו נרותיהן.

⁸ותאמרנה הבתולות הכסילות לחכמות תנו לנו משמנכם שנרותינו נדעכו.

⁹ותעננה החכמות לאמר לכו נא אל המוכרים וקנו לכן כי אין די בשמן שלנו ולכן. נירא שיחסר לנו.

¹⁰ויהי כאשר הלכו לקנות בא החתן והמוכנות באו עמו לחופה ונסגר השער.

¹¹ואח''כ באו הכסילות ותקראנה לשער לאמר אדוננו פתח לנו.

¹²ויען להן באמת אני אומר לכם איני יודע מי אתן.

¹³ועל כן השמרו לכם שלא תדעו היום והשעה שיבא החתן.

<u>פרק ק''ה</u>

¹⁴עוד אמר יש''ו לתלמידיו דמיון אחר מלכות שמים דומה לאדם הולך בדרך רחוקה ויקרא את עבדיו ויפזר להם ממונו.

¹⁵לאמר נתן חמשה זהובים לשני נתן שנים זהובים ולשלישי אחד איש כראוי לו נתן להם. וילך לדרכו.

¹⁶וילך המקבל החמשה זהובים והרויח חמשה אחרים.

¹⁷וכמו כן המקבל שנים הלך קנה ומכר והרויח חמשה אחרים.

¹⁸והמקבל האחד הלך וחפר בארץ ויטמון את ממון אדוניו.

¹⁹ואחר ימים רבים בא אדון העבדים ההם ויבקש מהם חשבון הממון.

²⁰ויגש המקבל החמשה זהובים אמר לו אדוני חמשה זהובים נתת לי והא לך חמשה אחרים אשר רוחתי.

²¹ויאמר לו אדוניו אמנם עבד טוב ונאמן אתה. ויען היית נאמן במעט אשימך על הרבה בא בשמחת אדוניך.

²²וגם המקבל שנים הזהובים נגש ויאמר אדוני שנים זהובים נתת לי והנה שנים אחרים אשר הרוחתי.

²³ויאמר לו אדוניו אמנם עבד טוב ונאמן אתה. וכי היית נאמן במעט אשימך על הרבה בא בשמחת אדוניך.

²⁴ויגש המקבל האחד ויאמר אדוני ידעתי שעז וקשה אתה תקצור אשר לא זרעת ותאסוף אשר לא פזרת.

²⁵ומיראתך הלכתי וטמנתי הזהוב שלך והא לך שלך.

²⁶ויען אדוניו ויאמר עבד רע ועצל אחרי שידעת שקוצר אני אשר לא זרעתי ואוסף אשר לא פזרתי

²⁷לזאת היית חייב לתת נכסי לשולחני ובבואי הייתי מקבל את שלי עם ריוח.

²⁸לזאת קחו ממנו הזהב וחנותו לאשר רווח החמשה זהובים.

²⁹לאשר יש לו תנתן לו ולאשר אין לו הראוי לו ילקח ממנו.

³⁰והעבד העצל השליכהו במחשכי תחתיות ושם יהיה לו בכי וחרוק שנים.

## פרק ק''ו

³¹עוד אמר יש''ו לתלמידיו ובבוא בן האדם במראהו עם מלאכיו אז ישב על כסא כבודו.

³²ויאספו לפניו כל הגוים ויפריד ביניהם כאשר יפריד הרועה בין הכשבים ובין העזים.

³³ויציג את הכשבים לימינו והעזים לשמאלו.

³⁴אז ידבר לאשר לימינו בואו ברוכים ברוכי אבי וירשו לכם ממלכות השמים המוכן לכם מבריאת העולם עד עתה.

³⁵כי רעבתי ונתתם לי לאכול צמאתי ונתתם לי לשתות אורח הייתי ותאספוני

³⁶ערום ותלבישוני חולה ותבקרוני בבית הסהר הייתי ותבואו אלי.

³⁷אז יענו הצדיקים אדוננו מתו ראינוך והשבענוך צמנו והשקתוך

³⁸ערום וכסיתוך

³⁹חולה ובקרנוך בבית הסהר ובאנו אליך.

⁴⁰ויען המלך ויאמר להם אמן אני אומר לכם שבכל הפעמים אשר עשיתם לאחד מאחד אלו הקטנים כאלו עשיתם לי.

⁴¹וגם ידבר לאשר לשמאלו סורו ממני ארורים ובאו באש

עולמית במקום מוכן לכם עם השטן ומלאכיו

⁴²שרעבתי ולא נתתם לי לאכול צמאתי ולא השקיתם לי

⁴³הייתי אורח ולא אספתם אותי ערום ולא כסיתם אותי חולה ובבית ולא בקרתם אותי.

⁴⁴אז יענו גם הם ויאמרו אליו מתי ראינוך אדוננו רעב וצמא או אורח וערום וחולה או בבית הסוהר ולא היינו עמך משרתים אותך.

⁴⁵ויענה אליהם ויאמר אני אומר לכם שכל הפעמים אשר לא עשיתם זאת לעני אחד מאלו הקטנים כאלו לא עשיתם אלי.

⁴⁶וילכו אלה לדראון עולם והצדיקים לחיי עולם.

## פרק ק''ז 26

¹ויהי כאשר כלה יש''ו לדבר כל הדברים האלה אמר לתלמידיו

²הלא תדעו שאחר שני ימים יהיה הפסח ובן האדם ימסר ביד היהודים לצליבה.

³אז נאספו סגני הכהנים וגדולי העם בחצר נגיד הכהנים ושמו קאיפש.

⁴ויועצו יחדיו לתפוש את יש''ו בערמה ולהורגו.

⁵ויאמרו לא יהיה בחג פן שאון יהיה בעם.

⁶ויהי כאשר היה יש''ו בכפר חנניה בבית סימון המצורע

⁷נגשה אליו אשה אחת בפך משיחה יקרה ותיצק אותו על ראשו והוא מסבה לשלחן.

⁸וירע להם מאד מדוע האבדון הזה

⁹יוכל למוכרה במחיר רב ולתת לעניים.

¹⁰ויש''ו היודע כל דבר לאיזה ענין נעשה אמר להם אתם מאשימים את האשה הזאת. באמת מעשה טוב ונפלא עשתה עמדי.

¹¹כי העניים יחיו עמכם תמיד ואני לא אהיה עמכם תמיד.

¹²ושמה זאת בגופי רומז לקבורתי.

¹³אמן אני אומר לכם בכל מקום אשר תקרא בשורה זו לעז אוונגיל בכל העולם יאמר אשר עשה זאת בזכרי.

## פרק ק"ח

$^{14}$אז הלך אחד מהשנים עשר ששמו יודא אשכריוטו לגדולי הכהנים.

$^{15}$ויאמר מה תתנו לי ואני אמסור יש"ו לכם. ויפסקו אתו שלשים כסף.

$^{16}$ומכאן ואילך בקש ענין למסור אותו.

$^{17}$וביום הראשון של חג המצות קרבו התלמידים ליש"ו לאמר אנה נכין לך אכילת הסדר הפסח.

$^{18}$ויאמר להם לכו אל העיר לאיזה איש שידברו לבו לעשות ואמרו לו כה אמר הרב זמני קרוב הוא עמך ויעשה פסח עם תלמידי.

$^{20}$ויהי לעת ערב והוא יושב לשלחן עם י"ב תלמידיו.

$^{21}$כאמר היו אוכלים אמר להם אומר אני לכם שאחד מכם ימסרני.

$^{22}$ויתעצבו מאד ויאמרו לו כל אחד לאמר אדוני האני זה.

$^{23}$ויען להם הטובל קרפס עמי בקערה הוא ימכרני. וכולם היו אוכלים בקערה אחת. לכן לא הכירוהו שאלו הכירוהו השמידוהו.

$^{24}$ויאמר להם יש"ו אמת שבן האדם הולך ככתוב בו אוי לאדם ההוא אשר בשבילו בן אדם ימסר. טוב לו שלא נולד לאיש ההוא.

$^{25}$ויען יודא אשר מכרו ויאמר לו רבי האני זה ויאמר אתה דברת.

## פרק ק"ט

$^{26}$המה אוכלים ויקח יש"ו מצה ויברך ויחלקהו ויתן לדלמידיו ויאמר קחו ואכלו זה הוא גופי.

$^{27}$ויקח את הכוס ויתן שבחים לאביו ויתן להם ויאמר שתו מזה כולכם.

$^{28}$זהו דמי מחלק מברית חדשה אשר ישפך בעבור הרבים לכפרת עונות.

$^{29}$אומר אני לכם לא אשתה אני מכאן ואילך מפרי הגפן הזאת

עד היום ההוא שאשתה אותו חדש עמכם במלכות שמים.
‏30‏וילכו ויצאו להר הזתים.

## פרק ק''י

‏31‏אז אמר יש''ו לתלמידיו באו כלכם התעצבו עלי הלילה שכן כתיב הך את הרועה ותפוצינה הרועים.
‏32‏ואחרי קומי מהמיתה אגלה לכם בגליל.
‏33‏ויען פיט''רוש ויאמר לו אם כלם יעצבו עליך אני לא אתעצב לעולם.
‏34‏ויאמר יש''ו אמן אני אומר לך שבזה הלילה קודם קריאת הגבר תכפור בי ג' פעמים.
‏35‏ויאמר לו פיט''רוש אם יתכן לי למות עמך לא אכפור בך. וכזה אמרו לו כל התלמידים.
‏36‏אז בא יש''ו עמהם לכפר גיא שמנים ויאמר שבו נא עד שאלך לשם ואתפלל.
‏37‏ויקח את פיטרוש ואת שני בני זבדאל והתחיל להתעצב ולהיות זעף.
‏38‏אז אמר להם נפשי מתעצבת עד מות סמכוני ושמרו עמי.
‏39‏וילך לאט לאט מעט ויפול על פניו ויתפלל ויאמר אם יוכל להיות הסר נא ממני הכוס הזה. אמנם לא כמו שאני רוצה יהיה אלא כרצונך.
‏40‏ויבא אל התלמידים וימצאם ישנים. ויאמר לפיט''רו כך האינך יכול לשמור עמדי שעה אחת.
‏41‏שמרו והתפללו פן תבאו בנסיון שהאמת שהרוח נכון לילד לו ראו את הבשר חלש וחולה.
‏42‏וילך שנית להתפלל לאמור אם לא תוכל להסיר הכוס הזה אלא שאשתהו יהיה עשי כרצונך.
‏43‏וישב אחרי כן וימצאם ישנים שהיו עיניהם כבדים.
‏44‏ויעזוב אותם וילך להתפלל פעם שלישית כדברים הראשונים.

## פרק קי''א

‏45‏אז בא יש''ו לגליל לתלמידיו ויאמר להם שנו ונוחו הנה הקרב

העת ובן האדם ימסר ביד החטאים.

⁴⁶קומו ונלך שהנו קרוב מי שימסרנו.

⁴⁷עודנו מדבר והנה אסכריוטא אחד מי׳׳ב תלמידיו בא. ועמו חבורה אחת רבה בחרבות ובשוטים שלוחים מאת גדולי הכהנים ושרי העם.

⁴⁸ואשר מסרוהו נתן להם אות אשר אשקנו הוא ותפשוהו.

⁴⁹ומיד נגש אל יש׳׳ו ויאמר לו שלום עליך רבי וישקהו.

⁵⁰ויאמר אליו יש׳׳ו אהובי מה עשית. ויקרבו וישלחו ידם בו ויתפשוהו.

⁵¹והנה אחד מאשר היה עם יש׳׳ו נטה ידו וישלוף חרבו ויך עבד אחד מעבדי הכהנים ויכרות אזנו.

⁵²ויאמר אליו יש׳׳ו השב חרבך אל נדנה שהשרופים חרב בחרב יפולו.

⁵³הלא תבין שאוכל לפגוע באויבי ואכן לי עתה יתר מי׳׳ב לגיונות של מלאכים?

⁵⁴ואיך ימלאון הכתובים? שכן ראוי לעשות.

⁵⁵אחר אמר יש׳׳ו לחבורה כמו אם היינו גנבים באתם לקחת אותי בחרבות ובשוטים. והלא בכל יום הייתי עמכם במקדש מלמדכם ולא עכבתוני?

⁵⁶אמנם כל זה נעשה יען ימלאו הכתובים מהנביאים. אז כל תלמידיו הניחוהו וברחו.

⁵⁷והם הוליכו ליש׳׳ו לבית קאיפש גדול הכהנים. ואז כל הסופרים והפרושים נקהלו.

⁵⁸ופיט׳׳רוש היה הולך אחריו מרחוק עד בית גדול הכהנים. ונכנס לבית וישב לו אצל האומנים עד יראה התכלית.

⁵⁹וגדולי הכהנים והפרושים היו רוצים עדי שקר נגד יש׳׳ו יען ימיתוהו.

⁶⁰ולא היו מוצאים ואחד אשר הכינו הרבה עדי שקר נגד יש׳׳ו. לסוף באו שני עדים שקרים.

⁶¹ויאמר זה אמר יש לי יכולת להשחית מקדש האל ואחר ג׳ ימים לתקן אותו.

⁶²וגדול הכהנים קם ויאמר לו אינך עונה דבר נגד העדות שאלו מעידים נגדך.

⁶³ויש''ו לא ענה דבר. וגדול הכהנים אמר לו משביעך אני באל חי שתאמר לנו אם אתה משיח בן האל.

⁶⁴ויען לו יש''ו אתה אומר ועוד אני אומר לכם עדין תראו בן האל יושב לימין גבורת האל בא בעבי שחקים.

⁶⁵אז גדול הכהנים קרע בגדיו ואמר זה ברך אלקים. ומה לנו צורך לעדים אחרים? והנה כולכם שמעתם איך ברך האל.

⁶⁶מה יראה לכם שיתכן לעשות? והם ענו שחייב מיתה.

⁶⁷ואז רקקו בפניו והלקוהו על שכמו ואחרים טבחו לו בפניו

⁶⁸אומרים אמור לנו המשיח מי הכך.

⁶⁹ופיט''רוש היה עומד לפתח החצר ונגשה אליו שפחה אחת ואומרת לו והאל אתה עם יש''ו הגלילי היית עומד.

⁷⁰ופיט''רוש כחש לה בפני הכל ואמר לה אשה איני יודע מה את אומרת.

⁷¹וכאשר עבר השער ראה שפחה אחרת ואמרת לעוברים שם זה האיש היה עומד עם יש''ו בנאצ''רת.

⁷²ופעם אחרת כחש יש''ו בשבועה שלא הכירו.

⁷³ואחר כן לזמן מעט נגשו אל פיט''רוש העומדים בחצר ויאמרו לו אתה הוא מחבורת זה הנביא שמדברך נכר שאתה מהם.

⁷⁴אז התחיל לכפור ולישבע שבשום זמן לא הכירו. ומיד קרא התרנגול.

⁷⁵ופיט''רוש נזכר מאשר אמר לו יש''ו שקודם קריאת הגבר יכפור בו ג' פעמים. ואז יצא לחוץ ובכה במרירות נפשו.

## פרק קי''ב 27

¹ויהי בבקר כל גדולי החכמים והקדמונים לקחו עצה נגד יש''ו שמכל וכל יהרגוהו.

²וקשור הוליכוהו לבית פו''טץ פילא''ט שהיה גזבר.

³ואז כאשר ראה יודא אסכריוטא שהיה נדון התחיל לשוב בתשובה. וחזר השלשים דינרים לגדול הכהנים ולזקני העם.

⁴אמר אני חטאתי ששפכתי דם נקי. והם אמרו לו מה לנו אתה תראה.

⁵וזרק המעות במקדש והלך לו ולקח חבל אחת ותלה עצמו.

⁶וגדולי הכהנים כאשר לקחו המעות אמרו לא יתכן שנשים אלו המעות במקדש שדמי דם הם שנתנו בעד דמי יש''ו.

⁷ויועצו ויתנו אותם בעד שדה אדם יוצר חרס בעד שיגברו שם הגרים.

⁸ולכן נקרא אותו שדה אהל דם היום הזה.

⁹אז נשלם מאמר זכריה הנביא ואומר להם אם טוב בעיניכם רבו שכרי ואם חדלו. וישקלו שכרי שלשים כסף. ויאמר ה'' אלי השליכו אל היוצר. וזהו מהאדם היוצר חרס ¹⁰כאשר אדוני צוה.

¹¹ויש''ו היה עומד לפני פילא''ט ושאל לו האתה הוא מלך היהודים. ויש''ו אמר אתה אומר.

¹²וכאשר יש''ו היה רודף בעד גדולי הכהנים וזקני העם לשום דבר שהיו אומרים עליו לא היה עונה.

¹³ופילא''ט אמר לו אינך רואה כמה עדיות יש נגדך.

¹⁴ויש''ו לא ענה אליו דבר ופילא''ט היה נפלא מזה מאד.

¹⁵וביום החג הנכבד של פסח היה מנהגם שגובר העיר היה לתת לעם אסור אחד מהאסורים אותו אשר ירצו.

¹⁶וביד פולא''ט היה חבוש אחד שהיה כמעט שוטה שמו ברבא''ש. ונלקח על רצחה ושם אותו בבור.

¹⁷וכאשר נאספו אמר להם פילא''ט איזה מאלו תרצו שאינח ברבא''ש או יש''ו שנקרא משיח.

¹⁸לפי שפילא''ט היה יודע שעל שנאת חנם נלקח.

¹⁹ובעודו יושב בכסא אשתו שלחה לו שליח לאמר אחילה אני ממך שבשום ענין לא תאמר דבר כנגד אותו צדיק שבזאת הלילה סבלתי ענינים רבים במראה בעדו.

²⁰וגדולי הכהנים וזקני הדת הקהילו לעם ישאלו את ברבאש ושיש''ו ימית.

²¹ויען להם פילא''ט איזה מהם תרצו שניח. והם אמרו

ברבאש.

<sup>22</sup>ויאמר להם פילאט א׳׳כ מה אעשה מיש׳׳ו הנקרא משיח. וכולם ענו שיתלה.

<sup>23</sup>ופילא׳׳ט אמר להם איזו רעה עשה. והם בחוזק היו זועקים יתלוהו יתלוהו יתלוהו.

<sup>24</sup>ופילאט׳׳וש בראותו שלא היה תקומה ולא יכול להשלים שום דבר עמהם קודם שיקום בעד זה קטטה גדולה בעם לקח מים ורחץ ידיו בפני העם ואמר אני נקי מהם. שמרו לכם מה תעשו.

<sup>25</sup>וענו כל העם ואמרו דמו יהיה עלינו ועל זרענו.

<sup>26</sup>ואז הניח לה ברבאש ומסר להם יש׳׳ו לקוי ומעונה שיתלוהו.

<u>פרק קי׳׳ג</u>

<sup>27</sup>אז פרשי החצר לקחו ליש׳׳ו במשמר ויקהלו בפני קהל רב מעמים רבים.

<sup>28</sup>וילבישוהו ליש׳׳ו בגדי משי ויעטפוהו מעיל משי ירוק.

<sup>29</sup>ועשו עטרה מקוצים וישימהו על ראשו ושמו לו קנה אחת ביד הימנית וכורעים היו מלעיגים ממנו שלום עליך מלך היהודים.

<sup>30</sup>ורוקקים לו בפניו והיו לוקיחם הקנה ומכים בראשו.

<sup>31</sup>וכאשר הלעיגו ממנו הפשיטו ממנו המעיל והלבישוהו מלבושו וצוו לתלותו.

<sup>32</sup>ועודם יוצאים מהעיר פגעו באיש ששמו שמעון הכנעני. ואנסוהו שיוליך הצליבה ר׳׳ל השתי וערב.

<sup>33</sup>ובאו למקים נקרא גולגוטא הוא הר קאלוואירי

<sup>34</sup>ונתנו לו יין מזוג במרה. וכאשר התחיל לשתות הרגישו ולא ירצה לשתות.

<sup>35</sup>ואחר כאשר שמוהו בצליבה חלקו בגדו בגורל.

36

<sup>37</sup>ואחר הניחו לו על ראשו מכתב אחד שהיה אומר זה יש׳׳ו נאזרת מלך ישראל.

<sup>38</sup>אז נתלו עמו שני גנבים האחר לימינו והאחד לשמאלו.

<sup>39</sup>והעוברים היו מלעיגים ממנו ומניעים ראש

<sup>40</sup>ואומרים ראה אפשר חרבת מקדש האל ובעוד שלשה ימים

תושיע עצמך ואם אתה בן האל רד מן הצליבה.

⁴¹וגדולי הכהנים וזקני העם היו מלעיגים ממנו ואומרים

⁴²האחרים הושיע ועצמו לא יוכל להושיע. אם מלך ישראל הוא ירד מן העץ ונאמין.

⁴³כי הוא נשען באל יושיעהו עתה אם ירצה שהוא אמר שהוא בן האלקים.

⁴⁴ואותם הדברים עצמם אמרו לו הגנבים שהיו נתלים עמו.

⁴⁵ולשעה ששית נעשו חשוכות בכל העולם ועמדו עד שעה תשיעית.

⁴⁶ויש''ו צעק בקול גדול אומר בלשון הקודש אלי אלי למה עזבתני.

⁴⁷ואחד מהעומדים שם אמר זה קורא לאליה.

⁴⁸ומיד לקח אספוג ומלאהו חומץ ונתן לו לשתות.

⁴⁹והאחרים היו אומרים נראה אם יבא אליה ויושיעהו.

⁵⁰ויש''ו צעק פעם אחרת בקול גדול ושלח נשמתו לאביו.

⁵¹ומיד נקרע פרכת המקדש לשני קרעים מלמעלה למטה ורעשה הארץ ונשתברו האבנים.

⁵²והקברים נפתחו ורבים מישיני אדמת עפר קמו.

⁵³ויצאו מקבורתם ואחר שחיו באו בעיר הקדש ונגלו לרבים.

⁵⁴ושר המאה והעומדים עמו לשמור יש''ו ראו הרעשת הארץ והדברים שנעשו ויפחדו מאד ואומרים באמת זה היה בן האלק.

⁵⁵והיו שם נשים רבות שהיו עומדות מרחוק מאותן אשר שמשו ליש''ו מהגליל עד כה.

⁵⁶ובכללן היתה מריאה מגדלינה ומרים אם יעקב ויוסף ואם בני זבדאל.

⁵⁷ולעת ערב בא אדם עשיר שהיה מכרנאסיאה. שמו יוסף והיה תלמיד מיש''ו.

⁵⁸והלך לפילא''ט ושאל לו הגוף מיש''ו. ופילא''ט צוה שיתנוהו לו.

⁵⁹ויוסף לקחו וכרכו בבגד משי חשוב מאד.

⁶⁰ושם אותו בקברו שהיה נחצב חדש מאבן ושם אבן גדולה על

פי הקבר.

61

62וממחרת הפסח גדולי הכהנים והפרושים באו לפילאט.

63ואמרו לרן אדוננו אנו מזכירים שזה השקרן היה אומר בעודו בחיים שלקץ שלשה ימים יעמוד ויחיה.

64ולכן צוה לשמור קברו עד יום השלישי שבאולי איזה מתלמידיו יבא ויגנוב אותו. ואחר יאמרו לעם שעמד מהמות. ואם זה יעשו גדל יהיה עון האחרון מן הראשון.

65ופילאט אמר להם בקשו שומרים שמרו היותר טוב שתוכלו.

66והם שלמו בנין הקבר וחתמוהו והניחו שם שומרים.

## פרק קי''ז 28

1וביום הראשון מהשבוע בהשכמה באו מרים מגדלינה ומרים אחרת לראות הקבר.

2ונרעשה הארץ שמלאך ה'' ירד מן השמים לקבר והפן האבן ועמד.

3ומראהו היה כשמש ובגדיו כשלג.

4ומפחדו נבהלו השומרים ועמדו המתים.

5וענה המלאך ואמר לנשים אל תפחדו שאני יודע שאתן מבקשות ליש''ו אשר נתלה.

6איננו כאן שכבר חי כמו שאמר. לכן בואו וראו המקום אשר עמד שם האדון.

7ולכו מיד ואמרו לתלמידיו שכבר עמד שם הארון. והוא יהיה לפניכם ושם תראוהו כאשר אמר לכם.

## פרק קט''ו

8ויצאו הנשים בפחד מהקבר בעבור ראות המלאך ובשמחה רבה לפי שהאדון עמד חי. וירוצו לאמר לתלמידיו.

9והמה הולכות ויש''ו עבר לפניהם אומר יושיעכן. והם קרבו אליו ויקדו לו.

10אז אמר להן יש''ו אל תפחדו אמרו לאחי שילכו לגליל ושמה יראוני.

<sup>11</sup>ובעוד שהן הולכות איזה מהשומרים באו לעיר והגידו לגדולי הכהנים כל הנעשה.

<sup>12</sup>ויעדו לעצה עם זקני העם. ויתנו ממון רב לפרשים.

<sup>13</sup>ואמרו להם אתם תאמרו שבאו תלמידיו לילה וגנבוהו בעודכם ישנים.

<sup>14</sup>ואם זה יבא לאוזן פילאט אנו נדבר עמו בענין יניחכם.

<sup>15</sup>והם לקחו המטבע ואמרו כן כמו שלמדום. וזה הדבר בסור בין היהודים עד היום הזה.

<sup>16</sup>ואחר זה כאשר השנים עשר תלמידיו הלכו לגליל נראה להם בהר

<sup>17</sup>אשר בו התפללו. וכאשר ראוהו השתחוו לו ויש מהם שנסתפקו בו.

<sup>18</sup>ויש''ו קרב אליהם ואמר להם

<sup>19</sup>לכו אתם

<sup>20</sup>ושמרו אותם לקיים כל הדברים אשר ציויתי אתכם עד עולם.

Printed by Amazon Italia Logistica S.r.l.
Torrazza Piemonte (TO), Italy

13164047R00405